Client/Server
Programming with
Java and CORBA

Second Edition

Robert Orfali • Dan Harkey

WILEY COMPUTER PUBLISHING

JOHN WILEY & SONS, INC.

New York   Chichester   Weinheim   Brisbane   Singapore   Toronto

Publisher: Robert Ipsen
Editor: Theresa Hudson
Managing Editor: Angela Murphy
Text Design & Composition: Robert Orfali and Dan Harkey
Graphic Art: David Pacheco

Designations used by companies to distinguish their products are often claimed as trademarks. In all instances where John Wiley & Sons, Inc. is aware of a claim, the product names appear in initial capital or all capital letters. Readers, however, should contact the appropriate companies for more complete information regarding trademarks and registration.

This text is printed on acid-free paper. ∞

This publication is designed to provide accurate and authoritative information in regard to the subject matter covered. It is sold with the understanding that the publisher is not engaged in rendering legal, accounting, or other professional service. If legal advice or other expert assistance is required, the services of a competent professional person should be sought.

The authors and publisher of this book have used their best efforts in preparing this book. The authors and publisher make no warranty of any kind, expressed or implied, with regard to the documentation contained in this book. The authors and publisher shall not be liable in any event for incidental or consequential damages in connection with, or arising out of the use of, the information in this book.

The product descriptions are based on the best information available at the time of publication. Product prices are subject to change without notice.

Some illustrations incorporate clip art from Corel Systems Corporation's Corel Draw 5.0 clip art library.

All the views expressed in this book are solely the authors' and should not be attributed to IBM or any other IBM employee. The two authors contributed equally to the production of this book.

Library of Congress Cataloging-in-Publication Data:

Client/server programming with Java and CORBA / Robert Orfali and Dan Harkey. — 2nd ed.
    p.   cm.
  Includes index.
  ISBN 0-471-24578-X (pbk. /CD-ROM: alk. paper)
  1. Client/server computing. 2. Java (Computer program language)
  3. CORBA (Computer architecture)
  I. Harkey, Dan
  QA76.9.C550558   1998   98-10456
  005.2'762--dc21   CIP

Printed in the United States of America
10 9 8 7 6 5

Foreword

by Zog the Martian

Captain Zog

Greetings, Earthlings! I'm Zog, the captain of the Martian team. My team and I have visited Earth several times to understand what client/server is all about. In our previous visits, we discovered **The Essential Client/Server Survival Guide** and **The Essential Distributed Objects Survival Guide**. These two books were absolutely vital in our mission to explore this new technology. We really like the concept of the Object Web; it has great potential for our Martian intergalactic network. So, we were very excited to hear about **Client/Server Programming with Java and CORBA** by the same authors. We returned to Earth to pick up a copy of the book and do some serious CORBA/Java programming. It was just what we were looking for.

So what did I like about this book? It felt like it was talking directly to me and to my crew in a friendly voice. That's very important when you're from a foreign planet. The artwork is absolutely wonderful. I like to see pictures of myself in books (and especially on the cover). The ubiquitous scenarios show how objects really interact with each other. It's not that inert boring stuff you read in the textbooks. It makes objects come to life.

Mars has adopted Java as its programming language and *JavaBeans* as its component model. This is the first programming book to cover client/server computing and distributed objects with Java. It contains a lot of good working programs that give us a jump-start on how to use these distributed objects on our intergalactic client/server webs. Hopefully, our CORBA objects will be able to talk to yours.

This second edition is very timely. It explains how CORBA, JavaBeans, and Enterprise JavaBeans are coming together. It answers many of our questions about how to mix-and-match these technologies. We love the new JavaBeans version of Club Med. And, we appreciate the work the authors did to rewrite their programs using the new Java/IDL language mapping; it makes us more ORB-independent. We Martians cherish our independence.

The benchmarks are nice because they help us understand the trade-offs we face in the design of our distributed software. There are so many choices. You Earthlings don't make it any easier with all your competing middleware—DCOM/ActiveX, RMI,

Servlets, CORBA, Caffeine, Sockets, and HTTP/CGI. Why don't you just build applications instead of fighting middleware wars? As usual, the Soapboxes help us understand the issues and what the latest Earthling debates are all about. We like to hear strong opinions instead of just sterilized information.

After our last trip to Earth, we Martians standardized on CORBA; it's our distributed object bus. Now we're trying to get CORBA and Java to work together. Once we do, we can start building our intergalactic applications. So, I strongly recommend this Second Edition to my fellow Martians. It's must reading for anyone who wants to write intergalactic beans using CORBA and Java. Through this foreword, I highly recommend this book to you Earthlings. If I can program in Java and CORBA, so can you. Of course, if you wait another year, you may not even have to program any more. You may just be assembling your CORBA/JavaBeans via drag-and-drop. This book already demonstrates some of what you can do with visual assembly tools today.

Zog

Preface

The next shift catalyzed by the Web will be the adoption of enterprise systems based on distributed objects and IIOP (Internet Inter-ORB Protocol). IIOP will manage the communication between the object components that power the system. Users will be pointing and clicking at objects available on IIOP-enabled servers. We expect to distribute 20 million IIOP clients over the next 12 months and millions of IIOP-based servers over the next couple of years. We'll put the platform out there so that people can start developing for it.

> — Marc Andreessen,
> Netscape Cofounder

Marc Andreessen eloquently describes the *Object Web*—or the morphing of distributed objects and the Web. The Object Web is the latest paradigmatic shift in the distributed software industry. It is redefining the way we develop, deploy, maintain, package, and sell our client/server applications. Objects break up the client and server sides of an application into smart components that can play together and roam across networks. The Web and intranets provide the intergalactic networks where these components live. Java provides the mobile code infrastructure. And, it also provides the beans.

Is CORBA/Java Ready for Client/Server Prime Time?

The Object Web is still under construction. It seems that everyone in the software business is building a piece of it today. In this book, we look at two of the Object Web's core technologies: Java and CORBA/IIOP. Java provides the mobile code foundation; CORBA provides the distributed object infrastructure. They are both foundations of the Object Web.

So, what is the state of these two foundation technologies? Can we use CORBA and Java today to deploy a new generation of Web-based client/server applications? Are they ready for mission-critical prime time? What is the state of the CORBA/Java integration? What role do *JavaBeans* and *Enterprise JavaBeans* play? These are the questions we try to answer in this book.

We found that the best way to get a reality check on where things stand is to write lots of working code. Currently, most Java applications have been standalone

demos, but the real value of Java is when you build portable clients to much larger transactional systems. This is where CORBA and JavaBeans come into the picture. We hope to show you in this book that you can use CORBA and Java today to create some dynamite client/server applications. So we will put CORBA and JavaBeans through the wringer by running benchmarks. We will also be developing industrial-strength client/server applications using CORBA and Java. Finally, we will look at some of the alternatives—including DCOM/ActiveX, RMI, HTTP/CGI, Servlets, and Sockets.

The CORBA/Java Integration Story

You've probably already heard about CORBA; otherwise, you wouldn't be reading this book. And, of course, you've heard of Java or you wouldn't be from this planet. We assume that you think that CORBA and Java are important new technologies, which is why you purchased this book. So what could be left to say about CORBA and Java? It may come as a surprise, but very little has been said about how CORBA and Java play together. And, even less has been said about how CORBA and JavaBeans play together. This entire book is about the intersection of these two important object models.

We must warn our Java readers that CORBA is a lot more than just an ORB—it is also a complete distributed object platform. CORBA extends the reach of your applications across networks, languages, component boundaries, and operating systems. CORBA supplements Java with a rich set of distributed services that includes introspection, dynamic discovery, transactions, relationships, security, naming, and so on. CORBA provides the missing link between the Java mobile code environment and the world of intergalactic objects.

Now, we must warn our CORBA readers that Java is much more than just another language with CORBA bindings. Java is a mobile object system; it's a portable operating system for running objects. Soon, Java will allow your CORBA objects to run on everything from mainframes to network computers and cellular phones. JavaSoft seems to be defining new portable services every day—including server-side components, transactions, security, persistence, and system management. Like CORBA, Java is in the process of building a gigantic object infrastructure.

Luckily, these two object infrastructures complement each other well. Java starts where CORBA leaves off. CORBA deals with network transparency, while Java deals with implementation transparency. Java simplifies code distribution in large CORBA systems—its bytecodes let you ship object behavior around. Java is an almost ideal language for writing both client and server objects. Its built-in multithreading, garbage collection, and error management make it easier to write robust networked objects.

In the past, OMG has kept its distance from implementation and language issues (except for bindings). Consequently, CORBA is a language-independent object model, which is a good thing. However, Java solves some thorny implementation problems that have stood in the way of developing a truly portable distributed object market, which is also a good thing.

What This Book Covers

This book explains the intersection of CORBA and Java in depth. It is also a gentle guide to client/server programming with CORBA and Java. The book introduces CORBA to Java programmers. However, we do not introduce Java to CORBA programmers. We assume that you have a working knowledge of the Java language. If you don't, there are dozens of books that provide introductions to Java. Our book starts with the JDK 1.1 (or above); we give detailed explanations of anything that has to do with the new JDK system facilities—for example, RMI, JDBC, JavaBeans, Enterprise JavaBeans, sockets, serialization, security, and reflection.

This book consists of eight Parts that build on each other:

■ **Part 1** starts with an overview of what CORBA and Java do for each other. We explain the 3-tier *Object Web* client/server model. We provide a bird's-eye view of CORBA/IIOP for Java programmers. If you come from a client/server background, this discussion will help you understand what the Object Web is all about. We conclude Part 1 by picking a CORBA/Java ORB for this book.

■ **Part 2** starts our exploration of the CORBA/Java programming model. We develop a small client/server Ping that serves as a mini crash-course in core CORBA/Java programming. This simple program can be surprisingly useful. In Part 2, we use it to do the following performance comparisons: local invocations versus remote invocations, Java applets versus Java client applications, JIT compilers versus interpreters, and C++ ORBs versus Java ORBs. Finally, we use the program to show you how to call a C++ object from Java, and vice versa.

■ **Part 3** starts out with a rewrite of our Count program using the new *portable* server-side CORBA APIs as well as the standard CORBA *Naming Service*. This move gives us an ORB-independent, standards-based platform that we use to write the rest of the programs in this book. We then show you how to program CORBA's dynamic object facilities. The dynamic CORBA lets you create very flexible systems where clients and servers discover each other at run time. We look at two very versatile programming mechanisms: *dynamic invocations* and *callbacks*. With CORBA's dynamic invocations, any Java client can construct a remote method call on-the-fly, and then invoke it. With callbacks, clients can also be servers. Callbacks let servers call Java clients wherever they are. You will learn how to create multithreaded Java objects that are both clients and servers. This chapter also provides Ping performance numbers for CORBA's dynamic facilities.

■ **Part 4** compares CORBA/Java with its competitors: 1) *legacy Internet middleware*—including Java Sockets, Servlets, and CGI/HTTP, and 2) *non-CORBA Java ORBs*—including JavaSoft's RMI and Microsoft's DCOM. We also cover *Caffeine*, which is the Netscape/Visigenic answer to RMI; it provides an RMI-like programming environment on top of CORBA/IIOP. Caffeine lets you write CORBA distributed objects without CORBA IDL. It demonstrates a pure Java alternative to the traditional CORBA development process. In addition to the programming examples, we provide in-depth tutorials on each of these technologies. We also run Ping benchmarks to give you a feeling for their relative performance. It's not every day that you see the same Java client/server program running over Sockets, Servlets, HTTP/CGI, RMI, DCOM, and CORBA.

■ **Part 5** is about the "existential" CORBA. We explain CORBA's Interface Repository and introspection facilities. We show you how an object discovers its intergalactic universe. We also cover CORBA's activation services—including the new CORBA 3.0 *Portable Object Adapter (POA)*. An ORB must provide the illusion that all of its objects—and there can be millions of them—are up and running and active all the time, even though they are not. This illusion keeps the client code simple but it shifts the implementation burden to the server side. You must write code that cooperates with the ORB when you start and stop your objects or when the ORB starts up or shuts down. Finally, we cover in detail the new CORBA *IDL-to-Java* mapping. This is the mapping that lets us write very portable ORB-independent applications. We also cover the *Java-to-IDL* mapping. It lets you write CORBA code without IDL. Instead, you use RMI semantics. This mapping is very important because it unifies the CORBA and RMI worlds.

■ **Part 6** is about 2-tier and 3-tier client/server programming using Java, CORBA, and JDBC. In some circles, client/server is synonymous with SQL databases. This is not too surprising considering that SQL database is the most prevalent application model for client/server today. So one way to determine if CORBA and Java are ready for client/server prime time is to see how well they do database. Part 6 starts out with the world's longest tutorial chapter on JDBC. Then we develop a Debit-Credit benchmark that compares the performance of 2-tier versus 3-tier client/server systems using CORBA, Java, and JDBC. We will also compare the performance of static SQL versus dynamic SQL, JDBC-style. You will learn—in a fun way—some of the architectural trade-offs of the client/server discipline.

■ **Part 7** is about beans—including JavaBeans, CORBA Beans, and Enterprise JavaBeans. We first go over the JavaBeans component model in depth. Next, we explain the new CORBA component initiative—the so-called *CORBA Beans* (or JavaBeans++). Then, we cover *Enterprise JavaBeans (EJBs)*. The EJB specification defines a contract between a server-side JavaBean and an *Object Transaction Monitor (OTM)*. The OTM manages server-side beans in a scalable way using transactions, state management, and automatic activation and deactivation. EJB was designed from ground zero to be 100% CORBA-compatible. It augments CORBA by defining the interfaces between a server-side component (or bean) and its *container*. The beauty of the EJB framework is that it lets you declaratively define most of your server-side, run-time attributes. So you can use visual tools to administer, package, and set the properties of your server-side components—including their transactional, security, and state management policies.

■ **Part 8** concludes—in grand finale style—with a Web-based, *Club Med* client/server application. This Part brings it all together. We write a bean-based client applet that associates GUI events with method invocations on CORBA/Java server objects. In this 3-tier client/server application, the middle-tier objects interact with both the Web-applet clients and the Club Med JDBC database. We also include a poor man's TP Monitor for managing multithreaded server objects. We assemble our Club Med beans using three visual tools: Symantec's *Visual Cafe PDE*, Borland's *JBuilder C/S*, and IBM's *VisualAge for Java*. We show you how much visual client/server assembly you can do with these tools today. We even create a simple delegate class that makes our CORBA server-side objects look like ordinary beans.

A lot of this material covers previously uncharted territory. As far as we know, this is the first book that puts through the wringer client/server systems that use CORBA, JavaBeans, and JDBC. Consequently, we will develop complete 3-tier client/server frameworks for these technologies from scratch.

What Are the Boxes For?

We use shaded boxes as a way to introduce concurrent threads in the presentation material. It's the book's version of multitasking. The *Soapboxes* introduce strong opinions or biases on some of the more controversial topics of distributed object computing. Because the discipline is so new and fuzzy, there's lots of room for interpretation and debate—so you'll get lots of Soapboxes that are just another opinion (ours). The *Briefing* boxes give you background or tutorial type information. You can safely skip over them if you're already familiar with a topic. The *Detail* boxes cover some esoteric area of technology that may not be of interest to the general readership. Typically, the same readers that skip over the briefings will find the details interesting (so you'll still get your money's worth). Lastly, we use *Warning* boxes to let you know where danger lies—this is, after all, previously uncharted territory.

How to Read This Book

As we recommend in all our books, it's best to ask your boss for a one-week, paid sabbatical to go sit on a beach and read this book. Tell him or her that it's the

cheapest way to revitalize yourself technically and find out all there is to know about distributed objects, CORBA, and JavaBeans. Note that this time you should also take a laptop with you to run all the programs that come with the CD-ROM. One of the benefits of local/remote transparency is that you can run all the client and server programs on the same machine—including the ORB. So once you sink into that comfortable chair overlooking the ocean, we think you'll find the book a lot of fun— maybe even downright relaxing. If you do somehow become bored, simply jump to the next Part until you find something you like. But before jumping around, you need to read Chapter 4. It also helps to read Part 1.

What's New in This Edition

We thank our readers for keeping the first edition of this book at the top of the bestselling charts for over six consecutive months. As a result of this phenomenal success, our publisher asked us to do a "minor" update to bring this book up-to-date. Much to our surprise, this update became a major nine-month effort.

Over half of this book contains entirely new material—including the chapters on JavaBeans, CORBA Beans, Enterprise JavaBeans, Servlets, Java-to-IDL, IDL-to-Java, POA, Portable Count, CORBA Naming, and the JavaBeans version of Club Med. All the programs in the book were completely updated to comply with JDK 1.1, the new CORBA/Java mapping, VisiBroker 3.1, and the latest Netscape and Microsoft products. We also updated the chapter on the Object Web to reflect the latest in Internet middleware.

This book is at the bleeding edge of two technologies—JavaBeans and CORBA. Both are moving at bullet-train speeds. So there's no stability in sight. Writing code in this kind of environment is an ongoing struggle; it just doesn't sit still. Our students in the CORBA/Java graduate program suffer with us as we constantly look for this stable cross-section of technology where it all works together—they need it for their projects. Nirvana is where it all comes together. The collection of products and standards we use in this second edition represents the current Nirvana; it's a stable point. We hope you can put this stable point to good use. Also, be sure to visit our Web site for the latest updates and fixes to our software.

Who Is This Book For?

This book is for anyone involved with client/server programming, distributed objects, Java, or JavaBeans. It's particularly important for the following readers:

- Java programmers who need to understand client/server computing, distributed objects, CORBA/IIOP, JavaBeans, and JDBC. This book prepares you for the brave new world of distributed components and Enterprise JavaBeans.

- CORBA programmers who need to understand Java, JavaBeans, and Enterprise JavaBeans. This book is all about CORBA/Java integration. We also cover the latest Java-related CORBA standards and work-in-process—including IDL-to-Java, Java-to-IDL, RMI/IDL, Java/POA, Objects-by-Value, and CORBA Components.

- MIS programmers who are evaluating distributed components, CORBA, Java, JavaBeans, Enterprise JavaBeans, and intranets. This book provides you with tons of benchmarks and apple-to-apple comparisons with other forms of middleware—including DCOM, HTTP/CGI, RMI, Servlets, and Sockets. We also give you a feel for the state-of-the-art in visual client/server assembly using off-the-shelf JavaBeans tools.

■ Client/server architects who are thinking about using CORBA, JavaBeans, and Enterprise JavaBeans on their platforms. This is the first book that exhaustively looks at Java as a client/server platform. You'll get the good, the bad, and the ugly.

Eventually, every programmer will have to write a JavaBean component or distributed object program. So you'll find that reading this book is time well spent. If nothing else, it will give you a jump-start for programming the Object Web. Non-programmers can read the tutorials, benchmarking chapters, and the detailed comparisons. However, you may be better off reading one of our other books (see the next section). This one is really for programmers.

How Does This Book Compare With Our Other Books?

Here's what we cover in the other three books:

■ **The Essential Client/Server Survival Guide, Second Edition** (Wiley, 1996) provides an overview of the entire field of client/server computing—including NOSs, SQL databases, data warehouses, TP Monitors, groupware, the Internet, system management, tools, and distributed objects. The book also includes a 100-page introduction to the *Object Web*.

■ **The Essential Distributed Objects Survival Guide** (Wiley, 1996) covers distributed objects in-depth. The book also covers components and business objects. However, it's not a programming book.

■ **Instant CORBA** (Wiley, 1997) is a 300-page quick introduction to CORBA and its Object Services—including Security, Trader, and Transactions. Again, it's not a programming book. It's an introduction for people who are in a hurry.

We borrowed about 80 pages of relevant material from the two Survival Guides to make this book stand on its own. We also include some material from **Instant CORBA**.

CD-ROM and Book Web Site

The CD-ROM in our first edition was quite bare. In contrast, this CD-ROM is full of great evaluation software. Borland even created an evaluation copy of *JBuilder*

Client/Server especially for this book. Here's some of the software you'll find on this CD-ROM:

✔ Source code for all the programs in this book
✔ Borland/Visigenic *VisiBroker for Java 3.1*
✔ Borland/Visigenic *VisiBroker for C++ 3.1*
✔ Borland/Visigenic *CORBA Naming Service*
✔ Symantec *Visual Café PDE*
✔ IBM *VisualAge for Java*
✔ Borland *JBuilder Client/Server*
✔ JavaSoft *JDK 1.1*
✔ Connect Software *FastForward* JDBC driver
✔ Netscape *Enterprise Server* and *Communicator*
✔ InstallShield *InstallShield Java Edition*

With *InstallShield*, you should have no trouble installing the programs on your favorite platform.

Because all this area is in flux, we will continue to maintain a Web site with FAQs and code updates. So visit us at **http://www.corbajava.engr.sjsu.edu**.

A Personal Note

Despite the frustrations that come with exploring uncharted territory, we really enjoyed writing this book. Java has brought the fun back into client/server programming. JavaBeans is making it even better. We hope that you'll enjoy the tutorials, code, and Soapboxes. Drop us a line if you have something you want to "flame" about. We'll take compliments, too. We're relying on word-of-mouth to let people know about the book, so if you enjoy it, please spread the word. Finally, we want to thank you, as well as our Martian friends, for trusting us to be your guides.

Acknowledgments

It's impossible to thank all the hundreds of people that helped us with this book. But, we'll give it a try:

- To Deans Don Kirk and Nabil Ibrahim of San Jose State University for providing us with a world-class CORBA/Java integration lab and for helping us set up a graduate research program around it. To IBM for giving us time to work on this CORBA/Java lab. To Microsoft for their generous donations to our lab—thank you, Jim Gray. And, to HP for their generous donation of equipment.

- To Patty Dock, Ken Ausich, and their team of distributed object gurus for their ongoing support.

- To Visigenic and Netscape for making an early version of VisiBroker for Java available to us. To Tim Lopez of Symantec for getting us early versions of Visual Café.

- To the technical people in different companies who helped us make some sense out of this difficult topic—including Cory Adams, Marc Andreessen, Mark Baker, Jeff Bauer, Tim Berners-Lee, Mark Betz, Cedric Beust, Jim Black, Jeff Bonar, Nitin Bonwankar, Grady Booch, Ken Burgett, Kevin Butler, Larry Cable, Rick Cattell, Dan Chang, Lee Chang, David Christie, Brian Cottman, David Curtis, Alain Demour, Paul Daly, Dimitri Dimov, Jeri Edwards, Ron Emrick, Rod Fatoohi, Richard Finkelstein, Shel Finkelstein, Ira Forman, Bob Garnero, Nick Gault, Hisham Ghazouli, Jim Gray, Gene Guglielmo, Martin Haeberli, Jake Hamby, Mark Hapner, Pat Helland, Pete Homan, David Huntley, Adam Ip, Ivar Jacobson, Jim Johnson, Ralph Johnson, Jeff Jones, Mike Lee, Geoff Lewis, Farid Khoujinian, Charlie Kindel, Geoff Lewis, Marie Lenzi, Hal Lorin, Vlada Matena, Joe McIntyre, Timo Metsaportti, Domingo Mihovilovic, Jeff Mischkinsky, Tom Mowbray, Simon Nash, Jeff Nelson, Terry Okamoto, Annrai O'Toole, Ron Resnick, Mark Ryland, Chris Rygaard, Mary Rygaard, Ashvin Radiya, Bob Ringo, Roger Sessions, Jon Siegel, Oliver Sims, Colin Smith, Richard Soley, Nick Stier, Dave Stodder, Chris Stone, David Stryker, Guiling Sui, Rob Sward, John Tibbetts, Don Vines, Jon Udell, Walter Utz, Satya Vardharajan, Alan Warren, Andrew Watson, Kofi Weusi-Puryear, Jonathan Wilcox, Jonathan Weedon, Ron Zahavi, and May Zhang.

- To the marketing directors and managers who fed us with up-to-the-minute information on their latest and greatest products—including Aaron Alpar, David Andrews, Suzanne Anthony, Allen Bannon, Michael Barton, Barbara Bernstein, Karen Boucher, Nan Borreson, Anthony Brown, David Butler, Marty Cagan, David F. Carr, Sam Cece, Suresh Challa, Mala Chandra, Bill Coleman, Steve Dinwittie, Rick Fleischman, Bjorne Frogner, Phil Garrett, Michel Gerin, Barbara Hanscome, Basil Hashem, Scott Hebner, Randy Hietter, Scott Johnston, Jennifer King, James Lucky, Tim Lopez, Cynthia McFall, John Montgomery, David Pann, John Parenica, Larry Perlstein, Cliff Reeves, Dave Stodder, Nikhyl Singhal, James Utzschneider, David Vaskevitch, and David Weiden.

- To our graduate students. Your energy was contagious.

- To Dave Pacheco for creating the wonderful technical illustrations in this book (the cartoons are still by Jeri).

- To our tireless copy editor, Larry Mackin

- To our proof reader, Shelley Flannery.

- To the people at Wiley that had to deal with our pickiness—especially Terri Hudson, Frank Grazioli, Angela Murphy, Mike Sosa, Bob Ipsen, Sandy Bontemps, Ellen Reavis, and Tom Hyland.

- To the more than 400,000 readers of our previous books. Without your continued support we couldn't write these books.

Contents

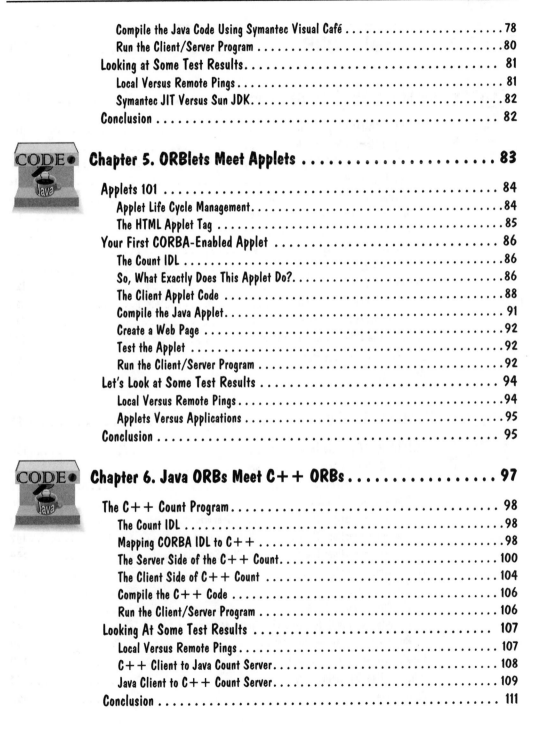

Chapter 11. HTTP/CGI Versus CORBA/Java ORBs. 231

Chapter 12. Servlets Versus CORBA/Java ORBs 255

Chapter 13. RMI Versus CORBA/Java ORBs 281

Chapter 14. Caffeine: The "Pure" CORBA/Java ORB 313

Chapter 15. DCOM Versus CORBA/Java ORBs 331

Chapter 16. And the Winner Is... 373

Part 5. The Existential CORBA 381

Chapter 17. How Do I Find My ORB? 383

Chapter 18. Who Activates My Objects? 389

Chapter 21. The CORBA Java-to-IDL Mapping 485

Chapter 22. The Introspective CORBA/Java Object 501

Part 6. JDBC 2-Tier Versus 3-Tier 519

CONCEPTS Chapter 23. JDBC Primer 521

Chapter 24. The JDBC Debit-Credit Benchmark. 575

Chapter 25. 2-Tier Debit-Credit with JDBC 599

Part 7. From JavaBeans To Enterprise JavaBeans 651

Chapter 29. The Event-Driven JavaBean 683

Chapter 30. The Propertied JavaBean 711

Part 8. Grand Finale: Club Med with CORBA/JavaBeans . 885

Chapter 35. The Club Med 3-Tier Client/Server 887

Part 1
CORBA Meets Java

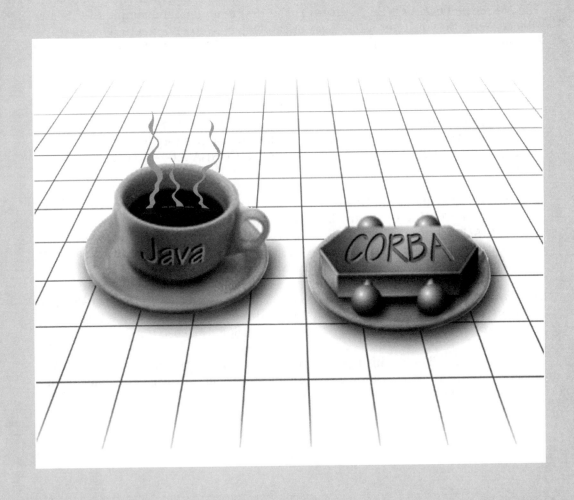

An Introduction to Part 1

You've probably already heard a lot about CORBA or you wouldn't be reading this book. And, of course, you've heard of Java or you wouldn't be from this planet. We assume that you think that CORBA and Java are important new technologies, which is why you purchased this book. So what could be left to say about CORBA and Java? It may come as a surprise, but very little has been said about the CORBA/Java relation. This entire book is about the intersection of these two important object models, and how they play together. We use programs to demonstrate the concepts and to serve as reality checks. But first you need to see the big picture, which is why there's a Part 1.

We start Part 1 with a gentle tour of CORBA for the Java programmer. If you know all about CORBA, you can skip over this material. Next, we explore the CORBA/Java integration issues. We explain how the Java and CORBA object models complement each other. The next big wave of client/server computing will be catalyzed by the marriage of distributed objects and the Web. We call this marriage the *Object Web*. The *Netscape ONE* CORBA platform is the first commercial example of this new Object Web. So you'll get a big dose of the Object Web and where it's going. We conclude Part 1 by going on a shopping tour for a CORBA/Java ORB.

Here's a brief description of the chapters in Part 1:

- *Chapter 1* provides a bird's-eye tour of CORBA 2.0. It's the world's fastest introduction to CORBA. It covers the ORB, IIOP, CORBA Services, and CORBA Business Objects. Then we give you a dose of 3-tier intergalactic client/server computing, CORBA-style. Finally, we look at CORBA 3.0—the next-generation ORB.

- *Chapter 2* is about the Object Web—the CORBA/Java killer app. We first tell you what CORBA does for Java, and vice versa. Next, we look at what CORBA/Java do for the Web. Then, we explain the Object Web 3-tier client/server architecture in some detail. Finally, we use a shopping mall analogy to introduce the CORBA/Java Object Web players. It's quite a crowd.

- *Chapter 3* is about CORBA/Java ORBs. These are the latest and greatest ORBs written entirely in Java. We look at the top three: Borland/Visigenic's *VisiBroker for Java 3.1*, Iona's *OrbixWeb 3.0*, and JavaSoft's *Java IDL*.

We hope that you'll enjoy this big-picture tour, even if you're a hard-core CORBA or Java programmer. Yes, we know it's "abstract stuff," but it provides the background you'll need to understand the rest of this book.

Chapter 1

Client/Server, CORBA-Style

The *Common Object Request Broker Architecture (CORBA)* is the most important (and ambitious) middleware project ever undertaken by our industry. It is the product of a consortium—called the Object Management Group (OMG)—that includes over 800 companies, representing the entire spectrum of the computer industry. The notable exception is Microsoft, which has its own competing object broker called the *Distributed Component Object Model (DCOM)*. For the rest of our industry, the next generation of middleware is CORBA. The CORBA object bus defines the shape of the components that live within it and how they interoperate. Consequently, by choosing an open object bus, the industry is also choosing to create an open playing field for components.

What makes CORBA so important is that it defines middleware that has the potential of subsuming every other form of existing client/server middleware. In other words, CORBA uses objects as a unifying metaphor for bringing existing applications to the bus. At the same time, it provides a solid foundation for a component-based future. The magic of CORBA is that the entire system is self-describing. In addition, the specification of a service is always separated from the implementation. This lets you incorporate existing systems within the bus.

CORBA was designed to allow intelligent components to discover each other and interoperate on an object bus. However, CORBA goes beyond just interoperability.

It also specifies an extensive set of bus-related services for creating and deleting objects, accessing them by name, storing them in persistent stores, externalizing their states, and defining ad hoc relationships between them.

CORBA lets you create an ordinary object and then make it transactional, secure, lockable, and persistent by making the object multiply-inherit from the appropriate services. This means that you can design an ordinary component to provide its regular function, and then insert the right middleware mix when you build it or create it at run time. So, welcome to the age of flexible "made-to-order" middleware. There is nothing like it for any other form of client/server computing.

This chapter is about the CORBA object bus and the object system services that extend the bus. We start with an overview of CORBA and what it does for intelligent components. We then cover the CORBA object model and the architecture that ties it all together. Finally, we will put the whole thing in a familiar client/server perspective. As you will see, some key distributed object pieces are still lacking. So we will also look at what's brewing in the upcoming OMG specifications.

DISTRIBUTED OBJECTS, CORBA-STYLE

Perhaps the secret to OMG's success is that it creates interface specifications, not code. The interfaces it specifies are always derived from demonstrated technology submitted by member companies. The specifications are written in a neutral *Interface Definition Language (IDL)* that defines a component's boundaries— that is, its contractual interfaces with potential clients. Components written to IDL should be portable across languages, tools, operating systems, and networks. And with the adoption of the CORBA 2.0 specification in December 1994, these components should be able to interoperate across multivendor CORBA object brokers.

What Is a Distributed CORBA Object?

CORBA objects are blobs of intelligence that can live anywhere on a network. They are packaged as binary components that remote clients can access via method invocations. Both the language and compiler used to create server objects are totally transparent to clients. Clients don't need to know where the distributed object resides or what operating system it executes on. It can be in the same process or on a machine that sits across an intergalactic network. In addition, clients don't need to know how the server object is implemented. For example, a server object could be implemented as a set of C++ classes, or it could be implemented with a million lines of existing COBOL code—the client doesn't know the difference. What the client needs to know is the interface its server object publishes. This interface serves as a binding contract between clients and servers.

Everything Is in IDL

As we said earlier, CORBA uses IDL contracts to specify a component's boundaries and its contractual interfaces with potential clients. The CORBA IDL is purely declarative. This means that it provides no implementation details. You can use IDL to define APIs concisely, and it covers important issues such as error handling. IDL-specified methods can be written in and invoked from any language that provides CORBA bindings—currently, C, C++, Ada, Smalltalk, COBOL, and Java (Objective C is in the works). Programmers deal with CORBA objects using native language constructs. IDL provides operating system and programming language independent interfaces to all the services and components that reside on a CORBA bus. It allows client and server objects written in different languages to interoperate (see Figure 1-1).

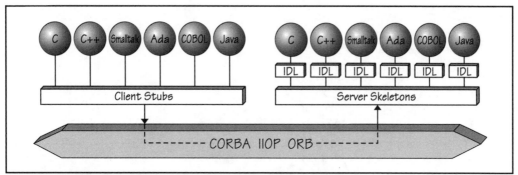

Figure 1-1. CORBA IDL Language Bindings Provide Client/Server Interoperability.

You can use the OMG IDL to specify a component's attributes, the parent classes it inherits from, the exceptions it raises, the typed events it emits, and the methods its interface supports—including the input and output parameters and their data types. The IDL grammar is a subset of C++ with additional keywords to support distributed concepts; it also fully supports standard C++ preprocessing features and pragmas.

The ambitious goal of CORBA is to "IDL-ize" all client/server middleware and all components that live on an ORB. OMG hopes to achieve this goal by following two steps: 1) it will turn everything into nails, and 2) it will give everyone a hammer.

■ The "nail" is the CORBA IDL. It allows component providers to specify in a standard definition language the interface and structure of the objects they provide. An IDL-defined contract binds the providers of distributed object services to their clients. For one object to request something from another object, it must know the target object's interface. The CORBA *Interface Repository* contains the definitions of all these interfaces. It contains the *metadata* that lets components discover each other dynamically at run time. This makes CORBA a self-describing system.

■ The "hammer" includes the set of distributed services OMG providers will supply. These services will determine which objects are on the network, which methods they provide, and which object interface adapters they support. The location of the object should be transparent to the client. It should not matter whether the object is in the same process or across the world.

Does this all sound familiar? It should. We're describing the "object wave" of client/server computing; this time it's between cooperating objects as opposed to cooperating processes. The goal of this new wave is to create multivendor, multiOS, multilanguage "legoware" using objects. Vendors such as Oracle, Sun, HP, IBM, BEA, Novell, Netscape, Tandem, and NCR are all using CORBA as their standard IDL-defined interface into the object highway. The IDL is the contract that brings it all together.

CORBA Components: From System Objects to Business Objects

Notice that we've been using the terms "components" and "distributed objects" interchangeably. CORBA distributed objects are, by definition, components because of the way they are packaged. In distributed object systems, the unit of work and distribution is a component. The CORBA distributed object infrastructure makes it easier for components to be more autonomous, self-managing, and collaborative. This undertaking is much more ambitious than anything attempted by competing forms of middleware. CORBA's distributed object technology allows us to put together complex client/server information systems by simply assembling and extending components. You can modify objects without affecting the rest of the components in the system or how they interact. A client/server application becomes a collection of collaborating components. In addition, CORBA is incorporating many elements of the JavaBeans component model, which should help make CORBA components more toolable.

The ultimate "Nirvana" in the client/server components business are supersmart components that do more than just interoperate—they collaborate at the semantic level to get a job done. Programmers can easily get things to collaborate by writing code for the two sides of the collaboration. The trick, however, is to get components that have no previous knowledge of each other to do the same. To get to that point, you need standards that set the rules of engagement for different component interaction boundaries.

OMG'S OBJECT MANAGEMENT ARCHITECTURE

In the fall of 1990, the OMG first published the *Object Management Architecture Guide (OMA Guide)*. It was revised in September 1992. The details of the Common Facilities were added in January 1995. Figure 1-2 shows the four main elements of the architecture: 1) *Object Request Broker (ORB)* defines the CORBA object bus; 2) *CORBAservices* define the system-level object frameworks that extend the bus; 3) *CORBAfacilities* define horizontal and vertical application frameworks that are used directly by business objects; and 4) *Application Objects* are the business objects and applications—they are the ultimate consumers of the CORBA infrastructure. This section provides a top-level view of the four elements that make up the CORBA infrastructure.

The Object Request Broker (ORB)

The *Object Request Broker (ORB)* is the object bus. It lets objects transparently make requests to—and receive responses from—other objects located locally or remotely. The client is not aware of the mechanisms used to communicate with, activate, or store the server objects. The CORBA 1.1 specifications—introduced in 1991—only specified the IDL, language bindings, and APIs for interfacing to the ORB. So, you could write portable programs that could run on top of the dozens of CORBA-compliant ORBs on the market (especially on the client side). CORBA 2.0 specifies interoperability across vendor ORBs.

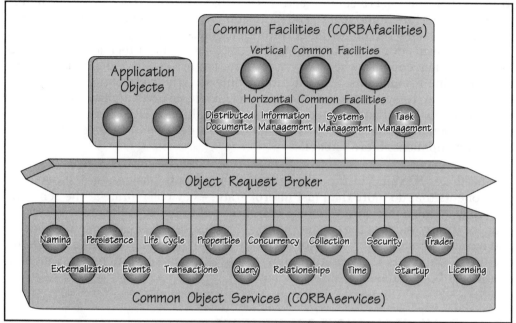

Figure 1-2. The OMG Object Management Architecture.

A CORBA ORB provides a wide variety of distributed middleware services. The ORB lets objects discover each other at run time and invoke each other's services. An ORB is much more sophisticated than alternative forms of client/server middleware—including traditional Remote Procedure Calls (RPCs), Message-Oriented Middleware (MOM), database stored procedures, and peer-to-peer services. In theory, CORBA is the best client/server middleware ever defined. In practice, CORBA is only as good as the products that implement it.

To give you an idea of why CORBA ORBs make such great client/server middleware, we offer the following "short" list of benefits that every CORBA ORB provides:

- **Static and dynamic method invocations**. A CORBA ORB lets you either statically define your method invocations at compile time, or it lets you dynamically discover them at run time. So you either get strong type checking at compile time or maximum flexibility associated with late (or run-time) binding. Most other forms of middleware only support static bindings.

- **High-level language bindings**. A CORBA ORB lets you invoke methods on server objects using your high-level language of choice. It doesn't matter what language server objects are written in. CORBA separates interface from implementation and provides language-neutral data types that make it possible to call objects across language and operating system boundaries. In contrast, other types of middleware typically provide low-level, language-specific, API libraries. And they don't separate implementation from specification—the API is tightly bound to the implementation, which makes it very sensitive to changes.

- **Self-describing system**. CORBA provides run-time metadata for describing every server interface known to the system. Every CORBA ORB must support an *Interface Repository* that contains real-time information describing the functions a server provides and their parameters. The clients use metadata to discover how to invoke services at run time. It also helps tools generate code "on-the-fly." The metadata is generated automatically either by an IDL-language precompiler or by compilers that know how to generate IDL directly from an OO language. For example, Visigenic/Netscape's *Caffeine* generates IDL directly from Java bytecodes. To the best of our knowledge, no other form of client/server middleware provides this type of run-time metadata and language-independent definitions of all its services. As you will discover later in this book, business objects and components require all the late-binding flexibility they can get.

- **Local/remote transparency**. An ORB can run in standalone mode on a laptop, or it can be interconnected to every other ORB in the universe using CORBA 2.0's *Internet Inter-ORB Protocol (IIOP)* services. An ORB can broker inter-object calls within a single process, multiple processes running within the same machine, or multiple processes running across networks and operating systems. This is completely transparent to your objects. Note that the ORB can broker among fine-grained objects—like C++ classes—as well as more coarse-grained objects. In general, a CORBA client/server programmer does not have to be concerned with transports, server locations, object activation, byte ordering across dissimilar platforms, or target operating systems—CORBA makes it all transparent.

- **Built-in security and transactions**. The ORB includes context information in its messages to handle security and transactions across machine and ORB boundaries.

- **Polymorphic messaging**. In contrast to other forms of middleware, an ORB does not simply invoke a remote function—it invokes a function on a target object. This means that the same function call will have different effects, depending on the object that receives it. For example, a *configure_yourself* method invocation behaves differently when applied to a database object versus a printer object (also see the following Briefing box).

- **Coexistence with existing systems**. CORBA's separation of an object's definition from its implementation is perfect for encapsulating existing applications. Using CORBA IDL, you can make your existing code look like an object on the ORB, even if it's implemented in stored procedures, CICS, IMS, or COBOL.

This makes CORBA an evolutionary solution. You can write your new applications as pure objects and encapsulate existing applications with IDL wrappers.

ORB Versus RPC

Briefing

So how are ORB method invocations different from RPCs? The mechanisms are very similar, but there are some important differences. With an RPC, you call a specific function (the data is separate). In contrast, with an ORB, you're calling a method within a specific object. Different object classes may respond to the same method invocation differently through the magic of polymorphism. Because each object manages its own private instance data, the method is implemented on that specific instance data (see Figure 1-3).

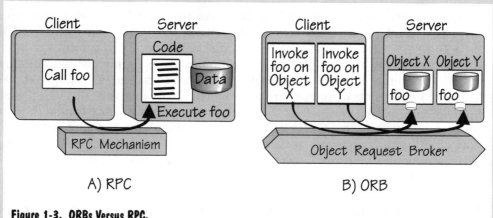

Figure 1-3. ORBs Versus RPC.

ORB method invocations have "scalpel-like" precision. The call gets to a specific object that controls specific data, and then implements the function in its own class-specific way. In contrast, RPC calls have no specificity—all the functions with the same name get implemented the same way. There's no differentiated service here. ❑

The Anatomy of a CORBA 2.0 ORB

A CORBA 2.0 *Object Request Broker (ORB)* is the middleware that establishes the client/server relationship between objects. Using an ORB, a client object can

transparently invoke a method on a server object, that can be on the same machine or across a network. The ORB intercepts the call and is responsible for finding an object that can implement the request, pass it the parameters, invoke its method, and return the results. The client does not have to be aware of where the object is located, its programming language, its operating system, or any other system aspects that are not part of an object's interface. It is very important to note that the client/server roles are only used to coordinate the interactions between two objects. Objects on the ORB can act as either client or server, depending on the occasion.

Figure 1-4 shows the client and server sides of a CORBA ORB. The light areas are new to CORBA 2.0. Even though there are many boxes, it's not as complicated as it appears to be. The key is to understand that CORBA, like SQL, provides both static and dynamic interfaces to its services. This happened because the OMG received two strong submissions to its original ORB *Request For Proposal (RFP)*: one from HyperDesk and Digital based on a dynamic API, and one from Sun and HP based on static APIs. The OMG told the two groups to come back with a single RFP that combined both features. The result was CORBA. The "Common" in CORBA stands for this two-API proposal, which makes a lot of sense because it gives us both static and dynamic APIs.

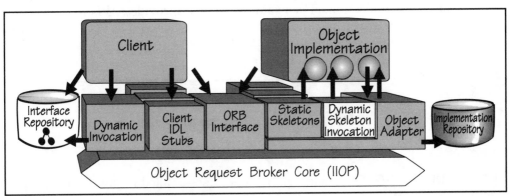

Figure 1-4. The Structure of a CORBA 2.0 ORB.

Let's first go over what CORBA does on the client side:

■ **The Client IDL Stubs** provide the static interfaces to object services. These precompiled stubs define how clients invoke corresponding services on the servers. From a client's perspective, the stub acts like a local call—it is a local *proxy* for a remote server object. The services are defined using IDL, and both client and server stubs are generated by the IDL compiler. A client must have an IDL stub for each interface it uses on the server. The stub includes code to perform *marshaling*. This means that it encodes and decodes the operation and its parameters into flattened message formats that it can send to the server.

It also includes header files that enable you to invoke the method on the server from a higher-level language like C, C++, Java, or Smalltalk without worrying about the underlying protocols or issues such as data marshaling. You simply invoke a language method from within your program to obtain a remote service.

- **The Dynamic Invocation Interface (DII)** lets you discover methods to be invoked at run time. CORBA defines standard APIs for looking up the metadata that defines the server interface, generating the parameters, issuing the remote call, and getting back the results.

- **The Interface Repository APIs** allow you to obtain and modify the descriptions of all the registered component interfaces, the methods they support, and the parameters they require. CORBA calls these descriptions *method signatures*. The *Interface Repository* is a run-time distributed database that contains machine-readable versions of the IDL-defined interfaces. Think of it as a dynamic metadata repository for ORBs. The APIs allow components to dynamically access, store, and update metadata information. This pervasive use of metadata allows every component that lives on the ORB to have self-describing interfaces. The ORB itself is a self-describing bus (see the next Briefing box).

- **The ORB Interface** consists of a few APIs to local services that may be of interest to an application. For example, CORBA provides APIs to convert an object reference to a string, and vice versa. These calls can be very useful if you need to store and communicate object references.

FYI

CORBA 2.0 Global Repository IDs

Briefing

With CORBA 2.0, ORBs provide global identifiers—called *Repository IDs*—to uniquely and globally identify a component and its interface across multivendor ORBs and repositories. The Repository IDs are system-generated, unique strings that are used to maintain consistency in the naming conventions used across repositories—no name collisions are allowed. Repository IDs are generated via *pragmas* in IDL. The pragma specifies whether to generate them via DCE *Universal Unique Identifiers (UUIDs)* or via a user-supplied, unique prefix appended to IDL-scoped names. The Repository ID itself is a string consisting of a three-level name hierarchy. ❑

The support for both static and dynamic client/server invocations—as well as the Interface Repository—gives CORBA a leg up over competing middleware. Static invocations are easier to program, faster, and self-documenting. Dynamic invocations provide maximum flexibility, but they are difficult to program; they are very useful for tools that discover services at run time.

The server side cannot tell the difference between a static or dynamic invocation; they both have the same message semantics. In both cases, the ORB locates a server object adapter, transmits the parameters, and transfers control to the object implementation through the server IDL stub (or skeleton). Here's what CORBA elements do on the server side of Figure 1-4:

■ The **Server IDL Stubs** (OMG calls them *skeletons*) provide static interfaces to each service exported by the server. These stubs, like the ones on the client, are created using an IDL compiler.

■ The **Dynamic Skeleton Interface (DSI)**—introduced in CORBA 2.0—provides a run-time binding mechanism for servers that need to handle incoming method calls for components that do not have IDL-based compiled skeletons (or stubs). The Dynamic Skeleton looks at parameter values in an incoming message to figure out who it's for—that is, the target object and method. In contrast, normal compiled skeletons are defined for a particular object class and expect a method implementation for each IDL-defined method. Dynamic Skeletons are very useful for implementing generic bridges between ORBs. They can also be used by interpreters and scripting languages to dynamically generate object implementations. The DSI is the server equivalent of a DII. It can receive either static or dynamic client invocations.

■ The **Object Adapter** sits on top of the ORB's core communication services and accepts requests for service on behalf of the server's objects. It provides the run-time environment for instantiating server objects, passing requests to them, and assigning them object IDs—CORBA calls the IDs *object references*. The Object Adapter also registers the classes it supports and their run-time instances (i.e., objects) with the *Implementation Repository*. CORBA 2.0 specifies that each ORB must support a standard adapter called the *Basic Object Adapter (BOA)*. Servers may support more than one object adapter. CORBA 3.0 introduces a portable version of BOA called the *Portable Object Adapter (POA)*.

■ The **Implementation Repository** provides a run-time repository of information about the classes a server supports, the objects that are instantiated, and their IDs. It also serves as a common place to store additional information associated with the implementation of ORBs. Examples include trace information, audit trails, security, and other administrative data.

■ The **ORB Interface** consists of a few APIs to local services that are identical to those provided on the client side.

This concludes our panoramic overview of the ORB components and their interfaces.

CORBA 2.0: THE INTERGALACTIC ORB

CORBA 1.1 was only concerned with creating portable object applications; the implementation of the ORB core was left as an "exercise for the vendors." The result was some level of component portability, but not interoperability. CORBA 2.0 added interoperability by specifying a mandatory *Internet Inter-ORB Protocol (IIOP)*. The IIOP is basically TCP/IP with some CORBA-defined message exchanges that serve as a common backbone protocol. Every ORB that calls itself CORBA-compliant must either implement IIOP natively or provide a *half-bridge* to it. Note that it's called a half-bridge because IIOP is the "standard" CORBA backbone. So any proprietary ORB can connect with the universe of ORBs by translating requests to and from the IIOP backbone.

In addition to IIOP, CORBA supports *Environment-Specific Inter-ORB Protocols (ESIOPs)* for "out-of-the-box" interoperation over specific networks. CORBA 2.0 specifies DCE as the first of many optional ESIOPs (pronounced "E-SOPs"). The DCE ESIOP provides a robust environment for mission-critical ORBs (see the next Briefing box).

You can use inter-ORB bridges and IIOPs to create very flexible topologies via federations of ORBs. Figure 1-5 shows an IIOP backbone with various proprietary ORBs feeding into it via half-bridges. Note the presence of the DCE ESIOP. You can segment ORBs into domains based on administrative needs, vendor ORB implementations, network protocols, traffic loads, types of service, and security concerns. Policies on either side of the fence may conflict, so you can create firewalls around

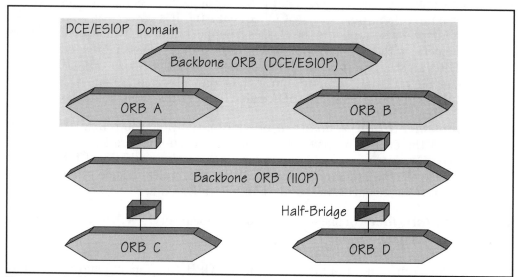

Figure 1-5. An Intergalactic Federation of Multivendor ORBs.

the backbone ORB via half-bridges. CORBA 2.0 promotes diversity and gives you total mix-and-match flexibility, as long as you use IIOP for your global backbone.

CORBA 2.0: The Inter-ORB Architecture

Briefing

The choice of ORB interoperability solutions does not impact application software. Interoperability is an issue between ORB vendors, not between vendors and users. Few, if any, developers will ever be involved in programming with GIOPs and ESIOPs.

> — Tom Mowbray et al., Authors
> The Essential CORBA
> (Wiley, 1995)

Even though few application developers need to worry about how ORBs interoperate, it is interesting to understand the mechanics. So despite what Mowbray says, we'll dive into CORBA 2.0 interoperability. Figure 1-6 shows the elements of the CORBA 2.0 inter-ORB architecture. Here's a description of what each of these elements provides:

■ The ***General Inter-ORB Protocol (GIOP)*** specifies a set of message formats and common data representations for communications between ORBs. The GIOP was specifically built for ORB-to-ORB interactions. It is designed to work directly over any connection-oriented transport protocol. GIOP defines seven message formats that cover all the ORB request/reply semantics. No format negotiations are needed. In most cases, clients send a request to objects immediately after they open a connection. The *Common Data Representation (CDR)* maps data types defined in OMG IDL into a flat, networked message representation. The CDR also takes care of inter-platform issues such as byte ordering (no byte swapping is needed) and memory alignments.

■ The ***Internet Inter-ORB Protocol (IIOP)*** specifies how GIOP messages are exchanged over a TCP/IP network. The IIOP makes it possible to use the Internet itself as backbone ORB through which other ORBs can bridge. It was designed to be simple and provide "out-of-the-box" interoperation for TCP/IP based ORBs. The GIOP may eventually be mapped to different transports. To be CORBA 2.0 compatible, an ORB must support GIOP over TCP/IP (or connect to it via a half-bridge). Note that both the IIOP and DCE/ESIOP have built-in mechanisms for implicitly transmitting context data that is associated with the transaction or security services. The ORB takes care of passing these requests without your application's involvement. Better

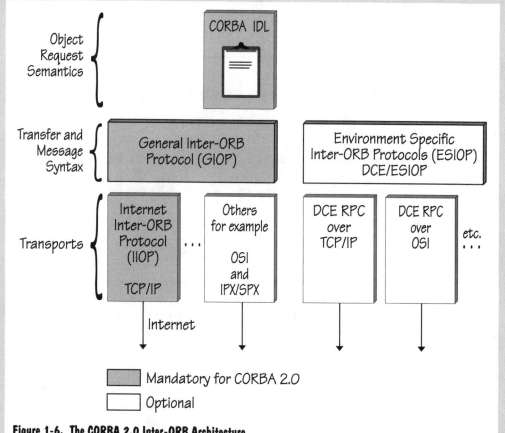

Figure 1-6. The CORBA 2.0 Inter-ORB Architecture.

yet, this information can also be passed across heterogeneous CORBA ORBs via bridges. The CORBA 2.0 standard does a good job specifying the location of this context data in an ORB-generated message.

■ The **_Environment-Specific Inter-ORB Protocols (ESIOPs)_** are used for "out-of-the-box" interoperation over specific networks. CORBA 2.0 specifies DCE as the first of many optional ESIOPs. Like GIOP, DCE/ESIOP supports IORs using a DCE tagged profile (we explain IORs later in this box). The DCE/ESIOP uses the GIOP CDR to represent OMG IDL data types over the DCE RPC. This means that DCE IDL is not required. Instead, OMG IDL and CDR types are mapped directly into DCE's native _Network Data Representation (NDR)_. The DCE ESIOP currently provides a robust environment for mission-critical ORBs. It includes advanced features such as Kerberos security, cell and global directories, distributed time, and authenticated RPC. DCE also lets you transmit large amounts of data efficiently, and it supports multiple underlying transport protocols, including TCP/IP. Finally, with DCE

> you can use both connection and connectionless protocols for your ORB communications.
>
> GIOP also defines a format for *Interoperable Object References (IORs)*. An ORB must create an IOR (from an object reference) whenever an object reference is passed across ORBs. IORs associate a collection of *tagged profiles* with object references. The profiles describe the same object, but they each describe how to contact the object using a particular ORB's mechanism. More precisely, a profile provides self-describing data that identifies the ORB domain to which a reference is associated and the protocols it supports. ❑

CORBAservices

CORBAservices are collections of system-level services packaged with IDL-specified interfaces. You can think of object services as augmenting and complementing the functionality of the ORB. You use them to create a component, name it, and introduce it into the environment. OMG has published standards for fifteen object services:

■ The **Life Cycle Service** defines operations for creating, copying, moving, and deleting components on the bus.

■ The **Persistence Service** provides a single interface for storing components persistently on a variety of storage servers—including Object Databases (ODBMSs), Relational Databases (RDBMSs), and simple files.

■ The **Naming Service** allows components on the bus to locate other components by name; it also supports federated naming contexts. The service also allows objects to be bound to existing network directories or naming contexts—including ISO's *X.500*, OSF's *DCE*, Sun's *NIS+*, Novell's *NDS*, and the Internet's *LDAP.*

■ The **Event Service** allows components on the bus to dynamically register or unregister their interest in specific events. The service defines a well-known object called an *event channel* that collects and distributes events among components that know nothing of each other.

■ The **Concurrency Control Service** provides a lock manager that can obtain locks on behalf of either transactions or threads.

■ The **Transaction Service** provides two-phase commit coordination among recoverable components using either flat or nested transactions.

- The ***Relationship Service*** provides a way to create dynamic associations (or links) between components that know nothing of each other. It also provides mechanisms for traversing the links that group these components. You can use the service to enforce referential integrity constraints, track containment relationships, and for any type of linkage among components.

- The ***Externalization Service*** provides a standard way for getting data into and out of a component using a stream-like mechanism.

- The ***Query Service*** provides query operations for objects. It's a superset of SQL. It is based on the upcoming SQL3 specification and the Object Database Management Group's (ODMG) *Object Query Language (OQL)*.

- The ***Licensing Service*** provides operations for metering the use of components to ensure fair compensation for their use. The service supports any model of usage control at any point in a component's life cycle. It supports charging per session, per node, per instance creation, and per site.

- The ***Properties Service*** provides operations that let you associate named values (or properties) with any component. Using this service, you can dynamically associate properties with a component's state—for example, a title or a date.

- The ***Time Service*** provides interfaces for synchronizing time in a distributed object environment. It also provides operations for defining and managing time-triggered events.

- The ***Security Service*** provides a complete framework for distributed object security. It supports authentication, access control lists, confidentiality, and non-repudiation. It also manages the delegation of credentials between objects.

- The ***Trader Service*** provides a "Yellow Pages" for objects; it allows objects to publicize their services and bid for jobs.

- The ***Collection Service*** provides CORBA interfaces to generically create and manipulate the most common collections.

All these services enrich a distributed component's behavior and provide the robust environment in which it can safely live and play.

Figure 1-7 shows the *Request For Proposal (RFP)* schedules that OMG is using to develop the object service specifications. OMG RFPs are requests for a technology. They result in responses from members on how to implement a particular standard. Members must base their responses on existing products or products that are in development (some proof of concept is needed). Usually an RFP is met by merging the responses obtained from several organizations. From the time the OMG issues an RFP, it takes about 12 to 16 months to obtain a working standard. As you can see, the OMG has almost completed the work on its object services and ORB specifications.[1] The action has now shifted to CORBA/JavaBeans, CORBA domains, and Business Objects. In addition, OMG is getting ready to release CORBA 3.0 (more on this later in the chapter).

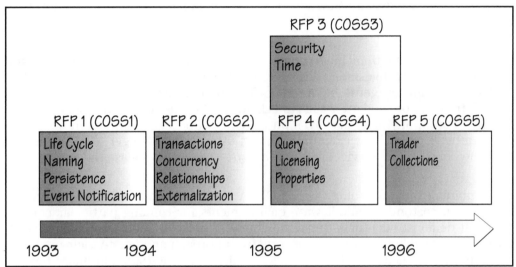

Figure 1-7. The OMG Road Map for Delivering Object Services.

Object Services: Build-to-Order Middleware

CORBA object services provide a unique approach for creating *build-to-order* middleware. It's unlike anything classical client/server systems provide today. With CORBA, component providers can develop their objects without any concern for system services. Then, depending on what the customer's needs are, the developer (or system integrator) can mix the original component with any combination of CORBA services to create the needed function. They do this by subclassing the original class, and then mixing it with the required object service classes via multiple inheritance. For example, you may develop a component called "car" and create a concurrent, persistent, and transactional version of car by multiply inheriting from the corresponding services.

In addition, object factories can use these services to compose a class at run time based on a client's request. You can create made-to-order classes by multiply

---

[1] The one exception is the *Persistence Object Service (POS)*. In early 1997, OMG issued an RFP for a POS2. In November 1997, it received a joint submission that is based on an automatic persistence model. It is similar to the model used in ODBMSs and Object-to-Relational mappers.

inheriting from existing object services. For example, the factory can take an ordinary component such as a "car" and make it transactional, lockable, and secure by multiply inheriting from existing object service classes. This approach is the ultimate form of made-to-order middleware. The beauty is that the original component provider may have known nothing about transactions, security, or locking. These services are dynamically added to the component at factory creation time based on the client's requirements.

If you don't like multiple inheritance, some ORB implementations let you add methods "on-the-fly" to existing classes. In particular, you can add *before* and *after* callbacks that are triggered before and after any ordinary method executes. You can use these before and after calls to call any of the existing CORBA services—or, for that matter, anything that lives on an ORB. You can even attach scripts to before/after triggers. For example, you can use a *before* trigger to obtain a lock from the concurrency service; you use the *after* trigger to release the lock.

By combining this technology with CORBA services, you will be able to create last-minute, customized middleware environments for running particular components. It demonstrates the ultimate flexibility of objects. Most component developers will probably take a more conservative approach and create their mixins at compile time or via a tool at build time. In either case, it's still a lot more flexible than anything you can do with today's client/server middleware.

CORBAfacilities

CORBAfacilities are collections of IDL-defined frameworks that provide services of direct use to application objects. Think of them as the next step up in the semantic hierarchy. The two categories of common facilities—*horizontal* and *vertical*—define rules of engagement that business components need to effectively collaborate.

The Common Facilities that are currently under construction include mobile agents, data interchange, workflow, firewalls, business object frameworks, and internationalization. Like the highway system, Common Facilities are an unending project. The work will continue until CORBA defines IDL interfaces for every distributed service we know of today, as well as ones that are yet to be invented. When this happens, CORBA will provide IDL-interfaces for virtually every networked service (many will be IDL-ized versions of existing middleware).[2]

---

[2] The Common Facilities work is now being done by the *ORB Services Task Force*; it seems they've moved up the food chain. Some of this work is also being done by the *Business Object Domain Task Force*. Yes, it's hard to keep up with OMG's reorganizations.

CORBA BUSINESS OBJECTS

Business objects provide a natural way for describing application-independent concepts such as customer, order, competitor, money, payment, car, and patient. They encourage a view of software that transcends tools, applications, databases, and other system concepts. The ultimate promise of object technology and components is to provide these medium-grained components that behave more like the real world does. Of course, somebody must first define the rules of engagement for these components to play, which is where the OMG comes into the picture.

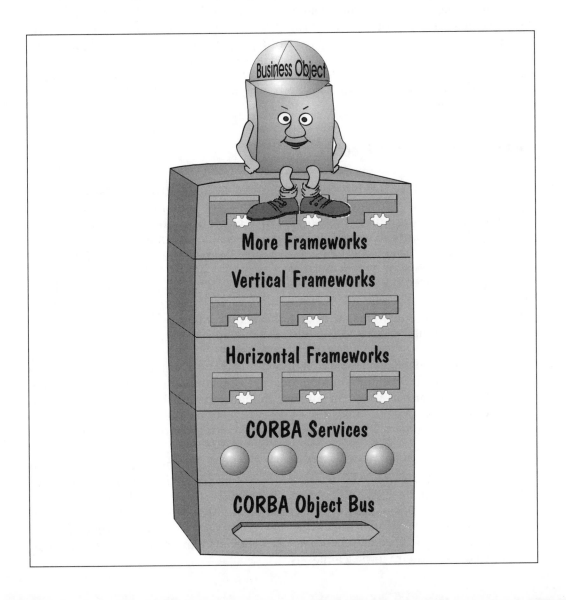

According to OMG's *Business Object Task Force*, a business object is an application-level component you can use in unpredictable combinations. A business object is, by definition, independent of any single application. Post-monolithic applications will consist of suites of business objects—the application simply provides the environment to execute these business objects. In other words, a business object is a component that represents a "recognizable" everyday life entity. In contrast, system-level objects represent entities that make sense only to information systems and programmers—they're not something an end user recognizes.

In a high-rise building, everyone's ceiling is someone else's floor until you get to the penthouse. Then the sky is your ceiling. You may think of the business object as the penthouse of components. According to the OMG definition, these top-level objects are recognizable to the end user of a system. The size of the object maps to "business" things like cars or tax forms. The word business is used in a very loose sense. A business object is a self-contained *deliverable* that has a user interface, state, and knows how to cooperate with other separately developed business objects to perform a desired task.

Cooperating Business Objects

Business objects will be used to design systems that mimic the business processes they support. In the real world, business events are seldom isolated to a single business object. Instead, they typically involve clusters of objects. To mimic their real-world counterparts, business objects must be able to communicate with each other at a semantic level. You can capture and describe these object interactions using most of the popular design methodology tools—including Ivar Jacobson's *use cases*, Ian Graham's *task scripts*, Grady Booch's *interaction diagrams*, and Jim Rumbaugh's *event traces*. All these methodologies use some form of scenario diagrams to show who does what to whom and when. These scenarios can document the full impact of specific business events.

Business objects must have late and flexible binding—and well-defined interfaces—so that they can be implemented independently. A business object must be capable of recognizing events in its environment, changing its attributes, and interacting with other business objects. Like any CORBA object, a business object exposes its interfaces to its clients via IDL and communicates with other objects using the ORB.

Figure 1-8 shows a suite of four business objects that are part of a car reservation system: *customer, invoice, car,* and *car lot*. Note that *car lot* is a business object that contains other business objects—cars. Clearly, these four business objects have some agreed-upon semantics for communicating with each other to perform business transactions. Under the cover, they could use the CORBA *Object Transaction Service* to synchronize their actions. They also know how to share a single window to display their views seamlessly.

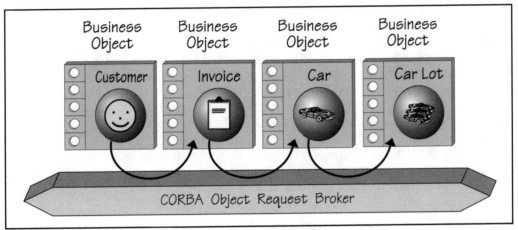

Figure 1-8. A Car Reservation System Using Cooperating Business Objects.

So how is this different from a traditional application? With very little work, you can reuse some of these business objects in another application context. For example, a car sales program could reuse most of these objects, especially if they were designed to work with more than one semantic suite. For example, the car, customer, and invoice objects could support multiple views to handle different business situations. In the extreme, the business objects could be specialized through inheritance to take into account the particularities of the car sales business. As you'll see in the next section, a business object is not a monolithic entity. It is factored internally into a set of cooperating objects that can react to different business situations. Business objects are highly flexible.

The Anatomy of a CORBA Business Object

A CORBA business object is a variation of the *Model/View/Controller (MVC)* paradigm. MVC is an object design pattern used to build interfaces in Smalltalk and in almost every GUI class library. MVC consists of three kinds of objects. The *model* represents the application object and its encapsulated data. The *view* represents the object visually on the screen. And the *controller* defines the way the user interface reacts to user input and GUI events.

In the CORBA model, a business object also consists of three kinds of objects (see Figure 1-9):

■ *Business objects* encapsulate the storage, metadata, concurrency, and business rules associated with an active business entity. They also define how the object reacts to changes in the views or model.

- **Business process objects** encapsulate the business logic at the enterprise level. In traditional MVC systems, the controller is in charge of the process. In the CORBA model, short-lived process functions are handled by the business object. Long-lived processes that involve other business objects are handled by the business process object—it's a specialization of the business object that handles long-lived processes and the environment at large. For example, it knows how to handle a workflow or long-lived transaction. The process object typically acts as the glue that unites the other objects. For example, it defines how the object reacts to a change in the environment. This type of change may be caused by the execution of a business transaction or by an incoming message from another business object. Note that some business objects may be entirely process-oriented and not associated with specific data or presentations.

- **Presentation objects** represent the object visually to the user. Each business object can have multiple presentations for multiple purposes. The presentations communicate directly with the business object to display data on the screen. And sometimes they communicate directly with the process object. The OMG also recognizes that there are non-visual interfaces to business objects.

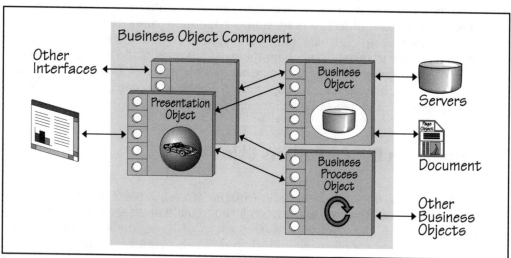

Figure 1-9. The Anatomy of a Business Object.

A typical business object component consists of a business object, one or more presentation objects, and a process object. Note that these entities act as a body. The underlying division of labor between the various objects is transparent to the users and clients of the business object. A business object also interacts with other servers and system-level objects but, again, in a totally encapsulated manner. The user only sees the aggregate business object. And clients of the object only deal with IDL-defined interfaces that are exposed by the aggregate business object.

The Anatomy of a Client/Server Business Object

Typically, a business object—like a car—may have different presentation objects spread across multiple clients. The business object and the process object may reside in one or more servers. The beauty of a CORBA-based architecture is that all the constituent objects have IDL-defined interfaces and can run on ORBs (see Figure 1-10). So it does not matter if the constituent objects run on the same machine or on different machines (ORBs provide local/remote transparency). As far as clients are concerned, they're still dealing with a single business object component, even though it may be factored into objects running in different machines. A well-designed business object builds on the CORBA services. For example, you can use the concurrency and transaction services to maintain the integrity of the business object's state. The ORB gives you these services for free, so you might as well use them.

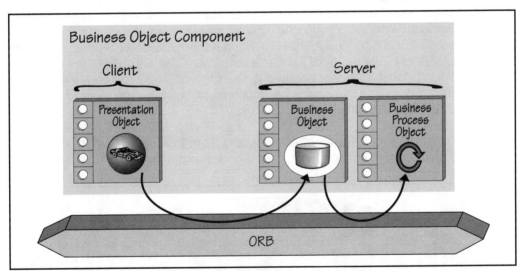

Figure 1-10. The Anatomy of a Client/Server Business Object.

CORBA Component Nirvana

Distributed objects are by definition components. The distributed object infrastructure is really a component infrastructure. Programmers can easily get things to collaborate by writing code for the two sides of the collaboration. The trick, however, is to get components that have no previous knowledge of each other to do the same. To get to this point, you need standards that set the rules of engagement for different component interaction boundaries. Together, these different interaction boundaries define a distributed component *infrastructure*.

At the most basic level, a component infrastructure provides an object bus—the *Object Request Broker (ORB)*—that lets components interoperate across address spaces, languages, operating systems, and networks. The bus also provides mechanisms that let components exchange metadata and discover each other. At the next level, the infrastructure augments the bus with add-on *system-level services* that help you create supersmart components. Examples of these services include licensing, security, version control, persistence, suite negotiation, semantic messaging, scripting, and transactions.

The ultimate goal is to let you create components that behave like *business objects*. These are components that model their real-world counterparts in some application-level domain. They typically perform specific business functions—for example, a customer, car, or hotel. You can group these business objects into visual suites that sit on a desktop but have underlying client/server webs.

So the ultimate Nirvana in the client/server components business are supersmart business object components that do more than just interoperate—they collaborate at the semantic level to get a job done. For example, roaming agents on a global network must be able to collaborate to conduct negotiations with their fellow agents. Agents are examples of business objects. The infrastructure provides application-level collaboration standards in the form of *application frameworks*. These frameworks enforce the rules of engagement between independent components and allow them to collaborate in suites.

Figure 1-11 shows the evolution of components from interoperability to collaboration. This evolution corresponds to the service boundaries of the component

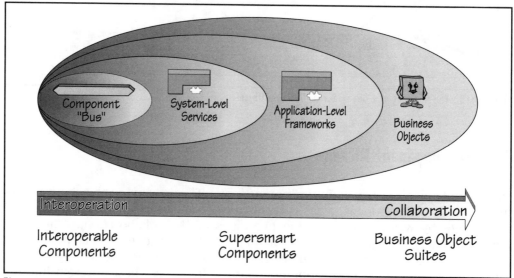

Figure 1-11. Component Evolution and Infrastructure Boundaries.

infrastructure. The component bus gives you simple interoperability, the system services give you supersmart components, and the application frameworks provide the application-level semantics for components to collaborate in suites.

3-TIER CLIENT/SERVER, OBJECT-STYLE

Business objects are ideal for creating scalable 3-tier client/server solutions because they are inherently decomposable. A business object is not a monolithic piece of code. Instead, it is more like a Lego of cooperating parts that you break apart and then reassemble along 3-tier client/server lines (see Figure 1-12). The first tier represents the visual aspects of the business object—one or more visual objects may each provide a different view. These visual objects typically live on the client. In the middle tier are server objects that represent the persistent data and the business logic functions. In the third tier are existing databases and legacy server applications. The partitioning of business objects is very dynamic. You should be able to decide where to host the different parts at run time.

Middle-tier server objects interact with their clients (the view objects) and implement the logic of the business object. They can extract their persistent state from multiple data sources—for example, SQL databases, HTML files, Lotus Notes, and TP Monitors. The server object provides an integrated model of the disparate data

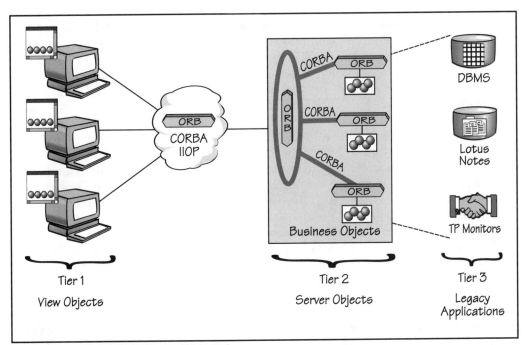

Figure 1-12. 3-Tiered Client/Server, Object-Style.

sources and back-end applications. Clients interact with business objects that naturally correspond to domain entities. They do not have to concern themselves with the hodgepodge of functions, stored procedures, and databases that live in the third tier. The business object hides all this nastiness.

The server object can cache the data it extracts in a local object database for fast subsequent access; or it may choose to directly update the third-tier data sources with fresh views from the object state. Clients must never directly interact with third-tier data sources. These sources must be totally encapsulated and abstracted by the middle-tier server objects. For example, you should be able to swap a database for another without impacting the clients.

The clients typically interact with the middle-tier server objects via an ORB. In addition, middle-tier objects can communicate with each other via a server ORB that they can use to balance loads, orchestrate distributed transactions, and exchange business events. This makes ORB-based business objects very scalable. Finally, server objects communicate with the third tier using traditional middleware. We will have a lot more to say about business objects throughout this book.

From Business Objects to CORBA Beans

As we go to press, OMG is still working on its *Business Object* RFP; it was issued in 1996. The idea behind this ambitious work is to bring CORBA to the masses. To do this, a *Business Object Framework (BOF)* must be able to hide from application programmers most of the CORBA system-level stuff (which is a lot of what this book covers). The programming masses should be able to write their intergalactic components using a minimal *surface area*—meaning the number of things they must understand to write a CORBA component.

So instead of turning everyone into a CORBA programmer, it may make more sense to embed CORBA within industry-specific frameworks that expose domain-level objects. To get there, OMG members are currently specifying domain frameworks for Manufacturing, Electronic Commerce, Transportation, Telecom, Healthcare, Insurance, Finance, and others. But, what do these frameworks build on? You may have guessed it: They build on another framework—the BOF. To be more exact, the BOF defines a generic CORBA component—or *business object*. It is the root object of all domain-specific business objects—they inherit all the CORBA functionality from this object (see Figure 1-13). In early 1997, the OMG received several strong submissions for the BOF. Together, they introduce the following new CORBA elements:

■ *A base CORBA business object.* This is an interoperable CORBA object that incorporates a variety of CORBA services such as Transactions, Life Cycle, Events, Externalization, and Licensing. It hides most of these services from the

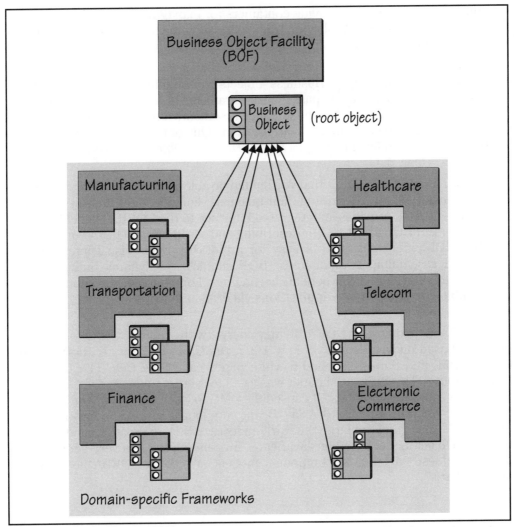

Figure 1-13. The Root Business Object.

application programmer. Domain-specific business objects are derived from this base object (or component). It's the root of all business objects.

- *A component definition language.* This is a superset of the CORBA IDL; it describes the semantics of a CORBA business object—including its properties, views, state, behavior, relationships, events, rules, roles, policies, triggers, persistence, initializers, constraints, and pre- and post-conditions.

- *The business object framework.* These are add-on services to support business objects. These services implement the IDL semantic extensions for components. They also provide containers for managing the Quality of Service of groups of objects. Finally, the framework should allow you to add objects to CORBA Collections and then query them via the Query Service.

- **Semantic messaging.** Business objects communicate via self-describing messages. The message is passed as a parameter in a regular CORBA method invocation. The data within the message is semantically tagged with names and values that are meaningful to an application. One of the BOF submissions calls these application-level messages *Semantic Data Objects (SDOs)*.

The central idea behind BOF is that you should be able to easily create and integrate CORBA components by describing their business semantics, not their system-level behavior. The BOF provides an integrated interface to the CORBA Object Services. You can think of BOF as a 4-GL for describing and assembling CORBA components. The BOF IDL extensions make it easy for a tool to provide visual interfaces for wiring and assembling components. BOF enables the dynamic integration of independently-developed components at run time. For example, you should be able to assemble components into applications via drag-and-drop.

So what happened to the BOF? It may merge with a new CORBA component initiative based on JavaBeans. In May 1997, the *Gang of Four (G4)*—Netscape, Oracle, IBM, and Sun—published a white paper called the *CORBA Component Imperatives*.[3] This influential paper was a call for action to marry the CORBA and JavaBeans component models. It caused the OMG to issue, one month later, an RFP to solicit technology for a CORBA/JavaBeans component model. So now it appears that the OMG is trying to merge the work on its two RFPs to create a single CORBA Business Object model based on JavaBeans. In general, this is a very good thing—the world doesn't need more component models. We cover CORBA JavaBeans in detail in Part 7.

CORBA 3.0: The Next Generation

CORBA seems to be perpetually under construction. It is now moving at bullet-train speeds just to keep up with the requirements of the *Object Web* (see the next chapter). CORBA must also maintain its headstart over DCOM—the ORB alternative from Microsoft. So there's no slowing down. In this section, we will look at the features that will most likely make it into CORBA 3.0 (due in 1998).[4]

---

[3] See OMG Document *orbos/97-05-25*.

[4] The OMG may deliver *CORBA 3.0* in two installments: a *CORBA 2.5* release that includes the ORB enhancements, and later a *CORBA 3.0* release that includes the component enhancements.

CORBA 3.0 is the umbrella name for the next-generation ORB technology. The ORB itself will be enhanced with several new features—including *Messaging*, *Multiple Interfaces*, *Objects-by-Value*, *IIOP Proxy* for firewall support, and *CORBA/DCOM Interoperability*. The server side of CORBA will be enhanced with a *Portable Object Adapter (POA)* that lets you write portable server applications. In addition, we expect to see a new CORBA *Persistence Service* that supports automatic persistence. Many of these features have been under construction for several years now.

At a higher level, CORBA will be augmented with a Common Facility for *Mobile Agents*, a JavaBeans-based *Business Object Framework*, and a *Workflow Facility*. At the domain level, we expect to see industry-specific frameworks for Manufacturing, Electronic Commerce, Transportation, Telecom, Healthcare, Finance, and the Internet.

Figure 1-14 shows how CORBA is evolving. Yes, it's a moving target. There's a ton of new stuff coming down the object pipe. Some ORB vendors (and book authors) are complaining that they can't keep up with the pace of innovation. But there's no stopping in this fast-moving industry. For vendors, it's either stay ahead of this fast-moving train or get out of this business.

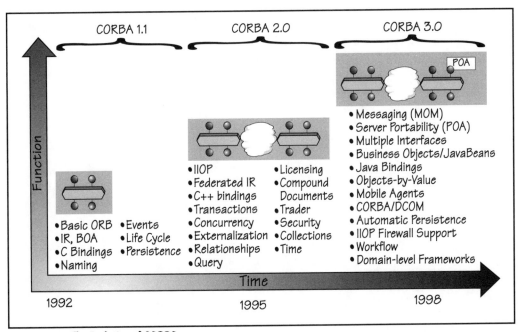

Figure 1-14. The Evolution of CORBA.

CONCLUSION

Distributed CORBA objects—modeled as business objects—are an excellent fit for 3-tier client/server architectures. They provide scalable and flexible solutions for intergalactic client/server environments and for the Internet and intranets. Business objects can be naturally decomposed and split across multiple tiers to meet an application's needs. They are self-describing and self-managing blobs of intelligence that you can move around and execute where it makes the most sense. Most importantly, business objects are evolutionary—they don't force you to throw away your existing server applications and start from scratch. You can encapsulate what you already have and incrementally add new intelligence, one component at a time. The next few chapters describe the Java mobile object infrastructure and how it complements CORBA.

Chapter 2

The Object Web: CORBA Meets Java

The next generation Web—in its Internet, intranet, and extranet incarnations—must be able to deal with the complex requirements of multistep business-to-business and consumer-to-business transactions. To do this, the Web must evolve into a highly-interactive medium that can run your line-of-business applications. The current HTTP/CGI paradigm is flawed and is running out of steam. The various CGI extensions—such as cookies, ISAPI, NSAPI, and ASP—are simply band-aids. To move to the next step, the Web needs distributed objects. We call this next wave of Internet innovation the *Object Web*.

The CORBA/Java story is really about the Object Web. Without the Object Web, CORBA and Java would just be esoteric technologies—mostly of interest to the enterprise client/server market and to object aficionados. As it turns out, CORBA and Java are having a shotgun wedding. Their marriage must be consummated for the higher good of the Object Web. The anxious parents—the ones with the shotguns—are a broad coalition of vendors that include almost everyone in the software industry but Microsoft. In this case, Microsoft is building its own Object Web—based on its ActiveX/DCOM component technology. This may explain the sense of urgency behind the CORBA/Java wedding. In this chapter, we'll first do the introductions and then tell you all about the CORBA/Java Object Web.

CORBA MEETS JAVA

CORBA is lot more than just an *Object Request Broker (ORB)*—it is also a very comprehensive distributed object platform. CORBA extends the reach of your Java applications across networks, languages, component boundaries, and operating systems. CORBA also supplements Java with a rich set of distributed services—for example, distributed introspection, dynamic discovery, transactions, relationships, security, and naming.

Of course, Java is much more than just another language with CORBA bindings. Java is a *mobile code system*; it is a portable operating system for running objects. Java provides a simpler and newer way to develop, manage, and deploy your client/server applications. You can access the latest version of an application by simply clicking on the mouse. You can distribute an application to millions of clients by putting it on a Web server. Distribution is immediate. And, you don't have to concern yourself with installation and updates. Java is also very good for servers. It lets you dynamically move services to where they're needed most.

So what does all this do for CORBA? Eventually, Java will allow your CORBA objects to run on everything from mainframes and network computers to cellular phones. Java simplifies code distribution in large CORBA systems—its bytecodes let you ship object behavior around, which opens up exciting new possibilities for CORBA agenting. We found Java to almost be the ideal language for writing our client and server CORBA objects. Its built-in multithreading, garbage collection, and error management make it easier to write robust networked objects.

The bottom line is that these two object infrastructures complement each other well. Java starts where CORBA leaves off. CORBA deals with network transparency, while Java deals with implementation transparency. CORBA provides the missing link between the Java portable application environment and the world of intergalactic objects.

Why the Shotguns?

So why isn't this marriage made in Heaven? Why were there so many shotguns at the wedding? Until recently, the problem was one of establishing clean divisions between the work of OMG and JavaSoft—both of these organizations believe they are in the business of defining object standards, which can sometimes lead to overlaps. For example, JavaSoft started to get into the ORB business when it defined its *Remote Method Invocation (RMI)* for Java-to-Java communications across Virtual Machines. It really stepped squarely on OMG's toes with that one— the 800-plus members of the OMG gave it the mission to develop distributed object standards. So, we're talking about really big toes.

The good news is that this turf war appears to be over. JavaSoft adopted CORBA as its distributed object model; it will run the RMI APIs on top of CORBA/IIOP with help from the OMG. This June 1997 announcement has done a lot to heal the rift between the CORBA and Java camps. Here's how JavaSoft plans to make CORBA part of the Java core:

- ***Include a CORBA/IIOP ORB as part of the JDK 1.2 core***. This is an all-Java ORB called *Java IDL*; it includes a development environment for generating CORBA stubs and skeletons from IDL. JDK 1.2 also includes an all-Java version of the CORBA *Naming Service*.

- ***Implement Java RMI on top of CORBA IIOP***. JavaSoft is also working with OMG on an RMI/IDL subset that allows RMI applications to talk to CORBA objects written in different languages, and vice versa.

- ***Deliver Enterprise JavaBeans***. Enterprise JavaBeans uses the CORBA Java/IDL subset for its distributed object model. In addition, Enterprise JavaBeans is built on top of the *Java Transaction Service (JTS)*—the Java implementation of the CORBA *Object Transaction Service (OTS)*.

These developments are very significant for both the low-end and the high-end of the CORBA/Java market. At the low-end, you will be able to get from your JDK provider (perhaps, even from Microsoft) a free CORBA/Java ORB as well as an IDL development environment. At the high-end, you will be able to get transactional JavaBeans. Transactions provide ACID protection for beans. They also serve as the glue that you can use to synchronize independently developed beans. As a result of all this, what started as a shotgun wedding may be turning into a love affair.

FYI

CORBA/Java ORBs

Briefing

What can you do with CORBA/Java today, given that JDK 1.1 doesn't include it? The answer is that you can do quite a lot. In the next chapter, we will go shopping for off-the-shelf CORBA/Java ORBs that you can use today to create very sophisticated 3-tier client/server applications with CORBA, Java, and JDBC. So you can start developing CORBA/Java solutions now. You don't have to wait for the next JDK. We will write our code using the new CORBA/Java bindings, which are supported by all the Java ORBs and will be in JDK 1.2. So your code should be quite portable. ❏

The Evolution of the Web

The Web was built on open, cross-platform, intergalactic client/server standards. To be intergalactic, the technology must run across multiple networks, OSs, languages, and computer platforms.

Figure 2-1 shows the progression of Web technologies. The Web first started out as a giant—and very trendy—unidirectional medium for publishing and broadcasting static electronic documents. The predominant HTTP client/server middleware was primarily designed to serve documents. Consequently, the Web became a giant URL-based file server. In late 1995, the Web evolved into a more interactive medium with the introduction of 3-tier client/server, CGI-style. The *Common Gateway Interface (CGI)* protocol lets Web servers route the content of your HTML forms to back-end server applications. CGI is now used to access every known server environment.

CGI: The Protocol That Won't Go Away

HTTP with CGI is a slow, cumbersome, and stateless protocol; it is not suitable for writing modern client/server applications. CGI is not a good match for object-oriented Java clients. In a sense, the Web server lives in the middle ages, while the

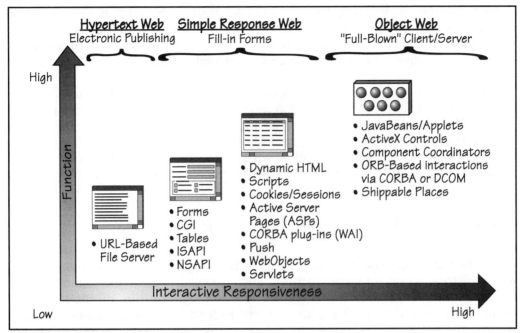

Figure 2-1. The Evolution of Web Technologies.

clients are postmodern. Web server vendors have gone through contortions to work around the limitations of HTTP/CGI. Their solutions are usually in the form of proprietary server frameworks and APIs. Examples of such frameworks include Netscape's *NSAPI*, Microsoft's *ISAPI*, NeXT/Apple's *WebObjects*, JavaSoft's *Servlets*, *WinCGI*, and *Fast CGI*.

To get around HTTP's statelessness, some of these frameworks may require that clients pass *cookies* (meaning server data held on the client) to identify their state. Others, like Microsoft *Active Server Pages (ASPs)*, extend cookies with session objects on the servers to represent their clients. These attempts are mostly proprietary and have serious flaws.

In addition, CGI is slow; it launches a new process to service each incoming client request. To get around this limitation, many of the vendor extensions provide memory-resident workarounds—such as in-process DLLs, server plug-ins, Java servlets, and even ORB-based objects. In general, the server side will do almost anything it can to keep the services in memory across invocations. As a result, they introduce another slew of non-standard—and sometimes platform-specific—extensions.

Recently, Microsoft introduced *Active Server Pages (ASPs)* that contain server-side scripts, which in turn invoke objects. You invoke these pages via HTTP using the infamous submit button. The server page typically executes a server-side script that knows how to instantiate and invoke objects. In addition, the client side now has enough intelligence to interact with the user without going to the server every time. You do this using either applets or scripts—for example, with *Dynamic HTML*, every element in an HTML page is a scriptable object.

The main problem with these approaches is that they require HTTP and the Web server to mediate between objects running on the client and objects running on the server. There is no way for a client object to directly invoke a server object. The HTTP form you submit is still the basic unit of client/server interaction. This clumsy workaround is not suitable for full-blown client/server applications that require highly interactive conversations between components. It also does not scale well.

CORBA/Java and the Web: Look Ma, No Cookies

To get the full benefits of object-to-object interactions, the Web must be augmented with a distributed object infrastructure. ORBs specialize in intercomponent communications across all kinds of boundaries—including client-to-client, client-to-server, server-to-client, and server-to-server. Java applets were the first step toward creating a client/server Object Web. Java is a necessary but not sufficient step toward creating the Object Web; Java needs to be complemented with a distributed object infrastructure, which is where CORBA comes into the picture.

The Object Web was officially born in June 1997 when Netscape shipped *Communicator* with a CORBA/Java ORB. On the server side, Netscape shipped both a CORBA/C++ and CORBA/Java ORB with every copy of the *Enterprise Server 3.0*. The intersection of Java and CORBA object technologies is the first step in the evolution of the Object Web.

Figure 2-2 shows how a typical Web-based client interacts with its server on the Object Web:

1. ***Web browser downloads HTML page***. In this case, the page includes references to embedded Java applets.

2. ***Web browser retrieves Java applet from HTTP server***. The HTTP server retrieves the applet and downloads it to the browser in the form of bytecodes.

3. ***Web browser loads applet***. The applet is first run through the Java run-time security gauntlet and then loaded into memory.

4. ***Applet invokes CORBA server objects***. The Java applet can include IDL-generated client stubs, which let it invoke objects on the ORB server. The session between the Java applet and the CORBA server objects will persist until either side decides to disconnect. Note that you will need an IIOP-savvy firewall to

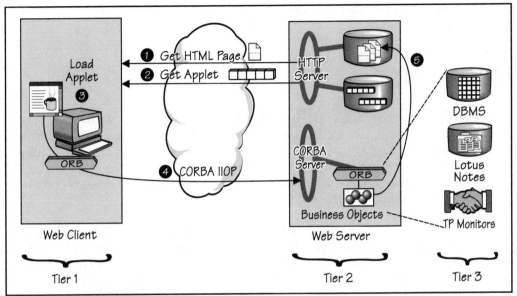

Figure 2-2. How HTTP, CORBA, and Java Play Together.

make this work. Today, you can use either Iona's *WonderWall* or Visigenic/Borland's *IIOP Gatekeeper*. By the time you read this, Netscape may have shipped its own IIOP firewall.

5. ***Dynamically generate the next page.*** Server objects can optionally generate the next HTML page for this client. This dynamic HTML generation on the server side is needed less frequently with the Object Web. In this new environment, a client application is typically packaged as a single HTML page with embedded components such as applets (or JavaBeans via the *Object* tag). CORBA then lets you interact with the server by clicking on any of the components embedded in the HTML layers without switching out of the page's context to obtain each response. So you don't have to dynamically generate an HTML page for each response.

As you will see in later chapters, the technology we just described performs surprisingly well today. However, the Object Web is still under construction. Some key pieces of technology must become available before we can declare it ready for mission-critical prime time. We explain some of these key pieces later in this chapter.

HOW CORBA/JAVA AUGMENT TODAY'S WEB

Augmenting the Web infrastructure with CORBA/Java provides two immediate benefits: 1) it gets rid of the CGI bottleneck on the server, and 2) it provides a scalable and robust server-to-server Web infrastructure. We briefly explain what this means.

Life Without CGI

CORBA/IIOP bypasses the CGI bottleneck and replaces it with ORB based object-to-object interactions. In the client/server interaction we just described, clients (applets or beans) directly invoke methods on a server. The client passes the parameters directly using precompiled stubs, or it generates them on-the-fly using CORBA's dynamic invocation services. In either case, the server receives the call directly via a precompiled skeleton.

With CORBA, you can invoke any IDL-defined method on the server. In addition, you can pass any typed parameter instead of just strings. This means there's very little client/server overhead, especially when compared with HTTP/CGI. With CGI, you must start a new instance of a program every time an applet invokes a method on a server; with CORBA, you don't.

CGI does not maintain state between client invocations; CORBA does. With CORBA, Java clients and applets can invoke a wide variety of IDL-defined operations on the server. In contrast, HTTP clients are restricted to a limited set of operations. Server-side applications are regular CORBA objects. Consequently, they are available on a permanent basis. There is no need to go through the overhead of spawning a CGI script for every invocation. As you will see in Part 4, we found CORBA pings to be over 100 times faster than their HTTP/CGI equivalents.

Scalable Servers

CORBA provides a scalable server-to-server infrastructure. Pools of server business objects can communicate using the CORBA ORB. These objects can run on multiple servers to provide load-balancing for incoming client requests. The ORB can dispatch the request to the first available object and add more objects as the demand increases. CORBA allows the server objects to act in unison using transaction boundaries and related CORBA services. In contrast, a CGI application is a bottleneck because it must respond to thousands of incoming requests; it has no way to distribute the load across multiple processes or processors.

What CORBA Brings to Java

Table 2-1 summarizes the differences between today's Java-to-CGI client/server approach and a solution based on CORBA's IIOP protocol. CORBA was designed

from the start to provide powerful 3-tier client/server solutions. In contrast, client/server interactions were wedged into HTTP and CGI; it's more of an afterthought. CORBA naturally extends Java's object model for distributed environments.

CORBA also makes it easier to split Java applets and beans into components that can be distributed along client/server lines. This means that the client side of the bean can remain small, which reduces the download time.

Without CORBA, Java on the Web is simply a competitor to Dynamic HTML; it's just a way to create a fancy page. With CORBA, the Java client becomes a rich object front-end to a mission-critical client/server system. It doesn't make much sense to use Dynamic HTML to invoke methods on server objects; it makes a lot more sense to use JavaBeans.

Table 2-1. Java Clients With CORBA IIOP Versus HTTP-CGI.

Feature	Java With CORBA ORB	Java With HTTP-CGI
State preservation across invocations	Yes	No
IDL and Interface Repository	Yes	No
Metadata support	Yes	No
Dynamic invocations	Yes	No
Transactions	Yes	No
Security	Yes	Yes
Rich object services	Yes	No
Callbacks	Yes	No
Server/server infrastructure	Yes	No
Server scalability	Yes	No
IDL-defined methods	Yes	No

This highly uneven comparison clearly demonstrates why the Java Web needs CORBA. However, CORBA is not the only distributed object model to extend the Web. The other serious contender is Microsoft's *DCOM*. We cover DCOM in Part 4.

What Java Brings to CORBA

In a sense, the Java infrastructure starts where CORBA ends. CORBA provides a distributed object infrastructure that lets applications extend their reach across networks, languages, component boundaries, and operating systems. Java provides a portable object infrastructure that works on every major operating system. CORBA deals with network transparency, while Java deals with implementation transparency. Here's a short list of what Java does for CORBA:

■ *Java allows CORBA to move intelligent behavior around.* Java's mobile code facilities let you dynamically move intelligence across the intergalactic CORBA infrastructure to where you need it most. This allows both clients and servers to dynamically gain intelligence. You can partition an application at run time to run on clients and servers without recompiling.

■ *Java complements the CORBA Life Cycle and Externalization services.* It makes it possible for a CORBA ORB to move around an object's behavior as well as its state.

■ *Java is making CORBA ubiquitous on the Web.* The Object Web may be the CORBA killer app. For example, Netscape is bundling Visigenic's *VisiBroker for Java*—a CORBA-compliant Java ORB—in all its browsers and servers. This makes CORBA IIOP the distributed object model for both the Internet and Java. The Netscape browser may be the most popular client application in existence, with over 40 million users.

■ *Java simplifies code distribution in large CORBA systems.* Java code can be deployed and managed centrally from the server. You update your code once on the server and then let the clients receive it when and where they need it. In theory, this should make it easier for you to manage large client/server intranet installations; it doesn't require that you manually update each individual desktop or laptop.

■ *Java complements CORBA's agenting infrastructure.* CORBA is defining an agenting framework for distributed objects. This framework will let *roaming objects* move from node to node based on rules you define. A roaming object typically carries its state, itinerary, and behavior in its travels. Java bytecodes are ideal for shipping behavior around. Java is becoming ubiquitous; consequently, the agents can safely assume that a Java Virtual Machine will be present on every node they visit.

■ *Java is a great language for writing CORBA objects.* Java is almost the ideal language for writing both client and server objects. Java's built-in multi-threading, garbage collection, and error management make it easier to write robust networked objects. Java's object model complements CORBA's; they both use the concept of interfaces to separate an object's definition from its implementation.

■ *Java complements CORBA's component services.* As you know by now, CORBA is adopting a JavaBeans-based component model. This will do wonders for the toolability of CORBA client/server applications. You will be able to use visual assembly tools to easily customize your CORBA beans. You will be able to create n-tier client/server applications by simply wiring together client and server beans. In addition, Enterprise JavaBeans complements CORBA by defining the interfaces between a managed server-side object and an *Object Transaction Monitor (OTM)*. CORBA augments the JavaBeans/EJB model with a distributed component infrastructure that includes support for transactions; it also provides cross-language support.

In summary, Java solves many thorny problems that have stood in the way of creating a truly portable distributed object market. Java lets you run portable applications that will one day be able to run on any machine in the galaxy. CORBA provides an intergalactic distributed object infrastructure over the Internet. Currently, most Java applications have been standalone demos, but the real value of Java is when you build portable clients to much larger transactional systems. This is where CORBA comes into the picture.

THE CORBA/JAVA OBJECT WEB

All new applications on the Object Web will be built and packaged as components. You can use CORBA IDL to wrapper existing code—written in almost any language—with object interfaces. For example, you can use CORBA to magically make a million lines of existing COBOL code look like an object (and eventually even masquerade it as a CORBA/JavaBean). Any IDL-described object can now play on the Object Web in a first-class manner. This magic works because CORBA—like Java—maintains a clean separation between the interface of an object and its implementation.

CORBA and JavaBeans

A *component* is a Lego-like piece of code that plays in ensembles with other components. Components require a thriving ecosystem to be commercially viable. The Object Web provides an ecosystem of intergalactic proportions. The major computing companies—including Sun, IBM/Lotus, Netscape, Oracle, Sybase, Novell, and BEA—are betting their shops on this killer app. They have chosen both CORBA IIOP and JavaBeans as the common way to provide a high level of plug-and-play between their products. For example, using CORBA/IIOP and JavaBeans, you should be able to mix-and-match groupware products from Netscape, Novell, and Lotus. In our industry, this is nothing short of a miracle.

The 3-Tier CORBA/Java Object Web

To understand what is going on, let's go over the 3-tier client/server architecture of this emerging Object Web (see Figure 2-3).

The first tier belongs to traditional Web browsers and the new Web-centric desktops. As opposed to today's static Web pages, the new content will have more the look-and-feel of real objects—for example, you'll be seeing places that contain people, things and other places. This very dynamic content is provided by ensembles of JavaBeans embedded in mobile containers such as HTML pages or JARs that contain *shippable places*. You will interact with these objects via drag-and-drop and other forms of direct manipulation. Client beans will be able to interact with other client beans in the container as well as with server beans. In addition, server beans will be able invoke methods on client beans using CORBA events and callbacks. Note that both IIOP and HTTP can run on the same networks. HTTP is used to download Web pages, JARs, and images; CORBA is used for Java client-to-server and server-to-client communications.

The second tier runs on any server that can service both HTTP and CORBA clients. This CORBA/HTTP combination is supported on almost every server OS platform—including Unixes, NT, OS/2, NetWare, MacOS, OS/400, MVS, and Tandem NonStop Kernel. CORBA objects—which could eventually be packaged as Enterprise JavaBeans—act as middle-tier application servers; they encapsulate the business logic. These objects interact with client JavaBeans via CORBA/IIOP. Less scalable applications can also call these objects via scripts that run in HTML server pages.

The CORBA objects on the server interact with each other using a CORBA ORB. They can also talk to existing server applications in the third tier using SQL/JDBC or any other form of middleware. You can even use the CORBA/IIOP server backbone as a general-purpose data bus. This is the technology Oracle is building for its data plug-ins. JDBC-on-IIOP data backbones are available today from both I-Kinetics and Borland/Visigenic.

The second tier must also provide a server-side component coordinator—also known as an *Object Transaction Monitor (OTM)*. These component coordinators are TP Monitors built on ORBs. Instead of managing remote procedures, they manage objects. The component coordinator prestarts pools of objects, distributes loads, provides fault tolerance, and coordinates multi-component transactions. Without these component coordinators, you cannot manage millions of server-side objects—a key requirement of the Object Web. Examples of CORBA-based compo-

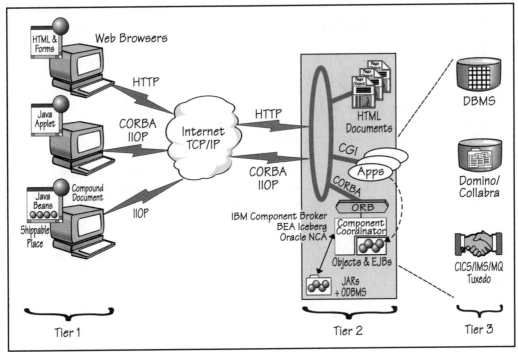

Figure 2-3. The 3-Tier CORBA/Java Object Web.

nent coordinators are IBM's *Component Broker* and BEA's *Tuxedo/Iceberg* (we provide a much longer list of CORBA OTM vendors in the Enterprise JavaBeans chapter).

But, what is a *server component*? In this case, it's a CORBA server object that also implements a minimum set of component services. Two good examples of this are *Enterprise JavaBeans* and Oracle *Cartridges*. They are CORBA objects augmented with component features such as declarative transactions and security (more on this in Part 7).

A server component must also be toolable. This means that it must provide introspective interfaces that let you assemble it using visual tools. For example, the object can provide an icon that represents it to the tool. When you click on the icon, the object will display the methods it supports, the events it emits, and properties such as its transactional and instance management capabilities.

So you will be able to wire object ensembles by connecting output events to input methods. This toolable server-side component technology will be provided by CORBA *Enterprise JavaBeans*. The CORBA/JavaBean technology is being integrated in visual builder tools from Borland, Symantec, Penumbra, ParcPlace, IBM/Taligent, Netscape, Lotus, and Sybase (we provide a much longer list in Part 7).

In a CORBA/Java Object Web, the second tier also acts as a store of component titles, HTML pages, and shippable places. These can be stored in *shippable compound files*—for example, Java JARs—that are managed by an ODBMS or DBMS. ODBMSs are better suited for the task. An ODBMS can treat a compound file as just another user-defined data type; an SQL database must support object extenders to provide the same kind of service. An ODBMS can transparently cache active compound document files in memory. So when a client requests a shippable place or component Web page, the ODBMS can service the request almost instantaneously by shipping a compound file that's in-memory. You will be able to get this technology on a CORBA/Java platform from vendors such as ODI and Gemstone.

The third tier is almost anything a CORBA object can access. This includes procedural TP Monitors, MOMs, DBMSs, ODBMSs, Lotus Notes, and e-mail. So the CORBA business objects replace CGI applications in the middle tier, which is good. Eventually, you will use CORBA/Java components that encapsulate most of the third-tier functions. This is an area where CORBA's inter-language communications capabilities will come in handy. Look at some of the I-Kinetics work to understand what you can do today with these back-end components.[1]

Meet the Players

A new CORBA/Java coalition is building around the CORBA/Java Object Web. The Web transforms CORBA/Java from a set of standards to a set of products that fulfill an intergalactic need. To use a shopping mall analogy, the anchor stores of the CORBA Object Web are Netscape, Oracle, JavaSoft, and IBM/Lotus (the press calls them the "Gang of Four"). This mall is also populated with hundreds of software vendors that provide the boutiques and specialty stores—including specialized ORBs, tools, components, and services. There should be enough critical mass to attract the shoppers with the dollars—ISVs, IT shops, and consumers of software. Let's take a quick look at what each of these players provides:

- **Netscape** is making CORBA ubiquitous on the client. It is bundling the *VisiBroker for Java* ORB with every browser. Netscape is also using CORBA for its server-to-server infrastructure. Potentially, Netscape can distribute over 40 million CORBA ORBs on the client and over a million CORBA ORBs on the server. CORBA also allows Netscape servers to play with other servers on the enterprise.

---

[1] See *http://www.i-kinetics.com/wp/cwvision/CWVision.htm.*

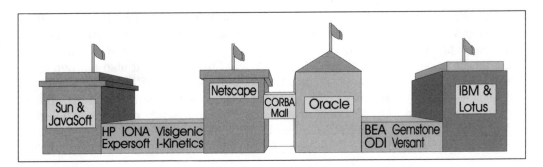

- **Oracle** has adopted CORBA/Java as the platform for its *Network Computing Architecture*. Oracle's entire software line—from the database engines to stored procedures, tools, and the Internet—will be built on a CORBA object bus. For example, the database engine will be componentized using CORBA. Third parties will be able to extend the database using CORBA components called *Cartridges*. Oracle is building most of the CORBA Services on top of the Borland/Visigenic VisiBroker ORB; it also has its own server-side IIOP ORB. The first Oracle product to ship with this technology is *Application Server 4.0*.

- **JavaSoft** is making CORBA a core Java technology. We explained what JavaSoft is doing in this area earlier in the chapter. Sun recently adopted VisiBroker as its ORB technology (more on this in the next chapter).

- **IBM/Lotus** is building its cross-platform network computing infrastructure on CORBA/Java. IBM is bundling Java VMs in all its OS platforms. The IBM *VisualAge* tool will target CORBA/Java objects on both clients and servers across all the IBM platforms. The IBM *Component Broker* is a scalable server-side component coordinator for managing middle-tier CORBA/Java objects. Finally, the next Lotus Notes—*Domino 5.0*—is being built on an IIOP foundation.

- **The boutiques** come in all shapes. They include long-standing CORBA players like HP, Iona, Visigenic/Borland, Tandem, Novell, I-Kinetics, and Expersoft. This camp also includes the ODBMS vendors—for example, ODI, GemStone, and Versant. In addition, TP Monitor vendors are now morphing ORBs with traditional TP Monitors—for example, BEA is building a scalable CORBA-based TP Monitor on top of Tuxedo. The boutiques also include tool vendors—such as Symantec, ParcPlace, Borland, Penumbra, and Sybase. The latest arrivals are Web server vendors that are moving to scalable application servers—examples include NetDynamics, Kiva/Netscape, and BlueStone. Finally, the boutiques include the major ISVs that gravitate in the Netscape, IBM, JavaSoft, BEA, Novell, and Oracle orbits. So there will be quite a crowd.

In summary, this new CORBA/Java coalition is building around a killer app called the Object Web. CORBA and Enterprise JavaBeans provide the architectural glue that connects the products on this Object Web. For example, ORBs running in Netscape browsers can talk to middle-tier Oracle Cartridges that also happen to be Enterprise JavaBeans. Object Transaction Monitors—from IBM, BEA, Netscape, and Oracle—can synchronize and coordinate these server-side business objects because they all use CORBA OTS. JavaBeans from thousands of vendors will play on both the client and server sides. The CORBA bus is the foundation technology that brings together all these disparate pieces of software from multiple vendors.

The CORBA/Java Object Web will eventually draw in thousands of smaller software developers that will create specialized components that service this huge market. This is our industry's first attempt to provide plug-and-play at the software product level, which is the ultimate open system dream.

In parallel, Microsoft is building its own rendition of the Object Web; it is based on DCOM and ActiveX. The *Microsoft Transaction Server (MTS)* is the DCOM component coordinator; it is Microsoft's secret weapon for winning the Object Web. Currently, the Microsoft Web appears to be a single-anchor mall with tons of boutiques.

The Next Client/Server Wave

The good news is that once the Object Web technology takes off, it will subsume all other forms of client/server computing—including TP Monitors, Database, and Groupware. Distributed objects and the Web can do it all, and better. Objects will help us break large monolithic applications into more manageable multivendor components that can live and coexist on intergalactic networks. They are also our only hope for managing and distributing the millions of software entities that will live on these intergalactic networks. The CORBA/Java Object Web is the killer application that will bring CORBA to the masses of intranet and Internet programmers.

In our previous books, we offered Figure 2-4 as our answer to the question: Which way client/server? The Ethernet era of client/server saw a file-centric application wave (the NetWare wave) followed by a database-centric wave (the Oracle wave); TP Monitors and Groupware generated minor ripples. The Object Web is the next big wave.

This new threshold marks the beginning of a transition from *Ethernet* client/server to *intergalactic* client/server that will result in the irrelevance of proximity. The center of gravity is shifting from single-server, 2-tier, LAN-based departmental client/server to a post-scarcity form of client/server. Here, every machine on the global "information highway" can be both a client and a server. Table 2-2 contrasts these two eras of client/server computing.

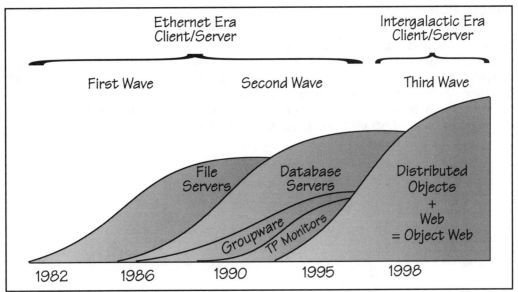

Figure 2-4. The Waves of Client/Server.

Table 2-2. Web Client/Server Versus Traditional Client/Server.

Application Characteristic	Intergalactic Era Client/Server	Ethernet Era Client/Server
Number of clients per application	Millions	Fewer than 100
Number of servers per application	100,000+	1 or 2
Geography	Global	Campus-based
Server-to-server interactions	Yes	No
Middleware	ORBs+OTMs on top of Internet	SQL and stored procedures
Client/server architecture	3-tier (or n-tier)	2-tier
Transactional updates	Pervasive	Very infrequent
Multimedia content	High	Low
Mobile agents	Yes	No
Client front-ends	OOUIs, WebTops, and shippable places	GUI
Timeframe	1998-2000	1985 till present

CONCLUSION

We're almost done painting the big picture. We hope to have convinced you that CORBA and Java were "made for each other." But enough of this abstract stuff. You're probably ready for some code that shows how all these pieces really work together. We hope to show you in this book that you can use CORBA and Java today to create some dynamite client/server applications. However, before we do this, we still need to pick a Java ORB, which is next chapter's topic.

Chapter 3

Meet the CORBA/Java ORBs

So what exactly is a CORBA/Java ORB? It's a CORBA IIOP ORB that's written entirely in Java for portability. The ORB must be able to generate Java language bindings from CORBA IDL. In addition, any code generated by the IDL compiler must be in pure Java; you should be able to download that code and run it on any machine hosting a Java run-time environment.

With a Java ORB, an ordinary Java applet can directly invoke methods on CORBA objects using the IIOP protocol over the Internet. The applet totally bypasses CGI and HTTP; the client and the server establish a direct communication link using the ORB. You should be able to load the CORBA-enabled applet into any commercial Java-enabled browser, and then execute it.

So where can you get one of these CORBA/Java ORBs? As we go to press, the "Big Three" CORBA/Java ORBs are: Iona's *OrbixWeb 3.0*, Borland/Visigenic's *VisiBroker for Java 3.1*, and JavaSoft's *Java IDL for JDK 1.2*. In the last year, the CORBA/Java ORBs from Visigenic and Iona have gone through at least two major revisions. Both companies now have Release 3 products on the market. It's a very competitive situation. In addition, JavaSoft is getting ready to ship its free *Java IDL* with JDK 1.2. It's hard to beat free. In this chapter, we go over the main features of these three ORBs. Then we pick an ORB for this book. Remember, we have code to write.

THE NEW CORBA JAVA/IDL MAPPING

From a programming perspective, a key difference between this book and its previous edition is that we now have a standard Java/IDL mapping. The good news is that the Big Three Java ORBs all comply with this standard. In some cases, they even implement elements of the standard before the OMG finalizes them—for example, POA/Java. In this section, we give you a quick overview of the new standard. Later, we explain how the new standard makes it so much easier to pick an ORB.

What These CORBA/Java Standards Cover

The CORBA/Java standards cover the following areas:

■ ***IDL-to-Java***. This is the standard that maps CORBA IDL to Java. The bulk of this standard is complete and already implemented in the Java ORBs—this is why they were going through so many revisions in the last year. The feature that is still under construction is the CORBA 3.0 *POA/Java*. In November 1997, OMG receive an initial submission for a POA/Java that is based on what the Big Three have already implemented in their products. It seems these ORB vendors are moving at Java speeds.

■ ***Java-to-IDL***. This is the CORBA/RMI convergence standard. It lets you specify your remote interfaces using Java RMI semantics instead of CORBA IDL. The compiler uses these semantics to automatically generate the CORBA IDL, stubs, and skeletons. The RMI/IDL subset allows RMI programs to be invoked by multilingual CORBA clients using IIOP; it also lets RMI programs call CORBA objects written in other languages. This standard is closely related to another CORBA standard called *Objects-by-Value*. It lets you pass the state of an object as a parameter of a remote method invocation. Currently, CORBA objects are only passed by reference. The original idea behind CORBA was that all objects could be remotely accessed. Consequently, you just pass the object reference instead of the object itself. Currently, Netscape/Visigenic's *Caffeine* implements all these features on top of *VisiBroker for Java*. However, their implementation is non-standard.

■ ***Enterprise JavaBeans***. The EJB specification includes a CORBA mapping. It is based on the RMI/IDL subset and CORBA transactions. It also maps JNDI to the CORBA Naming Service.

By the time you finish reading this book, these standards will become second nature. You will first use them in programs. We then formally introduce them to you in Parts 5 and 7.

The Just-in-Time CORBA/Java ORB

The new CORBA *IDL-to-Java* mapping is very complete. It eliminates most of the CORBA 2.0 portability potholes—on both the client and server. Consequently, your programs should be portable across any ORB that complies with this standard—in this case, the Big Three.

In addition, *IDL-to-Java* defines a standard interface for portable stubs and skeletons. It lets you have binary-compatible stubs and skeletons that run across vendor ORBs. This is a gift for developers. It means that we do not have to recompile our stubs and skeletons for different ORBs. The same stub bytecodes should run within any Java ORB that supports this interface. For example, you should be able to download and then run an OrbixWeb-generated stub into a Netscape browser that supports *VisiBroker for Java*. As a result, we do not have to generate ORB-specific Java stubs and skeletons.

There is even more good news. The specification defines a new property called *org.omg.CORBA.ORBClass*. This magic property lets a user dynamically swap CORBA/Java ORBs. For example, Visigenic/Borland claims that you can use this feature to replace, at run time, the JDK 1.2 *Java IDL* with *VisiBroker for Java*.

The last piece of good news is that CORBA/Java ORBs are 100% pure Java. Consequently, the ORB classes can be downloaded into the browser on demand just like any other set of Java classes. Most ORBs will only download the classes that a client needs so as not to incur unnecessary footprint penalties. These ORBs are packaged as JARs, which means that they take advantage of Java's archiving, compression, signing, and caching techniques.

So here's the bottom line. Netscape gives us a tremendous performance boost by baking *VisiBroker for Java* into every *Communicator* browser. If you can live with VisiBroker on both the client and the server, then you can't do any better. However, the reality of the Object Web is that you can't always depend on having a specific ORB baked inside a browser. So this is where the *IDL-to-Java* standard really helps. It lets us mix-and-match stubs across ORBs or even swap ORBs. Lastly, there are browsers that are totally ORB-less. In this case, you download the CORBA/Java ORB on-demand like any set of Java classes.

THE CORBA/JAVA ORBS

In this section, we cover the Big Three CORBA/Java ORBs: *VisiBroker for Java*, *OrbixWeb*, and *Java IDL*. We will tell you a little bit about their histories and then go over their current features.

JavaSoft's Java IDL

Java IDL has a colorful history (see the next Briefing Box). So what is *Java IDL*? It's a pure CORBA/Java ORB that provides: 1) IIOP client and server ORB functions, 2) a CORBA-compliant *Name Service*, and 3) a development environment—it includes an *IDL-to-Java* compiler that fully complies with the new CORBA Java/IDL mapping.

Java IDL is free, but it's also a minimalist CORBA ORB. On the positive side, it provides great online documentation and helps you get started with CORBA from within a JDK setting. So you can use *Java IDL* to write simple programs and learn all about CORBA. If you need to do serious CORBA/Java work, we suggest that you use the new swap option to replace the JDK's *Java IDL* with either *VisiBroker for Java* or *OrbixWeb*. Be warned that the material in this section is based on a beta version of *Java IDL*, so it may get better.

So what are these missing functions? As we go to press, *Java IDL* supports both static and dynamic CORBA invocations. However, it does not support a CORBA *Interface Repository*. This makes it almost useless for dynamic invocations. One workaround is to use some other vendor's Interface Repository. The second major shortcoming is that the Naming Service is volatile—you lose all the entries in your naming database every time the Name Server terminates. Obviously, this is not a good thing.

The third major shortcoming is the lack of CORBA add-on services—such as SSL-based CORBA security, firewall support, IIOP transaction propagation, dynamic servant activation, load-balancing, persistence, and automatic thread pooling. Both *VisiBroker* and *OrbixWeb* provide these services today. Finally, it's not clear how Java IDL will scale; it doesn't have the Version 3.0 maturity of its competitors.

Java IDL's Colorful History

Briefing

Sun—the creator of Java—was one of the six founding members of OMG. Consequently, Sun's client/server vision has always been "distributed objects everywhere." As you would expect, the integration of CORBA and Java is high on Sun's agenda. In Sun's view, you can use the Object Web for all client/server application development—including departments, intranets, and the Internet.

In September 1995, Sun announced *NEO*—a 3-tier client/server architecture that brings together Java, CORBA objects, and the Web. In January 1996, Sun first introduced CORBA IDL bindings for Java at the OMG meeting in San Diego; it also announced a Java ORB called *Joe*. In May 1996, JavaSoft renamed Joe *Java IDL* and announced that it is now part of *Java Enterprise*—a core Java framework. Java IDL will first ship with JDK 1.2 (it is freely downloadable now).

In December 1997, JavaSoft published the *Enterprise JavaBeans* specification based on the CORBA *Object Transaction Service (OTS)*. In January 1998, Sun dropped NEO in favor of *VisiBroker for Java* and *VisiBroker for C++*. JavaSoft now owns the *Java IDL* development effort; it appears that JavaSoft wants to fully control this ORB to fulfill its future enterprise vision. In any case, JavaSoft hasn't moved to *VisiBroker* yet (more on this in a later Soapbox). ❑

Iona's OrbixWeb 3.0

Iona is the leading provider of CORBA technology. Its C++ Orbix ORB now runs on over 20 operating systems—including 12 Unix variants, OS/2, NT, Windows 95, Macintosh System 7.5, OpenVMS, and MVS. Iona ORBs support both IIOP and the proprietary Orbix protocol. In July 1996, Iona released *OrbixWeb V1.0*—a client-side Java implementation of Iona's *Orbix* CORBA ORB. In late 1996, it shipped the server function with *OrbixWeb 2.0*. In December 1997, Iona shipped

OrbixWeb 3.0. This latest incarnation fully implements the new CORBA *IDL-to-Java* mapping.

OrbixWeb 3.0 is a fully-functional CORBA/Java ORB. The server supports thread-pooling and dynamic activation across Java VMs. The product provides SSL-based security as well as IIOP-proxy firewall support via Iona's *WonderWall*. Applets can call IIOP servers across firewalls, and servers can callback applets. Iona supports several CORBA services—including Naming, Trader, and Transactions. It also provides CORBA extensions for automatic object persistence.

Borland/Visigenic's VisiBroker for Java 3.1

Like *Java IDL*, *VisiBroker* also has a colorful history (see the next Briefing Box). In the first edition of this book, we used *VisiBroker for Java 1.2*. It was the first Java IIOP ORB to support both client and server functions; servers were also able to callback their clients. This early CORBA/Java ORB supported both static and dynamic invocations; it included a full CORBA *Interface Repository* written in Java. It also introduced a primitive version of the *IIOP Gatekeeper* firewall.

VisiBroker for Java comes with a fault-tolerant object-naming service called the *OSAgent*. Multiple OSAgents running in the same network locate each other and automatically partition the namespace among themselves. This lets you replicate and load-balance objects on different server machines. In the case of a crash, the ORB automatically re-routes the client calls to one of the replicas.

In March 1997, Visigenic released all-Java versions of the CORBA *Naming* and *Event* Services. In May, it shipped *VisiBroker 2.5*. This is an early release of *VisiBroker for Java 3.0*; it was released early to allow Netscape to embed it in *Communicator* and *Enterprise Server 3.0*.

VisiBroker 2.5 was the first release of VisiBroker to support the new CORBA *IDL-to-Java* mapping. It was also the first release that "officially" exposed *Caffeine*—the Netscape/Visigenic alternative to RMI. Caffeine is a Java-to-IIOP solution that lets you automatically generate CORBA stubs and skeletons using Java interfaces. Caffeine also lets you pass CORBA objects by value. In addition, it provides a URL-based name service for CORBA objects.

In September 1997, Visigenic finally shipped *VisiBroker for Java 3.0*. This release enhances the server by providing thread-pool and connection managers; it lets the ORB more dynamically manage system resources. The ORB allocates threads based on the incoming client requests. The 3.0 release also includes an add-on product called the *VisiBroker Developer SSL Pack for Java*; it supports SSL over IIOP. The product documentation also became world-class with this new release.

In November 1997, Visigenic shipped *VisiBroker for Java 3.1*. This minor update introduces elements of the POA/Java; it also repackages the ORB inside multiple JARs. Finally, the new *VisiBroker* is being supplemented with a set of graphical tools to help you monitor and manage the distributed object environment.

In December 1997, Visigenic announced the beta of the *Integrated Transaction Service (ITS)*—an OTS-based *Object Transaction Monitor (OTM)* for VisiBroker ORBs.

VisiBroker's Colorful History

Briefing

VisiBroker started life as PostModern's *Black Widow* ORB. It was the first CORBA/Java ORB to support both client and server Java objects. The ORB was written entirely in Java, which made it a downloadable ORBlet. In early 1996, PostModern was acquired by *Visigenic*—a leading vendor of database middleware. In July 1996, Visigenic changed the name of *Black Widow* to *VisiBroker for Java*; the C++ ORB is now called *VisiBroker for C++*. In November 1997, Visigenic was acquired by Borland.

VisiBroker has become the great equalizer of the CORBA industry; it's the closest thing to a ubiquitous ORB. Companies embedding the *VisiBroker* ORB into their products include Oracle, Hitachi, Netscape, Novell, SunSoft, NetDynamics, Novera, Sybase, Borland, Gemstone, Silicon Graphics, Hummingbird, Cincom, and Business Objects. *VisiBroker* is now baked into every Netscape browser, which makes it ubiquitous on clients. Borland may make *VisiBroker* even more ubiquitous by tightly incorporating it with its tools. This could open up CORBA to the programming masses in a big way. ❏

WHICH JAVA ORB?

As you can see, picking a CORBA/Java ORB can be a tough choice. Each of the Big Three ORBs have strong backers: *Java IDL* will be included with every copy of JDK 1.2; *VisiBroker* is included with every Netscape browser and server; and *OrbixWeb* is sold by Iona—the leading provider of ORBs to corporate IT shops.

Table 3-1 is the decision matrix we used to make our choice. We ended up picking *VisiBroker for Java 3.1*; it had the most stable *IDL-to-Java* mapping at the time we were writing this book. JavaSoft's *Java IDL* was not ready or scalable. *OrbixWeb 3.0* was still in beta.

Table 3-1. A Comparison of the CORBA/Java ORBs, Circa Late 1997

CORBA Feature	OrbixWeb 3.0	Java IDL	VisiBroker for Java 3.X
Static method invocations	Yes	Yes	Yes
Dynamic method invocations	Yes	Yes	Yes
Interface Repository	Yes	No	Yes
New IDL-to-Java Mapping	Yes	Yes	Yes
Server callbacks	Yes	Yes	Yes
Native Java over IIOP	Yes	Yes	Yes
Server-side Java	Yes	Yes	Yes
Dynamic Skeleton Invocation (DSI)	Yes	Yes	Yes
POA/Java	Yes	Yes	Yes
Tie	Yes	Yes	Yes
SSL-IIOP Security	Yes	No	Yes
Firewall support	Yes	No	Yes
Java-to-IIOP	No	No	Yes (Caffeine)
URL-based naming	No	No	Yes
CORBA-to-DCOM bridging	Yes	No	Yes
CORBA Naming Service	Yes	Yes (but volatile)	Yes
CORBA Event Service	Yes	No	Yes
CORBA Transactions	Yes	No	Yes
Ship date	December '97	June '98	September '97
Documentation	Very good	Very good	Excellent
Wide market support	Yes	Yes (via JDK 1.2)	Yes

Before you draw conclusions, you should consider this interesting angle. We picked *VisiBroker* because it gave us the most stable platform on which to write portable programs. By definition, these portable programs are secular and ORB-independent. With some luck, you should be able to run the programs in this book on any standards-compliant CORBA/Java ORB—including *VisiBroker 3.1*, *OrbixWeb 3.0*, and *Java IDL*. The beauty of the new CORBA/Java standard is that it gives you total freedom of choice. So the trick is to always write portable code. Then pick the *ORB du jour* that runs your code best.

Is JavaSoft Really Santa Claus?

Soapbox

We will use this Soapbox to answer the following question: Does Santa Claus really exist? If you read this chapter, you may have reached the conclusion that Santa is alive and well. JavaSoft's free CORBA/Java ORB (with JDK 1.2) is a wonderful gift to the CORBA community. JavaSoft also does a terrific job evangelizing its core APIs, which should further help popularize CORBA. Of course, as soon as these programmers become CORBA-savvy, they are very likely to use the new swap option to replace the JDK's *Java IDL* with either *VisiBroker for Java* or *OrbixWeb*. Some may even move to more scalable server-side CORBA ORBs like BEA's *Iceberg* or IBM's *Component Broker*.

So what does JavaSoft get from all this? We're in the middle of a Soapbox, which means we can indulge in some speculation (remember, we're just stating our opinion). We'll list some of JavaSoft's options and assign a probability to each (Gartner Group style):

- **JavaSoft goes into the middleware business (0.7)**. In this scenario, JavaSoft decides to stop being Santa and start selling software. There are two lucrative areas where JavaSoft can make some serious money: 1) *Embedded Java* (Java for TV sets, and so on) and 2) *Enterprise Java* (i.e., the server-side of the Object Web). In this second scenario, the CORBA/Java ORB becomes a key element of an Enterprise Java product offering—along with Enterprise JavaBeans, JNDI, JavaSpaces, and a few other things.

- **JavaSoft uses its ORB to do RMI over IIOP (0.6)**. The CORBA/Java ORB provides a great engine for doing RMI over IIOP. So JavaSoft continues to enhance it.

- **JavaSoft gives away the ORB to counter Microsoft (0.5)**. CORBA provides a layer of cross-platform distributed object glue that ties together the enterprise and the Object Web. In addition, CORBA is a foundation technology for *Enterprise JavaBeans*. JavaSoft understands this big picture and decides it must continue to give away its CORBA ORB. This strategy counters Microsoft's free version of DCOM.

■ *JavaSoft uses its ORB to negotiate a good deal (0.3).* In this scenario, JavaSoft wants out of the ORB business. It takes several hundred engineers to effectively compete ORB-for-ORB against Iona, Borland/Visigenic, BEA, or IBM. So JavaSoft wants out (just like SunSoft got out). However, it must first OEM a free CORBA/Java ORB that also does RMI. Of course, neither Visigenic nor Iona are in the business of giving away a free ORB. And neither company is particularly enamored with RMI. So the current ORB becomes a negotiating chip.

■ *JavaSoft is really Santa Claus (0.2).* In this scenario, JavaSoft (and Sun) get all their pleasure from giving away free software to programmers. So they continue to enhance their free ORB. It makes us happy; it makes them happy. Happiness is what life's all about.

Of course, we like the last scenario best. But the odds are not in its favor. ❑

CONCLUSION

Whew! We're glad this choice is behind us. The nice thing about the new CORBA/Java standard is that you'll always have more than one ORB to choose from. It's a very competitive market. In this case, Visigenic won by being slightly—about three months—ahead of the pack.

The good news is that we've now completed the big picture tour. Yes, it's time to jump into some code. If you feel this tour was not comprehensive enough, you may want to look at some of the references we list at the end of the book.

Part 2
Core CORBA/Java

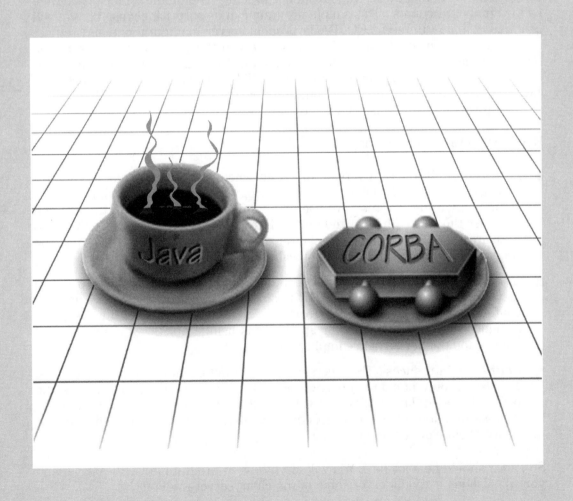

An Introduction to Part 2

In Part 2, we start our exploration of the CORBA/Java programming model by developing a small client/server example based on CORBA *static* invocations. Why static invocations? Because it's the bedrock of CORBA programming. The model should be very familiar to Java programmers; it lets you invoke methods on remote CORBA server objects just like you would on any ordinary Java object. Of course, before you can invoke methods on these server objects, you must first define them in CORBA IDL. So you will begin learning some IDL in Part 2, as well as how to develop CORBA clients and servers in Java. It's a mini crash-course in core CORBA/Java programming.

The plan for Part 2 is to develop a simple client/server Count program that invokes a single method on a server and gets back a response. The method increments a counter. As a result, we can use this program to measure the average performance of a CORBA Ping—in this case, it's the round-trip response time of a method invocation. We obtain the average response time by dividing the total elapsed time by the number of counts. This simple program can be surprisingly useful. We will use it to compare different CORBA/Java client/server configurations and remote method invocation techniques. In Part 3, we use the program to measure the response time of CORBA dynamic invocations; we also measure a POA-based Count. In Part 4, we will use it again to compare CORBA with its competitors—including Java RMI, Servlets, HTTP/CGI, DCOM, and Sockets. So we can get quite a bit of useful information from this simple program.

Here's what we will be covering in Part 2:

- **Chapter 4** introduces a version of Count where both clients and servers are Java applications. The client and server programs communicate using CORBA static method invocations. We use this configuration to measure the average response time for both local and remote interprocess communications. We also measure the effect of JIT compilation on performance. Finally, we use the program to demonstrate CORBA's local/remote transparency features.

- **Chapter 5** extends the Count client into a Java applet. The client applet and server still communicate using CORBA static method invocations. We use this configuration to measure the performance of applets as clients. If we're going to build our future client/server applications using applets, we might as well understand the performance implications.

- **Chapter 6** introduces a C++ version of the Count client and server programs. This is the only non-Java program in this book. We use it to compare the performance of Java ORBs and C++ ORBs. We also use this example to demonstrate how a C++ CORBA client can talk to a Java server and also how a Java client can talk to a C++ server.

So Part 2 should be a lot fun. You will learn how to program in CORBA/Java, and you will also get a good feel for some of the client/server tradeoffs.

Chapter 4

Your First CORBA Program

Let's dive right in and write our first client/server program using CORBA and Java. The server side is a simple CORBA object; it increments a counter and returns the current count whenever it receives a request from a client. The client communicates with the server by invoking methods across a CORBA ORB. In the next chapters, we create different versions of this client/server Count program to explain the principles of CORBA programming in Java. We'll use these examples to measure the time it takes for a client to invoke a request on a server and then get back a response. So we're measuring a round trip from the client to the server and back. It's very much like measuring the performance of a Ping.

In this chapter's incarnation of Count, the client and server communicate using CORBA's *static method invocations*. You will get a feel for the performance of interprocess communications—local and remote—using these static invocations. You will also get to see first-hand how well CORBA handles local/remote transparency. This chapter also serves as a crash course in CORBA development. By the time you complete this chapter, you'll know how to write the client and server sides of a CORBA program. And, you'll get some hands-on experience with CORBA IDL. Finally, you'll get your first glimpse of how objects and the ORB discover each other during initialization. It should be fun.

THE STATIC CORBA

This section gives you some background information on static versus dynamic programming with CORBA. We also go over the static compilation process. Before diving into *VisiBroker for Java*, let's go over the steps in the development process that are common to all CORBA ORBs. In the next few sections, you'll get some hands-on experience with this process using the VisiBroker ORB. In most cases, VisiBroker complies with CORBA to the letter. So we'll keep this section very brief.

CORBA Method Invocations: Static Versus Dynamic

Figure 4-1 shows the two types of client/server invocations that are supported by a CORBA ORB: static and dynamic. In both cases, the client performs a request by having access to an object reference (i.e., object ID) and invoking the method that performs the service (see the following Details box). The server can't tell the difference between static and dynamic invocations.

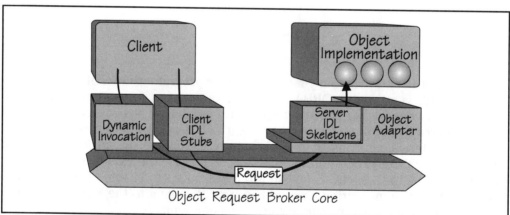

Figure 4-1. CORBA's Static and Dynamic Method Invocations.

Clients see the object interfaces through the perspective of a *language mapping*— or *binding*—that brings the ORB right up to the programmer's level. Client programs should be able to work without any source changes on any ORB that supports the language binding. They should be able to call any object instance that implements the interface. The implementation of the object, its object adapter, and the ORB used to access it is totally transparent to both static and dynamic clients.

The *static interface* is directly generated in the form of stubs by the IDL precompiler. It is perfect for programs that know at compile time the particulars of the operations they will need to invoke. The static stub interface is bound at compile time and provides the following advantages over the dynamic method invocation:

- *It is easier to program*—you call the remote method by simply invoking it by name and passing it the parameters. It's a very natural form of programming.

- *It provides more robust type checking*—the checking is enforced by the compiler at build time.

- *It performs well*—a single API call is issued to the stub, which takes it from there.

- *It is self-documenting*—you can tell what's going on by reading the code.

In contrast, the *dynamic* method invocation provides a more flexible environment. It allows you to add new classes to the system without requiring changes in the client code. It's very useful for tools that discover what services are provided at run time. You can write some very generic code with dynamic APIs. However, most applications don't require this level of flexibility and are better off with static stub implementations.

What's an Object Reference?

Details

An object reference provides the information you need to uniquely specify an object within a distributed ORB system—it's a unique name or identifier. The implementation of object references is not defined by the CORBA specification, which means it is implementation specific. Two CORBA-compliant ORBs may have different representations for object references. However, CORBA 2.0 now defines *Interoperable Object References (IOR)* that vendors must use to pass object references across heterogeneous ORBs. So how do you maintain client/server program portability in such an environment? You maintain it by using language bindings to insulate your programs from the actual representation of the object references (see Figure 4-2).

All ORBs must provide the same language binding to an object reference (usually referred to as an *object*) for a particular programming language. This means that the language provides the portability and allows you to reference objects that run on different ORBs from within your programs. What happens if your program is accessing object references on two different ORBs? According to CORBA, your programs should still work fine; it is up to the vendors to resolve—via IIOP IORs—any object reference conflicts that may be encountered by the client code.

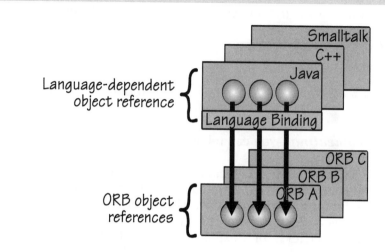

Language-dependent object reference {

Smalltalk

C++

Java

Language Binding

ORB C

ORB B

ORB A

ORB object references {

Figure 4-2. Language-independent Object References.

How do the client programs obtain object references? They usually receive them from a Naming Service or invocations on other objects to which they have references. You can convert an object reference to a string-name that you can store in files. The string-name can be preserved or communicated by different means, and then turned back into an object reference by the ORB that produced the string. CORBA defines two ORB interface functions—*object_to_string* and *string_to_object*—to help store, communicate, and retrieve object references. Client programs can use these two functions to obtain a string-name and convert it to an object reference, and vice versa.

We also expect the OMG to get into the business of allocating "well-known object references." The CORBA 2.0 Initialization specification already includes a few well-known objects. We cover ORB initialization in Part 5.

Finally, the ORB interface defines some operations that you can invoke on any object reference. These operations are directly implemented by the ORB on the object reference. This means that they're not passed to the object implementation. You can invoke the method *get_interface* on any object reference to obtain an Interface Repository object that provides type and metadata information for that object. You can invoke the method *get_implementation* on any object reference to obtain an *Implementation Repository* object that describes the implementation of that object. You'll see examples of how these methods are used later in this chapter and in Part 5. ❑

CORBA Static Method Invocations: From IDL to Interface Stubs

Figure 4-3 shows the steps you go through to create your server classes, provide interface stubs for them, store their definitions in the Interface Repository, instantiate the objects at run time, and record their presence with the Implementation Repository. Let's go through these steps one-by-one and see what's involved:

1. ***Define your server interfaces using the Interface Definition Language (IDL).*** The IDL is the means by which objects tell their potential clients what operations are available and how they should be invoked. The IDL definition language defines the types of objects, their attributes, the methods they export, and the method parameters.

2. ***Bind the interface definitions to the Interface Repository.*** Typically, you use a utility to bind—or, if you prefer, load—the IDL information in an Interface Repository that programs can access at run time.

3. ***Run the IDL file through a language precompiler.*** A typical CORBA precompiler is capable of generating at least three types of output files: 1) *client stubs* for the IDL-defined methods—these stubs are invoked by a client program that needs to statically access IDL-defined services via the ORB; and 2) *server*

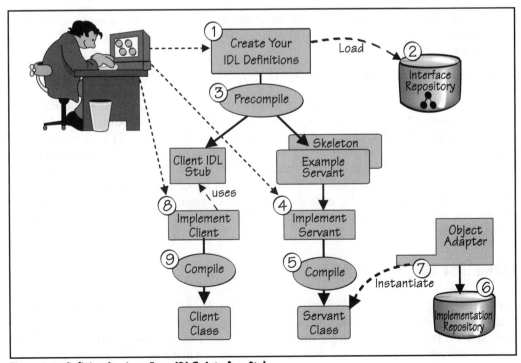

Figure 4-3. Defining Services: From IDL To Interface Stubs.

skeletons that call the methods on the server—they're also called *up-call interfaces*; and 3) a language-specific *example* class for your implementation. You must only provide the code that implements the server interface—CORBA 3.0 calls it a *servant* class. The automatic generation of stubs and skeletons frees developers from having to write them, and frees applications from dependencies on a particular ORB implementation.

4. **Add the servant implementation code.** You must supply the code that implements the methods in the servant. In other words, you must implement the business logic for your IDL-defined interfaces. Typically, you will start with the example file. Make sure to rename it.

5. **Compile the code.** You do this using a regular language compiler.

6. **Register the run-time objects with the Implementation Repository.** The Implementation Repository must know which servant classes are supported on a particular server. The ORB uses this information to locate active objects or to request the activation of objects on a particular server.

7. **Instantiate the objects on the server.** At startup time, a server *Object Adapter* may instantiate on demand server objects that service remote client method invocations. These run-time objects are instances of your implementation classes. CORBA specifies different Object Adapter strategies that are used to create and manage these run-time objects (more on this in Part 5).

8. **Implement the client code.** Your client invokes CORBA objects using language-specific bindings. The stubs take care of all the marshaling and unmarshaling.

9. **Compile the client code.** You do this using a regular language compiler.

The nine steps we just outlined are typical of most CORBA implementations. CORBA, of course, allows deviations. For example, it is not a requirement for IDL source code to be available, as long as the interface information is available in stub form or in an Interface Repository. You don't have to implement the server objects as classes as long as they're encapsulated by IDL stubs. Instead of inheriting from the skeletons directly, your implementations can be called via delegates (CORBA calls them Tie classes). In addition, the separation of the interface from the implementation enables you to incorporate existing legacy systems within an ORB environment.

YOUR FIRST CORBA PROGRAM

The Count program we will develop in this section is truly a minimalist client/server program; it doesn't get any simpler. As usual, we have a client and a server. In this case, the server exports a single method called *increment* (see Figure 4-4). This method simply increments by one the value of a variable called *sum* and then returns the value to the client.

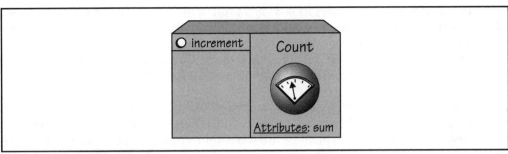

Figure 4-4. The Count Interface.

We declare *sum* to be a CORBA read/write *attribute*. This means your clients can access its value using CORBA's built-in *accessor* functions. The clients use these functions to set the initial state of *sum* and then again later to read its final state. We use this simple example to illustrate CORBA's powerful attribute accessor mechanism.

Our client program must do the following: 1) set the initial value of the *sum* attribute, 2) invoke the *increment* method 1000 times, and 3) display the final value of the *sum* attribute along with the average response time. The client must also be able to handle CORBA exceptions.

As you can see, this is a very minimalist client/server application. In Part 3, we introduce a more sophisticated version of Count that uses callbacks to synchronize the method invocations on multiple clients; it's like hitting a remote start button. We will also beef up the server to provide a more functional benchmarking environment. But, for now, let's keep it simple. We must first learn the CORBA/Java walk before we can run.

The Count IDL

The first step in the CORBA development process is for you to create language-independent IDL definitions of your server's interfaces. You can do this using any editor. The *count.idl* file contains the IDL for our **Count** interface.

Listing 4-1. Count.IDL: CORBA IDL Definition of the Count Interface.

```
module Counter
{ interface Count
  { attribute long sum;
    long increment();
  };
};
```

The CORBA IDL syntax should look very familiar to a C++ or Java programmer. We defined the **Count** interface within a CORBA module called **Counter**. Our interface has one method (or *operation* in CORBA terminology) and one attribute. The method returns the value of the count. Note that CORBA is a strongly-typed system. All variables, parameters, return values, and attributes are typed.

A *module* is the CORBA equivalent of a Java *package* or a C++ *namespace*. It provides a naming context for a set of related interfaces. Typically, these interfaces must trust each other. Names must be unique within a module's scoping context. The module's name is part of the scoped name of an interface. For example, the scoped name of our interface is **Counter::Count** (in Java, it maps to **Counter.Count**). We leave the details of CORBA IDL and how it maps into Java for Part 5.

Mapping CORBA IDL to Java

Now that we have an IDL file, we must map it into something that Java clients and servers can understand. So we will need an IDL-to-Java compiler. We just happen to have one—the VisiBroker *idl2java* compiler (or precompiler). Before you run the compiler make sure that you have properly installed VisiBroker and the Java binaries on your machine (we used both Symantec's Visual Café and JavaSoft's JDK 1.1). If you haven't done so already, please review the installation and setup instructions on the CD-ROM. After you complete the installation, run the idl2java compiler from the command prompt by entering:

```
prompt> idl2java count.idl -no_comments -no_tie
```

CORBA supports two styles of programming: *inheritance-based* and *delegation-based*. We use inheritance-style programming in most of our programs. Typically, you would use delegation to help you integrate with legacy code written in non-OO languages. The "-no_tie" option tells the compiler not to generate the extra delegation classes. Even so, the idl2java compiler is very prolific; it generates a Java package called **Counter** that contains five Java classes and one Java interface (see Figure 4-5).

The precompiler has done its part. Now the ball is back in our court. We must provide the code for the application logic. But before we do this, let's take a quick look at what the precompiler has just created for us:

■ **Counter._CountImplBase** is a Java class that implements the CORBA server-side skeleton for **Count**. It unmarshals the arguments for the **Count** object. In addition, this is the class that brings together the CORBA and Java object models. It does this by being a Java object that also implements the Java **org.omg.CORBA.Object** interface (OMG calls it **CORBA::Object**). This is the root CORBA interface; all CORBA objects must implement it. Your implementa-

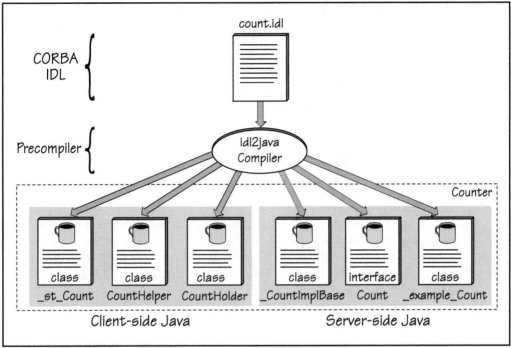

Figure 4-5. The Java Classes and Interfaces Generated by the Idl2java Compiler.

tion of **Count** will simply inherit this dual functionality by extending the compiler generated **_CountImplBase** class. We tell you more about the root CORBA classes in Parts 3 and 5.

■ **Counter._st_Count** is a Java class that implements the client-side stub for the **Count** object. It's really an internal implementation of the **Count** interface that provides marshaling functions. Make sure to include it with your client implementation.

■ **Counter.CountHelper** is a Java class that provides useful helper functions for **Count** clients. For example, the compiler automatically generates code for a *narrow* function that lets clients cast CORBA object references to the **Count** type. In addition to the required CORBA helper functions, the VisiBroker implementation provides a very useful, but non-standard, function called *bind*; it is used by clients to locate objects of this type. In this case, you use it to find remote objects that implement the **Count** interface.

■ **Counter.CountHolder** is a Java class that holds a public instance member of type **Count**. It is used by clients and servers to pass objects of type **Count** as *out* and *inout* parameters inside method invocations. Remember that Java natively only supports *in* parameters (i.e., parameters that are copied from the client to the server). We give you more details on Holders and Helpers in Part 5.

■ **Counter.Count** is a Java interface. It maps the **Count** interface to the corresponding Java interface (see below). We must provide code that implements this interface.

```
package Counter;
public interface Count extends org.omg.CORBA.Object
{
  public int  sum();
  public void sum(int _val);
  public int  increment();
}
```

■ **Counter._example_Count** is an example class for the **Count** object implementation. It contains constructors and example methods for the *sum* attribute and *increment* method that was defined in count.idl. With this example as a starting point, completing the **Count** object implementation is as easy as filling in the methods in the example. Here's the example file VisiBroker generates for **Count**:

```
package Counter;
public class _example_Count extends Counter._CountImplBase {
  public _example_Count(java.lang.String name) {
    super(name);
  }
  public _example_Count() {
    super();
  }
  public int increment() {
    // implement operation...
  }
  public void sum(int sum) {
    // implement attribute writer...
  }
  public int sum() {
    // implement attribute reader...
  }
}
```

The Server Side of Count

Every CORBA server must have some kind of main program that initializes the ORB environment and starts objects. We will write a class called **CountServer** to implement this main function. In addition, the server must provide implementations of the CORBA interfaces that are defined in the IDL. In this case, we only have one interface to implement: **Counter.Count**. We write a class called **CountImpl** to implement this interface. So, we only have two classes to write on the server side. Where do we start?

With the CORBA inheritance model, you always derive your server implementation class from the corresponding **_XXXImpBase** class. This is how your *servant* class inherits the functionality of both the CORBA and Java object models. You also inherit the skeleton function from this class. These are up-calls that allow the ORB to automatically invoke your object's methods. You do not write any dispatching code. This is part of the CORBA magic. So our task is simply to implement the **Counter.Count** interface. Your best bet is to start with the **_example_Count** template and use it as your model. Make sure to rename it. If not, the IDL compiler could later regenerate an example file and wipe out your work. Here's the implementation:

Listing 4-2. CountImpl: The Count Implementation.

```
// CountImpl.java: The Count Implementation
class CountImpl extends Counter._CountImplBase
{ private int sum;

  // Constructor
  CountImpl(String name)
  { super(name);
    System.out.println("Count Object Created");
    sum = 0;
  }
  // get sum
  public  int sum()
  { return sum;
  }

  // set sum
  public  void sum(int val)
  { sum = val;
  }

  // increment method
  public int increment()
  { sum++;
    return sum;
  }
}
```

In addition to implementing the **Count** interface functions, we also implemented a constructor for our **CountImpl** class. The constructor calls its *super*—in this case, the parent is the skeleton class—to create a named implementation object. This means that each instance of **CountImpl** will have a *persistent* name. If you invoke super without an argument, it will create an *anonymous*—or *transient*—object.

Now we must implement **CountServer**—the class that provides the main function on the server side. If you're dealing with a single object, this class may seem like a lot of overhead. In a more realistic situation, the main program will be managing multiple objects, each running in its own thread. In its simplest form, here's what the main program must do: 1) initialize the ORB, 2) initialize the BOA, 3) create a **CountImpl** object, 4) export to the ORB the newly created object, and 5) wait for incoming requests (see Figure 4-6).

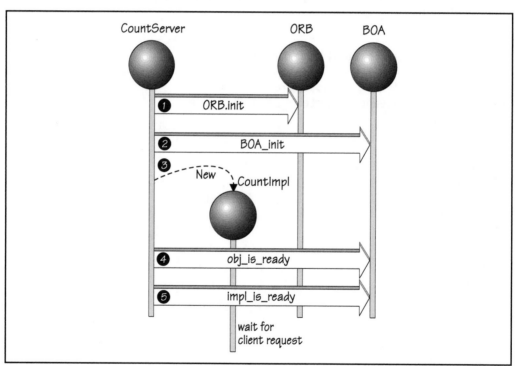

Figure 4-6. Object Interaction Diagram for Server-Side Count.

Here's the code that does it all:

Listing 4-3. CountServer: The Main Server Program.

```
// CountServer.java: The Count Server main program
class CountServer
```

```
{ static public void main(String[] args)
  { try
    { // Initialize the ORB
      org.omg.CORBA.ORB orb = org.omg.CORBA.ORB.init(args, null);

      // Initialize the BOA
      org.omg.CORBA.BOA boa = orb.BOA_init();

      // Create the Count object
      CountImpl count = new CountImpl("My Count");

      // Export to the ORB the newly created object
      boa.obj_is_ready(count);

      // Ready to service requests
      boa.impl_is_ready();
      }
      catch(org.omg.CORBA.SystemException e)
      { System.err.println(e);
      }
  }
}
```

The **org.omg.CORBA.ORB** class is part of the VisiBroker run time; it implements in Java most of the function that OMG specifies in the **CORBA::ORB** interface. Note that *org.omg.CORBA.ORB.init* is a Java class method. This means that you do not invoke it on a specific object. The method returns an object of type **org.omg.CORBA.ORB**. This method also lets you pass in the main program's command line arguments, which lets you set certain ORB-related properties at run time. So we now have a reference to the VisiBroker ORB object that we can invoke to initialize the BOA. The *BOA_init* call returns an object reference for BOA. We then use this reference to register with the BOA the newly created **CountImpl** object. Finally, we tell the BOA that our object is ready for business. The server-side is now complete. Notice that we did not write a do-forever loop to service incoming client calls. CORBA and the BOA automatically provide this function under-the-covers. We must just implement our interfaces and then register them with the ORB via BOA. In Part 5, you will get all the gory details about BOA and its newer incarnation called POA.

The Client Side of Count

The client program consists of a single Java class—**CountClient**. This class provides the *main* method; it must perform the following functions: 1) initialize the

ORB, 2) locate a remote **Count** object, 3) set the remote *sum* attribute to zero, 4) calculate the start time, 5) invoke the *increment* method 1000 times, 6) calculate the elapsed time, and 7) print the results (see Figure 4-7).

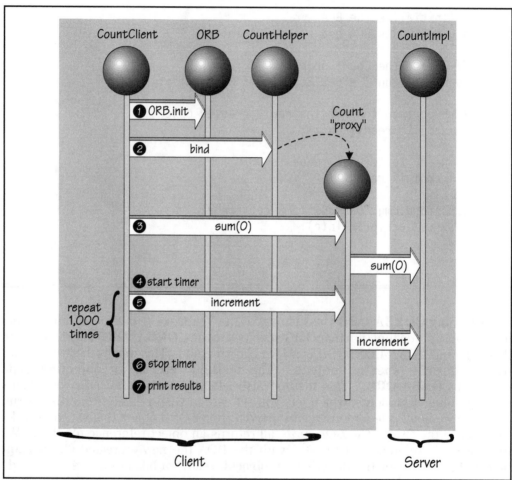

Figure 4-7. Object Interaction Diagram for Client-Side Count.

Here's the code that does it all:

Listing 4-4. CountClient: The Main Client Program.

```
// CountClient.java  Static Client, VisiBroker for Java
class CountClient
{ public static void main(String args[])
  { try
```

```
{ // Initialize the ORB
  System.out.println("Initializing the ORB");
  org.omg.CORBA.ORB orb = org.omg.CORBA.ORB.init(args, null);
  // Bind to the Count Object
  System.out.println("Binding to Count Object");
  Counter.Count counter = Counter.CountHelper.bind(orb, "My Count");

  // Set sum to initial value of 0
  System.out.println("Setting sum to 0");
  counter.sum((int)0);

  // Calculate Start time
  long startTime = System.currentTimeMillis();

  // Increment 1000 times
  System.out.println("Incrementing");
  for (int i = 0 ; i < 1000 ; i++ )
  { counter.increment();
  }

  // Calculate stop time; print out statistics
  long stopTime = System.currentTimeMillis();
  System.out.println("Avg Ping = "
                     + ((stopTime - startTime)/1000f) + " msecs");
  System.out.println("Sum = " + counter.sum());
} catch(org.omg.CORBA.SystemException e)
{ System.err.println("System Exception");
  System.err.println(e);
  }
 }
}
```

You can see how easy it is to invoke the remote Count object; it's just like calling a local Java object. And it's just as easy to manipulate the remote *sum* attribute. It's all part of the magic CORBA provides.

Of course, to invoke these methods, we must first obtain an object reference. This is where the *bind* method of the **Counter.CountHelper** class comes into play. Remember, this is one of the Java classes idl2java created for us. Make sure to package it with your client code.

Notice that we were able to specify—by name—the particular object instance we want. This means that you can always go back to the same named object—a very useful feature in client/server situations. We've completed our dissection of the client code, except for the next Briefing box.

CORBA Exceptions

Briefing

Client/server environments contain many moving parts; any of them can go wrong at any time. It only gets worse when you invoke methods across the Internet or across multivendor ORBs that run on different operating systems. Consequently, you must write your code in "baby steps," always looking over your shoulder to check for anything that can go wrong. Obviously, this can be very tedious. Luckily, CORBA and Java come to the rescue. Together they provide a very elegant mechanism for error-handling; it's based on the C++ *try-throw-catch* mechanism.

As shown in the code examples, exception-handling is a generic part of client/server programming with CORBA. It all starts with the idl2java compiler, which automatically generates the CORBA *system exceptions* a method can generate—these exceptions are typically generated by the ORB. You can also define in IDL the *user exceptions* your methods can *throw* (or *raise* in CORBA terminology). The idl2java will generate the appropriate Java exception classes for both types of errors. All exceptions have a name and an Interface Repository ID. Typically, the name of an exception is all you need to report most errors. The Repository ID provides additional information.

To take advantage of CORBA/Java error-handling, we must surround our code with standard Java *try* blocks. And, of course, we must provide the corresponding *catch* error-handling code. We must be able to handle all the possible exceptions that can be thrown at us. We do this using standard Java programming constructs. In general, you'll find that the exception-handling code in Java is a pleasure to read. It's self-documenting code that's easy to follow, which is very important in client/server situations. ❑

Compile the Java Code Using Symantec Visual Café

We're now ready to compile our Java programs. We chose the *Symantec Visual Café* development environment because the Symantec Java virtual machine includes a *Just-In-Time (JIT)* compiler. The JIT should give our classes an extra dose of caffeine (see the next Briefing box). The fastest JIT compiler—at the time we wrote this book—was the one that came with Visual Café. To compile the Java programs, first make sure Symantec Visual Café is installed on your machine. If not, just follow the instructions on the CD-ROM. You can compile the programs by running the *make.bat* file we provide with each directory. Or, you can type the following commands at the prompt:

```
prompt> javac -d \CorbaJavaBook.2e\classes CountClient.java
prompt> javac -d \CorbaJavaBook.2e\classes CountServer.java
prompt> javac -d \CorbaJavaBook.2e\classes CountImpl.java
```

The -d option tells the compiler to put the (.class) files it creates into the directory we specify—in this case, \CorbaJavaBook.2e\classes. If the compile is successful, you should have some compiled Java classes—(.class) files—that you can now run.

JIT Compilers

Briefing

A common complaint about Java is that it is slower than native-compiled languages such as C++. JIT compilers dramatically improve Java's performance by compiling the bytecodes "on-the-fly," as they execute. Instead of interpreting bytecodes one at a time, a JIT compiler compiles each bytecode once, and then reinvokes the compiled code repeatedly when the program executes. Internally, the JIT maintains links to the compiled code. When a bytecode comes up again, the JIT activates the link and runs the compiled code instead.

Java bytecodes are very close to machine-level instructions. Consequently, the JIT compilation is blazingly fast. For example, Microsoft claims that the VJ++ JIT compiler can compile a million lines of code per minute. In addition to JIT compilers, many vendors are developing build-time compilers for Java. These compilers will be able to generate executable files (.EXE) directly from Java source files (.java).

So, where do I get a JIT compiler from? The JIT compiler is part of a Java Virtual Machine (Java VM). It must be there at run time to compile your bytecodes "on-the-fly." The JavaSoft JDK 1.1 does not include a JIT compiler (there will be one in JDK 1.2). Consequently, we must use a third-party Java VM to obtain a JIT compiler. In this book, we use the Java VM that comes with Symantec Visual Café; it's also the one used by Netscape *Communicator* and JavaSoft's *Performance Pack*. In the DCOM chapter, we use the Java VM that comes with Microsoft's Visual J++.

> In the Symantec Java VM, you compile your bytecodes by invoking *javac*. You then run your bytecodes in Symantec's *java* machine. In the Microsoft Java VM, you compile your bytecodes by invoking *jvc*. You then run your bytecodes in Microsoft's *jview* machine. ❑

Run the Client/Server Program

To run the client/server program, first start the VisiBroker *OSAgent*. You can install an OSAgent on each machine. Or, you can tell your client and server programs where to find their OSAgent when you start them. Remember, the OSAgent provides fault-tolerant location services; it must be running on at least one machine in the LAN environment. You can run an OSAgent either by double-clicking on the fancy *Smart Agent* icon or by typing the following command at the prompt:

prompt> `start osagent -c`

Next, you must start the server. To run the server program, type the following command at the prompt:

prompt> `start java -DOAid=TSession CountServer`

We used the property OAid with a value of TSession to disable the VisiBroker server's default thread pooling. Thread pooling was introduced with VisiBroker 3.0; it substantially improves performance when you have heavily-loaded servers. In our current case—one server object with one client—it introduces extra overhead with no added benefit. Consequently, we disable it to make our tests consistent with the previous version of this book.

Now, you can finally fire off that client. Type the following command at the prompt:

prompt> `java CountClient`

You will see a screen output that looks like this:

```
Initializing the ORB
Binding to Count Object
Setting Sum to 0
Incrementing
Avg Ping = 3.884 msec
Sum = 1000
```

LOOKING AT SOME TEST RESULTS

We will run this client/server program in different situations to get a reading on the performance of CORBA static method invocations. The client performs 1000 method invocations during the elapsed time. The program calculates average response time in milliseconds by dividing the elapsed time by the number of invocations. We're measuring the equivalent of a Ping for CORBA static method invocations.

Local Versus Remote Pings

One of the wonderful features of CORBA is local/remote transparency. You write the client and server programs once and you can then run them either locally or remotely. Your clients can invoke objects on the same machine or across the intergalactic network. You don't have to rewrite a line of code. In the case of VisiBroker, OSAgent will find your objects wherever they are. It's part of the ORB magic.

So how does the ORB do its magic? Remember, with CORBA ORBs clients do not connect directly with servers as they do with an RPC. Instead, all requests are mediated by the ORB. The ORB is the broker that redirects the request to the appropriate server. This server can be in the same process, across processes, or across the network. The ORB makes it all transparent to the client.

In this test, we first run the client and server programs in the same machine—a 120-MHz Pentium running NT 4.0. Then we run them across a 10 Mbit/s Ethernet LAN. Table 4-1 compares the results.

Table 4-1. Local Versus Remote Static Counts: Java Client and Server.

Local Static Count Ping (interprocess)	Remote Static Count Ping (interprocess over 10 Mbit/s Ethernet)
3.9 msecs	3.6 msecs

You should be warned that these numbers deviate by 10% in either direction, even with the same setup. But the relative performance is more or less constant. In general, remote invocations are slightly faster than local ones. Why? The program runs on two machines instead of one. This appears to offset the network overhead. The Java virtual machine appears to be quite CPU-intensive. Of course, you can run the benchmarks and see for yourself. You have our code.

Symantec JIT Versus Sun JDK

Everybody in "Java Land" knows that the *Symantec Visual Café* JIT compiler is blazingly fast. So what exactly is blazingly fast? You can soon find out. Let's rerun these programs using the JavaSoft JDK 1.1 Virtual Machine (i.e., without the JIT). Install the JDK and then follow the instructions on the CD-ROM for running these programs using JDK 1.1. Table 4-2 shows the results.

Table 4-2. Java JIT Comparisons: Symantec Visual Café Versus Sun JDK.

	Symantec Visual Café JIT	Sun JDK (interpreted)
Local interprocess	3.9 msecs	6.7 msecs
Remote interprocess	3.6 msecs	5.6 msecs

You can see that the Symantec JIT compiler dramatically improves the performance.

CONCLUSION

This concludes our first Java/CORBA program. This chapter was rather long in relation to the size of the programs. This is typical for a first program; we had to set the stage and explain the new programming environment. In addition, we had to explain new CORBA concepts. In the next chapter, we continue with our Count example by developing an applet version of the client.

Chapter 5

ORBlets
Meet Applets

It's time for some fun stuff—Java applets. Applets are what made Java famous. They are now literally changing the dynamics of client/server computing. What makes these applets so irresistible? They let you create component-sized applications that servers can ship to clients via ordinary HTML pages. Once an applet lands in a Web browser, it becomes an instant front-end to the remote services you provide. So, in a sense, applets are "just-in-time" shippable clients. The server downloads the client application when and where it's needed.

But how does the applet efficiently communicate with its server? In Part 1 we made the case that CORBA over the Internet (or IIOP) provides the best solution for these new types of dynamic client/server interactions. But talk is cheap. Let's demonstrate—using code—exactly what CORBA can do for an applet.

In this chapter, we start our exploration by creating the applet version of the Count client. We will show you how an applet can statically invoke methods on a CORBA Count server. The server doesn't care if you invoke its methods from an applet or from regular application; it works just the same. As an extra benefit of this example, we will be able to compare the performance of an applet versus that of an ordinary Java client application.

APPLETS 101

Technically, an applet is a piece of code that inherits its behavior from the Java **Applet** class, which it then extends with new function. An applet is not a complete application. It's really a component that runs within a browser's environment. In this case, the browser acts as a framework for running Java components—or applets.

So what type of component framework services do browsers provide? A Web browser provides three useful services to its applets. First, it fully controls the applet's life cycle. Second, it supplies the applet with attribute information from the APPLET tag. And third, it serves as the main program or process within which the applet executes—it provides the *main* function. Let's quickly go over these services.

Applet Life Cycle Management

A Web browser manages all phases of an applet's life cycle. Remember, the browser first downloads the applet and then runs it within its environment. The browser is also kind enough to inform the applet of key events that happen during its life cycle. The Java **Applet** class and the **Runnable** interface define the methods that a browser can invoke on an applet during its life cycle (see Figure 5-1).

The browser invokes *init* when it loads your applet for the first time. The browser calls *start* whenever a user enters or returns to the page containing your applet. This lets your applet do whatever it has to do before running. The browser calls *stop* whenever the user moves off the page. Finally, the browser calls *destroy* before it shuts down normally. The last two calls should cause your applet to kill all its threads, stop executing, and release all resources.

To be highly interactive, your applet should implement a *run* method that executes inside a thread. Here's how you manage the lifecycle of the thread within your applet: 1) create the thread when your applet receives an *init*, 2) *run* the thread when your applet receives a *start*, and 3) destroy the thread when your applet receives a *stop* or *destroy* (see Figure 5-1).

The **Applet** class has a large number of methods that a browser calls in response to user actions, such as moving the mouse or manipulating the user interface. Most applets implement some level of event-handling code and paint functions. For example, you implement the *paint* method to draw and refresh the graphics in your applet. You implement *mouseMove* and *mouseDown* methods to handle mouse events. And, you implement the *action* method to service events from GUI controls. We could go on with this list.

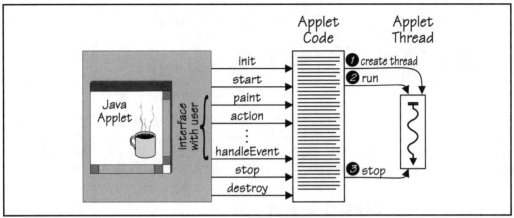

Figure 5-1. How a Browser Interacts With an Applet.

The key idea here is that the browser owns your applet. It provides your applet with a running environment that includes life cycle management. And, it calls your applet to handle events that require its attention.

The HTML Applet Tag

A Java applet's main role in life is to provide live content to Web pages displayed in a Java-enabled browser. In contrast, a Java application can run without a Web browser. You use the APPLET HTML tag to place an applet inside a Web page and describe its attributes and environment. The tag tells the browser where to find the applet to download. Java provides a set of methods that an applet uses to obtain information about its environment—including the embedded tag attributes and their values.

The APPLET tag provides the essential information that connects the Web browser to the embedded applet. It also lets you specify key attribute information; you can use these attributes to configure an applet and control its behavior without having to write a line of code. A well-designed applet will provide as many attributes as needed to let you control its behavior via HTML.

The APPLET tag contains the required attributes CODE, WIDTH, and HEIGHT; it also contains optional attributes such as CODEBASE and ALIGN. The CODE attribute specifies the (.class) file that contains the applet's bytecodes. This file is normally in the same directory as the URL document. However, you can use the optional CODEBASE attribute to specify a different location. The WIDTH and HEIGHT attributes specify the area within an HTML page that belongs to the applet. You can use the optional ALIGN attribute to tell the browser where you want it to place the applet (it's a relative placement). Here's an example of the APPLET tag:

```
<APPLET CODE=Hello.class CODEBASE="applets/myapps"
 WIDTH=300 HEIGHT=200  ALIGN=Left>
<PARAM NAME=Parm1  VALUE="Java is cool">
<PARAM NAME=Parm2  VALUE="Is there life without Java?">
</APPLET>
```

The PARAM attributes are specific to each applet. Each applet can define as many parameters as it needs. You must provide a PARAM tag for each parameter you want to pass to the applet via HTML; each tag contains a name/value pair. An applet can access any parameter—by name—by invoking the Java method *getParameter*.

YOUR FIRST CORBA-ENABLED APPLET

OK, enough applet basics. You're probably a seasoned Java programmer who just wants to understand how a Java applet calls a CORBA object server. So let's address your needs. We will first create the applet version of the **Count** client. We will then embed it inside an HTML page, which we download using a Web browser. And finally, we will use the applet to invoke methods on the **Count** server we developed in the last chapter. The client and server will communicate using CORBA's *static method invocations*.

The Count IDL

We will use the Count server class from the last chapter as is. Consequently, the IDL remains unchanged. This means we can use the client stubs that were generated the last time we ran idl2java—our applet can use both the **Counter._st_Count** and **Counter.CountHelper** classes as is. So the lesson here is that your client stubs remain valid as long as you don't change your server's interfaces. You can distribute these stubs to as many client programs as you want (see the next Warning box).

So, What Exactly Does This Applet Do?

Before we get into the code, let's look at a screen capture of the Count applet (see Figure 5-2). We call this the "minimalist cool" look. To interact with this minimalist applet, you enter a count number in the input field and then click on the "Run" button. The applet will then invoke the Count server's *increment* method "n" times, where n is the number you just entered. If you don't enter a number, the default is 1000. The applet displays the average response time in the output field. It will also display progress status in the browser's status line. This way you'll know what it's doing at all times.

Don't Break That Contract

Warning

We just saw how easy it is to distribute stubs to clients that invoke your objects' services. These stubs are hardcoded to work with the interfaces you defined via IDL. An interface is an iron-clad contract between the server and its clients. If your server breaks the contract by changing the IDL or the interface, then you must also refresh the stubs on all the clients. Obviously, this is not a very pleasant undertaking—especially in intergalactic environments.

So how do you work around this problem? How do you update an interface? The easiest solution is to publish a new interface with a different name while continuing to support the old one. This is the approach Microsoft takes with its *Distributed Component Object Model (DCOM)*. The second approach is to download the stubs along with the applet. This approach works well if your clients are Java applets. The third approach is for clients to use the CORBA *Dynamic Invocation Interface*. In this approach, clients build the request "on-the-fly." By doing so, they are guaranteed to work with the latest version of the interface. There are no stubs. Which approach is best? It's really the classical trade-off between flexibility and performance. We will return to this topic in Part 3—"The Dynamic CORBA." ❑

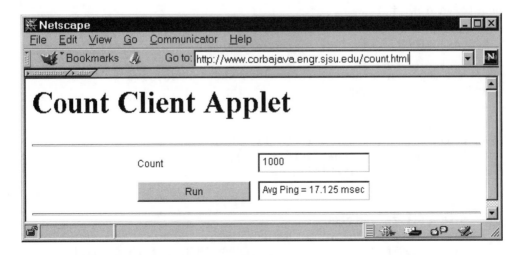

Figure 5-2. A Screen Capture of the Java Count Applet.

The Client Applet Code

The Count applet consists of a single Java class—**CountClientApplet**. This class extends **java.applet.Applet** and implements two methods: *init* and *action*. There is no main program. An applet must rely on the browser to tell it when things happen. The browser calls *init* after it loads the applet. The *init* method performs the following functions: 1) creates a user interface consisting of four widgets, 2) initializes the ORB, and 3) locates a remote **Count** object.

The browser calls *action* when the user clicks on the "Run" button. The *action* method performs the following functions: 1) sets the remote *sum* attribute to zero, 2) reads from an input field the number of times to count (the default is 1000), 3) calculates the start time, 4) invokes the *increment* method 1000 times (or the number you specify), 5) calculates the elapsed time, and 6) displays the results. Here's the code that does it all (the bold lines are CORBA-specific).

Listing 5-1. CountClientApplet: The Client Applet Program.

```
// CountClientApplet.java  Applet Client, VisiBroker for Java
import java.awt.*;

public class CountClientApplet extends java.applet.Applet
{ private TextField countField, pingTimeField;
  private Button runCount;
  private Counter.Count counter;

  public void init()
  { // Create a 2 by 2 grid of widgets
    setLayout(new GridLayout(2, 2, 10, 10));

    // Add the four widgets, initialize where necessary
    add(new Label("Count"));
    add(countField = new TextField());
    countField.setText("1000");
    add(runCount = new Button("Run"));
    add(pingTimeField = new TextField());
    pingTimeField.setEditable(false);

    try
    { // Initialize the ORB
      showStatus("Initializing the ORB");
      org.omg.CORBA.ORB orb = org.omg.CORBA.ORB.init(this, null);

      // Bind to the Count Object
```

```
      showStatus("Binding to Count Object");
      counter = Counter.CountHelper.bind(orb, "My Count");
    } catch(org.omg.CORBA.SystemException e)
    { showStatus("Applet Exception" + e);
    }
  }

  public boolean action(Event ev, Object arg)
  { if(ev.target == runCount)
    { try
      { // Set sum to initial value of 0
        showStatus("Setting sum to 0");
        counter.sum((int)0);

        // get data from and set value of applet fields
        showStatus("Incrementing");
        int stopCount = Integer.parseInt(countField.getText());
        pingTimeField.setText(" ");

        // Calculate Start time
        long startTime = System.currentTimeMillis();

        // Increment stopCount times
        for (int i = 0 ; i < stopCount ; i++ )
        { counter.increment();
        }

        // Calculate stop time; show statistics
        long stopTime = System.currentTimeMillis();
        pingTimeField.setText("Avg Ping = "
              + Float.toString((float)(stopTime- startTime)/stopCount)
              + " msecs");
        showStatus("Sum = " + counter.sum());
      } catch(org.omg.CORBA.SystemException e)
      { showStatus("System Exception" + e);
      }
      return true;
    }
    return false;
  }
}
```

The first thing to notice in this code is that there is no *main* function. Remember, the browser provides it. The second thing to notice is that the CORBA code—the bold lines—is identical to the code we developed in the last chapter. However, there is one important exception. You must now pass a reference to your applet in the *org.omg.ORB.init* call to comply with the new Java-to-IDL mapping.

So the only thing left for us to explain is the *Abstract Window Toolkit (AWT)* code, which should be old hat to most of our readers. You construct the user interface with various GUI building blocks when the *init* method is called. And, you provide code that responds to user interface events in the *action* method. You should note that *showStatus* lets you write text in the browser's status field.

Later in this book, we will show you how to create more sophisticated user interfaces. In this minimalist applet, we hardcode a user interface that consists of four component objects (or visual controls): a **Label**, a **Button**, and two **TextField** objects. AWT defines classes for most common GUI controls. These classes are all derived from the **Component** class. To create a user interface, you must populate a visual container—such as a window, frame, or panel—with the component instances you create. It's like populating a Visual Basic form.

AWT containers are GUI objects that group components inside a visual area. A Java applet is derived from the **Container** class (see Figure 5-3). Consequently, an applet is also a container. In AWT, you add a component object to a container by invoking the *add* method; you pass—as a parameter—the object you want to add. In our code, we create the object when we add it. This is just a convenience that saves us exactly one line of code for each *add*.

Notice that we do not specify the positions of the components in our code. Why? To make your code platform-independent, AWT requires that you do not specify any absolute layout positions. So who does the layout? AWT does—with some hints from you. AWT provides an elegant mechanism that lets you specify a *layout manager* class. You create an object of that class, and then let it manage the screen real-estate. It will place your components inside the container, resize them when necessary, and handle differences in display sizes.

AWT provides a number of predefined layout manager classes. We chose for our layout the **GridLayout** class. It uses a layout scheme that divides the display into a grid of equal-sized cells; it then resizes each component and gives it a cell's worth of visual real-estate. So you get to see rows and columns of equal-sized components. In the constructor of the grid object, you specify 1) the number of rows, 2) the number of columns, 3) the space between rows, and 4) the space between columns (the last two parameters are optional). We have four objects, so we specify a 2 by 2 grid. You add components, starting with the first entry in the first row, then the second entry in the first row, and so on. This is all there is to say about this applet code. The next step is to compile our class.

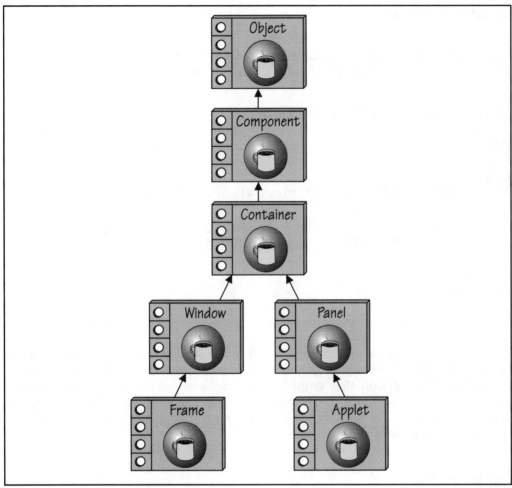

Figure 5-3. Java Container Class Hierarchy.

Compile the Java Applet

Type the following command at the prompt:

```
prompt> javac -d \CorbaJavaBook.2e\classes CountClientApplet.java
```

The -d option tells the compiler to put the (.class) files it creates into the directory we specify—in this case, \CorbaJavaBook.2e\classes. If the compile is successful, you should have some compiled Java programs—(.class) files—that you can now run.

Create a Web Page

The next step is to create a minimalist HTML Web page that embeds our applet. Open a file called count.html and enter the following:

Listing 5-2. Count.html: Web Page for Count Applet.

```
<h1>Count Client Applet</h1>
<hr>
<center>
<APPLET CODE=CountClientApplet.class WIDTH=300 HEIGHT=60
        CODEBASE=classes>
        <param name=org.omg.CORBA.ORBClass
               value=com.visigenic.vbroker.orb.ORB>

</APPLET>
</center>
<hr>
```

You may be wondering about the parameter in the shaded area. It causes whatever Visigenic ORB you have in your CODEBASE to be downloaded and then substituted for the baked-in version that comes with *Communicator*. As we go to press, Netscape uses *VisiBroker 2.5*. However, we expect them to upgrade to 3.1 by the time you read this. So, we force this download to make sure your programs are using the latest version of VisiBroker.

Test the Applet

To run the client/server program locally, first make sure that the *OSAgent* and Count server are up and running. Then do the following: 1) install a Java-enabled browser—for example, Netscape *Communicator*—on a client machine, 2) copy *count.html* and the Java applet files—including the stub classes—to a directory on this machine, 3) point your Web browser to the *count.html* file—your Web browser should display the applet shown in Figure 5-2 on page 87, 4) enter a count and then click on the Run button, and 5) observe the result in the lower-right field.

Run the Client/Server Program

If you got this far, your next step is to run the client/server program from an HTTP server. Here are the steps you follow (see Figure 5-4):

1. ***Install your applet on a Web server.*** Move your applet files—including the stub and CORBA classes—to a Web server. You must also un-JAR the *VisiBroker 3.1* ORB classes before you put them in the CODEBASE (see the CDROM for detailed instructions). Make sure that the (.class) files are in the same directory as the (.html) file. If you want to put your (.class) files in a separate directory, use the CODEBASE attribute to specify the new location.

   In addition, you must start the *IIOP Gatekeeper*, which acts as an IIOP firewall proxy. It lets an applet invoke an object server on a host other than the one from which the applet originated; it also lets the server invoke methods on the applet via callbacks. Gatekeeper also provides *HTTP tunnelling* to allow clients to communicate with object servers across firewalls that do not support the IIOP proxy. You must also start your Count server as described in Chapter 4.

2. ***Download the applet and CORBA classes.*** Point your Web browser to the URL of your Web page. The HTTP server will download the applet, the stub classes, and other CORBA classes—including the ORB if it's not already on your client. The minimalist applet should appear in the browser.

3. ***Set the count.*** The count field tells the applet how many times to invoke the Count server's *increment* method. We preset this number to 1000. If you want a different count, this is the time to change it.

4. ***Invoke the CORBA Count server 1000 times.*** Click on the Run button to invoke increments on the remote CORBA server.

5. ***Obtain the results.*** The lower right-hand field displays the average response time in milliseconds for an *increment* method (it's the equivalent of a Ping performance).

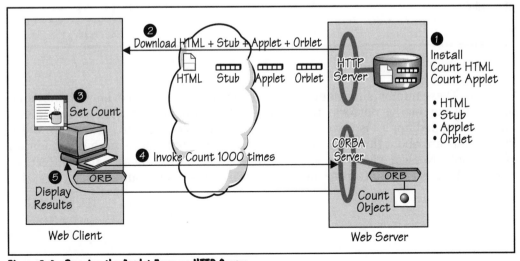

Figure 5-4. Running the Applet From an HTTP Server.

We also run the CORBA Count server on the same machine as the Web browser to measure local interprocess performance.

LET'S LOOK AT SOME TEST RESULTS

We will run this client/server program in different situations to get a reading on the performance of CORBA static method invocations. As usual, our client performs 1000 method invocations. The tests measure the average response time of Pings invoked from a Web browser applet using static CORBA method invocations. What a mouthful.

Local Versus Remote Pings

In this test, we first run the Web client and server programs in the same machine— a 120-MHz Pentium running NT 4.0. Then we run them across a 10 Mbit/s Ethernet LAN. Table 5-1 compares the average applet response times for a Ping (i.e., the *increment* method) using static CORBA method invocations. We used Netscape Communicator's JIT compiler to obtain the JIT-compiled applet numbers. To obtain the interpreted results, we disabled the default JIT compiler by renaming the *jit3240.dll* in Communicator's *program\java\bin* subdirectory.

Table 5-1. Local Versus Remote: Java Applet/CORBA Count Server.

	Local Static Count (interprocess, same machine)	Remote Static Count (interprocess, over 10 Mbit/s Ethernet)
JIT Compiled	17.6 msecs	16.1 msecs
Interpreted	30.2 msecs	23.3 msecs

Warning: These numbers may deviate by 10% in either direction even with the same setup. But the relative performance is more or less constant. As you would expect, the JIT-compiled applet is faster than its interpreted counterpart. However, these Ping results are about three times slower than their counterparts in the first edition of our book. Netscape is aware of this problem and is working on a fix. Of course, the best thing is for you to run the benchmarks and see for yourself.

Applets Versus Applications

Table 5-2 compares the remote performance of an applet client versus that of a Java application—compiled or interpreted. We use the remote results from Chapter 4 for the Java application.

Table 5-2. Remote Client: Java Applet Versus Java Application

	Java Applet	Java Application
JIT Compiled	16.1 msecs	3.6 msecs
Interpreted	23.3 msecs	5.6 msecs

As you can see, JIT-compiled Java client applications are about 400% faster than their applet counterparts; in the previous edition of our book they were only 40% faster. This is definitely a step in the wrong direction. Again, we made Netscape aware of the problem so we expect it to be fixed.

CONCLUSION

This concludes our second CORBA/Java program. The good news is that every Netscape browser is CORBA-enabled. This means you do not have to download the ORBlets along with the applet. It becomes much more efficient to invoke CORBA server objects from within your applets. This chapter gives you a headstart in this new style of client/server Web programming. The bad news is the performance got worse. It is now 4 times slower to invoke a remote object from within a browser than from within a Java application. As you will see in Part 4, this is still 50 times faster than the HTTP/CGI equivalent.

Chapter 6

Java ORBs Meet C++ ORBs

In this chapter, we will develop a C++ version of the Count client/server program. We will use this program to compare the performance of Java ORBs with their C++ counterparts. We keep hearing that Java is slow compared to C++; we'll soon find out if there's any truth to this. After writing the C++ version, we will be able to compare the performance of client/server Java objects with their C++ counterparts. We will also be able to tell how well an ORB written in Java performs by comparing it with a C++ implementation. Luckily, Borland/Visigenic provides a *VisiBroker for C++* (also in a Version 3.1 release). So we will be comparing products from the same vendor. It's one way to avoid lawsuits.

One of the many benefits of CORBA is that it lets your objects communicate across languages and operating systems. So, after we develop the C++ Count client and server programs, we will use them to talk to their Java counterparts. The Java client should be able to invoke C++ **Count** objects. And, the C++ client should be able to invoke Java **Count** objects. If we can demonstrate this miracle, we're sure you can put it to very good use. Think of the trillions of lines of existing code that you can encapsulate with CORBA interfaces and then make available to Java applets on the Internet and intranets.

Have we got your attention yet? If so, let's write some C++ code. This will be the only chapter in this book where you will see any C++ code. The rest of the book is pure Java—we promise! If you don't care about programming CORBA in C++, then skip to the end of this chapter and glance over the results.

THE C++ COUNT PROGRAM

The client/server program we will develop in this chapter is a C++ rewrite of the static Count program we introduced in Chapter 4. As usual, we have a client and a server. And, as usual, we must start with CORBA IDL. Because CORBA IDL is language-independent, we can use the count.idl from Chapter 4 without any changes.

The Count IDL

Listing 6-1. Count.IDL: CORBA IDL Definition of the Count Interface.

```
module Counter
{
  interface Count
  { attribute long sum;
    long increment();
  };
};
```

Mapping CORBA IDL to C++

Now that we have an IDL file, we must map it into something that C++ clients and servers can understand. So, we will need an IDL-to-C++ precompiler (or compiler). The one that comes with *VisiBroker for C++ 3.1* is called *idl2cpp*. Before you run the compiler, make sure that you have installed the VisiBroker for C++ on your machine. If you haven't done so already, please go to the CD-ROM and follow the installation and the setup instructions. After you complete the installation, run the compiler from the command prompt by entering:

prompt> idl2cpp -src_suffix cpp -no_tie

The "-no_tie" option tells the compiler not to generate delegation code stubs. Remember, we use inheritance-style programming. The "-src_suffix cpp" option tells the precompiler to use the (.cpp) suffix for any code file it generates. As in the Java case, the compiler is very prolific; it generates four C++ files from the IDL input (see Figure 6-1).

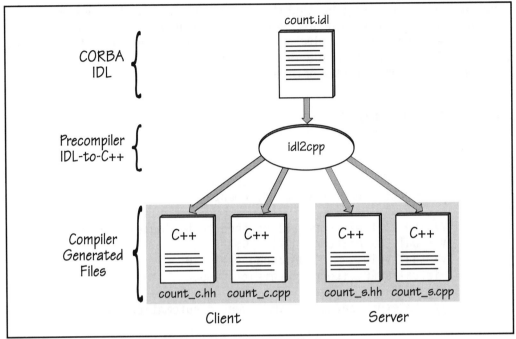

Figure 6-1. The C++ Files Generated by the Idl-to-C++ Compiler.

The precompiler has done its part. Now the ball is back in our court. We must provide the code for the application logic. But before we do this, let's take a quick look at what the precompiler has just created for us:

■ ***Count_s.cpp*** is the server skeleton for the methods of **Count** class. This is the code that unmarshals calls for the **Count** object and then invokes your implementation of the object.

■ ***Count_s.hh*** is a server header file that includes the class definitions for the server skeletons implemented in **count_s.cpp**.

■ ***Count_c.cpp*** contains a class called **Count** that serves as a proxy on the client for the **Count** object. It provides stubs and marshaling functions for all the methods defined in the **Count** interface. It also implements a *bind* method that helps the client locate a **Count** server.

■ ***Count_c.hh*** is a client header file that includes declarations and class definitions for the stub implementations in **count_c.cpp**.

The four files generated by the IDL compiler contain mostly functions that are private to VisiBroker. The compiler tells you very explicitly not to modify any of these files. And, ideally, you should never have to look inside these files. They're as ugly as C++ code ever gets. Unfortunately, the C++ ORB does not provide an example template. Consequently, you must look inside one of these files—count_s.hh—to get the C++ abstract virtual function definitions of the **Count** interface. These C++ virtual functions are analogous to a Java interface. Here's the code snippet that is of interest to us:

Listing 6-2. Count_s.hh Snippet.

```
class _sk_Counter
{   public:

    class _sk_Count : public Counter::Count
    {
        // The following operations need to be implemented by the server
        virtual CORBA::Long sum() = 0;
        virtual void sum(CORBA::Long val) = 0;
        virtual CORBA::Long increment() = 0;

        // Skeleton Operations implemented automatically
                        .
                        .

    };
};
```

This snippet shows the C++ mappings for the IDL interface—these are the server functions we must implement in C++. It's a good start. Too bad we had to wade through all the gunk the compiler produces to find them. The VisiBroker people could make life easier for C++ implementors by creating a separate file with a class declaration for the functions we must implement—just like they did for Java. Then we wouldn't have to look at all the gunk. On the other hand, the gunk makes it very clear why we need ORBs. It's messy system-level code that we thankfully don't have to write.

The Server Side of the C++ Count

Every CORBA server must have some kind of main program that initializes the ORB environment and starts objects. So we have to write a C++ main function that does this. In addition, the server must provide implementations of the CORBA interfaces that are defined in the IDL. In this case, we only have one interface to implement: **Counter::Count**. We write a C++ class called **CountImpl** to implement this interface.

So, where do we start? With VisiBroker, you derive your server implementation class from the corresponding skeleton class. This is how your servant class inherits the functionality of the CORBA object model; it is also how your class obtains the skeleton functions that allow the ORB to automatically invoke your object's methods. As usual, you do not write any dispatching code. This is part of the CORBA magic. So our task is simply to implement **CountImpl** and the main function.

The following listing shows our C++ header file with the class declaration. For our Java readers who are not familiar with C++, headers are a way of life with C++. This is where you declare the class definitions. You write your implementations in separate files and then include the headers. In contrast, with Java you declare variables and classes as you implement them.

Listing 6-3. Countimp.h: The Server-Side Header File.

```
// countimp.h  Count Implementation class definition, VisiBroker for C++

#include <count_s.hh>

class CountImpl: public _sk_Counter::_sk_Count
{
  private:
   long _sum;

  public:
   CountImpl(const char *object_name=NULL);
   CORBA::Long sum();
   void sum(CORBA::Long val);
   CORBA::Long increment();
};
```

We derived the **CountImpl** class definition from the snippet of code generated by the IDL compiler (see the last section). We added to this snippet a constructor for the class. As usual, the class is derived from its skeleton called the **_sk_Count** class. This is the IDL-generated class we described in the previous section.

Next, we must provide the server main program (server.cpp) and the implementation of our **CountImpl** class (CountImpl.cpp). Good C++ programming practice requires that we provide a separate implementation file for our Count object. The two listings follow.

Listing 6-4. Server.cpp: The C++ Count Server Implementation Code.

```cpp
// server.cpp  Count Server, VisiBroker for C++
#include "countimp.h"
int main(int argc, char* const* argv)
{ try
  { // Initialize the ORB
    CORBA::ORB_ptr orb = CORBA::ORB_init(argc, argv);

    // Initialize the BOA
    CORBA::BOA_ptr boa = orb->BOA_init(argc, argv);

    // Create the Count object
    Counter::Count_ptr count = new CountImpl("My Count");

    // Export the newly created object
    boa->obj_is_ready(count);

    // Ready to service requests
    boa->impl_is_ready();
  }
  catch(const CORBA::Exception& e)
  { cerr << e << endl;
  }
 return (0);
}
```

Listing 6-5. CountImpl: The C++ Count Implementation Code.

```cpp
// countimp.cpp  Count Implementation, VisiBroker for C++
#include "countimp.h"

// Constructor
CountImpl::CountImpl(const char *object_name)
                       : _sk_Counter::_sk_Count(object_name)
{ cout << "Count object created" << endl;
  this->_sum = 0;
}

// Get the value of the sum Attribute
CORBA::Long CountImpl::sum()
{ return this->_sum;
}
// Set the value the sum Attribute
```

```
void CountImpl::sum(CORBA::Long val)
{ this->_sum = val;
}
// Increment the sum
CORBA::Long CountImpl::increment()
{ this->_sum++;
  return this->_sum;
}
```

The main function is almost a carbon copy of its Java counterpart, except that the code is now in C++. Like its Java counterpart, the C++ *main* must: 1) initialize the ORB, 2) initialize the BOA, 3) create a **CountImpl** object, 4) export to the ORB the newly created object, and 5) wait for incoming requests. There are no surprises in this code. It should be very familiar to a C++ programmer (also see the next Details box).

The **CountImpl** C++ servant class is also similar to its Java counterpart. It implements in C++ the *increment* method and the accessor functions to the *sum* attribute. The only thing that may seem strange to a Java programmer is the constructor for this C++ class.

```
CountImpl::CountImpl(const char *object_name) :
                    _sk_Counter::_sk_Count(object_name)
{ cout << "Count object created" << endl;
  this->sum = 0;
}
```

In C++, you can specify from within the constructor's declaration the parent constructors you may want to call. In this case, our constructor calls its parent—the skeleton class—to create a named implementation object. This means that each instance of **CountImpl** will have a *persistent* name. If you invoke super without an argument, it will create an *anonymous—or transient—*object.

How C++ Represents CORBA Objects

Details

You may have noticed in the previous code that CORBA object references map to C++ pointer-like types—examples are CORBA::ORB_ptr, CORBA::BOA_ptr, and Counter::Count_ptr. The OMG C++ CORBA bindings specify two different ways to map object references:

- ■ **InterfaceName_ptr** provides a minimalist object reference type that has the semantics of a C++ pointer—for example, Count_ptr.

- ■ **InterfaceName_var** is a superset of (_ptr) that automatically releases its object reference when it is deallocated or when assigned a new object reference. For example, you declare objects that implement the **Count** interface to be of type Count_var.

Clients frequently use the less primitive (_var) object reference type because it does more of the housekeeping. For many operations, you can intermix data references of type (_var) and (_ptr) without any explicit casts. The final question is: Who creates these reference types? The IDL compiler creates them for you; it implements them as C++ classes. If you really must know, you can always scan through the stub and skeleton code to see how all this is done. ❑

The Client Side of C++ Count

The client side consists of a C++ *main* program and its header file. Like its Java counterpart, *main* must perform the following functions: 1) initialize the ORB, 2) locate a remote **Count** object, 3) set the remote *sum* attribute to zero, 4) calculate the start time, 5) invoke the *increment* method 1000 times, 6) calculate the elapsed time, and 7) print the results. Here's the code that does it all.

Listing 6-6. Client.cpp: The C++ Count Client.

```
// Client.cpp   Count Static Client, VisiBroker for C++

#include <count_c.hh>

#include <iostream.h>
#include <stdlib.h>
#include <time.h>
#include <sys\types.h>
#include <sys\timeb.h>

struct timeb timebuff;
double startTime, stopTime;

int main(int argc, char *const *argv)
{
  try
  { // Initialize the ORB
    cout << "Initializing the ORB" << endl;
```

```
    CORBA::ORB_ptr orb = CORBA::ORB_init(argc, argv);

    // Bind to the Count Object
    cout << "Binding to Count Object" << endl;
     Counter::Count_var Counter = Counter::Count::_bind("My Count");

    // Set sum to initial value of 0
    cout << "Setting sum to 0" << endl;
    Counter->sum((long)0);

    // Calculate Start time
    ftime(&timebuff);
    startTime = ((double)timebuff.time
                +((double)timebuff.millitm)/(double)1000);

    // Increment 1000 times
    cout << "Incrementing" << endl;
    for (int i=0; i<1000; i++)
    { Counter->increment();
    }

    // Calculate stop time; print out statistics
    ftime(&timebuff);
    stopTime = ((double)timebuff.time
                +((double)timebuff.millitm)/(double)1000);
    cout << "Avg Ping = " << (stopTime - startTime) << " msecs" << endl;
    cout << "Sum = " << Counter->sum();
  }
  catch(CORBA::SystemException& excep)
  { cout << "System Exception" << endl;
    cout << excep;
    return(1);
  }

  return(0);
}
```

The C++ client is very similar to its Java counterpart. Again, CORBA performs its magic. This time it allows you to invoke remote objects using ordinary C++ invocation semantics. And it's as easy to manipulate the remote *sum* attribute. Of course, to invoke these methods, we must first obtain an object reference. This is where the *bind* method comes into play. This method is automatically implemented by the local C++ **Count** proxy class.

Notice that we're using the **Count_var** type for our references instead of **Count_ptr**. We recommend that you use this reference on the client side because it takes care of memory deallocation (see the previous Details box). To use these compiler-generated C++ bindings from within our code, we must import *count_c.hh*.

This completes our dissection of the C++ code. We must still compile it and then run it.

Compile the C++ Code

We're now ready to compile our programs. You can use most C++ compilers on Unix or NT platforms to compile this code. For example, to use Visual C++ on NT, perform the following steps: 1) install Visual C++ 5.X on your machine, 2) install *VisiBroker for C++ 3.1* (see instructions on the CD-ROM), and 3) run the *nmake* utility—it will pick a file called *makefile* that we provide in the *\CorbaJava-Book.2e\CPP\Count* subdirectory. To run *nmake*, enter the following command at the prompt:

```
prompt> nmake
```

The make file builds the client and server programs. It links the client with the stub files and the server with the skeleton files. Note that with C++ we enabled thread-pooling; it provides better results for the local invocations.

Run the Client/Server Program

To run the client/server program, first start the VisiBroker *OSAgent*. You can install an OSAgent on each machine. Or, you can tell your client and server programs where to find their OSAgent when you start them. You run an OSAgent by either double-clicking on the fancy *Smart Agent* icon or by typing the following command at the prompt:

```
prompt> start osagent -c
```

Next, you must start the server. To run the server program, type the following command at the prompt:

```
prompt> start server
```

Now you can finally fire off that client. Type the following command at the prompt:

prompt> client

You should see a screen output that looks like this:

```
Initializing the ORB
Binding to Count Object
Setting sum to 0
Incrementing
Avg Ping time = 2.270 msecs
Sum = 1000
```

LOOKING AT SOME TEST RESULTS

We will run this client/server program in different situations to get a reading on the performance of C++ CORBA static method invocations. As usual, the client performs 1000 method invocations during the elapsed time. The program calculates average response time in milliseconds by dividing the elapsed time by the number of invocations.

Local Versus Remote Pings

In this test, we first run the client and server programs in the same machine—a 120-MHz Pentium running NT 4.0. Then we run them across a 10 Mbit/s Ethernet LAN. Table 6-1 compares the average response times.

Table 6-1. Local Versus Remote Static Counts: C++ Client and Server.

Local Static Count Ping (interprocess, same machine)	Remote Static Count Ping (interprocess over 10 Mbit/s Ethernet)
2.3 msecs	3.9 msecs

So it looks like C++ remote invocations are significantly slower than local ones. This is the opposite of what we saw with Java; it indicates that the Java VM is very CPU-intensive.

If you compare these numbers to the Java numbers in Chapter 4, they indicate that C++ ORBs are about 41% faster than their Java counterparts for local Pings, but are slightly slower for remote Pings. Of course, you can run the benchmarks and see for yourself. You have our code.

C++ Client to Java Count Server

In this test, we run the C++ client against the Java Count server we developed in Chapter 4. The test will demonstrate that a C++ ORB on the client side can talk to a Java ORB on the server side via IIOP. The test also demonstrates that ORBs allow you to transparently invoke objects across languages. In this case, the C++ client transparently calls a Java server object without requiring any changes to either side (see Figure 6-2). The proof is that we're mixing and matching programs that we developed in two separate chapters.

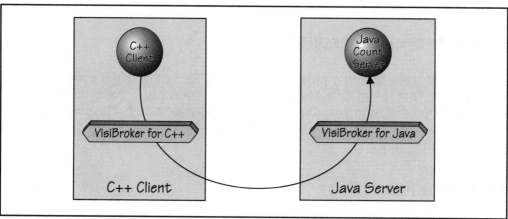

Figure 6-2. C++ Client Invoking Java Count Server.

We will first run the C++ client and Java server programs in the same machine—a 120-MHz Pentium running NT 4.0. Then we run them across a 10 Mbit/s Ethernet LAN. The OS Agent finds the Java server without any problem—whether it's running on the same machine as the client or across the network. Table 6-2 compares the average response times.

Table 6-2. Local Versus Remote Static Counts: C++ Client and Java Server.

Local Static Count Ping (interprocess, same machine)	Remote Static Count Ping (interprocess, over 10 Mbit/s Ethernet)
3.6 msecs	3.4 msecs

The results show the local interprocess performance to be slightly slower than the remote performance. However, the mind-blowing news is that Java makes a better remote server for C++ clients. Java servers are slightly faster than their C++ counterparts when servicing C++ clients. This should make the six o'clock news.

Java Client to C++ Count Server

In this test, we reverse directions and have the Java client from Chapter 4 call the C++ Count server from this chapter. This test demonstrates that Java and C++ ORBs can interoperate via IIOP. It also demonstrates that Java clients can use CORBA to transparently call objects written in other languages—in this case, C++ (see Figure 6-3). Again, we're mixing and matching programs.

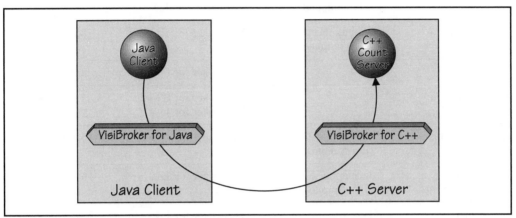

Figure 6-3. Java Client Invoking C++ Count Server.

We will first run the Java client and its C++ server in the same machine—a 120-MHz Pentium running NT 4.0. Then we run them across a 10 Mbit/s Ethernet LAN. The OSAgent finds the C++ server without any problem—whether it's running on the same machine as the client or across the network. Table 6-3 compares the average response times.

Table 6-3. Local Versus Remote Static Counts: Java Client and C++ Server.

Local Static Count Ping (interprocess, same machine)	Remote Static Count Ping (interprocess, over 10 Mbit/s Ethernet)
5.7 msecs	4.3 msecs

The local Pings are significantly slower than remote ones. However, note that the Pings are significantly faster for C++ clients to Java servers versus Java clients to C++ servers. Why? We don't have a clue. If you do, please send us a note.

Tables 6-4 and 6-5 rank the Ping results for CORBA static invocations. We rank the results from the last three chapters for remote and local invocations. As you can see, interpreted Java is not the way to go. JIT is free, so you should always use it.

The results also show that Java can hold its ground against C++, especially for remote invocations.

Table 6-4. A Comparison of Remote CORBA Static Pings.

Client Platform	Server Platform	ORB	Ping Performance
C++	Java application (JIT compiled)	VisiBroker for C++ VisiBroker for Java	3.4 msecs
Java application (JIT compiled)	Java application (JIT compiled)	VisiBroker for Java	3.6 msecs
C++	C++	VisiBroker for C++	3.9 msecs
Java application (JIT compiled)	C++	VisiBroker for C++ VisiBroker for Java	4.3 msecs
Java application (interpreted)	Java application (Interpreted)	VisiBroker for Java	5.6 msecs
Java applet (JIT compiled)	Java application (JIT compiled)	VisiBroker for Java	16.1 msecs
Java applet (interpreted)	Java application (Interpreted)	VisiBroker for Java	23.3 msecs

Table 6-5. A Comparison of local CORBA Static Pings.

Client Platform	Server Platform	ORB	Ping Performance
C++	C++	VisiBroker for C++	2.3 msecs
C++	Java application (JIT compiled)	VisiBroker for C++ VisiBroker for Java	3.6 msecs
Java application (JIT compiled)	Java application (JIT compiled)	VisiBroker for Java	3.9 msecs
Java application (JIT compiled)	C++	VisiBroker for C++ VisiBroker for Java	5.7 msecs
Java application (interpreted)	Java application (interpreted)	VisiBroker for Java	6.7 msecs
Java applet (JIT compiled)	Java application (JIT compiled)	VisiBroker for Java	16.1 msecs
Java applet (interpreted)	Java application (JIT compiled)	VisiBroker for Java	30.2 msecs

CONCLUSION

This chapter demonstrates that IIOP ORBs provide a very clean way for Java to interoperate with programs written in other languages. We showed Java clients talking to C++ servers and C++ clients talking to Java servers.

The performance results were astonishing. First, we showed that C++ local invocations are faster than their remote counterparts, which is what you would expect. Of course, with Java the reverse is true. Java remote object invocations are faster than local ones, which is counter intuitive. However, it does tell us that the Java Virtual Machine is very CPU-intensive.

The big news in this chapter is that Java ORBs are as fast as their C++ counterparts for remote invocations. The even bigger news is that Java provides a better server platform for remote C++ clients.

Does this all mean that Java ORBs are generally as fast as their C++ counterparts? *VisiBroker for C++ v3.1* is among the fastest C++ ORBs we tested in our lab. It's also a seasoned product that has been fine-tuned over time. Given this track record, *VisiBroker for Java v3.1* is blazingly fast, especially for remote invocations. We believe it can take on any C++ ORB on the market.

Part 3
The Dynamic CORBA

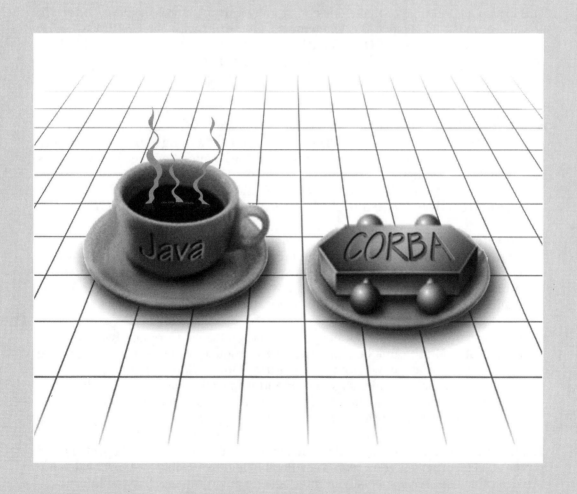

An Introduction to Part 3

In addition to static method invocations, CORBA also provides a dynamic distributed object foundation. The dynamic CORBA lets you create very flexible systems where clients and servers discover each other at run time. Servers offer new services and interfaces whenever they become available. Clients discover these interfaces and dynamically invoke them using CORBA's *Dynamic Invocation Interface (DII)*, *Trader Services*, and *Interface Repositories*.

In Part 3, we explore dynamic CORBA by looking at two versatile programming mechanisms: *dynamic invocations* and *callbacks*. With CORBA's dynamic invocations, any Java client can construct a remote method call on-the-fly, and then invoke it. With callbacks, clients can also be servers. Callbacks let servers call Java clients wherever they are. For example, callback messages from your favorite server could magically appear within your applets at any time. Callbacks extend the Java client's reach to include events generated by remote servers.

This is also a good time to make our code totally portable across vendor ORBs. To do this we must: 1) replace the Visigenic-specific *bind* with the CORBA *Naming Service*, and 2) replace BOA-related calls with the portable CORBA 3.0 POA semantics. So we will start Part 3 with a portable version of Count.

Here's what we will be covering in Part 3:

- *Chapter 7* introduces a portable version of Count. We start with a tutorial on the CORBA *Naming Service*. Then we tell you something about POA. Finally, we convert Count to use POA semantics and the Naming Service. In theory, this Portable Count should work with any CORBA ORB that complies with the new *IDL-to-Java mapping*—including JavaSoft's *Java IDL* (JDK 1.2 Edition), Iona's *OrbixWeb 3.0*, and Borland/Visigenic's *VisiBroker for Java 3.1*.

- *Chapter 8* introduces a dynamic version of the Count client. The Java client class uses CORBA's DII to invoke remote methods on a Count server. The server code remains unchanged. We will use this program to demonstrate CORBA programming, DII-style. The program will also help us understand the performance implications of these dynamic invocations. Yes, freedom comes at a price.

- *Chapter 9* is about callback magic. We use callbacks to remotely control the clients of a MultiCount benchmark. We introduce a new server—called the Coordinator—that knows how to orchestrate industrial-strength benchmarks. The Coordinator uses callbacks to start and stop all the players, and collect their statistics. At the end of Chapter 9, you will learn how to create multithreaded Java objects that are both clients and servers.

The CORBA DII and callback mechanisms extend the reach of your Java client and server objects. They let you create very flexible and extensible systems, which are two desirable features, especially in intergalactic environments like the Internet.

Chapter 7

The Portable Count

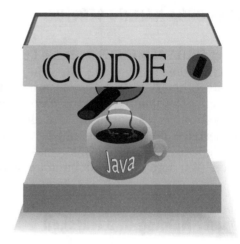

In this chapter, we create a more portable version of **Count**. With some luck, you should be able to run it on all the commercial Java ORBs—including *VisiBroker 3.1*, *OrbixWeb V3.0*, and the JDK 1.2 version of *Java IDL*. We will make the Count portable by first replacing the Visigenic-specific *bind* with the CORBA *Naming Service*, which is supported by all the CORBA ORBs on the market; it is also part of JDK 1.2. Second, we will replace the BOA-specific code in Count with POA semantics.

POA stands for the *Portable Object Adapter*; it's the CORBA 3.0 technology that makes the server side of your applications portable across multivendor ORBs. Again, all three ORBs support POA semantics (but not the full POA). In this chapter, we explain the POA semantics you'll need for Count. We provide a more detailed explanation of POA in Part 5.

So the plan for this chapter is to first give you a detailed tutorial of the CORBA Naming Service. You will discover it is a very flexible naming system you can use to create namespaces that span across multiple servers. The CORBA Naming Service does not introduce its own string-based naming conventions. Instead, it uses generic structures to compose compound names. Consequently, it can be made to work with existing global naming conventions such as URLs, domain names, DCE, JNDI, LDAP, NDS, Unix files, NT files, and others. After the tutorial on the Naming Service we will jump right into the code. We will explain the new POA APIs when we encounter them.

THE CORBA NAMING SERVICE

The CORBA *Naming Service* is like the telephone white pages for objects; it lets you find objects by name. It is the principal mechanism for objects on an ORB to locate other objects. Names are humanly recognizable values that identify an object. The naming service maps these human names to object references. A name-to-object association is called a *name binding*. A *naming context* is a namespace in which the object's name is unique. Every object has a unique reference. You can optionally associate one or more names with an object reference. You always define a name relative to its naming context.

Object Naming in a Nutshell

The Object Naming Service became an OMG standard in September 1993. It was designed to transparently encapsulate existing name and directory services such as the DCE CDS, ISO X.500, Sun NIS+, and the Internet's LDAP. The idea was not to reinvent the wheel. The Naming Service lets you create naming hierarchies. Clients can navigate through different naming context trees in search of the object they want. Name contexts from different domains can be used together to create federated naming services for objects. A CORBA naming hierarchy does not require a "universal" root.

The Naming Service has no dependencies on other CORBA object services. But if your clients need to perform complex searches, you can register naming characteristics for your object with the CORBA *Properties Service*. Clients can then use the CORBA *Query Service* to look for object names with certain externally visible characteristics—for example, objects whose *time_last_modified* date is greater than 1/1/96.

What's in a CORBA Object Name?

You can reference a CORBA object using a sequence of names that form a hierarchical naming tree (see Figure 7-1). In the figure, each dark node is a *naming context*. An object's name consists of a sequence of names (or components) that form a *compound name*. Each component—except for the last one—is used to name a context. The last component is the object's *simple* name.

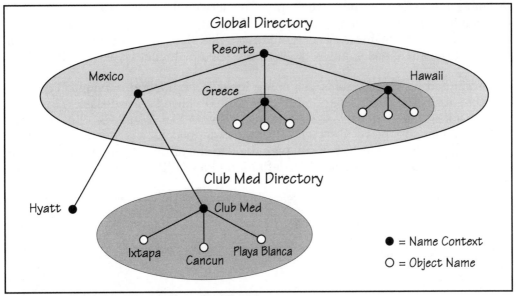

Figure 7-1. CORBA Objects Support Hierarchical Naming.

In Figure 7-2 we show a compound name that consists of a simple name—*Playa Blanca*—and three context names: *Resorts, Mexico,* and *Club Med*. The compound name defines a path for resolving context names until you get to the simple name. You can start from any context and use a sequence of names to resolve an object. To *resolve* a name means to find the object associated with the name in a given context. To *bind* a name is to create a name-to-object association for a particular context. A *binding* is a name-to-object association. A Naming Service maintains a database of *bindings* between names and object references.

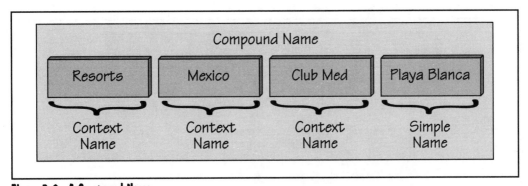

Figure 7-2. A Compound Name.

Each named component is a structure with two attributes: 1) *identifier* is the object's name string; 2) *kind* is a string in which you can put a descriptive attribute for your name—for example, a file type. The service designers prefer that you do not encode meanings directly into names. Instead, they want you to use the *kind* attribute to qualify names. The Naming Service does not interpret, assign, or manage these attributes in any way. They are used by higher levels of software.

All distributed naming systems use some form of compound naming. Typically, these are strings of slash-separated names. So you have forward-slash (/) naming systems like Unix and back-slash naming systems like Windows. In contrast, CORBA names are more abstract. They are defined as a sequence of named components. Consequently, you can map them to the different naming conventions that are in use today. Here's the IDL definition of a CORBA name:

```
// IDL
typedef sequence <NameComponent> Name;

struct NameComponent
{
  Istring id;
  Istring kind;
};
```

How Does It Work?

Figure 7-3 shows the two interfaces—**NamingContext** and **BindingIterator**—that implement the Naming Service. **NamingContext** objects contain a set of name-to-object bindings in which each name is unique. These objects may also be bound to names in other naming context objects to be part of a name hierarchy.

○ resolve	NamingContext	○ bind
○ list		○ rebind
○ destroy		○ bind_context
○ new_context		○ rebind_context
○ unbind		○ bind_new_context

○ next_one	BindingIterator
○ next_n	
○ destroy	

Figure 7-3. The Object Naming Service Interfaces.

You invoke the *bind* method in the **NamingContext** interface to associate an object's name with a binding context. The *rebind* method is the same as *bind* except that it does not return an error if the name has already been bound to another object; it simply rebinds the object to the new name. This is how you create a naming hierarchy. You invoke *unbind* to remove a name from a binding context. The *new_context* method returns the naming context. The *bind_new_context* method creates a new context and binds it to a name you supply. The *destroy* method lets you delete a naming context.

You can find any named object using the *resolve* method; it retrieves an object bound to a name in a given context. The *list* method lets you iterate through a returned set of names (it returns a **BindingIterator** object). You iterate by invoking *next_one* and *next_n* on the returned **BindingIterator** object. You invoke *destroy* to free the iteration object.

Naming Service: The CORBA IDL

The CORBA Naming Service interfaces let you manage namespaces for objects, and then query and navigate them. Like all of CORBA, the interfaces to the Naming Service are language-neutral. Clients written in different languages can use these interfaces to access CORBA Name Servers over the ORB. Also, it does not matter what language vendors use to implement these name servers. In this section, we present the IDL for the CORBA Naming Service. In the next section, we show you the corresponding Java API mapping.

Listing 7-1. CosNaming: The NamingContext Interface.

```
// CORBA IDL
interface NamingContext
{

  Object resolve(in Name n)
        raises(NotFound, CannotProceed, InvalidName);
  void list(in unsigned long how_many,
           out BindingList bl,
           out BindingIterator bi);
  void destroy() raises(NotEmpty);
  NamingContext new_context();
  void unbind(in Name n)
        raises(NotFound, CannotProceed, InvalidName);
  void bind(in Name n, in Object obj)
        raises(NotFound, CannotProceed, InvalidName, AlreadyBound);
```

```
void rebind(in Name n, in Object obj)
      raises(NotFound, CannotProceed, InvalidName);
void bind_context(in Name n, in NamingContext nc)
      raises(NotFound, CannotProceed, InvalidName, AlreadyBound);
void rebind_context(in Name n, in NamingContext nc)
      raises(NotFound, CannotProceed, InvalidName);
NamingContext bind_new_context(in Name n)
      raises(NotFound, AlreadyBound, CannotProceed, InvalidName);
};
```

Listing 7-2. CosNaming: The BindingIterator Interface.

```
//CORBA IDL
interface BindingIterator
{
 boolean next_one(out Binding b);
 boolean next_n(in unsigned long how_many, out BindingList bl);
 void destroy();
};
```

Listing 7-3. CosNaming: Data Structures.

```
// CORBA IDL
module CosNaming
{
 struct NameComponent
 {
   Istring id;
   Istring kind;
 };

 typedef sequence <NameComponent> Name;

 enum BindingType {nobject, ncontext};

 struct Binding
 {
   Name binding_name;
   BindingType binding_type;
 }
};
```

Naming Service: The Java Interfaces

The Java APIs to the Naming Service are defined using the new CORBA *IDL-to-Java* mapping. The ORB vendors simply had to compile the IDL from the previous section using their IDL-to-Java compilers. The compilers will automatically generate the Java interfaces. In addition, they generate the typical CORBA support classes—including stubs, servants, Helpers, Holders, and Tie. Of course, the CORBA vendors must still implement the Naming Service itself. Most have. In addition, it will be part of the core JDK 1.2 *CosNaming* package. So you have a wide choice of commercial implementations. We will be using the CORBA Naming Service from Borland/Visigenic.

What follows are the vendor-independent Java interfaces and classes to the Naming Service. To save a few trees, we do not show all the support classes, but they're all there.

Listing 7-4. The org.omg.CosNaming NamingContext Interface.

```Java
// Java
public interface NamingContext extends Object
{
  Object resolve(NameComponent[] n)
          throws NotFound, CannotProceed, InvalidName;
  void list(int how_many, BindingListHolder bl, BindingIteratorHolder bi);
  void destroy() throws NotEmpty;
  NamingContext new_context();
  void unbind(NameComponent[] n)
          throws NotFound, CannotProceed, InvalidName;
  void bind(NameComponent[] n, Object obj)
          throws NotFound, CannotProceed, InvalidName, AlreadyBound;
  void rebind(NameComponent[] n, Object obj)
          throws NotFound, CannotProceed, InvalidName;
  void bind_context(NameComponent[] n, NamingContext nc)
          throws NotFound, CannotProceed, InvalidName, AlreadyBound;
  void rebind_context(NameComponent[] n, NamingContext nc)
          throws NotFound, CannotProceed, InvalidName;
  NamingContext bind_new_context(NameComponent[] n)
          throws NotFound, AlreadyBound, CannotProceed, InvalidName;
}
```

Listing 7-5. The org.omg.CosNaming BindingIterator Interface.

```Java
// Java
public interface BindingIterator extends Object
```

```java
{
// Methods
public abstract boolean next_one(BindingHolder b);
public abstract boolean next_n(int how_many,
                                   BindingListHolder bl);
public abstract void destroy();
}
```

Listing 7-6. The org.omg.CosNaming NameComponent Class.

```java
// Java
public final class NameComponent extends Object
{
// Variables
public String id;
public String kind;

// Constructors
public NameComponent();
public NameComponent(String identifier String kind);
}
```

Listing 7-7. The org.omg.CosNaming Binding Class.

```java
// Java
public final class Binding extends Object
{

// Variables
public NameComponent[] binding_name;
public BindingType binding_type

// Constructors
public Binding(NameComponent[] name, BindingType type);
}
```

Listing 7-8. The org.omg.CosNaming BindingType Class.

```java
// Java
public final class BindingType extends Object
{
// Variables
public static final int _nobject;
```

```
public static final int _ncontext;
public static final BindingType nobject;
public static final BindingType ncontext;

// Methods
public int value();
public static final BindingType from_int(int i) throws BAD_PARAM;
}
```

Client/Server Naming Scenarios

Figure 7-4 shows a simplified view of the client/server naming interactions (the scenarios will provide more details). Here's what happens: 1) a server invokes *bind* to associate a logical name with an object reference, 2) the Name Server adds this obj_ref/name binding to its namespace database, 3) a client application invokes *resolve* to obtain an object reference with this name, and 4) the client uses the object reference to invoke methods on the target object. So the Name Server services both clients and servers. Servers export name/object bindings to the Name Server; clients then find these objects.

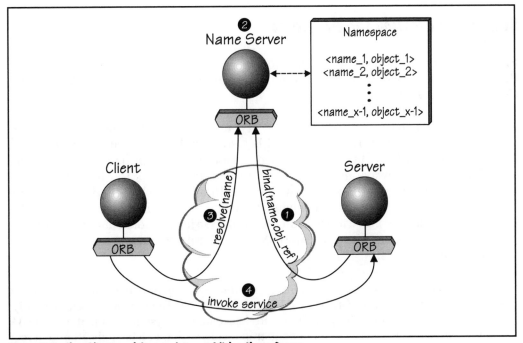

Figure 7-4. How Clients and Servers Interact With a Name Server.

Clients navigate the namespace to find object references by name. The namespace API lets you organize your object references under different naming contexts (or paths). It's like a file system for objects. In this analogy, the naming context nodes are like directories. Objects can belong to more than one context (or path). This lets you tailor the namespace to accommodate different views and needs.

In this section, we develop two usage scenarios. The first is a server-side scenario where we create the partial namespace shown in Figure 7-5. In the second scenario, a client traverses the namespace to find an object reference. The nodes *Resorts* and **Club Med** are naming contexts. *Playa Blanca* and *Cancun* are names of CORBA objects. These are objects that implement the **ClubMed** interface we develop in Part 8.

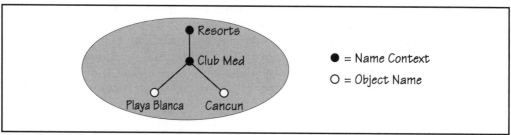

Figure 7-5. The Scenario's Naming Context Graph.

Scenario 1: Creating the Namespace

Figure 7-6 shows how a server application creates the namespace in Figure 7-5. In this scenario, the server binds its two club objects to the names *Playa Blanca* and *Cancun*. Let's walk through the steps:

1. ***Obtain the initial naming context.*** Typically, the initial context is passed to a server when it is started. The OMG is also working on defining a well-known bootstrap port (port 900) that is used to obtain an initial naming context via IIOP.[1] You will always invoke *resolve_initial_references* to obtain the initial naming context, regardless of how the ORB finds it. This method is part of the standard CORBA bootstrap mechanism, which we cover in Part 5. This **ORB** method returns a generic reference of type **Object**. Consequently, we must *narrow* (or typecast) it to the more derived **NamingContext** type. Here's the code that does this:

---

[1] The OMG is currently working on an *Interoperable Naming Service* that was proposed by IBM, SunSoft, Netscape, Oracle, and Visigenic (see OMG Document *orbos/97-06-03*). In a nutshell, these companies propose a URL-based naming system on top of the CORBA Naming Service as well as a common bootstrap mechanism that lets applications share a common initial naming context.

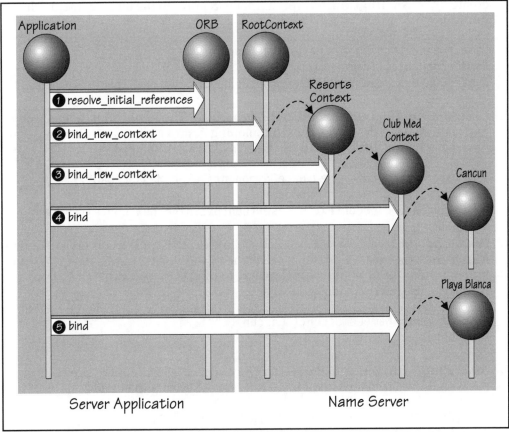

Figure 7-6. CORBA Naming Scenario 1: Creating the Namespace.

```
org.omg.CORBA.Object objRef =
        orb.resolve_initial_references("NameService");
org.omg.CosNaming.NamingContext rootContext =
        org.omg.CosNaming.NamingContextHelper.narrow(objRef);
```

The **NamingContextHelper** is a helper object. The CORBA compiler automatically generates these Helper classes for each CORBA interface. Helpers provide additional helper methods like *narrow* that are type-specific but don't deal with the business logic. The *org.omg.CosNaming* package contains Helpers and Holders for all the Naming Service classes; it also contains Java client stubs for the remote interfaces.

2. *Create a naming context called Resorts.* The application first creates a **NameComponent** object for *Resorts*; it uses a constructor that takes two string arguments: id and kind. You can pass an empty string for the kind component, as we show in this example. The application invokes *bind_new_context* to

create a new **NamingContext** for this name relative to the initial context. Here's the code:

```
NameComponent comp1 = new NameComponent("Resorts", "");
NameComponent [] name = {comp1};
NamingContext resortContext = rootContext.bind_new_context(name);
```

3. ***Create a naming context called Club Med.*** The application goes through the same steps to create a *Club Med* naming context relative to *Resorts*. This time we add an "ORG" value to the kind field. Here's the code:

```
NameComponent comp1 = new NameComponent("Club Med", "ORG");
NameComponent [] name = {comp1};
NamingContext clubContext = resortContext.bind_new_context(name);
```

4. ***Bind Cancun to its object reference***. Again, the application creates a new **NameComponent** that contains the name of the object; in this case, *Cancun*. It then invokes *bind* on the **clubContext** to bind *Cancun* with a CORBA object reference. Here's the code:

```
name[0] = new NameComponent("Cancun", "");
clubContext.bind(name, club1Ref);
```

5. ***Bind Playa Blanca to its object reference***. It's just like the previous step, but with different names and object references. Here's the code:

```
name[0] = new NameComponent("Playa Blanca", "");
clubContext.bind(name, club2Ref);
```

This concludes our first scenario. We now have a namespace. In Java, a CORBA name maps to an array of **NameComponent** objects. So we could have made our code a little bit more compact by combining steps 2 and 3 above. Here's code that creates a new name context using a compound name:

```
NameComponent comp1 = new NameComponent("Resorts", "");
NameComponent comp2 = new NameComponent("Club Med", "ORG");
NameComponent [] name = {comp1, comp2};
NamingContext clubContext = rootContext.bind_new_context(name);
```

The bottom line is that you can create namespaces that come in all shapes. Different parts of the namespace can run on different Name Servers. A naming context is an object. Consequently, it can be bound to a name in a naming context just like any other object. Because a naming context can contain other naming contexts, it is similar to a directory. A compound name contains a sequence of one or more naming contexts with the last component denoting the object. This is similar to the

way a pathname contains one or more directories with the last name being the file name.

From a programmer's perspective, the general rule is to use *bind_new_context*, *bind_context*, and *rebind_context* to create and navigate naming contexts. Use *bind* and *rebind* to bind names that are objects.

Scenario 2: Finding Objects

The scenario in Figure 7-7 shows how a client finds an object (or resolves a name) in the namespace we just created. Our client will navigate the naming context to find an object reference for the Cancun Club Med. Let's walk through the steps:

1. ***Obtain the initial naming context.*** The client obtains a reference to this context by invoking the **ORB** object's *resolve_initial_references* and then narrowing the result. Here's code that does this:

```
org.omg.CORBA.Object objRef =
                orb.resolve_initial_references("NameService");
NamingContext rootContext = NamingContextHelper.narrow(objRef);
```

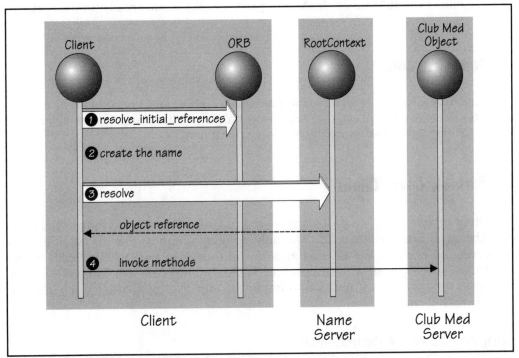

Figure 7-7. CORBA Naming Scenario 2: Finding Objects.

2. **Create the composite name you're after.** We're looking for Cancun. So we create a compound name for Cancun as follows:

```
NameComponent comp1 = new NameComponent("Resorts", "");
NameComponent comp2 = new NameComponent("Club Med", "ORG");
NameComponent comp3 = new NameComponent("Cancun", "");
NameComponent [] name = {comp1, comp2, comp3};
```

3. **Find the object with this name.** Invoke *resolve* to obtain the object reference associated with the name we just created. You must then *narrow* the objectRef to a **ClubMed** CORBA object. Remember, the Naming Service returns generic CORBA objects; you must *narrow* them to a more derived class. Here's the code:

```
org.omg.CORBA.Object objRef = rootContext.resolve (name);
ClubMed clubRef = ClubMedHelper.narrow (objRef);
```

4. **Invoke methods on the target object.** It's CORBA as usual. You can dynamically or statically invoke methods on the Cancun **ClubMed** object using the object reference you just obtained. To statically invoke methods you must have a stub for this object.

This concludes our tutorial on the Naming Service. We're now ready for the Portable Count.

THE PORTABLE COUNT

With this Name Service tutorial behind us, the Portable Count is going to be a piece of cake. There are two areas that are new in this code: the Naming Service and the POA calls. So let's go over the code to see what's new.

The Portable Count Client

The client consists of a single Java class called **CountPortableClient**. This class does the usual Count client stuff. The only thing new here is how the client locates its server objects (see the shaded area in the following code). We replaced the VisiBroker-specific *bind* with calls to the CORBA Naming Service. This code is very similar to the tutorial, so there's nothing left to say. Notice that we did add some error-handling code.

Listing 7-9. The CountPortableClient Class.

```
// CountPortableClient.java  Static Client, VisiBroker for Java
```

```java
import org.omg.CosNaming.*;

class CountPortableClient
{ public static void main(String args[])
  { try
    { // Initialize the ORB
      System.out.println("Initializing the ORB");
      org.omg.CORBA.ORB orb = org.omg.CORBA.ORB.init(args, null);

      // Get a reference to the Naming service
      org.omg.CORBA.Object nameServiceObj =
                orb.resolve_initial_references ("NameService");
      if (nameServiceObj == null)
      {
        System.out.println("nameServiceObj = null");
        return;
      }

      // Narrow the object
      org.omg.CosNaming.NamingContext nameService =
          org.omg.CosNaming.NamingContextHelper.narrow(nameServiceObj);
      if (nameService == null)
      {
        System.out.println("nameService = null");
        return;
      }

      // Locate an object called countName
      // relative to initial namecontext
      NameComponent[] countName = {new NameComponent("countName", "")};
      CounterPortable.Count counter =
          CounterPortable.CountHelper.narrow(
                nameService.resolve(countName));

      // Set sum to initial value of 0
      System.out.println("Setting sum to 0");
      counter.sum((int)0);

      // Calculate Start time
      long startTime = System.currentTimeMillis();

      // Increment 1000 times
      System.out.println("Incrementing");
      for (int i = 0 ; i < 1000 ; i++ )
      { counter.increment();
```

```
    }

    // Calculate stop time; print out statistics
    long stopTime = System.currentTimeMillis();
    System.out.println("Avg Ping = "
                    + ((stopTime - startTime)/1000f) + " msecs");
    System.out.println("Sum = " + counter.sum());
  } catch(Exception e)
  { System.err.println("Exception");
    System.err.println(e);
  }
 }
}
```

The Portable Count Server

The server side of the Portable Count consists of the CORBA IDL interface and two classes. The **CountPortableImpl** class implements the **Count** interface; it provides the servant code. The **CountPortableServer** class provides the *main* that initializes the server and then instantiates a single **CountPortableImpl** object. Here's the code:

Listing 7-10. The Count IDL.

```
// Count.idl

module CounterPortable
{
  interface Count
  { attribute long sum;
    long increment();
  };
};
```

Listing 7-11. The CountPortableImpl Class.

```
// CountPortableImpl.java: The Count Implementation
class CountPortableImpl extends CounterPortable._CountImplBase
{ private int sum;
  // Constructors
  CountPortableImpl()
  { super();
    System.out.println("Count Object Created");
```

```
     sum = 0;
  }

  // get sum
  public synchronized int sum()
  { return sum;
  }

  // set sum
  public synchronized void sum(int val)
  { sum = val;
  }

  // increment method
  public synchronized int increment()
  { sum++;
    return sum;
  }
}
```

Listing 7-12. The CountPortableServer Class.

```
// CountPortableServer.java: The Count Server main program
import org.omg.CosNaming.*;

class CountPortableServer
{ static public void main(String[] args)
  { try
    { // Initialize the ORB
      org.omg.CORBA.ORB orb = org.omg.CORBA.ORB.init(args, null);

      // Create the Count object
      CountPortableImpl count = new CountPortableImpl();
      // Export the newly created object
      orb.connect(count);

      // Get a reference to the Naming service
      org.omg.CORBA.Object nameServiceObj =
                  orb.resolve_initial_references ("NameService");
      if (nameServiceObj == null)
      {
        System.out.println("nameServiceObj = null");
        return;
      }
```

```
org.omg.CosNaming.NamingContext nameService =
    org.omg.CosNaming.NamingContextHelper.narrow(nameServiceObj);
if (nameService == null)
{
  System.out.println("nameService = null");
  return;
}

// bind the Count object in the Naming service
NameComponent[] countName = {new NameComponent("countName", "")};
nameService.rebind(countName, count);

// wait forever for current thread to die
Thread.currentThread().join();
```

```
  } catch(Exception e)
  { System.err.println(e);
  }
 }
}
```

The good news is that there are no changes in the IDL or the object implementation—it's a carbon copy of the code in Chapter 4. All the changes are in the *main* server program (see shaded area in Listing 6-12). So what's new in this code? First, we replaced the VisiBroker-specific *bind* with calls to the CORBA Naming Service; no surprises here. Second, we replaced the BOA calls in the code with POA semantics. So, what is POA? And, why did we remove the BOA calls from our portable code?

The *Portable Object Adapter (POA)* is the CORBA 3.0 version of BOA. It defines a portable API for registering your objects with the ORB and activating them on demand. The problem is that the original BOA was underspecified. Consequently, ORB vendors introduced their own BOA extensions to fill-in-the-blanks. This led to many inconsistencies in the way server programs interface with the ORB. Consequently, it made our server code not portable across vendor ORBs. POA fixes this problem (we cover the POA in detail in Part 5).

So how does POA affect your existing applications? The good news is that you won't have to rewrite your existing implementation objects; you only have to rewrite the code that interfaces with the ORB. For example, *BOA.obj_is_ready* has now been replaced by *ORB.connect* in the new OMG mappings; *BOA.deactivate_obj* has been replaced by *ORB.disconnect*. In addition, your server objects automatically become POA servants by extending **ImplBase** (we already do this).

COMPILE THE CLIENT/SERVER PROGRAM

We're now ready to compile our Java programs. To compile the Java programs, first make sure Symantec Visual Café is installed on your machine. If not, just follow the instructions on the CD-ROM. You can compile the programs by running the *make.bat* file we provide with each directory. Or, you can type the following commands at the prompt:

```
prompt> javac -d \CorbaJavaBook.2e\classes CountPortableClient.java
prompt> javac -d \CorbaJavaBook.2e\classes CountPortableServer.java
prompt> javac -d \CorbaJavaBook.2e\classes CountPortableImpl.java
```

The -d option tells the compiler to put the (.class) files it creates into the directory we specify—in this case, \CorbaJavaBook.2e\classes. If the compile is successful, you should have some compiled Java classes—(.class) files—that you can now run.

To run the client/server program, first start the VisiBroker *OSAgent*. OSAgent is only used by the Naming Service under the covers. You can run an OSAgent either by double-clicking on the fancy *Smart Agent* icon or by typing the following command at the prompt:

```
prompt> start osagent -c
```

Next, start the CORBA Naming Service using the following command:

```
prompt> java -DORBservices=CosNaming -DSVCnameroot=CorbaJava
    -DJDKrenameBug com.visigenic.vbroker.services.CosNaming.ExtFactory
    CorbaJava namingLog
```

Next, you must start the server. When running a Java program that uses the naming service, you must provide a parameter to add *CosNaming* to the bootstrap list of initial services and the name of the root context. Our root context name is *CorbaJava*. To run the server program, type the following command at the prompt:

```
prompt> start java -DORBservices=CosNaming
    -DSVCnameroot=CorbaJava CountPortableServer
```

Now, you can finally fire off that client. Type the following command at the prompt:

```
prompt> java -DORBservices=CosNaming
    -DSVCnameroot=CorbaJava CountPortableClient
```

You will see a screen output that looks like this:

```
Initializing the ORB
Setting Sum to 0
Incrementing
Avg Ping = 3.625 msec
Sum = 1000
```

LOOKING AT SOME TEST RESULTS

We will run this client/server program in different situations to get a reading on the performance of portable CORBA. The client performs the usual 1000 method invocations during the elapsed time. We're measuring the Ping performance for portable CORBA static method invocations. In this test, we first run the client and server programs in the same machine—a 120-MHz Pentium running NT 4.0. Then we run them across a 10 Mbit/s Ethernet LAN. Table 7-1 compares the results.

Table 7-1. Local Versus Remote Static Counts: Java Client and Server.

Local Static Count Ping (interprocess)	Remote Static Count Ping (interprocess over 10 Mbit/s Ethernet)
3.7 msecs	3.5 msecs

You should be warned that these numbers deviate by 10% in either direction, even with the same setup. As usual, remote invocations are slightly faster than local ones. The Portable Count performs slightly better than its Visigenic-specific counterpart from Chapter 4. So this is good news. Interestingly, the Visigenic documentation warns that you could incur a performance penalty by moving to the portable version. This doesn't appear to be the case. At least not for Pings. Anyway, try it out and see what you come up with.

CONCLUSION

This chapter finally moves us to a fully portable CORBA/IIOP platform. We are now totally compliant with the new CORBA *IDL-to-Java* standard. In theory, this Portable Count should work as is with the two other CORBA/Java ORBs: JavaSoft's *Java IDL* and Iona's *OrbixWeb 3.0*. Give it a try: you have the code. From here on we will use this portable platform to build all our CORBA programs. In addition, the CD-ROM contains a portable version of the CORBA applet from Chapter 5. So all the code we create in this book should be portable across CORBA-compliant ORBs.

Chapter 8

The Dynamic Count

In all the examples we've seen so far, clients needed a precompiled stub to invoke operations on a server object. We supplied a stub for each interface the client used. Applets are more dynamic than this. They can download the stub's bytecodes at run time—when they need to invoke an operation on a server object. However, they still need a stub to get to that server. So, is there any way for clients to get to the millions of objects on the network without requiring a precompiled stub for each server interface? The answer must be yes, or we wouldn't have written this chapter.

In this chapter, we introduce a stubless run-time binding approach—the CORBA *Dynamic Invocation Interface (DII)*. CORBA's DII lets a client pick any target object at run time and then dynamically invoke its methods. Your client can invoke any operation on any object without requiring precompiled stubs. This means that your client discovers interface-related information at invocation time; it requires no compile-time knowledge.

In the client/server world, the DII is the closest thing we have to absolute freedom. Servers offer new services and interfaces whenever they become available. Clients will discover these interfaces at run time and know how to call them. It's all part of the CORBA magic. The DII provides a very dynamic environment that allows your systems to remain flexible and extensible. This is a very desirable feature, especially in intergalactic environments like the Internet.

But how do clients first discover these remote objects? They do this using a variety of mechanisms. In the simplest approach, you can provide the client with a "stringified" object reference. The client can then convert the string into a live object reference and make the connection. Clients can also look up objects by name using the CORBA *Naming Service*. Or, they can discover these objects via CORBA's Yellow Pages—the *Trader Service*.

In an Object Web environment, objects will be dynamically discovered by spiders, crawlers, bots, search engines, publish-and-subscribe services, and agents of all types. The Traders will keep them up-to-date with the latest and greatest. It's becoming a very dynamic world out there. Once clients discover these objects, they will need the CORBA DII to invoke their operations. The alternative is to download a Java applet with a prebuilt client for a particular service. There is room for both approaches.

In this chapter, we will start our exploration of Dynamic CORBA by creating a DII version of the Count client. Servers don't care whether their clients call them using the DII or via precompiled stubs. It's all the same to them. So, to accept DII calls we don't do anything special on the server. Consequently, we will just reuse the Count server from Chapter 7. But we must still write the dynamic client.

Everything in life is a trade-off. In this case, the trade-off is that we pay for our new-found freedom by writing more lines of code. The dynamic client is much more complex than its static counterpart. But once you get the hang of it, you may like it. As a side benefit, we will be able to compare the performance of a dynamic CORBA invocation with that of a static one. Now, that's something to anticipate.

CORBA 101: DYNAMIC INVOCATIONS

Before you can dynamically invoke a method on an object, you must first find the object and obtain its reference. Once you have the object reference, you can use it to retrieve the object's interface and dynamically construct the request. You must specify in the request the method you want to execute and its parameters. You typically obtain this information from an *Interface Repository (IR)*. A *Trader Service* can augment the IR. For example, it can specify the range of values a server expects.

Dynamic Invocations: The Big Picture

Let's assume that you acquired—by whatever means—a reference for the object you want to dynamically invoke. Here's a very high-level description of how you invoke a remote method on this object (see Figure 8-1):

1. ***Obtain the interface name.*** In our scenario, we have a reference for the server object. CORBA objects are introspective; they can provide you with quite a bit of information about themselves. Consequently, we can ask this object for the name of its interface by invoking the object's *get_interface* method. This call returns a reference to **InterfaceDef** object. This is an object inside an Interface Repository that describes this interface. We cover Interface Repository in Part 5.

2. ***Obtain the method description from the Interface Repository.*** We can use the **InterfaceDef** as an entry-point for navigating the Interface Repository. We can obtain all kinds of detailed information about the interface and the methods it supports. CORBA specifies about ten calls for navigating the Interface Repository and describing the objects it contains. In our example, the client issues a *lookup_name* to find the method it wants to invoke. It then issues a *describe* call to obtain the method's full IDL definition. Or you can issue a

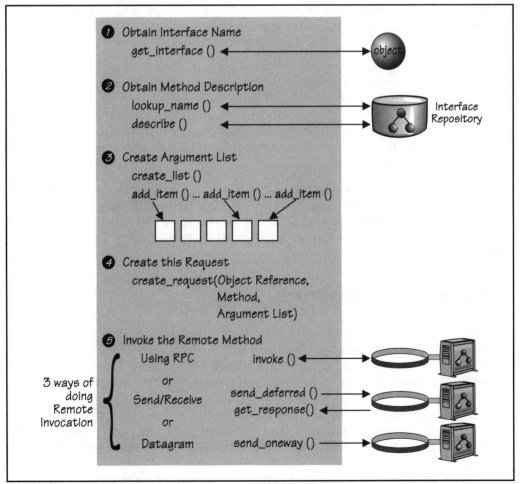

Figure 8-1. The CORBA Dynamic Invocation Process.

describe_interface to obtain a full description of the interface and find the method you want to invoke.

3. ***Create the argument list***. CORBA specifies a self-defining data structure for passing parameters, which it calls the *Named Value List*. You implement this list using an **NVList** pseudo-object. You create the list by invoking *create_list* and as many *add_item* calls as it takes to add each argument to the list. Alternatively, you can let the ORB create the list for you by invoking *create_operation_list* on a **CORBA::ORB** object. You must pass it the name of the operation for which it returns a list.

4. ***Create the request***. A request is a CORBA pseudo-object that contains the name of the method, the argument list, and the return value. You create a request by invoking *create_request*. You must pass it the name of the method to invoke, the **NVList**, and a pointer to the return value. Alternatively, you can create a short version of the request by invoking *_request* and passing it the name of the method you want to invoke. You use the short version to invoke methods that do not require parameters.

5. ***Invoke the request***. You can invoke a request in one of three ways: 1) the *invoke* call sends the request and obtains the results; 2) the *send_deferred* call returns control to the program, which must then poll for the response by issuing *poll_response* or *get_response*; and 3) the send call can be defined to be a datagram by issuing *send_oneway*—in this case, no response is needed. These three invocation styles are sometimes referred to as synchronous, deferred synchronous, and one-way.

As you can see, it takes quite a bit of effort to dynamically invoke a method. Actually, invoking the method is easy—the hard part is constructing the request. This task is made even more complicated by the different ways you can construct and invoke a remote method. As usual, you're trading off complexity and performance for added flexibility.

The Dynamic Invocation Interfaces

The services you need to dynamically invoke an object are part of the CORBA core. Unfortunately, the methods are dispersed across four interfaces in the CORBA module (see methods with light buttons in Figure 8-2). Here's a quick overview of the methods in these four interfaces that you use for dynamic invocation:

■ **CORBA::Object** is a pseudo-object interface that defines operations that every CORBA object must support.[1] It's the root interface for all CORBA objects. This interface includes three methods that you can use to construct dynamic invoca-

---

[1] These operations are performed by the ORB. You simply inherit them when you create your object.

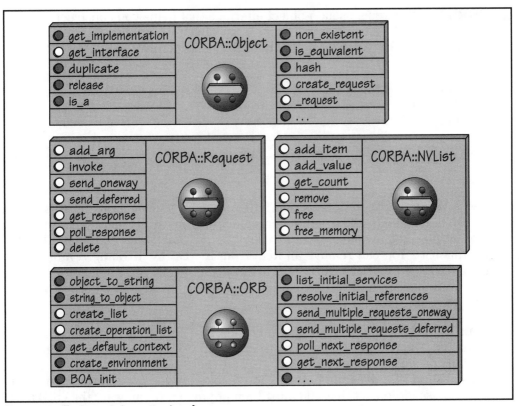

Figure 8-2. The Dynamic Invocation Interfaces.

tions. You invoke *get_interface* to obtain the interface an object supports. The call returns a reference to an **InterfaceDef**, which is an object inside an Interface Repository that describes this interface. You invoke *create_request* to create a **Request** object; you must pass it the method name and parameters for the remote invocation. Or, you can create a short version of the request object by invoking *_request*; you simply pass it the name of the method (or operation in CORBA-speak) that you want to remotely invoke.

■ **CORBA::Request** is a pseudo-object interface that defines the operations on a remote object. The *add_arg* method incrementally adds arguments to the request. The *invoke* method does a call/return. The *send_deferred* method returns control to your program after transmitting the request. You invoke *poll_response* to find out if there's any returned message. Then you invoke *get_response* to read the message. You can send a datagram by invoking *send_oneway*. You invoke *delete* to delete the **Request** object from memory.

- **CORBA::NVList** is a pseudo-object interface that helps you construct parameter lists. An **NVList** object maintains a list of self-describing data items called NamedValues. Here's the IDL that defines this structure:

```
struct NamedValue
{ Identifier  name;        //argument name
  any         argument;    //argument
  long        len;         //length/count of argument value
  Flags       arg_modes;   //in, out, or inout
};
```

The **NVList** interface defines operations that let you manipulate a list. You invoke *add_item* to add a parameter to the list. You can set its value by invoking *add_value*. You invoke *get_count* to obtain the total number of items allocated for this list. You can remove an item from the list by invoking *remove*. You invoke *free_memory* to free any dynamically allocated out-arg memory associated with the list. And you invoke *free* to free the list structure itself; it will call *free_memory* on your behalf.

- **CORBA::ORB** is a pseudo-object interface that defines general-purpose ORB methods. You can invoke these methods on an ORB pseudo-object from either a client or server implementation. Six of these methods are specific to the construction of a dynamic request. You invoke *create_list* to create an empty **NVList** pseudo-object that you must then populate. If you want the ORB to do the work for you, call *create_operation_list* instead. This method will create an **NVList** and automatically populate it with the descriptions of the arguments for the remote operation you specify. The **ORB** provides four operations for sending and receiving multiple requests. You invoke *send_multiple-_requests_oneway* to send a multiple datagrams. You invoke *send_multiple-_requests_deferred* to send multiple request/reply messages. You poll for replies by invoking *poll_next_response*; you invoke *get_next_response* to read the next response.

In addition to these four interfaces, you also use Interface Repository objects to construct a remote invocation. It's quite an undertaking.

Dynamic Invocation Scenarios

Are you getting overwhelmed by all these interfaces? If you are, don't feel bad. You're not alone. We discovered that the best way to decipher this stuff is to walk through three object interaction diagrams that show how the pieces play together. Why three? Because there is more than one way to skin this cat. We call the first scenario the "Do-It-Yourself." It shows how to do a remote invocation the hard way.

We call the second scenario "ORB-Can-Help." It shows the one small thing an ORB can do to help you. Finally, the third scenario shows a different technique for doing it the hard way; we'll call it "Yet-Another-Way." We don't want to turn this into a Soapbox, but it appears that the CORBA designers had one too many espressos when they were designing the Dynamic Invocation Interface.

Dynamic Invocation: The Do-It-Yourself Scenario

As we said earlier, creating a request is the hardest part of a dynamic invocation. In this scenario, we assemble the request without any help from the ORB. Here's a step-by-step description of the object interactions shown in Figure 8-3:

1. ***Ask the object for its interface definition***. You can invoke *get_interface* on any CORBA object to obtain an **InterfaceDef** object that fully describes this interface in the Interface Repository.

2. ***Look up the method you're interested in.*** You invoke *lookup_name* on the **InterfaceDef** object to obtain an **OperationDef** object that fully describes the method you want to dynamically invoke.

3. ***Obtain the method's description.*** You invoke *describe* on the **OperationDef** object to obtain a full description of the method.

4. ***Create an empty NVList***. You invoke *create_list* on the ORB object to create an empty **NVList**. You must specify the number of items to allocate for this list.

5. ***Populate the NVList.*** You invoke *add_item* and *add_value* for each argument in the method.

6. ***Create the request object***. You invoke *create_request* on the object reference to create a **Request** object. You must pass it: 1) the name of the method, 2) the **NVList**, and 3) a **NamedValue** to receive the result.

7. ***Invoke the remote operation.*** You issue *invoke* to call the method on the remote object. This is a synchronous invocation. The results will appear in the **Request** object.

8. ***Free the request object.*** You issue *delete* to destroy the **Request** object. Yes, it breaks our heart to do this after all the effort it took to assemble it, but that's life.

9. ***Free the NVList***. You invoke *free* to release the space associated with the **NVList**.

As you can see, it takes quite a bit of work to dynamically create a request. In the next scenario, we let the ORB do some of this work for us.

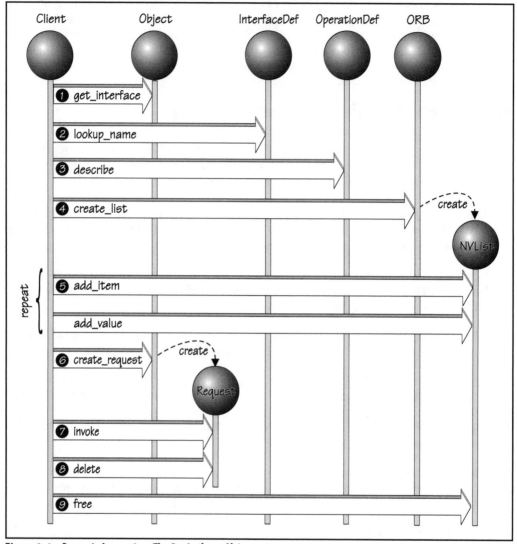

Figure 8-3. Dynamic Invocation: The Do-It-Yourself Scenario.

Dynamic Invocation: The ORB-Can-Help Scenario

This scenario is slightly easier because we will let the ORB assemble the parameter descriptions for us. Here's a step-by-step description of the object interactions shown in Figure 8-4:

1. ***Ask the object for its interface definition***. You can invoke *get_interface* on any CORBA object to obtain an **InterfaceDef** object that fully describes this

interface in the Interface Repository.

2. ***Look up the method you're interested in.*** You invoke *lookup_name* on the **InterfaceDef** object to obtain an **OperationDef** object that fully describes the method you want to dynamically invoke.

3. ***Tell the ORB to create and populate an NVList***. You invoke *create_operation_list* to let the ORB create an **NVList** that it populates with the name and data types of the arguments; you must pass it the **OperationDef**.

4. ***Set the values for your arguments***. You invoke *add_value* to set the value of each argument in the **NVList**.

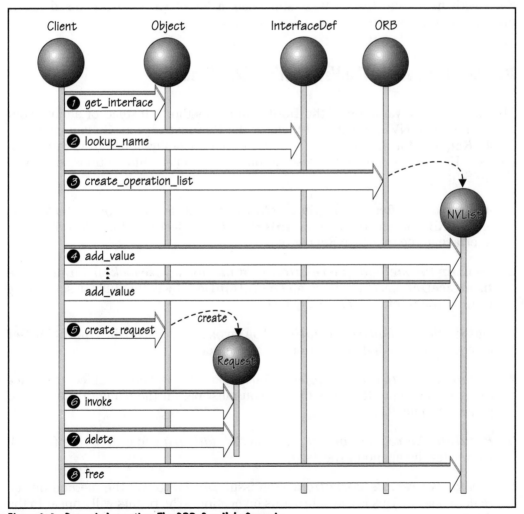

Figure 8-4. Dynamic Invocation: The ORB-Can-Help Scenario.

5. **Create the request object**. You invoke *create_request* on the object reference to create a **Request** object. You must pass it: 1) the name of the method, 2) the **NVList**, and 3) a **NamedValue** to receive the result.

6. **Invoke the remote operation**. You issue *invoke* to call the method on the remote object. This is a synchronous invocation. The results will appear in the **Request** object.

7. **Free the request object**. You issue *delete* to destroy the **Request** object.

8. **Free the NVList**. You invoke *free* to release the space associated with the **NVList**.

Even with help from the ORB, it still takes a lot of work to do this dynamic invocation. But it's a step in the right direction.

Dynamic Invocation: The Yet-Another-Way Scenario

This scenario is a variation of the Do-It-Yourself method. Instead of adding your arguments to an **NVList**, you add them to the **Request** object. So you create an empty **Request** for an operation. You then incrementally populate it with arguments. Here's a step-by-step description of the object interactions shown in Figure 8-5:

1. **Ask the object for its interface definition**. You can invoke *get_interface* on any CORBA object to obtain an **InterfaceDef** object that fully describes this interface in the Interface Repository.

2. **Look up the method you're interested in**. You invoke *lookup_name* on the **InterfaceDef** object to obtain an **OperationDef** object that fully describes the method you want to dynamically invoke.

3. **Obtain the method's description**. You invoke *describe* on the **OperationDef** object to obtain a full description of the method.

4. **Create an empty request object**. You invoke *_request* on the object reference to create an empty **Request** object; you must pass it the name of the method you want to invoke.

5. **Populate the request object**. You invoke *add_arg* and *add_value* for each parameter the method expects.

6. **Invoke the remote operation**. You issue *invoke* to call the method on the remote object. This is a synchronous invocation. The results will appear in the **Request** object.

7. ***Free the request object***. You issue *delete* to destroy the **Request** object.

As you can see, we took a step backwards. This was just another form of do-it-yourself construction. However, it can be useful in some situations. For example, when the method you invoke takes no parameters. Then you simply create a request and invoke it.

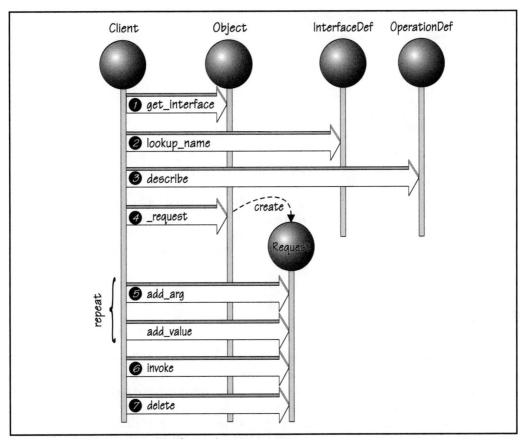

Figure 8-5. Dynamic Invocation: The Yet-Another-Way Scenario.

THE DYNAMIC COUNT

OK, it's time to write some code. In this section, we create the DII version of the Count client. After marinating you with all these scenarios, it should hopefully go down like a warm fudge brownie.

The Count IDL

We will use the Count server class from Chapter 7, as is. Consequently, the IDL remains unchanged. We list it here one more time for your convenience. It's probably engraved in your brain by now.

Listing 8-1. Count.IDL: CORBA IDL Definition of the Count Interface.

```
module Counter
{
  interface Count
  {
    attribute long sum;
    long increment();
  };
};
```

You do not need stubs for a dynamic client. However, we will create a mixed client that does both static and dynamic invocations. We will invoke *increment* dynamically and statically manipulate the *sum* attribute. The idea is to show you that you can mix the two invocation styles in your programs. We will use the stubs from Chapter 7 for the static manipulations.

The Client Side of Count

The client program consists of a single Java class—**CountClientDii**. This class provides *main* and must perform the following functions: 1) initialize the ORB, 2) locate a remote **Count** object, 3) set the remote *sum* attribute to zero, 4) calculate the start time, 5) build the dynamic request, 6) invoke the *increment* method 1000 times, 7) calculate the elapsed time, and 8) print the results. If you start the program with an argument called "loop_all," it will rebuild the dynamic request every time it invokes the method. Otherwise, it only loops on the method invocation. We did this to measure the average time it takes to prepare a request. You'll be surprised at the results. But we're getting ahead of our story. Here's the code:

Listing 8-2. CountClientDii: The Main Client Program.

```
// CountClientDii.java  Dynamic Client, VisiBroker for Java
import org.omg.CosNaming.*;

class CountClientDii
{ public static void main(String args[])
```

```java
{
  boolean loop_all = false;
  long startTime, stopTime;
  org.omg.CORBA.Request request;

  try
  { // Initialize the ORB
    System.out.println("Initializing the ORB");
    org.omg.CORBA.ORB orb = org.omg.CORBA.ORB.init(args, null);

    // Get a reference to the Naming service
    org.omg.CORBA.Object nameServiceObj =
                orb.resolve_initial_references ("NameService");
    if (nameServiceObj == null)
    {
      System.out.println("nameServiceObj = null");
      return;
    }

    // Narrow to the Name Service Object
    org.omg.CosNaming.NamingContext nameService =
        org.omg.CosNaming.NamingContextHelper.narrow(nameServiceObj);
    if (nameService == null)
    {
      System.out.println("nameService = null");
      return;
    }

    // Locate an object called countName
    // relative to initial namecontext
    NameComponent[] countName = {new NameComponent("countName", "")};
    CounterPortable.Count counter =
        CounterPortable.CountHelper.narrow(
                nameService.resolve(countName));

    // Set Sum to initial value of 0
    System.out.println("Setting Sum to 0");
    counter.sum((int)0);

    if ((args.length != 0) &&
        (args[0].compareTo("loop_all") == 0))
      loop_all = true;
    if (loop_all)
    {
      System.out.println("Starting IR lookup + invoke test");
```

```java
      // Calculate Start time
      startTime = System.currentTimeMillis();

      for (int i = 0 ; i < 1000 ; i++ )
      {
        request = buildRequest(counter);
        request.invoke();
      }
    }else
    {
      System.out.println("Starting invoke only test");
      request = buildRequest(counter);

      // Calculate Start time
      startTime = System.currentTimeMillis();

      // Increment 1000 times
      for (int i = 0 ; i < 1000 ; i++ )
      { request.invoke();
      }
    }
    // Calculate stop time; print out statistics
    stopTime = System.currentTimeMillis();
    System.out.println("Avg Ping = "
                       + ((stopTime - startTime)/1000f)
                       + " msecs");
    System.out.println("Sum = " + counter.sum());
  }
  catch(Exception e)
  { System.err.println("System Exception");
    System.err.println(e);
  }
}

public static org.omg.CORBA.Request buildRequest(
                               CounterPortable.Count counter)
{
  //get interface for Count object
  org.omg.CORBA.InterfaceDef CountInterface =
                               counter._get_interface();

  // describe interface for Count object
  org.omg.CORBA.InterfaceDefPackage.FullInterfaceDescription intDesc =
           CountInterface.describe_interface();
```

```
    if (intDesc.operations[0].name.compareTo("increment") == 0)
    { //create request object for dynamic increment
       org.omg.CORBA.Request request = counter._request("increment");
       // initialize result value
       request.result().value().insert_long(0);
       return request;
    } else
       System.out.println("Unknown method");
    return null;
  }
}
```

Notice that we're using a variation of the "Yet-Another-Way" scenario to build the dynamic request. The *increment* operation requires no parameters. Consequently, we can immediately invoke *_request* to create a **Request** object with no parameters.

We threw in two operations—*_get_interface and describe_interface*—to show you how they work. They're a bit of an overkill in this simple example. We poke inside the **FullInterfaceDescription** to look for the *increment* method. It's a sanity check—we make sure the interface supports this operation before we invoke it. An alternative way to do this is to use *create_operation_list*.

Note that *increment* has a return value. We must tell the **request** object the type of this return value. This is called "priming." In this case, we prime the return value for an integer and we set it to zero using *insert_long*. We could have retrieved this information from the description, but we wanted to keep this example short. This completes our overview of the DII code.

Compile the Java Code Using The Symantec Compiler

We're now ready to compile the DII client code. Make sure you have installed the Symantec Visual Café compiler; then enter the following command at the prompt:

prompt> javac -d \CorbaJavaBook.2e\classes CountClientDii

The -d option tells the compiler to put the (.class) files it creates into the directory we specify—in this case, \CorbaJavaBook.2e\classes. If the compile is successful, you should have some compiled Java classes—(.class) files—that you can now run.

Run the Client/Server Program

First start the OSAgent, the Naming Service, and the Count Server (follow the same steps as in Chapter 7). Next, you must start the Interface Repository and add the Count IDL to the repository. When you start the Interface Repository you can specify the name by which the repository will be known and the name of the file where it will store its information. Enter the following commands:

```
prompt> start irep myIR myIR.dat
prompt> idl2ir -replace count.idl
```

The *replace* option allows an interface definition already stored in the Interface Repository to be overwritten.

Now you can finally fire off that DII client. Type the following command at the prompt:

```
prompt> java -DORBservices=CosNaming
        -DSVCnameroot=CorbaJava CountPortableClient
```

You should see a screen output that looks like this:

```
Initializing the ORB
Binding to Count Object
Setting Sum to 0
Strting invoke only test
Avg Ping = 3.925 msec
Sum = 1000
```

To calculate the overhead of constructing the requests, type the following command at the prompt:

```
prompt> java -DORBservices=CosNaming
        -DSVCnameroot=CorbaJava CountClientDii loop_all
```

LOOKING AT SOME TEST RESULTS

We will run this client/server program in different situations to get a reading on the performance of CORBA dynamic method invocations. The client performs 1000 method invocations during the elapsed time. The program calculates the average response time in milliseconds by dividing the elapsed time by the number of invocations. We're measuring equivalent of a Ping for CORBA dynamic method invocations.

In this test, we first run the client and server programs in the same machine—a 120-MHz Pentium running NT 4.0. Next, we run them across a 10 Mbit/s Ethernet LAN. Finally, we repeat the local and remote tests with the "loop_all" parameter turned on. This adds the overhead associated with constructing the requests to our average response times. Table 8-1 compares the results.

Table 8-1. Local Versus Remote Dynamic Counts: Java DII Client and Server.

	Local Dynamic Count Ping (interprocess, same machine)	Remote Dynamic Count Ping (interprocess, over 10 Mbit/s Ethernet)
Invoke only	3.9 msecs	3.6 msecs
Prepare and invoke	61.4 msecs	57.8 msecs

The big surprise here is the huge overhead associated with constructing a request. It's definitely not cheap. Of course, we're doing several lookups against an Interface Repository every time we construct this request. It does chew up quite a few machine and disk cycles. But now we can put a price tag on freedom. Are you still willing to trade-off performance for flexibility? We're sure it's worth it in certain situations. But we're not planning to throw away our stubs soon (see next section).

WHEN TO USE DYNAMIC

With traditional CORBA, you have only two choices for your invocations: static precompiled stubs or dynamic invocations using DII. Java gives us a third choice: downloadable stubs. Remember, stub bytecodes are Java classes. You download them along with an applet. So, you get both the client code and the stubs—it's really a downloadable client technique. Now, which of these three techniques should you use? It depends on your usage patterns (see Table 8-2).

Table 8-2. DII Versus the Alternatives.

Usage Pattern	Recommended Invocation Technique
Client invokes server object frequently; server object does not change.	Use static precompiled stubs.
Client invokes server object infrequently.	Use dynamic invocations (DII).
Client discovers server object at run time.	Use dynamic invocations (DII).
Client runs within browser; it discovers new object.	Use downloadable applet and static stubs. Applet becomes the client for this object.

CONCLUSION

This concludes our Dynamic Count program. We spent most of this chapter in tutorial mode explaining the different DII techniques. The *increment* method was relatively easy to build and did not require all the sophistication DII provides. The big revelation in this chapter is that DII calls can be over 15 times slower than static invocations. The invocation itself is not very slow. The overhead comes from building the request.

Chapter 9

MultiCount: The Jazzed-Up Count

In this chapter, we develop a full-featured version of the Count program. We call it MultiCount. We use it to provide a benchmarking framework for Count that lets you start and stop multiple clients and obtain their results. In addition, the new MultiCount demonstrates *callbacks*, CORBA-style. So what's a callback? It's a call from a server to a client. A callback reverses the client and server roles; it allows a client to become a server. The *VisiBroker for Java* CORBA ORB is both a client and a server. Consequently, any client can automatically receive callbacks. Any server that has an object reference for the client's callback object can remotely invoke it.

As you will see in this chapter, you must first create a multithreaded client to receive callbacks. So we will show you how to write such a client using Java's threads. We will also introduce a new server—the Coordinator—that uses callbacks to remotely control clients. In this case, the Coordinator will orchestrate the Count benchmark. But you can use the Coordinator to orchestrate almost any type of client/server situation. We will also develop an applet that serves as a visual front-end to the Coordinator. We call it the MultiConsole.

Once you get the hang of it, you'll find that callbacks are extremely versatile. They let you create very dynamic client/server environments that fully complement Java. Callbacks extend the client's event-driven architecture to include messages from their servers. In our example, the server uses callbacks to tell its clients to start and stop incrementing Count. Surely, you'll find more exciting uses for this technology.

In general, servers invoke callbacks whenever they have something urgent to tell you. Callbacks from servers will soon magically pop up inside your applets or Java client applications (see Figure 9-1). This chapter should give you a taste for these forthcoming attractions. We're moving to a brave new world where every client is also a server.

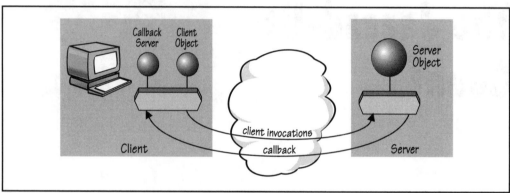

Figure 9-1. Callbacks, or When Servers Call Their Clients.

THE DESIGN OF MULTICOUNT

The minimalist Count of the previous chapters consisted of a single client talking to a server. We had no way to synchronize the starting and stopping of multiple clients on multiple machines. We also had no automatic way to collect statistics from multiple clients. In contrast to this minimalist Count, MultiCount introduces a Coordinator that synchronizes the invocation of *increment* methods across multiple clients on multiple machines. The Coordinator also collects statistics from clients and displays them via an applet. In addition, the new clients have visual interfaces that can display these statistics locally. We will use the MultiCount client to run static CORBA method invocations against the Count server. This is a multiclient version of the program we introduced in Chapter 7.

MultiCount is a complex system consisting of many parts. The good news is that none of the individual parts are by themselves very complex. In fact, each part uses CORBA and Java technology that should—by now—be old hat. Except for threads, we do not introduce any new programming concepts. What is new are the dynamic interactions between the client and server parts—for example, the use of callbacks.

You can think of these interactions as design patterns for client/server systems. You can use these patterns to create very sophisticated client/server systems.

The key is to understand how simple parts can play together to create a complex whole (or client/server ensemble). In this section, we first introduce the players and explain their parts. We then go over the CORBA interfaces that define each server part's contract with the outside world. Finally, we go over a scenario that shows how the client and server parts play together.

Meet the Players

Figure 9-2 shows the four types of programs that play in a MultiCount distributed system. Here's a brief description of what they each do:

■ **CountMultiClient** is a multithreaded version of the traditional Count client application. The multithread capability allows the client to receive callbacks on a separate thread. One thread invokes remote *increment* methods on the Count server, while the other waits on the Coordinator to tell it when to stop. So we have a hybrid that is both a client and a server. You can start as many of these hybrid clients as you want; in the next figure, we show three. The client application also has a simple GUI interface consisting of four AWT widgets.

■ **MultiConsole** is a client applet that also serves as our control panel for running the benchmark programs. You use this applet to tell the clients when to start and stop invoking remote increments. The applet also displays the benchmark results—including the average Ping for the server and that of each individual client.

■ **Count** is the unmodified version of our Count server. For the first time, we have multiple clients invoking its services. So we will be able to say something about its multithreaded capabilities. Note that they were always there.

■ **Coordinator** is a new server application that knows how to orchestrate and run races. In this case, it tells our clients when to start and stop issuing *increment* method invocations against the Count server. The clients must register with the Coordinator when they first come up. When you click on the "Run" button, the MultiConsole tells the Coordinator to start counting. The Coordinator then tells each registered client to start issuing *increment* methods; it does this via a callback. When you click on the "Stop" button, MultiConsole tells the Coordinator to stop counting. The Coordinator then tells each client to stop counting—again via callbacks. The clients return their individual counts as part of the callback. The Coordinator returns all this information to the Console, which then displays it.

Clearly, this is a more complex system than the minimalist Count of the previous chapters. In the distributed world, whenever you have complex systems you also have coordinators. They typically provide brokering functions to articulate the pieces. Our design is no exception.

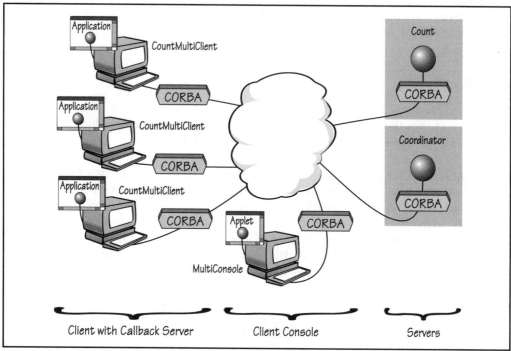

Figure 9-2. MultiCount: Meet the Players.

The MultiCount CORBA Interfaces

Figure 9-3 shows the CORBA IDL interfaces for the different parts of the MultiCount system. These are the methods you can remotely invoke via a CORBA ORB. We will later go over the classes that implement these methods. The **ClientControl** interface defines the two callback methods clients export to their **Coordinator** servers. A **Coordinator** invokes *start* to tell the client to start a loop that invokes *increment* methods on the Count server; it invokes *stop* to end the loop.

The **Coordinator** interface consists of three methods: *register*, *start*, and *stop*. Clients invoke *register* to register their **ClientControl** object references with the **Coordinator**. The MultiConsole applet invokes *start* to start the benchmark. This causes the **Coordinator** to invoke a *start* method on every **ClientControl** object that has registered with it. The applet invokes the *stop* method on the **Coordinator** to terminate the counting. This causes the **Coordinator** to invoke *stop* on all the **ClientControl** objects.

The **Count** interface is still the same. It exports that famous *increment* method. Clients spin in a loop invoking *increment* methods on **Count** when they receive a *start* callback. They break out of the loop when they receive a *stop*. So all the registered clients will concurrently (and continuously) invoke *increment* calls from the time you click on "Run" to the time you click on "Stop."

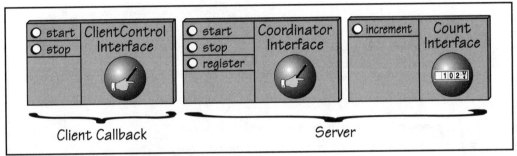

Figure 9-3. The MultiCount CORBA Interfaces.

A MultiCount Callback Scenario

It's time for a little scenario that shows how the parts play together. In this scenario, we treat each client as a monolithic entity. Later in this chapter, we break the client apart and go over its internal classes and threads. We will then present a more detailed scenario that includes the interactions between the client's internal objects and threads. Figure 9-4 shows a MultiCount scenario with two clients. In the scenario, the servers are up and running. Here's what happens when we start the client applications:

1. ***Client 1 registers with the Coordinator.*** You launch the Java client application and pass it a string that contains the client's number. This is our first client, so we'll give it a "1." The client then invokes the *register* method on the **Coordinator** and passes it two parameters: 1) a string with this client's number, and 2) the object reference of its **ClientControl** callback object. Note that you will see a window with "Run" and "Stop" buttons (see Figure 9-5). You can use this window to manually start and stop the Counts. In this scenario, the **Coordinator** will orchestrate the benchmark. So you shouldn't click on these buttons. The window also provides local feedback on this client's performance. However, you can obtain this same information from the MultiConsole applet. In our scenario, we try to do everything via remote control.

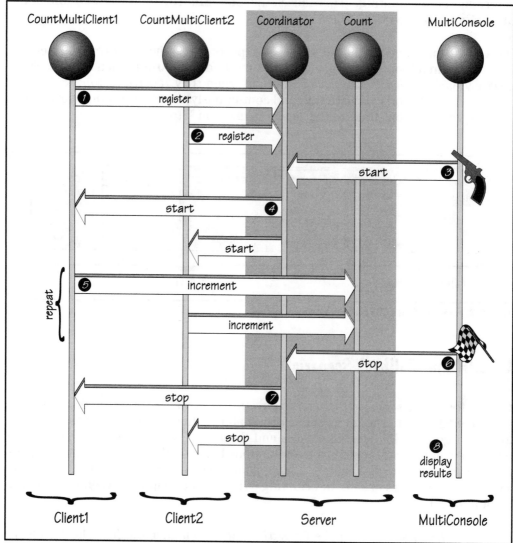

Figure 9-4. A MultiCount Scenario With Two Concurrent Clients.

Count Client Number 1	_ □ ×
Status	Sum = 2693, Avg Ping = 7.876346 msec:
Run	Stop

Figure 9-5. A Screenshot of the Client Window.

2. *Client 2 registers with the Coordinator.* You launch another instance of the Java client application and give it a different number, "2." The client will invoke the *register* method on the **Coordinator** and pass it all the relevant information. Note that you can start multiple clients on the same machine to simulate a network of clients. If you have the hardware, you should run each client on its own machine.

3. *Start counting.* You start the benchmark by clicking on the MultiConsole applet's "Run" button. The applet invokes the *start* method on the **Coordinator**. It also starts the timer.

4. *The Coordinator starts the clients.* The **Coordinator** invokes the *start* method on each client callback object that has registered with it. In this case, it knows of two clients. The ORB delivers each callback to a Java object that implements the IDL-defined **ClientControl** interface.

5. *The clients invoke increment calls.* Each of the clients goes into a loop that continuously invokes *increment* calls on the **Count** server.

6. *Stop counting.* You stop the benchmark by clicking on the MultiConsole applet's "Stop" button. The applet invokes the *stop* method on the **Coordinator**. It also stops the timer.

7. *The Coordinator stops each client.* The **Coordinator** invokes the *stop* method on each client callback object that has registered with it. In this case, it knows of two clients. The callback returns a string that contains the client's local count statistics.

8. *The applet displays the results.* The MultiConsole applet's status field will display the total number of counts and the average Ping response time for the Count server—it divides the elapsed time by the total number of counts. It also displays a listbox with the individual client results (see Figure 9-6).

You can see that we've included in the total elapsed time some coordination overhead. This added overhead becomes insignificant if you run the benchmark for more than a few minutes. So we recommend that you run the benchmark for at least 10 minutes to get representative numbers.

THE MULTICONSOLE APPLET

One of the benefits of IDL-defined distributed components is that they are self-contained entities. We can start our description of the code by looking at any of the components in no particular order. So we will start with the MultiConsole applet. We will first show you a screenshot of the applet and then go into the code.

What the Applet Looks Like

Figure 9-6 shows a screenshot of the MultiConsole Applet. It's your typical AWT grid with the following six components: two labels, two buttons, a listbox, and a text field. It's not very pretty, but it's functional. The status field shows the total benchmark results—including the total count and the average count response time. The listbox displays individual client results—including the number of counts this client issued, and the average response time for this client. You click on the "Run" and "Stop" buttons to start and stop the counting.

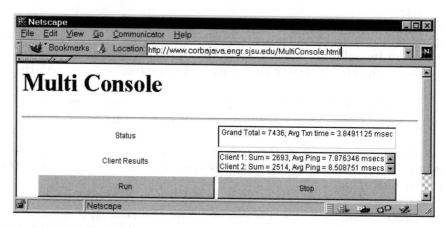

Figure 9-6. The MultiConsole Applet.

The MultiConsole Applet HTML

You can use the following HTML to run this applet:

```
<h1>Multi Console</h1>
<hr>
<center>
  <APPLET
    CODE=MultiConsoleApplet.class WIDTH=600 HEIGHT=120>
    <param name=org.omg.CORBA.ORBClass
           value=com.visigenic.vbroker.orb.ORB>
    <param name=ORBservices value=CosNaming>
    <param name=SVCnameroot value=JavaCorba>
  </APPLET>
</center>
<hr>
```

The MultiConsoleApplet Class

We implement the applet using a single class—**MultiConsoleApplet**. This class extends **java.applet.Applet** and implements four methods: *init, action, startCounting,* and *stopCounting.* The last two are private helper methods. The browser calls *init* after it loads the applet. The *init* method performs the following three functions: 1) creates a user interface consisting of six widgets, 2) initializes the ORB, and 3) locates a **Coordinator** object and obtains a reference to it.

The browser calls *action* when the user clicks on the "Run" or "Stop" buttons. The *action* method simply turns around and invokes its helper functions: *startCounting* and *stopCounting.* The *startCounting* method does the following: 1) clears the status field, 2) calculates the start time, and 3) invokes the *start* method on the remote **Coordinator** object.

The *stopCounting* method does the following: 1) invokes the *stop* method on the **Coordinator** and obtains its count statistics, 2) calculates the stop time, 3) displays the client statistics in the listbox, 4) pulls out the count from each client string, 5) calculates the total count, and 6) displays the total statistics in the Status field. Here's the code:

Listing 9-1. The MultiConsoleApplet Class.

```
// MultiConsoleApplet.java, Console for Multiclient performance tests
import org.omg.CosNaming.*;

import java.awt.*;
import java.util.*;

public class MultiConsoleApplet extends java.applet.Applet
{ private TextField statusField;
  private List clientStatusList;
  private Button run, stop;
  private MultiCoordinator.Coordinator myCoordinator;
  private long startTime, stopTime;

  public void init()
  {
    // Create a 3 by 2 grid of widgets.
    setLayout(new GridLayout(3, 2, 5, 5));

    // Add six widgets, initialize where necessary
    add(new Label("Status", Label.CENTER));
    add(statusField = new TextField());
```

```
statusField.setEditable(false);
statusField.setText("ready");
add(new Label("Client Results", Label.CENTER));
add(clientStatusList = new List(4, false));
add(run = new Button("Run"));
add(stop = new Button("Stop"));

try
{ // Initialize the ORB.
  statusField.setText("Initializing the ORB");
  org.omg.CORBA.ORB orb = org.omg.CORBA.ORB.init(this, null);

  // Get a reference to the Naming service
  statusField.setText("Finding the Name Service");
  org.omg.CORBA.Object nameServiceObj =
            orb.resolve_initial_references("NameService");
  if (nameServiceObj == null)
  {
    statusField.setText("nameServiceObj = null");
    return;
  }

  org.omg.CosNaming.NamingContext nameService =
            org.omg.CosNaming.NamingContextHelper.narrow (nameServiceObj);
  if (nameService == null)
  {
    statusField.setText("nameService = null");
    return;
  }

  // Resolving the Coordinator Object
  statusField.setText("Binding to the Coordinator");
  NameComponent[] countName =
                {new NameComponent("Coordinator", "Multi")};
  myCoordinator = MultiCoordinator.CoordinatorHelper.narrow(
                                    nameService.resolve(countName));
  if (myCoordinator == null)
  {
    statusField.setText("Failed to resolve coordinator");
    return;
  }

  statusField.setText("Ready");
} catch(Exception e)
{ statusField.setText("Exception" + e);
```

```
   }
}


public boolean action(Event ev, java.lang.Object arg)
{ if(ev.target == run)
    return startCounting();
  if(ev.target == stop)
    return stopCounting();
  return false;
}


private boolean startCounting()
{ statusField.setText("Running");
  clientStatusList.clear();
  try
  {
    // Calculate Start time
    startTime = System.currentTimeMillis();

    myCoordinator.start();
  } catch(org.omg.CORBA.SystemException e)
  { statusField.setText("Exception" + e);
  }
  return true;
}


private boolean stopCounting()
{ try
  {
    String clientStatus;
    StringTokenizer token1;
    String clientSum;

    String clientStatistics = myCoordinator.stop();
    stopTime = System.currentTimeMillis();

    StringTokenizer tokens = new StringTokenizer(clientStatistics, "\n");
    int totalSum = 0;

    while (tokens.hasMoreTokens())
    {
      // get status for one client, add to list box
```

```
    clientStatus = tokens.nextToken();
    clientStatusList.addItem(clientStatus);

    // extract sum for one client, add to total sum
    token1 = new StringTokenizer(clientStatus, " ,");
    token1.nextToken();   // Skip unwanted tokens
    token1.nextToken();
    token1.nextToken();
    token1.nextToken();
    clientSum = token1.nextToken();
    totalSum = totalSum + Integer.parseInt(clientSum);
  }

  String statistics = "Grand Total = " + totalSum +
      ", Avg Txn time = " +
      Float.toString((float)(stopTime - startTime)/(float)totalSum) +
      " msecs";
  statusField.setText(statistics);
  } catch(org.omg.CORBA.SystemException e)
  { statusField.setText("Exception" + e);
  }
  return true;
  }
}
```

The only strange thing in this code is the tokenizing function in *stopCounting*. Here's what's going on. The **Coordinator** returns a multiline *clientStatistics* string that could look like this:

```
Client 1: Sum = 2955, Avg Ping = 9.0344 msecs /n
Client 2: Sum = 4999, Avg Ping = 7.0221 msecs /n
     .
     .
Client N: Sum = 3425, Avg Ping = 6.0552 msecs /n
```

We need to extract from this returned string the sum of the counts for all clients. So we need to extract each returned sum value and get a grand total. To do this, the tokenizer reads in one line at a time using the newline character "/n" as its token separator. Then within each line it looks for the value of the sum. It finds it by tokenizing the contents of the line using a space or comma as a token separator. The value of the sum appears in the fifth token. We invoke the *Integer.parseInt* method to convert the string value of this token into an integer. We then add this value to the running total in the *totalSum* variable. So all we're doing here is a bit of arithmetic to obtain the total count for this benchmark. This is the number that we display in the Status field.

THE CLIENT

The client provides four functions: 1) it invokes CORBA *increment* methods on the **Count** server, 2) it allows itself to be remotely controlled by a **Coordinator** via callbacks, 3) it collects its local performance statistics and returns them to the **Coordinator**, and 4) it provides a minimalist user interface that uses four AWT widgets. The client consists of four classes that together provide a very reactive multithreaded environment. In this section, we first describe these four classes. Then we provide a scenario that shows how these classes work together and how they interact with the outside world. We conclude with the code.

Client Classes and Threads

The client consists of four Java classes. Three of these classes—**CountMultiClient**, **ClientCountThread**, and **ClientControlThread**—run in their own separate thread. This allows the client to walk and chew gum at the same time. It can receive callbacks from the server, respond to local user interactions, and pound the Count server with back-to-back *increment* method invocations. The fourth class—**ClientControlImpl**—implements the callback interface. Here's a description what these four classes do:

■ **CountMultiClient** provides the *main* method for the client program. This method calls the class constructor. It then resizes the window frame and displays its contents. The class constructor performs the following: 1) creates a user interface consisting of four widgets, 2) initializes the ORB, 3) locates a **Count** server object and obtains a reference to it, 4) creates a new **ClientControlThread** object, 5) starts the **ClientControlThread** in high-priority mode, 6) creates a new **ClientCountThread** object, and 7) starts the **ClientCountThread** thread.

In addition to *main*, **CountMultiClient** provides the following three methods: *actionPerformed*, *startCounting*, and *stopCounting*. The frame invokes the *actionPerformed* method when the user clicks on the "Run" or "Stop" buttons. When this happens, the method simply turns around and invokes its helper functions: *startCounting* and *stopCounting*. The *startCounting* method does the following: 1) resets the clientSum count field, 2) calculates the start time, and 3) invokes either *resume* or *start* on the **ClientCountThread** object.

The *stopCounting* method does the following: 1) invokes the *suspend* method on the **ClientCountThread**, 2) calculates the stop time, 3) displays the client's statistics in the status field, 4) formats the statistics, and 5) returns the formatted statistics.

- **ClientControlThread** extends the Java **Thread** class. It implements the *run* method that is invoked when the thread starts. Java implicitly calls *run* when you invoke a thread's *start* or *resume* methods. The *run* method provides the following functions: 1) initializes the ORB, 2) creates a **ClientControlImpl** object, 3) connects to the ORB, 4) registers the newly created object in the Naming Service, 5) locates a **Coordinator** server object, 6) invokes *register* on the **Coordinator** to register this client's callback object reference and client number, and 7) waits to service requests.

- **ClientControlImpl** implements the callback interface defined in the CORBA IDL. It behaves exactly like any other server object implementation—except that it's part of the client. Here's the CORBA IDL that defines the interface:

```
// ClientControl.idl
module Client
{ interface ClientControl
  { // start and stop opeations for controlling client counting
    boolean start();
    string  stop();
  };
};
```

ClientControlImpl implements the *start* method by simply invoking the *startCounting* method we described earlier. Likewise, it implements *stop* by invoking *stopCounting*. This allows a **Coordinator** to remotely control the local client. It's just like clicking on the local interface's "Run" and "Stop" buttons.

- **ClientCountThread** also extends the Java **Thread** class. It implements a *run* method that is invoked when you *start* or *resume* the thread. The *run* method implements a continuous loop that: 1) invokes the *increment* method on a remote **Count** server via static CORBA invocations, and 2) increments the client's local count. You can control the looping by suspending and resuming the thread.

It's definitely time for a scenario that shows how all these classes work together. So we'll provide a quick scenario and then jump into the code.

A Multithreaded Client/Server Scenario

Figure 9-7 shows how the different classes and threads within the client interact with each other and their servers. In this scenario, a single client is remotely controlled by a **Coordinator**. Here's a step-by-step explanation of what takes place within a client to make this happen:

1. *Create the callback thread*. The **CountMultiClient** constructor creates a new **ClientControlThread** object and runs it in a high-priority thread. This object creates a **ClientControlImpl** object that implements the IDL-defined callback interface the client exposes to its servers.

2. *Create the Count client thread*. The **CountMultiClient** constructor also creates a new **ClientCountThread** object and runs it in a regular-priority thread.

3. *Register the callback with the Coordinator*. The **ClientControlThread** object invokes the *register* method on the **Coordinator** and passes it the object reference to its callback interface.

4. *The Coordinator tells everyone to start counting*. You click on the MultiConsole applet's "Run" button to start the benchmark. The **Coordinator** will relay your command to all the clients that have registered with it by invoking their *start* method via a callback.

5. *Pass the command to the main thread*. The **ClientControlThread** invokes the *startCounting* method on the **CountMultiClient** object.

6. *Activate the ClientCountThread*. The main thread invokes the *start* method on the **ClientCountThread** object to activate its thread. If the thread had been previously activated and then suspended, it would invoke *resume* instead. Note that the **ClientCountThread** class inherits the *start*, *suspend*, and *resume* methods from its parent class, **Thread**.

7. *Invoke remote increments*. The active **ClientCountThread** spins in a do-forever loop that continuously invokes the *increment* method on a remote **Count** server. The client and server communicate using static CORBA method invocations.

8. *The Coordinator tells everyone to stop counting*. Eventually, you will click on the MultiConsole applet's "Stop" button. The **Coordinator** will then relay your command to all the clients that have registered with it by invoking their *stop* method. It's also a callback.

9. *Pass the command to the main thread*. The **ClientControlThread** invokes the *stopCounting* method on the **CountMultiClient** object.

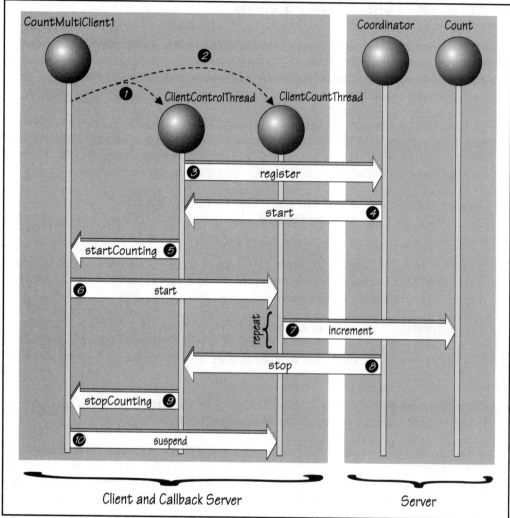

Figure 9-7. A Scenario of the Internal Workings of the Client.

10. **Suspend the ClientCountThread**. The main thread invokes the *suspend*
    method on the **ClientCountThread** object to suspend its thread. This is one
    way to stop the invocation of remote *increment* methods.

The Client Code

After this lengthy introduction and the last scenario, there should be no surprises
left in the client code. So here is the code without further ado.

Listing 9-2. Client Code: The CountMultiClient Class.

```java
// CountMultiClient.java

import java.awt.*;
import java.awt.event.*;
import org.omg.CosNaming.*;

public class CountMultiClient extends Frame
            implements ActionListener, WindowListener
{ public  TextField statusField;
  private Button run, stop;
  private org.omg.CosNaming.NamingContext nameService;
  public  CounterPortable.Count counter;
  public  long clientSum;
  private long startTime, stopTime;
  private Thread countThread;
  private boolean countThreadStarted;
  private Thread controlThread;
  public  String clientNumber;

  public CountMultiClient(String[] args)
  {
    setTitle("Count Client Number " + args[0]);
    // Create a 2 by 2 grid of widgets.
    setLayout(new GridLayout(2, 2, 5, 5));

    // Add the four widgets, initialize where necessary
    add(new Label("Status", Label.CENTER));
    add(statusField = new TextField());
    statusField.setEditable(false);
    statusField.setText("ready");
    add(run = new Button("Run"));
    run.addActionListener(this);
    add(stop = new Button("Stop"));
    stop.addActionListener(this);
    addWindowListener(this);

    try
    { // Initialize the ORB
      org.omg.CORBA.ORB orb = org.omg.CORBA.ORB.init(args, null);

      // Get a reference to the Naming service
      org.omg.CORBA.Object nameServiceObj =
                orb.resolve_initial_references ("NameService");
```

```
      if (nameServiceObj == null)
      {
        statusField.setText("nameServiceObj = null");
        return;
      }

      nameService =
            org.omg.CosNaming.NamingContextHelper.narrow (nameServiceObj);
      if (nameService == null)
      {
        statusField.setText("nameService = null");
        return;
      }

      // resolve the Count object reference
      NameComponent[] countName = {new NameComponent("countName", "")};
      counter = CounterPortable.CountHelper.narrow(
                              nameService.resolve(countName));
      if (counter == null)
      {
        statusField.setText("Failed to resolve countName");
        return;
      }

      clientNumber = args[0];
      controlThread = new ClientControlThread(this, args, nameService);
      controlThread.start();
      controlThread.setPriority(Thread.NORM_PRIORITY + 1);

    } catch(Exception e)
    { statusField.setText("Exception" + e);
    }

    countThread = new ClientCountThread(this);

  }



// used to handle events when window is being killed
public void windowClosing(WindowEvent event)
{ System.exit(0);
}

public void windowClosed(WindowEvent event) {}
```

```java
public void windowDeiconified(WindowEvent event) {}
public void windowIconified(WindowEvent event) {}
public void windowActivated(WindowEvent event) {}
public void windowDeactivated(WindowEvent event) {}
public void windowOpened(WindowEvent event) {}

public void actionPerformed(ActionEvent ev)
{
  String arg = ev.getActionCommand();
  if ("Run".equals(arg))
     startCounting();
  if ("Stop".equals(arg))
     stopCounting();
}


public boolean startCounting()
{ // initialize client sum, update status
  clientSum = 0;
  statusField.setText("Incrementing");

  // Calculate Start time
  startTime = System.currentTimeMillis();

  // start the count
  if (countThreadStarted)
  { countThread.resume();
  } else
  { countThread.start();
    countThreadStarted = true;
  }
  return true;
}


public String stopCounting()
{ countThread.suspend();

  // Calculate stop time; show statistics
  long stopTime = System.currentTimeMillis();
  String statistics =  "Sum = " + clientSum + ", Avg Ping = " +
      Float.toString((float)(stopTime - startTime)/(float)clientSum) +
      " msecs";
  statusField.setText(statistics);
  return "Client " + clientNumber + ": " + statistics;
```

```java
    }


  public static void main(String[] args)
  {
    CountMultiClient f = new CountMultiClient(args);
    f.setSize(480, 90);
    f.show();
  }
}


class ClientControlThread extends Thread
{
  private CountMultiClient thisClient;
  private MultiCoordinator.Coordinator myCoordinator;
  private String[] args;
  private org.omg.CosNaming.NamingContext nameService;


  ClientControlThread(CountMultiClient client, String[] myargs,
                      org.omg.CosNaming.NamingContext naming)
  { thisClient = client;
    args = myargs;
    nameService = naming;
  }

  public void run()
  { try
    { // Initialize the ORB
      org.omg.CORBA.ORB orb = org.omg.CORBA.ORB.init(args, null);

      // Create the ClientControl object
      ClientControlImpl control =
              new ClientControlImpl(thisClient);

      // Export the newly created object
      orb.connect(control);

      // resolve the Coordinator object reference
      NameComponent[] coordName =
                      {new NameComponent("Coordinator", "Multi")};
      myCoordinator = MultiCoordinator.CoordinatorHelper.narrow(
                                  nameService.resolve(coordName));
```

```
      // Register with Coordinator
      if (myCoordinator.register(thisClient.clientNumber,
                                 (Client.ClientControl)control))
         {
          System.out.println("Registration Succeeded");
          thisClient.statusField.setText("Ready");
         }
      else
         {
          System.out.println("Registration Failed");
          thisClient.statusField.setText("Registration Failed");
         }

      // Ready to service requests
      System.out.println("Control: Waiting for requests");
      Thread.currentThread().join();

     }
    catch(Exception e)
    { System.err.println("Exception in ClientControl: " + e);
    }
   }
  }
}
```

Listing 9-3. Client Code: The ClientControlThread Class.

```
class ClientCountThread extends Thread
{ CountMultiClient myClient;

  ClientCountThread(CountMultiClient client)
  { myClient = client;
  }

  public void run()
  { // increment count continually
    while (true)
    { try
       {
        myClient.clientSum++;
        myClient.counter.increment();
       } catch(org.omg.CORBA.SystemException e)
       { myClient.statusField.setText("System Exception" + e);
       }
```

```
    }
  }
}
```

Listing 9-4. Client Code: The ClientControlImpl Class.

```java
// ClientControlImpl.java
class ClientControlImpl extends Client._ClientControlImplBase
                        implements Client.ClientControl
{ private CountMultiClient thisClient;

  ClientControlImpl(Object client)
  {
    super();
    thisClient = (CountMultiClient)client;
    System.out.println("Client Control Object Created as client"
                       + thisClient.clientNumber);
  }

  public  boolean start()
  { return thisClient.startCounting();
  }

  public  String stop()
  { return thisClient.stopCounting();}
}
```

Listing 9-5. Client Code: The ClientCountThread Class.

```java
class ClientCountThread extends Thread
{ CountMultiClient myClient;

  ClientCountThread(CountMultiClient client)
  { myClient = client;
  }

  public void run()
  { // increment count continually
    while (true)
    { try
      {
        myClient.clientSum++;
        myClient.counter.increment();
      } catch(org.omg.CORBA.SystemException e)
```

```
      { myClient.statusField.setText("System Exception" + e);
      }
    }
  }
}
```

THE COORDINATOR

The Coordinator is a simple CORBA server that clients use to register their presence on the network. A client must pass the Coordinator object a reference to its callback interface. The Coordinator then uses these references to remotely control the execution of client threads. The Coordinator is the client of the callback. Or, if you prefer, the server invokes the client. The Coordinator in turn is controlled by the MultiConsole applet. So the applet user is really at the controls. The Coordinator simply relays commands from the applet to all its registered clients via callbacks (see Figure 9-8).

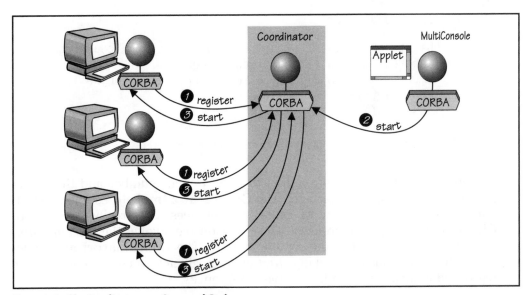

Figure 9-8. The Coordinator as a Command Broker.

The Coordinator is similar to a *publish-and-subscribe* system. In this case, the clients are the subscribers. The applet is the publisher. We use this publish-and-subscribe metaphor to remotely control the execution of the Count benchmark. However, this is a generic mechanism that you can use very effectively in a variety of event-driven or broadcast situations.

In this section, we first describe the classes that provide the Coordinator service. Then we go over the IDL. We conclude with the code.

The Coordinator Classes

We implement the Coordinator using two Java classes: **CoordinatorServer** and **CoordinatorImpl.** Here's a description of what they do:

■ **CoordinatorServer** provides the *main* method for the server program. It provides the following functions: 1) initializes the ORB, 2) creates a **CoordinatorImpl** object, 3) connects to the ORB, 4) registers the newly created object in the Naming Service, and 5) waits for requests.

■ **CoordinatorImpl** implements the **Coordinator** interface. Here's the CORBA IDL that defines this interface:

```
module MultiCoordinator
{ interface Coordinator

  { // object for registering and controlling client counting
    boolean register(in string clientNumber,
                     in Client::ClientControl clientObjRef);
    boolean start();
    string  stop();
  };
};
```

The client uses the *register* method to pass a client number and the object reference of its callback interface. The **CoordinatorImpl** stores this information in its in-memory array of callback references. It's really an array of **ClientControl** object references. The MultiConsole invokes the *start* and *stop* methods to start and stop the remote clients. The **CoordinatorImpl** implements these methods by invoking *start* or *stop* callbacks on every client that is registered in its array of callback object references.

The implementation of these two classes is quite straightforward. The code follows.

The Coordinator Code

Listing 9-6. Coordinator Code: The CoordinatorServer Class.

```
// CoordinatorServer.java
```

```java
import org.omg.CosNaming.*;

class CoordinatorServer
{ static public void main(String[] args)
  {
    try
    { // Initialize the ORB.
      org.omg.CORBA.ORB orb = org.omg.CORBA.ORB.init(args, null);

      // Create the Coordinator object.
      CoordinatorImpl coord =
                new CoordinatorImpl("Coordinator");

      // Export the newly create object
      orb.connect(coord);

      // Get a reference to the Naming service
      org.omg.CORBA.Object nameServiceObj =
                orb.resolve_initial_references ("NameService");
      if (nameServiceObj == null)
      {
        System.out.println("nameServiceObj = null");
        return;
      }

      org.omg.CosNaming.NamingContext nameService =
                org.omg.CosNaming.NamingContextHelper.narrow (nameServiceObj);
      if (nameService == null)
      {
        System.out.println("nameService = null");
        return;
      }

      // bind the Count object in the Naming service
      NameComponent[] coordName =
                {new NameComponent("Coordinator", "Multi")};
      nameService.rebind(coordName, coord);

      // Ready to service requests
      System.out.println("Coordinator waiting for requests");

      // wait forever for current thread to die
      Thread.currentThread().join();
    }
    catch(Exception e)
```

```java
     { System.err.println(e);
     }
  }
}
```

Listing 9-7. Coordinator Code: The CoordinatorImpl Class.

```java
// CoordinatorImpl.java

class CoordinatorImpl
      extends MultiCoordinator._CoordinatorImplBase
      implements MultiCoordinator.Coordinator
{
  int maxClients = 20;
  public  Client.ClientControl[] thisClient =
                      new Client.ClientControl[maxClients];

  CoordinatorImpl(String name)
  { super(name);
    System.out.println("Coordinator Object Created");
    for (int i=0; i  maxClients; i++)
    {
      thisClient[i] = null;
    }
  }

  public boolean register(String clientNumber,
                          Client.ClientControl clientObjRef)

  {
    try
    { System.out.println("Client " + clientNumber + " Registering");
      thisClient[Integer.parseInt(clientNumber)] = clientObjRef;
      System.out.println("Client " + clientNumber + " Registered");
      return true;
    } catch(Exception e)
    { System.out.println("Exception" + e);
      return false;
    }
  }


  public  boolean start()
  { try
```

```
    { System.out.println("Start");
      for (int i=0; i  maxClients; i++)
      {
        if (thisClient[i] != null)
          thisClient[i].start();
      }
      return true;
    } catch(org.omg.CORBA.SystemException e)
    { System.out.println("Exception" + e);
      return false;
    }
  }


  public  String stop()
  { String status = "";
    try
    {
      System.out.println("Stop");
      for (int i=0; i  maxClients; i++)
      {
        if (thisClient[i] != null)
          status = status + thisClient[i].stop() + "\n";
      }
    } catch(org.omg.CORBA.SystemException e)
    { System.out.println("Exception" + e);
    }
    return status;
  }
}
```

COMPILE THE CLIENT AND SERVER PROGRAMS

We're now ready to compile the MultiCount client and server programs. You should
first run the CORBA IDL compiler to generate the stubs and skeletons. To do this
go to the appropriate directory and type the following command at the prompt:

prompt> call idl2java Coordinator.idl -no_comments

Next, you must compile the code. So make sure you have installed the Symantec
Visual Café compiler or the Java JDK. To compile the code, run the make file. Or,
type the following commands at the prompt:

prompt> javac -d \CorbaJavaBook.2e\classes CountMultiClient.java

```
prompt> javac -d \CorbaJavaBook.2e\classes ClientControlImpl.java
prompt> javac -d \CorbaJavaBook.2e\classes CoordinatorServer.java
prompt> javac -d \CorbaJavaBook.2e\classes CoordinatorImpl.java
prompt> javac -d \CorbaJavaBook.2e\classes MultiConsoleApplet.java
```

The -d option tells the compiler to put the (.class) files it creates into the directory we specify. In this case, the *\CorbaJavaBook.2e\classes* subdirectory. If all goes well, you should have some compiled Java code—including stubs and skeletons—that you can now run.

RUN THE CLIENT/SERVER PROGRAMS

To run the MultiConsole program, first start the OSAgent, the Naming Service, and the Count Server (follow the same steps as in Chapter 7).

Next, you must start the servers. To run the Count server, first install your (.class) files on a server machine. Then type the following command at the prompt:

```
prompt> start java -DORBservices=CosNaming
        -DSVCnameroot=CorbaJava CountPortableServer
```

To run the Coordinator server, install your (.class) files on a server machine. Then type the following command at the prompt:

```
prompt> java -DORBservices=CosNaming -DSVCnameroot=JavaCorba
            CoordinatorServer
```

Next install the MultiConsole applet on an HTTP server. Make sure to include the stub (.class) and the html files. Next start the Gatekeeper. Point to the MultiConsole applet page from within the browser. The MultiConsole panel should appear within your browser.

You are now ready to run as many client programs as you require for this benchmark. You can run multiple client programs from the same machine. Or you can give each client its own machine. To start a client program, enter the following command at the prompt:

```
prompt> java CountMultiClient 1
```

You must give each client a number. The MultiConsole applet will use this number to display this client's statistics. If all goes well, you should see the client's panel on the screen. You can ignore it for now. You'll be running the benchmarks using the MultiConsole panel.

You're now ready to run the benchmarks. The results you obtain will depend on how you deploy your clients and servers. You can run everything on the same machine. Figure 9-9 shows a setup with three clients and the MultiConsole; the servers are on a separate machine. However, don't forget that each client runs in its own Java virtual machine, which can easily chew up your memory and CPU resources. So you're better off running the clients on separate machines. The results will also depend on the number of clients you start. The more the better.

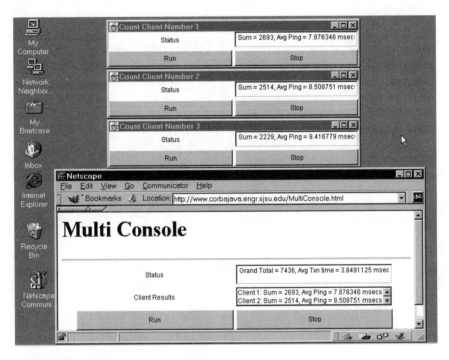

Figure 9-9. The Results of a Benchmark With 3 Clients.

CONCLUSION

The lesson to learn from this chapter is that CORBA callbacks are very useful. You can use them to create very dynamic client/server systems. We used callbacks to create a flexible benchmarking system that you can control from any remote browser. For example, we could be running the benchmarking machines in our lab, and you could be controlling them from your home over the Internet. This chapter also demonstrates that any client can also be a server—with a little bit of code. Of course, we got some help from Java's built-in threading facilities. Java threads complement CORBA callbacks beautifully. So, welcome to the world of dynamic client/server systems, CORBA/Java-style.

Part 4
CORBA and Its
Competitors

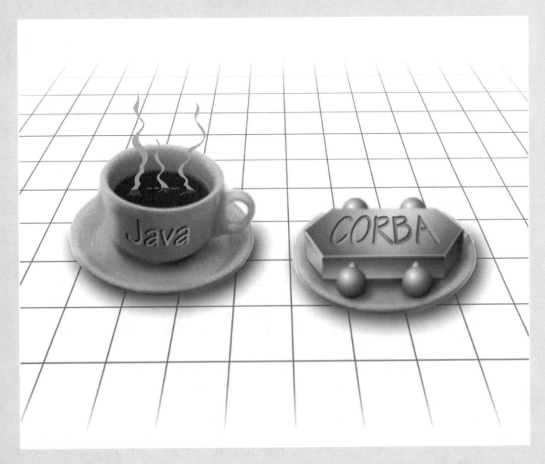

An Introduction to Part 4

Whenever there's serious money to be made, there's always serious competition. In the case of Java distributed objects, the prize is the Internet. And, it's winner take all. So it should come as no surprise that CORBA/Java ORBs face stiff competition from other forms of middleware. This competition comes from two directions: 1) *legacy Internet middleware*—including Java Sockets, CGI/HTTP, and Servlets; and 2) *non-CORBA Java ORBs*—including JavaSoft's RMI and Microsoft's DCOM.

So how do you determine which Java middleware solution is best for you? In Part 4, we help you understand the tradeoffs by performing an amazing feat. We create back-to-back versions of the minimalist Count client/server application using the following technologies:

■ *Java Sockets* is the substrate technology for Java network programming. Until recently, Sockets was the only way you could write a client/server application in Java. The Sockets Count will serve as our watermark for raw networking performance.

■ *HTTP/CGI* is the predominant model for creating 3-tier client/server solutions for the Internet today. HTTP provides simple RPC-like semantics on top of Sockets. CGI provides a protocol for delivering an HTTP command to a server application. The HTTP/CGI Count program will help you understand why the Internet badly needs ORBs.

■ *Servlets* are Java server-side plug-ins. They fix some of CGI's shortcomings. We'll see how well they do this.

■ *RMI* is a native Java ORB from JavaSoft. It introduces new distributed object semantics for Java. These semantics form the basis for the CORBA *Java-to-IDL* mapping. You'll get a taste of the RMI model.

■ *Caffeine* from Netscape/Visigenic provides an RMI-like programming environment on top of *VisiBroker for Java*. It lets you write CORBA distributed objects without IDL. The Caffeinated Count program shows you how it works.

■ *DCOM* is the industry's other leading ORB. DCOM is a formidable competitor to CORBA because Microsoft is including it with all its OSs. It's also the foundation technology for ActiveX and the Microsoft Internet. Microsoft's *Visual J++* introduced DCOM for Java; it lets a Java object remotely invoke another Java object using the DCOM ORB. The DCOM Count program will give you an idea of how all this works.

Yes, it's a three-ring circus for programmers. In addition to the programming examples, we provide in-depth tutorials on each of these technologies. We also run Ping benchmarks to give you a feeling for their relative performance. And, we compare each of these technologies with CORBA. Finally, we risk life and limb by declaring a winner. So this should be an exciting Part. It's not every day that you see the same Java client/server program running over Sockets, HTTP/CGI, Servlets, RMI, DCOM, and CORBA.

Chapter 10

Sockets Versus CORBA/Java ORBs

Before CORBA and RMI came along, the only way for a Java program to connect to the world at large was via the *java.net* package. This important package provides two very useful Internet communications services: 1) a set of classes that let you download and manipulate *URL objects*, and 2) a native Java implementation of *Berkeley sockets*. Together, these two services allowed Java to live up to its reputation as the programming language for the Internet. We cover sockets in this chapter and touch on URLs in the next.

The plan for this chapter is to return to the original Count program from Chapter 7. This minimalist Count allows us to focus on sockets programming without letting the bells and whistles get in the way. We will develop several versions of the Count program using Java sockets. As you will soon find out, sockets alone won't get us too far. We also need Java *streams*, which let us move data into and out of sockets using a file-like metaphor. With streams, you can send and receive data across networks as easily as you read and write data in files.

We begin this chapter by talking a little bit about Berkeley sockets. If sockets and ports are old news to you, you may want to jump directly to the Java sockets tutorial. Here, we cover both Java's datagram and stream-based sockets. We then cover the sockets-related stream classes that are part of the *java.io* package. We will use these classes to write four versions of the sockets Count program. Why four? First, we develop a version of Count that uses *datagram sockets*. Then we develop two versions of *streamed sockets—buffered* and *unbuffered*. Finally, we develop a *buffered data stream* version. We learned the hard way that there are extreme differences in performance between these implementations. We don't want you to fall into the same trap.

At the end of this chapter, we will give you statistics that compare the four implementations of Count using sockets. By today's standards, sockets are as close-to-the-wire as networked peer-to-peer protocols get. Think of sockets as the assembly language of network programming. So the numbers we collect in this chapter can serve as the watermark for raw networking performance. Consequently, by comparing CORBA with sockets, we can get a good feel for the overhead CORBA introduces. So fasten your seatbelts—we have a lot of important ground to cover in this chapter.

BERKELEY SOCKETS 101

Berkeley sockets are the premier peer-to-peer protocol for communicating over TCP/IP stacks. Sockets were introduced in 1981 as the Unix BSD 4.2 generic interface that would provide Unix-to-Unix *interprocess communications (IPC)*. In 1985, Sun introduced NFS and RPC over sockets. Today, sockets are supported on virtually every operating system. The Windows socket API, known colloquially as *WinSock*, is a multivendor specification that standardizes the use of TCP/IP under Windows. In BSD Unix systems, sockets are part of the kernel; they provide both a standalone and networked IPC service. Non-BSD Unix systems, MS-DOS, Windows, MacOS, and OS/2 provide sockets in the form of libraries. Java provides sockets as part of the core language classes. So it is safe to say that sockets provide the current *de facto* portable standard for network application providers on TCP/IP networks.

What Is a Socket?

A socket is a peer-to-peer communication *endpoint*—it has a name and a network address. From a programmer's perspective, a socket hides the details of the network. Typically, sockets come in three flavors: *stream, datagram,* and *raw*. Stream and datagram sockets interface to the TCP and UDP protocols, and raw sockets interface to IP or ICMP protocols. You specify the type of socket at creation time. In theory, you can extend the socket interface and you can define new types to provide additional services.

How Do You Like Your Socket?

Here are the characteristics of the three socket types:

- **Datagram sockets** provide an interface to the *User Datagram Protocol (UDP)*. UDP handles network transmissions as independent packets and provides no guarantees. UDP does include a checksum, but it makes no attempt to detect duplicate packets or to maintain any form of sequencing on multipacket transmissions. No acknowledgment of receipt is built into the protocol. You're on your own: data can be lost, duplicated, or received in the wrong order. You're in charge of retransmissions when an error occurs—UDP does not save your message either. On the plus side, datagrams are blazingly fast and introduce little overhead. On the minus side, datagrams impose a limit on the amount of data transferred—typically, 32 KBytes—and require that you provide all the reliability mechanisms (also see the next Briefing box).

- **Stream sockets** provide an interface to the reliable TCP transport protocol. TCP provides a session-based service that takes care of flow control, packet reassembly, and connection maintenance. The stream socket guarantees that packets are sent without errors or duplication and that they are received in the same order as they are sent. No boundaries are imposed on the data; it is considered to be a stream of bytes. On the plus side, TCP provides a reliable peer-to-peer mechanism. On the negative side, TCP is slower than UDP and requires more programming overhead. Be warned: *TCP knows nothing about the preservation of message boundaries.* This is to be expected because the Unix file system, whose semantics TCP models, knows nothing about record boundaries. We'll show you how to work around this when we get to the programming sections.

- **Raw sockets** provide an interface to the lower-layer protocols such as the IP network layer and the *Internet Control Message Protocol (ICMP)*. This raw interface does not provide traditional peer-to-peer services. It is used to test new protocols and access some of the more advanced facilities of an existing protocol.

 FYI

Datagrams Versus Sessions

Briefing

Connection-oriented protocols—also known as *session-based protocols, virtual circuits,* or *sequenced packet exchanges*—provide a reliable two-way connection service over a session. Each packet of information that gets exchanged over a session is given a unique sequence number through which it gets tracked and individually acknowledged. The session services detect and discard duplicate packets.

The price you pay for this reliable class of service is the overhead associated with creating and managing the session. If a session is lost, one of the parties must reestablish it. This can be a problem for fault-tolerant servers that require automatic switchovers to a backup server if the primary server fails. The backup server needs to reestablish all the outstanding sessions with clients. In addition, sessions are inherently a two-party affair and don't lend themselves well to broadcasting (one-to-many exchanges).

Datagrams—also known as *connectionless* protocols or *transmit and pray* protocols—provide a simple but unreliable form of exchange. The more powerful datagram protocols such as NetBIOS provide broadcast capabilities. NetBIOS allows you to send datagrams to a named entity, to a select group of entities (multicast), or to all entities on a network (broadcast). Datagrams are unreliable in the sense that they are not acknowledged or tracked through a sequence number. You "send and pray" that your datagram gets received. The recipient may not be there or may not be expecting a datagram (you will never know). Novell literature estimates that about 5% of datagrams don't make it. You may, of course, design your own acknowledgment schemes on top of the datagram service. Some stacks (for example, LAN Server's Mailslots) provide an acknowledged datagram service.

Datagrams are very useful to have in "discovery" types of situations. These are situations where you discover things about your network environment by broadcasting queries and learning who is out there from the responses. Broadcast can be used to obtain bids for services or to advertise the availability of new services. Broadcast datagrams provide the capability of creating electronic "bazaars." They support the creation of very dynamic types of environments where things can happen spontaneously. In situations where the name of the recipient is not known, broadcast datagrams are the only way to spread the message. The cost of broadcast datagrams is that, in some cases, recipients may get overloaded with "junk mail." The multicast facility helps alleviate this problem because broadcast mail can then be sent only to "special interest" groups. The alternative to broadcast is to use a network directory service.

Datagrams are also very useful in situations where there is a need to send a quick message without the world coming to an end if the message is not received. The typical situation is sending control-like information, such as telling a network manager "I'm alive." It doesn't make sense to go through all the overhead of creating a session with the network manager just to say "I'm alive." And, what if there are 500 nodes on the network? The manager will need 500 permanent sessions—an exorbitant cost in resources. This is where the datagram alternative comes in. With datagrams, you can send your "I'm alive" message. And if the manager misses your message once, it will get another one when you send your next heartbeat (provided you're still alive). ❏

Socket Ports

A socket address on a TCP/IP network consists of two parts: an IP address and a port address (see Figure 10-1). So what's an IP address? And what's a port?

Figure 10-1. Socket = Internet Address (IP) + Port Address.

An *Internet Address (IP)* is a 32-bit number, usually represented in a dotted string notation—for example, 206.26.48.100. Or it may be represented by its domain name—for example, *java.sun.com*. The IP address must be unique within an administered IP domain. A TCP/IP *host* (i.e., networked machine) may have as many IP addresses as it has network interfaces. IP addresses can also be assigned dynamically by a server.

A *port* is an entry point to an application that resides on a host. It is represented by a 16-bit number. Ports are commonly used to define entry points for server applications. TCP directory services also maintain lists of *well-known ports* that are reserved for specific services. For example, important commercial server programs—such as HTTP servers or Oracle DBMSs—have their own well-known ports. You should only use these reserved port numbers as a client or provider of one of the well-known services.

Java's InetAddress Class

The *java.net* package uses the **InetAddress** class to encapsulate an IP address. This class turns an IP address into an object that returns useful information. You obtain this useful information by invoking methods on an object of this class (see Figure 10-2). For example, *equals* returns true if two objects represent the same IP address. You invoke *getAddress* to obtain the IP address of an object. You invoke *getByName* to determine the IP address of a host, given its name. The host name can either be a machine name—such as *java.sun.com*—or a dotted string representing its IP address. You invoke *getAllByName* to obtain all the IP addresses associated with a host. You invoke *getHostName* to obtain the host name for this IP address. You invoke *getLocalHost* to obtain the IP address of your local host. The programming examples will show you how some of these methods are used.

Figure 10-2. The InetAddress Class.

Notice that the **InetAddress** has no public constructor. So how do you create objects of this class? You must invoke the class methods *getLocalHost*, *getByName*, or *getAllByName* to create a new **InetAddress** instance. In case you're interested in the details, here's the class declaration:

Listing 10-1. The Java InetAddress Class.

```
public final class InetAddress
    extends java.lang.Object implements serializable
{
    // No constructor
    // Class methods
    public static InetAddress getByName(String  host)
                            throws UnknownHostException;
    public static InetAddress[] getAllByName(String  host)
                              throws UnknownHostException;
    public static InetAddress getLocalHost()
                            throws UnknownHostException;
    // Public Instance methods
    public boolean equals(Object obj);
    public byte[] getAddress();
    public String getHostName();
    public String getHostAddress();
    public boolean isMulticastAddress();
    public int hashCode();
    public String toString();
}
```

The Anatomy of a Sockets Exchange

Before we dive into the mechanics of sockets, let's not lose track of why we're looking at all this. All the major ORBs and RPC protocols are built on top of sockets. One of the goals of a good ORB is to isolate you from all the networking issues we are about to cover. So we're looking at sockets to get a better understanding of what ORBs do for you and at what cost.

The best way to explain sockets is to go over a simple scenario that shows a client/server interaction. Figure 10-3 shows a stream socket interaction for a simple transaction. The client asks for Bob's balance. The server returns a balance of $300. Let's go over the steps that make this transaction happen:

1. **Create the socket endpoints.** Every process that uses sockets must first create and initialize a socket using the *socket* call.

2. **Establish a service port.** Server processes must *bind* their sockets to a unique port name to become known on the network.

3. **Listen for connection requests to arrive.** Server processes using stream sockets must issue a *listen* call to indicate their readiness to accept connections from clients. The server is now open for business on this socket. The call typically defines the size of the queue for incoming requests. Additional requests are ignored by the server.

4. **Connect to the server.** The client issues a *connect* call on a stream socket to initiate a connection to the port with the service. The client may optionally block until the connection is accepted by the server. On a successful return, the client socket is associated with the connection to the server.

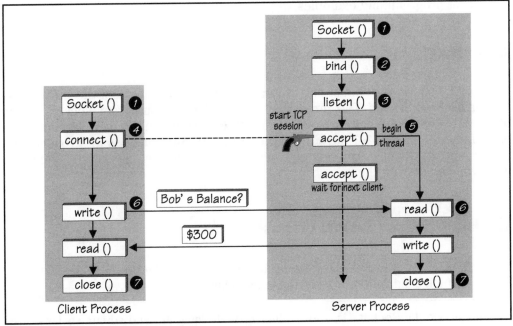

Figure 10-3. A Berkeley Socket Client/Server Scenario.

5. *Accept the connection*. The server side accepts the connection on a stream socket with the *accept* call. The call will optionally block if no connections are pending. If many connections are pending, it will pop the first one off the queue. In a multithreaded environment, the server starts a new thread to take care of the client's request on a separate socket. The original thread then reissues the *accept* call to service new clients on that socket.

6. *Conduct network business*. Clients and servers have many calls from which to choose for their data exchanges. Stream interactions are usually conducted using *read* and *write* calls. Datagram sockets use *send* and *receive* calls. In our scenario, the client issues a *write* to obtain Bob's balance. The server issues a *read* to receive the request. It then issues a *write* to return the balance. The client issues a *read* to obtain the balance.

7. *Close the socket*. Sockets are scarce resources. You must be able to reuse them. The client and server thread both issue *close* commands to terminate their side of the socket. Note that the original server socket thread is still alive and waiting for requests from clients.

Datagram sockets require less commands. The datagram server does not issue *listen* or *accept* calls because there is no incoming session to manage. In addition, datagrams use the more primitive *send* and *receive* semantics instead of *read* and *write*. Remember, read/write are associated with streams; datagrams do not use streams. You will be able to better understand all these subtleties after we go over the socket programming examples.

JAVA SOCKETS 101

Figure 10-4 shows the socket class hierarchy in *java.net*. Two of these classes—**DatagramSocket** and **DatagramPacket**—implement datagram sockets. The other three—**ServerSocket**, **Socket**, and **SocketImpl**—implement stream sockets.[1] In addition, JDK 1.1 introduced the **MulticastSocket** class for broadcasting datagrams. In the next few sections, we cover these socket classes and show you what you can do with them.

The Java Datagram Sockets Classes

Figure 10-5 shows the two classes that implement Java's datagram socket services. Here's a quick description of what these two classes do:

---

[1] You can use the **Socket** class to implement both datagram and stream sockets. The constructor lets you specify the mode. The default is to use this class with stream sockets.

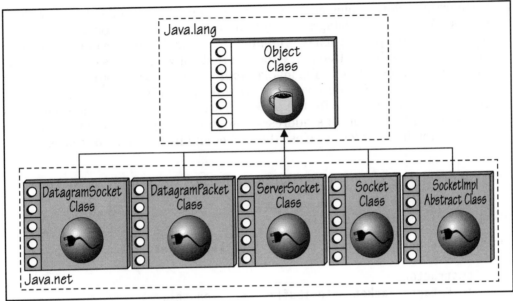

Figure 10-4. The Java.net Sockets Classes.

■ **DatagramPacket** implements a packet container object. You send or receive the packet over a network using a socket. You invoke the *DatagramPacket* constructor to create a send packet; you must specify the array of bytes you want to send as well as the destination address and port. You can also create a receive packet by invoking the receive *DatagramPacket* constructor; you must specify an array of bytes into which the data will be received. You retrieve the contents of a received packet by invoking *getData* and *getLength*. You invoke *getAddress* and *getPort* to retrieve the sender's address and port. You can also set any of these parameters via setter methods.

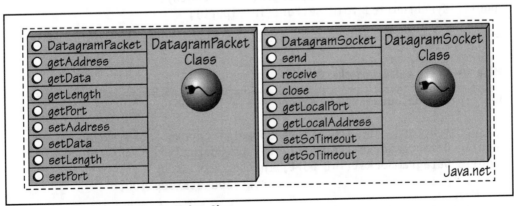

Figure 10-5. The Java.net Datagram Sockets Classes.

■ **DatagramSocket** implements a socket that you use to send and receive datagrams. You create a datagram socket by calling the class constructor *DatagramSocket* and passing it a port number. If you don't specify a port, the system automatically assigns a free port. You can find out what port is currently in use by invoking *getLocalPort*. You invoke *send* to send a **DatagramPacket** object through your socket. You invoke *receive* to wait for a packet to arrive at the socket. The system waits for the packet to arrive at the socket and then stores it—along with the sender's address—into the **DatagramPacket** object you specify. You invoke *close* to close the socket and free its port for reuse.

Here are the class declarations for **DatagramPacket** and **DatagramSocket**:

Listing 10-2. The DatagramPacket Class.

```
public class DatagramPacket extends java.lang.Object
{
  // Constructors
  public DatagramPacket(byte ibuf[], int ilength);
  public DatagramPacket(byte ibuf[],
                    int ilength,
                    InetAddress iaddr,
                    int iport);

  // Methods
  public synchronized InetAddress getAddress();
  public synchronized byte[] getData();
  public synchronized int getLength();
  public synchronized int getPort();
  public synchronized void setAddress(InetAddress iaddr);
  public synchronized void setData(byte ibuf[]);
  public synchronized void setLength(int ilength);
  public synchronized void setPort(int iport);
}
```

Listing 10-3. The DatagramSocket Class.

```
public class DatagramSocket extends java.lang.Object
{
  // Constructors  public DatagramSocket() throws SocketException;
  public DatagramSocket(int port) throws SocketException;
  public DatagramSocket(int port, InetAddress laddr)
                            throws SocketException;
  // Methods
  public void send(DatagramPacket p) throws IOException;
```

```
public synchronized void receive(DatagramPacket p) throws IOException;
public void close();
public int getLocalPort();
public InetAddress getLocalAddress();
public synchronized void setSoTimeout(int timeout)
        throws SocketException;
public synchronized int getSoTimeout() throws SocketException;
}
```

A Java Datagram Scenario

It's time for a little scenario. Figure 10-6 shows how you use Java's datagram classes to create a simple client/server interaction. The client asks for Bob's balance. The server provides the balance. Let's walk through this scenario:

1. **Create the socket endpoints.** The client and server each creates a socket by issuing calls to the *DatagramSocket* constructor and passing it their respective port numbers.

2. **Server creates an incoming packet object.** The server invokes the constructor *DatagramPacket* to create a receiving **DatagramPacket** object.

3. **Client creates an outgoing packet object.** The client invokes the constructor *DatagramPacket* to create an outgoing **DatagramPacket** object. The client specifies the message to be sent—Bob's balance—and the target address and port.

4. **Server waits for incoming datagrams.** The server invokes *receive* and waits for clients to call it.

5. **Client sends a datagram.** The client invokes *send* on its socket object to transmit its outgoing packet object.

6. **Server receives the datagram.** The server invokes *getData* on the packet object to retrieve the contents of the datagram packet. It also invokes *getAddress* and *getPort* to retrieve the address and port of the calling client.

7. **Client creates an incoming packet object.** The client invokes the constructor *DatagramPacket* to create a receiving **DatagramPacket** object.

8. **Client waits for response from server.** The client invokes *receive* and waits for the server to call it.

9. **Server creates an outgoing packet object.** The server invokes the constructor *DatagramPacket* to create an outgoing **DatagramPacket** object. It returns

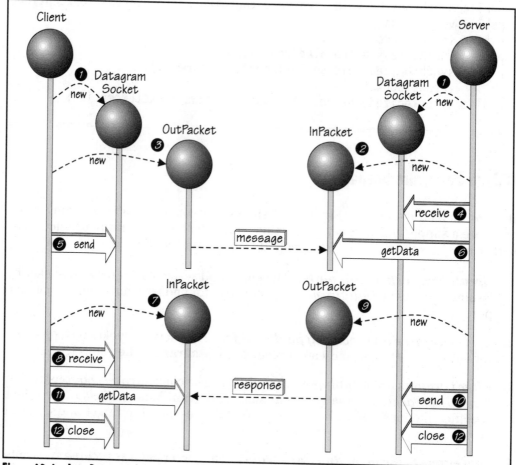

Figure 10-6. Java Datagram Scenario.

Bob's balance in the message buffer. The server also passes to the constructor the client's address and port number. Remember, it retrieved both of these values from the incoming datagram.

10. ***Server sends the response datagram***. The server invokes *send* on its socket object to transmit its outgoing packet object.

11. ***Client obtains the response***. The client invokes *getData* on the packet object to retrieve the contents of the incoming datagram packet.

12. ***Close the socket endpoints***. The client and server invoke *close* on their respective socket objects. These calls free the socket endpoints and release the client and server ports.

Later in this chapter, we will go over code that implements the datagram version of
Count. The code includes a request/reply exchange that is very similar to the
scenario we just covered.

The Java Stream Sockets Classes

Figure 10-7 shows the three classes that implement Java's stream sockets. The
Socket class is the workhorse that both clients and servers use to obtain their
socket services. In addition, servers use the **ServerSocket** class to listen for

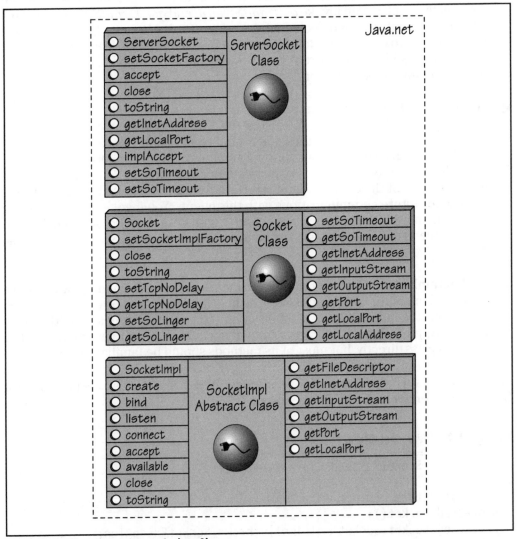

Figure 10-7. The Java.net Stream Sockets Classes.

connection requests from clients. Together, these two classes provide abstractions that hide many of the lower-level socket commands from your applications. If you're interested in the low-level implementation details, check the **SocketImpl** abstract class. This is the class that Java JDK licensees must implement—and possibly extend—for their respective platforms. Both the **Socket** and **ServerSocket** classes use these implementations.

Here's a short description of what these classes do:

■ **Socket** implements a streamed socket. You use one of eight *Socket* constructors to create a socket and pass it the destination port and address information. Once you create a socket, you invoke *getInputStream* and *getOutputSream* to return input and output stream objects that you use to read and write data. You invoke *getLocalPort* to obtain your local port. You invoke *getInetAddress* and *getPort* to obtain the address and port of your remote partner. You invoke *close* to close this socket and release its port.

■ **ServerSocket** implements a streamed server-side socket that listens for incoming connections from clients. You invoke the *ServerSocket* constructor to create a server-side socket that listens for a client connection on a local port you specify; you can also specify an optional amount of time to wait for a connection. The call to *ServerSocket* returns when a connection arrives. You can then invoke *accept* to accept the connection; it returns a **Socket** object that a server thread can use for future communications with this client. You invoke *getInetAddress* to return the address of the connecting client. You invoke *getLocalPort* to retrieve the local port number. You invoke *close* to close the socket and release the port.

■ **SocketImpl** is an abstract class that defines the socket methods JDK licensees must implement for their platforms. The licensees may even provide specialized extensions that are suitable for different environments. For example, they may provide AppleTalk or IPX/SPX versions of sockets. You will never have to deal with this class directly, but most of its methods should be familiar to you by now.

For our readers who prefer to see plain code, here are the class declarations for **Socket**, **ServerSocket**, and **SocketImpl**:

Listing 10-4. The Socket Class.

```
public class Socket extends java.lang.Object
{
  // Constructors
  protected Socket();
  protected Socket(SocketImpl impl) throws SocketException;
  public Socket(String host, int port)
```

```
                    throws UnknownHostException, IOException;
   public Socket(InetAddress address, int port)
                    throws IOException;
   public Socket(String host, int port, InetAddress localAddr,
                    int localPort) throws IOException;
   public Socket(InetAddress address, int port, InetAddress localAddr,
                    int localPort) throws IOException;
   public Socket(String host, int port, boolean stream)
                    throws IOException;
   public Socket(InetAddress host, int port, boolean stream)
                    throws IOException;


   // Class methods
   public static synchronized void
                    setSocketImplFactory(SocketImplFactory fac)
                    throws IOException;


   // Methods
   public synchronized void close() throws IOException;
   public String toString();
   public void setTcpNoDelay(boolean on) throws SocketException;
   public boolean getTcpNoDelay() throws SocketException;
   public void setSoLinger(boolean on, int val)
                         throws SocketException;
   public int getSoLinger() throws SocketException;
   public synchronized void setSoTimeout(int timeout)
                         throws SocketException;
   public synchronized int getSoTimeout() throws SocketException;
   public InetAddress getInetAddress();
   public InputStream getInputStream() throws IOException;
   public OutputStream getOutputStream() throws IOException;
   public int getPort();
   public int getLocalPort();
   public InetAddress getLocalAddress();
}
```

Listing 10-5. The ServerSocket Class.

```
public final class ServerSocket
    extends java.lang.Object
{
        // Constructors
    public ServerSocket(int port) throws IOException;
    public ServerSocket(int port, int backlog) throws IOException;
```

```
public ServerSocket(int port, int backlog, InetAddress bindAddr)
                    throws IOException;

    // Class Methods
public static synchronized void setSocketFactory(SocketImplFactory fac)
      throws IOException, SocketException;

    // Instance methods
public Socket accept() throws IOException;
public void close() throws IOException;
public String toString();
public InetAddress getInetAddress();
public int getLocalPort();
protected final void implAccept(Socket s) throws IOException;
public synchronized void setSoTimeout(int timeout)
                    throws SocketException;
public synchronized int getSoTimeout() throws IOException;
}
```

Listing 10-6. The SocketImpl Class.

```
public abstract class SocketImpl extends java.lang.Object
{
    // Fields
    protected InetAddress address;
    protected FileDescriptor fd;
    protected int localport;
    protected int port;

    // Constructors
    public SocketImpl();

// Methods
protected abstract void create(boolean stream) throws IOException;
protected abstract void bind(InetAddress host, int port)
                            throws IOException;
protected abstract void listen(int backlog) throws IOException;
protected abstract void connect(String host, int port)
                            throws IOException;
protected abstract void connect(InetAddress address, int port)
                            throws IOException;
protected abstract void accept(SocketImpl s) throws IOException;
protected abstract int available() throws IOException;
protected abstract void close() throws IOException;
```

```
public String toString();
protected FileDescriptor getFileDescriptor();
protected InetAddress getInetAddress();
protected abstract InputStream getInputStream() throws IOException;
protected abstract OutputStream getOutputStream() throws IOException;
protected int getPort();
protected int getLocalPort();
}
```

JAVA STREAMS 101

We're not through with our explanation of stream sockets. We must still explain the "stream" in the stream socket. Streams provide the data transfer mechanism on top of sockets. To use a telephone analogy, sockets are like the telephone connection and streams are like voice exchanges. When you speak to a friend on the telephone, you create an output stream; your voice is picked up on the receiving end by an input stream—in this case, your friend's ear. Operating systems use streams to transfer data between programs as well as between programs and external devices such as files, network connections, and printers.

Streams provide a uniform input/output mechanism that hides the devices. You simply write data in one end of a stream and the recipient reads it from the other end. It's like a data pipe. You will find that it is typically easier to write to a stream than to read from it. The writer simply writes to the stream and puts the data in the pipe. The reader, on the other hand, must be prepared to deal with slow writers without blocking an entire program waiting for data to arrive. The reader must also be able to detect the end of a stream. Streams must also provide protocols that allow readers and writers to exchange more complex data—this means anything more than a simple array of bytes. In addition, they must provide mechanisms that allow readers to navigate the stream and randomly access its data. Finally, the better stream packages allow you to filter data and repackage the data as it moves from one stream to another. Programming with streams can be a lot of fun, if you know what you're doing.

The *java.io* package provides a large number of classes—most are derived from the **InputStream** or **OutputStream** abstract classes. These extended classes provide a rich assortment of stream classes that you can use with your sockets. Stream classes are almost always paired—there is usually a corresponding output stream for each input stream type. Figure 10-8 shows the stream classes in *Java.io* that you can use with your stream sockets. The most important of these classes are the derived classes at the bottom. They let you create buffered streams and data-typed streams. The latter preserves the Java data types inside your messages.

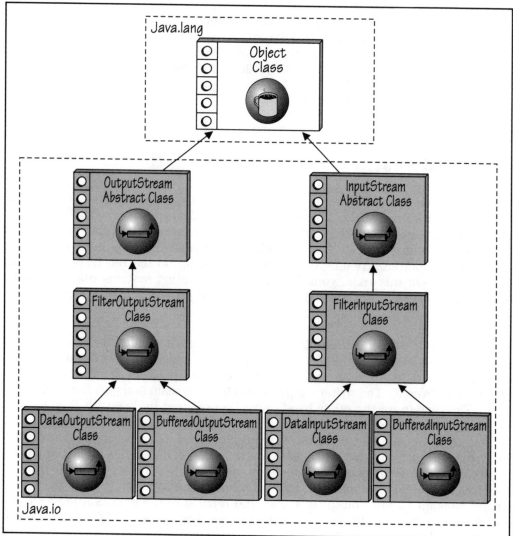

Figure 10-8. The Java.io Sockets-Related Stream Classes.

But how do sockets and streams come together in the first place? You may recall that the **Socket** class provides two methods that let you associate a socket with a pair of streams—*getOutputStream* and *getInputStream*. The first method returns an **OutputStream** object, and the second returns an **InputStream** object. You can then extend these objects to support any of the specialized input/output stream pairs we show in Figure 10-8. Here's a snippet of code that adds a **DataInput-Stream** filter to a socket's **InputStream**:

```
InputStream in_plain = mySocket.getInputStream();
DataInputStream in_data;
in_data = new DataInputStream(in_plain);
```

After you do this, any data the socket receives will be delivered via a **DataInput-Stream** stream. As you will see in the next sections, the extended streams provide added value.

The Java Output Stream Classes

Figure 10-9 shows the sockets-related output stream class hierarchy. All the output stream classes are derived from the **OutputStream** abstract class. The two classes that interest us the most are **DataOutputStream** and **BufferedOutputStream**. They are both filtering streams derived from **FilterOutputStream**. Filtering streams let you chain together streams to produce composite streams of greater power. The buffered and data streams classes are examples of such filters. Let's go over the functions these classes provide:

- **OutputStream** is the abstract class that defines the basic output methods that all output stream classes must provide. You invoke *write* to write a single byte or an array or subarray of bytes. You invoke *flush* to force any buffered data to be sent. Finally, you invoke *close* to close the stream and free up the system resources it owns.

- **FilterOutputStream** is the class that lets you chain together and filter output streams. The class simply overrides all methods of **OutputStream** with versions that pass all requests to the underlying output stream. Subclasses of **FilterOut-putStream** may further override some of these methods as well as provide additional methods and fields.

- **DataOutputStream** is the class that implements a filtered stream enabling you to write Java primitive data types to an output stream in their binary representations. A recipient application uses a **DataInputStream** to read the data back into Java. You invoke the constructor *DataOutputStream* to create a data output stream filter; you must specify the **OutputStream** object to be filtered. You invoke *size* to obtain the number of bytes you wrote so far. You invoke *write* to write a single byte. You can *write* multiple bytes by specifying an offset within a buffer and the number of bytes to write. The class provides methods for writing all the basic Java types to a stream in their binary representation. These methods are self-explanatory except for *writeUTF.* You invoke *writeUTF* to write a Java string of Unicode characters using an ASCII-compatible encoding scheme called UTF-8.

■ **BufferedOutputStream** is the class that implements a buffered output stream filter. Instead of calling the stream for each byte you write, it stores the data in a buffer. It then writes the data to the output stream if the buffer reaches its capacity. You can explicitly flush a buffer's contents by invoking *flush* or *close*. You invoke the constructor *BufferedOutputStream* to create a buffered stream filter; you must specify the **OutputStream** object to be filtered. The constructor provides a 512-byte default buffer that you can optionally override with a size you specify. You invoke *write* to write a single byte; you can *write* multiple bytes by specifying an offset within a buffer and the number of bytes to write. So why are we doing all this? In theory, a buffered filter should give you better performance; it lets you write data to streams in chunks instead of writing it one byte at a time.

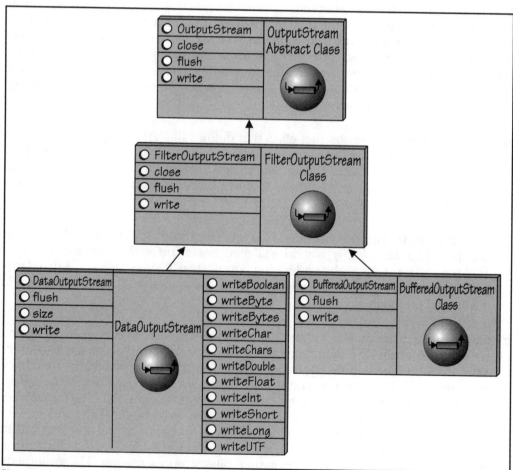

Figure 10-9. The Java.io Sockets-Related Output Stream Classes.

For our readers who enjoy the look-and-feel of plain code, here are the class declarations for **OutputStream**, **FilterOutputStream**, **DataOutputStream**, and the **BufferedOutputStream**:

Listing 10-7. The OutputStream Class.

```
public abstract class OutputStream
    extends java.lang.Object
{
        // Constructors
    public OutputStream();

        // Instance Methods
    public void close() throws IOException;
    public void flush() throws IOException;
    public void write(byte b[]) throws IOException;
    public void write(byte  b[], int off, int len) throws IOException;
    public abstract void write(int b) throws IOException;
}
```

Listing 10-8. The FilterOutputStream Class.

```
public class FilterOutputStream
    extends java.io.OutputStream
{
        // Fields
    protected OutputStream out;

        // Constructors
    public FilterOutputStream(OutputStream  out);

        // Instance Methods
    public void close() throws IOException;
    public void flush() throws IOException;
    public void write(byte b[]) throws IOException;
    public void write(byte b[], int off, int len) throws IOException;
    public void write(int b) throws IOException;
}
```

Listing 10-9. The DataOutputStream Class.

```
public class DataOutputStream
    extends java.io.FilterOutputStream
    implements java.io.DataOutput
```

```
{
        // Fields
    protected int written;

        // Constructors
    public DataOutputStream(OutputStream out);

        // Instance Methods
    public void flush() throws IOException;
    public final int size();
    public synchronized void write(byte b[], int off, int len)
            throws IOException;
    public synchronized void write(int b) throws IOException;
    public final void writeBoolean(boolean v) throws IOException;
    public final void writeByte(int v) throws IOException;
    public final void writeBytes(String s) throws IOException;
    public final void writeChar(int v) throws IOException;
    public final void writeChars(String s) throws IOException;
    public final void writeDouble(double v) throws IOException;
    public final void writeFloat(float v) throws IOException;
    public final void writeInt(int v) throws IOException;
    public final void writeLong(long v) throws IOException;
    public final void writeShort(int v) throws IOException;
    public final void writeUTF(String str) throws IOException;
}
```

Listing 10-10. The BufferedOutputStream Class.

```
public class BufferedOutputStream
    extends java.io.FilterOutputStream
{
        // Fields
    protected byte buf[];
    protected int count;

        // Constructors
    public BufferedOutputStream(OutputStream out);
    public BufferedOutputStream(OutputStream out, int size);

        // Instance Methods
    public synchronized void flush() throws IOException;
    public void write(byte b[], int off, int len) throws IOException;
    public void write(int b) throws IOException;
}
```

The Java Input Stream Classes

Figure 10-10 shows the sockets-related input stream class hierarchy. All the input stream classes are derived from the **InputStream** abstract class. The two classes that interest us the most are **DataInputStream** and **BufferedInputStream**. They are both filtering streams derived from **FilterInputStream**. Filtering lets you chain together streams to produce composite streams of greater power. The buffered and data stream classes are examples of such filters. Let's go over the functions these classes provide:

■ **InputStream** is the abstract class that defines the basic input methods that all input stream classes must provide. You invoke *read* to read the next byte from the stream. If you pass *read* an array, it will fill it as much as possible with data from the stream and then return the number of bytes it actually read. You can also specify an offset to start reading from, as well as the number of bytes you want to read. You invoke *available* to obtain the number of bytes that are already in the stream. You invoke *skip* to skip over the next number of bytes within a stream. You invoke *mark* to mark the current position within a stream; you can specify the number of bytes to be read before the mark position is invalidated. You can subsequently invoke *reset* to reposition the stream to the marked position. You invoke *markSupported* to check if the stream supports marking; it will return true if it does. Finally, you invoke *close* to close the stream and free up the system resources it consumes.

■ **FilterInputStream** is the class that lets you chain together and filter input streams. The class simply overrides all methods of **InputStream** with versions that pass all requests to the underlying input stream. Subclasses of **FilterInputStream** may further override some of these methods as well as provide additional methods and fields.

■ **DataInputStream** is the class that implements a filtered stream that lets you read Java primitive data types from an input stream. You invoke the constructor *DataInputStream* to create a data input stream filter; you must specify the **InputStream** object to be filtered. You invoke *read* to read a single byte. You can *read* multiple bytes by specifying a buffer and the number of bytes to read. The method will block until some input is available; it will then return the number of bytes actually read. You invoke *readFully* to read data into an array of bytes; it will block until all the data is available. The class also provides methods for reading all the basic Java types from a stream in their binary representation. These methods are self-explanatory, except for two—*readLine* and *readUTF*. The *readLine* method reads characters from a stream until it encounters a newline or a carriage return. The *readUTF* method reads a Java string of Unicode text encoded in the UTF-8 format.

■ **BufferedInputStream** is the class that implements a buffered input stream filter. It reads in data and stores it in a buffer. When you request data, it is usually available in the buffer. The idea is to block data fetches and avoid dipping into the stream for each byte you request. You invoke the constructor *Buffered-InputStream* to create a new buffered input stream filter; you must pass it the **InputStream** object to be filtered and an optional buffer size (the default is 512 bytes). You invoke *read* to read a single byte, or you can *read* multiple bytes by specifying an offset within a buffer and the number of bytes to read. Again, the reason we're doing all this is to improve stream performance by reading in chunks of data instead of reading in one byte at a time.

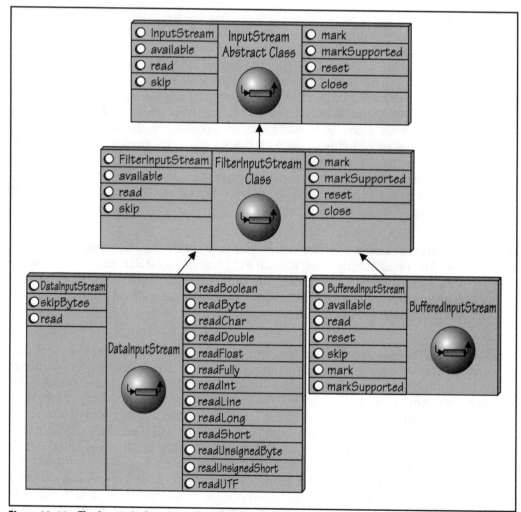

Figure 10-10. The Java.io Sockets-Related Input Stream Classes.

For our readers who prefer to see plain code, here are the class declarations for **InputStream**, **FilterInputStream**, **DataInputStream** and **BufferedInput-Stream**:

Listing 10-11. The InputStream Class.

```
public abstract class InputStream
    extends java.lang.Object
{
        // Constructors
    public InputStream();

        // Instance Methods
    public int available() throws IOException;
    public void close() throws IOException;
    public synchronized void mark(int readlimit);
    public boolean markSupported();
    public abstract int read() throws IOException;
    public int read(byte b[]) throws IOException;
    public int read(byte b[], int off, int len) throws IOException;
    public synchronized void reset() throws IOException;
    public long skip(long n) throws IOException;
}
```

Listing 10-12. The FilterInputStream Class.

```
public class FilterInputStream
    extends java.io.InputStream
{
        // Fields
    protected InputStream in;

        // Constructors
    protected FilterInputStream(InputStream  in);

        // Instance Methods
    public int available() throws IOException;
    public void close() throws IOException;
    public synchronized void mark(int readlimit);
    public boolean markSupported();
    public int read() throws IOException;
    public int read(byte b[]) throws IOException;
    public int read(byte b[], int off, int len) throws IOException;
    public synchronized void reset() throws IOException;
```

```
    public long skip(long n) throws IOException;
}
```

Listing 10-13. The DataInputStream Class.

```
public class DataInputStream
    extends java.io.FilterInputStream
    implements java.io.DataInput
{
    // Constructors
    public DataInputStream(InputStream in);

    // Class Methods
    public final static String readUTF(DataInput in) throws IOException;

    // Instance Methods
    public final int read(byte b[]) throws IOException;
    public final int read(byte b[], int off, int len) throws IOException;
    public final boolean readBoolean() throws IOException;
    public final byte readByte() throws IOException;
    public final char readChar() throws IOException;
    public final double readDouble() throws IOException;
    public final float readFloat() throws IOException;
    public final void readFully(byte b[])
                throws IOException;
    public final void readFully(byte b[], int off, int len)
                throws IOException;
    public final int readInt() throws IOException;
    public final String readLine() throws IOException;
    public final long readLong() throws IOException;
    public final short readShort() throws IOException;
    public final int readUnsignedByte() throws IOException;
    public final int readUnsignedShort() throws IOException;
    public final String readUTF() throws IOException;
    public final static String readUTF(DataInput in) throws IOException;
    public final int skipBytes(int n) throws IOException;
}
```

Listing 10-14. The BufferedInputStream Class.

```
public class BufferedInputStream
    extends java.io.FilterInputStream
{
    // Fields
```

```
protected byte buf[];
protected int count;
protected int marklimit;
protected int markpos;
protected int pos;

    // Constructors
public BufferedInputStream(InputStream in);
public BufferedInputStream(InputStream in, int size);

    // Instance Methods
public int available() throws IOException;
public void mark(int readlimit);
public boolean markSupported();
public int read() throws IOException;
public int read(byte b[], int off, int len) throws IOException;
public void reset() throws IOException;
public long skip(long n) throws IOException;
}
```

A Java Buffered-Stream Socket Scenario

Are you suffering from class overload? Is it getting too confusing? It's time for a scenario. The scenario we will develop consists of a simple client/server exchange using buffered-stream sockets. The client asks for Bob's balance; the server returns that infamous $300. Unfortunately, the page is not wide enough to show both the client and server sides of the exchange. So we will show you the client and server sides separately. Figure 10-11 shows the client side of this interaction; Figure 10-12 shows the server side. Let's first go over the client side of this interaction:

1. *Create a client socket*. Invoke the *Socket* constructor and pass it the server's host name and port address.

2. *Obtain an OutputStream*. The client invokes *getOutputStream* on the **Socket** object to obtain its **OutputStream** object.

3. *Create a buffered output filter for sending messages*. The client invokes the *BufferedOutputStream* constructor and passes it the **OutputStream** object—this is the object on which it creates the buffered output filter.

4. *Obtain an InputStream*. The client invokes *getInputStream* on the **Socket** object to obtain its **InputStream** object.

5. *Create a buffered input filter for receiving messages*. The client invokes

the *BufferedInputStream* constructor and passes it the **InputStream** object—this is the object on which it creates the buffered input filter.

6. ***Write to the buffered output stream***. The client invokes *write* and passes it an array of bytes requesting Bob's balance.

7. ***Flush the stream***. The client invokes *flush* to force the stream to deliver the message. This is how you enforce message boundaries on socket streams.

8. ***Read from the buffered input stream***. The client invokes *read*. The input

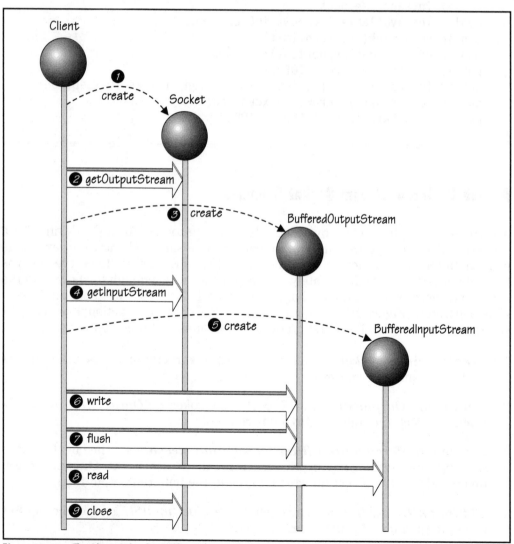

Figure 10-11. The Client Side of a Buffered-Stream Socket Scenario.

stream should contain a reply message from the server that states Bob's balance.

9. ***Close the socket***. The client invokes *close* to close the socket and release its resources.

Now we must change hats and role-play the server. Isn't this fun? Figure 10-12 shows the server side of this interaction. The server receives a request for Bob's balance. It retrieves the balance and returns it to the client. Let's go over the steps:

1. ***Create a server socket***. The server invokes the *ServerSocket* constructor and passes it a port address for this banking service.

2. ***Wait for a client to call***. The server invokes *accept*; it will block and wait for an incoming connection. In this scenario, the client eventually calls the server.

3. ***Accept the call***. Accept returns a new **Socket** object that the server uses to communicate with this client. You would typically create a new thread and pass it the socket. The current thread can then reissue *accept* to intercept new requests from clients.

4. ***Obtain an OutputStream***. The server invokes *getOutputStream* on the **Socket** object to obtain its **OutputStream** object.

5. ***Create a buffered output filter for sending messages***. The server invokes the *BufferedOutputStream* constructor and passes it the **OutputStream** object—this is the object on which it creates the buffered output filter.

6. ***Obtain an InputStream***. The server invokes *getInputStream* on the **Socket** object to obtain its **InputStream** object.

7. ***Create a buffered input filter for receiving messages***. The server invokes the *BufferedInputStream* constructor and passes it the **InputStream** object—this is the object on which it creates the buffered input filter.

8. ***Read from the buffered input stream***. The server invokes *read*. The input stream should contain a request for Bob's balance.

9. ***Write to the buffered output stream***. The server invokes *write* and passes it an array of bytes that contain Bob's balance.

10. ***Flush the stream***. Invoke *flush* to force the stream to deliver the message.

11. ***Close the socket***. Invoke *close* to close the socket and release its resources.

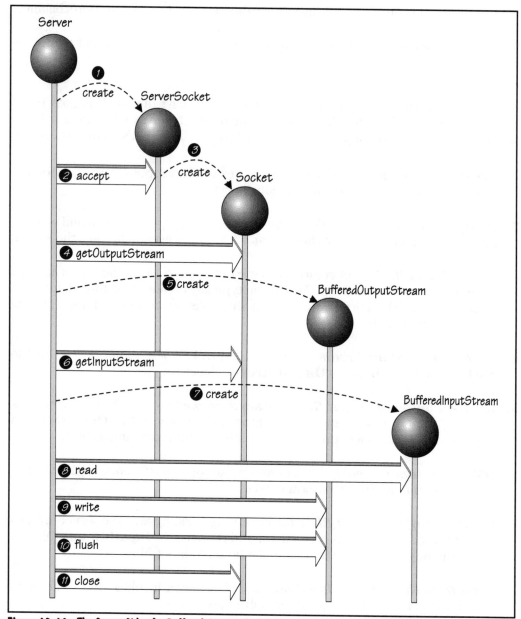

Figure 10-12. The Server Side of a Buffered-Stream Socket Scenario.

After this very lengthy tutorial, you should be more than ready for some code. We won't disappoint you. In the next sections, we create four socket versions of Count: 1) using datagrams, 2) using data streams, 3) using buffered streams, and 4) using buffered data streams.

THE JAVA DATAGRAM SOCKET COUNT

We build our first version of the Sockets Count using datagrams. The code follows very closely the datagram scenario we presented in Figure 10-6. The program consists of two Java classes: a **Client** class and a **Server** class. So how do we avoid naming collisions in our four implementations? We put each implementation in a separate Java package. We call the package for the datagram implementation *SocketDatagram* (see Figure 10-13).

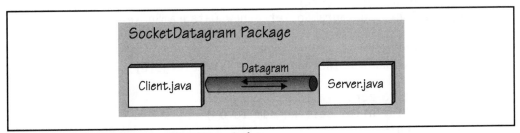

Figure 10-13. The SocketDatagram Client/Server Package.

The Datagram Socket Count Client

The client program consists of a single Java class called **Client**. This class provides a *main* function that does the following: 1) creates a **DatagramSocket**, 2) obtains the Inet address of the server, 3) sets the remote sum value to zero, 4) calculates the start time, 5) sends an increment request n times, 6) calculates the elapsed time, and 7) prints the results. You must pass to the program the name of a server host and an increment count number. Here's the code:

Listing 10-15. The Datagram Socket Count Client.

```java
// Client.java,  Java Sockets Client using datagrams

package SocketDatagram;
import java.net.*;
import java.io.*;

public class Client
{ public static void main(String args[])
  {
    byte[] buffer = new byte[10];
    String sumString = "";
    String myOperation;
    DatagramPacket inPacket = null;
```

```java
DatagramPacket outPacket = null;

try
{ if(args.length != 2)
  {
    System.out.println("Usage java Client <host> <count>");
    return;
  }

  // Create datagram socket
  DatagramSocket datagramSocket = new DatagramSocket(250);

  // Get inet addr of server
  InetAddress addr = InetAddress.getByName(args[0]);

  // set sum to zero
  System.out.println("Setting sum to 0");
  myOperation = "set_sum";
  buffer = myOperation.getBytes();
  outPacket = new DatagramPacket(buffer, myOperation.length(),
                                 addr, 251);
  datagramSocket.send(outPacket);
  inPacket = new DatagramPacket(buffer, buffer.length);
  datagramSocket.receive(inPacket);
  buffer = inPacket.getData();
  sumString = new String(buffer, 0, inPacket.getLength());
  System.out.println("sum = " + sumString);

  // get count, initialize start time
  System.out.println("Incrementing");
  int count = new Integer(args[1]).intValue();
  long startTime = System.currentTimeMillis();

  // perform increment "count" number of times
  for(int i = 0; i < count; i++)
  { myOperation = "increment";
    buffer = myOperation.getBytes();
    outPacket = new DatagramPacket(buffer, myOperation.length(),
                                   addr, 251);
    datagramSocket.send(outPacket);
    inPacket = new DatagramPacket(buffer, buffer.length);
    datagramSocket.receive(inPacket);
    buffer = inPacket.getData();
    sumString = new String(buffer, 0, inPacket.getLength());
  }
```

```
      // display statistics
      long stopTime = System.currentTimeMillis();
      System.out.println("Avg Ping = "
            +  ((stopTime - startTime) / (float)count) + " msecs");
      System.out.println("Sum = " + sumString);
    }
    catch(Exception e)
    { System.err.println(e);
    }
   }
 }
}
```

Notice that we created our own conventions for passing the request names and their arguments. We put everything in string form, and we do our own marshaling. We also don't check for lost messages or duplicate ones. It's transmit-and-pray. The only good news is that the code should be easy to follow, especially if you read the tutorial.

The Datagram Socket Count Server

The server program consists of a single Java class—**Server**. This class provides a *main* function that does the following: 1) creates a **DatagramSocket**, 2) waits for client requests, 3) decodes and executes the requested operation, 4) sends back a reply, and 5) waits for new requests to arrive. It's your classical do-forever server loop. Here's the code:

Listing 10-16. The Datagram Socket Count Server.

```
// Server.java,  Java Sockets Server using datagrams

package SocketDatagram;
import java.net.*;
import java.io.*;

public class Server
{ public static void main(String[] args)
   {
     byte[] buffer = new byte[10];
     int sum = 0;
     String sumString = "";
     DatagramSocket datagramSocket = null;
     DatagramPacket inPacket = null;
     DatagramPacket outPacket = null;
```

```java
    InetAddress addr = null;

    try
    { // create socket
      datagramSocket = new DatagramSocket(251);

      // wait for request packets
      System.out.println("Waiting for client requests");

      // execute client requests
      while(true)
      {
        inPacket = new DatagramPacket(buffer, buffer.length);
        datagramSocket.receive(inPacket);
        buffer = inPacket.getData();
        addr   = inPacket.getAddress();   // addr for reply packet

        String myOperation = new String(buffer, 0,
                                        inPacket.getLength());

        // perform increment operation
        if (myOperation.equals("increment"))
          sumString = String.valueOf(++sum);
        else
          // perform set sum operation
          if(myOperation.equals("set_sum"))
          { sum = 0;
            sumString = String.valueOf(sum);
            System.out.println("Sum = " + sumString);
          }

        buffer = sumString.getBytes();
        outPacket = new DatagramPacket(buffer, sumString.length(),
                                       addr, 250);
        datagramSocket.send(outPacket);
      }
    } catch (Exception e)
    { System.err.println("Closing DatagramSocket");
      if (datagramSocket != null)
        datagramSocket.close();
    }
  }
}
```

Notice that the code is very similar to the datagram scenario we presented earlier. So there should be no surprises. Again, notice that we're using a roll-your-own convention for interpreting requests and their arguments. It's really a very primitive protocol.

THE BUFFERED SOCKET COUNT

We build our second socket Count using buffered streams. The code follows very closely the buffered-stream scenario we presented in Figures 10-11 and 10-12. The program consists of two Java classes: a **Client** class and a **Server** class. To avoid naming collisions, we put each of our client/server socket implementations in a separate Java package. This one goes in a package called *SocketBuffered* (see Figure 10-14).

Figure 10-14. The SocketBuffered Client/Server Package.

The Buffered Socket Count Client

Again, the client program consists of a single Java class called **Client**. This class provides a *main* function that does the following: 1) creates a new client **Socket**, 2) creates the input and output streams, 3) sets the remote sum value to zero, 4) calculates the start time, 5) sends an increment request n times, 6) calculates the elapsed time, and 7) prints the results. You must pass the program the name of a server host and an increment count number. Here's the code:

Listing 10-17. The Buffered Socket Count Client.

```
// Client.java,  Java Sockets Client, Buffered Streams

package SocketBuffered;
import java.net.*;
import java.io.*;

public class Client
```

```java
{ public static void main(String args[])
  { byte[] buffer = new byte[10]; // buffer for sockets transfers
    int bytesRead;                // variable for bytes read
    String sumString = "";        // variable for storing current sum
    String myOperation;           // variable for byte to string conversion

    try
    { if(args.length != 2)
      {
        System.out.println("Usage java Client <host> <count>");
        return;
      }

      // Create socket connection
      System.out.println("Opening socket and creating streams");
      String host = args[0];
      Socket socket = new Socket(host, 250);

      // create streams
      BufferedOutputStream ostream =
                new BufferedOutputStream(socket.getOutputStream());
      BufferedInputStream istream =
                new BufferedInputStream(socket.getInputStream());

      // set sum to zero
      System.out.println("Setting sum to 0");
      myOperation = "set_sum";
      buffer = myOperation.getBytes();
      ostream.write(buffer, 0, myOperation.length());
      ostream.flush();
      bytesRead = istream.read(buffer, 0, 10);
      sumString = new String(buffer, 0, bytesRead);

      // get count, initialize start time
      System.out.println("Incrementing");
      int count = new Integer(args[1]).intValue();
      long startTime = System.currentTimeMillis();

      // perform increment "count" number of times
      for(int i = 0; i < count; i++)
      { myOperation = "increment";
        buffer = myOperation.getBytes();
        ostream.write(buffer, 0, myOperation.length());
        ostream.flush();
        bytesRead = istream.read(buffer, 0, 10);
```

```
        sumString = new String(buffer, 0, bytesRead);
      }

      // display statistics
      long stopTime = System.currentTimeMillis();
      System.out.println("Avg Ping = "
                       + ((stopTime - startTime) / (float)count) + " msecs");
      System.out.println("Sum = " + sumString);
    }
    catch(Exception e)
    { System.err.println(e);
    }
  }
}
```

Notice that we create our own conventions for passing the request names and their arguments. We also do our own marshaling by stuffing everything in a buffer. It's not very elegant, but welcome to life at the socket level.

The Buffered Socket Count Server

The server program consists of a single Java class—**Server**. This class provides a *main* function that does the following: 1) creates a **ServerSocket**, 2) waits for a client connection, 3) obtains a new **Socket** object, 4) creates buffered input and output streams, 5) decodes and executes client requests, 6) sends back a reply, and 7) waits for new requests to arrive. It's your classical do-forever server loop. Here's the code:

Listing 10-18. The Buffered Socket Count Server.

```
// Server.java,  Java Sockets Server, Buffered Streams

package SocketBuffered;
import java.net.*;
import java.io.*;

public class Server
{ public static void main(String[] args)
  {
    ServerSocket serverSocket = null;
    Socket socket = null;
    byte[] readBuffer = new byte[40];  // buffer for sockets transfers
    byte[] writeBuffer = new byte[40];  // buffer for sockets transfers
```

```java
int bytesRead;                // bytes read to/from buffer
int sum = 0;                  // current sum value
String sumString = "";        // for byte to string conversion

// create socket
try
{
  serverSocket = new ServerSocket(250);
} catch (Exception e)
{ System.err.println("Exception Creating Socket");
}

while (true)
{ try
  { // wait for connection then create streams
    System.out.println("Waiting for client connection");
    socket = serverSocket.accept();
    BufferedOutputStream ostream =
        new BufferedOutputStream(socket.getOutputStream());
    BufferedInputStream istream =
        new BufferedInputStream(socket.getInputStream());

    // execute client requests
    while(true)
    { bytesRead = istream.read(readBuffer, 0, 40);
      String myOperation = new String(readBuffer, 0, bytesRead);

      // perform increment operation
      if(myOperation.equals("increment"))
        sumString = String.valueOf(++sum);
      else
        // perform set sum operation
        if(myOperation.equals("set_sum"))
        { sum = 0;
          sumString = String.valueOf(sum);
          System.out.println("Sum = " + sumString);
        }
      writeBuffer = sumString.getBytes();
      ostream.write(writeBuffer, 0, sumString.length());
      ostream.flush();
    }
  } catch (Exception e)
  { System.err.println("Closing Socket connection");
    if (socket != null)
      try
```

```
        { socket.close();
          serverSocket = new ServerSocket(250);
        } catch (IOException ex) {}
    }
  }
 }
}
```

This code is very similar to the scenario we presented earlier, so there should be no surprises. Again, notice that we're using a roll-your-own convention for interpreting requests and their arguments. It's the best we could do with sockets.

THE DATA STREAM SOCKET COUNT

We build our third socket Count using nonbuffered data streams. The code is similar to the buffered-stream scenario we presented in Figures 10-11 and 10-12. Both examples deal with streamed sockets. The major difference is the stream type. In this example, we use data streams instead of buffered streams. As usual, the socket program consists of two Java classes: a **Client** class and a **Server** class. This implementation is in a package called *SocketDataStream* (see Figure 10-15).

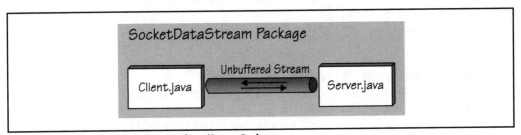

Figure 10-15. The SocketDataStream Client/Server Package.

The Data Stream Socket Count Client

Again, the client program consists of a single Java class called **Client**. This class provides a *main* function that does the following: 1) creates a new client **Socket**, 2) creates the input and output data streams, 3) sets the remote sum value to zero, 4) calculates the start time, 5) sends an increment request n times, 6) calculates the elapsed time, and 7) prints the results. You must pass to the program the name of a server host and an increment count number. Here's the code:

Listing 10-19. The Data Stream Socket Count Client.

```java
// Client.java,  Java Sockets Client, Data Streams

package SocketDataStream;
import java.net.*;
import java.io.*;

public class Client
{ public static void main(String args[])
  {
    String sumString = "";          // variable for storing current sum

    try
    { if(args.length != 2)
      {
        System.out.println("Usage java Client <host> <count>");
        return;
      }

      // Create socket connection
      System.out.println("Opening socket and creating streams");
      String host = args[0];
      Socket socket = new Socket(host, 250);

      // create streams
      DataOutputStream ostream =
          new DataOutputStream(socket.getOutputStream());
      DataInputStream istream =
          new DataInputStream(socket.getInputStream());

      // set sum to zero
      System.out.println("Setting sum to 0");
      ostream.writeUTF("set_sum");
      ostream.flush();
      sumString = istream.readUTF();

      // get count, initialize start time
      System.out.println("Incrementing");
      int count = new Integer(args[1]).intValue();
      long startTime = System.currentTimeMillis();

      // perform increment "count" number of times
      for(int i = 0; i < count; i++)
      { ostream.writeUTF("increment");
```

```
      ostream.flush();
      sumString = istream.readUTF();
    }

    // display statistics
    long stopTime = System.currentTimeMillis();
    System.out.println("Avg Ping = "
                    + ((stopTime - startTime) / (float)count) + " msecs");
    System.out.println("Sum = " + sumString);
  }
  catch(Exception e)
  { System.err.println(e);
  }
  }
 }
}
```

We're still dealing with sockets. Consequently, we create our own conventions for passing the request names and their arguments. We also do our own marshaling. Notice that we're using *writeUTF* to write to the output stream. We invoke *readUTF* on the input stream to receive results. This is a little bit more elegant than stuffing buffers, but it's still quite primitive.

The Data Stream Socket Count Server

The server program consists of a single Java class—**Server**. This class provides a *main* function that does the following: 1) creates a **ServerSocket**, 2) waits for a client connection, 3) obtains a new **Socket** object, 4) creates input and output data streams, 5) decodes and executes client requests, 6) sends back a reply, and 7) waits for new requests to arrive. It's very similar to the buffered-stream program. The only difference is in the type of stream we use. Here's the code:

Listing 10-20. The Server Side of the Data Stream Socket Count.

```
// Server.java,  Java Sockets Server, Data Streams

package SocketDataStream;
import java.net.*;
import java.io.*;

public class Server
{ public static void main(String[] args)
  {
    ServerSocket serverSocket = null;
```

```
Socket socket = null;
int sum = 0;                        // current sum value
String sumString = "";

// create socket
try
{
  serverSocket = new ServerSocket(250);
} catch (Exception e)
{ System.err.println("Exception Creating Socket");
}

while (true)
{ try
  { // wait for connection then create streams
    System.out.println("Waiting for client connection");
    socket = serverSocket.accept();
    DataOutputStream ostream =
        new DataOutputStream(socket.getOutputStream());
    DataInputStream istream =
        new DataInputStream(socket.getInputStream());

    // execute client requests
    while(true)
    { String myOperation = istream.readUTF();

      // perform increment operation
      if(myOperation.equals("increment"))
         sumString = String.valueOf(++sum);
      else
         // perform set sum operation
         if(myOperation.equals("set_sum"))
         { sum = 0;
           sumString = String.valueOf(sum);
           System.out.println("Sum = " + sumString);
         }

      ostream.writeUTF(sumString);
      ostream.flush();
    }
  } catch (Exception e)
  { System.err.println("Closing Socket connection");
    if (socket != null)
       try
       { socket.close();
```

```
        } catch (IOException ex) {}
    }
  }
 }
}
```

Again, notice that we're using our roll-your-own convention for interpreting requests and their arguments. The big improvement is that we extract string data from our input stream using *readUTF*. And we write to the output stream using *writeUTF*. Instead of just stuffing buffers, data streams allow us to directly read and write any of the primitive Java data types. This is definitely a step in the right direction. But before you throw away your buffered sockets, you should consider the buffered data stream combination that we present in the next section.

THE BUFFERED DATA STREAM COUNT

We build our last socket Count using a buffered data stream combination. To create a buffered data stream, you simply replace the create stream filters in the previous non-buffered example, with the following filters:

```
DataOutputStream ostream =
        new DataOutputStream(new BufferedOutputStream(
                                 socket.getOutputStream()));
DataInputStream istream =
        new DataInputStream(new BufferedInputStream(
                                 socket.getInputStream()));
```

You must do this on both the client and the server. The rest of the code is unchanged, so we won't repeat it here (it's on the CD-ROM).

COMPILE THE SOCKET COUNTS

We're now ready to compile the sockets code. Make sure you have installed the Symantec Visual Café compiler. The code for each of the sockets implementations is in its own subdirectory—for example, datagrams are in the *SocketDatagram* directory. To compile the datagram client/server code, go to the appropriate directory and type the following commands at the prompt:

```
prompt> javac -d \CorbaJavaBook.2e\classes Client.java
prompt> javac -d \CorbaJavaBook.2e\classes Server.java
```

The -d option tells the compiler to put the (.class) files it creates into the directory we specify—in this case, \CorbaJavaBook.2e\classes. If the compile is successful, you should have some compiled Java classes—(.class) files—that you can now run.

RUN THE CLIENT/SERVER PROGRAMS

To run the datagram server program, type the following command at the prompt:

prompt> `start java SocketDatagram.Server`

To run the datagram socket client, type the following command at the prompt:

prompt> `java SocketDatagram.Client corbajava.engr.sjsu.edu   1000`

Make sure to enter your server's host name in the place of *corbajava.engr.sjsu.edu*. Of course, you're always welcome to use our lab. Note that the number of increments (or Pings) for this test run is 1000. If all goes well, you'll see a screen output that looks like this:

```
Opening socket and creating streams
Setting Sum to 0
Incrementing
Avg Ping = 4.200 msecs
Sum = 1000
```

Repeat these steps to compile and run the other three versions of the sockets program—buffered, data stream, and buffered data stream.

LOOKING AT SOME TEST RESULTS

We will run these four client/server programs in different situations to get a reading on the performance of Java's socket types. In all cases, the Count client performs 1000 method invocations during the elapsed time. The program calculates the average response time in milliseconds by dividing the elapsed time by the number of invocations. We're measuring the equivalent of Ping performance using Java sockets.

We first run the client and server programs in the same machine—a 120-MHz Pentium running NT 4.0. Then we run them across a 10 Mbit/s Ethernet LAN. We run this local/remote test using the four socket programs. Table 10-1 compares the results. Buffered data stream sockets are relatively a screamer. They provide the typed benefits of data streams without the performance penalty.

Table 10-1. Local Versus Remote Counts Using Java Sockets.

	Local Sockets (interprocess)	Remote Sockets (interprocess over 10 Mbit/s Ethernet)
Datagram sockets	4.2 msecs	3.9 msecs
Buffered stream sockets	3.7 msecs	3.9 msecs
Buffered data stream sockets	1.7 msecs	2.1 msecs
Data stream sockets	400.6 msecs	300.5 msecs

SOCKETS VERSUS CORBA IIOP

We've shown you sockets in their best light—the Count server only supports two operations with a simple return parameter. Instead, imagine a simple server that exposes a dozen or so interfaces to its clients. Let's say that each interface consists of a dozen methods that each require five or six parameters with different data types. Can you see yourself implementing this service using the roll-your-own socket messaging schemes we introduced in this chapter? We're talking about a major maintenance and programming nightmare here. This is why you need an ORB. ORBs hide these nasty details and let you program at a higher level of abstraction. Table 10-2 compares the sockets and CORBA programming models.

Table 10-2. CORBA IIOP Versus Java Sockets.

Feature	CORBA IIOP	Java Sockets			
		Datagram	Buffered	Data Stream	Buffered Data Stream
Reliable communications	Yes	No	Yes	Yes	Yes
Parameter marshaling	Yes	No	No	No	No
Interface descriptions	Yes (via IDL)	No	No	No	No
Dynamic discovery	Yes (via IR and DII)	No	No	No	No
Parameter data typing	Yes (Language and OS neutral binary interchange format)	No	No	Yes (Java-to-Java only)	Yes (Java-to-Java only)

Table 10-2. CORBA IIOP Versus Java Sockets. (Continued)

Feature	CORBA IIOP	Java Sockets			
		Datagram	Buffered	Data Stream	Buffered Data Stream
Ping Performance	Fast (3.5 msecs)	Fast (3.9 msecs)	Fast (3.9 msecs)	Very slow (300.5 msecs)	Very Fast (2.1 msecs)
Security	Yes (via CORBA and SSL)	Yes (via SSL)	Yes (via SSL)	Yes (via SSL)	Yes (via SSL)
Transactions	Yes	No	No	No	No

Sockets are really a lower-level programming model. It's like programming in assembler when you have a high-level language—in this analogy, CORBA.

CONCLUSION

This concludes another very long chapter. The big revelation here is that programming sockets with data streams is something you want to avoid. They're extremely slow. In addition, we showed that the sockets programming model is very primitive. If you're given a choice, you should avoid programming Java client/server applications with sockets and streams. In Java's pre-CORBA and pre-RMI days there was no choice—it was sockets or nothing. Luckily, we have more choices now.

So was this a waste of time? Absolutely not. You should understand the socket/stream programming model because most higher-level middleware packages—including ORBs—build on top of it. Sometimes a socket-related error may pop out of nowhere—for example, "host unknown." Also, it's very likely that you will encounter streams—of one type or another—in your Java programs. So you should also understand how they work. The next chapter shows you how to use streams and sockets to create HTTP/CGI Internet programs.

Chapter 11

HTTP/CGI Versus CORBA/Java ORBs

HTTP/CGI is currently the predominant model for creating 3-tier client/server solutions over the Internet. The *Hypertext Transfer Protocol (HTTP)* provides simple RPC-like semantics on top of sockets. You can use it very effectively to access resources that live in URL space. Everyone knows that URLs point to HTML pages. However, URLs also provide a consistent intergalactic naming scheme that you use to identify all Web resources—including Web pages, documents, images, sound clips, applets, and programs. So you can use URLs within an HTTP message to locate a server program anywhere on the Internet.

So what happens after HTTP locates a program identified by a URL? On the receiving end, the typical Web server only knows how to handle HTML documents. When it receives a request for a program, it simply turns around and invokes the resource named in the URL and tells it to take care of the request. The server passes the method request and its parameters to the back-end program using a protocol called the *Common Gateway Interface (CGI)*. You can write your CGI server programs in any language that can read standard input and write to standard output—including Java. The HTTP server will launch the Java application and virtual machine whenever a client submits an HTTP request for that application. The application executes and returns the results in HTML/HTTP format to the server. The server turns around and returns the results to the client.

HTTP clients and servers use the Internet's MIME data representations to describe (and negotiate) the contents of messages. HTTP defines protocols for invoking common commands and passing their parameters. Consequently, HTTP/CGI provide all the pieces you need to create Web-based client/server applications in Java. Of course, all the client/server interactions must first pass through an HTTP server to get to the CGI program. Some people may consider this to be added goodness—system administrators are very familiar with CGI and HTTP servers. So how does the HTTP client/server model compare with CORBA's? You will soon find out.

The plan for this chapter is to develop the HTTP/CGI version of the minimalist Count. We begin this chapter by talking a little bit about HTTP and CGI. If these topics are old news to you, you may want to jump directly to the programming section. If you haven't done so yet, make sure to read Chapter 10; the CGI version of Count uses sockets everywhere. By the end of this chapter, you will have a good idea of the overhead HTTP servers and CGI introduce. You will also understand why CORBA is a better 3-tier client/server platform for the Internet than HTTP/CGI.

HTTP 101

The *Hypertext Transfer Protocol (HTTP)* has been in use on the Web since 1990. The first version of HTTP—referred to as HTTP/0.9—was a simple protocol for raw data transfer across the Internet. HTTP/1.0 improved the protocol by introducing self-describing messages using a variant of the Internet Mail's MIME protocol.

HTTP 1.1—developed by the original authors of HTTP, Tim Berners-Lee, Roy Fielding, and Henrik Frystyk Nielsen—is backwards-compatible with HTTP/1.0, but it includes more stringent requirements to ensure that its features are implemented reliably. Further on the horizon is HTTP-NG, which promises to evolve HTTP 1.X into a more efficient protocol.

So What Exactly Is HTTP?

As we mentioned earlier, HTTP is the Web's RPC on top of TCP/IP. You use it to access and retrieve URL-named resources. The HTTP RPC is stateless. The client establishes a connection to the remote server. Next, it issues a request. The server first processes the request, returns a response, and then closes the connection. A client—typically a Web browser—requests a hypertext page and then issues a sequence of separate requests to retrieve any images referenced in the document. Once the client has retrieved the images, the user will typically click on a hypertext link and move to another document. HTTP typically sets up a new connection for each request. The client must wait for a response before sending out a new request.

HTTP Data Representations

An important feature of HTTP is that it lets you pass self-describing data over the RPC. The protocol allows Web browsers to inform their server about the data representations they can understand. Clients and servers must negotiate their data representations every time a connection is made. This adds to the connection overhead. Why don't the servers keep track of their clients' attributes? Remember, HTTP servers are stateless, which means they have no recollection of previous client connections. HTTP's statelessness works well in simple client/server environments. It allows servers to function very efficiently. They pick up connections, fulfill the request, and quickly drop the connection. Note, however, that state is needed in all but the simplest client/server interactions. So this can be a problem with the current HTTP protocol. There are some very clumsy workarounds to this problem; we cover them later in the chapter.

So What Does an HTTP Request Look Like?

An HTTP client/server interaction consists of a single request/reply interchange. Figure 11-1 shows the syntax of an HTTP request. It consists of a *request line*, one or more optional *request header fields*, and an optional *entity body*. The lines are separated by a carriage-return/line-feed (crlf). The entity body is preceded by a blank line. Here are the details:

■ *The request line* consists of three text fields, separated by white spaces. The first field specifies the method—or command—to be applied to a server resource. The most common method is GET, which asks the server to send a copy of the resource to the client. The second field specifies the name of the target resource; it's the URL stripped of the protocol and server domain name. The third field identifies the protocol version used by the client—for example, HTTP/1.0.

■ *The request header fields* pass additional information about the request and about the client itself to the server. The fields act like RPC parameters. Each header field consists of a name followed by a colon (:) and the field value. The order in which you transmit the header fields is not significant.

■ *The entity body* is sometimes used by clients to pass bulk information to the server.

The bottom of Figure 11-1 is an example of an archetypical HTTP GET request—the client requests a file called file.html from the server. The first *accept* header field tells the server that the client knows how to handle text HTML files. The second *accept* field tells the server that the client can also handle all audio formats. Finally, the *user-agent* field lets the server know that the client is a MacWeb

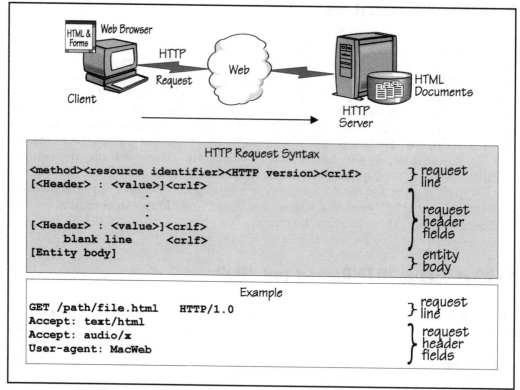

Figure 11-1. The HTTP Request Format.

browser. So, the various accepts tell the server which data types the client can handle; user-agent gives the implementation name of the client.

So What Does an HTTP Response Look Like?

Figure 11-2 shows the syntax of an HTTP response. It consists of a *response header line*, one or more optional *response header fields*, and an optional *entity body*. The lines are separated by a carriage-return/line-feed (crlf). The entity body must be preceded by a blank line. Here are the details:

■ ***The response header line*** returns the HTTP version, the status of the response, and an explanation of the returned status.

■ ***The response header fields*** return information that describe the server's attributes and the returned HTML document to the client. Each header field consists of a name followed by a colon (:) and the field value. The order in which the server returns the header fields is not significant.

■ *The entity body* typically contains an HTML document that a client has requested.

The bottom of Figure 11-2 shows a typical server's response to a GET request. The result code 200 indicates that the request was successful. The *server* header field identifies the server as a NCSA/1.3. The *MIME-version* field indicates that the server supports MIME 1.0 (see the next Details box). The *content-type* field describes the returned object as being a text/HTML document. The *content-length* field indicates the document length. This is followed by the HTML document itself—the object of the request. The server sends the requested data and then drops the TCP/IP connection. That's all there is to it. Congratulations, you're now a bona fide HTTP expert.

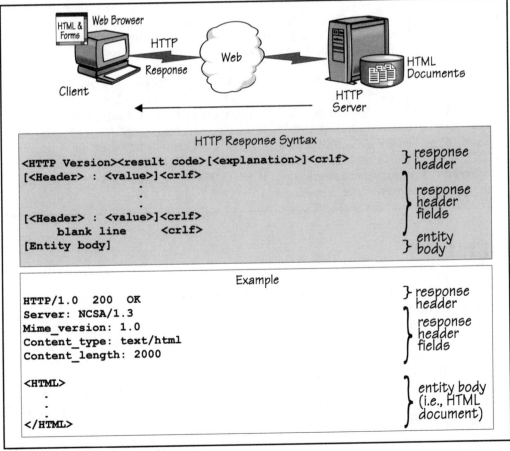

Figure 11-2. The HTTP Response Format.

HTTP and MIME

Details

HTTP borrows heavily from the *Internet Mail* (RFC 822) and the *Multipurpose Internet Mail Extensions (MIME)* (RFC 1521), which provides extensible mechanisms for transmitting multimedia e-mail. In case you're interested, RFC 822 deals mostly with the headers that appear at the top of your Internet Mail, but it does very little to describe the contents of the mail. MIME supplements RFC 822 by specifying additional headers that describe what sorts of data the message body contains. For example, MIME defines several headers that are used to specify if a message consists of multiple parts and how these parts are separated. A MIME header uses the familiar format "content-type: type/subtype" as in "content-type: text/html." MIME currently supports seven data types— plain text; audio; video; still images; message, which can point to an external message; multipart messages, in which each part can have a different type; and application-specific data. Each MIME type can also have subtypes.

It should come as no surprise that HTTP's content-type headers are very MIME-like. However, HTTP itself is not a MIME-compliant application. HTTP's RPC-like performance requirements differ substantially from those of Internet Mail. Consequently, the HTTP architects chose not to obey the constraints imposed by RFC 822 and MIME for mail transport. But even though HTTP is not MIME-compliant, you can include a *MIME-version* header field in a message to indicate what version of the MIME protocol was used to construct the message content-type headers. ❑

CGI 101

Web browsers are the modern renditions of yesterday's 3270 terminals. Yes, we're going back into the future. But where are the 3270 "fill-out forms?" These are the computer equivalents of the paper forms that we fill out every day of our life. It so happens that the Web is teeming with forms. They're everywhere. In case you haven't seen one, a *Web form* is an HTML page with one or more data entry fields and a mandatory "Submit" button. You click on the Submit button to send the form's data contents to a Web server. This causes the browser to collect all the inputs from the form, stuff them inside an HTTP message, and then invoke either an HTTP GET or POST method on the server side.

On the receiving end, the typical Web server does not know what to do with a form— it's not your ordinary HTML document. So the server simply turns around and invokes the program or resource named in the URL and tells it to take care of the request. The server passes the method request and its parameters to the back-end program using a protocol called the *Common Gateway Interface (CGI)*.

The back-end program executes the request and returns the results in HTML format to the Web server using the CGI protocol. The Web server treats the results like a normal document that it returns to the client. So, in a sense, the Web server acts as a conduit between the Web client and a back-end program that does the actual work.

Figure 11-3 shows the elements of this 3-tier client/server architecture, Web-style. The first tier is a Web browser that supports interactive forms; the second tier is a vanilla HTTP server augmented with CGI programs; and the third tier consists of traditional back-end servers.

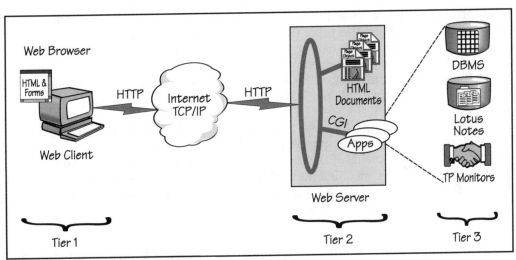

Figure 11-3. 3-Tier Client/Server, Web-Style.

The CGI technology makes it possible for Internet clients to update databases on back-end servers. In fact, updates and inserts are at the heart of online electronic commerce. However, most online service providers will not let you update their databases without some form of iron-clad client/server security. This is where protocols like *Secure Sockets Layer (SSL)*, *Secure HTTP (S-HTTP)*, and Internet firewalls come into the picture. They provide one more technology that's needed to turn the Internet into the world's largest shopping mall.

Software vendors are using the technology we just described to connect Web browsers to virtually every form of client/server system—including SQL databases, TP Monitors, groupware servers, MOM queues, e-mail backbones, distributed object brokers, and so on. All these systems now provide gateways that accept CGI requests. And they all provide *transformers* to dynamically map their data into HTML so that it can be displayed within Web browsers. In other words, the servers build a Web page "on-the-fly" to display their results.

As they said in the movie *Field of Dreams*, "If you build it, they will come." In the case of the Web, they built the universal client and then the servers all came. Unfortunately, as you will soon discover, these servers live on the other side of a bottleneck called CGI.

HTML FORMS

Forms are used to gather information for a CGI-based server application. Creating a form is a three-step process. First, you must create the HTML for the input form. Second, you must write the server CGI application that acts on the data from the input form. Finally, you must design the reply document a user sees after submitting the form; the HTML for the reply document is dynamically generated by the CGI program. A reply document can be very simple or quite elaborate. A simple reply may say, "We received your request; thank you very much." An elaborate reply may return thousands of table rows from an SQL database; you may have to generate an HTML table "on-the-fly" to display the results in a row-column format.

The HTML <FORM> tag has two mandatory attributes: METHOD and ACTION. The METHOD can be either an HTTP GET or POST; it specifies how the data entered in the various fields of the form is transmitted to the CGI server application. The ACTION attribute specifies the URL to which you send the form's contents; it must be the name of a server CGI program (or script) that can process the form's data. Here's an example of a FORM tag:

```
<FORM METHOD="POST" ACTION="HTTP://www.mylab.org/cgi-bin/sampleform">
```

So what is *cgi-bin*? It's the name of a special executable directory where CGI programs reside. This directory is usually under the direct control of a Webmaster—you don't want the average user tampering with programs on your server. The /cgi-bin/ directory in a URL indicates to a Web server that the incoming HTTP request is for a CGI program. In this example, the URL causes the server to invoke—via the CGI protocol—an external program called *sampleform*.

3-Tier Client/Server, CGI-Style

So how is a form's data passed to a program that hangs off an HTTP server? It gets passed using an end-to-end client/server protocol that includes both HTTP and CGI.

The best way to explain the dynamics of the protocol is to walk you through a POST method invocation. As we explain later, you should avoid at all cost using GET even though it is the default method for submitting forms.

Figure 11-4 shows how the client and server programs play together to process a form's request. Here's the step-by-step explanation of this interaction:

1. ***User clicks on the form's Submit button***. This causes the Web browser to collect the data within the form, and then assemble it into one long string of

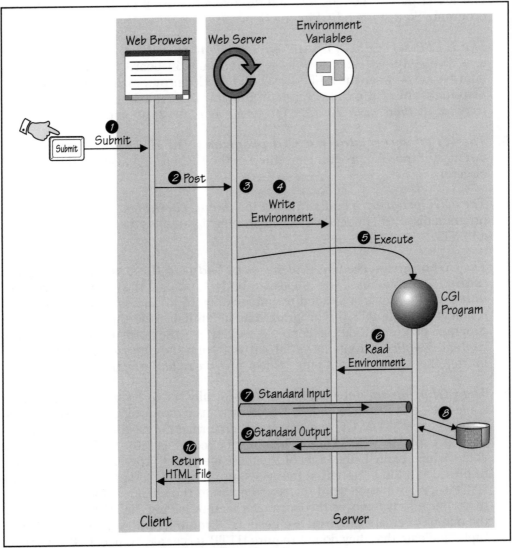

Figure 11-4. HTTP POST: An End-to-End Client/Server Scenario.

name/value pairs, each separated by an ampersand (&). The browser translates spaces within the data into plus (+) symbols. Yes, it's not very pretty.

2. ***The Web Browser invokes a POST HTTP method***. This is an ordinary HTTP request that specifies a POST method, the URL of the target program in the "cgi-bin" directory, and the typical HTTP headers. The message body—HTTP calls it the "entity"—contains the form's data. This is the string: *name=value&name=value&...*

3. ***The HTTP server receives the method invocation via a socket connection***. The server parses the message and discovers that it's a POST for the "cgi-bin" program. So it starts a CGI interaction.

4. ***The HTTP server sets up the environment variables***. The CGI protocol uses *environment variables* as a shared bulletin board for communicating information between the HTTP server and the CGI program. The server typically provides the following environmental information: *server_name*, *request_method*, *path_info*, *script_name*, *content_type*, and *content_length*.

5. ***The HTTP server starts a CGI program***. The HTTP server executes an instance of the CGI program specified in the URL; it's typically in the "cgi-bin" directory.

6. ***The CGI program reads the environment variables***. In this case, the program discovers by reading the environment variables that it is responding to a POST.

7. ***The CGI program receives the message body via the standard input pipe (stdin)***. Remember, the message body contains the famous string of *name=value* items separated by ampersands (&). The *content_length* environment variable tells the program how much data is in the string. The CGI program parses the string contents to retrieve the form data. It uses the *content_length* environment variable to determine how many characters to read in from the standard input pipe. Cheer up—we're half way there.

8. ***The CGI program does some work***. Typically, a CGI program interacts with some back-end resource—like a DBMS or transaction program—to service the form's request. The CGI program must then format the results in HTML or some other acceptable MIME type. This information goes into the HTTP response entity, which really is the body of the message. Your program can also choose to provide all the information that goes into the HTTP response headers. The HTTP server will then send the reply "as is" to the client. Why would you do this? Because it removes the extra overhead of having the HTTP server parse the output to create the response headers. Programs whose names begin with "nph-" indicate that they do not require HTTP server assistance; CGI calls them *nonparsed header (nph)* programs.

9. *The CGI program returns the results via the standard output pipe (stdout).* The program pipes back the results to the HTTP server via its standard output. The HTTP server receives the results on its standard input. This concludes the CGI interaction.

10. *The HTTP server returns the results to the Web Browser.* The HTTP server can either append some response headers to the information it receives from the CGI program, or it sends it "as is" if it's an nph program.

As you can see, a CGI program is executed in real time; it gets the information and then builds a dynamic Web page to satisfy a client's request. CGI makes the Web more dynamic. In contrast, a plain HTML document is static, which means the text file does not change. CGI may be clumsy, but it does allow us to interface Web clients to general-purpose back-end services as well as to Internet search utilities such as *Yahoo!* and *Alta Vista.* You can even stretch CGI to its limits to create general-purpose client/server programs like the Federal Express package-tracking Web page.

CGI and State

So how does CGI maintain information from one form to the next? Well, it doesn't. As we explained earlier, the protocol is totally stateless. The server forgets everything after it hands over a reply to the client. However, the nice thing about the Internet is that there is always some "kludge" that you can use to work around problems. In this case, the kludge is to use *hidden* fields within a form to maintain state on the client side.

Hidden fields are basically invisible; they contain values that are not displayed within a form. They are used to store information a user enters and then resubmit that information in subsequent forms. The user doesn't have to reenter it or even be aware that the information is being passed around. In other words, the hidden fields act as variables that maintain state between form submissions. So how does this information get passed from one form to another? It gets passed through the CGI program.

Figure 11-5 shows an electronic transaction that requires multiple form submissions, which lead to an electronic payment. The first set of forms lets you pick the merchandise that you place on your electronic shopping cart. The next form requests a delivery address and time. The last form presents you with the bill and requests some form of payment.

How is the state of this transaction maintained across form invocations? Here's how: The CGI program processes a form and then presents you with the next form; this continues until you make your final payment or abort the transaction. The trick here is that the CGI program uses invisible fields to store information from the previous forms in the next form. For example, it writes inside the invisible fields

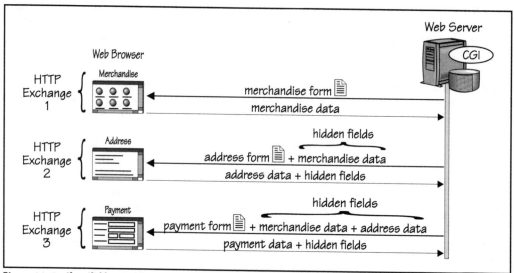

Figure 11-5. How Hidden Fields Maintain State Across Web Invocations.

the goods you selected in the previous forms. You never see the contents of these hidden fields. You never know they're there, unless you view the document's HTML. However, when you submit the form, all these hidden fields are passed right back to the CGI program along with any new data.

So, in essence, the CGI program stores the state of the transaction in the forms it sends back to the client instead of storing it in its own memory. What do you think of this workaround? We did warn you that it was going to be a real work of art.

Cookies provide another variation of this hidden field approach. A cookie is a small piece of data that is stored in the client on behalf of a server. In essence, a cookie is an invisible field that is stored on the client for a specified time. Typically, servers use cookies to store user IDs or basic configuration information. The cookie is sent back to the server in subsequent page requests from this client. By default, cookies are only returned to the server that creates them. Of course, there are ways to change this default.

Stay Away From GETs

Warning

Even though GET is the default HTTP method for submitting a form's contents, we strongly recommend that you *always* use POST instead. The best way to understand why is to look at an end-to-end GET interaction. On the client side,

GET causes the set of "name=value" contents of the form to be appended to the URL after a separating question mark (?). In contrast, POST appends the contents to the body of the HTML message.

On the receiving side, GET causes the HTTP server to parse the URL and insert the entire string of name/value pairs that follow the question mark (?) into the *query-string* environment variable. The server is really fooled into thinking that it received a query. The CGI program reads the *query-string* environment variable to obtain the contents of the form.

So what's wrong with this picture? It's deadly. Here's why: Most operating systems limit their environment variables to between 256 and 1024 characters *total*. This means that any data that exceeds this maximum size will either be truncated or cause the operating system to blow up. But as we explained earlier, there's no way to limit the amount of data from a multiline input field. For this reason, you should always use POST with forms; don't even think of using GET. ❏

THE HTTP/CGI COUNT

OK, it's time to write some code. In this section, we create the HTTP/CGI version of the Count client/server program. The client Java applet is very similar to the one we developed in Chapter 5. The difference is that it uses HTTP/sockets instead of CORBA to interact with the server. On the server side, we use a standard Netscape *Enterprise Server 3.0* HTTP server to run the CGI version of Count. This means we don't have to create a server daemon. Of course, we must still write code for the CGI Count server. Figure 11-6 shows how the pieces play together.

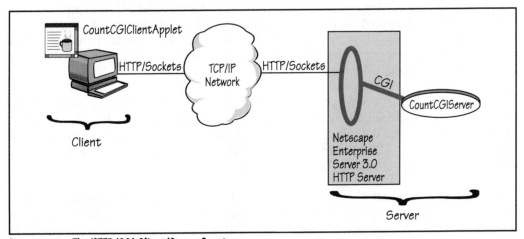

Figure 11-6. The HTTP/CGI Client/Server Count.

The CGI Count Client Applet

Before we get into the code, let's look at a screen capture of the Count applet (see Figure 11-7). As you can see, this applet looks almost identical to the one we developed in Chapter 5. To interact with this minimalist applet, you enter a count number in the input field and then click on the Run button. The applet will then increment the CGI Count server "n" times, where n is the number you just entered. If you don't enter a number, the default is 1000. The applet displays in its output field the average time it takes to do an increment, or Ping. It will also display progress status.

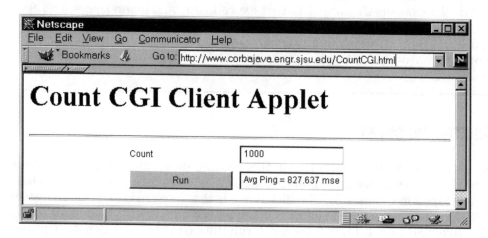

Figure 11-7. A Screen Capture of the Java CGI Count Applet.

The Count applet consists of a single Java class—**CountCGIClientApplet**. This class extends **java.applet.Applet** and implements three methods: *init*, *action*, and *increment*. There is no main program. Applets must rely on the browser to tell them when things happen. The browser calls *init* after it loads the applet. The *init* method creates a user interface consisting of four widgets.

The browser calls *action* when the user clicks on the "Run" button. The *action* method performs the following functions: 1) reads from an input field the number of times to count (the default is 1000), 2) calculates the start time, 3) invokes the *increment* method 1000 times (or the number you specify), 4) calculates the elapsed time, and 5) displays the average response time.

The *increment* method does the following: 1) creates a client **Socket** object that points to our HTTP Netscape Web server—port 80 is a well-known port for HTTP, 2) creates a buffered data stream socket filter, 3) builds an HTTP POST request, 4) writes the request to the output stream, 5) reads the response from the input stream,

6) returns the last line—it contains the actual response from the CGI program, and 7) closes the socket.

As you can see, we're recreating the Web browser's HTTP POST mechanism. Why? Because we need to measure the end-to-end response time of an HTTP/CGI client/server interaction. To do this, we must control the point of invocation. If Web browsers gave us hooks into their socket invocation mechanism, we could have saved ourselves some work. But they don't. So we have to recreate this code. Luckily, we're all socket pros by now, so it should be a piece of a cake. Here's the code that does it all.

Listing 11-1. CountCGIClientApplet: The Client Applet Program.

```java
// CountCGIClientApplet.java, Java CGI Applet

import java.awt.*;
import java.io.*;
import java.net.*;
import java.util.*;

public class CountCGIClientApplet extends java.applet.Applet
{
  private TextField countField, pingTimeField;
  private Button runCount;

  public void init()
  {
    // Create a 2 by 2 grid of widgets.
    setLayout(new GridLayout(2, 2, 10, 10));

    // Add the four widgets, initialize where necessary
    add(new Label("Count"));
    add(countField = new TextField());
    countField.setText("1000");
    add(runCount = new Button("Run"));
    add(pingTimeField = new TextField());
    pingTimeField.setEditable(false);
  }

  public boolean action(Event ev, Object arg)
  {
    if(ev.target == runCount)
    { try
      { String sum = "0";
```

```java
      // get count, initialize start time
      showStatus("Incrementing");
      int count = new Integer(countField.getText()).intValue();
      long startTime = System.currentTimeMillis();

      // Increment count times
      for (int i = 0 ; i < count ; i++ )
      { sum = increment(sum);
      }

      // Calculate stop time; show statistics
      long stopTime = System.currentTimeMillis();
      pingTimeField.setText("Avg Ping = "
        + ((stopTime - startTime) / (float)count) + " msecs");
      showStatus("Sum = " + sum);
    } catch(Exception e)
    { showStatus("System Exception" + e);
    }
    return true;
  }
  return false;
}


public String increment(String currentSum)
{ String script = "/cgi-bin/Count.bat";
  Socket socket = null;
  String rdata = "";
  String line = "";
  String lastLine = "";

  try
  {
    socket = new Socket(getCodeBase().getHost(), 80);
    PrintWriter ostream
      = new PrintWriter(socket.getOutputStream());
    BufferedReader istream = new BufferedReader(
                        new InputStreamReader(
                                socket.getInputStream()));

    ostream.print("POST " + script
      + " HTTP/1.0\r\n"
      + "Content-type: text/plain\r\n"
      + "Content-length: "
      + ("increment " + currentSum).length() + "\r\n\r\n");
```

```
        ostream.print("Increment " + currentSum + "\r\n");
        ostream.flush();

        try
        {
          while ((line = istream.readLine()) != null)
          { lastLine = line;
          }
        } catch (  SocketException e )
        {
          istream.close();
          ostream.close();
        }
      }
    catch (Exception e)
    {
      System.out.println("Error " + e);
      if (socket != null)
        try
        {
          socket.close();
        }
        catch (IOException ex) {}
    }
    return lastLine;
    }
}
```

Most of the code implements the HTTP POST protocol on top of socket data streams. The POST causes the HTTP server at the other end to call the CGI program—*/cgi-bin/Count.bat*. This is the batch file that invokes our CGI **Count-CGIServer** class. We will tell you all about this batch file in the next section. Notice that we pass the count value along with the increment command. Why? HTTP servers are stateless. In this case, they can't remember the count from one invocation to another. So the client passes them the count. In a more realistic scenario, the server could store the count in a database between invocations. We didn't want to put a database in the loop. It would skew the benchmark numbers. We would be measuring a database access instead of just the Ping-like invocation.

The other thing to notice in the code is that we're ignoring the information the server returns, except for that last line. Why? The HTTP server thinks it's talking to a browser. So it creates all the HTTP header information we introduced in the tutorial. This is all very nice, but all we care about is our return value, which is the application-specific part of the message. In this case, we know we have a very short response that will fit in a single line. So we go after this last line without parsing the rest of the message. As a result, we don't add any parsing overhead to the CGI Ping response time calculation.

The CGI Count Server

The server-side the CGI count consists of three programs: 1) Netscape's *Enterprise Server 3.0* HTTP server, 2) the *Count.bat* batch file, and 3) the **CountCGIServer** Java class. *Enterprise Server* is an off-the-shelf HTTP server. Note that you can use any HTTP server for this job; it doesn't have to be *Enterprise Server*.

The HTTP server invokes the batch file when it receives a POST message from our client applet. The *Count.bat* file contains a single line:

```
c:\java\bin\java CountCGIServer
```

Make sure to place this file in the *cgibin* subdirectory where the HTTP server can find it. The batch file simply starts the Java virtual machine and invokes the **CountCGIServer** class. We must write code that implements this class.

The **CountCGIServer** class provides a *main* function that does the following: 1) creates input and output buffered data stream filters on top of the standard input and output streams, 2) receives the client request in the input data stream, 3) executes the client request, 4) sends back a reply in the data output stream, and 5) closes the input and output streams. Here's the code:

Listing 11-2. CountCGIServer.java: The CGI Count Server.

```
// CountCGIServer.java, Java CGI Server Program

import java.io.*;
import java.util.*;

class CountCGIServer
{ public static void main(String[] args)
  { int count;
    String line;

    try
    { // create streams
      BufferedReader istream = new BufferedReader(
                          new (InputStreamReader(System.in));
      PrintWriter ostream = new PrintWriter(System.out);
```

```
      // execute client requests
      line = istream.readLine();
      StringTokenizer tokens = new StringTokenizer(line);
      String myOperation = tokens.nextToken();

      // perform increment operation
      if(myOperation.equals("increment"))
        { String countString = tokens.nextToken();
          count = Integer.parseInt(countString);
          count++;
          ostream.println(Integer.toString(count));
          ostream.flush();
        }

      // close streams
      istream.close();
      ostream.close();
    }
  catch (Exception e)
    { System.out.println("Error " + e);
    }
  }
}
```

The **StringTokenizer** class is part of the *java.util* package. You create an instance of this class to break a string into tokens separated by delimiters. You can optionally specify the delimiting characters in the constructor. If you don't specify a delimiter, the default is a whitespace delimiter. You invoke the object's *countTokens* method to obtain the number of tokens in the string. You invoke *nextToken* to access a token. Finally, you invoke *hasMoreTokens* to check if the string contains more tokens.

The **Integer** class is part of *java.lang*. It provides an object wrapper around the *int* primitive data type. The wrapper includes many useful methods for converting strings to integers, and vice versa. In this case, we used *parseInt* to convert the string token into an *int* that we could then increment.

COMPILE THE CLIENT/SERVER PROGRAM

We're now ready to compile the CGI client/server program. Make sure you have installed the Symantec Visual Café compiler. To compile the code, go to the appropriate directory and type the following commands at the prompt:

```
prompt> javac -d \CorbaJavaBook.2e\classes  CountCGIClientApplet.java
prompt> javac -d \CorbaJavaBook.2e\cgi-bin  CountCGIServer.java
```

The -d option tells the compiler to put the (.class) files it creates into the directory we specify. In this case, the client code goes into the *CorbaJavaBook.2e\classes* subdirectory. The server code goes in the *CorbaJavaBook.2e\cgi-bin* subdirectory. If all goes well, you should have some compiled Java classes—(.class) files—that you can now run.

CREATE A WEB PAGE

The next step is to create a minimalist HTML Web page that embeds our applet. Open a file called count.html and enter the following:

Listing 11-3. Count.html: Web Page for the CGI Count Applet

```
<h1>Count CGI Client Applet</h1>
<hr>
<center>
  <APPLET CODE=CountCGIClientApplet.class
  CODEBASE=classes width=300 height=60>
  </APPLET>
</center>
```

Note that we use the CODEBASE attribute to point to a *classes* subdirectory that hangs off the HTTP server. This is the subdirectory that contains the **CountCGIClientApplet** class.

RUN THE CLIENT/SERVER PROGRAMS

To run the CGI client/server programs, you need a Java-enabled Web browser and an HTTP server. We used Netscape *Communicator 4.0* as our browser and Netscape *Enterprise Server 3.0* as our HTTP server. Many vendors provide equivalent software that you can also use to run this benchmark. Next, follow these steps (see Figure 11-8):

1. **Install the code on a Web server.** Move the applet (.class) files and the (.html) file to the Web server. Use the CODEBASE attribute to place them in separate subdirectories. You must also place both the **CountCGIServer** (.class) file and the *Count.bat* in the server's *cgi-bin* subdirectory.

2. **Download the applet.** Point your Web browser to the URL of your Web Count page. The HTTP server will download the applet class. The minimalist applet

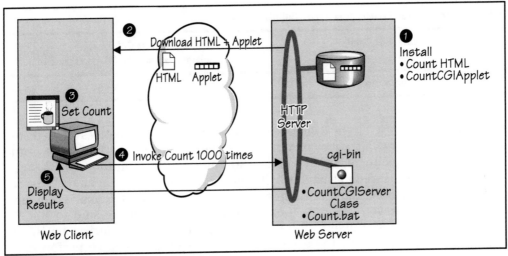

Figure 11-8. Running the CGI Count.

should appear in the browser.

3. **Set the count.** The count field tells the applet how many times to invoke the Count server's *increment* method. We preset this number to 1000. If you want a different count, this is the time to change it.

4. **Invoke the CGI Count server 1000 times.** Click on the Run button to invoke increments on the remote CGI server.

5. **Obtain the results.** The lower right-hand field displays the average response time in milliseconds for an *increment* method (it's the equivalent of a Ping performance).

We also run the CGI Count server on the same machine as the Web browser to measure local interprocess performance.

LOOKING AT SOME TEST RESULTS

We ran this client/server program in different situations to get a reading on the performance of CGI method invocations. As usual, our client performs 1000 method invocations. The tests measure the average response time of CGI Pings. We first run the Web client and server programs in the same machine—a 120-MHz Pentium running NT 4.0. Then we run them across a 10 Mbit/s Ethernet LAN. Table 11-1 compares the average response times.

Table 11-1. Local Versus Remote: Java Applet/CGI Count Server.

Local CGI Count (interprocess, same machine)	Remote CGI Count (interprocess, over 10 Mbit/s Ethernet)
865.3 msecs	827.9 msecs

The numbers show CGI to be dramatically slower than the alternatives we've tested so far. In some cases, it's over two orders of magnitude slower than some of the alternatives. For example, CGI is about 230 times slower than the CORBA static invocations we measured in Chapter 4; it is about 50 times slower than the browser invocations we demonstrated in Chapter 5. This should definitely make headlines in *PC Week*. However, before you call "Spencer the Cat," make sure to run the programs and see for yourself. You may find that the numbers deviate by 10% in either direction, even with the same setup. However, the relative performance should remain more or less constant.

You may also want to share with Spencer the CORBA/CGI comparison in Table 11-2.

Table 11-2. CORBA IIOP Versus CGI/HTTP.

Feature	CORBA IIOP	HTTP/CGI
Reliable communications	Yes	Yes
State across invocations	Yes	No
Parameter marshaling	Yes	No
Interface descriptions	Yes (via IDL)	No
Dynamic discovery	Yes (via IR and DII)	No
Parameter data typing	Yes (Language and OS neutral binary format)	No
Performance	Fast (3.6 msec Ping)	Very Slow (827.9 msec Ping)
Security	Yes (via CORBA)	Yes (via SSL or S-HTTP)
Transactions	Yes	No

CONCLUSION

This concludes another very long chapter. The message is that the CGI/HTTP protocol is clumsy, stateless, and extremely slow. In this chapter, we show CGI's Ping performance to be drastically slower than CORBA IIOP. The bottom line is that programming Internet client/server applications with CGI is a very poor choice. The bad news is that CGI is the premier 3-tier client/server application model for the Internet today. The good news is that the leading Internet architects are well aware of CGI's shortcomings and are starting to migrate to saner alternatives. For example, Netscape's Marc Andreessen anticipates that CORBA/IIOP will very soon replace HTTP/CGI as the backbone for the Internet. Netscape is doing its part to accelerate this move by bundling a CORBA ORB with every browser.

Chapter 12

Servlets Versus CORBA/Java ORBs

In mid-1997, JavaSoft shipped the *Java Web Server* (previously known as *Jeeves*). This product had two claims to fame: 1) it was the first implementation ever of a Java-based Web server, and 2) it introduced *servlets*—a new all-Java plug-in architecture for servers. JavaSoft also provides a *Java Servlet Development Kit*, which lets you run servlets on the more popular Web servers—including *Apache*, Netscape *Enterprise Server*, and Microsoft *IIS*. This kit includes a set of classes and interfaces that define exactly how a Web server must interact with a servlet.

A servlet is a small piece of Java code that a Web server loads to handle client requests. Unlike a CGI application, the servlet code stays resident in memory when the request terminates. In addition, a servlet can connect to a database when it is initialized and then retain its connection across requests. A servlet can also chain a client request to another servlet. This is called *servlet chaining*. All these features make servlets an excellent workaround for many of CGI's limitations.

In this chapter, we look at servlets as a CGI extension. We will show you how they fix some of the CGI shortcomings we encountered in the last chapter. We will also compare servlets with the pure CORBA/IIOP alternative. Note that you can implement servlets as CORBA or RMI objects. But as you will see, they still don't provide the full power of distributed object interfaces—you must interact with a servlet via a generic API. However, it's precisely this constraint that makes servlets convenient for simple applications. For example, servlets make good replacements for CGI-bin scripts. They are good at accepting form input, interacting with a single database, and then dynamically generating an HTML response page. So there may still be a place for servlets in your Java server-side arsenal.

SERVLETS 101

To develop servlets, you will need to run a servlet-enabled Web server. You will also need the freely downloadable *Java Servlets Development Kit (JSDK)*. In this section, we will go over the basic servlet interfaces and classes that are part of the **javax.servlet** and **javax.servlet.http** packages. These interfaces will become part of the Java JDK 1.2 extensions. We will not be covering the Sun-specific Java Web Server packages.

The Life Cycle of a Servlet

A servlet is a body of Java code that implements the *servlet API*; it is loaded into and then runs inside a network service, such as a Web server. A Web server uses this generic callback API to control the life cycle of a servlet, invoke its *service* method, and exchange standard requests and replies. A server must first load a servlet and then invoke its *init* method. Then the servlet can continuously service requests. A servlet is deactivated when it either receives a *destroy* call or when its server terminates. Note that servlets typically run inside multithreaded servers, so you are responsible for synchronizing access to shared resources.

The Core Servlet Interfaces

Figure 12-1 shows the core servlet interfaces and classes that are part of *javax.servlet*. The package consists of five interfaces and three helper classes. Life starts with the JavaSoft-provided **GenericServlet** class. This helper class implements both the **Servlet** and **ServletConfig** interfaces. Typically, your servlet implementations will simply extend this class. Note that CORBA or RMI objects that act as servlets must directly implement these interfaces.

Here's a brief description of the *javax.servlet* core interfaces and classes:

■ The **Servlet** interface defines standard methods all servlets must implement. To create a servlet, you typically extend either the **GenericServlet** class or its more specialized descendent called **HttpServlet** (see the next section). A server initializes a servlet by calling its *init* method. This method passes to a servlet a **ServletConfig** object; it contains the servlet's startup configuration and initialization parameters. A server invokes the *service* method to pass to the

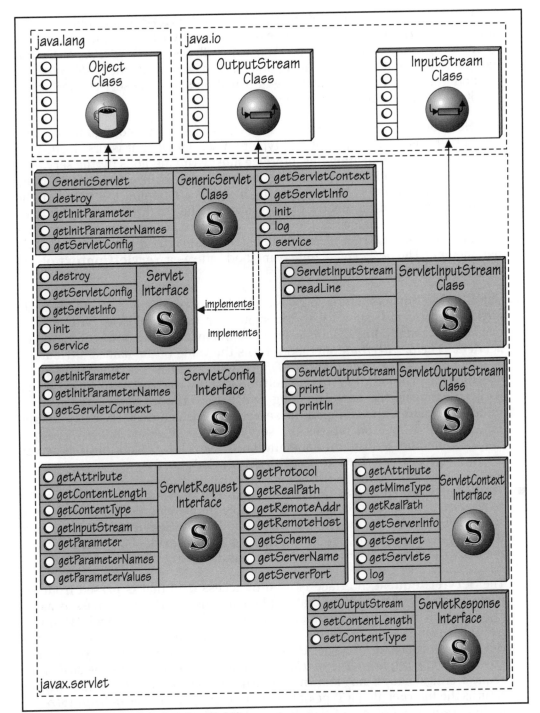

Figure 12-1. The Javax.servlet Interfaces and Classes.

servlet requests for service; this method takes a **ServletRequest** object for its input and returns a **ServletResponse** object. Finally, a server can kill a servlet by invoking its *destroy* method. You can call a servlet's *getServletConfig* method to obtain its **ServletConfig** object. You can invoke the *getServletInfo* method to obtain a string containing information about the servlet—for example, its author, version, and copyright.

- The **ServletConfig** interface gives a servlet access to its configuration data. The server passes an object of this type to a servlet when it is first loaded. A service writer implementing this interface must write methods for the servlet to use to get its initialization parameters and the context in which it is running. The *getInitParameter* method returns a string containing the value of the named initialization parameter of the servlet. The *getInitParameterNames* method returns the names of the servlet's initialization parameters as an enumeration of strings; it returns an empty enumeration if there are no initialization parameters. The *getServletContext* method returns a **ServletContext** object that contains this servlet's context.

- The **ServletContext** interface gives a servlet access to information about its environment; it also allows it to log significant events. Servlet writers must decide what data to log. The interface is implemented by servers and used by servlets. The *getAttribute* method returns the value of the named attribute of the network service. The *getMimeType* method returns the mime type of the specified file. The *getRealPath* method applies alias rules to the specified virtual path and returns the corresponding real path. The *getServerInfo* method returns the name and version of the server under which this servlet is running. The *getServlet* method returns the servlet of the specified name. The *getServlets* method returns an enumeration of **Servlet** objects on this server. Finally, *log* lets you write a message to the servlet's log file.

- The **GenericServlet** class implements both the **Servlet** and **ServletConfig** interfaces. This class provides both a simple implementation of the life cycle methods *init* and *destroy*, as well as the methods in the **ServletConfig** interface. It also implements the *log* method as defined by the **ServletContext** interface. Servlet writers must override and implement the abstract *service* method.

- The **ServletRequest** interface is used to access data that is passed from the client to the servlet; objects that implement this interface are passed as an argument of the *service* method. The data contained in a **ServletRequest** object includes parameter names and values, attributes, and a **ServletInputStream**. The *getAttribute* method returns the value of a named attribute in the request. The *getContentLength* method returns the size of the request entity data; if not known it returns -1. The *getContentType* method returns the Internet Media Type of the request entity data. The *getInputStream* method returns an object of type **ServletInputStream**; you use it as an input stream for reading the request body.

The *getParameter* method returns a string containing the value of the specified parameter. The *getParameterNames* method returns the parameter names for this request as an enumeration of strings. The *getParameterValues* returns the values of the specified parameter for the request as an array of strings. The *getProtocol* method returns the protocol and version of the request. The *getRemoteAddr* method returns the IP address of the client that sent the request. The *getRemoteHost* method returns the fully qualified host name of the client that sent the request. The *getScheme* method returns the scheme of the URL used in this request—for example, http, https, or ftp. The *getServerName* method returns the host name of the server that received the request. Finally, the *getServerPort* method returns the port number on which this request was received.

- The **ServletResponse** interface is used by a servlet to return response data to the client. A **ServletResponse** object is passed as an argument to the *service* method. The *getOutputStream* method returns an output stream that a servlet uses to write the response data. The *setContentLength* method is used by the servlet to set the content length for this response. The *setContentType* method is used to set the content type for this response.

- The **ServletInputStream** class provides an input stream that servlets use to read incoming requests and data. This class defines an abstract *readLine* method. It lets you read an array of bytes at the specified offset. The method reads into an array either the number of characters you request or the number of characters before a newline (\n) is encountered.

- The **ServletOutputStream** class provides an output stream for writing servlet responses. The overloaded *print* method lets you write to the stream basic Java types such as booleans, characters, floats, and ints. The *println* method lets you write these same basic types, followed by a CRLF.

Here are the more detailed class descriptions:

Listing 12-1. The Javax.servlet Servlet Interface.

```
public interface Servlet
{
    // Methods
    public abstract void init(ServletConfig config) throws ServletException;
    public abstract ServletConfig getServletConfig();
    public abstract void service(ServletRequest req, ServletResponse res)
                                throws ServletException, IOException;
    public abstract String getServletInfo();
    public abstract void destroy();
}
```

Listing 12-2. The Javax.servlet ServletConfig Interface.

```
public interface ServletConfig
{
  // Methods
  public abstract ServletContext getServletContext();
  public abstract String getInitParameter(String name);
  public abstract Enumeration getInitParameterNames();
}
```

Listing 12-3. The Javax.servlet ServletContext Interface.

```
public interface ServletContext
{
  // Methods
  public abstract Servlet getServlet(String name)
                              throws ServletException;
  public abstract Enumeration getServlets();
  public abstract void log(String msg);
  public abstract String getRealPath(String path);
  public abstract String getMimeType(String file);
  public abstract String getServerInfo();
  public abstract Object getAttribute(String name);
}
```

Listing 12-4. The Javax.servlet GenericServlet Class.

```
public abstract class GenericServlet extends Object
implements Servlet, ServletConfig
{ // Constructor
  protected GenericServlet();

  // Methods
  public ServletContext getServletContext();
  public String getInitParameter(String name);
  public Enumeration getInitParameterNames();
  public void log(String msg);
  public String getServletInfo();
  public void init(ServletConfig config) throws ServletException;
  public ServletConfig getServletConfig();
  public abstract void service(ServletRequest req, ServletResponse res)
                              throws ServletException, IOException;
  public void destroy();
}
```

Listing 12-5. The Javax.servlet ServletRequest Interface.

```
public interface ServletRequest
{
  // Methods
  public abstract int getContentLength();
  public abstract String getContentType();
  public abstract String getProtocol();
  public abstract String getScheme();
  public abstract String getServerName();
  public abstract int getServerPort();
  public abstract String getRemoteAddr();
  public abstract String getRemoteHost();
  public abstract String getRealPath(String path);
  public abstract ServletInputStream getInputStream()
                              throws IOException;
  public abstract String getParameter(String name);
  public abstract String[] getParameterValues(String name);
  public abstract Enumeration getParameterNames();
  public abstract Object getAttribute(String name);
}
```

Listing 12-6. The Javax.servlet ServletResponse Interface.

```
public interface ServletResponse
{
  // Methods
  public abstract void setContentLength(int len);
  public abstract void setContentType(String type);
  public abstract ServletOutputStream getOutputStream()
                          throws IOException;
}
```

Listing 12-7. The Javax.servlet ServletInputStream Class.

```
public abstract class ServletInputStream extends InputStream
{
  // Constructor
  protected ServletInputStream();

  // Methods
  public int readLine(byte b[], int off, int len) throws IOException;
}
```

Listing 12-8. The Javax.servlet ServletOutputStream Class.

```
public abstract class ServletOutputStream extends OutputStream
{
  // Constructor
  protected ServletOutputStream();

  // Methods
  public void print(String s) throws IOException;
  public void print(boolean b) throws IOException;
  public void print(char c) throws IOException;
  public void print(int i) throws IOException;
  public void print(long l) throws IOException;
  public void print(float f) throws IOException;
  public void print(double d) throws IOException;
  public void println() throws IOException;
  public void println(String s) throws IOException;
  public void println(boolean b) throws IOException;
  public void println(char c) throws IOException;
  public void println(int i) throws IOException;
  public void println(long l) throws IOException;
  public void println(float f) throws IOException;
  public void println(double d) throws IOException;
}
```

The HTTP Servlet Interfaces

Figure 12-2 shows the HTTP servlet interfaces and classes that are part of the *javax.servlet.http* package. It consists of two classes and two interfaces. Together, they define servlet extensions for the HTTP protocol. It's the servlet version of CGI. The heart of this package is the **HttpServlet** abstract class; it extends the **Generic-Servlet** class and provides a support for HTTP 1.0 requests. The **HttpServlet-Request** and **HttpServletResponse** interfaces are HTTP extensions of the **ServletRequest** and **ServletResponse** interfaces; they let you pass HTTP-specific parameters. The **HttpUtils** class provides a set of HTTP helper functions.

Here's a brief description of the servlet HTTP interfaces and classes:

■ The **HttpServlet** abstract class extends the **GenericServlet** with six new HTTP-related methods. You must subclass this abstract class and override at least one method. Typically, you will override *doPost* to handle HTTP POSTs and *doGet* to handle HTTP GETs. If you need to manage resources held over the lifetime of a servlet, you will need to override the inherited life cycle methods

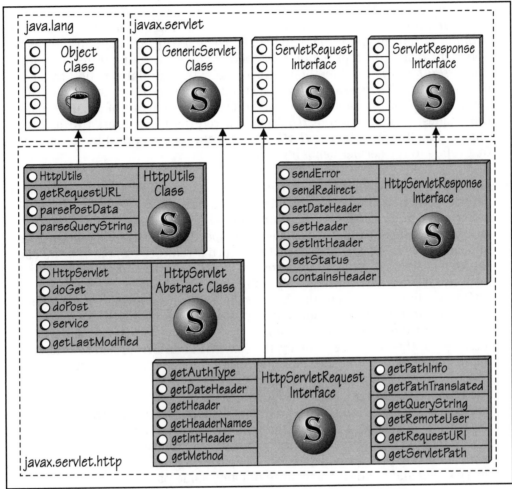

Figure 12-2. The Javax.servlet.http Interfaces and Classes.

init and *destroy*. To support HTTP 1.1 commands—such as OPTIONS, PUT, DELETE, or TRACE—you must override the *service* method and handle these additional HTTP methods directly. Note that only the *service* method is public; it delegates calls to the other methods defined in this interface. The *getLastModified* method facilitates the caching of GET requests; it returns the time the requested entity was last modified.

■ The **HttpServletRequest** interface represents an HTTP servlet request. It provides methods to extract HTTP header information. The *getAuthType* method returns the authentication scheme of the request. The *getDateHeader* method returns the value of a date header field. The *getHeader* method returns the value of a header field. The *getHeaderNames* method returns an enumeration of strings representing the header names for this request. The *getIntHeader* method returns the value of an integer header field. The *getMethod* returns the HTTP command. The *getPathInfo* method returns the optional extra path information that follows the servlet's path in the request. The *getPathTranslated* method returns the extra path information translated to a real path. The *getQueryString* method returns the query string part of the servlet URI. The *getRemoteUser* method returns the name of the user making this request. The *getRequestURI* method returns the request URI as a URL object. Finally, the *getServletPath* method returns the part of the request URI that refers to the servlet being invoked.

■ The **HttpServletResponse** interface represents an HTTP servlet response. It defines helper methods to dynamically generate an HTTP response; it also defines constants for the HTTP return codes. You invoke *sendError* to return an error response to the client using the specified status code and a default message. You invoke *sendRedirect* to return a redirect response to the client specifying the new URL. You invoke *setDateHeader* to add a date field to the response header; you must specify a field name and a date value. You invoke *setHeader* to add a field to the response header with a given name and value. You invoke *setIntHeader* to add a field to the response header with a given name and integer value. You invoke *setStatus* to specify the status code and a default message for this response. Finally, the *containsHeader* method returns true if the response message header has a field with the name you specify.

■ The **HttpUtils** class provides a useful collection of HTTP utility methods. The *getRequestURL* method takes as its input an **HttpServletRequest**; it returns the URL the client used to make the request. The *parsePostData* takes as its input a **ServletInputStream**; it then parses it and returns the POST's form data in a **Hashtable** of name/value pairs. The *parseQueryString* method parses a query string and builds a **Hashtable** of name/value pairs.

Here are the more detailed class descriptions:

Listing 12-9. The Javax.servlet.http HttpServlet Class.

```
public abstract class HttpServlet extends GenericServlet
{
  // Constructor
  protected HttpServlet();

  // Methods
  protected void doGet(HttpServletRequest req, HttpServletResponse resp)
                  throws ServletException, IOException;
  protected void doPost(HttpServletRequest req, HttpServletResponse resp)
                  throws ServletException, IOException;
```

```
  protected void service(HttpServletRequest req, HttpServletResponse resp)
                  throws ServletException, IOException;
  public void service(ServletRequest req, ServletResponse res)
                  throws ServletException, IOException;
  protected long getLastModified(HttpServletRequest req);
}
```

Listing 12-10. The Javax.servlet.http HttpServletRequest Interface.

```
public interface HttpServletRequest extends ServletRequest
{
  // Methods
  public abstract String getMethod();
  public abstract String getRequestURI();
  public abstract String getServletPath();
  public abstract String getPathInfo();
  public abstract String getPathTranslated();
  public abstract String getQueryString();
  public abstract String getRemoteUser();
  public abstract String getAuthType();
  public abstract String getHeader(String name);
  public abstract int getIntHeader(String name);
  public abstract long getDateHeader(String name);
  public abstract Enumeration getHeaderNames();
}
```

Listing 12-11. The Javax.servlet.http HttpServletResponse Interface.

```
public interface HttpServletResponse extends ServletResponse
{
  // Constants -- status return codes
  public static final int SC_OK;
  public static final int SC_CREATED;
  public static final int SC_ACCEPTED;
  public static final int SC_NO_CONTENT;
  public static final int SC_MOVED_PERMANENTLY;
  public static final int SC_MOVED_TEMPORARILY;
  public static final int SC_NOT_MODIFIED;
  public static final int SC_BAD_REQUEST;
  public static final int SC_UNAUTHORIZED;
  public static final int SC_FORBIDDEN;
  public static final int SC_NOT_FOUND;
  public static final int SC_INTERNAL_SERVER_ERROR;
  public static final int SC_NOT_IMPLEMENTED;
```

```
public static final int SC_BAD_GATEWAY;
public static final int SC_SERVICE_UNAVAILABLE;

// Methods
public abstract void setStatus(int sc, String sm);
public abstract void setStatus(int sc);
public abstract void setHeader(String name, String value);
public abstract void setIntHeader(String name, int value);
public abstract void setDateHeader(String name, long date);
public abstract void sendError(int sc, String msg)
                        throws IOException;
public abstract void sendError(int sc)
                        throws IOException;
public abstract void sendRedirect(String location)
                        throws IOException;
public abstract boolean containsHeader(String name);
}
```

Listing 12-12. The Javax.servlet.http HttpUtils Class.

```
public class HttpUtils extends Object
{
  // Constructor
  public HttpUtils();

  // Methods
  public static Hashtable parseQueryString(String s);
  public static Hashtable parsePostData(int len,
                                ServletInputStream in);
  public static StringBuffer getRequestURL(HttpServletRequest req);
}
```

Servlet Scenario 1: A Simple HTTP Request-Response

It's time for a scenario that shows how the servlet pieces come together. Figure 12-3 demonstrates the mechanics of a simple servlet request/response invocation via HTTP. Let's walk through the steps:

1. *The server creates a new servlet*. This servlet extends the **HttpServlet** class and understands the Web's HTTP protocol. You must put it in a *servlets* directory on the server. Servlets can be dynamically loaded when a request from a client arrives. In addition, an administrator can force load them at server startup time.

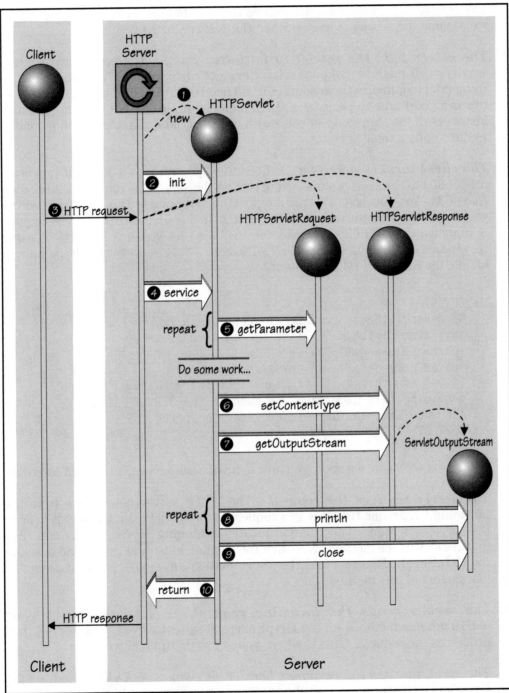

Figure 12-3. Servlet Scenario 1: A Simple HTTP Request-Response.

The normal Java class-loading facilities are used in both cases. In our scenario, we assume the servlet is loaded when the server starts up.

2. ***The server tells the servlet to initialize itself.*** The server invokes the servlet's *init* method and passes it a **ServletConfig** object. This is a signal to the servlet to initialize the resources it will need during its lifetime—for example, this is a good time to perform a JDBC connection. Note that you can initialize instances of the same servlet class with different data. They are then managed as differently named servlets.

3. ***The client invokes a servlet.*** It does this by creating a URL with */servlet/* prepended to the servlet name. Note that on the server the directory, it is called */servlets*. Yes, this last "s" is not a typo. You can point to this URL from within your browser to see the output of the servlet. In our scenario, the servlet request is tunneled over HTTP. Some servers will also let you invoke servlets using server-side includes inside an S-HTML page. These servers should be able to handle the following HTML syntax:

```
<SERVLET
  Name=ServletName  Code=ServletCode.class
  initParam1=initArg1   initParam2=initArg2 ...>
  <param name=param1   value=val1>
  <param name=param2   value=val2>
  If you see this text, it means that the web server
  providing this page does not support the SERVLET tag.
  Ask your Internet Service Provider to upgrade!
</SERVLET>
```

In the next scenario, we show you how to invoke the servlet via a client program.

4. ***The server receives the request***. The HTTP server determines from the incoming URL name that this is a request for a servlet. So it hands it over to the servlet daemon. The daemon locates a running servlet object and then invokes its *service* method. Note that the daemon must first create and initialize the **HttpServletRequest** and **HttpServletResponse** objects that it passes as parameters of this method.

5. ***The servlet reads the incoming request***. It does this by invoking *getParameter* methods on the **HttpServletRequest** object. The servlet then processes the request. This is where you get to do the real work.

6. ***The servlet writes the response header***. It invokes *setXXX* methods on the **HttpServletResponse** to set the HTTP response header. In this scenario, we invoke *setContentType* to indicate that the response body will contain an HTML/text response.

7. ***The servlet obtains a response stream***. It invokes *getOutputStream* method on **HttpServletResponse** to obtain a **ServletOutputStream**. It will use this stream to write the HTML text.

8. ***The servlet generates the HTML response page***. It repeatedly invokes *println* to dynamically generate the body of the HTML response page.

9. ***The servlet releases the output stream***. It invokes the *close* method on the **ServletOutputStream** object to release it.

10. ***The client gets the response***. The daemon returns the result to the HTTP server, which then returns it to the client. In contrast to its CGI counterparts, this servlet stays in memory, waiting to service the next request.

As you can see from this scenario, servlets provide a more convenient CGI-like mechanism.

Servlet Scenario 2: The Client/Server Count

This second object interaction scenario shows the servlet version of the client/server Count program (see Figure 12-4). This time we will concentrate on the client side and leave out the details of the server-side object interactions. Let's go over the steps:

1. ***Create a URL object***. The client creates a new **java.net.URL** object that points to a **CountServlet**; it also passes a parameter called operation and sets its value to *reset*. This is private command that we pass to this servlet type. Here's the format:

```
http://www.corbajava.sjsu.edu/servlet/CountServlet?operation=reset
```

2. ***Obtain a URLConnection object***. The client invokes the **URL** object's *openConnection* method; it returns a **java.net.URLConnection** object that represents a connection to the remote object referred to by the URL.

3. ***Set up the parameters for this connection***. A URL connection can be used for input and/or output. To make this an input/output connection, we invoke the *setDoOutput* and *setDoInput* methods with their flag set to True. This is also a good time to disable the caches; it will give you better performance. You do this by invoking the methods *setDefaultUseCaches* and *setUseCaches* with the flag set to False. We do not show these last two methods in the figure.

4. ***Connect to the remote object***. The client invokes the *connect* method to open a communications link to the resource referenced by this URL.

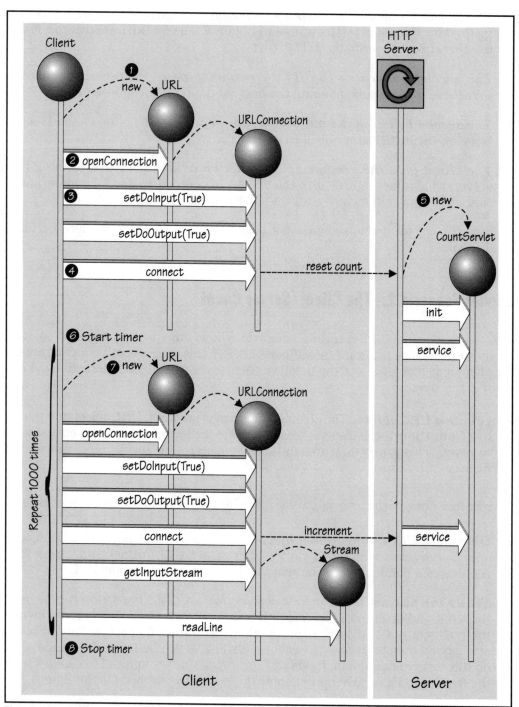

Figure 12-4. Servlet Scenario 2: The Client/Server Count.

5. ***The servlet is invoked***. This is the first time the **CountServlet** is invoked, so the server loads this class. Then it creates a new servlet instance and invokes the new object's *init* method. Finally, it invokes the servlet's *service* method and passes it the remote request. The servlet deciphers the request and discovers that it contains a *reset* parameter (this is a command we invented). Consequently, it resets the remote count to zero.

6. ***Start the timer***. This is the start of the elapsed time.

7. ***Invoke the remote increment 1000 times***. The client creates a new **URL** object with the following format:

```
http://www.corbajava.engr.sjsu.edu/servlet/CountServlet?operation=increment
```

Notice that we're using this URL to invoke the **CountServlet** and tell it to do an *increment* (this is another one of our commands). The client follows the same steps we described earlier to invoke the remote servlet and tell it to increment; it repeats these steps 1000 times.

8. ***Stop the timer***. The client obtains the elapsed time and then uses it to calculate the average Ping performance of an HTTP servlet.

In the next section, we develop the code that implements this scenario.

THE SERVLET COUNT

In this section, we will develop the client and server sides of the Servlet Count program. The client is an applet and the server is a servlet. The applet runs inside a Netscape *Communicator* browser; the servlet runs inside Netscape's *Enterprise Server 3.0* (see Figure 12-5). So, you get to see how an applet talks to a servlet over a standard HTTP infrastructure.

The Servlet Count Client

The client applet consists of a single class called **CountServletApplet**. The AWT code in this applet is identical to its CGI counterpart. The main difference is that this applet uses the **URL** and **URLConnection** classes to interact with the HTTP server. These are the two *java.net* classes we introduced in Scenario 2. Here's the code that implements this scenario:

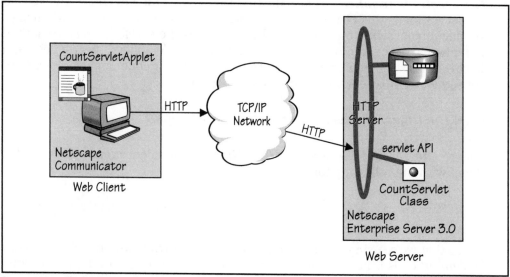

Figure 12-5. The Applet/Servlet Client/Server Count.

Listing 12-13. CountServletApplet: The Servlet Count Client.

```java
// CountServletApplet.java, Java Servlet Applet

import java.awt.*;
import java.io.*;
import java.net.*;

public class CountServletApplet extends java.applet.Applet
{
  private TextField countField, pingTimeField;
  private Button runCount;
  private Counter.Count counter;

  private URLConnection connect;
  String sum = "0";

  public void init()
  {
    // Create a 2 by 2 grid of widgets.
    setLayout(new GridLayout(2, 2, 10, 10));

    // Add the four widgets, initialize where necessary
    add(new Label("Count"));
    add(countField = new TextField());
    countField.setText("1000");
```

```
    add(runCount = new Button("Run"));
    add(pingTimeField = new TextField());
    pingTimeField.setEditable(false);
}

public boolean action(Event ev, Object arg)
{
    if(ev.target == runCount)
    { try
        {
            System.out.println("Resetting count");

            connect = new URL(getDocumentBase(),
                        "/servlet/CountServlet?operation=reset");
            connect.openConnection();
            connect.setDefaultUseCaches(false); //for future connections
            connect.setUseCaches(false); //for this one
            connect.setDoInput(true);
            connect.setDoOutput(true);
            connect.connect();

            DataInputStream in =
                        new DataInputStream(new BufferedInputStream(
                                            connect.getInputStream())));
            String response = in.readLine();
            in.close();

            // get count, initialize start time
            showStatus("Incrementing");
            int count = new Integer(countField.getText()).intValue();
            long startTime = System.currentTimeMillis();

            // Increment count times
            for (int i = 0 ; i < count ; i++ )
            { sum = increment(sum);
            }

            // Calculate stop time; show statistics
            long stopTime = System.currentTimeMillis();
            pingTimeField.setText("Avg Ping = "
                + ((stopTime - startTime) / (float)count) + " msecs");
            showStatus("Sum = " + sum);
        } catch(Exception e)
        { showStatus("System Exception: " + e);
            System.out.println("System Exception " + e);
```

```
      }
    return true;
    }
  return false;
  }

  public String increment(String currentSum)
  {

    try      .
    {
      connect = (new URL(getDocumentBase(),
                "/servlet/CountServlet?operation=increment");
      connect.openConnection();
      connect.setDefaultUseCaches(false); //for future connections
      connect.setUseCaches(false); //for this one
      connect.setDoInput(true);
      connect.setDoOutput(true);
      connect.connect();
      DataInputStream in =
              new DataInputStream(new BufferedInputStream(
                                    connect.getInputStream()));
      String response = in.readLine();
      return response;
    } catch (Exception e)
    { showStatus("Error " + e);
      return "";
    }
  }
}
```

The Servlet Count Server

The server side consists of a single class called **CountServlet**. This class extends the **HttpServlet** abstract class and implements two of its methods: *init* and *service*. Remember that a servlet uses the HTTP Server as its framework. The framework manages the life cycle of the servlet and calls its methods via the servlet API.

The **CountServlet** will reset the count when the framework invokes its *init* method. And it will service a client's request when its *service* method is called. In our client/server Count application, *service* executes remote commands from the client that are passed via a parameter we call *operation*. We support two commands: *reset* and *increment*. Here's the code:

Listing 12-14. CountServlet: The Servlet Count Server.

```java
// CountServlet.java, Java HTTP Servlet
import java.io.*;
import javax.servlet.*;
import javax.servlet.http.*;

public class CountServlet extends HttpServlet
{ int count;

  public void init(ServletConfig conf) throws ServletException
  {
    super.init(conf);
    count = 0;
  }

  public void service(HttpServletRequest req, HttpServletResponse res)
                              throws IOException
  { try
    {
      String myOperation;
      myOperation = req.getParameter("operation");

      // perform increment operation
      if(myOperation.equals("increment"))
      { count++;
        ServletOutputStream out = res.getOutputStream();
        res.setContentType("text/html"); //Required for HTTP
        out.println("" + count);
        out.close(); //Close the output stream
      }
      else
       if(myOperation.equals("reset"))
       { count=0;
         ServletOutputStream out = res.getOutputStream();
         res.setContentType("text/html"); //Required for HTTP
         out.println("" + count);
         out.close(); //Close the output stream
       }
    } catch (Exception e)
    { System.out.println("Error " + e);
    }
  }
}
```

COMPILE THE CLIENT/SERVER PROGRAM

We're now ready to compile the Servlet Count client/server program. Make sure you have installed the Symantec Visual Café compiler. You will also need to download from the JavaSoft site either an evaluation copy of the *Java Web Server* or the *Java Servlets Development Kit (JSDK)*. If you are using Netscape's *Enterprise Server* like we did to run your servlets, you need to make additions from the *Servlets Development Kit* to your Web server. Follow the detailed instructions in the *readme.netscape* file in the root directory of your JSDK installation.

To compile the code, go to the appropriate directory and type the following commands at the prompt:

```
prompt> javac -d \CorbaJavaBook.2e\classes CountServletApplet.java
prompt> javac -d \CorbaJavaBook.2e\servlets CountServlet.java
```

The -d option tells the compiler to put the (.class) files it creates into the directory we specify. In this case, the client code goes into the *\CorbaJavaBook.2e\classes* subdirectory. The server code goes into the *\CorbaJavaBook.2e\servlets* subdirectory. If all goes well, you should have some compiled Java classes—(.class) files—that you can now run.

CREATE A WEB PAGE

The next step is to create a minimalist HTML Web page that embeds our applet. Open a file called *CountServlet.html*; then enter the following:

Listing 12-15. CountServlet.html: Web Page for the Servlet Count Applet.

```
<h1>Count Servlet Applet</h1>
<hr>
<center>
  <APPLET CODE=CountServletApplet.class
   CODEBASE=classes width=300 height=60>
</APPLET>
</center>
<hr>
```

Note that we use the CODEBASE attribute to point to a *classes* subdirectory that hangs off the HTTP server. This is the subdirectory that contains the **CountServletApplet** class.

RUN THE CLIENT/SERVER PROGRAM

To run the client/server Servlet Count, you need a Java-enabled Web browser and a HTTP server. We used Netscape *Communicator 4.0* as our browser and Netscape *Enterprise Server 3.0* as our HTTP server. Many vendors provide equivalent software that you can also use to run this benchmark. You will also need to install the *Java Servlets Development Kit*. Next, follow these steps (see Figure 12-6):

1. *Install the code on a Web server*. Move the applet (.class) files and the (.html) file to the Web server. Use the CODEBASE attribute to place them in a separate subdirectory. You must also place the **CountServlet** (.class) file in the server's *servlets* subdirectory.

2. *Download the applet*. Point your Web browser to the URL of your Web Count page. The HTTP server will download the applet class. The minimalist applet should appear in the browser.

3. *Set the count*. The count field tells the applet how many times to invoke the Count server's increment method. We preset this number to 1000. If you want a different count, this is the time to change it.

4. *Invoke the servlet server 1000 times*. Click on the Run button to invoke increments on the remote Servlet.

5. *Obtain the results*. The lower right-hand field displays the average response time in milliseconds for an *increment* method (it's the equivalent of a Ping performance).

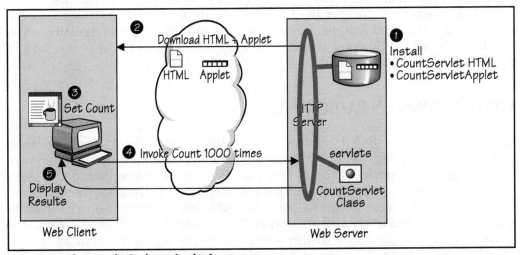

Figure 12-6. Running the Applet-to-Servlet Count.

We also run the Servlet Count server on the same machine as the Web browser to measure local interprocess performance. To compare apples with apples, we also run a Java application version of the servlet Count client; we include the code for this application in the CD-ROM.

LOOKING AT SOME TEST RESULTS

We ran this client/server program in different situations to get a reading on the performance of CGI method invocations. As usual, our client performs 1000 method invocations. The tests measure the JIT-enabled average response time of HTTP/Servlet Pings. We first run the Web client and server programs in the same machine—a 120-MHz Pentium running NT 4.0. Then we run them across a 10 Mbit/s Ethernet LAN. We also run the client application version. Table 12-1 compares the average response times.

Table 12-1. Local Versus Remote Count Servlets.

	Local Servlet Count (interprocess, same machine)	Remote Servlet Count (interprocess, over 10 Mbit/s Ethernet)
Applet-to-Servlet	103.9 msecs	92.9 msecs
Application-to-Servlet	61.7 msecs	55.6 msecs

The numbers show servlets to be extremely slow. With the exception of CGI, servlets are much slower than any of the alternatives we've seen so far. They appear to be more than 15 times slower than the CORBA static invocations we measured in Chapter 7. If it's any consolation, servlets are an order of magnitude faster than CGI. Before you call "Spencer the Cat," be sure to run the programs and see for yourself. You may find that the numbers deviate by 10% in either direction, even with the same setup. However, the relative performance should remain more or less constant.

SERVLETS VERSUS CORBA/IIOP

Table 12-2 compares HTTP servlets with CORBA/IIOP. Like CGI and sockets, servlets provide a very primitive form of middleware. You must do your own marshaling and unmarshaling of parameters. Servlets do not support typed interfaces. Consequently, you must create your own command formats. Note that even our simple code example started to look quite ugly—there were two operations with a simple return parameter. Like we said in the Sockets chapter, imagine if you had to implement a simple server that exposes a dozen or so interfaces to its clients. Then let's say that each interface consists of a dozen methods that each require five or six parameters with different data types. You will find that even something that simple can turn into quite a nasty undertaking if you use servlets.

So what are servlets really good for? Without turning this into a Soapbox, servlets appear to be about one notch better than CGI (or sockets) in the Web middleware hierarchy. They provide a simple callback API to a Web server. In addition, they include useful helper functions that let you extract HTTP name/value pairs and compose a dynamic HTTP response.

The simplistic API servlets provide is a two-edged sword. It's a good fit for a CGI-like request/response paradigm. However, it's also a crippled distributed object solution; it does not take advantage of interfaces to provide higher levels of abstractions to the services your write.

Servlets also lack many of the important features you would expect from a scalable server-side component infrastructure. For example, they do not support transactions, which are now a standard feature of the CORBA/Enterprise JavaBeans and DCOM/MTS server-side component models. In addition, servlets do not support a dynamic deactivation mechanism.

Table 12-2. CORBA IIOP Versus HTTP/Servlets.

Feature	CORBA/IIOP	HTTP/Servlets
Reliable communications	Yes	Yes
State across invocations	Yes	Yes (with great difficulty)
Parameter marshaling	Yes	No
Interface descriptions	Yes (via IDL)	No
Remote Dynamic discovery	Yes (via IR and DII)	No
Parameter data typing	Yes	No
Performance	Fast (3.5 msec Ping)	Slow (55.6 msec Ping)
Security	Yes	Yes
Transactions	Yes	No

CONCLUSION

A servlet is simply a Java class that supports the servlet API; it provides a level of middleware abstraction that's only a notch higher than sockets. Obviously, this is not the level of abstraction you would expect from a server-side component model.

To end this chapter on a positive note, servlets provide a simple, no-frills component model for running Java classes from within a Web server. You may find them useful as a CGI replacement—they provide an all-Java solution that is many times faster than CGI counterparts. However, if you're looking for a scalable server-side component model, servlets are not your answer. Instead, you should be looking at either CORBA/EJBs or Viperized DCOM/ActiveXs.

Chapter 13

RMI Versus CORBA/Java ORBs

The *Remote Method Invocation (RMI)*—now part of JDK 1.1—was designed from ground zero to seamlessly support remote method invocations on objects across Java virtual machines. RMI directly integrates a distributed object model into the Java language. It makes the ORB almost transparent to the client by adding some new implementation requirements on the server. RMI also extends Java's security net to include the dynamic downloading of stubs.

We start this chapter by giving you a tutorial on RMI. We introduce RMI's distributed object model and explain how you use it to create client/server applications. We then go over RMI's main classes and interfaces. We follow this with a scenario that illustrates how you would use these classes to invoke methods on remote objects. We then write the RMI version of Count. At the end of the chapter, we will provide Ping numbers for RMI. We will be able to compare the RMI performance with CORBA IIOP. So this should be a lot of fun.

RMI 101

An RMI object is a remote Java object whose methods can be invoked from another Java Virtual Machine, even across a network. You can invoke methods on the remote RMI object like you would on a local Java object. In this respect, RMI is very much like CORBA. And like CORBA, RMI lets you pass a reference to a remote object in an argument or return it as a result. This section explains the RMI object model in some detail. We also look at some of the new RMI features in JDK 1.2.

How RMI Extends Local Java Calls

Like their CORBA counterparts, RMI clients interact with remote objects via their published interfaces. They never directly interact with the classes that implement these interfaces.

Unlike a local Java call, an RMI invocation passes local objects in parameters by copy, instead of by reference—this is also called *pass-by-value*. Why pass-by-value? Because a reference to a local object is only useful within a single virtual machine. RMI uses the Java 1.1 *object serialization* service to flatten a local Java object's state into a serial stream that it can then pass as a parameter inside a message. On the other hand, you can access remote objects over the network. So RMI—like CORBA—passes a remote object by reference, not by copying the actual remote implementation.

RMI provides new interfaces and classes that let you find remote objects, load them, and then run them securely. Currently, RMI provides a very primitive, non-persistent naming service that lets you locate remote objects. It also provides a class loader that lets clients download stubs from the server. Like its CORBA counterpart, an RMI stub serves as a proxy on the client for the remote object. RMI provides some extra security to ensure that these proxies are well-behaved. Finally, RMI defines new marshaling classes that let you pass these stubs as parameters inside your method invocations.

Distributed objects fail in more mysterious ways than their local counterparts. So you must be able to handle the additional exceptions that can occur during a remote method invocation. To help you, RMI extends the Java exception classes to deal with remote failures. The new classes extend error-handling across Java virtual machines. We cover the RMI remote exception model later in this chapter.

RMI's Garbage Collection of Remote Objects

In a distributed system, a garbage collector must be able to automatically delete remote objects that are not referenced by any client. A good garbage collector frees you from having to keep track of which client connections are still active. RMI uses a reference-counting garbage-collection scheme that keeps track of all external *live references* to server objects within a Java virtual machine. In this case, a live reference is just a client/server connection over a TCP/IP session.

As long as a reference to a remote object exists, it cannot be garbage-collected. You can pass references as arguments in remote calls. The remote client to which a reference is passed is added to the referenced set. Every time a client obtains a reference, the object's reference count is incremented by one; it is decremented by one when the client stops referencing the object. When the reference count reaches zero, RMI puts the server object on the *weak reference* list. The Java garbage collector can now discard this object.

A reference to a remote object is *leased* for a period of time by the client holding the reference. The lease period starts when the *dirty* call is received. It is the client's responsibility to renew the leases by making additional *dirty* calls on the remote references it holds before such leases expire. If the client does not renew the lease before it expires, the distributed garbage collector assumes that the remote object is no longer referenced by the client.

As in the local Java case, the Java garbage collector calls the object's *finalize* method before deleting it from memory. In addition, an object can implement the **java.rmi.server.Unreferenced** interface to be notified when it is no longer being referenced. This interface defines a single method, *unreferenced*. RMI invokes this method when there are no live references to this remote object. For most implementations, *finalize* gives you all the notification you need; *unreferenced* may be overkill.

The Pitfalls of Remote Reference Counting

Warning

Network failures make it a lot trickier to implement a remote reference-counting algorithm that really works. It is much easier to implement reference-counting in local object environments. For example, a remote server object could be prematurely garbage-collected when a link fails. The reconnecting client would then hold a reference to a non-existent server object. Of course, RMI will generate a **RemoteException** to let you know when this happens. But you must still handle these exceptions in your application. The current version of RMI does not provide automatic rebinding. ❏

The RMI Development Process

Figure 13-1 shows the steps you must follow to create your RMI client and server classes, and then run them. Let's go through these steps one-by-one and see what's involved:

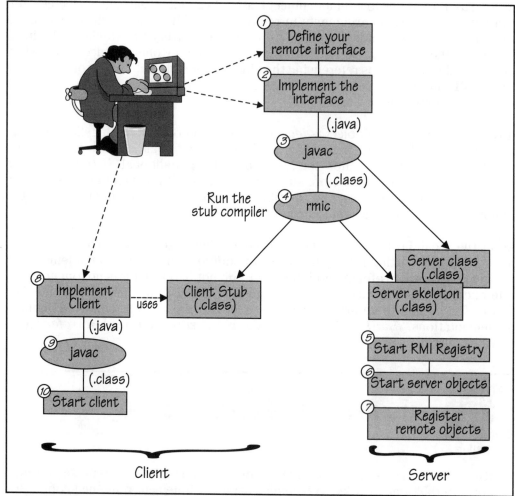

Figure 13-1. How to Write an RMI Client and Server Application.

1. ***Define a remote interface***. Your server object must declare its services via a remote interface. It does this by extending the **java.rmi.Remote** interface. Each method in a remote interface must *throw* a **java.rmi.RemoteException**.

2. ***Implement the remote interface***. You must provide a Java server class that implements the interface you published to the outside world. You must derive this class from **java.rmi.UnicastRemoteObject**.

3. ***Compile your server class***. You must compile your server class using *javac*.

4. ***Run the stub compiler***. RMI provides a stub compiler called *rmic*. You must run rmic against your (.class) files to generate client stubs and server skeletons for your remote classes. Like their CORBA counterparts, RMI stubs provide

client proxies for your server objects. They marshal remote calls and send them to the server. The RMI server skeleton receives the remote call, unmarshals the parameters, and then calls your implementation class. You run rmic by entering the following command at the prompt:

```
prompt> rmic classname
```

You must have previously compiled this class successfully using javac. The rmic stub compiler takes the same command-line arguments as javac. For example, you can specify the location of your classes using the CLASSPATH environment variable or via the *-classpath* command line argument. The compiled class files are placed in the current directory unless you specify a different location using the *-d* argument.

5. ***Start the RMI registry on your server.*** RMI defines interfaces for a non-persistent naming service called the *Registry*. RMI has a remote object implementation of this registry. It lets you retrieve and register server objects using simple names. Each server process can support its own registry, or you can have a single stand-alone registry that supports all the virtual machines on a server node. You start a registry object on your server by entering the following command at the prompt:

```
prompt> rmiregistry
```

Note that the registry database is empty when the server first comes up (or boots). You must populate it with the remote objects you create.

6. ***Start your server objects.*** You must load your server classes and then create instances of remote objects.

7. ***Register your remote objects with the registry.*** You must register all instances of remote objects with the RMI registry so clients can reach them. You use methods of the **java.rmi.Naming** class to bind a name to your server object. This class uses the underlying RMI registry to store the names. Your server objects are now ready to be invoked by clients.

8. ***Write your client code.*** The client consists mostly of ordinary Java code. You must use the **java.rmi.Naming** class to locate a remote object. You then invoke its methods via a stub that serves as a proxy for the remote object. These stubs are generated by rmic.

9. ***Compile the client code.*** You do this using *javac*.

10. ***Start the client.*** You must load the client classes and their stubs. RMI also provides security hooks that make it possible for clients to download stub classes from the server on demand.

You can see that RMI follows a very ORB-like development process. This shouldn't be too surprising—after all RMI is an ORB.

RMI INTERFACES AND CLASSES

The interfaces and classes that are responsible for specifying the remote behavior of the RMI system are defined in the following four packages: *java.rmi*, *java.rmi.server*, *java.rmi.dgc*, and *java.rmi.registry*. Together, these packages define over 25 interfaces and classes. This makes RMI a relatively large Java subsystem. The good news is that you only need to understand half of these interfaces to write your RMI client/server applications. The rest of these interfaces are primarily for system providers. They define the lower layers of the RMI subsystem.

In this book, we break down the RMI interfaces into four functional categories: 1) *RMI core* defines the interfaces you'll absolutely need to perform remote method invocations; 2) *RMI naming service* defines the interfaces and classes that implement the registry; 3) *RMI security* defines the new RMI security manager and class loader interfaces; and 4) *RMI marshaling* defines lower-level interfaces for serializing and marshaling remote objects and stubs. In the next sections, we cover the first three categories in detail. These are the interfaces you are most likely to use. The marshaling interfaces are extremely powerful, but they are mostly of interest to RMI system providers. So we will briefly tell you why these marshaling interfaces are great without getting into all the gory details.

The RMI Core

The RMI core consists of six classes and interfaces. Together, they define the stub and skeleton infrastructure for remote invocations. They also define extensions for remote error-handling. Figure 13-2 shows the relationships between these core Java interfaces and classes. All the remote interfaces either directly or indirectly extend **Remote**. This interface is really a flag; it does not define any new methods. Its main purpose is to flag the existence of your remote classes to rmic.

Your RMI clients invoke remote methods using service-specific stubs. These stubs are generated by the *rmic* stub compiler. They inherit their function from the **RemoteStub** class. On the server side, your RMI classes must extend the **Unicast-RemoteObject** class. RMI dispatches and unmarshals client calls to your remote server objects using rmic-generated skeletons. The rmic compiler implements a skeleton class for each server interface you define.

Here's a brief description of the Java RMI core interfaces and classes:

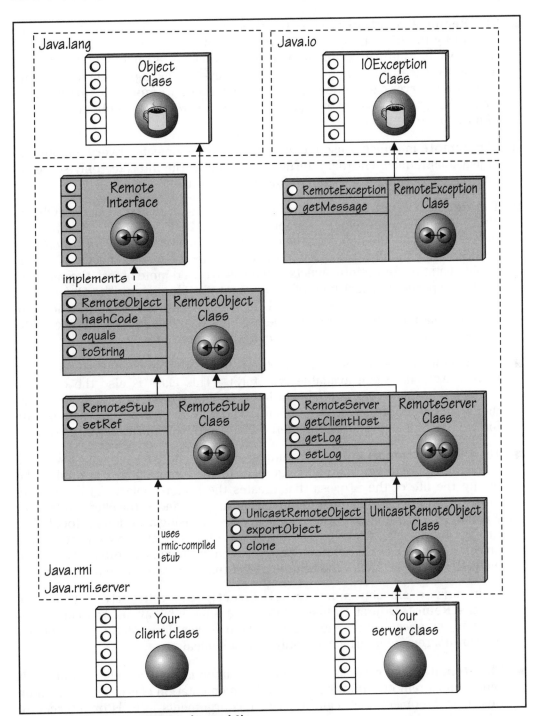

Figure 13-2. The Core Java RMI Interfaces and Classes.

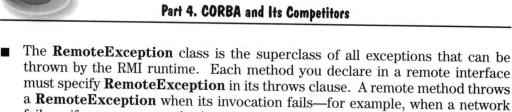

- The **RemoteException** class is the superclass of all exceptions that can be thrown by the RMI runtime. Each method you declare in a remote interface must specify **RemoteException** in its throws clause. A remote method throws a **RemoteException** when its invocation fails—for example, when a network fails or if a server cannot be found. You construct a **RemoteException** object by invoking the class constructor. You invoke *getMessage* to obtain the cause of a remote exception.

- The **Remote** interface is used to identify all remote objects. Every remote RMI object must implement this interface. Of course, the interface only serves to flag remote objects; it does not define any methods.

- The **RemoteObject** class provides a remote version of the Java root **Object** class. It implements remote versions of the methods *hashCode*, *equals*, and *toString*. You should note that the default implementation for *Object.getClass* is appropriate for all Java objects, local or remote; the method needs no special implementation for remote objects. When used on a remote object, the *getClass* method reports the exact type of the generated stub object. The *Object.wait* and *Object.notify* methods are used for thread waiting and notification. In remote situations, these methods operate on the client's local reference to the remote object, not on the actual object at the remote site.

- The **RemoteServer** class defines methods to create server objects and export them (i.e., make them available remotely). This class is also the common superclass to all server implementations. The *getClientHost* method returns the host address of the invoking client. The *getLog* method returns a stream for the RMI call log. The *setLog* method logs RMI calls to an output stream.

- The **UnicastRemoteObject** class implements a remote server object with the following characteristics: 1) all references to the remote object are only valid during the life of the process that creates the remote object; 2) the remote protocol requires a TCP connection-based transport; and 3) the client and server communicate parameters, invocations, and results using a stream protocol. The *exportObject* method returns a stub that serves as a local proxy for the remote object. Clients use this method to dynamically download stubs. The *clone* method returns a clone of the remote object that is distinct from the original.

  Your server classes must either directly or indirectly extend the **UnicastRemoteObject** class and inherit its remote behavior. You can implement any number of remote interfaces in your server class. Methods that do not appear in a remote interface are only available locally.

- The **RemoteStub** class is the common superclass to all client stubs. It represents a remote stub for a specified implementation class. Either the stub object or the object itself can be passed as arguments in calls or returned to clients. During marshaling, if a reference to a remote object is passed, a lookup is performed to find the matching remote stub. The stub is what gets passed or returned, not the object itself. Of course, the proper security safeguards must be in place to distribute these stubs. The *setRef* method specifies a remote reference

To write your RMI programs, your server objects must simply extend the **Unicast-RemoteObject** class to inherit its remote semantics. Your client objects use the RMI naming service to locate a remote object. Then, they invoke its methods using a stub that serves as a proxy for the remote object.

For our readers who really want to see the gory details, here are the class definitions of the RMI core:

Listing 13-1. The Java.rmi RemoteException Class.

```
public class RemoteException extends java.io.IOException
{
    // Variables
  public Throwable detail;

    // Constructors
  public RemoteException();
  public RemoteException(String s);
  public RemoteException(String s, Throwable ex);

    // Methods
  public String getMessage();
}
```

Listing 13-2. The Java.rmi Remote Interface.

```
public interface Remote
{
}
```

Listing 13-3. The Java.rmi.server RemoteObject Class.

```
public class RemoteObject extends Object implements Remote, Serializable
{
    // Variables
  protected RemoteRef ref;

    // Constructors
  protected RemoteObject();
  protected RemoteObject(RemoteRef newref);
```

```
    // Methods
  public int hashCode();
  public boolean equals(Object obj);
  public String toString();
}
```

Listing 13-4. The Java.rmi.server RemoteServer Class.

```
public class RemoteServer extends RemoteObject
{
    // Constructors
  protected RemoteServer();
  protected RemoteServer(RemoteRef ref);

    // Class Methods
  public static String getClientHost() throws ServerNotActiveException;
  public static PrintStream getLog();
  public static void setLog(OutputStream out);
}
```

Listing 13-5. The Java.rmi.server UnicastRemoteObject Class.

```
public class UnicastRemoteObject extends RemoteServer
{
    // Constructor
  protected UnicastRemoteObject() throws RemoteException;

    // Class methods
  public static RemoteStub exportObject(Remote obj)
     throws RemoteException;

    // Instance methods
  public Object clone() throws CloneNotSupportedException;
}
```

Listing 13-6. The Java.rmi.server RemoteStub Class.

```
public class RemoteStub extends RemoteObject
{
    // Constructors
  protected RemoteStub();
  protected RemoteStub(RemoteRef ref);
    // Class Methods
```

```
protected static void setRef(RemoteStub stub,
                             RemoteRef ref);
}
```

The Java RMI Naming Service

Before they can invoke a remote object's method, clients must first obtain a reference to this object. Typically, the client obtains its reference to a remote object as a return value in a method call. RMI also provides a simple naming service that lets you obtain references to server objects by name.

RMI defines its naming service using two classes and one interface (see Figure 13-3). You will typically interact with the **Naming** class to obtain the services of the RMI registry. The RMI registry is defined by the **Registry** interface. Notice that the registry is a remote RMI server object. This means that you can access its services across a network using remote method invocations. The **LocateRegistry** class helps you find a registry.

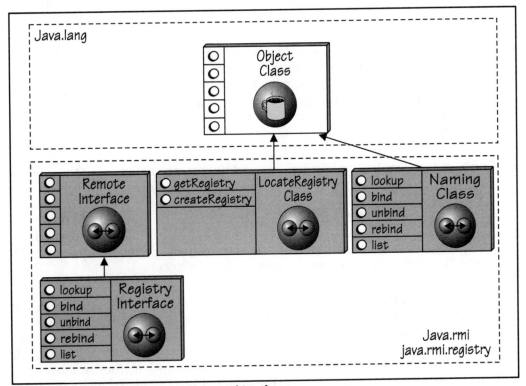

Figure 13-3. The RMI Naming Service Classes and Interfaces.

JavaSoft provides a very simple implementation of the **Registry** interface. This non-persistent implementation only supports flat names and it forgets all its contents when you restart the server. In this simple implementation, remote clients can only invoke the *lookup* and *list* methods. Clients must run on the same machine as the registry to invoke the *bind*, *unbind*, and *rebind* methods. Note that you can store a remote object reference using a URL-based naming scheme that we later describe.

Here's more information on what these classes and interfaces do:

- The **Registry** interface defines methods that let you update entries in a registry and list its contents. You invoke *bind* to map a remote object to a human-readable name. You invoke *rebind* to update the mapping between a name and a remote object; the registry will discard any previous binding of the name. You should always invoke *rebind* instead of *bind* to avoid receiving an **AlreadyBoundException**, if the object was previously bound to a name. You invoke *lookup* to obtain an object that is bound to the name you specify. If the returned object is remote, you must cast it to its expected remote interface. You invoke *unbind* to remove the mapping between the name and the remote object. You invoke *list* to obtain the list of object names in the registry. The call returns the names in an array of strings.

- The **LocateRegistry** class provides a set of overloaded *getRegistry* static methods to help you find a registry. You can retrieve a registry on a host you specify. You can also specify the port on a particular host, or you can rely on a default well-known port for a registry. The method will return a remote **Registry** object if it finds one. You can also invoke *createRegistry* to create a new **Registry** object.

- The **Naming** class lets you retrieve and define remote objects using the familiar URL syntax. The class uses the registry services to perform its operations. You specify an RMI URL as follows: *rmi://host:port/name*. The *host* is the host name of the registry; it defaults to the current host. The *port* is the port number of the registry; it defaults to the registry's well-known port number (port 1099). The *name* is the name of the remote object. Here's an example: *rmi://www.corbajava.engr.sjsu.edu:2001/MyObject*.

The *lookup* method returns the remote object for this URL name. In our example, the *lookup* method would return a file called **MyObject**. The *bind* method associates the URL name you specify with the remote object. The *rebind* method always binds the URL name to the object, even if the name is already bound—the old binding is lost. The *unbind* method removes the binding between the URL name and the remote object. The *list* method returns an array of strings containing a snapshot of the URL names in the registry.

Most of us will only be working with the **Naming** class. However, it doesn't hurt to understand the underlying classes it uses to perform its service. For our readers who are itching to see some code, the class descriptions follow.

Listing 13-7. The Java.rmi.registry Registry Interface.

```
public interface Registry extends Remote
{
    // Methods
  public abstract Remote lookup(String name)
                throws RemoteException, NotBoundException,
                     AccessException;
  public abstract void bind(String name, Remote obj)
                throws RemoteException, AlreadyBoundException,
                     AccessException;
  public abstract void unbind(String name)
                throws RemoteException, AccessException;
  public abstract void rebind(String name, Remote obj)
                throws RemoteException, AccessException;
  public abstract String[] list()
                throws RemoteException, AccessException;

}
```

Listing 13-8. The Java.rmi.registry LocateRegistry Class.

```
public class LocateRegistry extends Object
{
    // Class Methods
  public static Registry getRegistry() throws RemoteException;
  public static Registry getRegistry(int port) throws RemoteException;
  public static Registry getRegistry(String host)
                throws RemoteException, UnknownHostException;
  public static Registry getRegistry(String host, int port)
                throws RemoteException, UnknownHostException;
  public static Registry createRegistry(int port) throws RemoteException;
}
```

Listing 13-9. The Java.rmi Naming Class.

```
public final class Naming extends Object
{
    // Class Methods
  public static Remote lookup(String name)
                throws NotBoundException, MalformedURLException,
```

```
                          UnknownHostException, RemoteException;
public static void bind(String name, Remote obj)
            throws AlreadyBoundException, MalformedURLException,
                   UnknownHostException, RemoteException;
public static void unbind(String name)
            throws RemoteException, NotBoundException,
                   MalformedURLException, UnknownHostException;
public static void rebind(String name, Remote obj)
            throws RemoteException, MalformedURLException,
                   UnknownHostException;
public static String[] list(String name)
            throws RemoteException, MalformedURLException,
                   UnknownHostException;
}
```

RMI's Dynamic Stub Loading Classes

So what is dynamic stub loading? RMI extends Java's on-demand class loading mechanism to the loading of stub bytecodes. The idea is that clients can dynamically download stubs that reference remote objects from the server. This "just-in-time" downloading of stubs is called **dynamic stub-loading**. In extreme situations, the stub code for a remote implementation could be generated on-the-fly at the server site and then shipped to the client.

A client resorts to dynamic stub-loading when the stub it needs is not on its local machine. Remember, without the appropriate stub class for a service, there is no way for the client to invoke the remote interface. In addition, RMI uses stubs to return arguments that reference a remote object interface.

Of course, when you start downloading arbitrary classes into clients or servers, you open yourself to potential security threats. Without proper safeguards, the dynamic stub-loading environment can quickly turn into a giant incubator of viruses. So be sure to read the next Warning box.

RMI's dynamic stub downloading requires three functions: 1) a Java class loader, 2) a security manager, and 3) an object serialization mechanism to transmit classes over the wire. A request to dynamically load a stub class is first handed to the local file system using the CLASSPATH environment variable. If the class is not in the local file system, RMI needs to know where to find the class. It uses one of two mechanisms to find these remote stub classes. In the first mechanism the server tells the client where to find the stub by making the stub's URL available as part of the object reference. In the second mechanism, the stubs are loaded from a URL

Download at Your Own Risk

Warning

When you download classes from untrusted sources, you expose your clients, servers, and ultimately everything on the network to a broad range of attacks. JavaSoft recommends that you disable RMI class downloading, unless you understand and accept the potential risks. You can disable downloading by setting the property *java.rmi.server.useCodebaseOnly* to true; it forces classes to be loaded from the locally-defined codebase only. ❏

that you specify in the client's local *java.rmi.server.codebase* property; it's a form of static configuration.

So how do RMI servers tell their clients where to find these remote stubs? They do it using RMI marshaling. When a remote object reference is passed as a parameter inside a message, a URL that specifies where the stub code resides can be passed along with the object reference. The marshaling stream that transmits the reference also embeds the URL. The client uses this URL to locate and load the stub code.

Any class that you load from the network must be controlled and restricted by a security manager. If you don't like this, you can always load your stubs dynamically from the local file system without any security manager restrictions.

In contrast to the client side, all the server code is typically loaded from the local file system. Consequently, the loading of server classes is not restricted by a security manager. But what happens if a remote object is passed to a server for which there is no corresponding stub code? In this case, the server becomes a client. The RMI marshaling stream contains the location from which the classes for that remote object can be loaded. What happens next depends on how you configured your server. RMI defines a set of properties that let you control whether remote classes can be loaded on a server. You can also specify the locations from which these classes can be loaded. The RMI system will operate within these policy constraints. RMI enforces the policies you define via its security manager and stub loader.

The **RMIClassLoader** and **RMISecurityManager** classes implement methods that can help you keep viruses in check on both clients and servers. They allow clients to locate and load remote stubs in a controlled manner. RMI uses the **RMIClassLoader** to load classes from a remote server as needed; it is similar in function to the Applet class loader (see the next Briefing box).

The security manager must be started as the first action of a Java program so that it can regulate all subsequent actions. Any class that loads successfully is then regulated by the security manager. Classes can only be loaded if a security manager is present, even if the server supplies a URL for the stub; the server must also provide a *java.rmi.server.codebase* property. If any of these conditions are missing, you're plain out of luck. Your only other recourse is to invoke the *Class.forName* method and let the default class loader load the stub from the local CLASSPATH.

Applets Have Their Own Loaders

Briefing

You can only use the RMI security classes to constrain the actions of Java applications, not applets. Applets have their own class loaders and security mechanisms. For example, the applet environment is exclusively controlled by the **AppletSecurityManager** and **AppletClassLoader** classes. An applet can load remote stubs—as well as parameters that return object classes—from its home server. You must first install the appropriate stub classes on the applet's home server. ❑

Figure 13-4 shows the **RMIClassLoader** and **RMISecurityManager** classes and their methods. Here's what they do:

■ The **RMIClassLoader** class is used by the RMI runtime to load stubs and skeletons via a URL. The class loader will first try to load locally available classes and stubs. It will download classes over a network only if the required stubs are not locally available and if a security manager is present. When it loads a stub, any class it references will be loaded from the same host, subject to the same security restrictions. A server must declare to the RMI runtime the URL location of the stubs that will be available to its clients using the *java.rmi.server.codebase* property. You invoke the *loadClass* method to find and load a class you specify by name. You can specify the URL as the base to locate the class file. When everything else fails, you can always invoke *Class.forName* to load your class.

■ The **RMISecurityManager** class provides a simple security manager that is responsible for the actions of remotely-loaded stubs and classes (not applets). For code loaded as a stub, the security manager disables all functions except class definition and access. To enable a security manager, you invoke the *System.setSecurityManager* method, passing it an **RMISecurityManager**

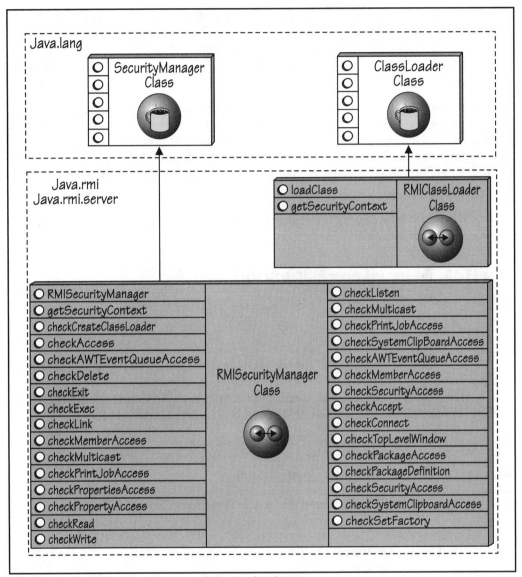

Figure 13-4. The RMI Security Manager and Class Loader Classes.

object. If no security manager is enabled, RMI will load stub classes only from the local file system as defined by CLASSPATH. You cannot download classes—even if a security manager is in place—when you set *java.rmi.server.useCodebaseOnly* to true; it forces classes to be loaded only from a local codebase.

The only variable that currently determines whether a stub can perform certain operations is the host from which it originated. You can obtain the host context by invoking *getSecurityContext*. The *checkXXX* methods let you discover the capabilities of a loaded stub. You invoke *checkRead* and *checkWrite* to determine if a stub is allowed to read or write to the file you specify. You invoke *checkConnect* to determine if the stub is allowed to connect to the host and port you specify. You invoke *checkPackageAccess* to check if the stub can access a package.

The current version of RMI prevents stubs from doing the following: 1) accept connections, 2) listen on any port, 3) manipulate threads outside their thread groups, 4) fork processes, 5) create class loaders, 6) link to DLLs, 7) exit from a Java virtual machine, 8) access properties, and 9) open file descriptors. If you find these policies too restrictive, you can always define your own security manager.

For our readers who need to program the security manager and class loader, the class descriptions follow.

Listing 13-10. The Java.rmi.server RMIClassLoader Class

```java
public class RMIClassLoader extends java.lang.ClassLoader
{
    // Class Methods
    public static Class loadClass(String name)
                throws MalformedURLException, ClassNotFoundException;
    public static Class loadClass(URL codebase, String name)
                throws MalformedURLException, ClassNotFoundException;
    public static Object getSecurityContext(ClassLoader loader);
}
```

Listing 13-11. The Java.rmi RMISecurityManager Class

```java
public class RMISecurityManager extends java.lang.SecurityManager
{
    // Constructors
    public RMISecurityManager();

    // Methods
    public Object getSecurityContext();
    public synchronized void checkCreateClassLoader();
    public synchronized void checkAccess(Thread t);
    public synchronized void checkAccess(ThreadGroup g);
    public synchronized void checkExit(int status);
    public synchronized void checkExec(String cmd);
    public synchronized void checkLink(String lib);
    public synchronized void checkPropertiesAccess();
    public synchronized void checkPropertyAccess(String key);
```

```
public synchronized void checkRead(String file);
public synchronized void checkRead(String file, URL base);
public void checkRead(String file, Object context);
public synchronized void checkRead(FileDescriptor fd);
public synchronized void checkWrite(String file);
public synchronized void checkWrite(FileDescriptor fd);
public void checkMulticast(InetAddress maddr);
public void checkMulticast(InetAddress maddr, byte ttl);
public void checkPrintJobAccess();
public void checkSystemClipboardAccess();
public void checkAwtEventQueueAccess();
public void checkMemberAccess(Class class, int which);
public void checkSecurityAccess(String provider);
public synchronized void checkListen(int port);
public synchronized void checkAccept(String host, int port);
public synchronized void checkConnect(String host,
                                      int port);
public void checkConnect(String host, int port,
                         Object context);
public synchronized boolean checkTopLevelWindow(Object window);
public synchronized void checkPackageAccess(String pkg);
public synchronized void checkPackageDefinition(String pkg);
public synchronized void checkSetFactory();
public void checkDelete(String file);
}
```

The RMI Marshaling Objects

JDK 1.1's serialization provides a lightweight object persistence service; you can also use it to serialize the contents of Java objects to streams and sockets. RMI uses the new serialization classes—now part of *java.io*—to marshal arguments in remote calls and to return values. These classes provide methods to write and read an object to and from a stream. The *writeObject* method lets you write the state of an object to an **ObjectOutputStream**. The *readObject* method lets you internalize the object from an **ObjectInputStream**. These methods extend the functions of *java.io*'s **DataOutputStream** and **DataInputStream**. They let you serialize objects—including arrays, Strings, and any class you write.

Typically, you will let Java's default mechanisms handle the serialization of your objects to streams and to marshaling objects. You can override the class's default serialization by implementing private versions of the *writeObject* and *readObject* methods. If you don't provide a private method, the Java default mechanism writes all the fields of the object—except for transient and static fields—to the **ObjectOutputStream**.

Generally, you will not be concerned with all this serialization activity. It's just something that happens under the cover. The one exception is when you need to do your own serialization. For example, you may have a class that stores its state in an RDBMS or ODBMS. In this case, you may have to implement versions of *writeObject* and *readObject* that save and restore the object's state to and from an RDBMS or ODBMS. We anticipate that ODBMS vendors will make this process seamless. After all, the idea behind a good ODBMS is to provide object persistence within the semantics of an object language like C++, Smalltalk, and now Java. (We cover Java Serialization in Part 7.)

RMI-Over-IIOP

As we explained in Part 1, JavaSoft and the OMG are currently working on a convergence of the CORBA and RMI object models. This convergence is happening in the following two areas:

- **RMI-over-IIOP.** JavaSoft will offer a version of RMI that works on top of the IIOP transport. IIOP provides the following benefits to RMI: 1) built-in support for the propagation of transactions, 2) ORB-based firewall support via the IIOP proxy (no HTTP tunneling), 3) interoperability with objects written in other languages via the RMI/IDL subset, and 4) an open distributed object standard.

- **RMI/IDL.** The CORBA *Java-to-IDL* standard is also the CORBA/RMI convergence standard. It lets Java programmers specify CORBA interfaces using Java RMI semantics instead of CORBA IDL. The compiler uses these semantics to automatically generate the CORBA IDL, stubs, and skeletons. The RMI/IDL subset allows RMI programs to be invoked by multilingual CORBA clients using IIOP; it also lets RMI programs call CORBA objects written in other languages. This standard is closely related to another CORBA standard called *Objects-by-Value*. *Enterprise JavaBeans* uses this RMI/IDL subset.

Without turning this into a Soapbox, *RMI-over-IIOP* appears to be a good thing for the CORBA/Java camp. It brings together two powerful technologies and avoids the splintering that was so endemic in the Unix world.

The JDK 1.2 RMI

The JDK 1.2 implementation of RMI introduces some CORBA-like features that make it easier to implement RMI-over-IIOP. Here's the list of new RMI enhancements:

■ ***Support for persistent object references.*** Today, a reference to an RMI object is transient. The reference is only valid while the object is active; RMI cannot re-establish a reference to an object after a system crashes. The JDK 1.2 version of RMI introduces a CORBA-like persistent object reference that allows a client to reconnect to the same object at a later time.

■ ***Support for remote object activation.*** Persistent references enable the JDK 1.2 version of RMI to introduce a CORBA-like activation framework (we describe CORBA activation in Part 5). The idea is that you can't have a million server objects active all the time. So the server must be able to deactivate some objects to let others execute. However, clients must be given the illusion that all server objects are active all the time. The new RMI will let clients transparently re-activate an object on demand. The RMI ORB will then re-initiate the object's execution inside an appropriate Java VM.

The JDK 1.2 RMI activation system uses a form of *lazy activation*, which means that the object is activated only after a client first invokes it. The object reference contains a *unique identifier* that points to an **ActivationDesc** object. This is a serializable object that contains: 1) a group identifier that specifies a VM in which the object is activated, 2) the object's class name, 3) a **java.security.CodeSource** that specifies from where to load the object's class code, and 4) some object-specific data in marshaled form—for example, the name of a file containing the object's data. The activator loads the class of the object and then instantiates the object itself using a special constructor that takes several arguments—including the previously registered activation descriptor.

■ ***Support for custom socket types.*** A remote object can now specify the custom socket type that RMI will use for remote calls to that object. For example, RMI over a secure transport (such as SSL) can be supported using custom socket types.

■ ***Minor API enhancements.*** These include unexporting a remote object, obtaining the stub for an object implementation, obtaining a local object implementation from a stub, and exporting an object on a specific port.

We cover object activation in detail in Part 5 (and also in Part 7 in the *Enterprise JavaBeans* chapter).

RMI SCENARIO

It's time for a scenario that shows how these interfaces play together. Figure 13-5 shows the client and server sides of an RMI interaction. The server object exports a remote **Count** object interface. The client sets the count to zero and invokes the

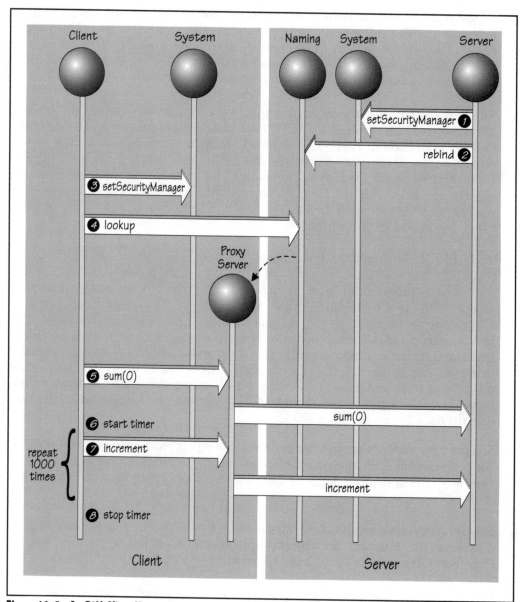

Figure 13-5. An RMI Client/Server Scenario.

increment method 1000 times. It's the RMI version of Count. Let's walk through the steps:

1. ***The server enables the RMI security manager.*** The server creates a new **RMISecurityManager** object. It then passes it to the **System** object by invoking the *setSecurityManager* method. The **System** class is implemented

in *java.lang*; it implements platform-independent system functions via its class methods. You do not instantiate a **System** object.

2. ***The server registers with the RMI Naming service***. The server invokes *rebind* to associate the remote server object with a URL-based name.

3. ***The client enables the RMI security manager***. The client creates a new **RMISecurityManager** object. It then invokes the *setSecurityManager* method to pass it to the **System** object.

4. ***The client locates the remote object***. The client invokes the *lookup* method on the **Naming** object and passes it the URL name of the remote object. The method returns a proxy reference to the remote object. It will also download a stub for that object, if it's not already on the local machine.

5. ***The client sets the remote count to zero***. The client invokes the *sum* method on the remote object and passes it a value of zero.

6. ***The client starts the timer***. This is the start of the elapsed time.

7. ***The client invokes the remote increment 1000 times***. The client invokes the *increment* method on the proxy server object 1000 times. Of course, the proxy forwards the call to the remote server object via its stub.

8. ***The client stops the timer***. The client obtains the elapsed time and then uses it to calculate the average Ping performance of an RMI server.

Notice that the RMI style of remote invocation is very similar to CORBA's. In the next section, we show some RMI code that implements the scenario we just covered.

THE RMI COUNT

OK, it's time to write some code. In this section, we create the RMI version of the Count client/server program. The client is a regular Java application. It is very similar to the one we developed in Chapter 7 for CORBA. On the server side, we provide the RMI version of the infamous Count server. Figure 13-6 shows how the pieces play together.

The RMI Count Client

The client program consists of a single Java class—**CountRMIClient**. This class provides a *main* method that performs the following functions: 1) installs an RMI security manager, 2) locates a remote **Count** object, 3) sets the remote *sum* attribute to zero, 4) calculates the start time, 5) invokes the *increment* method

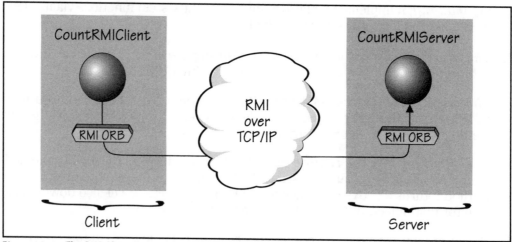

Figure 13-6. The RMI Client/Server Count.

1000 times, 6) calculates the elapsed time, and 7) displays the average RMI Ping performance. It's a textbook implementation of the scenario in Figure 13-5. Here's the code:

Listing 13-12. CountRMIClient: The RMI Count Application Client.

```java
// CountRMIClient.java  RMI Count client

import java.rmi.*;
import java.rmi.registry.*;
import java.rmi.server.*;

public class CountRMIClient
{ public static void main(String args[])
  { // Create and install the security manager
    System.setSecurityManager(new RMISecurityManager());

    try
    { CountRMI myCount = (CountRMI)Naming.lookup("rmi://"
                        + args[0] + "/" + "my CountRMI");

      // Set Sum to initial value of 0
      System.out.println("Setting Sum to 0");
      myCount.sum(0);

      // Calculate Start time
      long startTime = System.currentTimeMillis();
```

```
    // Increment 1000 times
    System.out.println("Incrementing");
    for (int i = 0 ; i < 1000 ; i++ )
    { myCount.increment();
    }

    // Calculate stop time; print out statistics
    long stopTime = System.currentTimeMillis();
    System.out.println("Avg Ping = "
                    + ((stopTime - startTime)/1000f)
                    + " msecs");
    System.out.println("Sum = " + myCount.sum());
  } catch(Exception e)
  { System.err.println("System Exception" + e);
  }
  System.exit(0);
 }
}
```

Like CORBA, RMI makes remote invocations appear almost seamless to the client. It's like calling a local Java object. Of course, the client must first locate the remote object before it can invoke its methods. The client obtains a reference to the remote object by invoking the *lookup* method on the **Naming** object; it uses RMI's URL-based naming scheme to specify the remote object.

The RMI Count Server

The server-side of the RMI Count consists of one interface and two classes. The **CountRMIImpl** class implements the **CountRMI** remote interface. The **CountRMIServer** class provides a *main* method that initializes the server and then instantiates a single **CountRMIImpl** object. Here's the code:

Listing 13-13. The CountRMI Interface.

```
// CountRmi Interface

public interface CountRMI extends java.rmi.Remote
{
    int sum() throws java.rmi.RemoteException;
    void sum(int _val) throws java.rmi.RemoteException;
    public int increment() throws java.rmi.RemoteException;
}
```

Listing 13-14. The CountRMIImpl Class.

```java
// CountRMIImpl.java, CountRMI implementation

import java.rmi.*;
import java.rmi.server.UnicastRemoteObject;

public class CountRMIImpl extends UnicastRemoteObject
        implements CountRMI
{

  private int sum;


  public CountRMIImpl(String name) throws RemoteException
  {
    super();
    try
    {
      Naming.rebind(name, this);
      sum = 0;
    }
    catch (Exception e)
    { System.out.println("Exception: " + e.getMessage());
      e.printStackTrace();
    }
  }


  public int sum() throws RemoteException
  { return sum;
  }


  public  void sum(int val) throws RemoteException
  { sum = val;
  }


  public int increment() throws RemoteException
  { sum++;
    return sum;
  }
}
```

Listing 13-15. The CountRMIServer Class.

```
// CountRMIServer.java

import java.rmi.*;
import java.rmi.server.*;

public class CountRMIServer
{

  public static void main(String args[])
  {

    // Create and install the security manager
    System.setSecurityManager(new RMISecurityManager());

    try
    {
      // Create CountRMIImpl
      CountRMIImpl myCount = new CountRMIImpl("my CountRMI");
      System.out.println("CountRMI Server ready.");
    }
    catch (Exception e)
    { System.out.println("Exception: " + e.getMessage());
      e.printStackTrace();
    }
  }
}
```

As shown in the code, the **CountRMI** interface extends **Remote** and defines the remote methods. The **CountRMIImpl** class implements these methods and extends **UnicastRemoteObject**. In addition, **CountRMIImpl** implements a constructor that registers the newly created object's name with the RMI **Naming** class.

The **CountRMIServer** class provides the server's *main* method. It provides the following functions: 1) creates a new **RMISecurityManager** object, 2) registers the stub security manager with the local **System** object, and 3) instantiates a named **CountRMIImpl** object. If you're dealing with a single object, this class may seem like a lot of overhead. In a more realistic situation, the main program will be managing multiple RMI objects, each running in its own thread. This completes the code for the RMI client and server sides.

COMPILE THE CLIENT/SERVER PROGRAM

We're now ready to compile the RMI client/server program. Make sure you have installed the Java JDK. To compile the code, go to the appropriate directory and enter the following commands at the prompt:

```
prompt> javac -d \CorbaJavaBook.2e\classes CountRMI.java
prompt> javac -d \CorbaJavaBook.2e\classes CountRMIImpl.java
prompt> javac -d \CorbaJavaBook.2e\classes CountRMIClient.java
prompt> javac -d \CorbaJavaBook.2e\classes CountRMIServer.java
```

The -d option tells the compiler to put the (.class) files it creates into the directory we specify, in this case, the *\CorbaJavaBook.2e\classes* subdirectory. Next, you must generate the stubs and skeletons using rmic. To do this, enter the following command at the prompt:

```
prompt> rmic -d \CorbaJavaBook.2e\classes CountRMIImpl
```

If all goes well, you should have some compiled Java RMI code—including a stub and skeleton—that you can now run.

RUN THE CLIENT/SERVER PROGRAMS

First, start the RMI registry. Enter the following command at the prompt:

```
prompt> start rmiregistry
```

Next, run the RMI server. Enter the following command at the prompt:

```
prompt> start java CountRMIServer
```

Then run the client. Enter the following command at the prompt:

```
prompt> java CountRMIClient <server-hostname>
```

You should see a screen output that looks like this:

```
Setting Sum to 0
Incrementing
Avg Ping = 3.275 msec
Sum = 1000
```

LOOKING AT SOME TEST RESULTS

We run this client/server program in different situations to get a reading on the performance of RMI method invocations. As usual, our client performs 1000 method invocations. The tests measure the average response time of RMI Pings. We first run the Web client and server programs in the same machine—a 120-MHz Pentium running NT 4.0. Then we run them across a 10 Mbit/s Ethernet LAN. Table 13-1 compares the average response times.

Table 13-1. Local Versus Remote: RMI Invocations (JIT Compiled).

Local RMI Count (interprocess, same machine)	Remote RMI Count (interprocess, over 10 Mbit/s Ethernet)
3.1 msecs	3.3 msecs

The numbers for RMI have greatly improved since our last book. RMI remote Pings are 3.3 msecs. In contrast, the remote Portable CORBA was 3.5 msecs. However, Pings provide the best-case performance numbers for RMI's native protocol—the *Remote Method Protocol (RMP)* because they do not pass any parameters. The performance of RMP starts to degrade when you pass arguments; it uses Java serialization to marshal and unmarshal each argument.

RMI-OVER-IIOP VERSUS RMI-OVER-RMP

As we explained earlier, RMI and CORBA are converging. In this section, we compare the forthcoming *RMI-over-IIOP* with today's *RMI-over-RMP*. From a programming perspective, you probably won't see too much of a difference. The RMI/IDL subset is very complete (see Part 5); it also supports the passing of objects by value using the new CORBA *Objects-by-Value* specification.

An open issue is whether CORBA will support the passing around of bytecodes (or behavior) inside parameters. Technology is not the issue here. CORBA *Pass-by-Value* lets you pass the state of an object hierarchy; it also supports the downloading of code via codebases (see Part 5). As we go to press, *Java-to-IDL* is not taking advantage of this last feature—this is why it's called the RMI/IDL subset. It seems the CORBA architects are making a conscious decision not to pass around behavior inside method calls; Caffeine has also adopted this self-imposed restriction. Why?

In the case of Caffeine, the Netscape/Visigenic designers felt that most installations would disable the code download feature for security reasons. Consequently, programmers can't assume that the missing code for a class will be automatically downloaded. This means that you must write tricky error-recovery code to compensate for cases where the code download is disabled and the class is not present on the target machine. So they may be doing us a favor by not implementing this "feature." Anyway, the first version of *RMI-over-IIOP* will probably be based on the RMI/IDL subset used in *Enterprise JavaBeans*. Currently, it does not include the passing of behavior.

RMI VERSUS CORBA/IIOP

Table 13-2 compares *RMI-over-IIOP* and *RMI-over-RMP*. This comparison shows that IIOP augments RMI by providing an intergalactic infrastructure. In the short run, *RMI-over-RMP* will continue to live; it will be used by programmers who need RMI's code-passing feature. Eventually, JavaSoft (and OMG) may incorporate this feature into RMI/IDL. If this happens, then RMI/IDL won't be a subset any longer. So it won't make much sense for JavaSoft to continue to enhance its proprietary RMP protocol.

Table 13-2. CORBA IIOP Versus RMI.

Feature	RMI-Over-IIOP	RMI over RMP
Parameter marshaling	Yes	Yes
Parameter passing	in, out, and in/out	in
Dynamic stub downloads	Yes (via codebase)	Yes
Dynamic class downloads	Maybe	Yes
Objects can be passed by value	Yes (via Pass-by-Value)	Yes
Garbage collection	Yes (via POA and ORB)	Yes (via language)
Interface descriptions	Yes (via Java interfaces)	Yes (via Java interfaces)
Distributed Dynamic discovery	Yes (via IR)	No
Distributed Dynamic invocations	Yes (via DII)	No

Table 13-2. CORBA IIOP Versus RMI. (Continued)

Feature	RMI-Over-IIOP	RMI over RMP
Wire-level security context	Yes (via CORBA Security)	No
SSL-based Security	Yes	Yes (with JDK 1.2)
Wire-level transaction context	Yes (via CORBA OTS)	No
Persistent naming	Yes	No
URL-based naming	Yes (non-volatile)	Yes (volatile)
Persistent object references	Yes	Yes (with JDK 1.2)
Multilingual invocations	Yes (with RMI/IDL subset)	No
Language-neutral wire protocol	Yes (via canonical IIOP data types)	No
Intergalactic scaling	Yes (via IORs, DSI, GUIDs, IIOP, and inter-ORB federations)	No
Standard ORB wire protocol	Yes (IIOP)	No
Enterprise JavaBeans Support	Yes	Unknown

CONCLUSION

The design of RMI has had a very strong influence on CORBA (see Part 5). RMI is really a new kind of ORB that builds on the Java object model. As an ORB, RMI introduces five key innovations: 1) it lets you move code in addition to data, 2) it makes a serious attempt to ensure that the code you download is safe to run, 3) it lets you pass objects by value, 4) it uses Java both as an interface definition language and as an implementation language, and 5) it uses a URL-based naming scheme.

RMI can be very attractive to Java programmers. It makes the ORB transparent, and it naturally extends Java's reach. With RMI, you do not have to deal with CORBA IDL or Java-to-CORBA type translations. RMI provides ORB-like facilities from within the Java object model. You do everything from within Java, period. However, with today's RMI—or *RMI-over-RMP*—you miss the boat on CORBA's intergalactic infrastructure, which is a shame. This is exactly why JavaSoft (with help from OMG) is developing *RMI-over-IIOP*; it will eventually let us have our cake and eat it, too. So you'll get the best of the CORBA and RMI worlds. In the next chapter, we introduce *Caffeine*—an RMI-like system built on top of CORBA IIOP. With Caffeine, you can *immediately* have your cake and eat it, too.

Chapter 14

Caffeine: The "Pure" CORBA/Java ORB

Caffeine—from Netscape and Visigenic—is a "pure Java" solution for CORBA IIOP developers. Caffeine provides an RMI-like programming environment on top of *VisiBroker for Java*. Caffeine includes the following: 1) a *Java2IIOP* code generator that takes Java interface files as input and automatically produces IIOP-compliant stubs and skeletons, 2) a *Java2IDL* compiler that automatically produces CORBA IDL from your Java code, and 3) a *URL-based* CORBA Naming Service. Caffeine makes the CORBA IDL totally transparent to Java programmers.

Caffeine gives you all the benefits of CORBA from within the Java object model. You simply write ordinary Java classes using RMI-like semantics to make them remote. Your objects are then automatically made CORBA-compliant. How? The Netscape/Visigenic implementation discovers your remote Java classes by reading bytecodes. You can even ask Caffeine to generate the CORBA IDL interfaces from your Java classes. You can then access the IDL descriptions from an Interface Repository.

In contrast to today's RMI, Caffeine's underlying *VisiBroker for Java* ORB lets your Java objects communicate with all the objects in the CORBA/IIOP universe— including C, C++, and Smalltalk objects. Caffeine also implements a default URL-based naming scheme using VisiBroker's OSAgent and CORBA Naming Services. Caffeine runs on CORBA/IIOP. Consequently, it gives your Java objects the benefits of CORBA transactions, security, introspection, and intergalactic connectivity. You're in the CORBA Magic Kingdom.

This chapter starts out with a brief tutorial on Caffeine. We explain how you use Caffeine to create client/server applications. We write the Caffeinated version of Count, and then run it. So, you'll be able to compare the Caffeinated CORBA performance with that of CORBA "on-the-rocks." The good news is that you already have almost everything you need to understand Caffeine. Consequently, this is a relatively short chapter.

CAFFEINE 101

This section goes over the Caffeine highlights. We explain *Java2IIOP, Java2IDL*, and the Caffeine development process. We also look at some of the ways Caffeine extends CORBA.

Java2IIOP—Look Ma, No IDL

Like RMI, Caffeine uses Java both as an interface definition language and as an implementation language. And like RMI, the Caffeine development process starts with a Java interface. You declare your Java interface to be remote by extending it—either directly or indirectly—from **org.omg.CORBA.Object**. You must compile your interfaces using *javac* and then run the output through *Java2IIOP*.

For each remote Java interface *Java2IIOP* encounters, it creates a package with the following four classes:

■ A client-side stub class called **_st_XXX**, where XXX is the name of your interface.

■ A server-side skeleton class called **_XXXImplBase**, where XXX is the name of your interface.

■ Helper and Holder classes for your interface.

These classes are identical to the ones *idl2java* generates (see Chapter 7). The difference is that *idl2java* starts with CORBA IDL input and then generates the IIOP stubs and skeletons. In contrast, *Java2IIOP* starts with Java interfaces and then generates the same IIOP stubs and skeletons. In this sense, Caffeine provides a "pure Java" alternative for creating *VisiBroker for Java* CORBA objects.

Java2idl: CORBA IDL Without Pain

The good news is that Caffeine creates CORBA IIOP objects directly from Java. You don't have to write a single line of CORBA IDL to create these objects. But, what if you want to tap into all the good stuff CORBA IDL provides—including self-describing objects, language-neutral interface repositories, and dynamic invocations? Again, Caffeine lets you have your cake and eat it, too. Hold on: You haven't seen the last miracle yet.

The other trick in the Caffeine arsenal is called *Java2IDL*. This precompiler parses your Java code looking for remote interfaces. It then generates CORBA IDL (.idl) files. You can load this IDL into a CORBA Interface Repository using VisiBroker's *IDL2ir* utility. The CORBA IDL serves as a language-neutral specification for your Java classes. If you do not use pass-by-value, your Caffeinated Java objects can be invoked from CORBA/IIOP clients written in a multiplicity of languages—including C, C++, Ada, Smalltalk, and COBOL (also see the next Details box). In contrast, RMI-over-RMP objects can only be called by other Java RMI objects. In addition, your Caffeinated Java clients can call multilingual server objects on a CORBA/IIOP ORB, but RMI objects can only call other RMI Java objects.

How Exactly Are CORBA Objects Passed-By-Value?

Details

You may recall that RMI lets you pass-by-value local objects that are *in* parameters in a remote method invocation. This means that the actual state of the object is copied in the call. In contrast, CORBA only supports pass-by-value for non-object types.

CORBA 2.0 lets you specify both object types and non-object types as *in, out*, and *inout* arguments of IDL-specified methods (or *operations*, in CORBA-speak). CORBA non-object types can be *basic* or *constructed* (see Figure 14-1). We cover CORBA types—including how they map to Java types—in Part 5.

CORBA copies the values of *in* parameters from the client to the server; it copies the values of *out* parameters from the server to the client—as part of a reply. Finally, it copies *inout* parameters in both directions—during the invocation and the reply. However, CORBA only passes an object's reference; it does not copy the state of the object. So the issue here is that CORBA does not currently copy-by-value the object's state; it only copies by value non-object types.

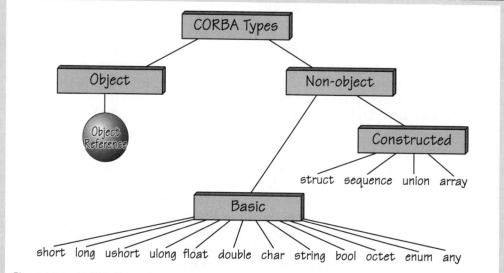

Figure 14-1. CORBA Types: Basic, Constructed, and Object References.

CORBA builds on the idea that all objects are remotable. Consequently, they can be accessed via their object reference. So you just pass object references in a call, not the object itself. If you create your remote applications starting from CORBA IDL, you won't have any problems. IDL won't let you pass objects by value. However, if you use Caffeine, you face the following problem: Java interfaces can define method invocations that include parameters that reference local objects. These references to local Java objects are only useful within a single virtual machine. So the ORB must copy these objects across Java virtual machines.

What is the solution to this problem? Here are your three options: First, you can refrain from passing local objects as parameters in remote Java invocations. If you must pass an object, make it remotable. Second, you can wait for Caffeine to implement the OMG's new *Objects-by-Value* standard for objects. In mid-1996, the OMG did issue such an RFP—it's called ORBOS RFP2 (see Part 5). Your third option is to use *VisiBroker for Java* right now. This ORB lets you pass objects by value using a non-standard extension to IIOP; it is the basis for the new OMG standard, but with modifications.

How does VisiBroker pass objects by value without breaking IIOP? It does this using something called *extensible structs*, which are upwardly-compatible extensions of CORBA *structs* (or structures); the new standard calls them *value* types. You can use these structs to pass objects by value with all CORBA language mappings, not just Java. In theory, you should be able to pass an object's state across languages such as OO-COBOL, C++, Smalltalk, and Java.

If you really must know, an extensible struct adds the following functions to an ordinary CORBA struct: 1) support for arbitrary recursive definitions that let you pass graphs of objects, 2) the use of nested encodings, and 3) an outer encoding that can represent the extensible struct as an opaque sequence of octets—this makes the struct transportable on IIOP ORBs that are not struct-aware.

In plain English, an extensible struct is simply a way to flatten the state of an object and all its parent objects. The flattened object can then be transported on any IIOP ORB. VisiBroker for Java uses these structs to flatten a Java object by writing to the extensible struct all the fields of an object—from the first field of the base class to the last field of the most derived class. These fields are stored using normal IIOP encodings. The sender marshals the struct; the receiver must unmarshal it and reconstruct the state of the object field-by-field. VisiBroker stubs and skeletons know exactly how to marshal and unmarshal these extensible structs. It's all done transparently. Note that both the Visigenic implementation and the new standard use a single-inheritance graph. This is good for Java, but it may not be good for C++. ❏

The Caffeine Development Process

Figure 14-2 shows the steps you must follow to create your Caffeine client and server classes, and then run them. Let's go through these steps one-by-one and see what's involved:

1. ***Define a remote interface***. Your server object must declare its services via a remote Java interface. It does this by extending **org.omg.CORBA.Object**. Each method in a remote interface must *throw* either a CORBA system or user exception.

2. ***Optionally, generate CORBA IDL.*** Run your Java interfaces through *Java2IDL* to generate CORBA IDL. You can also run your Caffeine clients and servers without CORBA IDL.

3. ***Compile your interface.*** You must compile your interface using *javac*.

4. ***Create the IIOP stubs and skeletons***. Run the Caffeine *Java2IIOP* compiler (or postprocessor) against the (.class) files to generate client stubs and server skeletons for your remote classes. The stubs provide IIOP proxies for your server objects. They marshal remote calls and send them to the server. The server skeleton (the **_XXXImplBase**) receives the remote call, unmarshals the parameters, and then calls your implementation class. The *Java2IIOP* compiler also creates Helper and Holder classes for your interface.

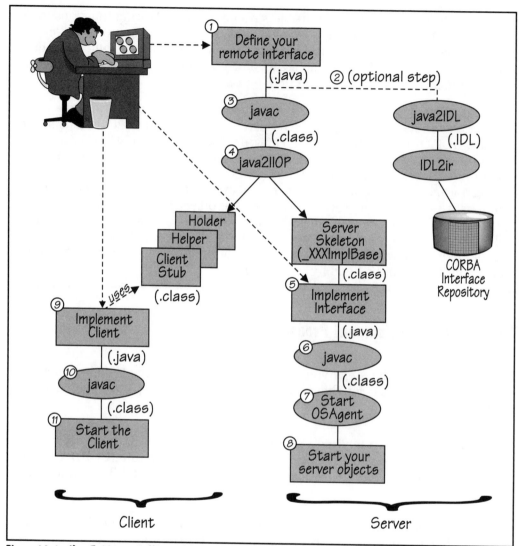

Figure 14-2. How To Write a Caffeinated Client and Server Application.

5. ***Implement the remote interface***. You must provide a Java server class that implements the interface you published to the outside world. You must derive this class from the **_XXXImplBase** class.

6. ***Compile your server class***. You must compile your server class using *javac*.

7. ***Start the VisiBroker Naming Service***. Start *OSAgent*. You can also use Caffeine's URL-based Naming Service. (Note that Netscape does not use OSAgent.)

8. **Start your server objects**. You must load your server classes and then create instances of remote objects.

9. **Write your client code**. The client consists mostly of ordinary Java code. You use a Naming Service to locate a remote object. You then invoke its methods via a stub that serves as a proxy for the remote object. These stubs are also generated by *Java2IIOP*.

10. **Compile the client code**. You do this using *javac*.

11. **Start the client**. You must load the client classes and their stubs.

You can see that Caffeine follows a very RMI-like development process. You develop in Java, and then use CORBA/IIOP as your ORB. If you're a Java developer, you get the best of the two worlds. CORBA developers may prefer to start with IDL.

The Caffeine URL Name Service

You can use a variety of Naming Services with Caffeine. Visigenic offers three services: OSAgents (or SmartAgents), CORBA COS Naming Service, and a URL-based name service. In addition, Netscape provides its own version of the URL Name Service. It is built on top of Netscape's own implementation of the CORBA COS Naming Service. Consequently, it does not require the Visigenic *OSAgent* engine. In this section, we cover the Netscape version of the URL-based naming scheme; it is part of *Enterprise Server 3.0c* with the WAI patch (or later).

What Is WAI and WAS?

Details

WAI—which stands for *Web Application Interface (WAI)*—lets you write server-side application extensions to *Enterprise Server 3.X*. WAI is based on CORBA; it is Netscape's primary API to extend *Enterprise Server 3.X* functionality. A *Web Application Server (WAS)* is a WAI application that you write using either Java or C++. It's like a CORBA Servlet. ❑

You can use the Netscape URL-based Naming Service to bind and resolve CORBA object references to URLs. The Netscape URL Name Server can be accessed by applications written in Java, JavaScript, or C++. These applications can be CORBA clients—running in either browsers or standalone mode—or CORBA servers. The runtimes are available on both the *Communicator* and *Enterprise Server 3.X*.

The API to the URL-based Naming Service is provided by the Netscape-defined **netscape.WAI.Naming** class (see Figure 14-3).

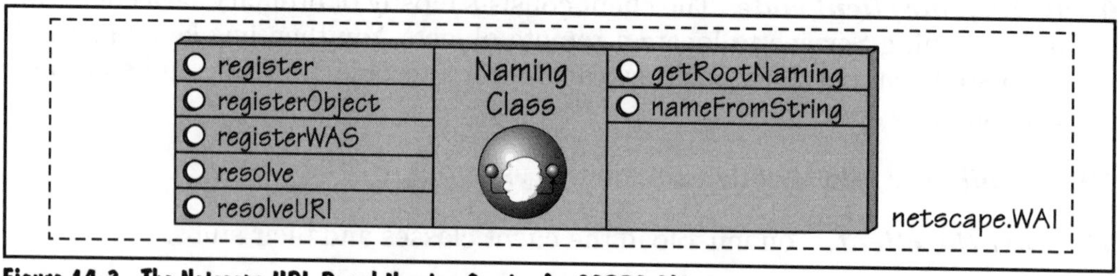

○ register	Naming	○ getRootNaming
○ registerObject	Class	○ nameFromString
○ registerWAS		
○ resolve		
○ resolveURI		netscape.WAI

Figure 14-3. The Netscape URL-Based Naming Service for CORBA Objects.

You invoke *register, registerObject,* or *registerWAS* to associate a CORBA object with a URL string. These methods help you create different URL naming structures. For example, *register* automatically inserts a */NameService* string between the host and the path/object name; *registerWAS* introduces an extra */WAS* subdirectory. Ordinary CORBA objects map to URLs with the following structure:

```
http://hostAndPort/NameService/Name
```

WAI objects must support an extra subdirectory:

```
http://hostAndPort/NameService/WAS/Name
```

You invoke *resolve* and *resolveURI* to obtain the CORBA object reference associated with this URL. The *resolve* call automatically inserts a */NameService* string between the host and the path/object name. In contrast, with *resolveURI*, you must explicitly put the */NameService* in your URL string.

The *getRootNaming* method returns the CORBA root **NamingContext** object. Remember, Netscape's URL naming is built on top of the CORBA Naming Service. So you can use this call to get to the underlying CORBA service. You can create a CORBA **Name** structure from a string by invoking *nameFromString*; you must pass it a string as well as a separator character. Here's the more detailed class description:

Listing 14-1. The Java netscape.WAI.Naming Class.

```
public class netscape.WAI.Naming
{
   public static void register(String url,
                               org.omg.CORBA.Object obj);
```

```
public static boolean registerObject(String hostAndPort,
                                     String uri,
                                     org.omg.CORBA.Object obj);
public static boolean registerWAS(String hostAndPort,
                                  String objectName,
                                  org.omg.CORBA.Object obj);
public static org.omg.CORBA.Object resolve(String url);
public static org.omg.CORBA.Object resolveURI(String protocol,
                                              String host,
                                              int port,
                                              String uri);
public static CosNaming.NamingContext getRootNaming(String host,
                                                    int port);
public static CosNaming.NameHolder nameFromString(String s,
                                                  String sepchar);
}
```

A URL-Naming Scenario

Figure 14-4 shows the client and server sides of a URL-naming scenario. Let's walk through the steps:

1. **_The server gives URL names to its objects._** The server invokes _register_ for every object reference it wants to associate with a URL name. For each object, the server must pass a URL string and an object reference. Here's a code example:

```
// Create CORBA Object
HelloImpl hi = new HelloImpl("Howdy");

// Register the URL of this object
netscape.WAI.Naming.register("http://mikelee:80/Howdy", hi);
```

2. **_The client binds to the URL._** The client invokes _resolve_ on the Name Server and passes it the URL of the remote object. The method returns the object reference associated with this URL. You must then typecast the generic CORBA object that is returned to its interface type. Here's a code example:

```
// Find the CORBA object ref for this URL
String url = "http://mikelee/NameService/Howdy";

// Resolve object
org.omg.CORBA.Object o =netscape.WAI.Naming.resolve( url );
```

```
// Typecast it to a Hello Type
Hello hi = HelloHelper.narrow(o);
```

3. ***Invoke methods on the server object.*** It's business as usual. The client invokes methods on the remote server object via its local proxy stub.

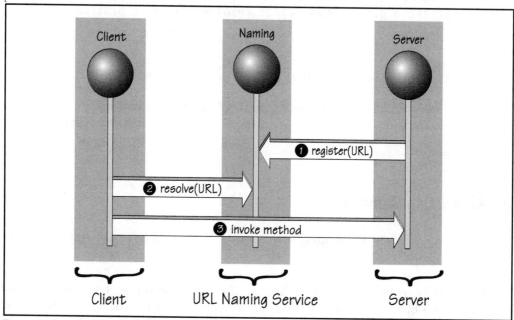

Figure 14-4. A URL Naming Scenario.

As you can see, the Netscape URL-based Naming Service provides a layer on top of the regular CORBA Naming Service. Instead of dealing with CORBA Naming Contexts and generic data structures, you use URL strings. The Service then translates these URLs into CORBA name bindings and contexts. These bindings are stored in the Netscape Name Server's database.

You may remember from Chapter 7 that the OMG is currently working on an *Interoperable Naming Service*; it was proposed by IBM, SunSoft, Netscape, Oracle, and Visigenic (see OMG Document *orbos/97-06-03*). One of the key elements in this new service is a URL-based naming system on top of the CORBA Naming Service. The Netscape URL-based Naming Service may become this standard (also see the next Briefing).[1]

---

[1] For more information on Netscape's URL-based naming, see Mike Lee's excellent technote at: *http://developer.netscape.com/library/technote/components/corba/naming.htm.*

The VisiBroker URL Naming Service

Details

Visigenic also provides a URL-based Naming Service; it's part of the Caffeine **URLNaming** package. The functions in this package are very similar to the Netscape service. However, there are two differences. First, VisiBroker uses different API semantics: *register_URL* instead of *register*; *locate_URL* instead of *resolve*. Second, the implementation is not very scalable. VisiBroker uses an HTTP server for its naming database. It first creates a file with the URL name on an HTTP server. Then it writes to the file the "stringified" IOR for a particular object reference. This practice is very resource intensive; it costs you one file per object URL on the HTTP server. Consequently, it doesn't scale well. In contrast, Netscape stores the URLs in a regular database. So it's a more scalable solution. ❑

THE CAFFEINATED COUNT

The good news is that the URL-Naming Service is the only new interface Caffeine introduces. So we can jump right in and write some code. Caffeine is just another way to develop CORBA code. Yes, the Caffeine Count is almost a carbon copy of the code we developed in Chapter 7. There are some minor differences that we will point out as we walk through the code.

The Caffeinated Count Client

The client program consists of a single Java class—**CountCaffeineClient**. This class provides a *main* method that performs the following functions: 1) initializes the ORB, 2) locates and then obtains a reference to a Count server object, 3) invokes the *setSum* method to reset the remote Sum attribute, 4) calculates the start time, 5) invokes the *increment* method 1000 times, 6) calculates the elapsed time, and 7) displays the average Caffeinated Ping performance.

First, notice that we're using a URL-based naming scheme to locate a reference to the remote object. Second, notice that we invoke the *setSum* method instead of setting an attribute. Why? Because you can't automatically declare accessor functions using Java interfaces. They don't support the equivalent of a CORBA attribute. So, you must define your own get and set accessor methods for all the instance variables you want to expose. In this case, Java programmers must do more work than their CORBA counterparts. But it allows Caffeine to remain true to the Java programming model. Remember, the idea is not to surprise Java programmers with new CORBA constructs.

Listing 14-2. CountCaffeineClient: The Caffeine Count Client.

```java
// CountCaffeineClient.java  Static Client, VisiBroker for Java

class CountCaffeineClient
{ public static void main(String args[])
  { try
    { // Initialize the ORB
      System.out.println("Initializing the ORB");
      org.omg.CORBA.ORB orb = org.omg.CORBA.ORB.init(args, null);

      // resolve URL to get Count object reference
      System.out.println("Resolving the CountCaffeine Name");
      org.omg.CORBA.Object obj =  netscape.WAI.Naming.resolve(
              "http://www.corbajava.engr.sjsu.edu/CountCaffeine");
      CounterCaffeine.CountCaffeine counter =
              CounterCaffeine.CountCaffeineHelper.narrow(obj);

      // Set sum to initial value of 0
      System.out.println("Setting sum to 0");
      counter.setSum((int)0);

      // Calculate Start time
      long startTime = System.currentTimeMillis();

      // Increment 1000 times
      System.out.println("Incrementing");
      for (int i = 0 ; i < 1000 ; i++ )
      { counter.increment();
      }

      // Calculate stop time; print out statistics
      long stopTime = System.currentTimeMillis();
      System.out.println("Avg Ping = " + ((stopTime - startTime)/1000f)
                  + " msecs");
      System.out.println("Sum = " + counter.getSum());
    } catch(org.omg.CORBA.SystemException e)
    { System.err.println("System Exception");
      System.err.println(e);
    }
  }
}
```

The Caffeinated Count Server

The server-side of the Caffeine Count consists of one Java interface and two classes. The **CountCaffeineImpl** class implements the **CountCaffeine** remote interface. The **CountCaffeineServer** class provides a *main* method that initializes the server and then instantiates a single **CountCaffeineImpl** object. Here's the code:

Listing 14-3. The CountCaffeine Interface.

```
package CounterCaffeine;
public interface CountCaffeine extends org.omg.CORBA.Object
{
  public int  getSum();
  public void setSum(int val);
  public int  increment();
}
```

Listing 14-4. The CountCaffeineImpl Class.

```
// CountCaffeineImpl.java: The CountCaffeine Implementation
class CountCaffeineImpl extends CounterCaffeine._CountCaffeineImplBase
{
  private int sum;

  CountCaffeineImpl(String name)
  { super(name);
    System.out.println("CountCaffeine Object Created");
    sum = 0;
  }

  public  int getSum()
  { return sum;
  }

  public  void setSum(int val)
  { sum = val;
  }

  public int increment()
  { sum++;
    return sum;
  }
}
```

Listing 14-5. The CountCaffeineServer Class.

```java
// CountCaffeineServer.java
import netscape.WAI.Naming;

class CountCaffeineServer
{ static public void main(String[] args)
  { try
    { // Initialize the ORB
      org.omg.CORBA.ORB orb = org.omg.CORBA.ORB.init(args, null);

      // Create the CountCaffeine object.
      CountCaffeineImpl count = new CountCaffeineImpl("My CountCaffeine");

      // Export to the ORB the newly created object
      orb.connect(count);

      // register the server with the Web Naming Service
      String host = java.net.InetAddress.getLocalHost().getHostName();
      String url = "http://" + host + "/CountCaffeine";
      System.out.println("URL = " + url);
      Naming.register(url, count);
      System.out.println("CountCaffeine registered");

      // wait forever for current thread to die
      Thread.currentThread().join();
    } catch(Exception e)
    { System.err.println(e);
    }
  }
}
```

As shown in the code, the **CountCaffeine** interface extends **org.omg.CORBA. Object** and defines the remote methods. The **CountCaffeineImpl** class implements these methods and extends the skeleton class, **_CountCaffeineImplBase**. In addition, **CountCaffeineImpl** implements a constructor that registers the newly created object's name with CORBA via its super.

The Java interface file is in a package called CounterCaffeine. The *Java2IIOP* compiler places all the classes it generates in this package—including the stub, skeleton, Helper, and Holder classes.

The **CountCaffeineServer** class provides the server's *main* method. It is very similar to its CORBA on-the-rocks counterpart from Chapter 7, except that it uses a URL-based naming scheme. The class provides the following functions: 1) initializes the ORB, 2) creates a new **CountCaffeineImpl** object, 3) connects to the ORB, 4) invokes *register* to associate the IOR of the **Count** object with a URL-based name, and 5) waits for requests.

The code is almost a carbon copy of the *main* from Chapter 7, except for URL-naming. Caffeine also lets you use the naming scheme from Chapter 7. But, we wanted to show you this new URL-Naming Service in action. This completes the code for the Caffeine client and server sides.

COMPILE THE CLIENT/SERVER PROGRAM

We're now ready to compile the CORBA Caffeine client/server program. Make sure you have installed VisiBroker for Java 3.0, the Symantec Visual Café compiler, and the Java JDK. You also need to have Netscape Enterprise Server 3.0c or later installed, and you must include the *nisb.zip* file in your CLASSPATH (see the instructions on the CD-ROM for details).

To compile the Java interface, go to the appropriate directory and enter the following command at the prompt:

```
prompt> javac CounterCaffeine\CountCaffeine.java
```

Next, you must generate the stubs and skeletons using *Java2IIOP*. To do this enter the following command at the prompt:

```
prompt> java2iiop CounterCaffeine\CountCaffeine -no_comments
```

You can optionally generate CORBA IDL. To do this, enter the following command at the prompt:

```
prompt> java2idl CounterCaffeine\CountCaffeine >CountCaffeine.idl
```

Next, you must compile the code for the client and server. To do this, run the make file we provide in the subdirectory. Or, enter the following commands at the prompt:

```
prompt> javac -d \CorbaJavaBook.2e\classes CountCaffeineClient.java
prompt> javac -d \CorbaJavaBook.2e\classes CountCaffeineServer.java
prompt> javac -d \CorbaJavaBook.2e\classes CountCaffeineImpl.java
```

The -d option tells the compiler to put the (.class) files it creates into the directory we specify, in this case, the *CorbaJavaBook.2e**classes* subdirectory.

If all goes well, you should have some compiled Java code—including a stub and skeleton—that you can now run.

RUN THE CLIENT/SERVER PROGRAMS

To run the Caffeine client/server programs, you must have Enterprise Server 3.0 running, and your server program must have the authority to make updates to Web Naming (again, see the CD-ROM for details). From this point, running your Caffeinated Count is similar to running the static Count program of Chapter 4.

Next, you must start the server. To run the server program, enter the following command at the prompt:

prompt> `start java CountCaffeineServer`

Now you can finally start the client. Enter the following command at the prompt:

prompt> `java CountCaffeineClient`

You should see a screen output that looks like this:

```
Initializing the ORB
Resolving the CountCaffeine Name
Setting sum to 0
Incrementing
Avg Ping = 3.612 msecs
Sum = 1000
```

LOOKING AT SOME TEST RESULTS

We run this client/server program in different situations to get a reading on the performance of Caffeinated CORBA method invocations. As usual, our client performs 1000 method invocations. The tests measure the average response time of Caffeinated CORBA Pings. We first run the client and server programs in the same machine—a 120-MHz Pentium running NT 4.0. Then we run them across a 10 Mbit/s Ethernet LAN. Table 14-1 compares the average response times.

Table 14-1. Local Versus Remote CORBA Caffeine Static Invocations.

Local Caffeine Count (interprocess, same machine)	Remote Caffeine Count (interprocess, over 10 Mbit/s Ethernet)
4.0 msecs	3.6 msecs

The numbers show that Caffeine performs the same across the network and on the same machine. The numbers also show that Caffeine's performance is equivalent to the CORBA on-the-rocks performance numbers from Chapter 7. So Caffeine does not introduce any performance penalties. But, make sure to run the programs and see for yourself. You may find that the numbers deviate by 10% in either direction, even with the same setup. However, the relative performance should remain more or less constant.

CONCLUSION

Caffeine provides three key innovations that make CORBA ORBs more friendly to Java developers: 1) it lets you pass local objects by value, 2) it lets you use Java both as an interface definition language and as an implementation language, and 3) it supports a persistent URL-based naming scheme. In contrast, the RMI URL Name Server is volatile; you lose all your name bindings when the Name Server process terminates.

Without turning this into a Soapbox, we believe that Caffeine provides an excellent pure Java solution on top of CORBA/IIOP today. It is the current CORBA alternative to *RMI-over-RMP*. Eventually, Caffeine and RMI will converge when they both implement the new CORBA *RMI-over-IIOP* semantics. In the next chapter, we cover the industry's other ORB—Microsoft's DCOM. You'll get to see how DCOM does Java.

Chapter 15

DCOM Versus CORBA/Java ORBs

If CORBA is the industry's leading standard for distributed objects, then Microsoft's *Distributed Component Object Model (DCOM)* is the de facto "other standard." What makes DCOM so important? Microsoft. Everything Microsoft is doing and will do is based on DCOM. Today, DCOM is shipping with NT 4.0. It will soon ship with every copy of Windows 98. DCOM is the foundation for Microsoft's Internet and component strategy. An *ActiveX* is simply a DCOM object. In early 1997, the *Microsoft Transaction Server (MTS)*—née *Viper*—shipped on the NT platform; it's a server-side component coordinator for transactional COM components. MTS appears to be the DCOM kingpin for the enterprise; it could eventually provide the scalability and robust intercomponent coordination that DCOM sorely lacks.

So what does this all have to do with Java client/server? Everything! DCOM is the ORB CORBA/Java must beat. In October 1996, Microsoft shipped its *Visual J++* development tool for Java. Among other things, Visual J++ includes Java language bindings for DCOM. Microsoft went the extra mile to make sure that Java is tightly integrated with DCOM—it is much more so than with Visual C++. In mid-1997, Microsoft shipped Visual J++ V1.1; it fixes many of the shortcomings of the first release. As you will see in this chapter, your Java clients can use DCOM to invoke remote Java objects as well as COM components written in other languages. With a bit of effort, you can even make an ActiveX look like a remote Java class.

This unusually tight integration between Java and DCOM leads us to believe that Microsoft is very serious about distributed Java objects. However, its solution is not based on the JavaSoft RMI/CORBA model. Instead, Microsoft is pushing DCOM as the alternative for its distributed Java. In the past, Microsoft treated DCOM as a binary interoperability standard; it did not provide good high-level language bindings. Visual J++ v1.1 provides very usable Java bindings for DCOM. In addition, the Microsoft Java Virtual Machine can make Java applets look like scriptable COM components. In the other direction, it makes all DCOM objects appear to a Java program as standard Java classes. For all these reasons, we believe that DCOM is the most serious contender to CORBA/Java.

This chapter starts out with a tutorial on DCOM. We introduce DCOM's distributed object model and explain how you use it to create client/server applications. We then go over the Visual J++ DCOM bindings for Java. We give you a step-by-step explanation of how to create Java client/server applications using DCOM. We then write the DCOM version of the Count client/server program. At the end of the chapter, we will have Ping numbers for DCOM. We will be able to compare the DCOM performance with CORBA IIOP. So once again, this is something to look forward to.

DCOM 101

This section presents a tutorial on DCOM. We will later show you how Visual J++ v1.1 simplifies some of DCOM's more tedious programming aspects. It makes DCOM more Java-like. If you come from a classical object background (or from the world of CORBA), be prepared for some culture shock. DCOM looks and feels like classical objects, yet it is very different. DCOM provides some of the same functions as CORBA, but it is done very differently. DCOM introduces its own terminology and object jargon. Because we've been so heavily absorbed with CORBA in this book, we first explain in this section the DCOM ORB in CORBA terms. Then we explore each function using DCOM terms. This should help ease you into the new culture. If you make it through this chapter, you may even start thinking like a DCOM/ActiveX programmer.

Looking at DCOM Through CORBA Eyes

Like CORBA, DCOM separates the object interface from its implementation and requires that all interfaces be declared using an Interface Definition Language (IDL). Microsoft's IDL is based on DCE—it is, of course, not CORBA-compliant. Microsoft also provides an IDL for OLE automation, called the *Object Definition Language (ODL)*. The ODL and IDL were merged for NT 4.0.

Unlike CORBA, DCOM does not support IDL-specified multiple inheritance. However, a DCOM component can support multiple interfaces and achieve reuse by encapsulating the interfaces of inner components and representing them to a client. So with DCOM, you achieve object reuse via containment and aggregation instead of inheritance.

A DCOM object is not an object in the OO sense. DCOM interfaces do not have state and cannot be instantiated to create a unique object—meaning an object that has a unique object reference. A DCOM interface is simply a group of related functions. DCOM clients are given a pointer to access the functions in an interface—this pointer is not related to state information. A DCOM client cannot reconnect to exactly the same object instance with the same state at a later time. It can only reconnect to an interface pointer of the same class. In other words, DCOM objects do not maintain state between connections (see next Briefing box). This can be a big problem in environments where you have faulty connections—for example, the Internet.

Like CORBA, DCOM provides both static and dynamic interfaces for method invocations. The *Type Library* is the DCOM version of an Interface Repository. DCOM precompilers can populate the Type Library with descriptions of ODL-defined objects—including their interfaces and parameters. Clients can query the Type Library to discover what interfaces an object supports and what parameters are needed to invoke a particular method. DCOM also provides a registry and some object look-up services that are similar to a CORBA Implementation Repository.

COM Monikers

Briefing

CORBA has persistent objects that also have persistent object references. DCOM has transient stateless objects that you can associate with a context via a *moniker*. A DCOM moniker is an object that acts as a persistent alias name for another object. Monikers can provide aliases for distributed filenames, database queries, a paragraph in a document, a range of spreadsheet cells, a remote computer, and so on. The intelligence of how to work with a particular name is encapsulated inside the name itself. The name becomes a "moniker object" that implements name-related interfaces. A moniker is really a patch for DCOM's lack of support for object identifiers. ❏

DCOM Style Interfaces

A DCOM *interface* is a collection of function calls—also known as methods or member functions. Like its CORBA equivalent, a DCOM interface serves as a client/server contract. It defines functions independently from their implementation. DCOM clients interact with each other and with the system by calling interface member functions. Like CORBA, a DCOM interface is language-independent and can call functions across address spaces and networks. DCOM simply defines a binary interoperability specification for how to access its interfaces using pointers and remote proxies. Microsoft provides DCOM language bindings for all of its development environments—including Visual C++, Visual Basic, and Visual J++. Borland's Delphi provides DCOM bindings for Pascal.

A DCOM interface is defined as a low-level binary API based on a table of pointers. To access an interface, DCOM clients use pointers to an array of function pointers—also known as a *virtual table* (or *vtable*). The functions that are pointed to by the vtable are the server object's implementation methods (see Figure 15-1). Each DCOM object has one or more vtables that define the contract between the object implementation and its clients.

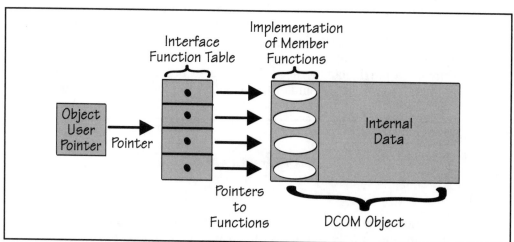

Figure 15-1. A DCOM Interface: The Pointer to a Vtable Representation.

The convention in DCOM (and OLE) is to represent an interface with a plug-in jack extending from an object (see Figure 15-2). These drawings are also called "bullet-and-stick" diagrams. Here, each bullet or plug-in jack represents an interface—meaning a group of semantically-related functions. It seems vtables make objects look rather intimidating. Plug-in jacks are more user-friendly; they use the metaphor of stereo system components that plug into each other.

An interface is, by convention, given a name starting with a capital "I"—for example, **IUnknown**. However, this name only has symbolic meaning (usually to a source-level programming tool). At run time, each interface is really known by its unique *Interface Identifier (IID)*. An IID is a DCOM-generated *globally-unique identifier (GUID)* for interfaces.

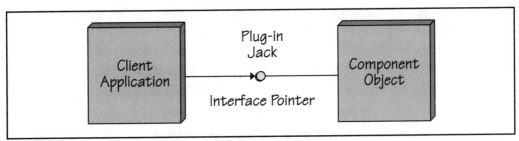

Figure 15-2. A DCOM Interface: The Plug-In Jack Representation.

GUIDs—pronounced goo-ids—are unique 128-bit IDs you generate by calling the DCOM API function *CoCreateGuid*. This function executes an algorithm specified by the OSF DCE. If you must really know, this algorithm calculates a globally unique number using the current date and time, a network card ID, and a high-frequency counter. There's almost no chance for this algorithm to create duplicate GUIDs. The IID allows a client to unambiguously ask an object if it supports the interface. Clients ask questions using a *QueryInterface* function that all objects support through a ubiquitous interface called **IUnknown** (we cover this interface in a later section). Interfaces are meant to be small contracts that are independent of each other—they're the smallest contractual unit in DCOM.

So, What's a DCOM Object?

A DCOM object—also known as an *ActiveX* object—is a component that supports one or more interfaces, as defined by that object's class. A DCOM interface refers to a predefined group of related functions. A DCOM class implements one or more interfaces and is identified by a unique 128-bit *Class ID (CLSID)*. A DCOM object is a run-time instantiation of a class. A particular object will provide implementations of the functions for all the interfaces its class supports. For convenience, the word "object" is used to refer to both an object class and an individual instantiation of a class.

Clients always deal with DCOM objects through interface pointers; they never directly access the object itself. Note that an interface is not an object in the classical sense. DCOM objects do not support unique object IDs (or CORBA-like persistent object references). You cannot ask to be connected to a particular DCOM object (also see the next Details box).

All DCOM objects must implement the **IUnknown** interface through which the client can control the lifetime of an object. Clients also use it for interface negotiations—a client can ask an object what interfaces it supports and obtain pointers to them. To use the stereo system analogy, the client must have the right kind of plug to fit into an interface jack so that it can talk to an object through that particular interface. By convention, **IUnknown** is shown as a plug-in jack that extends from the top of an object (see Figure 15-3).

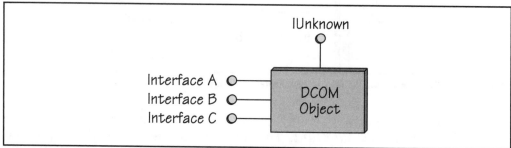

Figure 15-3. A DCOM Object Implements All the Interfaces Its Class Supports.

What? An Object With No ID?

Details

In a classical object system—like CORBA—each instantiated object has a unique identification (ID) that's a fundamental property of an object. The object ID—called an *object reference* in CORBA—is used by naming and trading services to locate a unique object. The ID is also used to track an object throughout its lifetime. Persistent services use it to save an object's state so that it can be reactivated at a later time. As we explain in Part 5, the object reference of a persistent CORBA object encapsulates an identifier (or unique key); it can be used to re-load the state of an object when it is reactivated. CORBA provides a set of APIs for converting an object ID to a string and vice versa. This lets you pass object IDs to other objects. Clients use the object ID to connect to a particular object. So, the concept of a unique object ID is fundamental to the classical object model.

In contrast, DCOM does not support the concept of an object ID. With DCOM, clients obtain a pointer to an interface and not a pointer to an object with state. DCOM clients cannot reconnect to that exact same object instance with the same state at a later time. Instead, clients have transient pointers to particular interfaces of an object. DCOM objects with the same set of interfaces and the same implementations for each are often loosely called instances of the same class. However, all access to the instances of the class by clients will only be through these transient interfaces; clients know nothing about an object other than that it supports certain interfaces. As a result, object instances play a much less significant role in DCOM than they do in classical object systems. ❏

What's a DCOM Server?

A DCOM *server* is a piece of code—a DLL, an EXE, or a Java class—that houses one or more object classes each with its own CLSID. When a client asks for an object of a given CLSID, DCOM loads the server code and asks it to create an object of that class. The server must provide a *class factory* for creating a new object. Once an object is created, a pointer to its primary interface is returned to the client. The server is not the object itself. The word "server" in DCOM is used to emphasize the serving agent. The phrase "server object" is used specifically to identify an object that is implemented in a server.

So a DCOM server provides the necessary structure around an object to make it available to clients (see Figure 15-4). More specifically a DCOM server must:

- **Implement a class factory interface**. The server must implement a class factory with the **IClassFactory** interface for each supported CLSID. The class factory creates instances of a class. If a class supports licensing, then it must implement the **IClassFactory2** interface. This interface creates an object only if a valid license file is present or a license key is provided.

- **Register the classes it supports**. The server must register a CLSID for each class it supports with the *NT Registry*. For each CLSID, it must create one or more entries that provide the pathname to the server DLL or EXE (or to both). This information is recorded using the NT Registry APIs. Typically, the classes are registered at installation time.

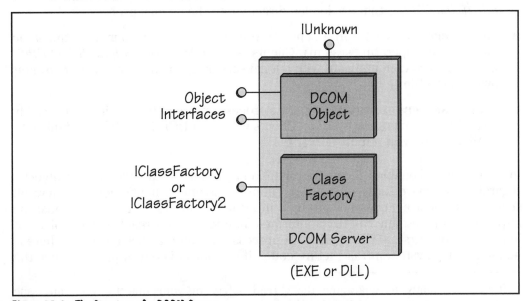

Figure 15-4. The Structure of a DCOM Server.

- **Initialize the DCOM library.** The server issues a call to the DCOM API *CoInitialize* to initialize DCOM.[1] The DCOM library provides run-time services and APIs. These are functions with the *Co* prefix, which stands for component.

- **Verify that the library is of a compatible version.** The server does this by calling the API *CoBuildVersion*.

- **Provide an unloading mechanism.** The server must provide a way to terminate itself when there are no active clients for its objects.

- **Uninitialize the DCOM library.** The server calls the DCOM API *CoUninitialize* when it is no longer in use.

The implementation of the server—including registration, the class factory, and the unloading mechanism—will differ depending on whether the server is packaged as a DLL, EXE, or (.class) file.

DCOM Local/Remote Transparency

You can implement a DCOM server in one of many flavors. The actual flavor depends on the structure of the code module and its relationship to the client processes that will be using it. DCOM defines three flavors of servers (see Figure 15-5):

- **In-process servers** execute in the same process space as their clients. Under Microsoft Windows and Windows NT, these are implemented as *Dynamic Link Libraries (DLLs)* that are loaded directly into the client's process.

- **Local servers** execute in a separate process from their clients on the same machine (and operating system). Clients use DCOM's *Lightweight RPC (LRPC)* mechanism to communicate with a local server. Local servers execute in their own (.EXE) file.

- **Remote servers** execute in a separate process on a remote machine and possibly on a different operating system. Clients will use a DCE-like RPC mechanism to communicate with remote servers.

In theory, DCOM enables clients to transparently communicate with server objects, regardless of where these objects are running. From a client's point of view, all server objects are accessed through interface pointers. A pointer must be in-process. In fact, any call to an interface function always reaches some piece of in-process code first. If the object is in-process, the call reaches it directly; there is no intervening system-infrastructure code. If the object is out-of-process, then the

---

[1] If you are ready to guarantee the thread safety of your objects, you can issue *CoInitializeEx*, instead of *CoInitialize*.

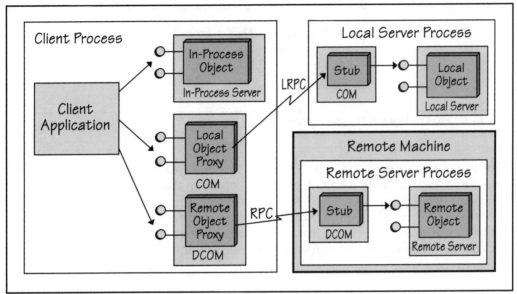

Figure 15-5. DCOM's Client/Server Boundaries.

call first reaches what is called a *proxy* object provided by DCOM itself. This object generates the appropriate remote procedure call to the other process or the other machine. The DCOM element that locates servers and gets involved with RPC invocations between clients and servers is called the *Service Control Manager (SCM)*—better known as "Scum."

From a server's point of view, all calls to an object's interface functions are made through a pointer to that interface. Again, a pointer only has context in a single process, so the caller must always be some piece of in-process code. If the object is in-process, the caller is the client itself. Otherwise, the caller is a *stub object* provided by DCOM that picks up the remote procedure call from the *proxy* in the client process and turns it into an interface call to the server object. Clients and servers always communicate using some in-process or local code (again, see Figure 15-5). The DCOM proxy and stub mechanism is very similar to the way CORBA implements local/remote transparency using static stubs on the client side and interface skeletons on the server side.

The Ubiquitous IUnknown Interface

The **IUnknown** interface is the heart of DCOM. It is used for run-time interface negotiations, life cycle management, and aggregation. Every DCOM interface must implement the three **IUnknown** member functions: *QueryInterface*, *AddRef*, and *Release* (see Figure 15-6).

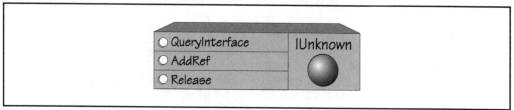

Figure 15-6. DCOM's Ubiquitous IUnknown Interface.

IUnknown supports interface negotiations through *QueryInterface*. And it supports the life cycle management of an interface instance through *AddRef* and *Release*. Because all DCOM interfaces derive from **IUnknown**, you can call *QueryInterface, AddRef*, and *Release* using any interface pointer. In other words, **IUnknown** is a base interface from which all other interfaces inherit these three functions and implement them in a polymorphic manner.

Interface Negotiations Using QueryInterface

When a client initially gains access to a DCOM object, by whatever means, it is given one—and only one—interface pointer in return. The client obtains the rest of the interfaces by calling *QueryInterface*, which forms the basis for interface negotiations. The *QueryInterface* function allows clients to discover at run time whether an interface—specified by an IID—is supported by an object. If the object supports this interface, the function returns the appropriate interface pointer to the client. After the client obtains an interface pointer, DCOM gets out of the way and lets the client directly interact with the server by invoking member functions of its interface.

So the unit of client/server negotiation is an interface, not an individual function. All clients must first obtain a pointer to an interface before they can interact with an object's services. The object can refuse service to a client by not returning a pointer. The *QueryInterface* function returns a failure code if the interface is not supported or if the server refuses to service a client.

QueryInterface supports the capability of returning pointers to the other interfaces a DCOM object supports, which is key to making aggregation work. DCOM requires that a *QueryInterface* call for a specific interface always return the same actual pointer value, no matter through which interface derived from **IUnknown** it is called. As a result, a client can perform an identity test to determine whether two pointers point to the same interface.

QueryInterface also lets components add new interfaces and lets clients discover them. This allows new interfaces to be added to an object's class as its function evolves. A client can ask an object: "Do you support Interface X?" An old object can answer the question with a "No," while a newer object can answer "Yes." This test allows clients to invoke the function only if an object supports it. In this manner, the client maintains compatibility with objects written before and after Interface X was available. This run-time negotiation is the cornerstone of DCOM's version control.

Life Cycle Management With Reference Counts

Briefing

In non-distributed object systems, the life cycle of objects—meaning the issues surrounding the creation and deletion of objects—is handled implicitly by the language or explicitly by application programmers. In a single program, there's always something—for example, the startup and shutdown code of a language runtime—that knows when objects must be created and when they should be deleted.

However, in distributed object systems, it is no longer true that someone or something always knows how to deal with the life cycle of objects. Object creation is still relatively easy—an object is created whenever a client with the right privileges requests it. But object deletion is another story: How do you know when an object is no longer needed? Even when the original client is done with the object, it can't simply shut the object down because it probably has passed a reference to the object to some other client in the system. So who's in charge of garbage-collection in a distributed object system?

There are different approaches for dealing with the distributed object garbage-collection issue. The first approach is to ignore garbage collection and rely on the operating system to kill objects during system shutdown. This approach may be acceptable to clients, but it is not workable on servers. The second approach is to let the ORB keep track of outstanding connections. This approach may work, especially if it is combined with ORB-mediated object caching and load-balancing. The third approach is to let an object keep track of its usage using *reference counts*; the clients must cooperate by telling an object when they are using it and when they are done. This solution is based on having all objects maintain reference counts and having objects delete themselves when they are no longer in-use. In a strange twist, the Java version of DCOM uses the first approach—it depends on Java for its garbage collection. The C++ version of DCOM uses the third approach. CORBA ORBs use the second approach.

The C++ version of DCOM makes reference counting ubiquitous by adding that function to **IUnknown** through the member functions *AddRef* and *Release*. An interface's *AddRef* function is called when a client requests a pointer to that interface or passes a reference to it. An interface's *Release* function is called when the client no longer uses that interface. The internal implementation of the interface must increment the reference count every time *AddRef* is called and decrement it every time *Release* is called. C++ DCOM implementations are required to support at least a 32-bit counter to keep track of reference counts.

The reference-counting mechanism equates the lifetime of an object with references to it. It makes the following existential statement: "I'm being used; therefore, I exist." On the positive side, reference counting allows independently developed components to obtain and release access to a single object without having to coordinate with one another on life cycle management issues. On the negative side, it places an extra burden on every object implementation and assumes that clients are well-behaved—they must play by the rules. Reference counting is a cooperative client/server effort. ❏

IClassFactory2: Object Creation and Licensing

Every DCOM class must implement a class factory that a DCOM server can invoke to create instances of that class. A DCOM class factory is an implementation of either the **IClassFactory** or **IClassFactory2** interfaces. **IClassFactory2** is an extension of **IClassFactory** that enforces licensing at object creation time (see Figure 15-7). It was introduced in late 1994 with OLE custom controls to enforce the licensing of OCXs. In addition to the ubiquitous **IUnknown** functions, **IClassFactory2** provides two member functions of the old **IClassFactory** interface and three new member functions that enforce licensing. When a DCOM server is initially loaded, it must instantiate a class factory for each of its classes and register them with DCOM by invoking the *CoRegisterClassObject* API call.

Although the class factory is an interface, it is not the root interface of the component. Every instance of a class factory is associated with a single CLSID and exists strictly to facilitate the creation of an object of that CLSID. As shown in Figure 15-7, the **IClassFactory2** interface implements two functions for creating a new instance of a class: *CreateInstance* and *CreateInstanceLic*. These two functions are like the C++ *new* operator. They both create an uninitialized instance of the object associated with the class factory and return an interface pointer of a requested IID. The *LockServer* function allows a client to keep a server object resident in memory even when it is not being used by clients—it keeps the object from getting automatically unloaded from memory when its reference count reaches zero.

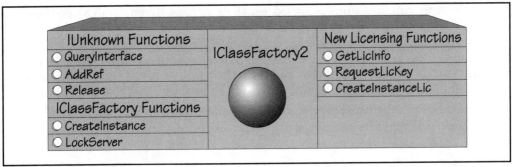

Figure 15-7. The IClassFactory2 Interface.

DCOM considers a machine to be fully licensed when a *license file* is installed on that machine. Otherwise, the client must supply a special *license key* when it instantiates the component. If the license key is not provided, the server will not instantiate the component. You can think of a license file as providing global permission to use a component on a machine, while the license key is a specific permission to use the component on another machine. License keys are used by applications that are assembled with third-party components. The development machine is fully licensed because we assume the components were purchased in the first place. The license key makes it possible to use these components on other machines. It's a piece of information that must be extracted from a component in the development environment and then provided at run time on the target machine.

The *GetLicInfo* function returns the type of licensing a component supports. It answers the questions: Is a license key required and, if so, is it available? The *RequestLicKey* function is used by a client to request a license key to use the component on a different machine. The client can use *CreateInstance* if a global license file is installed on a target machine. Otherwise, the client must invoke *CreateInstanceLic*, passing it the license key as one of its arguments. To repeat, a licensed component can only be created if a license key is provided by the client or if a global license file is available on the machine. The **IClassFactory2** implementation will validate the key or the license file before creating an instance of a component.

The DCOM licensing implementation is very primitive. The license file is simply a text file installed with the component itself, and a license key is, typically, the first line of that text file. There's no protection against forgeries, and there's no way to meter the use of licenses. In addition, it's a system management nightmare to keep track of license files for thousands of disparate components.

Note that in addition to licensing, Windows NT 4.0 lets you control access to CLSIDs using the NT Registry. You can configure the registry to: 1) disallow the launching of servers of a given CLSID based on the client's access token, 2) disallow client connections to running objects based on their access token, and 3) configure a given CLSID to always run as a specific user.

Here's how it works. You invoke *CoCreateInstance* with a CLSID. This results in a call to "scum," which verifies that you have the proper access rights for this class. Scum will impersonate you in a call to the NT Registry's *RegQueryValue* method; it will pass it your access rights. If the call succeeds, you will be able to instantiate an instance of this class.

A DCOM Object Creation Scenario

It's time to go over a scenario that shows how all these DCOM interfaces play together. We will assume that a class called **MyClass** was registered in the NT registry. This class supports a single interface called **IMyInterface** and is being serviced by a local server called *MyServer.exe*. The registry will contain an entry under the CLSID for **MyClass** that looks like: *LocalServer32 = c:\MyDir\MyServer.exe*. Our scenario starts right after DCOM finds MyServer.exe in the registry and loads it into memory. In the scenario, a client creates an instance of **MyClass** and obtains a pointer to **IMyInterface**. Let's walk through the steps (see Figure 15-8):

1. ***The client requests a pointer to the class factory.*** The client calls the DCOM API *CoGetClassObject* to obtain an **IClassFactory2** pointer for the **MyClass** CLSID.

2. ***The server instantiates a class factory and registers it.*** As soon as MyServer.exe is loaded, it must instantiate all its class factories and register them with DCOM. In this scenario, there's only one class: **MyClass**, which provides a factory with an **IClassFactory2** interface. The server instantiates the factory interface and passes DCOM a pointer to it by invoking the API *CoRegisterClassObject*. Now DCOM knows where to find the factory for that CLSID.

3. ***The client requests an instance of this object.*** The client calls the *CreateInstanceLic* function to create an instance of **MyClass** and passes it the IID for **IMyInterface** as well as a license key. Note that the client can also create an instance of an object by directly calling the DCOM API *CoCreateInstanceEx*. This new function—introduced with Windows NT 4.0—lets you pass an explicit remote host name; it also lets you receive more than one interface pointer to the newly created object. This cuts down on subsequent network traffic by eliminating the need for multiple *QueryInterface* calls to bind each interface.

4. ***The factory creates an instance of the class.*** The factory creates an instance of **MyClass** and returns to the client a pointer for the requested interface—in this case, it's **IMyInterface**.

5. ***The client interacts with the interface.*** The client can use its pointer to

IMyInterface to invoke whatever services this interface provides.

6. *The client releases IMyInterface.* The client invokes the *Release* function (derived from **IUnknown**) to decrement the reference count and release the pointer. This matches the *AddRef* count that was implicitly issued when the client obtained a pointer to **IMyInterface**.

7. *The client releases IClassFactory2.* The client invokes the *Release* function (derived from **IUnknown**) to decrement the reference count and release the pointer. This matches the *AddRef* count that was implicitly issued when the client obtained a pointer to **IClassFactory2**.

8. *The server is shut down.* During shutdown, the server must call the API *CoRevokeClassObject* to tell DCOM that the previously registered class factory is now out of service.

As you can see from the scenario, **IClassFactory2** eliminates the need for clients to know the exact name of the creation function for some type of component—the

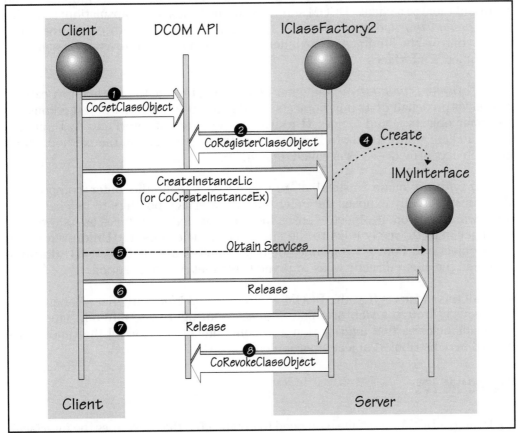

Figure 15-8. A DCOM Scenario: Creating an Instance of a Class.

client only needs to know a CLSID that can be retrieved from the registry. Also note that when clients create DCOM components, they're totally uninitialized—they have no persistent state. The client must help the component initialize its state by passing it a pointer to a storage unit. Finally, the scenario shows the client interacting directly with the class factory to initialize the component. Clients must interact directly with the class factory when dealing with a licensed component. But with non-licensed components, a client can use DCOM-provided wrapper functions like *CoCreateInstance* that isolate it from the class factory.

DCOM Style Inheritance: Aggregation and Containment

Unlike CORBA and Java, DCOM does not support multiple interface inheritance. However, a DCOM component can support multiple interfaces. By issuing *QueryInterface* calls, DCOM clients can determine at run time which group of interfaces a component supports. These two mechanisms allow developers to create outer components that encapsulate the services of inner components and represent them to a client. DCOM supports two methods of encapsulation: *containment/delegation* and *aggregation* (see Figure 15-9). In both cases, the outer object controls the lifetimes of the inner objects, and its **IUnknown** represents the inner object's interfaces.

In *containment/delegation*, the outer object must reissue the method invocations it receives on behalf of its inner objects. In Figure 15-9, the outer object A contains the inner objects B and C. A's **IUnknown** knows about interfaces A, B, and C. When a client wants to talk to B or C, the outer object calls on the methods these inner objects provide—this is called *delegation*.

In *aggregation* mode, instead of re-issuing each call, the outer component's **IUnknown** directly exposes the inner object's interface pointers to its clients. In other words, the outer object exposes the inner object's interfaces as its own. So the inner object directly talks to the client, but it delegates its **IUnknown** to the outer object. In Figure 15-9, inner objects B and C are part of A's **IUnknown**. However, the client directly talks to B and C without A's intervention.

What all this means is that the DCOM environment is inherently flat. "Inheritance" is achieved through a web of pointers that link or aggregate different interfaces. Microsoft believes that aggregation and containment provide all the reuse that's needed in a distributed object environment.

The DCOM IDL

To develop a DCOM interface, you need to create a file that describes the interface's methods and their arguments using DCOM's version of IDL. You must then run this

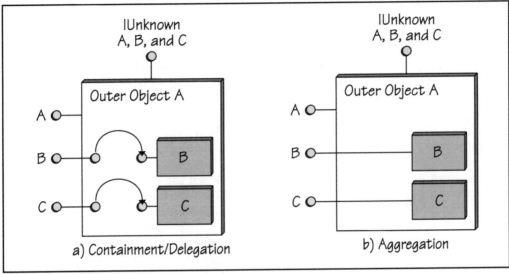

Figure 15-9. DCOM's Delegation Versus Aggregation.

file through the *Microsoft IDL (MIDL)* compiler to create the client proxies, the server stubs, and the code that marshals arguments between them.

The MIDL is more accurately a precompiler that turns text descriptions of an interface into code for both proxies and stubs. The MIDL compiler also creates header files that contain the interface definition. To finish the job, you must implement, compile, link, and register the server code.

DCOM's Dynamic Invocation Facilities

DCOM—like CORBA—provides dynamic invocation and metadata facilities. These facilities provide the foundation for OLE automation—now simply called *automation*. It allows client programs to dynamically invoke methods that manipulate the contents of scriptable objects. The DCOM *Type Library*, like the CORBA Interface Repository, allows clients to dynamically discover the methods and properties a DCOM automation server exposes. You must describe these interfaces using the DCOM *Object Definition Language (ODL)*. DCOM ODL is a now subset of the Microsoft IDL; you use it to define class metadata (also see the next Briefing box).

DCOM programmers must describe their automation objects—including their method names and parameter types, as well as object properties—using ODL. They can use either the *MIDL* or *MKTYPLIB* utilities to compile the ODL file into a type library. Also tools—like *Visual Basic* and *Visual J++*—can automatically emit type libraries.

Figure 15-10 shows how the DCOM automation pieces come together. An automation server is a DCOM object that implements a specific interface called **IDispatch**. This interface provides the late-binding mechanism through which an object exposes its functions—including its incoming and outgoing methods and properties. These late-bound functions are called *dispatch interfaces,* or more simply, *dispinterfaces.* A *property* is like a CORBA *attribute.* The server's interfaces, methods, and properties are maintained in the type libraries, which act as a run-time repository.

Automation controllers—meaning clients—can learn the names of the methods and properties an object supports using the **ITypeLib** interface. The type library, like the CORBA Interface Repository, lets you access this information without having to run the object. Finally, using the *IDispatch::Invoke* method, clients can create or obtain automation objects, get and set the properties they expose, and execute their methods.

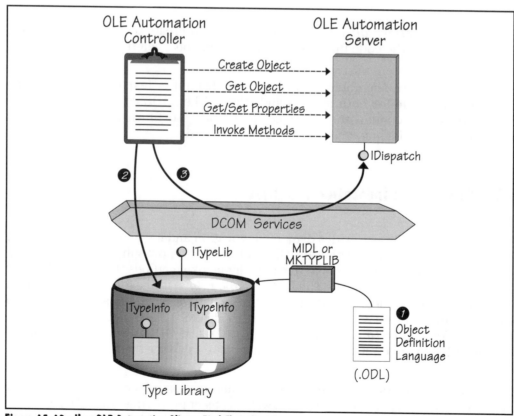

Figure 15-10. How OLE Automation Clients Find Their Servers.

What's a Dispinterface?

If you come from the world of CORBA, a *dispinterface* is the equivalent of a CORBA *dynamic skeleton interface*. The DCOM server decides at run time which method to invoke based on an identifier (the dispID) that it reads from the incoming message. In contrast, DCOM's static interfaces export their functions through vtable pointers that are compiled into the client source code. This means the client must be early-bound to a function based on its location in the vtable.

So how do clients invoke a particular dispinterface method or attribute? They do this by calling a single function—*IDispatch::Invoke*—and passing it a *dispatch identifier (dispID)* that uniquely identifies a method or property. How are these dispIDs generated? They're specified and generated using the DCOM ODL. Here's a snippet that should help you understand what we mean.

```
dispinterface Dog
   {
   properties:
   [id(0)] long Age;

   methods:
   [id(1)] long Bark;
   [id(2)] long Sit;
   [id(3)] long Run;
   };
```

As you can see, the *Age* property has a dispID of 0, the *Bark* method has a dispID of 1, and so on.

Only the *IDispatch::Invoke* method is compiled. The *invoke* method, at run time, uses the dispIDs to dispatch method calls and invoke gets or puts on properties. So, the server object must resolve at run time which method or property is invoked. In addition to the dispID, the *Invoke* method's arguments include a structure that defines the dispID method parameters and their types.

The IDispatch Interface

IDispatch provides mechanisms to access and retrieve information about an object's methods and properties as well as the *invoke* method (see Figure 15-11). In addition to the member functions inherited from **IUnknown**, you need to implement the following member functions within the class definition of each **IDispatch** object you expose:

■ *Invoke* maps an incoming dispID to a method call or a property access. Consequently, it lets you dynamically invoke the methods exposed by the object's dispinterface, and then access its properties.

■ *GetIDsOfNames* converts text names of properties and methods—including parameters—into a corresponding set of dispIDs, which may then be used on subsequent calls to *Invoke*.

■ *GetTypeInfoCount* returns whether there is type information available for this dispinterface.

■ *GetTypeInfo* retrieves the type information for this dispinterface. Type information is metadata that describes the interface.

As you can see, three of the four member functions of **IDispatch** are only there to help clients get the run-time information they need to issue the *Invoke* method.

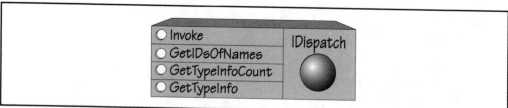

Figure 15-11. The IDispatch Member Functions.

 DCOM IDL Versus DCOM ODL

Briefing

If you come from the world of CORBA, you're used to running a single IDL file through a precompiler to generate language-specific bindings as well as run-time proxies (stubs) and skeletons. These are for marshaling and unmarshaling remote invocations and their parameters across address spaces. The CORBA IDL also produces metadata that goes into an *Interface Repository*. This metadata consists of language-independent descriptions of the method calls and their parameters.

In contrast to CORBA's single IDL, DCOM started out with two definition languages—*IDL* for generating remote stubs and proxies, and *ODL* for generating class metadata. Microsoft also provided two precompilers—*MIDL* for processing IDL, and *MKTYPLIB* for generating metadata. Because of its DCE heritage, the IDL syntax was C-like; MIDL turned C-like descriptions of an interface into C code for both proxies and stubs.

In contrast to IDL, ODL is more language-neutral. ODL also introduces a more general syntax for describing components. For example, you can use ODL to describe both static and dynamic interfaces and the overall structure of a DCOM class. MKTYPLIB turns these language-neutral class descriptions into type library (.TLB) files for your interfaces.

In September 1996, Microsoft declared ODL to be a subset of IDL; MKTYPLIB was also declared "dead." The newly released MIDL 3.0—bundled with VC++ and the Win32 SDK—can now process both (.IDL) and (.ODL) files. It even lets you embed ODL within IDL files. The MIDL treats ODL as a subset of IDL. So, you can now use the same precompiler to generate both metadata and proxy/stubs. How does MIDL handle local calls? You can use the *local* attribute to suppress the generation of proxy/stubs for non-remote calls.

So how does MIDL recognize the ODL within an IDL file? As you will see in the next section, the top-level element of the ODL syntax is the *library* statement (or library block). All ODL statements appear within a library block. In contrast, IDL lets you embed ODL-like libraries along with other IDL statements; the IDL statements can appear outside the scope of a library. When MIDL sees a library statement, it generates a type library in the same way that MKTYPLIB does. The statements found in the library block follow essentially the ODL syntax.

A DCOM IDL file consists of one or more interface definitions. Each interface consists of two parts: the *interface header* and the *interface body*. The interface header—delimited by brackets—contains information about the interface as a whole, such as its IID. The header also contains the keyword *object*, indicating that this interface is a DCOM interface, not a DCE interface. DCOM interfaces are derived from **IUnknown**. Here's an example of an IDL header and interface:

```
CODE = [
    object,
    uuid(7ACC12C3-C4BB-101A-BB6E-0000C09A6549),
    pointer_default(unique),
    oleautomation
]

interface IMyInterface : IUnknown
{
    import "unknwn.idl";
    HRESULT MyMethod(void);
}
```

The uuid attribute specifies the unique identifier for the interface. The *pointer_default* attribute specifies the default IDL type for all pointers. The *oleautomation* attribute indicates that an interface is compatible with OLE Automation. This means that the parameters and return types you specify for its member functions and attributes must be automation-compatible types (see Table 15-1).

The interface body contains declarations for data members, prototypes for all methods, and other information such as directives to the preprocessor. The *import* attribute allows an interface to reference constructs defined in other IDL files.

Because **IMyInterface** derives from **IUnknown**, the unknwn.idl file must be included. **IMyInterface** has only one method that takes no parameters; few interfaces will be this simple. With MIDL 3.0, all remote DCOM methods must return an *HRESULT*—this is a 32-bit error return value with several fields of encoded information.

Note that if an interface is derived from **IDispatch** or **IUnknown**, and it has the *oleautomation* attribute, it is automation-compatible. Every *dispinterface* is implicitly automation-compatible. Consequently, you must not use the *oleautomation* attribute on dispinterfaces. ❑

Table 15-1. The Automation-Compatible DCOM Types.

Type	Description
boolean	Unsigned char.
unsigned char	8-bit unsigned data item.
double	64-bit IEEE floating-point number.
float	32-bit IEEE floating-point number.
int	Integer whose size is system dependent.
long	32-bit signed integer.
short	16-bit signed integer.
BSTR	Length-prefixed string.
CY (or CURRENCY)	8-byte fixed-point number.
DATE	64-bit floating-point fractional number of days since December 30, 1899.
SCODE	Built-in error type.

Table 15-1. The Automation-Compatible DCOM Types. (Continued)	
Type	**Description**
enum	Signed integer whose size is system-dependent.
IDispatch *	Pointer to **IDispatch** interface.
IUnknown *	Pointer to **IUnknown** interface.

The DCOM ODL

As we said earlier, you must use DCOM ODL to generate metadata about the interfaces an object supports—including the automation dispinterfaces. The ODL is a normal text file that you can generate manually.

Figure 15-12 shows the main sections of an ODL file. Let's go over them:

- **Library** uniquely identifies and names an ODL. The library names a body of ODL—everything between the curly braces. An ODL is identified by the unique *type library* to which it belongs. A library has a name, unique global identifier (GUID), help context, and some defining attributes. The more interesting attributes include: *lcid*, the national language locale; *hidden*, meaning the library should never be displayed by a browsing tool; *restricted*, meaning the functions within the library can't be called; and *version*, which specifies a version number.

- **Importlib** brings in information from another type library (.TLB) file. To pull in automation types, servers with dispinterfaces must always import *stdole32.tlb*—an OLE-provided library.

- **Interfaces** define the signatures of the member functions that are part of a static vtable. Each function must have a name, return type, and a list of parameters. The list can be void or contain a sequence of *[attributes]* *<type>* *<name>* entries separated by a comma. The more interesting interface attributes include: *hidden*, meaning the interface should never be displayed by a browsing tool; *restricted*, meaning the member functions within that interface can't be invoked; and *dual*, meaning the interface is both static and dynamic. Interfaces can also have a GUID (also called the IID for Interface ID) and help context. The attributes on each function in the interface include: *propget* and *propput*, which indicates a get/put property function; *vararg*, which indicates the function can take a variable number of parameters; and *id(n)*, which assigns a dispID to the member. You can also denote a hidden function with a leading underscore—for example, *_Bark*. Finally, parameters themselves can each have attributes like *in*, *out*, and *optional*.

```
[uuid(<GUID>), <helpinfo>, <attributes>]                    ┌─────────────────┐
library <name>                                              │ Everything has a │
    {                                                       │ globally unique ID│
                                                            └─────────────────┘
    importlib("stdole32.tlb");                              ┌─────────────────┐
                                                            │ The name of your │
    [uuid(<GUID>), <helpinfo>, <attributes>]                │ type library    │
    interface <name>                                        └─────────────────┘
        {                                                   ┌─────────────────┐
        [<attributes>] <return type> [calling convention]   │ Imports OLE's standard│
            <function name>(<paramters>);                   │ automation types│
        ...                                                  └─────────────────┘
        }                                                   ┌─────────────────┐
                                                            │ Defines your in/out│
    [uuid(<GUID>), <helpinfo>, <attributes>]                │ static interfaces│
    dispinterface <name>                                    └─────────────────┘
        {                                                   ┌─────────────────┐
        Properties:                                         │ Defines your    │
            [<attributes>] <type> <name>;                   │ dynamic interfaces│
        ...                                                  └─────────────────┘
        Methods:
            [<attributes>] <return type> <name>(<paramters>);
            ...
        }

    [uuid(<GUID>), <helpinfo>, <attributes>]
    dispinterface <name>                                    ┌─────────────────┐
        {                                                   │ Defines a static/dynamic│
        interface <name>;                                   │ interface       │
        }                                                   └─────────────────┘

    [uuid(<GUID>), <helpinfo>, <attributes>]
    coclass                                                 ┌─────────────────┐
        {                                                   │ Lists all of the │
        [<attributes>] dispinterface <dispinterface name>;  │ class's interfaces│
        ...                                                 └─────────────────┘
        [<attributes>] interface <interface name>;
        }
    };
```

Figure 15-12. The Structure of DCOM ODL.

■ **Dispinterfaces** define the dynamic methods and properties of a dispatchable interface. Figure 15-12 shows two formats for dispinterfaces. The first format lets you specify individual methods and properties. The second format simply picks up the functions in some interface and makes a dispinterface out of it. A dispinterface can have a GUID (also called the IID) and help context. Each property and method can have an *id(n)* attribute that specifies a dispID for that member. A property can have a *read-only* attribute. Each method and the parameters of those methods can have the same attributes as interface (see previous bullet). Note that the two formats for dispinterface were necessary before dual interfaces were introduced. Dual interfaces let you specify that an interface is both static and dynamic using the *dual* attribute.

■ *Coclass* lists all the incoming and outgoing interfaces a DCOM class supports. It provides the metadata that lets you enumerate all the incoming and outgoing interfaces that a COM class supports. A class is identified by a GUID representing a unique Class ID. Coclass introduces some important new attributes: *appobject* identifies a class as an application object in the automation hierarchy; *control* identifies the class as an ActiveX control; and *licensed* indicates that the class must be instantiated using a **IClassFactory2**. Classes can be *hidden* and have a *version*. In addition, each interface or dispinterface in coclass can include a *source* attribute that marks it as an outgoing interface or event set. Finally, an interface may have a *default* attribute, marking it as the most important interface in a class. You typically have one default incoming interface and one default outgoing interface (also called the primary event set).

Building and Registering Type Libraries

You create a type library by running your ODL through the *MIDL 3.0* compiler. You can also use the older *MKTYPLIB* compiler. The MIDL compiler reads your ODL and compiles it. The end result is a type library (.TLB) file.

You can ship the (.TLB) file with an object or attach it as a resource in a DCOM server's EXE or DLL. You can also store it inside a compound file's stream, or make it available through a shared file on a network server. Regardless of how it gets there, the information in these type libraries must be made available to automation objects and DCOM clients. In addition to creating registry entries for a DCOM server, an installation program must also create entries for the corresponding type libraries using the API function *RegisterTypeLib*. If you use automation-compatible interfaces, then COM uses type libraries to do on-the-fly marshaling. This is called *type library driven* marshaling.

Finding and Loading a Type Library

To obtain the metadata they need, automation clients must first be able to locate a type library and load its contents into memory. So how does the client find the type library in the first place? By looking for it in the registry. The client invokes the COM API *QueryPathOfRegTypeLib* and passes it the ID of the type library it wants. The API returns the path of a registered type library. Now that the client has the library's file name, it can load it by invoking the COM API *LoadRegTypeLib*. This function uses the registry information to load the type library. COM also provides the function *LoadTypeLibFromResource* to extract a type library from a resource attached to a DLL or EXE. Both load functions return a **ITypeLib** interface pointer through which a client can navigate the entire library.

DCOM AND JAVA

As you can see, programming in DCOM is not for the faint of heart. Like CORBA, DCOM is a complete object system. This tutorial only covered the DCOM core. So we only scratched the surface. At this point, you may be wishing for something that makes DCOM more Java-friendly. The good news is that Microsoft's *Visual J++ v1.1* (with the *SDK for Java v2.0*) hides some of DCOM's nastiness from Java developers. It makes DCOM objects behave and look like Java classes. This section gives you a tutorial on DCOM for Java.

The DCOM for Java Development Process

Figure 15-13 shows the process you must follow to create client/server applications using DCOM and Java. To create a DCOM server object in Java you need to:

1. *Create DCOM IDL (and ODL) for your object*. You must define all the interfaces for your class. You can declare regular vtable interfaces to make them callable from Java, Visual Basic, or VC++. However, make sure you mark your class with the *oleautomation* attribute. And, don't use anything but automation-compatible types. Your interfaces can be either *dual* or *dispinterface* to be called from a late-bound scripting language—like VBScript or JavaScript. The default interface on your *coclass* must be a *dispinterface*.

2. *Generate GUIDs for your IDL interfaces*. You must create GUIDs and UUIDs for each class and interface you define in your IDL. You can generate these GUIDs using the GUID-generation utility that comes with the VJ++ (or VC++) Microsoft Developer Studio (see Figure 15-14 on page 365). You must then cut-and-paste the GUIDs into your IDL file.

3. *Create the type library file*. You must run your IDL through the MIDL 3.0 compiler to generate the type library (.TLB) files for your classes.

4. *Create Java wrappers for the DCOM class*. You must run your TLB file through the *JavaTLB* tool to generate Java (.class) files based on your type library. The tool generates (.class) files for each of your DCOM interfaces. It also generates a *summary.txt* file that contains a Java interface definition template for your DCOM class.

5. *Implement your DCOM class in Java*. You must create a Java class that implements all the interfaces you defined in the IDL. You should use the interfaces in *summary.txt* as your template. You must implement all the methods you defined in the IDL. It's not mandatory, but you should use the same name for the Java class as your IDL *coclass*; it will make your code more readable.

6. *Compile your implementation*. You must compile your Java (.java) classes

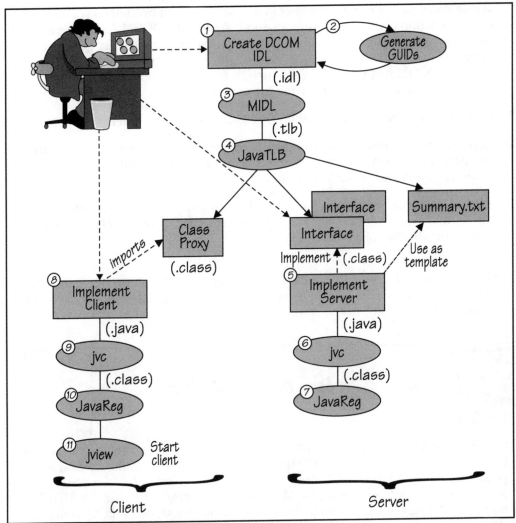

Figure 15-13. How to Write a Java Client/Server Application Using DCOM.

using the *jvc* compiler; it's the Java compiler that comes with VJ++. If your class does not implement all the methods you defined in the IDL, the compiler generates an error.

7. ***Register your Java class.*** You must run the *JavaReg* v2.0 tool from the command line to register your Java class as a DCOM class. You must assign a GUID for this class that matches the CLSID in your IDL. The *JavaReg* tool creates an NT Registry entry for your class. If you distribute your class, you must provide an installation program that invokes *JavaReg* with the *surrogate* option to register your class on the target machine. Also make sure that your Java class is in CLASSPATH.

8. ***Write your client code***. The client consists mostly of ordinary Java code. The only restriction is that you cannot use an instance of a DCOM Java class directly. You must always use it through an interface. So, you must first typecast to an interface and then use the class. Behind the scenes, the Visual J++ run time calls the DCOM API *CoCreateInstance* to bind to the server object. Note that you must also import the proxy for the server class.

9. ***Compile the client code***. You do this using the *jvc* compiler.

10. ***Register the client***. This area has been greatly simplified since we ran this program in the first edition of our book. Just run JavaReg v2.0 with the *remote:<machine-name>* option.

11. ***Start the client***. Start the client class from *jview*—this is Microsoft's Java VM for NT and Windows 95. Note that you don't start the server class; Scum does this automatically for you.

The bottom line is that you define the DCOM interface in IDL, compile it into a type library, and then import it into Java as if it were a standard Java (.class) file (also see next Briefing box).

The Java-to-DCOM Mapping

Briefing

The Microsoft *Java SDK 2.0* introduces a non-documented feature which, in theory, could let you create DCOM-enabled code directly from Java—no IDL required. Charlie Kindel of Microsoft calls it *Auto Dispatch*. The idea is that you should be able to export a DCOM class by: 1) writing a Java class with public members, 2) running it through *JavaReg 2.0* on the server, and 3) running it through *JavaReg /remote* on the client. This process only supports Java classes not interfaces; the client must issue a COM *coCreateInstance* to instantiate an object of this class. However, even with Charlie's help we were not able to get this feature to work by the time we went to press. We could not instantiate the remote server via *coCreateInstance*. In any case, the whole thing looked like it was still under construction. If you find a way to make it work, drop us a note an we'll post it on our Web site.

Auto Dispatch appears to be Microsoft's alternative to RMI and Caffeine. It is also a prelude for *COM+* which Microsoft plans to ship in late 1998. This version of COM uses directives inside the programming language itself to specify the remote interfaces and attributes of a component—for example, security, activation, persistence, and transactions. The compiler (with help from the OS) generates all the system "gunk." COM+ is the Microsoft alternative to the *Enterprise JavaBeans* declarative component model. ❑

DCOM Programming: Java Vs. C++

DCOM programming is much simpler in Java than in C++. For those of you who are familiar with DCOM programming in C++, this section compares it with Java. If you're not familiar with DCOM for C++, then just skip over this section and move on to the Count code example.

First, let's look at how you allocate DCOM objects in both C++ and Java. In C++, you create a new DCOM object using code that looks like this:

```
IMyInterface  pMyInterface;
CoCreateInstance (CLSID_MyInterface, NULL, CLSCTX_SERVER,
                  IID_IMyInterface, (void**)&pMyInterface);
```

The equivalent Java code looks like this:

```
IMyInterface  mystuff = (IMyInterface) new MyClass ();
```

Behind the scenes, this line performs a call to the DCOM API function *CoCreateInstance* instead of simply allocating space on the run-time heap. Note that you cannot use an instance of the class directly; you must always use it through an interface. Also note that as a Java programmer, you never refer to GUIDs—including IIDs, CLSIDs, CATIDs—directly. Instead, you refer to the names—within a type library—that are attached to these GUIDs.

What happens when a class supports more than one interface? DCOM objects must implement the *IUnknown::QueryInterface* function to switch between the object's supported interfaces. Here's how you switch between interfaces in C++:

```
// pMyobject points to an object that supports two interfaces:
// IMyFirstInterface and IMySecondInterface
IMyFirstInterface  *pMyFirstInterface;
IMySecondInterface *pMySecondInterface;

// Point to the first interface
pMyobject->QueryInterface (IID_MyFirstInterface,
                           (void **)&pMyFirstInterface);
```

```
// Point to the second interface
pMyobject->QueryInterface (IID_MySecondInterface,
                           (void **)&pMySecondInterface);
```

In Java, you switch between interfaces by doing a typecast. The equivalent Java code looks like this:

```
// To point to the first interface
IMyFirstInterface  myfirst = (IMyFirstInterface) new MyClass ();

// To point to the second interface
IMySecondInterface  mysecond = (IMySecondInterface) myfirst;
```

In C++, every object must handle its own reference counting. You must call *IUnknown::AddRef* when you create a new reference to an object; you must call *IUnknown::Release* when you stop using a reference to an object. In the Java version, DCOM depends on the Java Virtual Machine's garbage collector to automatically keep track of references to an object. Obviously, this doesn't work for distributed garbage collection. We still don't know how Microsoft plans to handle the remote case. The DCOM spec talks about implementing session Pings to check if a connection is still active. If a session breaks, DCOM will automatically invoke a *Release* on behalf of a client. But what happens if the client later tries to reconnect to the same object? We suspect that Microsoft is relying on MTS to eventually take care of every problem DCOM can't handle on its own.

Every Java DCOM interface is derived from the **com.ms.com.IUnknown** class. This is the class that provides the DCOM object model. The good news is that Java programmers never have to explicitly call any of this class's functions. This alone makes Java a superior programming environment for writing DCOM objects and ActiveXs.

For DCOM to activate an object, it must have a class identifier (CLSID) associated with it, and it must support a class factory. In Java, you do this by specifying a coclass that describes the DCOM-related attributes of the class. The coclass attribute is part of the IDL language, and it is stored in a type library. It allows a programmer to assign a CLSID to a particular class. Here's an example:

```
// extract from MyStuff.IDL
...
[uuid(2CFB1F60-9150-11cf-B63C-0080C792B782]
coclass MyClass
{
        interface ISomeInterface;
```

```
       interface ISomeOtherInterface;
};
```

You use a Java import directive in your code to import a type library that contains the coclass name as the name of a Java class. This tells the Java compiler—and VM—that this Java class is a DCOM class object. The Java VM will then automatically provide a class factory for the class. The following code illustrates this:

```
import project.MyStuff.*;
```

The Java class called **MyClass** has a "coclass" statement in the MyStuff type library imported in the previous code snippet. The coclass specifies the class's CLSID as well as a base set of interfaces implemented by the class.

In summary, the steps you follow to import a DCOM class into Java are: 1) put a coclass statement into an IDL file, 2) compile this IDL file into a type library using MIDL, and 3) import the resulting type library into a Java compilation unit—you use the coclass name as the name of a Java class. Of course, you must also take care of all the DCOM client configuration issues.

DCOM/Java Mappings

A Java program can access almost any DCOM construct that you can specify in IDL or in a type library. This also means that any construct that cannot be defined via DCOM IDL is by definition not accessible to Java programs. Remember, type libraries are generated from IDL. The *summary.txt* files describe the DCOM constructs that are exposed in Java by each of your DCOM IDL classes and interfaces. Table 15-2 shows how the DCOM IDL elements map into Java.

Table 15-2. How DCOM IDL Elements Map to Java.

DCOM IDL Element	Java Type
coclass	public class
interface	public interface
dispinterface	public interface
typedef struct	public final class
typedef enum	public final class
typedef union	public final class
properties	get<property>, put<property> accessors

Table 15-3 shows how the DCOM automation data types map to their Java counterparts. Note that jvc automatically implements **IUnknown** and **IDispatch** for every Java DCOM class. The **IDispatch** dispinterface contains the public methods that are on the "default" interface for the class. At run time, the Microsoft Java VM automatically provides type information for this **IDispatch** implementation—via *IDispatch::GetTypeInfo*.

Table 15-3. How DCOM IDL Types Map to Java Types.

DCOM IDL Type	Java Type
boolean	boolean
char	char
double	double
int	int
int64	long
float	float
long	int
short	short
unsigned char	byte
BSTR	**java.lang.String**
CY (or CURRENCY)	long
DATE	double
HRESULT	int (via **com.ms.com.ComException**)
VARIANT	**com.ms.com.Variant**
SAFEARRAY	**com.ms.com.SafeArray**
IUnknown	**com.ms.com.IUnknown**
IDispatch	**java.lang.Object**

THE DCOM JAVA COUNT

OK, it's time to develop the DCOM version of Count. As you will see, Microsoft's Java does a good job of hiding the programming complexity of DCOM.

The DCOM Count Client

The client program consists of a single Java class—**CountDCOMClient**. This class
provides a *main* method that performs the following functions: 1) binds to the
ICount interface on a Count server, 2) invokes the *set_sum* method to reset the
remote Sum attribute, 3) calculates the start time, 4) invokes the *increment* method
1000 times, 5) calculates the elapsed time, and 6) displays the average DCOM Ping
performance. The code follows:

Listing 15-1. CountDCOMClient: The DCOM Count Client.

```java
// CountDCOMClient.java

import count.*;

class CountDCOMClient
{ public static void main(String args[])
  { try
    {
      // Bind to the Count object
      System.out.println("Creating Count Object");
      ICount counter = (ICount)new count.Count();

      // Set sum to initial value of 0
      System.out.println("Setting sum to 0");
      counter.set_sum((int)0);

      // Calculate Start time
      System.out.println("Incrementing");
      long startTime = System.currentTimeMillis();

      // Increment 1000 times
      for (int i = 0 ; i < 1000 ; i++ )
      { counter.increment();
      }

      // Calculate stop time; print out statistics
      long stopTime = System.currentTimeMillis();
      System.out.println("Avg Ping = "
                    + ((stopTime - startTime)/1000f)
                    + " msecs");
      System.out.println("Sum = " + counter.get_sum());
    } catch(Exception e)
    { System.err.println("System Exception");
```

```
            System.err.println(e);
        }
    }
}
```

You should notice two things about this code. First, we import the count package generated by JavaTLB (see the next section). This is how the client binds to a proxy class for the remote server. Second, we bind to the remote object's **ICount** interface. We do this by typecasting the interface, DCOM-style. It is very important that you include this cast. DCOM uses it to generate a *CoCreateInstance* call. Note that you cannot bind to a unique object using DCOM. It has no concept of a unique object reference that you can later reconnect with. You just bind to a stateless interface, not to an object. Everything else in the code is very Java-like.

The DCOM Count IDL

The first step in developing a DCOM server class is to create its IDL. Of course, we're talking about DCOM IDL, not CORBA. Here's the DCOM IDL for our **Count** server class:

Listing 15-2. Count.idl: The DCOM IDL for Count.

```
// Count.idl

[
        uuid(1689CB21-2ADE-11d0-892E-00A024638502),
        version(1.0)
]
library Counter
{
    [
      object,
      uuid(1689CB22-2ADE-11d0-892E-00A024638502),
      pointer_default(unique),
      oleautomation
    ]
    interface ICount : IUnknown
    {
      import "oaidl.idl";

      HRESULT set_sum([in] int val);
      HRESULT get_sum([out, retval] int* retval);
      HRESULT increment([out, retval] int* retval);
```

```
   };

   importlib("stdole32.tlb");
   [
      uuid(1689CB23-2ADE-11d0-892E-00A024638502),
   ]
   coclass Count
   {
      [default] interface ICount;
   };
};
```

The long number strings are DCOM GUIDs for our class and interface. We generate these GUIDs using the Microsoft Developer Studio's *Create GUID* menu (see Figure 15-14). As a shortcut, you can generate one GUID and then increment the eighth digit to get the next ones.

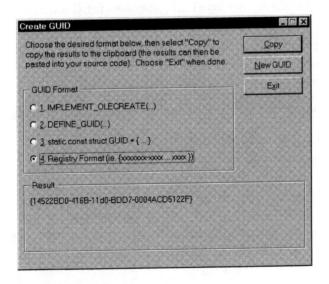

Figure 15-14. The Microsoft Developer Studio Create GUID Utility.

Run MIDL and JavaTLB

You must then run the MIDL 3.0 compiler against the IDL. You do this by entering the following command at the prompt:

prompt> `midl count.idl`

Next, you must register the type library and generate a template for the interface file. You do this by entering the following command at the prompt:

prompt> `javatlb /U:T count.tlb`

The following is the console output that JavaTLB generates:

```
import count.*;
C:\WINNT\java\trustlib\count\summary.txt(1): Class summary information
created
```

This output tells you two things: 1) the import statement to use in your class implementation, and 2) the location of a summary.txt file that has the Java interface definition template.

Here's the summary.txt file that javaTLB generates for Count:

```
public class count/Count extends java.lang.Object
{
}

public interface count/ICount extends com.ms.com.IUnknown
{
    public abstract void set_sum(int);
    public abstract int get_sum();
    public abstract int increment();
}
```

This is the template we use to implement the server class. Also, javaTLB generates two class files in the C:\WINNT\java\trustlib\count subdirectory: Count.class and ICount.class.

The DCOM Count Server

The server-side of the DCOM Count consists of a single class **Count**. This class implements a single interface, **ICount**. Note that JavaTLB generates the **ICount** class file (see previous section). So where is the *main* method? It is something DCOM takes care of. You don't provide it. But, you must provide method implementations for all the interfaces your class supports. Here's the code for the **Count** class:

Listing 15-1. The Count Java Server.

```java
// Count.java: The Count Implementation
import com.ms.com.*;
import count.*;

class Count implements ICount
{
  private int sum;

  public  int get_sum() throws ComException
  { return sum;
  }

  public  void set_sum(int val) throws ComException
  { sum = val;
  }

  public int increment() throws ComException
  { sum++;
    return sum;
  }
}
```

Note that we did not have to provide a constructor for the class. DCOM provides a default factory implementation for our Java class. The *import com.ms.com.* * is for exceptions. Each DCOM method must throw a **ComException**.

COMPILE THE CLIENT/SERVER PROGRAM

We're now ready to compile the DCOM client/server Count program. Make sure you have installed Microsoft's Visual J++ v1.1 and the SDK for Java 2.0. To compile the Count server, go to the appropriate directory and type the following command at the prompt:

prompt> jvc -d C:\winnt\java\trustlib Count.java

Note that there are three program subdirectories under C:\winnt\java:

```
classes  - contains java runtime classes
lib      - contains untrusted classes
trustlib - contains trusted classes
```

There are several statements in the registry that the MS Java VM uses to find classes:

```
Classpath - c:\winnt\java\classes\classes.zip;c:\winnt\java\classes;
LibsDirectory - c:\winnt\java\lib;
TrustedClasspath - c:\winnt\java\trustlib\tclasses.zip;
TrustedLibsDirectory - c:\winnt\java\trustlib;
```

Next, you must register the Java class. Enter the following command at the prompt:

prompt> `javareg /register /class:Count`
`/clsid:{1689CB23-2ADE-11d0-892E-00A024638502} /surrogate`

You can now compile the client code. Enter the following command at the prompt:

prompt> `jvc -d C:\winnt\java\trustlib CountDCOMClient.java`

If all goes well, you should have some compiled Java code that you can now run.

RUN THE CLIENT/SERVER PROGRAMS

To run the server, you must configure DCOM via JavaReg. When scum receives a remote invocation, it will instantiate an instance of your server class.

To run the client on the server's machine just enter the following command at the prompt:

prompt> `jview CountDCOMClient`

This runs the Count object as an *Inprocess Server*. We could not find a way to run the Java client as a *Local Server* on the same machine. DCOM uses either CLSCTX_INPROC_SERVER or CLSCTX_LOCAL_SERVER for *CoCreateInstance*. It seems the Inprocess Server configuration always gets precedence. And, you can't force it to run Local Server by deleting the Inprocess Server information from the object's CLASSID registry entry; it seems the Local Server surrogate also reads information from the Inprocess Server Registry. The bottom line is that we won't be able to obtain results for the local interprocess calls.

To run the client on a remote machine, you run JavaReg with the *remote* option at the client machine to specify the remote machine. Here's an example:

prompt> `javareg /register /class:Count`
`/clsid:{1689CB23-2ADE-11d0-892E-00A024638502} /remote:myServer`

Again, you run your client by entering:

prompt> `jview CountDCOMClient`

LOOKING AT SOME TEST RESULTS

We will run the DCOM client/server program using the remote configuration only. We could not get the local one to work. As usual, our client performs 1000 method invocations. The tests measure the average response time of DCOM remote Pings. We ran the client and server programs on two 120-MHz Pentiums running NT 4.0. They are connected across a 10 Mbit/s Ethernet LAN. Table 15-4 shows the results.

Table 15-4. Local Versus Remote DCOM Invocations.

Local RMI Count (interprocess, same machine)	Remote DCOM Count (interprocess, over 10 Mbit/s Ethernet)
N.A. (couldn't run local count)	3.8 msecs

The numbers show that DCOM is only slightly slower than the VisiBroker for Java CORBA/IIOP ORB. You should run the test and see for yourself.

DCOM VERSUS CORBA/IIOP

Table 15-5 compares DCOM with the Caffeinated CORBA IIOP. *VisiBroker for Java* is written in Java, which makes it very portable. A year ago, Microsoft announced it was working on an all-Java version of DCOM, but it never materialized. DCOM for Java uses native calls from within the Microsoft Java VM; it is not a Java/ORB, as we defined it in Chapter 3.

CORBA objects have unique and persistent references; they also have state. DCOM objects are pointers to stateless interfaces; monikers are a patch. The DCOM/DTC transaction model uses explicit invocations to propagate the transactional context. In contrast, CORBA IIOP implicitly propagates the transaction context. This means the ORB propagates the transaction, not the programmer. It is easier and less error-prone. Both DCOM and CORBA are good at late-binding and dynamic discovery. However, the CORBA Interface Repository provides a better intergalactic multi-ORB solution.

CORBA ORBs—now in their third generation—have a proven technology for inter-operabilty. Federations are inherent in the CORBA architecture. For example, CORBA IIOP goes to great lengths to specify inter-ORB references, inter-ORB repositories, and inter-ORB security. In contrast, DCOM is just starting to play in federations. CORBA ORBs run on all the major OS platforms—including Windows. DCOM appears to be primarily a Windows-first solution. Software AG is porting DCOM to different platforms. However, it will always be a generation behind the NT version. Also, DCOM requires the *Microsoft Transaction Server (MTS)* to scale on the server side; Software AG is not porting MTS. Consequently, with Software AG, Unix becomes a client to NT servers, not vice versa. CORBA is open in the sense that is controlled by a standards body. DCOM is semi-open. Microsoft has submitted a subset of the DCOM specification to the Open Group; it is also creating a DCOM advisory board.

Table 15-5. Caffeinated CORBA IIOP Versus DCOM.

Feature	CORBA IIOP with Caffeine	DCOM
ORB written in Java	Yes	No
Java Platforms	All Java platforms (including Microsoft)	Jview (Java VM for Windows 95 and NT)
Parameter marshaling	Yes	Yes
Parameter passing	in, out, and in/out	in, out, and in/out
Configuration	Easy	Easy
Objects can be passed-by-value	Yes	No
Interface descriptions	Yes (via Java interfaces or CORBA IDL)	Yes (via DCOM IDL and Auto Dispatch)
Dynamic discovery	Yes (via CORBA IR)	Yes (via type libraries)
Dynamic invocations	Yes (via DII)	Yes (via IDispatch)
Performance	Very fast (3.5 msec Ping)	Very fast (3.8 msec Ping)
Wire-level security context	Yes (via CORBA Security)	Yes (via NT security)
Wire-level transaction context	Implicit (via CORBA OTS)	Explicit (via COM/DTC)
Persistent naming	Yes	No (unless you use monikers)

Table 15-5. Caffeinated CORBA IIOP Versus DCOM. (Continued)

Feature	CORBA IIOP with Caffeine	DCOM
URL-based naming	Yes	Yes (via URL monikers)
Persistent object references	Yes	No
Multilingual invocations	Yes	Yes
Language-neutral wire protocol	Yes (via canonical IIOP data types)	Yes (via DCE Network Data Representation)
Intergalactic scaling	Yes (via IORs, DSI, GUIDs, IIOP, and inter-ORB federations)	No
Standard ORB wire protocol	Yes (IIOP)	Maybe (via the Open Group)

For now CORBA appears to have a solid headstart in distributed objects. It holds the upper ground. However, in the long run, DCOM is a formidable challenger. Microsoft is moving into Java in full force. It also understands the Internet and components. DCOM's secret weapon is called MTS—the transaction coordinator for server-side COM components. In our opinion, the DCOM/CORBA war is just starting. This chapter shows how this war is being played out on the Java front.

CONCLUSION

For better or for worse, DCOM is our industry's other ORB. And, it's here to stay. So, we must learn to live with it. This chapter shows that the current version of DCOM is not a big threat to the CORBA camp—at least, in the short run. In the long run, DCOM is a very serious competitor—especially if Microsoft delivers on its COM+ vision. As you saw in this chapter, DCOM is deeply embedded inside the Microsoft Java VM; it provides the distributed Java engine. It is Microsoft's answer to both RMI and CORBA. As a Java licensee, Microsoft will inherit a CORBA ORB with the Java JDK 1.2. It remains to be seen what Microsoft will do with this ORB. We can only guess. In the meantime, Microsoft is very serious about the DCOM/Java integration. But, as we saw in this chapter, they will do it their way.

Chapter 16

And the Winner Is... CONCEPTS

The last six chapters were a technology marathon. We covered the top six contenders for building the Object Web—including Sockets, HTTP/CGI, Servlets, Java RMI, CORBA/IIOP with Caffeine, and DCOM/ActiveX. The winner will provide the intergalactic infrastructure on which we will build the majority of our client/server applications over the next five years. The stakes are huge—especially for application developers like us. The winning technology will shape the way we develop and deploy the majority of our software. Once you invest in an infrastructure, you cannot easily walk away from it. So, it is important to make a careful choice.

We hope the last six chapters were a good learning experience. They should have given you a chance to bypass the hype and get some hands-on experience with each of the competing technologies. By writing the same client/server application on each competing platform, we can put together a report card that compares the following aspects of each system: 1) the client/server development process, 2) the Java integration facilities, 3) installation and deployment, 4) Ping performance, and 5) intergalactic reach.

We believe that Java is the client and server language of the Web. So it's important to evaluate how seamlessly each environment integrates with Java. But Java is not alone in the universe. Java objects must be able to seamlessly integrate with everything else on the intergalactic network—from C++ and Smalltalk objects to legacy COBOL systems. So, we must evaluate how each solution integrates with other languages and operating system environments.

The plan for this short chapter is to create a report card that compares the different platforms. This will give us a chance to consolidate our thoughts and observations in one place. Of course, everyone knows that report cards are very subjective. You will be getting our biases. In a sense, this whole chapter is a Soapbox. However, you have all the information you need to run the programs and form your own conclusions. Also, keep in mind that we're presenting a snapshot of the technologies as they stand today. The Object Web is like a fast-moving bullet train. It's very hard to pin it down for too long. But, you'll be getting our best shot of this moving train.

THE REPORT CARD

Table 16-1 shows our "Michelin rating" of the six contending Object Web technologies. Four stars is the highest rating. A hollow star is the worst rating; it means the function is not there. At this point, there should be no major surprises. The table provides a bird's-eye view of the comparisons that appeared in the last six chapters. But let's quickly review the categories:

- *Abstraction level:* The higher the level of abstraction, the less work your application must do. For example, Sockets present the lowest level of abstraction; you must create your own conventions for passing the request names and their arguments. You also do your own marshaling. It's like programming in assembler. The three ORBs—CORBA, DCOM, and RMI—provide the highest level of abstraction. They hide all these nasty details from your applications. HTTP/CGI and Servlets are somewhere in between Sockets and the ORBs.

- *Seamless Java integration:* CORBA/Caffeine and RMI provide the most seamless distributed programming environment for Java. They both use remote Java interfaces to expose their services; it doesn't get better. DCOM introduces its own IDL, which it eventually integrates with the Java object model. HTTP/CGI, Servlets, and Sockets provide lower-level Java class libraries. They do not extend the Java object model.

- *Operating system platform support:* CORBA, HTTP/CGI, and Sockets run on all the major client and server OSs: including Java OS, OS/2 Warp, OS/400, NetWare, MacOS, MVS, and all the Unixes. RMI is written in Java; it runs on all the OS platforms that support the Java OS. DCOM runs as a first-class citizen on NT and Windows 95 only. The Software AG port of DCOM to Unix lacks some critical server-side elements—for example, MTS. DCOM/Java is closely tied to the Microsoft VM. We give DCOM only two stars because—except for NT—it doesn't have a good server-side story.

Table 16-1. Comparing Java/CORBA ORBs and Their Competition.

Feature	CORBA/IIOP	DCOM	RMI/RMP	HTTP/CGI	Servlets	Sockets
Abstraction level	★★★★	★★★★	★★★★	★★	★★	★
Seamless Java integration	★★★★	★★★★	★★★★	★★	★★	★★
OS platform support	★★★★	★★	★★★★	★★★★	★★★★	★★★★
All-Java implementation	★★★★	★	★★★★	★★	★★★★	★★★★
Typed parameter support	★★★★	★★★★	★★★★	★	★	★
Ease of configuration	★★★	★★★	★★★	★★★	★★★	★★★
Distributed method invocations	★★★★	★★★	★★★	☆	☆	☆
State across invocations	★★★★	★★★	★★★	☆	★★	★★
Dynamic discovery and metadata support	★★★★	★★★	★★	☆	★	☆
Dynamic invocations	★★★★	★★★★	★	☆	☆	☆
Performance (remote Pings)	★★★ 3.5 msecs	★★★ 3.8 msecs	★★★ 3.3 msecs	☆ 827.9 msecs	★ 55.6 msecs	★★★★ 2.1 msecs
Wire-level security	★★★★	★★★★	★★★	★★★	★★★	★★★
Wire-level transactions	★★★★	★★★	☆	☆	☆	☆
Persistent object references	★★★★	★	☆	☆	☆	☆
URL-based naming	★★★★	★★	★★	★★★★	★★★★	★★★
Multilingual object invocations	★★★★	★★★★	☆	★★★	☆	★★★★
Language-neutral wire protocol	★★★★	★★★★	☆	★★★★	★★★★	☆
Intergalactic scaling	★★★★	★★	★	★★	★★	★★★★
Open standard	★★★★	★★	★★	★★★★	★★	★★★★

■ ***All-Java solution:*** There are commercial all-Java implementations of CORBA, Sockets, Servlets, RMI, and CGI/HTTP. However, DCOM is written in C/C++; Microsoft provides Java adapters for DCOM within its own Java VM on Windows 95 and NT. You can't run DCOM on other Java OSs.

- **Typed parameter support:** All three ORBs provide typed parameter support. DCOM and CORBA let you pass in, out, and in/out parameters. RMI only supports in parameters, but it lets you pass classes as arguments. HTTP/CGI and Servlets provide minimal parameter support; they use MIME to describe the message contents. Sockets provide no typed parameter support. However, Java lets you associate your Sockets with typed-streams.

- **Ease of configuration:** Everyone get three stars but you must bear in mind that configuring client/server systems is never a joy.

- **Distributed method invocations:** Only the three ORBs can perform distributed method invocations. We give CORBA a higher mark because it supports unique object references, so you can reactivate objects on-demand.

- **Maintain state across invocations:** The lack of state is one of the things that's killing HTTP/CGI. Sockets maintain state across invocations, but there is no notion of object state. The three ORBs maintain state and handle object state within a session. However, only CORBA supports the concept of a unique object. Consequently, CORBA can also maintain state across sessions. CORBA lets you reconnect to the same object (with the same state) at a later time. Servlets let you reconnect to the same instance within a server session.

- **Dynamic discovery and metadata support:** Only CORBA and DCOM support object introspection. Both ORBs let you dynamically discover an object's interfaces. CORBA also supports inter-ORB Interface Repositories. DCOM only supports local repositories for type libraries. RMI and Servlets support local Java reflection. To the best of our knowledge, you can't introspect an RMI class remotely. You can, however, download a stub for an RMI class that you can then introspect. But it's not a substitute for an Interface Repository.

- **Dynamic invocations:** Only CORBA and DCOM support dynamic invocations. This form of late-binding lets you construct a method on-the-fly. In theory, you could download an RMI stub and then invoke a method on it using Java reflection; it's a clumsy approach, but we'll give it one star.

- **Ping performance:** Sockets has the best Ping performance. The three ORBs come next. Finally, there are Servlets and HTTP/CGI. You can use the MultiCount benchmark framework from Chapter 9 to conduct your own tests. If you find something newsworthy, please send us a note. We will include it in the next revision of this book.

- **Wire-level security:** Sockets provides wire-level security via the *Secure Socket Layer (SSL)*. HTTP provides security via *Secure-HTTP (S-HTTP)* as well as SSL. DCOM incorporates NT domain-level security; it will include DCE-level security in the future. CORBA defines a complete Security Service that is built into the ORB and into the IIOP message structures.[1] CORBA security can also work with SSL. RMI security is based on SSL; RMI also provides security controls for downloading classes.

■ **Wire-level transactions:** Only CORBA and DCOM provide support for distributed transactions. The DCOM *Distributed Transaction Coordinator (DTC)* provides a transaction framework for DCOM ORBs. Its CORBA counterpart is the *Object Transaction Service*. We give CORBA four stars because it uses an implicit transaction model. The IIOP messaging protocol automatically propagates CORBA transactions; it requires no intervention on your part. In contrast, you must explicitly ask the DCOM transaction dispenser for a transaction reference. You must then explicitly pass this reference in all your subsequent calls.

■ **Persistent object references:** Only CORBA has persistent objects that also have persistent object references. DCOM has transient stateless objects that you can associate with a context via a *moniker*. A moniker is really a patch for DCOM's lack of support for object identifiers. So, let's give monikers one star for their patchwork. RMI will support persistent object references and CORBA-like object activation in its JDK 1.2 version. So we'll upgrade them to four stars in the next edition of this book.

■ **URL-based naming:** This can be a useful feature on Internets and intranets. URL naming was pioneered by HTTP/CGI. Socket ports are integrated in the URL naming scheme. However, Sockets are low-level entities. RMI and CORBA (via Caffeine) provide URL-naming schemes that let you associate an object with a URL. This means that you can click on a URL and bind it to a live object. The RMI URL-naming scheme is not persistent; the CORBA one is. DCOM supports URLs via monikers.

■ **Multilingual object invocations:** By now, all computer languages support Sockets. And, most support HTTP/CGI. RMI only works with Java. CORBA and DCOM support object invocations across languages. CORBA defines standard high-level language bindings. In contrast, DCOM is a binary protocol that is widely supported by Microsoft compilers (and tools). There are no standard language mappings for DCOM.

■ **Language-neutral wire protocol:** Both DCOM and CORBA provide a canonical message format for representing a rich variety of data types inside messages. The self-describing data is independent of any operating system, machine, or language representation. The CORBA language mappings bind the data types to the corresponding language representations. DCOM does it in a more ad hoc fashion based on the OLE automation types. HTTP also supports self-describing

---

[1] We provide an overview of the CORBA Services in **Instant CORBA** (Wiley, 1997).

data via MIME. However, it provides very limited data typing. Servlets support HTTP.

- **Intergalactic scaling:** Sockets via TCP/IP supports intergalactic federations of networks. However, this support is at a very low level of abstraction. In contrast, CORBA supports loose federations of ORBs. CORBA's IIOP defines protocols for propagating security and transactions across mulivendor ORB domains. It also supports interoperable objects across ORB domains. And, it defines an infrastructure for federated Interface Repositories, namespaces, and other ORB services. CORBA's secret weapon for intergalactic scalability is its infrastructure for loosely-coupled federations of ORBs.

- **Open standard:** An intergalactic platform must be an open, level-playing field. No single vendor should be allowed to control the platform. CORBA, Sockets, and HTTP/CGI are open—they are each controlled by a standards body. DCOM is controlled by Microsoft and then passed to a standards body—in this case, the *Open Group*. Likewise, JavaSoft controls the RMI and Servlets standards, which ISO may then ratify. We'll give Microsoft and JavaSoft two stars each for being semi-open.

And the Winner Is...

Soapbox

We expect that over the next few years IIOP will become as ubiquitous as HTTP and CGI. IIOP provides a comprehensive system through which objects can request services from one another across the wide variety of platforms or database systems they're built on. Just as Web technology has helped companies simplify and centralize the distribution of information, distributed objects will help them simplify and centralize their enterprise applications....Now that we have standard ways to build networks and run services on them, we have an opportunity that never existed before—to build network applications. Let's take advantage of it.

— **Marc Andreessen, Netscape Cofounder**

By sheer coincidence, Marc Andreessen picked the same winner we did—CORBA/IIOP. Yes, CORBA is inevitable. Why? Table 16-1 says it all. If you're not convinced, just read the previous six chapters. CORBA's only real competition is DCOM. RMI is currently a niche ORB; this will change when it runs on IIOP. Sockets is just a low-level protocol. And, HTTP/CGI just doesn't cut it. So, it's CORBA versus DCOM. As we explained in the last chapter, CORBA won the first round. But the battle will continue for the remainder of the century.

From past wars, we have learned—the hard way—never to underestimate Microsoft. We also learned that superior technology alone doesn't always win—especially in the face of a superior marketing machine. So why does the CORBA/Java camp stand a better chance against Microsoft where many others have failed?

In the last year, the CORBA camp was joined by fast-moving newcomers. This new guard looks at CORBA as a way to build products, not just standards. The new guard includes some agile pure-software companies like Netscape, Oracle, JavaSoft, BEA, and NetDynamics. They join long-standing CORBA players like IBM, Novell, Borland/Visigenic, SunSoft, Iona, Tandem, and Expersoft. Together, these companies form a formidable bloc. They have the support of hundreds of other software vendors as well as some major IT shops.

This new CORBA coalition is building around a killer app called the Object Web. The Web transforms CORBA from a set of standards to a set of products that fulfill an intergalactic need. CORBA becomes a powerful architecture that ties together products that form the Object Web. JavaBeans and Enterprise JavaBeans provide the component foundation and tool support. This a very potent combination of intergalactic technologies. The CORBA/Java camp has what it takes to give Microsoft a run for their money. ❏

Part 5
The Existential
CORBA

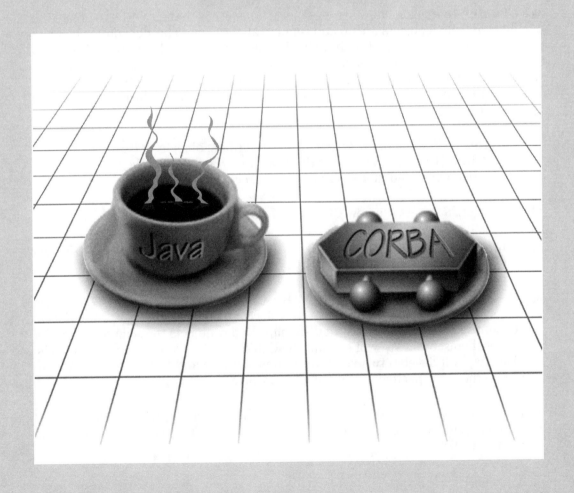

An Introduction to Part 5

This Part is about the "existential" CORBA. We explain CORBA's Interface Repository and Introspection facilities. We show you how an object discovers its intergalactic universe. We also cover CORBA's activation services. An ORB must provide the illusion that all of its objects—and there can be millions of them—are up and running and active all the time, even though they are not. This illusion keeps the client code simple, but it requires that you do more on the server side. This is also the Part where we finally introduce the new CORBA/Java standards—including *IDL-to-Java*, *Java-to-IDL*, and *Objects-by-Value*. Here's what we cover in Part 5:

- **Chapter 17** is about how you find your ORB and then use it to discover the universe of CORBA objects. The CORBA 2.0 *Initialization Protocol* ensures that an object can find its ORB, BOA, Interface Repository, Trader, Naming Service, and whatever else it needs to bootstrap itself into the intergalactic distributed object universe. We also briefly cover the *Trader Service*.

- **Chapter 18** explains how server objects conspire with their ORBs to create the illusion that all objects are up and running all the time. This conspiracy benefits the clients. Of course, this shifts the implementation burden to the server. You must write code that cooperates with the ORB when you start and stop your objects or when the ORB starts up or shuts down. This chapter covers the CORBA activation services—including the current BOA and the new CORBA 3.0 *Portable Object Adapter (POA)*.

- **Chapter 19** is about *metadata*—or self-describing objects. We explain in detail the CORBA IDL. We then cover the *Interface Repository*. We tell you how it stores IDL-generated metadata and how you can retrieve it.

- **Chapter 20** covers the new CORBA *IDL-to-Java* standard in detail.

- **Chapter 21** covers the new CORBA *Java-to-IDL* standard as well as *Objects-by-Value*. These are the RMI/CORBA convergence standards.

- **Chapter 22** is about the CORBA/Java introspection services. CORBA/Java objects are doubly introspective—they derive from both the CORBA and Java **Object** classes. As a result, they are supersmart objects that can tell you a lot about themselves. We will explain the CORBA and Java introspection models. Then we will develop two small programs—*AskMe* and *WalkIR*—that demonstrate the introspective powers of CORBA/Java objects.

You will find that CORBA's existential services let you create very flexible and extensible systems. They can also be a lot of fun. But first you must understand what they're all about.

Chapter 17

How Do I Find My ORB?

CONCEPTS

In this very short chapter we look at the CORBA 2.0 initialization protocol. We answer the following question: How does a newly activated object discover its ORB and the universe of CORBA objects? The CORBA 2.0 initialization protocol ensures that an object can find its ORB, BOA, Interface Repository, Trader, Naming Service, and whatever else it needs to bootstrap itself into the intergalactic distributed object universe. Before CORBA 2.0, this bootstrapping was left as an exercise for the ORB vendors. The results were non-portable solutions.

THE CORBA 2.0 INITIALIZATION INTERFACE

CORBA 2.0 defines a set of initialization methods that all ORBs must provide to help an object bootstrap itself into the distributed environment. These methods are implemented by the **CORBA::ORB** pseudo-object. You may recall from Chapter 8 that **CORBA::ORB** is one of the ORB's core interfaces.

As we explained in Chapter 8, **CORBA::ORB** is a pseudo-object interface that defines general-purpose ORB methods. A *pseudo-object* is an object that the ORB directly creates, but you can invoke it like any other object. The ORB itself is a pseudo-object. You can invoke methods on an **ORB** pseudo-object from either a client or server implementation. Three of these methods are specific to object initialization: *BOA_init*, *list_initial_services*, and *resolve_initial_references* (see Figure 17-1). In Java, the ORB pseudo-object maps to the **org.omg.CORBA. ORB** class.

You've already seen CORBA initialization in action. If you use BOA, you must invoke *BOA_init* to obtain a reference to your **BOA** pseudo-object. You'll need this reference to register your objects with the ORB. You invoke *list_initial_services* to obtain a list of names for well-known services. Think of it as the ORB's mini-naming service. It's your welcome package to the CORBA intergalactic universe. You invoke *resolve_intial_references* to convert the string names of services to object references.

So how do you obtain a reference to your ORB object? In CORBA 2.0, you issue the API call *ORB_init* to inform the ORB of your presence and to obtain a reference to an ORB *pseudo-object*. In Java, you use the *init* static method (or class method) instead. You can assume that an instance of **org.omg.CORBA.ORB** is already running in your environment. Invoking this class method is equivalent to the *ORB_init* API call. They both return a reference to a newly-initialized ORB object.

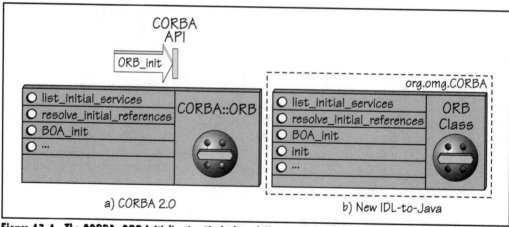

Figure 17-1. The CORBA::ORB Initialization Methods and Their Java Mapping.

AN INITIALIZATION SCENARIO

In essence, the initialization service provides a barebones naming service that allows objects to find the services they need to function on an ORB. Figure 17-2 shows the typical calls an object must invoke to bootstrap itself. Let's walk through this initialization scenario:

1. ***Obtain an object reference for your ORB***. You issue the CORBA API call *ORB_init* to inform the ORB of your presence and to obtain a reference to an ORB *pseudo-object*. Note that we issued an API call and not a method

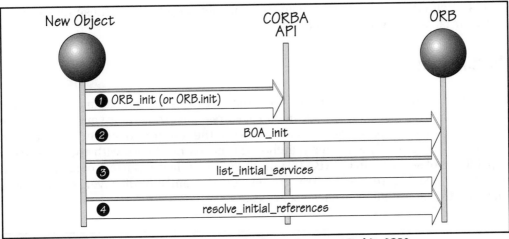

Figure 17-2. CORBA 2.0 Initialization Service—Or, How Does a Component Find Its ORB?

invocation. To invoke a method, you must first bootstrap yourself into the CORBA world. In Java, you must instead invoke the *org.omg.CORBA.ORB.init* static method.

2. ***Obtain a pointer to your Object Adapter***. If you use BOA, then you must invoke the method *BOA_init* on the ORB pseudo-object to tell the BOA you're there and to obtain its object reference (BOA is also a pseudo-object).

3. ***Discover what initial services are available***. You invoke the method *list_initial_services* on the ORB pseudo-object to obtain a list of well-known objects—for example, the Interface Repository, Trader, and the Naming Service. These well-known objects are returned in a list of string names.

4. ***Obtain object references for the services you want***. You invoke the method *resolve_initial_references* to obtain object references for the services you want. You're now a well-connected, first-class citizen on the CORBA ORB.

You should note that an object can initialize itself in more than one ORB.

HOW YOU FIND YOUR OTHER OBJECTS

The initialization service is just a bootstrap Naming Service. It gives you a list of well-known services—for example, the Trader and Naming Services. You can then use these services to find any object in the intergalactic ORB universe. The *Naming Service* is like a telephone White Pages for objects; it lets you look up other objects by name. You can also discover new objects via CORBA's Yellow Pages—the *Trader Service*. In an Object Web environment, objects can also be dynamically discovered by spiders, crawlers, bots, search engines, publish-and-subscribe services, and agents of all types. The Traders can dynamically keep track of these new objects and their latest and greatest services.

CORBA Trader 101

So what's a Trader? A *Trader* is an object that provides "matchmaking" services for other objects. *Exporters*—or service providers—advertise their services with the trader. *Importers*—or service consumers—use the trader to discover services that match their needs. The Trader matches the needs of clients with the advertised capabilities of servers. In CORBA terminology, it matches exporters of services with importers (see Figure 17-3). Traders let you dynamically discover services and facilitate the late binding to these services.

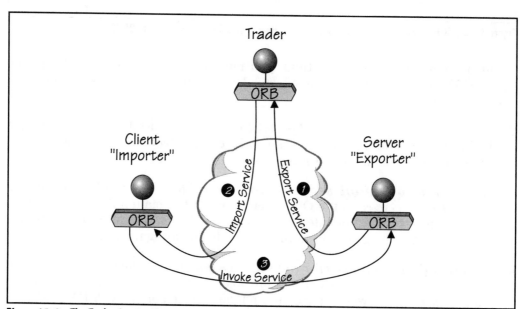

Figure 17-3. The Trader Service: Importers Meet Exporters.

A new service provider will first register its service with the trader. Then it will provide the following relevant information:

- **An object reference.** This is the reference clients use to connect to the advertised service and invoke its operations. It's the object reference to the interface that provides the service.

- **The service type name.** A service type includes information on the names of the operations (or methods) to which the service will respond along with their parameters and result types. It also includes distinguishing properties of the service.

- **The properties of the service**. These are name-value pairs that define the offer. This is how you advertise application-level information. Properties describe the capabilities of a service. An exporter specifies the values for properties of the service it is advertising. A property can be mandatory or optional. The exporter must specify values for all mandatory properties.

The Trader maintains a repository of *service types*. For example, you can have a service type called *restaurant*. The restaurant type would include the interfaces to the service and a set of properties that describe individual restaurants. For example, a restaurant has a menu, specials, a street address, business hours, reviews, and so on. In true CORBA fashion, types can extend other types via multiple inheritance.

The trader stores type descriptions in its *ServiceTypeRepository*. It also maintains a database of service objects that are instances of these types. These are the objects you advertise via the trader. Clients—or importers—can get in touch with the trader to find out what services are listed or to ask for a service by its type. It's like the telephone Yellow Pages. The trader will find the best match for the client based on the context of the requested service and the offers of the providers. A matching service will have a type that matches the client's request. It also has properties that match a client's criteria for a service.

Traders from different domains can create *federations* and pool their offers. This lets systems in different domains advertise their services in a pool while maintaining control of their own policies and services. This loose federation of traders is like an electronic bazaar. When a trader links to other traders, it makes the offer spaces of those other traders implicitly available to its own clients.

Each trader's horizon is limited to traders to which it is explicitly linked. But the target traders may in turn be linked to yet more traders. This means that you can reach a large number of traders from your starting trader. The total offer space of a set of linked traders can potentially be very large. The trader service lets you prune a search via *policies*, *constraints*, and *preferences*. It's really a very elaborate system for fine-tuning the dynamic discovery of objects.[1]

Here's a quick explanation of what they each do:

- **Policies** let you define the scope of the search. You specify a policy using a name-value pair. A policy identifies the set of service offers to examine. You specify how the search is to be performed instead of what services to pursue. Each policy partly determines the behavior of the trader. For example, you can set a *hop_count* policy to limit the number of trader links traversed during a

---

[1] We cover the Trader Service (and other CORBA Services) in more detail in **Instant CORBA** (Wiley, 1997).

search. *Scoping policies* allow you to specify the upper bounds of offers to be searched or returned. You can also use policies to limit a search to a single trader or to specify a starting trader. You set default policy values using the trader's **Admin** interface. You can then always override these defaults when you submit an import request.

■ *Constraints* let you specify the search criteria. An importer selects a service type and then specifies a constraint. So what exactly is a constraint? It is a well-formed expression conforming to a constraint language. The Trader Service defines a standard constraint language for interworking between traders. You can specify a different constraint language by including its name between << >> at the start of a constraint expression. For example, you can specify SQL to be your constraint language; you then pass an SQL statement in the constraint string.

■ *Preferences* let you specify the order in which the matching offers are returned. If you do not specify a preference string, the default is *first*—meaning the trader will return the offers in the order it discovers them. Valid preferences are *max*, *min, random,* and *with constraint*. You can specify a preference language by preceding the string with the name of that language—for example, <<SQL>>.

The bottom line is that you use policies to identify the set of service offers to examine. You then specify the search criteria using the service type and constraint. The search is applied against the set of service offers. The trader will then order the results using your preferences.

CONCLUSION

This short chapter explains how an object first discovers its ORB and then uses it to discover the rest of the CORBA universe. It's a classical bootstrap. After it bootstraps, an object can go to its Trader or Naming servers to find other objects. CORBA's Federated Traders have the potential to transform the Object Web into a gigantic online bazaar for objects. At the minimum, you can use Traders to create very powerful publish-and-subscribe systems for Web objects.[2] In the next chapter, we look at how the ORB activates its objects.

---

[2] In one of our CORBA/Java graduate classes, we assigned a class project to implement a minimalist CORBA Trader Service. Most students were able to complete their project in one semester working in groups of three. They created 3-tier client/server versions of the Trader Service using CORBA, Java, and JDBC. So, we know it can be done. In mid-1997, Iona became the first CORBA vendor to ship a full implementation of the Trader Service.

Chapter 18

Who Activates My Objects?

In all of our examples so far, we had to manually prestart the **Count** server objects before the client could connect to them. But what happens if a server supports millions of objects? We shouldn't have to prestart all of them before clients can connect to them. If we did, even the largest supercomputer could be brought to its knees. The CORBA philosophy is to keep the client side simple. In this case, simple means that the clients must view all objects on the server as being up and running all the time. These server objects must appear to be always actively waiting on the client to invoke their operations (or methods).

CORBA does not even provide an explicit command for a client to start up a server object.[1] Consequently, it falls upon the server side of the ORB to provide the illusion that all its objects—and there can be millions of them—are up and running and active all the time, even though they are not. This illusion keeps the client code simple, but it shifts the implementation burden to the server side. You must write code that cooperates with the ORB when you start and stop your objects or when the ORB starts up or shuts down. In other words, you must help the ORB provide an automatic startup function. The ORB should be able to either prestart an object or start it on demand when clients invoke it.

---

[1] The one exception is when the client creates a new object via a CORBA *factory*. The new object is then implicitly started by the factory.

Your implementation must also cooperate with a *Persistence Service* to save and restore the state of your server objects; you must do it in a way that is totally transparent to the client. For example, the client must be able to pass around an object reference, store it in a string format in a database or naming service, and then be able—perhaps many years later—to use the reference to retrieve the same object. Your server object must be able to resurrect itself in the same state the client left it in. Of course, if the object is shared, its state can be modified by another client in the interim. But you get the idea.

This chapter looks at the ORB activation (and deactivation) policies. We explain how your server objects conspire with the *Basic Object Adapter (BOA)* to give clients the illusion that every object they know of is always available. We then look at the *VisiBroker for Java* activation policies. Finally, we cover the CORBA 3.0 *Portable Object Adapter (POA)*. POA is a key element of the CORBA server-side portability story. POA lets you control and fine-tune—via policies—almost every aspect of the server run time; it provides the foundation for writing very scalable server applications. In addition, POA complements *Enterprise JavaBeans*, and vice versa. The EJB framework starts out where POA leaves off. We've been using aspects of POA in our programs starting with Part 3. This chapter tells you what's under-the-hood.

THE SERVER SIDE OF CORBA

POA is overhauling the server-side of CORBA. However, most CORBA programmers are still using BOA today. So, we started with BOA programs and then migrated to POA in Part 3. In this section, explain how BOA really works. You will need to understand this material to get a better appreciation of POA, which we cover later in this chapter. So we recommend that you read this section on BOA even if you are a POA practitioner.

The CORBA::BOA Interface

The BOA in OMG terminology is a *pseudo-object*. It is an object that is created directly by the ORB, but you can invoke it like any other object. The BOA provides operations that your server-object implementations can access. It also interfaces with the ORB core and with the implementation skeletons through private interfaces, which means they're ORB-specific. This is an area that the OMG also addressed in its second round of server standardization.

Figure 18-1 shows the methods (or operations) that OMG defines for the **CORBA::BOA** interface. You use this interface to create or destroy object references and to query or update the information the BOA maintains for an object reference. The BOA maintains a registry of the active objects and implementations that it controls. You use the **BOA** interface to communicate with this registry and tell the ORB about your objects. You can think of this protocol as a conspiracy between your server objects and the ORB to create the illusion that all server objects are active all the time.

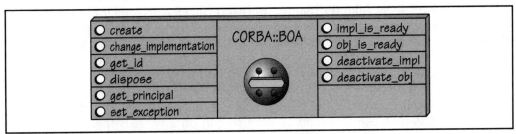

Figure 18-1. The CORBA::BOA Interface.

Let's quickly go over the operations the BOA supports. You invoke *create* to describe the implementation of a new object instance to the BOA and obtain a reference to it. You create the actual object via a language constructor or a factory. You must pass to the ORB three pieces of information it needs to bind the object with a new object reference: 1) an *interface name* that is described in the Interface Repository, 2) an *implementation name* that is described in the Implementation Repository, and 3) some unique *reference data* (or ID) that you define. The reference data is implementation-specific; it is totally opaque to the ORB. You typically use the ID to distinguish between objects or to specify a *Persistent ID (PID)* that points to where the object stores its state. The ORB doesn't care what you do with this ID. Note that POA calls it *Object Id*.

You can update the implementation information associated with an existing object by invoking *change_implementation*. You invoke *get_id* to obtain the reference data associated with this object. You invoke *dispose* to destroy the object reference. You must separately delete the object's resources using the CORBA *Life Cycle Service* or a destructor. You can also let the Java garbage collector do it for you.

The *get_principal* operation has been superseded by the CORBA Security Service; it should return a null. You invoke *set_exception* to tell the ORB that something went wrong. Servers and ORBs use the last four operations—*impl_is_ready, obj_is_ready, deactivate_impl,* and *deacivate_obj*—to activate and deactivate implementations and the objects that run within them. We describe these activation methods in the next section.

BOA and Other Object Adapters

An *Object Adapter* defines how an object is activated. You can do this by creating a new process, creating a new thread within an existing process, or by reusing an existing thread or process. A server could support a variety of object adapters to satisfy different types of requests. For example, an Object Database (ODBMS) may want to implicitly register all the fine-grained objects it contains without issuing individual calls to the Object Adapter. In such a case, it doesn't make sense for an Object Adapter to maintain a per-object state. The ODBMS may want to provide a special-purpose Object Adapter that not only interfaces with the ORB core but also meets its special requirements. However, OMG prefers not to see a proliferation of Object Adapter types. To avoid this proliferation, CORBA 2.0 specifies a *Basic Object Adapter (BOA)* that "can be used for most ORB objects with conventional implementations."

CORBA 2.0 requires that a BOA adapter be available in every ORB. Object implementations that use it should be able to run on any ORB that supports the required language bindings. CORBA requires that the following functions be provided in a BOA implementation:

- An Implementation Repository that lets you install and register an object implementation. It also lets you provide information describing the object.

- Mechanisms for generating and interpreting object references, activating and deactivating object implementations, and invoking methods and passing them their parameters.

- Activation and deactivation of implementation objects.

- Method invocations through skeletons.

BOA supports traditional and object-oriented applications. It does not specify how methods are packaged or located—this could be done through DLLs or a system call at startup that identifies the location of the methods.

CORBA 2.0 makes a clear distinction between a server and its objects. A *server* is an execution unit; it's a process. An *object* implements an interface. A server can contain one or more objects. It can even contain objects of different classes. In the other extreme, a server can contain code that only implements a single method, instead of an entire interface. In all cases, objects get activated within their servers. To get the widest application coverage, CORBA 2.0 defines four activation policies—*shared server, unshared server, server-per-method*, and *persistent server*. These policies specify the rules a given implementation follows for activating objects. Think of them as scheduling policies.

BOA Shared Server

In a *shared server* activation policy, multiple objects may reside in the same program (or process). The BOA activates the server the first time a request is

invoked on any object implemented by that server (see Figure 18-2). After the server has initialized itself, it notifies the BOA that it is prepared to handle requests by calling *impl_is_ready*. All subsequent requests are then delivered to this server process; BOA will not activate another server process for that implementation.

When the process is ready to terminate, it notifies BOA by issuing a *deactivate_impl* call. At this point, all the objects that are running within the process are automatically deactivated. You can also deactivate an individual object at any time by issuing *deactivate_obj*. You may want to do this when there are no active client references to your object. You should note that CORBA does not require that shared server objects invoke *obj_is_ready* when they first come up. However, most ORB implementations—including VisiBroker—require it. CORBA also mentions that objects can be instantiated on demand when an invocation is received. But it leaves the implementation of this concept as an exercise for the ORB vendors. Consequently, it is very non-standard. Later in this chapter, we explain how VisiBroker handles activation. And, you will see how POA provides a standard solution.

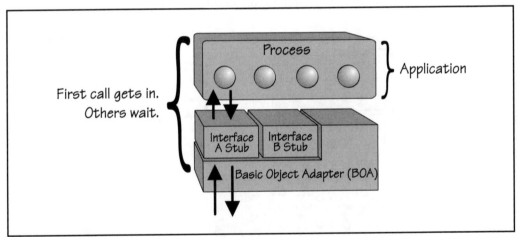

Figure 18-2. The BOA Shared Server Activation Policy.

Most CORBA servers are of the shared server variety. So how do you run multiple objects concurrently within the same process? You do this using threads. You should be warned that this whole area is very implementation-dependent. Because Java supports threads (and its libraries are thread-safe), we recommend that you use a thread to represent each active object instance. You can even use multiple threads to represent the same object to multiple clients. If you do this, you must serialize the access to the state information—for example, you can maintain the state in a multiuser database or treat it as a Java synchronized method. Make sure your ORB is thread-safe. *VisiBroker for Java* is thread-safe. The skeletons it creates also have enough smarts to direct an upcall to an object that's running in its own thread. We will show you how to write multithreaded server objects in Parts 6 and 8.

BOA Unshared Server

In an *unshared server* activation policy, each object resides in a different server process (see Figure 18-3). A new server is activated the first time a request is invoked on the object. When the object has initialized itself, it notifies BOA that it is prepared to handle requests by calling *obj_is_ready*. A new server is started whenever you request an object that is not yet active, even if a server for another object with the same implementation is active. A server object remains active and will receive requests until it calls *deactivate_obj*.

So where would you use an unshared server? You typically use this kind of activation in situations that require a dedicated object. For example, you could have a dedicated object represent a printer or a robot on a manufacturing line. Instead of managing multiple objects, the implementation only handles a single object.

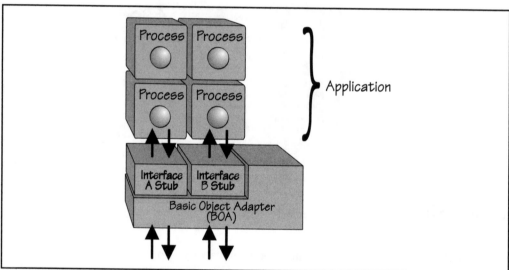

Figure 18-3. The BOA Unshared Server Activation Policy.

BOA Server-per-Method

In a *server-per-method* activation policy, a new server is always started each time a request is made. The server runs only for the duration of the particular method (see Figure 18-4). Several server processes for the same object—or even the same

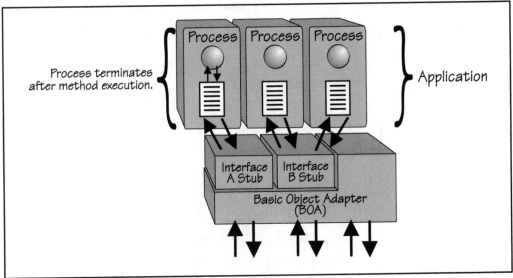

Figure 18-4. The BOA Server-per-Method Activation Policy.

method of the same object—may be concurrently active. A new server is started for each request, so it's not necessary for the implementation to notify BOA when an object is ready or deactivated. BOA activates a new process for each request, whether or not another request for that operation or object is active at the same time.

So where would you use a server-per-method? This is probably the most infrequently used activation policy. The best use of this activation policy is for running scripts or utility programs that execute once and then terminate.

BOA Persistent Server

In a *persistent server* activation policy, servers are activated by means outside BOA (see Figure 18-5). Typically you start the server application, which then notifies BOA that it's ready to accept work by means of an *impl_is_ready* call. BOA treats all subsequent requests as shared server calls; it sends activations for individual objects and method calls to a single process. If no implementation is ready when a request arrives, an error is returned for that request.

So where would you use a persistent server? The persistent server is really just a special case of the shared server. The difference is that the server activation is not handled by the ORB. Generally, you would expect a DBMS, ODBMS, TP Monitor, or Web Server to be up all the time. So these would be good candidate applications for the persistent server policy. All the programs we ran so far are persistent

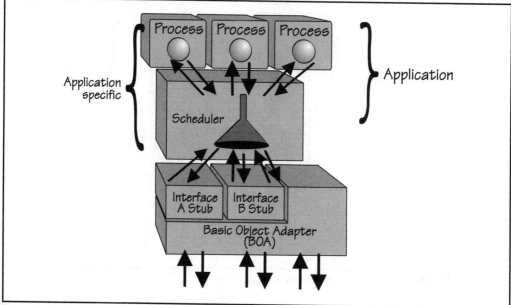

Figure 18-5. The BOA Persistent Server Activation Policy.

servers; we started them from the command line. You may want to create your own scripts to start a server.

An Object Activation Scenario

We will now take you through a shared server scenario that shows how to activate a new object as well as an existing object (see Figure 18-6). Here are the steps a shared server follows:

1. ***The server creates two object instances***. The server either invokes a CORBA factory or a Java constructor to create new instances of the objects.

2. ***The new object registers with the BOA***. Your new server object must invoke *BOA::create*. The object must pass the BOA its *interface name, implementation name,* and some unique *reference data* (or ID) that you define. The *create* call returns an object reference for this new object that you can then pass to *obj_is_ready* to let the ORB know that your object is ready for business.

   Note that *VisiBroker for Java* does not require that you explicitly call *create*. Instead, it requires that your class constructor invoke its *super* and provide it with a name for your object. The super is the skeleton CORBA object from which your class is derived. It provides factory-like services. If this is a new object, the super implicitly invokes the BOA's *create* method. The VisiBroker

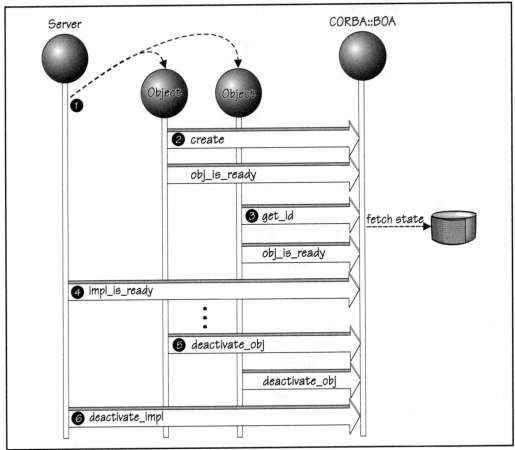

Figure 18-6. A Shared Server Activation Scenario.

OSAgent also keeps track of names of existing objects. In our scenario, the first object is totally new. The second object is known to the OSAgent; it's an existing object that is being reactivated for this scenario.

3. *The existing object registers with the BOA*. Your existing server object already has an object reference. You can use this object reference to obtain the Persistent ID (PID) that is associated with this object. You can then use this PID to load the object's state from a persistent store—for example, an ODBMS or RDBMS. Your object then invokes *obj_is_ready* to let the ORB know that it is ready for business. Note that VisiBroker for Java lets you reactivate an existing object by passing either an object reference or a persistent name.

4. *The server says it's ready for business*. The server has started all its objects. So it invokes *impl_is_ready* to tell the ORB that it's ready to accept client invocations. This starts a do-forever loop for this server.

5. **The objects deactivate**. In our scenario, each object deactivates itself by invoking *deactivate_obj*. There are a variety of strategies for when an object should invoke this method. You may want to issue a *deactivate_obj* when the Object Transaction Service issues a *commit*. The object can then store its state—or, you can issue *deactivate_obj* when the object's thread terminates. Finally, you can issue *deactivate_obj* when no clients are referencing this particular object.

6. **The server shuts down**. The server invokes *deactivate_impl* to tell the ORB that it will not accept subsequent requests.

This scenario demonstrates how server objects cooperate with their ORB to create an illusion that all objects are always active. A new breed of Object TP Monitors can also participate in this conspiracy to provide load-balancing, fault-tolerance, and scalability. We will need these TP Monitors to transparently manage millions of server objects. The TP Monitor will activate and deactivate the objects that it controls as well as manage their state (more on this in the *Enterprise JavaBeans* chapter).

THE VISIBROKER ACTIVATION DAEMON

The first thing to note about VisiBroker is that there is no separate ORB process. The ORB is linked with your client and server code; it runs in the same address space. This means that the ORB is very fast. You do not incur the overhead of an interprocess communication. So who starts this ORB? You start it when you run your program or when an *activation daemon* starts your program. The daemon is a separate program that you can run on your machines to provide automatic activation.

So how does this daemon work? The daemon—with help from the OSAgent—keeps track of all object implementations that are currently active. It also tracks objects that you can activate on demand. When a client invokes a method on an object, the OSAgent and daemon determine if the object is already running. If it is, the client can start communicating with the object directly. If the object is not active, the daemon will automatically activate the server implementation based on its activation policy. After the initial handshake between the object implementation and the daemon, the client can invoke requests on the object directly (see Figure 18-7).

So how do you tell VisiBroker about your objects? In the easiest case, you simply start all your objects when VisiBroker activates the process in which they live. You must issue an *obj_is_ready* call for each object you start. VisiBroker expects you to issue an *impl_is_ready* call when all the objects are ready. Your objects will remain active until the server process terminates or until you issue a *deactivate_obj* call to deactivate a particular object.

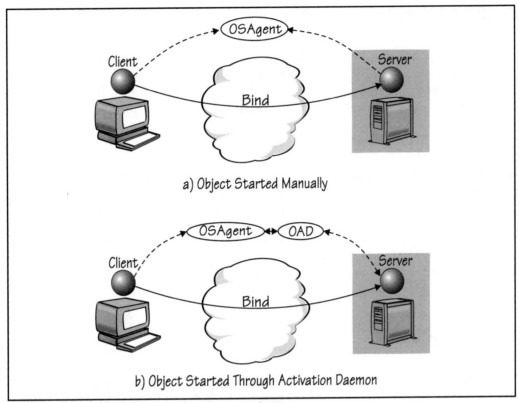

a) Object Started Manually

b) Object Started Through Activation Daemon

Figure 18-7. The VisiBroker for Java Object Activation Runtime.

But what if the activated process contained thousands of objects? In this case, instantiating all these objects in memory at start-up time could be a very costly and wasteful proposition. It is much more efficient to activate an object only when a client invokes it. Think of it as "just-in-time" activation. VisiBroker uses a modified version of *obj_is_ready* to pass a second argument that specifies an **Activator** for this object. This is a special class that implements two methods: *activate*, and *deactivate*. The activate method is called by the BOA when the object is invoked; it's an upcall from the BOA. The *deactivate* method is called when the server shuts down.

VisiBroker also provides a distributed Implementation Repository. Look for a file called *impl_rep* that hangs off the directories where the ORB is installed. This file contains implementation definitions for all objects registered with the BOA and activation daemons.

You use the *listimpl* command to read the contents of an Implementation Repository. You can list all the registered interfaces, object instance names, the pathnames of each implementation's executables, server activation modes, and the arguments and environment variables to be passed to each server when it is activated.

CORBA 3.0'S POA

As we mentioned earlier in this chapter, the client side of CORBA 2.0 is very portable, but the server side isn't. The problem is that the original BOA was underspecified. Consequently, ORB vendors introduced their own BOA extensions to fill in the blanks. This led to implementation inconsistencies in key areas such as: object activation/deactivation, the naming of base skeleton classes, and object registration with the ORB.

In June 1995, OMG issued an RFP for a Portable Server-Side ORB. In June 1997, it adopted the *ORB Portability Joint Submission*, jointly authored by all the major ORB vendors—including BEA, Iona, IBM, Visigenic, Expersoft, SunSoft, and HP. This standard also includes language bindings for C, C++, and Cobol.[2] In November 1997, OMG received an initial submission for the Java server-side bindings (or *POA/Java*).[3] This "preliminary" POA/Java is now partially implemented in the big three Java ORBs—*VisiBroker for Java 3.1*, *OrbixWeb V 3.0*, and the JDK 1.2 version of *Java IDL*.

Is It Goodbye BOA?

The CORBA designers had two choices: 1) fix the BOA, or 2) toss it away and start from scratch. They picked the second approach. Why? It turns out that the vendor BOA extensions were too diverse to reconcile. Consequently, fixing the existing BOA would have led to incompatibilities with existing ORBs. Instead of creating a gigantic migration problem, the CORBA designers chose not to touch the existing BOA—it continues to live "as is." In addition, they defined a portable version of BOA called the *Portable Object Adapter (POA)*. Originally, they were also going to define the higher-level *Server Framework Adapters (SFAs)*. The SFAs were replaced with short chapters that cover language-specific constructs in the POA.

So what does this do to your existing applications? The good news is that you won't have to rewrite your existing server objects; you only have to rewrite the code that interfaces to the ORB. For example, *obj_is_ready* has now been replaced by *connect* in the new OMG mappings for portable server implementations (the POA); *deactivate_obj* has been replaced by *disconnect*. In addition, your server objects automatically become POA servants by extending **_XXXImplBase**. We went through this transition earlier in this book; it wasn't too traumatic. Finally, POA opens up the internals of a CORBA server to system programmers; it lets you finely control almost every aspect of the CORBA server environment.

---

[2] See OMG document *orbos/97-05-15*.
[3] See OMG document *orbos/97-11-12*.

Most vendors will continue to maintain their BOA (alongside the POA) for many years to come. Remember that ORBs are designed to support multiple object adapters. So most ORBs will allow BOA and POA semantics to coexist for some time. Eventually, POA will completely replace BOA.

POA: The Big Picture

The POA is simply the BOA done right. Its design incorporates several years of experience by ORB vendors and users. Like BOA, the POA deals with the transparent activation of objects (remember the big conspiracy). And like BOA, POA can start: 1) a server program for each method, 2) a separate program for each object, and 3) a shared program for all instances of an object type. An implementation can also specify its own activation technique. Finally like BOA, the POA supports both IDL-generated static skeletons and DSI.

POA supports objects that are either *transient* or *persistent*. Transient objects only live within the process that creates them; they require minimal programming effort and overhead. Persistent objects typically have state; their life extends beyond the process that creates them. From the perspective of a client holding an object reference, a persistent object spans multiple server lifetimes.

POA also introduces some new concepts. You can optionally choose to supply a *servant manager* for each implementation of an object interface (or *implementation type*). These are callback objects that create *servants* on demand. Remember, a servant is a running instance of a particular implementation. So the POA invokes operations on servant managers to create, activate, and deactivate servants. You can think of these callback objects as *instance managers* that assist the POA in the management of your server-side objects. Of course, you can choose not to implement a servant manager and let the POA implicitly activate and deactivate your servants. The ORB vendors will provide default servant managers as well as servant managers that implement different activation/deactivation policies.

You must register your servant managers with the POA so that it can create instances of your objects. The POA maintains a map of active servant managers. It also maintains a map of the Object Ids of all active objects (or servants) called the *Active Object Map*; it maps Object Ids to running servants. An active object is identified by its object reference that, in turn, encapsulates an *Object Id*. A POA servant can simultaneously support multiple Object Ids. As usual, the client only sees an object reference; it uses it to invoke operations on a target object. On the server side, the ORB, POA, and servant manager cooperate to deliver the incoming request to a particular servant (see Figure 18-8).

POA provides a very flexible architecture that allows ORB vendors to tailor their CORBA servers to fit a variety of application needs. Notice in the figure that a single

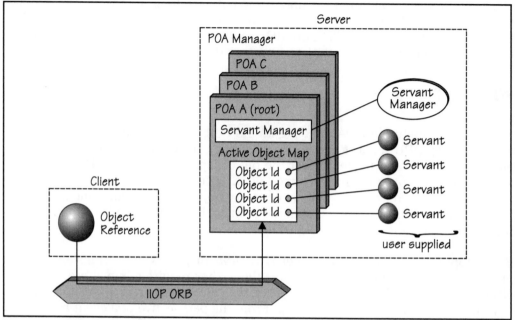

Figure 18-8. POA: The Big Picture.

server can support multiple POAs that are derived from a distinguished POA object called the *root POA*. The ORB vendor provides this root POA. Your server applications can then use it to create more specialized child POAs. Each POA instance can be configured to implement a different set of server-side policies. Here's how a server-side application discovers its root POA:

```
// get the root POA object
org.omg.CORBA.Object object =
            orb.resolve_initial_references("RootPOA");

// Cast it to a POA
org.omg.PortableServer.POA rootpoa =  POAHelper.narrow (object);
```

You can then use this reference to create or destroy new POAs by invoking *create_POA* and *destroy*. You can also use it to customize your POA (more on this later).

Persistent Object References

Your implementation can control a persistent object's behavior by: 1) specifying the data that defines the object's identity, 2) determining the relationship between the object's identity and the object's state, 3) managing the storage and retrieval of the object's state, 4) providing the code that will be executed in response to requests, and 5) determining whether or not the object exists at any point in time.

The *Object Id* is a value that your implementation and the POA use to identify a particular abstract CORBA object. The Object Id values may be assigned and managed by the POA, or they may be assigned and managed by your implementation. In both cases, they are hidden from clients and encapsulated by CORBA object references. Objects Ids have no standard form; they are managed by the POA as uninterpreted octet sequences. The Object Ids must be unique within a POA namespace. CORBA Object references encapsulate both the POA and the Object Id, which makes them unique.

Typically, your server programs will assign their own Object Ids to point to the state of their objects. For example, your Object Id could contain the key for a record in a DBMS that contains the object's state. Or you could let the POA generate these Ids for you by specifying a SYSTEM_ID policy. The POA will then transparently activate your servants and assign them Object Ids.

Servant Managers

You can control almost every aspect of your server's behavior by explicitly specifying a POA's policies. You can also register with the POA your own *servant manager* objects. This lets you control the creation, activation, deactivation, and destruction of your objects. The servant manager can even preload the state of an object instance and use it to initialize the object.

A servant manager is associated with a POA; it must be local to the process containing the POA. A servant manager lets a POA activate objects on demand when the POA receives a request targeted at an inactive object. A servant manager is registered with a POA as a callback object, which means it is invoked by the POA when necessary. An application server that activates all its objects at server startup does not need a servant manager.

If present, servant managers are responsible for managing the association of an object (as characterized by its Object Id value) with a particular servant, and for determining whether an object exists. A servant manager can implement one of two callback interfaces: **ServantActivator** or **ServantLocator**. The one you use depends on the policies you have in place. **ServantActivator** typically handles persistent objects that the POA also tracks in its *Active Object Map*. **Servant-Locator** deals with transient objects—they are not tracked by the POA. Each servant manager type contains two operations; the first is called to find and return a servant, and the second to deactivate a servant. The two types of servant managers correspond to the POA's RETAIN policy (**ServantActivator**) and to the

NON_RETAIN policy (**ServantLocator**). We explain these policies in the next section.

POA Policies

Together, the POA and servant managers enforce policies that let you intimately control the run-time environment of a servant. These policies let you specify the following behaviors for each POA: the thread management model, object life span, Object Id uniqueness, Id assignment technique, servant retention, and the activation model.

Table 18-1 lists the different POA policies. We also show the default policies of the root POA. If you find these default policies suitable, you can then create your objects using the root POA. Otherwise, you must create new POAs with the policies you specify. If you do this, you are then responsible for creating and initializing your POA objects at server start-up time.

You get to specify policies when you invoke *create_POA* on an existing POA to create a new POA. You must first create the **Policy** objects by invoking *create_XXX_policy* factory methods on any pre-existing POA—for example, the root POA. You then pass these **Policy** objects as a parameter of the *create_POA* operation. You cannot change a policy on an existing POA. In addition, a POA cannot inherit the policies of its parent.

You may find that creating your own POA (and its associated servant manager) gives you a tremendous amount of control over the behavior of your persistent objects. Typically, specialized POAs will be provided in the form of *Object Transaction Monitor (OTM)* frameworks (more on this in the *Enterprise JavaBeans* chapter). So you may not be doing this work yourself.

Table 18-1. The POA Polices.

Policy Type	Policy Description and Choices
Thread	This policy specifies the threading model you use with this POA. You can specify the following values: ■ **ORB_CTRL_MODEL**: The POA is responsible for assigning requests to threads. In a multithreaded environment, concurrent requests may be delivered using multiple threads. ■ **SINGLE_THREAD_MODEL**: The POA will process requests sequentially. In a multithreaded environment, all upcalls made by the POA to your implementation code will be made thread-safe. In this environment, the POA only uses the main thread. Root POA Default: **ORB_CTRL_MODEL**

Table 18-1. The POA Polices. (Continued)

Policy Type	Policy Description and Choices
Lifespan	This policy specifies the persistence model for this POA. You can specify the following values: ■ **TRANSIENT**: Your objects in this POA cannot outlive the process in which they are first created. ■ **PERSISTENT**: Your objects in this POA can outlive the process in which they are first created. Root POA Default: **TRANSIENT**
Object Id Uniqueness	This policy specifies whether the servants activated in this POA have unique Object Ids. You can specify the following values: ■ **UNIQUE_ID**: Servants activated with this POA support exactly one Object Id. ■ **MULTIPLE_ID**: A servant activated with this POA may support one or more Object Ids. Root POA Default: **UNIQUE_ID**
Id Assignment	This policy specifies whether the Object Ids in this POA are generated by the application or by the POA. You can specify the following values: ■ **USER_ID**: Objects are assigned Object Ids only by the application. ■ **SYSTEM_ID**: Objects are assigned Object Ids only by the POA. If the POA also has the **PERSISTENT** policy in effect, the assigned Object Ids must be unique across all instantiations of the same POA. Root POA Default: **SYSTEM_ID**
Servant Retention	This policy specifies whether this POA will retain active servants in an *Active Object Map*. You can specify the following values: ■ **RETAIN**: The POA will retain active servants in its *Active Object Map*. ■ **NON_RETAIN**: Servants are not retained by the POA. In this case, you must also enable either the **USE_DEFAULT_SERVANT** or **USE_SERVANT_MANAGER** policies. Root POA Default: **RETAIN**
Activation	This policy specifies if this POA supports the implicit activation of objects. You can specify the following values: ■ **IMPLICIT_ACTIVATION**: This POA will support implicit activation. ■ **NO_IMPLICIT_ACTIVATION**: This POA will not support implicit activation. Root POA Default: **IMPLICIT_ACTIVATION**
Request Processing	This policy specifies how requests are processed in this POA. You can specify the following values: ■ **USE_ACTIVE_OBJECT_MAP_ONLY**: If this POA does not find an Object Id in its map, it returns an exception to the client. The POA must also be using the **RETAIN** policy.

Table 18-1. The POA Polices. (Continued)

Policy Type	Policy Description and Choices
Request Processing (continued)	■ **USE_DEFAULT_SERVANT**: If this POA does not find the Object Id in its map or if the **NON_RETAIN** policy is present, it will dispatch the call to a default servant. You must have previously registered this default servant with the POA using *set_servant*. ■ **USE_SERVANT_MANAGER**: If this POA does not find the Object Id in its map or if the NON_RETAIN policy is present, it will dispatch the call to a servant manager. You must have previously registered this servant manager with the POA using *set_servant_manager*.
	Root POA Default: **USE_ACTIVE_OBJECT_MAP_ONLY**

Playing the Policy Game

You can create some interesting server behaviors by combining POA policies. Here are some examples:

■ *RETAIN and USE_ACTIVE_OBJECT_MAP_ONLY*. This is a good combination for servers that manage a finite number of pre-started objects—for example, services that must execute continuously (or as long as the server is executing). At servant start-up, your main program can create all the available servants, and load their state and identities from some persistent store. Your application must explicitly activate all objects served by this POA. You do this by either invoking *activate_object* or *activate_object_with_id* on the POA object. You can also use this combination to prestart well-known objects that act as initial points of contact that clients can use to access other objects—for example, factories. This approach always ensures that your objects are available when the POA is active, and it doesn't require writing servant managers. However, it has severe practical limitations for applications that must service a large number of objects.

■ *RETAIN and USE_SERVANT_MANAGER*. This combination is ideal for servers that manage a large number of persistent objects. At server start-up, your application invokes *activate_object* or *activate_object_with_id* on the **POA** to register well-known servants in its *Active Object Map*. You must also invoke *set_servant_manager* to register a servant manager of type **ServantActivator**. Later, if the POA doesn't find a servant in its *Active Object Map*, it invokes the *incarnate* method on the **ServantActivator** to activate this object on-demand.

■ *RETAIN and USE_DEFAULT_SERVANT*. This combination is ideal for servers that support a large number of transient objects; it introduces a minimal amount of per-object overhead. The POA uses a default servant to handle all requests involving unknown objects. At server start-up, your application invokes the **POA** *activate_object* or *activate_object_with_id* methods to register well-known servants in the *Active Object Map.* You also invoke *set_servant* to register the default servant with the POA. Later, the POA first tries to find a servant object in its map. If it fails, it invokes the default servant.

- *NON_RETAIN and USE_SERVANT_MANAGER.* This combination is ideal for situations where one servant is used per method call. For each remote invocation, the POA calls *preinvoke* on a servant manager of type **ServantLocator.**

As you can see, the POA policies let you control many key aspects of a server's run-time environment. However, POA does not currently support declarative policies for transactions. This is an area where *Enterprise JavaBeans* complements POA very nicely (more on this in the EJB chapter).

POA: Creating Object References

Servers create object references that can be exported to clients. You create references in the following ways:

- *By explicitly invoking the POA's factory methods.* A server application can directly create a reference by invoking the *create_reference* and *create_reference_with_id* methods on a POA object. These operations collect the necessary information to create the object reference—either from information associated with the POA or as parameters to the operation. Note that these operations only create the object reference. They do not associate the reference with an active servant. This decoupling is useful in situations where you do not have to create an object reference and a servant at the same time.

- *Explicitly at object activation.* A server application can explicitly activate a servant and then associate it with an Object Id by invoking the *activate_object* or *activate_object_with_id* methods on a POA object. The application can explicitly generate references for its objects by invoking the POA's *create_reference* or *create_reference_with_id* methods. Or, it can obtain the object reference of an active server by invoking the POA's *servant_to_reference* or *id_to_reference* methods.

- *Implicitly at object activation.* A server can cause a servant to implicitly activate itself by creating a POA that supports the IMPLICIT_ACTIVATION policy. If an attempt is made to obtain an object reference for an inactive servant, the POA automatically generates a unique Object Id for this servant and activates the resulting object. You can always obtain the reference either by invoking the

POA's *servant_to_reference* method or by performing a typecast from a programming language CORBA mapping that supports this conversion.

Once the server creates an object reference, it can make it available to clients in a variety of ways. First, it can advertise it using the CORBA Naming and Trading Services. Second, it can convert it to a string via *object_to_string* and publish it in some way that allows the client to discover the string and convert it to a reference using *string_to_object*. Third, it can return the reference as the result of a method invocation.

Once a client obtains a reference, it becomes the identity of the object from the client's perspective. As long as the client holds this reference, it can use it to invoke requests that the ORB sends to the same object. Of course, the server side has to go through a little dance to create this illusion, as we explain in the next sections.

Object Activation, POA-Style

As you saw in the previous section, the POA makes a clear distinction between the creation of object references and the activation of servants. At any point in time, a CORBA object may or may not be associated with an active servant. If the POA has a RETAIN policy, the servant and its associated Object Id are entered into the appropriate POA's *Active Object Map*. The object is then activated. This activation can occur in one of the following ways:

■ ***Explicitly, via calls to the POA.*** Your server application can explicitly activate individual objects by invoking the POA's *activate_object* or *activate_object_with_id* methods. Typically, you do this if your implementation has a reasonably small number of servants and you want to keep them all active continuously. When the server initializes, your main program can create all the available servants.

■ ***On-demand using a servant manager.*** The server application instructs the POA to activate objects on demand by invoking a user-supplied servant manager. You must first register this servant manager with the POA by invoking its *set_servant_manager* method.

■ ***Implicitly.*** If the IMPLICIT_ACTIVATION policy is in effect, the POA will implicitly activate an object when it receives a call for a servant that is not already active, which means it is not associated with an Object Id. The USE_DEFAULT_SERVANT policy instructs the POA to activate unknown objects by invoking the same servant no matter what the Object Id is. You must first register this servant with the POA by invoking the *set_servant* method. The NON_RETAIN policy will cause the POA to activate a servant only for the duration of a method invocation. For each request, the POA locates an active servant using either a default servant or a servant manager.

Finding the Target Object

An ORB request contains the Object Id of the target object as well as the identification of the POA that created the target object reference. When a client issues a request on an object reference, the ORB first locates an appropriate server (perhaps starting one if needed). Then it locates the appropriate POA within that server.

If the POA does not exist in the server process, the application has the opportunity to recreate the required POA by using an *adapter activator*. This is another user-implemented callback object that you can associate with a POA. It is invoked by the ORB when a request is received for a non-existent child POA. Activator objects must implement the POA-defined **AdapterActivator** interface; it consists of a single method.

Once the ORB locates the appropriate POA, it hands it the request. The POA then processes the request based on the policies that are in effect. Here's what may happen:

- If the POA has a RETAIN policy, it will look in its *Active Object Map* to determine if there is a servant associated with the Object Id from this request. If it finds one, it invokes the incoming method on that servant.

- If the POA has a NON_RETAIN policy or has a RETAIN policy but can't find a servant in its *Active Object Map*, it then does one of the following: 1) invokes the method on a default servant if the USE_DEFAULT_SERVANT policy is in effect, or 2) invokes an *incarnate* or *preinvoke* method on a servant manager if the USE_SERVANT_MANAGER policy is in effect.

In addition to raising the standard CORBA exceptions, a servant manager is capable of raising a **ForwardRequest** exception. This exception includes an object reference to which the ORB must forward this request. Typically, you would use this type of exception to notify the client that an object has moved to a new location.

POA/Java

In Java, the base **Servant** type is mapped to the Java **org.omg.CORBA.portable. ObjectImpl** class. It is the base class of all **xxxImplBase** servant skeletons. Remember, a CORBA compiler generates one of these classes for each of your IDL interfaces. The skeleton provides the default servant behavior that you then inherit in your implementations (or servants). All the skeleton classes provide a *_this* method. Your servant can invoke _this_ to obtain the CORBA object reference that it is incarnating in this request.

POA/Java defines four new **ORB** helper functions: _connect, disconnect, init,_ and _set_parameters_. These functions should be familiar to you by now. In POA terms, the _connect_ function is equivalent to calling _activate_object_ on the root POA. You invoke it to add your object (or servant) to the POA's _Active Object Map_. You invoke _disconnect_ to deactivate your object; it is equivalent to calling _deactivate_object_ on the root POA.

Finally, the **AdapterActivator**, **ServantActivator**, and **ServantLocator** interfaces map to Java like any other CORBA interfaces.

The POA Interfaces

Figure 18-9 shows the key POA-related interfaces. In addition, we show the POA-related methods in the **ORB** interface. Most of us will use the ORB interface to register our servants with the POA. We will then let the ORB deal with the POA. All our portable implementations extend the CORBA-generated **xxxImplBase** skeletons. Consequently, they are POA-aware, which means they behave like servants from day one. In any case, this is all we can do with today's ORBs.

As we go to press, none of the Java ORBs expose the POA interfaces. This may change, however, by the time you read this. In the meantime, just keep in mind that your ORBs are built on a set of well-defined POA objects. Soon, you will be able to use the POA interfaces to customize your server environments.

Of course, the POA will be your key interface. However, servant managers are just as important. You need to provide them to manage your persistent objects and activate them on demand. We expect that CORBA _Enterprise JavaBeans_ servers will make full use of these callback objects.

Like we said earlier, there are two kinds of servant managers: **ServantActivator** and **ServantLocator**. The type you use depends on the POA policies that are in effect. In general, you will use the **ServantActivator** to activate persistent objects and the **ServantLocator** to activate transient objects. Both interfaces inherit from **ServantManager**, which is an empty interface; it serves as a flag.

POA Scenario 1

This POA presentation wouldn't be complete without a couple of usage scenarios. In the first scenario, we will build a server environment that supports one perma-

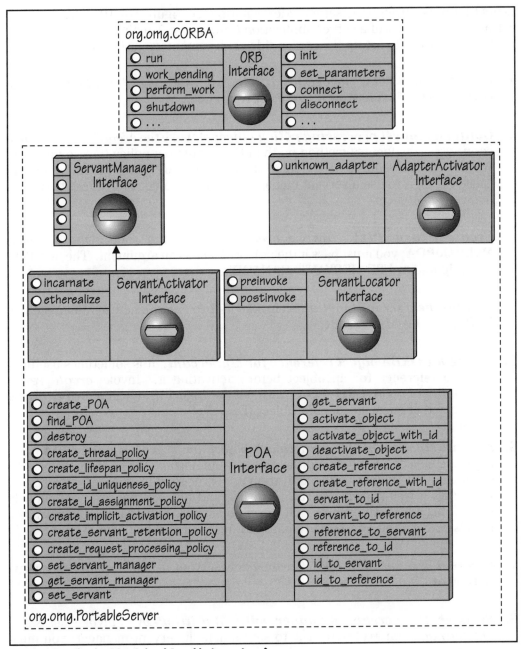

Figure 18-9. The Key POA-Related Portable Server Interfaces.

nently activated servant. We will also provide a servant manager that can activate new servants on demand. In the second scenario, we show how clients interact with this server.

Lets's first walk through the server-side scenario (see Figure 18-10). This scenario is from the viewpoint of a server application (your server's main). Here's what you must do at startup to set up the server-side environment we just described:

1. **Find the root POA.** Invoke *resolve_initial_references("RootPOA")* on the **ORB** object. Then narrow it to a **POA** reference.

2. **Obtain a request processing policy object.** Invoke the *create_request_pro-cessing_policy* factory method on the POA to obtain a policy that you can set. We will set the request policy value to USE_SERVANT_MANAGER. This will cause the POA to use a servant manager to activate objects it cannot find in its *Active Object Map*.

3. **Create a new POA.** Invoke *create_POA* on the root POA to create **MyLittlePOA**; you must pass it the policy object as an argument. The new POA is configured to USE_SERVANT_MANAGER.

4. **Create a new servant instance.** Invoke *new* to create a new servant instance. Its Object ID is **MyServant**.

5. **Create a CORBA object reference for MyServant.** It is sometimes useful to create a reference for an object before activating it. Invoke *create_refer-ence_with_id* on **MyLittlePOA** passing it the Object ID; it will return an object reference that encapsulates the Object ID.

6. **Activate MyServant.** Invoke *activate_object_with_id* on **MyLittlePOA** passing it the Object ID; it will add the object to its *Active Object Map*. This is an example of an explicit object activation at server start-up time. Typically, you will activate well-known objects, factories, and objects that are continuously used. This approach ensures that these objects are always available when the POA is active. And, it doesn't require writing a servant manager.

7. **Create a servant manager.** Create a new servant manager of type **Servant-Activator**.

8. **Register the servant manager with MyLittlePOA.** Invoke *set_serv-ant_manager* on **MyLittlePOA** to set its default servant manager; you must pass it the **ServantActivator** object.

9. **Start the daemon.** Invoke *run* on the **ORB** to start receiving calls.

In the next scenario, we will invoke objects on this server.

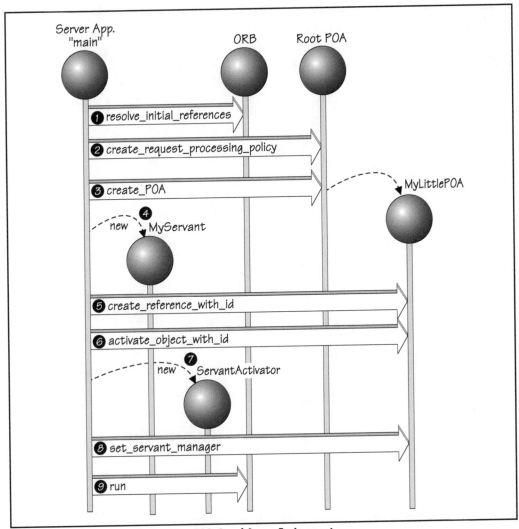

Figure 18-10. Scenario 1: Setting Up a POA-Based Server Environment.

POA Scenario 2

Figure 18-11 shows what happens when a client invokes objects on the POA we just created. This client will invoke the already active **MyServant** as well as an inactive object called **MyOtherServant**. We assume the client obtained references to these two objects by some means. Let's walk through this client/server scenario:

1. ***The client invokes doSomething on MyServant***. The object reference of **MyServant** contains the name of the POA that manages this object. So the ORB

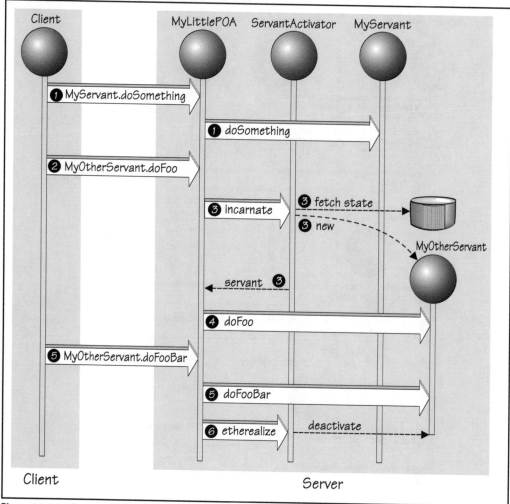

Figure 18-11. Scenario 2: Client Invocations on a POA-Managed Server.

locates **MyLittlePOA**. Then it hands it the method invocation. Next, **MyLittle-POA** extracts the Object ID from the object reference; it discovers that **MyServant** is already active and registered in its *Active Object Map*. So **MyLittlePOA** does an upcall and invokes *doSomething* on **MyServant**.

2. *The client invokes doFoo on MyOtherServant*. Again, the ORB finds **MyLittlePOA** and hands it the method invocation. This time, **MyLittlePOA** doesn't find the Object Id for **MyOtherServant** in its *Active Object Map*. However, this POA is configured to USE_SERVANT_MANAGER; it has a servant manager of type **ServantActivator**.

3. *MyLittlePOA tells its servant manager to activate this object*. It invokes

the *incarnate* method on the **ServantActivator** and passes it the Object Id for **MyOtherServant**. It previously extracted this Object Id from the object reference. The **ServantActivator** will recreate in memory the object with its previous state. It does this by following these steps: 1) retrieves the state from a DBMS using the Object Id as a key, 2) creates a servant of the appropriate implementation class, 3) initializes the servant with the state it retrieved from the DBMS, and 4) returns a reference to the new servant instance to **MyLittlePOA**—it's the return value of the *incarnate* call. **MyLittlePOA** can now add this servant to its *Active Object Map*.

4. **MyLittlePOA invokes the method**. It invokes *doFoo* on **MyOtherServant**.

5. **The client invokes doFooBar on MyOtherServant**. This time **MyLittlePOA** finds **MyOtherServant** in its Active Object Map. So it invokes *doFooBar* directly on the object without involving the servant manager.

6. **MyLittlePOA deactivates the servant**. **MyLittlePOA** decides for whatever reason to remove **MyOtherServant** from its Active Object Map. For example, this could be part of a garbage-collection scheme, or it may be based on the number of active objects reaching some limit. You can also explicitly tell a POA to deactivate an object by invoking *deactivate_object*. Regardless of the reason, **MyLittlePOA** invokes *etherealize* on the **ServantActivator** passing it an Object Id. The servant manager deactivates the object. Typically, it will first tell the object to save its state and release its resources. Activation/deactivation is another area where *Enterprise JavaBeans* complements POA. It introduces a standard callback interface that allows a container to explicitly notify the object when it is being created, activated, deactivated, and destroyed (more on this in the EJB chapter).

This concludes our second scenario. Again, be warned that the existing ORBs don't surface this part of the POA yet. So we can't use these facilities in our code, which is a pity. Perhaps it will be in the next edition of this book.

CONCLUSION

This conceptual chapter was mostly for server-side CORBA developers. We wanted you to be aware of the services an ORB provides to activate and deactivate your objects. The POA is a giant step in the right direction. It opens up the CORBA server and lets you control—using policies—almost every aspect of the server run time. We assume the full-function commercial implementations of the POA will work as advertised. Also, POA needs to be augmented with *Enterprise JavaBeans* before CORBA ORBs can be declared ready for client/server prime time. As you will see in Part 7, the EJB framework starts out where POA leaves off. So we will continue this discussion there.

Chapter 19

Metadata: Who Am I?

Metadata is the ingredient that lets us create agile client/server systems. An agile system is self-describing, dynamic, and reconfigurable. The system helps components discover each other at run time; it provides information that lets them interoperate. An agile system lets you write client software without hardcoding all calls to particular servers. Finally, it provides metadata information that application tools can use to create and manage components.

An agile system differentiates itself from a traditional client/server system by its pervasive use of metadata to consistently describe all available services, components, and data. Metadata allows independently developed components to dynamically discover each other's existence and to collaborate. The pervasive dissemination of metadata is a key ingredient in a distributed component infrastructure. Without it, you have a hard-coded client/server system with no flexibility.

CORBA is such an agile system. To be CORBA-compliant, any component you write must be self-describing. Every system-level object or service that lives on a CORBA bus must also be self-describing. Even the CORBA bus itself is self-describing. As a result, CORBA is a totally self-describing system. The CORBA metadata language is the *Interface Definition Language (IDL)*. The CORBA metadata repository is the *Interface Repository*. It's nothing more than a run-time database that contains the interface specifications of each object an ORB recognizes. Think of the

Interface Repository as a queryable and updatable run-time database that contains IDL-generated information.

The IDL precompiler and the Interface Repository are basic ORB services that are shipped with every CORBA-compliant ORB. The pervasive use of IDL and the Interface Repository makes CORBA more self-describing than any other form of client/server middleware. This chapter covers the CORBA IDL and the Interface Repository. We also cover in detail the new services CORBA 2.0 defines to make the Interface Repository metadata available across multivendor ORBs.

THE CORBA IDL: A CLOSER LOOK

As we said in Chapter 1, IDL is a contractual language that lets you specify a component's boundaries and its interfaces with potential clients. The CORBA IDL is language neutral and totally declarative. This means it does not define the implementation details. The IDL provides operating system and programming language independent interfaces to all services and components that reside on a CORBA bus.

What Does an IDL Contract Cover?

An IDL contract includes a description of any resource or service a server component wants to expose to its clients. Server components must support two kinds of clients: 1) run-time clients that invoke their services, and 2) developers who use IDL to extend an existing component's functions by subclassing. In both cases, IDL is required to specify the component's interfaces so that the implementation can be treated as a black box (or binary code).

You can use CORBA IDL to specify a component's attributes (or public variables), the parent classes it inherits from, the exceptions it raises, typed events, pragmas for generating globally unique identifiers for the interfaces, and the methods an interface supports—including the input and output parameters and their data types. The IDL grammar is a subset of C++ with additional keywords to support distributed concepts; it also fully supports standard C++ preprocessing features.

The IDL is a descriptive language; it supports C++ syntax for constant, type, and operation declarations. However, IDL does not include any procedural structures or variables. Note that because it separates implementation from specification, IDL is a good notational tool for software architects. Most notational languages only provide descriptions of interfaces. In contrast, CORBA IDL provides a direct path between a software architecture—defined by its interfaces—and the compiled code that implements it. From IDL descriptions, a precompiler can directly generate client stubs and server implementation skeletons. IDL also provides a great way to encapsulate low-level APIs and legacy software. Client/server architects will find CORBA IDL to be a very useful and versatile tool.

The Structure of the CORBA IDL

The Interface Repository contains metadata that is identical to the components you describe in IDL. In fact, the Interface Repository is simply an active database that contains compiled versions of the metadata information captured via IDL. So, before we jump into the structure of the Interface Repository, let's take a quick look at what's inside a CORBA IDL file.

Figure 19-1 shows the main elements that constitute the CORBA IDL. Let's go over the pieces:

■ *Modules* provide a namespace to group a set of class descriptions (or *interfaces* in OMG terminology). A module is identified by the keyword *module*. A module has a *scoped* name that consists of one or more *identifiers*. This means simple name strings. The identifiers are separated by the characters "::". So the main

```
module <identifier> ←─────────────────────────    Defines a
                                                   naming context
{

 <type declarations>;
 <constant declarations>;
 <exception declarations>;

     interface <identifier> [:<inheritance>] ←    Defines a
         {                                         CORBA class
             <type declarations>;
             <constant declarations>;
             <attribute declarations>;
             <exception declarations>;

             [<op_type>]<identifier>(<parameters>)←   Defines a
             [raises exception][context];            method
                     .
                     .
                     .

             [<op_type>]<identifier>(<parameters>)←   Defines a
             [raises exception][context];            method
                     .
                     .

         }

     interface <identifier> [:<inheritance>]←    Defines a
                     .                            CORBA class
                     .
}
```

Figure 19-1. The Structure of a CORBA IDL File.

purpose of a module is to introduce an additional level of hierarchy in the IDL namespace.

■ **Interfaces** define a set of methods (or *operations* in OMG terminology) that a client can invoke on an object. Think of it as a class definition, but without the implementation section. An interface can declare one or more *exceptions* that indicate an operation did not perform successfully. An interface may have *attributes*. These are values for which the implementation automatically creates *get* and *set* operations. You can declare an attribute read-only, in which case the implementation only provides the *get* function. An interface can be derived from one or more interfaces, which means IDL supports multiple interface inheritance. You define inheritance relationships using a C++-like syntax.

- **Operation** is the CORBA equivalent of a method. It denotes a service that clients can invoke. The IDL defines the operation's *signature*, which means the method's parameters and the results it returns. A parameter has a *mode* that indicates whether the value is passed from client to server (*in*), from server to client (*out*), or both (*inout*). The parameter also has a *type* that constrains its possible values. The *op_type* is the type of the return value. The method signature optionally defines the exceptions that a method *raises* when it detects an error. An optional *context* expression contains a set of attribute values that describe a client's context. It lets a client pass information to a server that describes its local environment.

- **Data types** are used to describe the accepted values of CORBA parameters, attributes, exceptions, and return values. These data types are named CORBA objects that are used across multiple languages, operating systems, and ORBs. CORBA supports two categories of types: *basic* and *constructed*. CORBA's basic types include short, long, unsigned long, unsigned short, float, double, char, boolean, and octet. CORBA's constructed types include enum, string, struct, array, union, sequence, and any. The *struct* type is similar to a C++ structure; it lets you create any complex data type using *typedefs* (meaning type definitions). The *sequence* type lets you pass a variable-size array of objects, but you must still specify a maximum number of items that can be placed in a sequence. The *any* type is very useful in dynamic situations because it can represent any possible IDL data type—basic, constructed, or object reference. This means you can use any to pass any type of information. Each CORBA IDL data type is mapped to a native data type via the appropriate language bindings.

The CORBA IDL is very comprehensive and concise. The entire language is described in 36 pages.[1] This includes the definition of the IDL grammar and all the CORBA data types.

An IDL Example

Was that too much material to digest in one reading? The answer is probably yes. So let's see if we can help make it "perfectly clear" with a quick example. Let's create some IDL to describe the interfaces in Figure 19-2. In the figure, we define two new CORBA interfaces—**Dog** and **Cat**—in a module called *MyAnimals*. Figure 19-3 shows the IDL file that creates these two interfaces.

---

[1] See **CORBA: Architecture and Specification** (OMG, 1996). The CORBA references are listed in the back of this book.

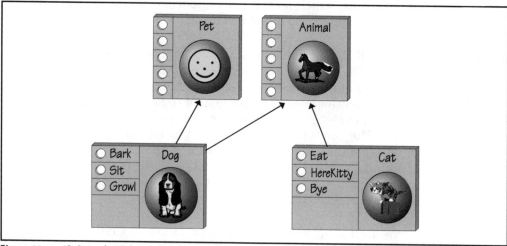

Figure 19-2. MyAnimals With Two Interfaces: Dog and Cat.

```
module MyAnimals
{
    /* Class Definition of Dog */
    interface Dog:Pet, Animal
    {
        attribute integer age;
        exception NotInterested {string explanation};

        void Bark(in short how_long)
            raises (NotInterested);

        void Sit(in string  where)
            raises (NotInterested);

        void Growl(in string  at_whom)
            raises (NotInterested);
    }

    /* Class Definition of Cat */
    interface Cat: Animal
    {
        void Eat();
        void HereKitty();
        void Bye();
    }
} /* End MyAnimals */
```

Figure 19-3. IDL Module MyAnimals With Two Interfaces: Dog and Cat.

The MyAnimals IDL module listed in Figure 19-3 defines two interfaces: **Dog** and **Cat**. **Dog** is derived from the parent classes **Pet** and **Animal**. **Dog** has an attribute called *age* for which the implementation automatically provides *get* and *set* methods. **Dog** supports three methods (or operations): *Bark*, *Sit*, and *Growl*. It *raises* an exception when the dog is not in the mood to obey the master. **Cat** is derived from **Animal** and supports the methods: *Eat*, *HereKitty*, and *Bye* (of course, cats are also pets, but we don't show it in the interface hierarchy).

Type Codes: CORBA's Self-Describing Data

CORBA defines *type codes* that represent each of the IDL-defined data types. You use these type codes to create self-describing data that can be passed across operating systems, ORBs, and Interface Repositories. Each type code has a globally unique Repository ID. Type codes are used in any CORBA situation that requires self-describing data. For example, they are used:

- *By Dynamic Invocation Interfaces* to indicate the data types of the various arguments.

- *By Inter-ORB Protocols*—including IIOP and DCE/ESIOP—to specify the data types of arguments within messages that get passed across ORBs and operating systems. So it serves as a canonical data representation.

- *By Interface Repositories* to create ORB-neutral IDL descriptions.

- *By the any data type* to provide a self-describing generic parameter.

The CORBA **TypeCode** interface defines a set of methods that let you operate on type codes, compare them, and obtain their descriptions (see Figure 19-4). For example, you can invoke a *content_type* operation on arrays or sequences to obtain

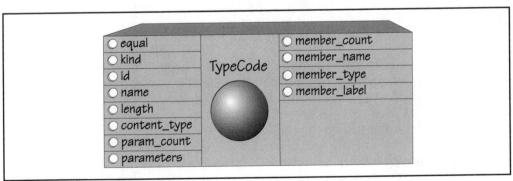

Figure 19-4. The CORBA TypeCode Interface.

the element type they contain. Note that many of the operations are data-type specific. For example, you can only invoke the member operations on structures, unions, and enumerated data types.

THE CORBA 2.0 INTERFACE REPOSITORY

CORBA 2.0 not only greatly enhances the functions of the CORBA 1.1 Interface Repository, it also broadens their inter-ORB scope. So, you can now create federations of Interface Repositories that operate across ORBs while maintaining the autonomy of local administrators. CORBA 2.0 introduces two new features that make this possible: 1) a set of new methods for *incrementally* updating the contents of an Interface Repository at run time, and 2) globally unique *Repository IDs* that can be used in a distributed namespace. This section covers the Interface Repository in some detail. If it gets too detailed, just fast-forward to the next section.

What's an Interface Repository?

A CORBA 2.0 *Interface Repository* is an on-line database of object definitions. You can capture these definitions directly from an IDL-compiler or through the CORBA Interface Repository write functions—CORBA doesn't care how the information gets there. The CORBA specification, however, does detail how the information is organized and retrieved from the repository. It does this creatively by specifying a set of classes whose instances represent the information that's in the repository. The class hierarchy mirrors the IDL specification. The result is a highly flexible object database that keeps track of collections of objects organized along the same lines as the IDL. Of course, all the objects in the repository are compiled versions of the information that's in an IDL source file.

Why Is an Interface Repository Needed Anyway?

An ORB needs to understand the definition of the objects it is working with. One way to get these definitions is by incorporating the information into the stubs. The other way to get this information is through a dynamically accessible Interface Repository. What does an ORB do with the information in the repository? It can use the object definitions to do the following:

■ *Provide type-checking of method signatures*. The parameter types are checked regardless of whether the request is issued using dynamic APIs or through a stub. Signatures define the parameters of a method and their type.

- ■ ***Help connect ORBs together.*** A multi-ORB "federation" of Interface Repositories is used to translate objects that go across heterogeneous ORBs. Note that you must use the same Repository ID to describe these objects. You must define the interfaces of these intergalactic objects in all ORB repositories.

- ■ ***Provide metadata information to clients and tools.*** Clients use the Interface Repository to create "on-the-fly" method invocations. Tools—such as class browsers, application generators, and compilers—can use the information to obtain inheritance structures and class definitions at run time.

- ■ ***Provide self-describing objects.*** You can invoke the *get_interface* method on any CORBA object to obtain its interface information (after that information is installed in the Interface Repository).

Interface Repositories can be maintained locally or managed as departmental or enterprise resources. They serve as valuable sources of metadata information on data structures and component interfaces. An ORB may have access to multiple Interface Repositories.

Interface Repository Classes: The Containment Hierarchy

The Interface Repository is implemented as a set of objects that represent the information in it. These objects must be persistent, which means they must be stored on a non-volatile medium. CORBA groups the metadata into modules that represent naming spaces. The repository object names are unique within a module. CORBA defines an interface for each of its eight IDL structures:

- ■ ***ModuleDef*** defines a logical grouping of interfaces. Like an IDL file, the Interface Repository uses modules to group interfaces and to navigate through groups by name. So you can think of a module as providing a namespace.

- ■ ***InterfaceDef*** defines the object's interface; it contains lists of constants, typedefs, exceptions, and interface definitions.

- ■ ***OperationDef*** defines a method on an object's interface; it contains lists of parameters and exceptions raised by this operation.

- ■ ***ParameterDef*** defines an argument of a method.

- ■ ***AttributeDef*** defines the attributes of an interface.

- ■ ***ConstantDef*** defines a named constant.

- ■ ***ExceptionDef*** defines the exceptions that can be raised by an operation.

- ■ ***TypeDef*** defines the named types that are part of an IDL definition.

In addition to these eight interfaces that represent IDL structures, CORBA specifies a **Repository** interface that serves as the root for all the modules contained in a repository namespace. Each Interface Repository is represented by a global root repository object. Figure 19-5 shows the containment hierarchy for objects that belong to these interfaces (or classes). You'll notice that some of the objects—for example, instances of the **Repository** class—contain other objects. Some objects—for example, instances of the **ModuleDef** class—are both contained and containers. Finally, some objects—for example, instances of the **ExceptionDef** class—are always contained in other objects, but they don't contain objects of their own.

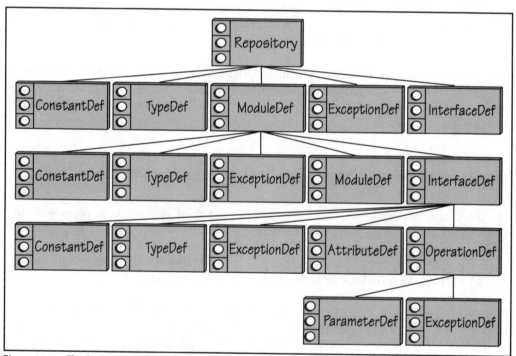

Figure 19-5. The Containment Hierarchy for the Interface Repository Classes.

The Interface Repository Class Hierarchy

The CORBA Interface Repository architects noticed these containment hierarchies, and then defined three abstract superclasses—or classes that cannot be instantiated—called **IRObject**, **Contained**, and **Container** (see Figure 19-6). Notice that this figure shows an inheritance hierarchy as opposed to a containment hierarchy. All Interface Repository objects inherit from the **IRObject** interface, which is new to CORBA 2.0. This interface provides an attribute operation for identifying the actual type of an object as well as a *destroy* method. Objects that are containers

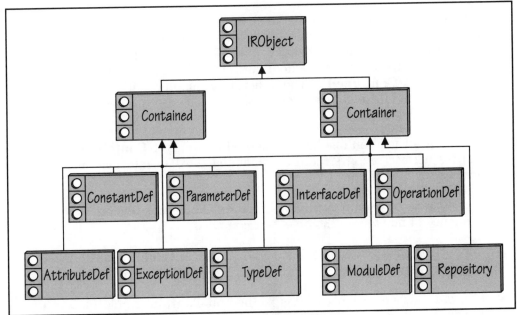

Figure 19-6. The Inheritance Hierarchy of the Interface Repository Classes.

inherit navigation operations from the **Container** interface. The **Contained** interface defines the behavior of objects contained in other objects. All the repository classes are derived from **Container**, from **Contained**, or from both through multiple inheritance. This clever scheme allows the repository objects to behave according to their containment relationships (also see the next Details box).

The Interface Repository: A Closer Look

Details

Figure 19-7 shows a class hierarchy of the more important Interface Repository classes (and their interfaces). The rest of the classes simply inherit from these interfaces; they are not shown here. The Interface Repository classes provide operations that let you read, write, and destroy metadata that's stored in a repository. The *destroy* operation deletes an object from the repository; if you apply this operation on a container object, it will destroy all its contents. The **Contained** interface provides a *move* operation to remove an object from its current container and add it to a target container. The write, destroy, and move operations are new to CORBA 2.0.

You access Interface Repository metadata by invoking methods polymorphically on different object types. Because of this clever design, you can navigate and extract information from repository objects with only nine methods (see Figure 19-7). Five of these methods are derived from the ancestor classes **Container** and **Contained**. The other four methods are specific to the **InterfaceDef** and **Repository** interfaces. Here's a description of the read and navigation methods:

- *Describe*—when you invoke this method on a target **Contained** object, it returns a Description structure containing the IDL information that "describes" the object.

- *Lookup*—when you invoke this method on **Container** objects, it returns a sequence of pointers to the objects it contains.

- *Lookup_name*—you invoke this method on a **Container** object to locate an object by name.

- *Contents*—when you invoke this method on **Container** objects, it returns the list of objects directly contained or inherited by this object. You use this method to navigate through a hierarchy of objects. For example, you can start with a **Repository** object and list all the objects it contains, and so on.

- *Describe_contents*—when you invoke this method on a **Container** object, it returns a sequence of pointers to the content descriptions of the objects it contains. This method combines the *contents* and *describe* operations. You can limit the scope of the search by excluding inherited objects or by looking for a specific type of object (for example, of type InterfaceDef).

- *Describe_interface*—when you invoke this method on an **InterfaceDef** object, it returns a structure that fully describes the interface—including its name, Repository ID, version number, operations, attributes, and all the parent interfaces.

- *Is_a*—when you invoke this method on an **InterfaceDef** object, it returns TRUE if the interface is identical to or inherits directly from an interface that you specify in an input parameter.

- *Lookup_id*—you invoke this method on a **Repository** object to look up an object in a repository given its Repository ID.

- *Get_primitive*—you invoke this method on a **Repository** object to obtain a reference on a primitive object. This means an immutable object type that is owned by the repository. Examples of primitive objects include object references, principals, base data types, and type codes.

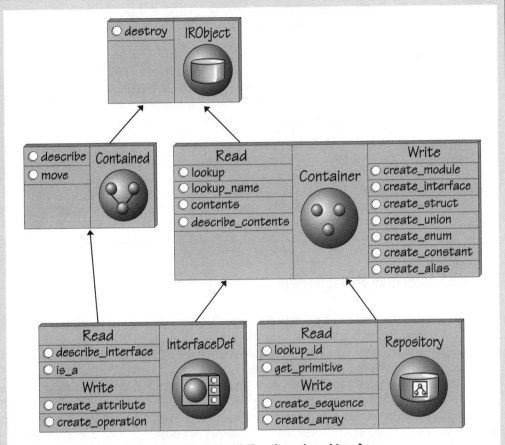

Figure 19-7. Interface Repository: The Top-Level Class Hierarchy and Interfaces.

Together, these method calls allow you to navigate through an Interface Repository. You can search through the namespaces of specific modules to look for objects that meet your search criteria. When you find an object, you use the *describe* method to retrieve the IDL information that defines it. Also, remember that **IRObject**, **Container**, and **Contained** are abstract classes, which means that you never deal with them directly. Instead, you invoke methods on Interface Repository objects that inherit their behavior from these abstract base classes.

How Do You Find an Interface in the First Place?

You can locate an object's interface in one of three ways:

1. ***By directly calling the Object::get_interface method.*** You can issue this call against any valid object reference. The call will return an **InterfaceDef** ob-

ject that fully describes the object's interface. This method is useful when you encounter an object whose type you do not know at compile time.

2. *By navigating through the module namespace using a sequence of names.* For example, if you know the name of the interface you're after, you can start by looking for it in the root module of the repository. When you find the entry, invoke the method *InterfaceDef::describe_interface* to obtain the metadata that describes that interface.

3. *By locating the InterfaceDef object that corresponds to a particular Repository ID.* You do this by invoking the method *Repository::lookup_id*.

Once you obtain an **InterfaceDef** object, you can invoke its interfaces to obtain the metadata you need. You can then use this metadata to dynamically invoke methods on that object. ❑

Federated Interface Repositories

With the new CORBA 2.0 enhancements, we can now create intergalactic federations of Interface Repositories that operate across multiple ORBs. To avoid name collisions, these repositories assign unique IDs—called *Repository IDs*—to global interfaces and operations. You can use these Repository IDs to replicate copies of the metadata across multiple repositories and still maintain a coherent view across them. This means that the unique identity of an interface is preserved across ORB and repository boundaries. For example, with a global Repository ID, you can obtain some metadata on an interface from a local repository. You can then obtain additional metadata on that *same* interface from a remote repository.

To ensure that IDL definitions in various repositories do not contain any duplicates, CORBA 2.0 defines the following naming conventions:

■ *Scoped names* uniquely identify modules, interfaces, constants, typedefs, exceptions, attributes, operations, and parameters within an Interface Repository. A scoped name consists of one or more identifiers separated by the characters "::".

■ *Repository IDs* globally identify modules, interfaces, constants, typedefs, exceptions, attributes, operations, and parameters. They are used to synchronize definitions across ORBs and Repositories.

The next section describes the mechanisms for creating these global Repository IDs.

What Does a Global Repository ID Look Like?

The *Repository ID* itself is a string consisting of a three-level name hierarchy. CORBA 2.0 defines two formats for specifying global Repository IDs:

■ ***Using IDL names with unique prefixes***. You create a Repository ID using an IDL name that consists of three components separated by colons ":". The first component is the string "IDL". The second component is a list of identifiers separated by "/" characters. The first identifier is a unique prefix, and the rest are the IDL identifiers that make up a scoped name. The third component consists of major and minor versions in decimal format separated by a period. For example, a valid Repository ID for the interface **Cat** in the module MyAnimals is "*IDL:DogCatInc/MyAnimals/Cat/:1.0*". In this case, *DogCatInc* is a unique prefix that denotes an organization. You can also use an Internet ID for a prefix (or any other unique name).

■ ***Using DCE Universal Unique Identifiers (UUIDs)***. DCE provides a UUID generator that calculates a globally unique number using the current date and time, a network card ID, and a high-frequency counter. There's almost no chance for this algorithm to create duplicate UUIDs. The DCE format for the Repository ID also consists of three components separated by colons ":". The first component is the string "DCE". The second component is a printable UUID. The third component is made up of a version number in decimal format. Note that there is no minor version. For example, a DCE Repository ID could look like "*DCE:700dc500-0111-22ce-aa9f:1*".

You can associate Repository IDs with IDL definitions in a variety of ways. For example, an installation tool might generate them for you. Or an IDL precompiler can generate them based on pragma directives that you embed in the IDL (see the next Details box).

Pragmas That Help You Create Repository IDs

Details

Pragmas are special directives to a compiler. In this case, pragmas tell an IDL precompiler how to generate the Repository IDs and associate them with a particular interface. CORBA 2.0 defines three new IDL pragmas that help you create Repository IDs:

■ The ***prefix pragma*** sets a prefix that will be appended to all subsequent IDL-formatted Repository IDs until a new prefix pragma is encountered. The

Chapter 20

The CORBA IDL-to-Java Mapping

In March 1997, the OMG completed the first pass of its CORBA IDL-to-Java mapping; POA/Java is still in the works. The good news is that Java ORBs already provide almost complete implementations of the new bindings—including *VisiBroker for Java* (starting with release 2.5), *OrbixWeb V3.0*, and JavaSoft's *JavaIDL*. You've already encountered some of these new bindings in the code we developed in previous chapters. In this very long chapter, we cover the rest of the gory details. You'll get a ton of reference material that you can always come back to when you need it.

Java programmers will be familiar with the language mappings for the basic CORBA types. However, the constructed types may leave you with a bad headache. They are based on C++ constructs that were deliberately removed from the Java language. Consequently, they are a little harder to digest—how do you represent a C++ union, typedef, or enumeration in Java? This journey into nostalgia is probably something you were hoping to leave behind forever when you moved on to Java. However, most of us still live in a multiplatform and multilanguage world. So until the world becomes 100% pure Java, we will have to live with the reality of distributed clients and servers developed using a variety of languages and platforms.

CORBA IDL is the lingua franca for describing multiplatform services in a heterogeneous world. One of the things IDL-to-Java does very well is map to Java constructs that have their roots in other languages. This mapping saves you from having to do all this work yourself, which is a good thing. So if a C++ client sends you a structure as an argument, the mappings provide Java code for that construct. But be warned: The mappings for constructed types can be convoluted. Consequently you should make it a practice to only use Java-like types in your distributed interfaces. If you can, avoid passing unions, structs, typedefs, and enumerations even if you find them to be elegant in certain situations. Of course, you can't tell this to a C++ programmer, which is why we have the mappings.

The new IDL-to-Java language mapping also defines an interface for portable stubs and skeletons that CORBA vendors must implement. This interface means that we do not have to recompile our stubs and skeletons for different ORBs. The same stub bytecodes should run within any Java ORB that supports this interface. For example, you should be able to download and then run an OrbixWeb-generated stub into a Netscape browser that supports *VisiBroker for Java*. As a result, you do not have to generate ORB-specific Java stubs and skeletons.

SUMMARY OF IDL-TO-JAVA MAPPINGS

Table 20-1 provides a quick summary of the CORBA IDL-to-Java mappings. The devil is in the details. We provide these devilish details in the sections that follow.

Table 20-1. The CORBA IDL to Java Mappings.

CORBA IDL	Java
General Constructs	
module	package
user exceptions	Java class—extends **org.omg.CORBA.UserException** which in turn extends **java.lang.Exception**
system exceptions	Java class **org.omg.CORBA.SystemException**— extends **java.lang.RuntimeException**
in parameters	normal Java parameters
out and inout parameters	Java Holder classes (IDL generated and then instantiated by client side)
typecasts (or narrow)	Java Helper classes
attributes	Java overloaded accessor and modifier methods with the same name as the attribute
Primitive Types	
const	public static final field
boolean, TRUE, FALSE	boolean, true, false

Table 20-1. The CORBA IDL to Java Mappings. (Continued)

CORBA IDL	Java
Primitive Types (continued)	
char, wchar	char
octet	byte
string, wstring	**java.lang.String**
short, unsigned short	short
long, unsigned long	int
long long, unsigned long long	long
float	float
double	double
Constructed Types	
interface	interface
sequence	array
array	array
struct	Java class with same name as struct type (includes instance variables and constructors for each field)
enum	Java class with same name as enum type
union	Java class with same name as union type class with get/set methods for fields
typedef	Java does not have a typedef construct. Mapped to simple IDL types or user-defined IDL types.
any	Java class **org.omg.CORBA.Any** (the ORB is the factory)
Server-Side Mapping	
server implementation using inheritance	Write an implementation class that extends the IDL-generated **_<interface_name>ImplBase** class
server implementation using delegation (i.e., Tie)	IDL-generated **_tie_<interface_name>** class that delegates calls to the implementation class you provide. The implementation class implements one or more IDL-defined interfaces (each represented by an IDL-generated **<interface_name>Operations** interface).
POA root servant class	Java class **org.omg.CORBA.portable.ObjectImpl**

Table 20-1. The CORBA IDL to Java Mappings. (Continued)

CORBA IDL	Java
Pseudo-Objects to Java Classes (see note)	
CORBA::ORB	Java class **org.omg.CORBA.ORB**
CORBA::Object	Java class **org.omg.CORBA.Object**
CORBA::NamedValue	Java class **org.omg.CORBA.NamedValue**
CORBA::NVList	Java class **org.omg.CORBA.NVList**
CORBA::Request	Java class **org.omg.CORBA.Request**
CORBA::ServerRequest (and DSI)	Java class **org.omg.CORBA.ServerRequest** (and DSI Mappings)
CORBA::TypeCode	Java class **org.omg.CORBA.TypeCode**
CORBA::TCKind	Java class **org.omg.CORBA.TCKind**

Note: We only list the most frequently used pseudo-objects.

GENERAL CONSTRUCTS

This section covers the CORBA-to-Java mappings for general CORBA constructs—including modules, exceptions, typecasts, attributes, and the passing of parameters.

CORBA Modules

A CORBA IDL *module* maps to a Java *package* with the same name as the IDL module. Here's a CORBA IDL example:

```
module MyStuff
{
   ....
};
```

Here's the corresponding Java code:

```
package MyStuff;
   ....
```

CORBA Exceptions

Figure 20-1 shows the CORBA exception hierarchy. CORBA defines two types of exceptions: 1) *system exceptions*, which are standard exceptions defined by CORBA, and 2) *user-defined exceptions*, which you define in your IDL. A user-defined exception is a structure that contains data fields. Note that any CORBA operation can implicitly generate a system exception; it does not have to be specified in the IDL signatures.

In the CORBA/Java mapping, the standard CORBA system exceptions derive indirectly from **java.lang.RuntimeException**. They map to final Java classes that

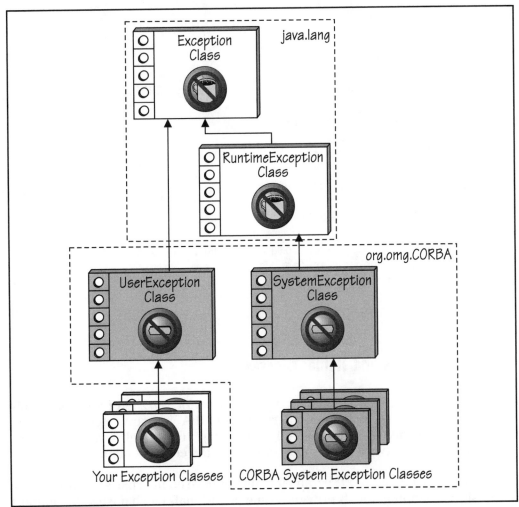

Figure 20-1. The CORBA Exception Class Hierarchy.

extend **org.omg.CORBA.SystemException**. These standard exception classes let you access the IDL major and minor exception codes, as well as a string describing the reason for the exception. The Java class name for each standard IDL exception is the same as its IDL name as declared in the *org.omg.CORBA* package.

User-defined exceptions map to final Java classes that extend **org.omg.CORBA. UserException**. The IDL compiler generates a Java class for each exception you define; this class provides instance variables for the fields of the exception as well as constructors. Here's a CORBA IDL example:

```
exception NotInterested
{
   string explanation;
};
```

Here's the corresponding Java code:

```
final public class NotInterested extends org.omg.CORBA.UserException
{
  public java.lang.String explanation;
  public NotInterested() {}
  public NotInterested(java.lang.String explanation)
  {
    this.explanation = explanation;
  }
  public java.lang.String toString()
  {
    org.omg.CORBA.Any any = org.omg.CORBA.ORB.init().create_any();
    NotInterestedHelper.insert(any, this);
    return any.toString();
  }
}
```

CORBA Parameters and Holder Classes

CORBA IDL defines three parameter passing modes: *in, out,* and *inout*. Java only supports *in*. Like their Java counterparts, CORBA *in* parameters implement call-by-value semantics. Consequently, they map to normal Java parameters. Similarly, IDL return types always map directly to the corresponding Java type.

In contrast, IDL *out* and *inout* parameters do not have counterparts in Java. So the IDL-to-Java mapping must provide some additional mechanisms to support call-by-value (and return result) for the IDL *out* and *inout* parameters. The mapping defines *Holder* classes, which serve as containers for all the IDL basic and user-defined types. These Holders implement the additional parameter passing modes in Java. The client must instantiate an instance of the appropriate Holder class that is passed by value for each IDL *out* or *inout* parameter. The contents of the Holder instance are modified by the server invocation. The client then uses the possibly changed contents after the invocation returns.

The ORB provides Holder classes for all the basic IDL data types as part of the *org.omg.CORBA* package. The Holder class name is the same as the Java type name with an appended Holder—for example, **ShortHolder**. Each Holder class has a constructor from an instance, a default constructor, and a public instance member called *value*. The default constructor sets the value field to the default value for the type as defined by the Java language—for example, false for boolean, zero for numeric and char types, null for strings, and null for object references.

Here's the code for the class **ShortHolder**:

```
final public class ShortHolder
{
  public short value;
  public ShortHolder() {}
  public ShortHolder(short initial)
  {
    value = initial;
  }
}
```

The following example shows how you would use this Holder. Here's CORBA IDL for a **Dog** interface with two methods that use both *in* and *out* parameters:

```
/* IDL Definition of Dog */

interface Dog
{
  void bark(out short times_barked) raises (NotInterested);
  void growl(in string  at_whom) raises (NotInterested);
};
```

Here's the corresponding Java interface:

```
public interface Dog extends org.omg.CORBA.Object
{
  public void bark(org.omg.CORBA.ShortHolder times_barked)
                              throws NotInterested;
```

```
  public void growl(java.lang.String at_whom) throws NotInterested;
}
```

As you can see, the CORBA *out* parameter is substituted with the corresponding Holder class. The client must instantiate an object of this class before invoking the method.

In addition, the IDL-to-Java compiler generates a Holder class for each user-defined IDL type and interface except the ones you define using typedefs. It constructs the class name by appending the suffix Holder to the name of the type—for example, **DogHolder**. To support portable stubs and skeletons, Holder classes for user-defined types also implement the **org.omg.CORBA.portable.Streamable** interface.

Here's the Holder class the Visigenic *IDL2Java* compiler generates for our **Dog** interface:

```
final public class DogHolder implements org.omg.CORBA.portable.Streamable
{
  public Dog value;
  public DogHolder() {}

  public DogHolder(Dog value)
  {
    this.value = value;
  }

  public void _read(org.omg.CORBA.portable.InputStream input)
  {
    value = DogHelper.read(input);
  }

  public void _write(org.omg.CORBA.portable.OutputStream output)
  {
    DogHelper.write(output, value);
  }

  public org.omg.CORBA.TypeCode _type()
  {
    return DogHelper.type();
  }
}
```

Notice that the Holder class also returns a **TypeCode** for the **Dog** interface.

CORBA Helper Classes

Helper classes contain methods that let you manipulate IDL types in various ways. The IDL-to-Java compiler generates a Helper Java class for each IDL type and interface that you define. The class is named with the suffix Helper appended to the type name—for example, **DogHelper**. The Helper class provides static methods that clients can use to manipulate the type. These include *Any* insert and extract operations for the type, getting the *repository ID*, getting the *typecode*, and reading and writing the type from and to a stream. In addition, the Helper class for a mapped IDL interface provides a static *narrow* method you can use for typecasts; it lets you locate server-side object references of a more derived type. The IDL exception CORBA::BAD_PARAM is thrown if the *narrow* fails.

In general, Helper classes provide CORBA-related methods that should not appear in the "regular" mapped classes. Here's the Helper class the Visigenic *IDL2Java* compiler generates for our **Dog** interface (we don't show the code that implements the methods):

```
abstract public class DogHelper
{
  public static Dog narrow(org.omg.CORBA.Object object)
  {
    ...
  }

  private static Dog narrow(org.omg.CORBA.Object object, boolean is_a)
  {
    ...
  }

  public static Dog bind(org.omg.CORBA.ORB orb)
  {
    ...
  }

  public static Dog bind(org.omg.CORBA.ORB orb, java.lang.String name)
  {
    ...
  }

  public static Dog bind(org.omg.CORBA.ORB orb,
                         java.lang.String name,
                         java.lang.String host,
                         org.omg.CORBA.BindOptions options)
```

```java
  {
    ...
  }

  private static org.omg.CORBA.ORB _orb()
  {
    ...
  }

  public static Dog read(org.omg.CORBA.portable.InputStream _input)
  {
    ...
  }

  public static void write(org.omg.CORBA.portable.OutputStream _output,
                           Dog value)
  {
    ...
  }

  public static void insert(org.omg.CORBA.Any any, Dog value)
  {
    ...
  }

  public static Dog extract(org.omg.CORBA.Any any)
  {
    ...
  }

  private static org.omg.CORBA.TypeCode _type;

  public static org.omg.CORBA.TypeCode type()
  {
    ...
  }

  public static java.lang.String id()
  {
    return "IDL:Dog:1.0";
  }
}
```

Think of this class as a gift from the ORB vendors; it's code you don't have to write or even look at. You just use these functions if you need them. *VisiBroker* and

OrbixWeb also include a set of *bind* methods with the Helper class to "help" you locate objects that implement this interface. The *bind* is a little easier to use than the standard CORBA Naming Service. With the exception of *bind*, everything else in this code is part of the standard CORBA bindings.

CORBA Attributes

CORBA IDL interfaces can have attributes, which are syntactic sugar for *set* and *get* operations for typed fields. Each attribute is mapped to a pair of overloaded Java accessor and modifier methods with the same name as the attribute. You can designate an IDL attribute as *readonly*—in this case, only the accessor operation is defined. Here's a CORBA IDL example:

```
attribute short age;
readonly attribute long salary;
```

Here's the corresponding Java code:

```
public void age(short age);
public short age();
public int salary();
```

This overloaded style for naming the attribute accessor functions is consistent with the CORBA C++ and Smalltalk mappings. However, it directly conflicts with the JavaBeans naming patterns for properties, which is a pity. The JavaBeans style is to name accessor functions by prepending *get* and *set* to the attribute name. The work-around is to explicitly define *get* and *set* functions in IDL instead of relying on attributes.

CORBA BASIC TYPES

This section covers the CORBA-to-Java mapping for the CORBA basic types—including const, boolean, char, wchar, octet, string, wstring, short, long, long long, float, and double.

CORBA Constants

CORBA *const* values declared within an IDL interface map to *public static final* fields in the corresponding Java interface. Constants not declared within an IDL interface map to a public interface with the same name as the constant. They contain a public static final field named value that holds the constant's value. Here's an example of CORBA IDL constants within an interface:

```
interface ConstantTypes
{
    const long MyLong = -12345;
    const boolean MyTrue = TRUE;
    const char MyChar = 'A';
    const short MyShort = -1;
    const unsigned short MyUnsignedShort = 15907;
    const unsigned long MyUnsignedLong = 901008;
    const string MyString = "Hello World";
};
```

Here's the corresponding Java code:

```
public interface ConstantTypes extends org.omg.CORBA.Object
{
    final public static int MyLong = (int) -12345;
    final public static boolean MyTrue = (boolean) true;
    final public static char MyChar = (char) 'A';
    final public static short MyShort = (short) -1;
    final public static short MyUnsignedShort = (short) 15907;
      final public static int MyUnsignedLong = (int) 901008;
    final public static java.lang.String MyString =
                                (java.lang.String) "Hello World";
}
```

Here's an example that shows how you would use this code:

```
// create variables and set them to an initial value from
// our IDL declared constants

int aLong = MyLong;
boolean thetruth = MyTrue;
char aChar = MyChar;
short aShort = MyShort;
short anUnsignedShort = MyUnsignedShort;
int anUnsignedLong = MyUnsignedLong;
java.lang.String aString = MyString;
```

```
// print out the values

System.out.println("aLong = " + aLong);
System.out.println("thetruth = " + thetruth);
System.out.println("aChar = " + aChar);
System.out.println("aShort = " + aShort);
System.out.println("anUnsignedShort = " + anUnsignedShort);
System.out.println("anUnsignedLong = " + anUnsignedLong);
System.out.println("aString = " + aString);
```

The CORBA Primitive Types

The rest of the CORBA basic types map very straightforwardly to their Java counterparts. Here's how:

- *Booleans*—The CORBA IDL *boolean* maps to the Java type *boolean*. The IDL constants TRUE and FALSE map to the Java constants true and false.

- *Characters*—The CORBA IDL *char* represents elements of the ISO 8859.1 character set. The CORBA *wchar* (for wide character) is used for 16-bit character representations such as Unicode. Java characters are represented in Unicode. The CORBA *char* and *wchar* both map to the Java type *char*.

- *Octets*—The CORBA IDL type *octet* is an 8-bit quantity that maps to the Java type *byte*.

- *Strings*—The CORBA IDL types *string* and *wstring* (for wide character strings) both map to the Java type **java.lang.String**.

- *Integers*—The CORBA IDL includes six integer data types: *short*, *long*, and *long long* in both signed and unsigned varieties. Java has three integer types: *short*, *int*, and *long*. The IDL integer data types map to the corresponding size Java integer data types.

- *Floating points*—The CORBA IDL floating-point types are *float* and *double*. They map to the corresponding Java floating-point types with the same names. Note that IDL also supports a *long double* type, which may eventually map to the **java.math.BigDecimal** type.

The CORBA basic types are used to type attributes, parameter values, initial values in constants, and fields of constructed types. Our previous code example shows how you can use these types.

CORBA CONSTRUCTED TYPES

The CORBA constructed types we cover in this section include user-defined types—such as *interface*, *union*, *struct*, and *enum*—as well as parameterized types—such as *array* and *sequence*. We also threw in the CORBA type *Any* because it can contain any type—constructed or basic.

CORBA Interface

A CORBA IDL type *interface* maps to a Java *interface* with the same name. The Java interface contains the mapped operation signatures. Methods are invoked on an object reference to this interface. Here's a CORBA IDL example:

```
interface Dog
{
    attribute short age;
    exception NotInterested
    {
      string explanation;
    };
    void bark(out short times_barked) raises (NotInterested);
    void growl(in string at_whom) raises (NotInterested);
};
```

Here's the corresponding Java code:

```
public interface Dog extends org.omg.CORBA.Object
{
  public void age(short age);
  public short age();
  public void bark(org.omg.CORBA.ShortHolder times_barked)
          throws DogPackage.NotInterested;

  public void growl(java.lang.String at_whom)
          throws DogPackage.NotInterested;
}
```

The IDL-to-Java compiler will also generate the following (.java) classes for this IDL interface: **DogHolder**, **DogHelper**, **DogStub**, **_DogImplBase**, and **DogExample**. If you enable the Tie option, it will also generate the **DogOperations** interface and the **_tie_Dog** class (we explain Tie later in this chapter).

CORBA Sequence

A *sequence* is a variable-sized one-dimensional array of elements, where the element can be of any IDL-defined type. An IDL sequence can optionally be *bounded* to a maximum length. You must name the sequence using an IDL typedef before you can use it as an IDL type.

A CORBA IDL type *sequence* maps to a Java *array* with the same name. CORBA sequences are either bounded or unbounded. The ORB checks the length of a bounded sequence when it marshals a parameter of this type. Here's a CORBA IDL example with both a bounded and unbounded sequence:

```
interface seqExample
{

// unbounded sequence of Dogs
typedef sequence< Dog > MyUnboundedSeq;

// bounded sequence with a maximum of 60
typedef sequence< Dog, 60 > MyBoundedSeq;

// sequence usage example
void seqtest(in MyBoundedSeq val1,
             in MyUnboundedSeq val2,
             out MyBoundedSeq val3);
};
```

Here's the corresponding Java code:

```
public interface seqExample extends org.omg.CORBA.Object
{
  public void seqtest(Dog[] val1,
                      Dog[] val2,
                      seqExamplePackage.MyBoundedSeqHolder val3);
}
```

The bounds for the bounded sequence are checked when the sequence argument is marshaled. The IDL-to-Java compiler also generates *Holder* and *Helper* classes for each sequence you define. It uses the sequence name with Holder and Helper suffixes appended to it.

CORBA Array

Like a sequence, a CORBA *array* can contain elements that are of any valid IDL type. Unlike a sequence, an array can be multidimensional, and it is always of fixed size. Because of its fixed size, an array can be a less flexible data structure than a sequence in certain situations.

A CORBA IDL type *array* maps the same way as a bounded sequence. The mapping lets you apply the Java subscripting operator to the mapped array. The bounds for the array are checked when the array is marshaled as an argument to an IDL operation. You can make the length of an array available in Java by bounding it with an IDL constant. Here's an IDL example of an array:

```
interface arrayExample
{
  const long ArrayBound = 60;
  typedef Dog MyArray[ArrayBound];
  void arraytest(in MyArray val1, out MyArray val2);
};
```

Here's the corresponding Java code:

```
public interface arrayExample extends org.omg.CORBA.Object
{
  final public static int ArrayBound = (int) 60;
  public void arraytest(Dog[] val1,
                    arrayExamplePackage.MyArrayHolder val2);
}
```

The IDL-to-Java compiler also generates *Holder* and *Helper* classes for each array you define; it uses the array name with the Holder and Helper suffixes appended to it.

CORBA Structs

A *structure* lets you package named fields of various types. The CORBA IDL type *struct* maps to a Java class with the same name. The Java class contains an instance variable for each field in the structure. There are two constructors for each structure. The first is a default constructor that sets all the fields in the structure to null. The second constructor takes the fields of the structure as arguments and initializes each field. Here's a CORBA IDL example:

```
struct MyStruct
{
  short age;
  string name;
};
```

Here's the corresponding Java code:

```
final public class MyStruct
{
   // Data members
  public short age;
  public java.lang.String name;

   // Constructors
  public MyStruct() {}
  public MyStruct(short age, java.lang.String name)
  {
   this.age = age;
   this.name = name;
  }

  public java.lang.String toString()
  {
    org.omg.CORBA.Any any = org.omg.CORBA.ORB.init().create_any();
    MyStructHelper.insert(any, this);
    return any.toString();
  }
}
```

The compiler also generates *Helper* and *Holder* classes for **MyStruct**, which it names **MyStructHelper** and **MyStructHolder**. The following snippet of code shows how you would use **MyStruct**:

```
// create a struct
MyStruct mystruct = new MyStruct(6, "Lassie");

// print out its values
System.out.println("mystruct.age = " + mystruct.age +
                   "mystruct.name = " + mystruct.name);
```

CORBA Enums

An *enumerated* type lets you assign identifiers to the members of a set of values. The CORBA IDL type *enum* maps to a Java class with that same name. The generated Java class includes the following: 1) two static data members per label, 2) a private constructor, 3) a *value* method that returns the integer value, 4) a *from_int* method that returns the enum with the specified value, and 5) a *toString* method.

Here's a CORBA IDL example:

```
enum MyEnum { yellow, red, blue };
```

Here's the corresponding Java code:

```
final public class MyEnum
{
  // One pair of static data members per label

  final public static int _yellow = 0;
  final public static MyEnum none = new MyEnum(_yellow);

  final public static int _red = 1;
  final public static MyEnum first = new MyEnum(_red);

  final public static int _blue = 2;
  final public static MyEnum second = new MyEnum(_blue);

  // A private constructor

  private int __value;

  private MyEnum(int value)
  {
    this.__value = value;
  }

  // A value method returns the integer value
  public int value()
  {
    return __value;
  }

  // A from_int method returns the enum with the specified value
```

```
public static MyEnum from_int(int $value)
{
  switch($value)
  {
    case _yellow:
      return yellow;
    case _red:
      return red;
    case _blue:
     return blue;
    default:
      throw new org.omg.CORBA.BAD_PARAM("Enum out of range:
                              [0.." + (5 - 1) + "]: " + $value);
  }
}

// toString
public java.lang.String toString()
{
  org.omg.CORBA.Any any = org.omg.CORBA.ORB.init().create_any();
  MyEnumHelper.insert(any, this);
  return any.toString();
}
}
```

The compiler also generates a *Helper* class for **MyEnum** called **MyEnumHelper**, and a *Holder* class called **MyEnumHolder**. The following snippet of code shows how you would use **MyEnum**:

```
// create an enumeration
MyEnum myenum = MyEnum.yellow;

// print out the value
System.out.println("myenum = " + myenum);
```

CORBA Union

A *discriminated union* lets you define a structure that references only one of several alternative data members at any given time (only one member is in-memory at any time). The union uses a *discriminator* label value to indicate which member of the union the value holds.

The CORBA IDL type *union* maps to a Java class with the same name. The mapped class includes the following: 1) a default constructor, 2) an accessor method for the discriminator, 3) an accessor method for each of the branches, 4) a modifier method for each of the branches, and 5) a *toString* method. The accessor and modifier methods for a branch have the same names but different signatures. Here's a CORBA union IDL example:

```
union AnimalUnion switch (short)
{
  case 1:  Dog dog;
  case 2:  Cat cat;
  default: Animal other;
};
```

Here's the corresponding Java code:

```
final public class AnimalUnion
{
  private java.lang.Object _object;
  private short   _disc;

  // constructor
  public AnimalUnion() {}

  // discriminator accessor
  public AnimalUnion discriminator()
  {
    return _disc;
  }

  // dog accessor
  public Dog dog()
  {
    // code not shown
    ....
  }

  // cat accessor
  public Cat cat()
  {
    // code not shown
    ....
  }
```

```
// default accessor
public Animal other()
{
   // code not shown
   ....
}

// dog modifier
public void dog (Dog value)
{
   // code not shown
   ....
}

// cat modifier
public void cat (Cat value)
{
   // code not shown
   ....
}

// default modifiers
public void other (Animal value)
{
   // code not shown
   ....
}

// toString method
public java.lang.String toString()
{
   org.omg.CORBA.Any any = org.omg.CORBA.ORB.init().create_any();
   AnimalUnionHelper.insert(any, this);
   return any.toString();
}
}
```

The underscores (_) are added to avoid naming conflicts with the mapped union name or fields.

The IDL compiler also generates a *Helper* class for **AnimalUnion** called **AnimalUnionHelper** and a *Holder* class called **AnimalUnionHolder**. The following snippet of code shows how you would use **AnimalUnion**:

```
// create a union
AnimalUnion aUnion = new AnimalUnion();

// initialize its value
aUnion.dog("Lassie");

// display a failure when the the wrong method is called
System.out.println("This works: aUnion.dog() = " + aUnion.dog());
System.out.println("This fails: aUnion.cat() = " + aUnion.cat());
```

The constructor leaves the union in an uninitialized state. Consequently, you must first initialize the union (or change it after initialization) by calling one of the branch modifier methods.

CORBA Typedef

Typedefs allow you to define new data type names—or aliases—for an IDL type. Java, of course, does not support a typedef-like construct. Consequently, CORBA *typedef* declarations for simple types are mapped to the original (mapped type) everywhere the typedef type appears. Typedefs for non-arrays and sequences are "unwound" to their original type until a simple IDL type or user-defined IDL type (of the non-typedef variety) is encountered. Here's the CORBA IDL for a typedef example:

```
struct DogFood
{
    string favorite;
    string leastFavorite;
};

typedef DogFood FoodItem;
```

Here's the corresponding Java code:

```
final public class DogFood
{
  public java.lang.String favorite;
  public java.lang.String leastFavorite;
  public DogFood() {}
  public DogFood(java.lang.String favorite,
                 java.lang.String leastFavorite)
  {
    this.favorite = favorite;
```

```
    this.leastFavorite = leastFavorite;
  }
  public java.lang.String toString()
  {
    org.omg.CORBA.Any any = org.omg.CORBA.ORB.init().create_any();
    DogFoodHelper.insert(any, this);
    return any.toString();
  }
}
```

The IDL-to-Java compiler generates *Helper* classes for all typedefs. If the type is a sequence or array, it will also generate a *Holder* class.

CORBA Any

The CORBA IDL type *Any* maps to the Java class **org.omg.CORBA.Any**. The Any is a self-describing data structure that retains its type. Any lets you extract and insert values of predefined IDL types at run time using type-safe conversion functions. You invoke *insert_XXX* methods to initialize or update the Any. You invoke *extract_XXX* functions to return a typed value contained in this Any. It then throws an exception if the value it contains does not match the return type of the extraction method.

The **ORB** is the factory for Any objects. The following snippet shows how you would create a new Any and then initialize it from a short:

```
org.omg.CORBA.Any x = orb.create_any();
x.insert_short((short)4);
```

You can then retrieve the value in the Any as follows:

```
short y = x.extract_short();
```

The **Any** class provides a pair of generic streamable methods to handle non-primitive IDL types. You invoke *create_input_stream* to create a stream containing the Any's value. You invoke *create_output_stream* to create an empty output stream. You invoke *read_value* to read an Any's value from the input stream. Finally, you invoke *write_value* to write an Any's value to an output stream. Note that each user-defined IDL type generates a Helper class that includes a pair of methods to convert it to and from an Any.

The values stored in an Any are defined by a TypeCode. The **Any** class provides a pair of overloaded *type* methods that let you access and set the type contained in the Any. This method is primarily used to set the Any for IDL out parameters. Note that the *insert_XXX* operations sets both the value you specify and the Any's typecode.

Here's the class definition of the **org.omg.CORBA.Any** class:

Listing 20-1. The org.omg.CORBA.Any Class.

```
abstract public class org.omg.CORBA.Any
{
  // insert primitive types into any
 abstract public void insert_short(short s);
 abstract public void insert_long(int i);
 abstract public void insert_longlong(long l);
 abstract public void insert_ushort(short s);
 abstract public void insert_ulong(int i);
 abstract public void insert_ulonglong(long l);
 abstract public void insert_float(float f);
 abstract public void insert_double(double d);
 abstract public void insert_boolean(boolean b);
 abstract public void insert_char(char c);
 abstract public void insert_wchar(char c);
 abstract public void insert_octet(byte b);
 abstract public void insert_string(String s);
 abstract public void insert_wstring(String s);
 abstract public void insert_any(org.omg.CORBA.Any a);

 // insert constructed IDL types into Any
 abstract public void insert_Streamable(
                    org.omg.CORBA.portable.Streamable s);

  // insert typecode into Any
 abstract public void insert_TypeCode(org.omg.CORBA.TypeCode t);

  // insert object type into Any
 abstract public void insert_Object(org.omg.CORBA.Object o);

  // insert and throw exception when typecode inconsistent with value
 abstract public void insert_Object(org.omg.CORBA.Object o,
                            org.omg.CORBA.TypeCode t)
                            throws org.omg.CORBA.MARSHAL;

  // insert Principal type into Any
 abstract public void insert_Principal(org.omg.CORBA.Principal p);
```

```
// extract primitive types from Any
abstract public short extract_short()
                            throws org.omg.CORBA.BAD_OPERATION;
abstract public int extract_long()
                            throws org.omg.CORBA.BAD_OPERATION;
abstract public long extract_longlong()
                            throws org.omg.CORBA.BAD_OPERATION;
abstract public short extract_ushort()
                            throws org.omg.CORBA.BAD_OPERATION;
abstract public int extract_ulong()
                            throws org.omg.CORBA.BAD_OPERATION;
abstract public long extract_ulonglong()
                            throws org.omg.CORBA.BAD_OPERATION;
abstract public float extract_float()
                            throws org.omg.CORBA.BAD_OPERATION;
abstract public double extract_double()
                            throws org.omg.CORBA.BAD_OPERATION;
abstract public boolean extract_boolean()
                            throws org.omg.CORBA.BAD_OPERATION;
abstract public char extract_char()
                            throws org.omg.CORBA.BAD_OPERATION;
abstract public char extract_wchar()
                            throws org.omg.CORBA.BAD_OPERATION;
abstract public byte extract_octet()
                            throws org.omg.CORBA.BAD_OPERATION;
abstract public org.omg.CORBA.Any extract_any()
                            throws org.omg.CORBA.BAD_OPERATION;
abstract public org.omg.CORBA.Object extract_Object()
                            throws org.omg.CORBA.BAD_OPERATION;
abstract public String extract_string()
                            throws org.omg.CORBA.BAD_OPERATION;
abstract public String extract_wstring()
                            throws org.omg.CORBA.BAD_OPERATION;

// extract typecode from Any
abstract public org.omg.CORBA.TypeCode extract_TypeCode()
                            throws org.omg.CORBA.BAD_OPERATION;

// extract Principal from Any
abstract public org.omg.CORBA.Principal extract_Principal()
                            throws org.omg.CORBA.BAD_OPERATION;

// create input and output streams
abstract public org.omg.CORBA.portable.InputStream
                            create_input_stream();
```

```
abstract public org.omg.CORBA.portable.OutputStream
                        create_output_stream();

  // read and write Any values to/from streams
  // throws exception when typecode inconsistent with value
abstract public void read_value(org.omg.CORBA.portable.InputStream is,
                        org.omg.CORBA.TypeCode t)
                        throws org.omg.CORBA.MARSHAL;
abstract public void write_value(org.omg.CORBA.portable.OutputStream os);

  // Any equality test
abstract public boolean equal(org.omg.CORBA.Any a);

  // Any type code getter
abstract public org.omg.CORBA.TypeCode type();

  // Any type code setter
abstract public void type(org.omg.CORBA.TypeCode t);

}
```

In summary, the CORBA Any lets you specify an attribute value, parameter, or return type which contains an arbitrary type that is determined at run time instead of at compile time. This makes it an incredibly powerful and useful type, but it can also be very dangerous. The Any gives you a rope to hang yourself because you can use it to pass anything you want. Also note that CORBA typecodes complement Any. They let you discover the data type at run time, which is what makes CORBA a highly self-describing system.

CORBA/JAVA SERVER-SIDE MAPPINGS

CORBA supports two server-side mappings for implementing an IDL interface: *ImplBase inheritance* and *Tie delegation*. The inheritance approach is a lot more prevalent. You implement the IDL interface using an implementation class that also extends the compiler-generated **xxxImplBaseClass** (or skeleton). With the delegation approach, you implement the IDL interface using two classes: 1) an IDL-generated Tie class that inherits from **xxxImplBaseClass**, but delegates all calls to an implementation class; and 2) a class that implements the IDL-generated **xxxOperations** interface—which defines the IDL function.

Inheritance: The ImplBase Approach

As you know from previous chapters, the IDL-to-Java compiler generates a Java skeleton base class—the *Servant Base Class*—for each IDL interface you define. The Java mapping defines the skeleton as follows:

```
public class _<interface_name>ImplBase implements <interface_name>{}
```

For each IDL interface, you must write a *servant* class that extends this base implementation class and implements the IDL-defined functions. For example, here's the IDL for a simple **Dog** interface:

```
/* IDL Definition of Dog */

interface Dog
{
    // attribute
    attribute short age;

    // methods
    void growl(in string  at_whom);
};
```

The IDL-to-Java compiler will generate a servant base class that looks like this:

```
public class _DogImplBase extends org.omg.CORBA.portable.ObjectImpl
{
  /* stuff you don't have to look at  */
}
```

Note that **org.omg.CORBA.portable.ObjectImpl** is the Java mapping of the POA root **Servant** class.

You must then provide a servant implementation that inherits from **_DogImplBase**. Here's a code snippet for a **DogImpl**:

```
public class DogImpl extends _DogImplBase
{
  public DogImpl(java.lang.String name)
  {
    super(name);
  }
  public DogImpl()
```

```
{
    super();
}
public void growl(java.lang.String at_whom)
{
    // implement operation...
}
public void age(short age)
{
    // implement attribute writer...
}   public short age()
{
    // implement attribute reader...
    return 0;
}
}
```

Notice that this servant implementation eats up its single Java inheritance by extending **_DogImplBase**. If this is a problem for you, then you may want to consider the CORBA delegation mechanism instead.

Delegation: The Tie Approach

As we go to press, the delegation mapping for Java is still under construction. This section is based on the initial *POA/Java* submission OMG received in November, 1997 (see OMG document *orbos/97-11-12*). Both *VisiBroker for Java 3.1* and *OrbixWeb 3.0* provide Java implementations of Tie that are carbon copies of the Tie mechanism described in the submission.

Here's how you tell VisiBroker's *idl2Java* to generate Tie classes for the **Dog** interface (Note: Don't include the -no_tie option):

```
idl2java dog.idl
```

This will cause *idl2Java* to generate one new Tie-related class and one new interface (see the checks in Figure 20-2).

The **_tie_Dog** is the *delegator class* for the **Dog** interface; it delegates every call to the real implementation class. You must pass to the Tie object—via its constructor—an instance of the real implementation class (the delegate) when you first initialize it. Here's the code *idl2java* generates for the **_tie_Dog** class:

```
public class _tie_Dog extends _DogImplBase
{
```

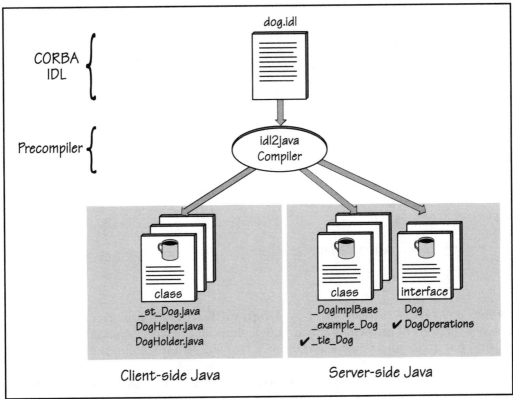

Figure 20-2. The Whole Works: Tie Plus Implementation Inheritance.

```
// variables
private DogOperations _delegate;

// constructors
public _tie_Dog(DogOperations delegate, java.lang.String name)
{
  super(name);
  this._delegate = delegate;
}
public _tie_Dog(DogOperations delegate)
{
  this._delegate = delegate;
}

// delegate accessor
public DogOperations _delegate()
{
  return this._delegate;
```

```
    }

    // IDL operations
    public void growl(java.lang.String at_whom)
    {
      this._delegate.growl(at_whom);
    }

    // IDL attributes
    public void age(short age)
    {
      this._delegate.age(age);
    }
    public short age()
    {
      return this._delegate.age();
    }
}
```

As you can see, the Tie class extends **_DogImplBase**, but it provides no implementation semantics of its own. Instead, it delegates all the work to an implementation object. Each Tie object stores a reference to a single implementation object.

We must now provide the implementation class. We do this by writing a class that implements the **DogOperations** interface. This is an interface the IDL compiler generates; it defines the minimum set of methods you must implement to support the IDL interface. Here's the **DogOperations** interface *idl2java* generates:

```
public interface DogOperations
{
  // attributes
  public void age(short age);
  public short age();

  // methods
  public void growl(java.lang.String at_whom);
}
```

As usual, you can use the example class as a template for your implementation. And, like before, you must rename the class. In the Tie implementation, you must also replace extends **_DogImplBase** with implements **DogOperations**. The following snippet shows the Tie version of **DogImpl**:

```
public class DogImpl implements DogOperations
{
```

```
// constructor
public DogImpl()
{
}
// IDL methods
public void growl(java.lang.String at_whom)
{
   // implement operation...
}

// IDL attributes
public void age(short age)
{
   // implement attribute writer...
}
public short age()
{
   // implement attribute reader...
   return 0;
}
}
```

Note that this delegate class will not eat up your precious inheritance tree.

Your implementation class can implement more than one interface, which is one way to implement multiple interface inheritance in Java. So, a single delegate could service Tie objects that represent different interfaces. In this case, the Tie objects are the POA *servants*. They just happen to delegate the work to other objects.

Finally, you must provide a main server program that instantiates an implementation object and a corresponding Tie object. You must also pass the implementation object as a parameter to the Tie constructor; for example:

```
public class DogServer
{ static public void main(String[] args)
  { try
    {
      org.omg.CORBA.ORB orb = org.omg.CORBA.ORB.init(args, null);

      // Create the Dog implementation object
      DogImpl new_dog = new DogImpl();

      // Create the Tie object and pass it the implementation object
      Dog dog = new _tie_Dog(new_dog, "My Dog");
```

```
    // Export the Tie object reference
    orb.connect(dog);

    // Register the dog object with the naming service

       ... Code omitted for brevity


    // wait forever for current thread to die
    Thread.currentThread().join();
  }
  catch(Exception e)
  { System.err.println(e);
  }
 }
}
```

Only Use Tie As a Last Resort

Warning

The Tie mechanism adds a level of indirection that may slow your server implementations. We find inheritance to be more intuitive and easier to use than Tie. With inheritance, the implementation object behaves and looks like the object reference. So we recommend you only use Tie if your implementation needs to inherit from a class other than **ImplBase**. You may also want to use Tie in situations that require the level of indirection Tie provides. For example, the *Enterprise JavaBeans* CORBA mapping uses Tie to create an intermediary layer that intercepts incoming calls and then provides add-on, framework-like functions to server-side objects. ❑

MAPPING CORBA PSEUDO-OBJECTS TO JAVA

Pseudo-objects are ORB-provided objects. They are specified in IDL, but they're language-specific objects. This section goes over the Java mappings for some of the more commonly used pseudo-objects. You must remember that a pseudo-object is not necessarily a remote CORBA object. It is typically a process-local programming language construct. In general, a pseudo-object has the following constraints: 1) it is not represented in the Interface Repository, 2) it does not generate *Helper* or *Holder* classes, and 3) it is mapped to a Java public abstract class that does not extend or inherit from any other classes or interfaces.

The predefined CORBA objects and data types are defined within an IDL module called CORBA. The Java mapping maps the CORBA module to a Java package called *org.omg.CORBA*. As you would expect, all pseudo-objects are mapped to the *org.omg.CORBA* Java package. It's as if they have the following IDL declaration:

```
module org {
  module omg {
    module CORBA {
```

CORBA::ORB Mapping

As you saw in earlier chapters, the **ORB** pseudo-object is the CORBA workhorse; it provides a set of core functions—including ORB initialization, object bootstrap, typecode factories, dynamic invocation support, and the translation of object references to and from strings. And, as you will soon see in this section, the new Java bindings introduce some additional ORB functions. Here's the CORBA pseudo-IDL for **ORB**:

```
pseudo interface ORB
{
  // exceptions
  exception InvalidName {};

  // typedefs
  typedef string ObjectId;
  typedef sequence<ObjectId> ObjectIdList;

  // operations

  // intialization methods
  ObjectIdList list_initial_services();
  Object resolve_initial_references(in ObjectId object_name)
                                    raises(InvalidName);
  boolean get_service_information(in ServiceType service_type,
                                  out ServiceInformation service_info);

  // object-to-string, and vice versa
  string object_to_string(in Object obj);
  Object string_to_object(in string str);

  // DII support methods
  NVList create_list(in long count);
  NVList create_operation_list(in OperationDef oper);
```

```
NamedValue create_named_value(in String name,
                             in Any value,
                             in Flags flags);
ExceptionList create_exception_list();
ContextList create_context_list();
Context get_default_context();
Environment create_environment();
void send_multiple_requests_oneway(in RequestSeq req);
void send_multiple_requests_deferred(in RequestSeq req);
boolean poll_next_response();
Request get_next_response() raises (wrongTransaction);

// deprecated — use resolve_initial_references
Current get_current();

// typecode creation methods
TypeCode create_struct_tc(in RepositoryId id,
                          in Identifier name,
                          in StructMemberSeq members);
TypeCode  create_union_tc(in RepositoryId id,
                          in Identifier name,
                          in TypeCode discriminator_type,
                          in UnionMemberSeq members);
TypeCode   create_enum_tc(in RepositoryId id,
                          in Identifier name,
                          in EnumMemberSeq members);
TypeCode create_alias_tc (in RepositoryId id,
                          in Identifier name,
                          in TypeCode original_type);
TypeCode create_exception_tc(in RepositoryId id,
                          in Identifier name,
                          in StructMemberSeq members);

TypeCode create_interface_tc (in RepositoryId id,
                             in Identifier name);
TypeCode create_string_tc (in unsigned long bound);
TypeCode create_wstring_tc(in unsigned long bound);
TypeCode create_sequence_tc (in unsigned long bound,
                             in TypeCode element_type);
TypeCode create_recursive_sequence_tc(in unsigned long bound,
                                      in unsigned long offset);

TypeCode create_array_tc (in unsigned long length,
                          in TypeCode element_type);
```

```
// additional operations for Java mapping
TypeCode get_primitive_tc(in TCKind tcKind);
Any create_any();
OutputStream create_output_stream();
void connect(Object obj);
void disconnect(Object obj);

// POA-Defined ORB Control
boolean work_pending();
void peform_work();
void shutdown(in boolean wait_for_completion);
void run();

// Dynamic Any Support
DynAny create_dyn_any(in any value);
DynAny create_basic_dyn_any(in TypeCode type)
                        raises(DynAny::InconsistentTypeCode);
DynStruct create_dyn_struct(in TypeCode type)
                        raises(DynAny::InconsistentTypeCode);
DynSequence create_dyn_sequence(in TypeCode type)
                        raises(DynAny::InconsistentTypeCode);
DynArray create_dyn_array(in TypeCode type)
                        raises(DynAny::InconsistentTypeCode);
DynUnion create_dyn_union(in TypeCode type)
                        raises(DynAny::InconsistentTypeCode);
DynEnum create_dyn_enum(in TypeCode type)
                        raises(DynAny::InconsistentTypeCode);
DynFixed create_dyn_fixed(in TypeCode type)
                        raises(DynAny::InconsistentTypeCode);

// Additional methods for ORB initialization - Java Specific

public static ORB init(Strings[] args, Properties props);
public static ORB init(Applet app, Properties props);
public static ORB init();
abstract protected void set_parameters(String[] args,
                                    java.util.Properties props);
abstract protected void set_parameters(Applet app,
                                    java.util.Properties props);
}
```

Here's the corresponding Java mapping:

Listing 20-2. The org.omg.CORBA.ORB Class.

```
package org.omg.CORBA;
public abstract class ORB
{
  // intialization methods
  String[] list_initial_services();
  org.omg.CORBA.Object resolve_initial_references(String object_name)
                        throws org.omg.CORBA.ORBPackage.InvalidName;
  public boolean get_service_information(short service_type,
                        ServiceInformationHolder service_info);
  // object-to-string, and vice versa
  String object_to_string(org.omg.CORBA.Object obj);
  org.omg.CORBA.Object string_to_object(String str);

  // DII support methods
  NVList create_list(int count);
  NVList create_operation_list(OperationDef oper);
  NamedValue create_named_value(String name, Any value, int flags);
  ExceptionList create_exception_list();
  ContextList create_context_list();
  Context get_default_context();
  Environment create_environment();
  void send_multiple_requests_oneway(Request[] req);
  void send_multiple_requests_deferred(Request[] req);
  boolean poll_next_response();
  Request get_next_response() throws wrongTransaction;

  // deprecated - use resolve_initial_references
  Current get_current();

  // typecode creation
  TypeCode create_struct_tc( String id, String name,
                        StructMember[] members);
  TypeCode create_union_tc( String id, String name,
                        TypeCode discriminator_type,
                        UnionMember[] members);
  TypeCode create_enum_tc( String id, String name,
                        EnumMember[] members);
  TypeCode create_alias_tc( String id, String name,
                        TypeCode original_type);
  TypeCode create_exception_tc( String id, String name,
                        StructMember[] members);
  TypeCode create_interface_tc( String name, String name);
  TypeCode create_string_tc( int bound);
```

```
TypeCode create_wstring_tc(int bound);
TypeCode create_sequence_tc(int bound, TypeCode element_type);
TypeCode create_recursive_sequence_tc(int bound, int offset);
TypeCode create_array_tc( int length, TypeCode element_type);

// additional methods for IDL/Java mapping
TypeCode get_primitive_tc(TCKind tcKind);
Any create_any();
org.omg.CORBA.portable.OutputStream create_output_stream();
void connect(org.omg.CORBA.Object obj);
void disconnect(org.omg.CORBA.Object obj);

// POA-Defined ORB Control
public boolean work_pending();
public void peform_work();
void shutdown(boolean wait_for_completion);
void run();

// Dynamic Any Support
public DynAny create_dyn_any(Any value);
public DynAny create_basic_dyn_any(TypeCode type)
        throws org.omg.CORBA.DynAnyPackage.InconsistentTypeCode;
public DynStruct create_dyn_struct(TypeCode type)
        throws org.omg.CORBA.DynAnyPackage.InconsistentTypeCode;
public DynSequence create_dyn_sequence(TypeCode type)
        throws org.omg.CORBA.DynAnyPackage.InconsistentTypeCode;
public DynArray create_dyn_array(TypeCode type)
        throws org.omg.CORBA.DynAnyPackage.InconsistentTypeCode;
public DynUnion create_dyn_union(TypeCode type)
        throws org.omg.CORBA.DynAnyPackage.InconsistentTypeCode;
public DynEnum create_dyn_enum(TypeCode type)
        throws org.omg.CORBA.DynAnyPackage.InconsistentTypeCode;
public DynFixed create_dyn_fixed(TypeCode type)
        throws org.omg.CORBA.DynAnyPackage.InconsistentTypeCode;

// additional static methods for ORB initialization
public static ORB init(Strings[] args, Properties props);
public static ORB init(Applet app, Properties props);
public static ORB init();
abstract protected void set_parameters(String[] args,
                                    java.util.Properties props);
abstract protected void set_parameters(Applet app,
                                    java.util.Properties props);
}
```

CORBA::Object Mapping

The CORBA **Object** is mapped to the Java **org.omg.CORBA.Object** interface and the corresponding *Helper* class. It provides methods for manipulating the type. A *Holder* class is also generated. The Java interface for each user-defined IDL interface extends **org.omg.CORBA.Object**. Here is the Java interface that represents CORBA objects:

Listing 20-3. The org.omg.CORBA.Object Interface.

```java
// Java
package org.omg.CORBA;
public interface Object
{
  // Core object methods
  boolean _is_a(String Identifier);
  boolean _is_equivalent(Object that);
  boolean _non_existent();
  int _hash(int maximum);
  org.omg.CORBA.Object _duplicate();
  void _release();

  // Introspection support methods
  ImplementationDef _get_implementation();
  InterfaceDef _get_interface();

  // DII support methods
  Request _request(String s);
  Request _create_request(Context ctx,
                          String operation,
                          NVList arg_list,
                          NamedValue result);
  Request _create_request(Context ctx,
                          String operation,
                          NVList arg_list,
                          NamedValue result,
                          ExceptionList exclist,
                          ContextList ctxlist);
}
```

In Java, this interface is implemented by the servant base class **org.omg.CORBA. portable.ObjectImpl**.

CORBA::NamedValue Mapping

As we explained in Chapter 8, a **NamedValue** pseudo-object describes a name-value pair. It is used in the DII and DSI to describe arguments and return values; it is also used to pass context property-value pairs. Here's the CORBA pseudo-IDL for a **NamedValue**:

```
// typedefs
typedef unsigned long Flags;
typedef string Identifier;
const Flags ARG_IN = 1;
const Flags ARG_OUT = 2;
const Flags ARG_INOUT = 3;
const Flags CTX_RESTRICT_SCOPE = 15;


// interface
pseudo interface NamedValue
{
  readonly attribute Identifier name;
  readonly attribute any value;
  readonly attribute Flags flags;
};
```

Here's the corresponding Java mapping:

Listing 20-4. The org.omg.CORBA.NamedValue Class and Related Interfaces.

```
package org.omg.CORBA;

// constant mappings
public interface ARG_IN
{
  public static final int value = 1;
}
public interface ARG_OUT {
  public static final int value = 2;
}
public interface ARG_INOUT {
  public static final int value = 3;
}
public interface CTX_RESTRICT_SCOPE {
  public static final int value = 15;
}
```

```
// interface mapping
public abstract class NamedValue
{
  public String name();
  public Any value();
  public int flags();
}
```

CORBA::NVList Mapping

As we explained in Chapter 8, the **NVList** pseudo-object maintains a list of **NamedValue** objects. It is used by the DII and DSI to describe arguments as well as context values. Here's the CORBA pseudo-IDL for an **NVList**:

```
pseudo interface NVList
{
  // attribute
  readonly attribute unsigned long count;

  // methods
  NamedValue add(in Flags flags);
  NamedValue add_item(in Identifier item_name, in Flags flags);
  NamedValue add_value(in Identifier item_name,
                       in any val,
                       in Flags flags);
  NamedValue item(in unsigned long index) raises (CORBA::Bounds);
  void remove(in unsigned long index) raises (CORBA::Bounds);
};
```

Here's the corresponding Java mapping:

Listing 20-5. The org.omg.CORBA.NVList Class.

```
package org.omg.CORBA;
public abstract class NVList
{
  // read accessor
  public int count();

  // methods
  public NamedValue add(int flags);
  public NamedValue add_item(String item_name, int flags);
```

```
public NamedValue add_value(String item_name,
                            Any val,
                            int flags);
public NamedValue item(int index)
                            throws org.omg.CORBA.Bounds;
public void remove(int index) throws org.omg.CORBA.Bounds;
}
```

CORBA::Request Mapping

As we also explained in Chapter 8, a **Request** pseudo-object lets you invoke DII operations on a remote server object. Here's the CORBA pseudo-IDL for a **Request**:

```
pseudo interface Request
{
  // attributes
  readonly attribute Object target;
  readonly attribute Identifier operation;
  readonly attribute NVList arguments;
  readonly attribute NamedValue result;
  readonly attribute Environment env;
  readonly attribute ExceptionList exceptions;
  readonly attribute ContextList contexts;
  attribute Context ctx;

  // methods
  any add_in_arg();
  any add_named_in_arg(in string name);
  any add_inout_arg();
  any add_named_inout_arg(in string name);
  any add_out_arg();
  any add_named_out_arg(in string name);
  void set_return_type(in TypeCode tc);
  any return_value();
  void invoke();
  void send_oneway();
  void send_deferred();
  void get_response() raises (wrongTransaction);
  boolean poll_response();
};
```

Here's the corresponding Java mapping:

Listing 20-6. The org.omg.CORBA.Request Class.

```java
package org.omg.CORBA;
public abstract class Request
{
  // accessor methods
  Object target();
  String operation();
  NVList arguments();
  NamedValue result();
  Environment env();
  ExceptionList exceptions();
  ContextList contexts();
  Context ctx();
  void ctx(Context c);

  // methods
  Any add_in_arg();
  Any add_named_in_arg(String name);
  Any add_inout_arg();
  Any add_named_inout_arg(String name);
  Any add_out_arg();
  Any add_named_out_arg(String name);
  void set_return_type(TypeCode tc);
  Any return_value();
  void invoke();
  void send_oneway();
  void send_deferred();
  void get_response() throws wrongTransaction;
  boolean poll_response();
}
```

CORBA::ServerRequest and the DSI Mappings

A **ServerRequest** pseudo-object is used—on the server side—to encapsulate a DSI-received invocation. Here's the CORBA pseudo-IDL for a **ServerRequest**:

```
pseudo interface ServerRequest
{
  readonly attribute Identifier operation;
  void arguments(inout NVList nv);
```

```
  Context ctx();
  void set_result(in Any val);
  void set_exception(in Any val);
};
```

CORBA 2.1 renamed most of the **ServerRequest** methods. So the Java mapping marks the previous methods as deprecated and defines them as calls to the new methods. Here's the Java mapping for the CORBA 2.1 **ServerRequest**, including the deprecated methods:

Listing 20-7. The org.omg.CORBA.ServerRequest Class.

```
package org.omg.CORBA;
public abstract class ServerRequest
{
  // CORBA 2.1 methods
  String operation();
  void arguments(NVList nv);
  Context ctx();
  void set_result(Any val);
  void set_exception(Any val);

  // Deprecated CORBA 2.0 methods
  String op_name();
  // replaced by operation()
  void params(NVList nv);
  // replaced by arguments(NVList nv)
  void result (Any val);
 // replaced by set_result(Any val)
  void except (Any val);
 // replaced by set_exception(Any val)
}
```

DSI allows a CORBA implementation object to receive requests from a client without requiring a precompiled skeleton object. So, you don't have to inherit from a specific **xxxImplBase** class. Instead, your DSI server class must extend the CORBA-defined **DynamicImplementation** class and implement the *invoke* method. Here's the Java mapping for this class:

Listing 20-8. The org.omg.CORBA.DynamicImplementation Class.

```
package org.omg.CORBA;
public abstract class DynamicImplementation
                    extends org.omg.CORBA.portable.ObjectImpl
```

```
{ // methods
  public void invoke(org.omg.CORBA.ServerRequest request);

  // POA support methods
  public String _primary_interface(byte[] oid,
                        org.omg.PortableServer.POA poa);
  public org.omg.CORBA.Object _this()
  {
   return _this_object();
  }
}
```

The client can't tell the difference between a DSI server object or an object that inherits from precompiled skeletons. The ORB presents the client's request to the DSI object by calling its *invoke* method and passing it a **ServerRequest** object.

Of course, implementing server-side objects with DSI requires a lot more work. Instead of performing an up-call to a particular method, the ORB simply hands the DSI implementation object a raw request. It's up to the object to unravel the arguments associated with the request and then invoke the appropriate method. In many cases, the DSI object may route the call to another server—for example, to provide a gateway-like service or to perform some form of load-balancing.

The following shows a code snippet of a DSI implementation of the **Dog** interface:

Listing 20-9. A DSI Implementation of Dog.

```
public class DogDSIImpl extends org.omg.CORBA.DynamicImplementation
{
  DogDSIImpl(String name)
  { super(name, "IDL:Dog:1.0");
  }

  public void invoke(org.omg.CORBA.ServerRequest request)
  {
    // make sure the operation name is correct
    if(!request.op_name().equals("growl"))
    { throw new org.omg.CORBA.BAD_OPERATION();
    }

    // create an empty parameter list
    org.omg.CORBA.NVList params = _orb().create_list(0);

    // create an Any for the at_whom parameter
    org.omg.CORBA.Any at_whomAny = _orb().create_any();
```

```
  // set the Any's type to be a string
  at_whomAny.type(_orb().get_primitive_tc(
                      org.omg.CORBA.TCKind.tk_string));

  // add "in" parameter to the parameter list
  params.add_value("at_whom", at_whomAny, org.omg.CORBA.ARG_IN.value);

  // obtain the parameter values from the request
  request.params(params);

  // get the at_whom parameter from the Any
  String at_whom = at_whomAny.extract_string();

  // invoke the growl operation
  this.growl(at_whom);
  }

  public synchronized void growl(String at_whom)
  {
    System.out.println("Grrrrr " + at_whom );
  }
}
```

Note that the VisiBroker implementation of this class provides a set of constructors that are not part of the CORBA mapping. In addition, VisiBroker 3.1 does not currently support the new CORBA 2.1 implementation of **ServerRequest**. As a result, our code uses the deprecated methods. You can tell *idl2Java* to generate the DSI base classes by enabling the *-portable* flag option:

```
idl2java -portable dog.idl
```

VisiBroker also requires that you register your DSI object implementation with the ORB in the normal way, using *connect*. Here's a server example:

Listing 20-10. A Server Class for Running DSI Objects.

```
public class DogDSIServer
{ static public void main(String[] args)
  { try
    { org.omg.CORBA.ORB orb = org.omg.CORBA.ORB.init();

      // Create the Dog object,
      DogDSIImpl dog = new DogDSIImpl("My Dog");
```

```
    // Export the object reference
    orb.connect(dog);

    // Register the dog object with the naming service

        ...  Code omitted for brevity

    // wait forever for current thread to die
    Thread.currentThread().join();

  } catch(Exception e)
  { System.err.println(e);
  }
 }
}
```

DSI Is Not for Everyone

Warning

CORBA's DII and DSI are really system-level APIs that let you dynamically marshal and unmarshal invocation requests. DII and DSI are totally independent of each other. Stub-based clients can invoke DSI; DII-based clients can invoke static skeletons. However, DII and DSI have the same look and feel because they both make use of the same low-level ORB facilities (like the **NVList** pseudo-object) to process messages.

CORBA's IDL-generated stubs and skeletons hide all these implementation details from your code. They provide a layer of abstraction that makes your remote calls look like ordinary method invocations. And, the compiler provides all the typechecking for free. Mere mortals should avoid writing code to either the DSI or DII interfaces. It's like writing in assembler instead of a high-level language. However, if you're a system programmer, DII and DSI are a dream come true. They both provide tremendous flexibility—one on the client, and the other on the server. ☐

CORBA::TypeCode

As we explained in the last chapter, all CORBA types have a typecode. The **TypeCode** pseudo-object provides methods to let you manipulate type codes. However, remember that some of these methods only apply to particular data types.

Note that the **org.omg.CORBA.ORB** class provides factories for typecodes. Here's the CORBA pseudo-IDL for a **TypeCode**:

```
pseudo interface TypeCode
{
  exception Bounds {};
  exception BadKind {};

  // for all TypeCode kinds
  boolean equal(in TypeCode tc);
  TCKind kind();

  // for objref, struct, union, enum, alias, and exceptions
  RepositoryID id() raises (BadKind);
  RepositoryId name() raises (BadKind);

  // for struct, union, enum, and exceptions
  unsigned long member_count() raises (BadKind);
  Identifier member_name(in unsigned long index)
                      raises (BadKind, Bounds);

  // for struct, union, and exceptions
  TypeCode member_type(in unsigned long index)
                      raises (BadKind, Bounds);

  // for union
  any member_label(in unsigned long index) raises (BadKind, Bounds);
  TypeCode discriminator_type() raises (BadKind);
  long default_index() raises (BadKind);

  // for string, sequence, and array
  unsigned long length() raises (BadKind);
  TypeCode content_type() raises (BadKind);
}
```

Here's the corresponding Java mapping:

Listing 20-11. The org.omg.CORBA.TypeCode Class.

```
package org.omg.CORBA;
public abstract class TypeCode
{
  // for all TypeCode kinds
  boolean equal(TypeCode tc);
```

```
TCKind kind();

// for objref, struct, union, enum, alias, and exceptions
String id() throws TypeCodePackage.BadKind;
String name() throws TypeCodePackage.BadKind;

// for struct, union, enum, and exceptions
int member_count() throws TypeCodePackage.BadKind;
String member_name(int index)
                    throws TypeCodePackage.BadKind;

// for struct, union, and exceptions
TypeCode member_type(int index) throws
                    TypeCodePackage.BadKind,
                    TypeCodePackage.Bounds;

// for union
Any member_label(int index) throws
                    TypeCodePackage.BadKind,
                    TypeCodePackage.Bounds;
TypeCode discriminator_type()
                throws TypeCodePackage.BadKind;
int default_index() throws TypeCodePackage.BadKind;

// for string, sequence, and array
int length()  throws TypeCodePackage.BadKind;
TypeCode content_type() throws TypeCodePackage.BadKind;
}
```

CORBA::TCKind

The predefined typecodes are defined by the pseudo-object **TCKind**. Here's the CORBA pseudo-IDL for **TCKind**:

```
enum TCKind
{
  tk_null, tk_void,
  tk_short, tk_long, tk_ushort, tk_ulong,
  tk_float, tk_double, tk_boolean, tk_char,
  tk_octet, tk_any, tk_TypeCode, tk_Principal, tk_objref,
  tk_struct, tk_union, tk_enum, tk_string,
  tk_sequence, tk_array, tk_alias, tk_except,
```

```
   tk_longlong, tk_ulonglong, tk_longdouble,
   tk_wchar, tk_wstring, tk_fixed
};
```

Here's the corresponding Java mapping:

Listing 20-12. The org.omg.CORBA.TCKind Class.

```
package org.omg.CORBA;
public final class TCKind
{
  public static final int _tk_null = 0;
  TCKind tk_null = new TCKind(_tk_null);

  public static final int _tk_void = 1;
  TCKind tk_void = new TCKind(_tk_void);

  public static final int _tk_short = 2;
  TCKind tk_short = new TCKind(_tk_short);

  public static final int _tk_long = 3;
  TCKind tk_long = new TCKind(_tk_long);

  public static final int _tk_ushort = 4;
  TCKind tk_ushort = new TCKind(_tk_ushort);

  public static final int _tk_ulong = 5;
  TCKind tk_ulong = new TCKind(_tk_ulong);

  public static final int _tk_float = 6;
  TCKind tk_float = new TCKind(_tk_float);

  public static final int _tk_double = 7;
  TCKind tk_double = new TCKind(_tk_double);

  public static final int _tk_boolean = 8;
  TCKind tk_boolean = new TCKind(_tk_boolean);

  public static final int _tk_char = 9;
  TCKind tk_char = new TCKind(_tk_char);

  public static final int _tk_octet = 10;
  TCKind tk_octet = new TCKind(_tk_octet);
```

```
public static final int _tk_any = 11;
TCKind tk_any = new TCKind(_tk_any);

public static final int _tk_TypeCode = 12;
TCKind tk_TypeCode = new TCKind(_tk_TypeCode);

public static final int _tk_Principal = 13;
TCKind tk_Principal = new TCKind(_tk_Principal);

public static final int _tk_objref = 14;
TCKind tk_objref = new TCKind(_tk_objref);

public static final int _tk_stuct = 15;
TCKind tk_stuct = new TCKind(_tk_stuct);

public static final int _tk_union = 16;
TCKind tk_union = new TCKind(_tk_union);

public static final int _tk_enum = 17;
TCKind tk_enum = new TCKind(_tk_enum);

public static final int _tk_string = 18;
TCKind tk_string = new TCKind(_tk_string);

public static final int _tk_sequence = 19;
TCKind tk_sequence = new TCKind(_tk_sequence);

public static final int _tk_array = 20;
TCKind tk_array = new TCKind(_tk_array);

public static final int _tk_alias = 21;
TCKind tk_alias = new TCKind(_tk_alias);

public static final int _tk_except = 22;
TCKind tk_except = new TCKind(_tk_except);

public static final int _tk_longlong = 23;
TCKind tk_longlong = new TCKind(_tk_longlong);

public static final int _tk_ulonglong = 24;
TCKind tk_ulonglong = new TCKind(_tk_ulonglong);

public static final int _tk_longdouble = 25;
TCKind tk_longdouble = new TCKind(_tk_longdouble);
```

```
public static final int _tk_wchar = 26;
TCKind tk_wchar = new TCKind(_tk_wchar);

public static final int _tk_wstring = 27;
TCKind tk_wstring = new TCKind(_tk_wstring);

public static final int _tk_fixed = 28;
TCKind tk_fixed = new TCKind(_tk_fixed);

public int value() {...}
private TCKind(int) {...}


}
```

In Chapter 22, we develop a program that demonstrates CORBA typecodes in action.

CONCLUSION

This concludes the CORBA IDL-to-Java mappings. It may seem overwhelming, but it really isn't. CORBA supports all the C++ types. Consequently, CORBA types are a superset of the Java types. In a sense, CORBA expands your distributed Java power. However, if you want to keep things simple, just use Java types. After all, Java was designed to provide a gentler, kinder C++.

The IDL-to-Java mappings will make you feel right at home, regardless of which vendor's Java ORB you use. For example, we found both *VisiBroker for Java V3.1* and *OrbixWeb 3.0* to be highly compliant with the new bindings. JavaSoft's *JavaIDL* is also very compliant. Consequently, you'll find it very easy to move your programs across these three environments. Finally, the new IDL-to-Java language mapping also defines an interface for portable stubs and skeletons. This means you don't have to recompile your stubs and skeletons to run on different vendors' ORBs.

Chapter 21

The CORBA Java-to-IDL Mapping

The Java programming community is currently forced to choose between three different distributed object paradigms: Java *Remote Method Invocation (RMI)*, Netscape/Visigenic's *Caffeine* over IIOP, and CORBA IDL. Both RMI and Caffeine have proven to be extremely popular because they don't require Java programmers to learn a separate interface definition language. However, RMI lacks interoperability with other languages—its current incarnation does not support standard wire protocols. This chapter is about the great unification of these three camps.

By the time you read this, OMG will have finalized its CORBA *Java-to-IDL* mapping. This is a reverse language mapping for Java. This means that it generates CORBA IDL from Java RMI semantics. You write Java RMI and then out comes IDL. The mapping attempts to unify the ease-of-programming of Java RMI with: 1) the cross-language support CORBA IDL provides, and 2) the standard wire protocol CORBA IIOP provides.

In short, *Java-to-IDL* unifies the different styles of distributed programming in Java. The industry can now converge on the use of IDL and IIOP. By supporting RMI semantics—instead of Caffeine—this mapping tries to address the needs of the existing RMI community. As you already know, JavaSoft plans to offer RMI over IIOP. By adopting RMI as the basis for its Java-to-IDL mapping, OMG is meeting JavaSoft half way.

In this chapter, we first go over the benefits RMI-to-IDL and RMI-to-IIOP provide to the programmer. Then we introduce the new OMG *Objects-by-Value* specification. The *Java-to-IDL* mapping is a heavy user of the new CORBA pass-by-value semantics. So we need to understand how they work. We conclude with the *Java-to-IDL* mapping.

RMI MEETS CORBA

Java programmers have a lot to gain from the merger of RMI with CORBA IDL and IIOP. In Part 4, we explained the advantages of the pure-Java distributed object programming environments like the ones RMI and Caffeine provide. In case you missed it, both of these environments let you define distributed objects using ordinary Java interfaces instead of IDL (see Figure 21-1). And they both let you pass objects-by-value in your method invocations. We won't repeat the benefits of RMI and Caffeine here. Instead, we will concentrate on what IDL and IIOP bring to RMI.

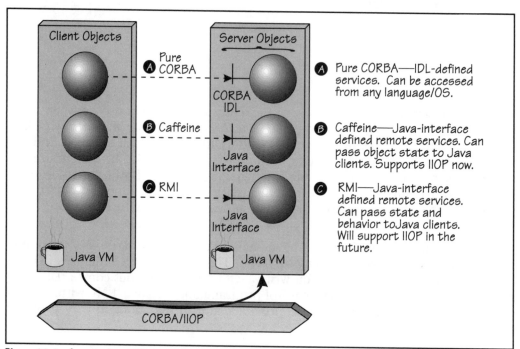

Figure 21-1. Java-to-Java ORB-based Communication Options.

Why RMI to IDL?

So what does this all mean to you as a CORBA/Java programmer? It means that you can use Java RMI semantics to define your CORBA interfaces, instead of IDL. A

Java-to-IDL compiler can then automatically create CORBA stubs and skeletons from your Java code. In addition, the compiler can optionally generate CORBA IDL from your RMI/Java source.

So what does the automatically-generated CORBA IDL buy you in this situation? The answer is quite a bit. Here's our short list:

- **Distributed access to metadata.** You can load the generated CORBA IDL into an Interface Repository to make it accessible over the network.

- **Dynamic method invocations.** Clients can use the IDL to dynamically invoke methods on your Java-specified remote interfaces.

- **Multilingual client access.** You can use the IDL to compile client stubs in CORBA-supported languages such as C, C++, Smalltalk, COBOL, and Ada. These clients can then invoke your Java-specified remote interfaces.

- **Tool support.** Tools—such as Rational Rose—can import the CORBA IDL and then use it to represent your objects.

- **Language-neutral documentation.** You can publish your remote interfaces in a language-neutral IDL format. Note that CORBA IDL is becoming the lingua franca for defining middle-tier services. So you get this consistency for free.

Like Caffeine and straight RMI, the new RMI-to-IDL CORBA mapping lets you write distributed applications from within the Java language. Like Caffeine, the RMI-to-IDL mapping provides all the advantages of IDL to Java (and RMI) programmers.

Why RMI Over IIOP?

We find it to be even more important that the new mapping lets you run your RMI-defined objects on top of CORBA/IIOP—the standard wire protocol for distributed object communications. Here's what RMI-over-IIOP provides:

- **Built-in support for the propagation of transaction and security contexts.** RMI programs can tap into these architected IIOP features to participate in global transactions and to implicitly pass security credentials.

- **Common firewall support.** The CORBA community is working on a common IIOP proxy that all firewall vendors will support. Currently, both Iona and Visigenic/Borland provide IIOP-based firewalls. By the time you read this,

Netscape may have shipped its own CORBA/IIOP firewall as part of *Enterprise Server 4.0*. RMI will benefit from all this work.

■ **Interoperability with objects written in other languages.** The RMI-to-IDL mapping defines an RMI subset that allows CORBA clients written in non-Java languages to invoke RMI services. Of course, a C++ program would not know what to do if it got hit in the head with a bucket of bytecodes. So this RMI feature may not be supported across languages, which is why we call it a subset.

■ **Support for open standards.** This is a key requirement in the distributed system world—even Microsoft had to play by this rule to get DCOM accepted (they put DCOM under the tutelage of the Open Group). IIOP will help deploy RMI on the Internet, intranets, and enterprise networks.

■ **A plug-and-play environment for ORB services.** Instead of getting all your RMI ORB technology from one vendor (JavaSoft), RMI-over-IIOP lets you pick the pieces from different ORB vendors—including BEA, IBM, Iona, Oracle, Netscape/Kiva, and Visigenic/Borland. These vendors are competing to provide IIOP ORBs, CORBA-based services, distributed system management, and scalable Object Transaction Monitors (OTMs).

■ **Bidirectional access to DCOM objects.** CORBA defines standard bi-directional gateways to COM and DCOM objects. Commercial COM/CORBA gateways are available from a number of vendors—including Visual Edge, Iona, BEA Systems, IBM, and Borland/Visigenic.

Without turning this into a Soapbox, RMI over IIOP is a good thing for both the CORBA and RMI camps. It brings together two powerful technologies and avoids the splintering that was so endemic in the Unix world.

CORBA's New Objects-By-Value

To maximize its compliance with RMI semantics, the *Java-to-IDL* mapping takes full advantage of CORBA's new pass-by-value features. Pass-by-value requires new IDL extensions that are defined in the *Objects-by-Value* submission to the OMG by BEA, IBM, Iona, Netscape, Novell, and Visigenic/Borland (see OMG document *orbos/97-11-11*). This submission is based on the *VisiBroker for Java* Caffeine extensions; JavaSoft also contributed a code download mechanism based on RMI's codebases. This section contains a brief overview of the new pass-by-value semantics.[1]

---

[1] Note that the *Objects-by-Value* submission was still not finalized as we went to press.

The Value Type

As you know from Part 4, today's CORBA does not let you pass objects-by-value inside a parameter. Caffeine is the exception; it supports the passing of objects-by-value using a non-standard CORBA extension. The design point of CORBA was stationary distributed objects that you can reach from anywhere. So you simply pass a reference to a remote object instead of the object itself. The *Objects-by-Value* proposal extends the CORBA object model to let you pass objects by value inside method parameters. To do this, it introduces a new IDL type called the *value* type.

A value type lets you specify an object that you can pass by value between clients and servers, even if they are implemented in different languages. When an ORB encounters an object of type *value* inside a parameter, it automatically passes a copy of that object's state to the recipient. In contrast, the ORB will pass by reference any object that you declare via an IDL *interface*.

You may find the value type to be quite useful in certain situations. For example, you can use a value type inside a parameter to copy the state of an object whose primary purpose is to encapsulate a data structure.

You can think of a value type as being half way between a regular IDL interface and a struct. The value IDL syntax lets you specify some additional implementation details—for example, *state*—that are not part of a regular CORBA interface. You can also specify local methods that operate on this state. Unlike IDL interfaces, a value's methods cannot be invoked remotely.

A stateful value type can only singly inherit from other stateful value types. But it can multiply inherit from pure interfaces. The data members of a value type can be either private or public. Note that the ORB will transmit all the data members in the hierarchy tree, starting with the highest base type and ending with the most derived type.

Here's an example of a value type called **Dog**:

```
module MyAnimals
{
   interface Animal {...};
   interface Pet {...};

   value Dog: Animal, Pet
   {
       /* local operations */
       void bark(in short how_long);
       void sit(in string  where);
```

```
    void growl(in string  at_whom);

    /* state */
    state
    {
      public string name; // the default is private
      short age;
    };
  };
}
```

Notice that **Dog** can multiply inherit from interfaces as well as other value types. Unlike an interface, a **Dog** value can specify its state. It can also specify local methods. However, note that you can only remotely invoke methods that are declared via ordinary CORBA interfaces.

Passing Objects By Value

When you pass an instance of a value type as a parameter, the ORB marshals its state and passes it to the receiver. On the receiving side, the ORB: 1) unmarshals the state, 2) finds an implementation of the type, 3) instantiates a new instance of the type, and 4) loads its state. If the ORB cannot find an implementation of the type on the receiving machine, it will try to download an implementation by calling back the sender. It does this by invoking a callback object on the sender called the **CodeBase**; the callback object's URL is passed along with the value. Note that the ORB will negotiate its support for code downloads as part of the *quality of service* it provides. Because of the security implications, you may find this feature to be often disabled.

Figure 21-2 shows how **Lassie** gets passed as a parameter in remote invocations across several machines. **Lassie** is an instance of the **Dog** value type. In the scenario, Machine B has a local **Dog** class that implements the IDL-defined **Dog** value; Machine C does not have an implementation. Here's what happens when **Lassie** is passed across these machines:

1. ***Lassie is passed in a remote invocation***. The ORB encounters a value parameter of type **Dog**. Consequently, it marshals the state of this object as part of the remote invocation. In this case, the state represents a **Dog** called **Lassie**. On the receiving end, the ORB locates a local **Dog** class. So it uses it to create a new instance of **Dog** and then loads its state. **Lassie** is now also running on Machine B.

2. ***Machine B passes Lassie by value to Machine C***. The ORB passes **Lassie** by value to C. However, this time it fails to find a local implementation of **Dog**.

3. ***The ORB downloads a Dog class from Machine B's CodeBase***. The ORB invokes the **CodeBase** object on B to download a **Dog** class to C. Note that this time the actual code gets copied.

4. ***Lassie now also runs on Machine C***. The ORB loads the newly downloaded **Dog** class into memory. It uses it to create a new instance of **Dog**. Then it loads the state (i.e., **Lassie**) into the new **Dog** object. So **Lassie** is now also running on Machine C.

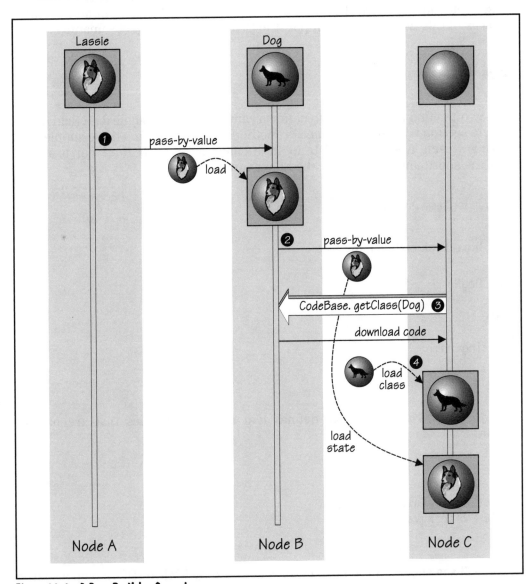

Figure 21-2. A Pass-By-Value Scenario

You should note that once a **Lassie** is passed-by-value, it runs as a separate object. There are no replica semantics in pass-by-value. If you update Lassie on one machine, the changes will not be automatically propagated to the other Lassies.

By default, value types are not regular CORBA objects—they do not inherit from **CORBA::Object**. Instead, they are derived from a new base type called **CORBA::ValueBase**. This type provides all the basic pass-by-value marshaling operations. In CORBA/Java, this base type maps to **java.io.Serializable**. Of course, you can always declare that a particular type inherits from an interface; instances of this type will then support the CORBA remote object semantics.

Boxed Values

You may often find it convenient to define a value type with a single data field inside the state section with no inheritance or methods. You can define these simple data containers using a shorthand IDL notation called a *boxed value*. For example, here's the shorthand for a value called **DogName**:

```
value DogName string;
```

This a boxed value shorthand for:

```
value DogName
{
 state
 {
   string name;
 };
};
```

The *Objects-by-Value* proposal defines two new boxed types that are part of CORBA:

```
module CORBA
{
  value StringValue string;
  value WstringValue wstring;
};
```

As you will see shortly, these boxed values are used by RMI-to-IDL to map a shared string that can also accept nulls.

Mapping Value Types to Java

A stateful value type will map directly to a usable class-like construct in each programming language CORBA supports; it may also generate some *Helper* classes. In Java, C++, and Smalltalk, the value will map to a concrete implementation class; in C, it will map to a struct. The classes must provide method implementations that implement the operations you specify in IDL. Each language mapping specifies an appropriate marshaling/unmarshaling protocol for passing values. The marshaling is typically implemented by the *Helper* class.

An IDL-to-Java compiler will map an IDL value type to a Java class with the same name; it will also generate a *Helper* class with the suffix **Helper** appended to the name. The mapped Java class will contain method definitions that correspond to the operations you defined in the IDL; you must provide the code that implements these methods. In addition, the Java class will contain instance variables that correspond to the IDL state fields. In Java, a value class must extend **java.io.serializable** either directly or indirectly. This interface serves as a flag; it lets the Java VM know that this class is automatically serializable (we cover Java Serialization in Part 7).

An Example

Here's the CORBA IDL for a value type called **Cat**:

```
value Cat
{
  /* local operations */
  void eat();
  void hereKitty();

  /* state */
  state
  {
    public long weight;
    long age;
  };
}
```

Here's the corresponding Java mapping:

```
public class Cat implements java.io.Serializable
{
```

```
// instance variables
public int weight;
private int age;

// local methods
public void eat() {...}            // implement this method
public void hereKitty() {...}      // implement this method
}
```

THE JAVA-TO-IDL MAPPING

In this section, we present a brief overview of the *Java-to-IDL* mapping. It probably contains more detail than you will ever need. After all, one of the primary ideas behind this mapping is to hide CORBA IDL from the Java programmer.[2]

RMI Meets CORBA

The *Java-to-IDL* mapping is fully compatible with current RMI semantics as well as with CORBA IDL and IIOP. The subset that meets these goals is called *RMI/IDL*; it is also the subset on which Enterprise JavaBeans are based. To meet the needs of the RMI and CORBA communities, the OMG architects (with lots of help from JavaSoft) defined RMI/IDL to be a strict subset of current Java RMI. They went out of their way to make RMI/IDL as large a subset of RMI as was practical—for example, they made full use of the CORBA *Objects-by-Value* features we describe in the previous section).

The Java-to-IDL Mapping at a Glance

Table 21-1 lets you see at-a-glance the new *Java-to-IDL* mapping. In general, this mapping goes out of its way to let you use CORBA from within your familiar Java setting. It even takes care of little details like mapping JavaBeans properties to CORBA attributes. We explain JavaBeans properties and their design patterns in Part 7.

The mapping of general constructs from Java to CORBA should be familiar by now. The only strange thing here is the mapping of overloaded methods. Here's the story.

---

[2] The material in this section is based on the updated *Java-to-IDL* joint submission from IBM, Netscape, Oracle, Sun, and Visigenic/Borland (see OMG document *orbos/97-11-29*). As we go to press, this specification is still not finalized. We expect the standard to be adopted by the time you read this.

Table 21-1. The Java to IDL Mapping.

Java	CORBA IDL
General Constructs	
package	module
overloaded methods	Yes, within same interface (via mangled names)
throws	raises
local exception classes	IDL exception containing a valuetype
RMI **RemoteException** classes	IDL standard exceptions
property (uses JavaBeans get/set semantics)	attribute
Primitive Types	
void	void
boolean	boolean
char	wchar
byte	octet
short	short
int	long
long	long long
float	float
double	double
Constructed Types	
java.lang.Object	any
java.lang.String	CORBA::WstringValue
java.lang.Array	Value type containing an unbounded sequence
Remote Interfaces	
remote interface (inherits from **java.rmi.Remote**)	interface implemented by CORBA::Object
Objects Pass-By-Value Types	
java.io.Serializable	CORBA::Value

Table 21-1. The Java to IDL Mapping. (Continued)

Java	CORBA IDL
Objects Pass-By-Value Types (continued)	
java.io.Externalizable	CORBA::Value
Non-remote interface	IDL value type (without state)
Local serializable objects passed as arguments	IDL value objects (inheritance tree preserved)

Like C++, Java supports overloaded methods—meaning that the same method name can have different signatures. CORBA, on the other hand, requires that each method name have a unique signature. To get around this limitation, the mapping creates mangled IDL signature names for overloaded methods. Again, you don't have to look at the IDL. So it doesn't really matter much. However, it's nice to know that they have found a workaround.

Notice in the table that the primitive Java data types map directly to their CORBA IDL counterparts. So there's nothing more to say here. The **java.lang.Object** maps to CORBA **any**. They can both be used to accommodate arbitrary data types. However, this doesn't mean that completely arbitrary Java objects can be passed across RMI/IDL interfaces (more on this in the next section).

Java supports a pointer model for strings. You can have null pointers for strings as well as several pointers to one string. The Java-to-IDL mapping could have simply mapped a Java **String** to a CORBA **wstring**. However, we would have lost both the null pointers and the pointer sharing when transmitting a graph of Java objects across IIOP. To get around this limitation, the **java.lang.String** is mapped to the new **CORBA::WstringValue**. This is the new CORBA type we told you about in the last section; it's a value object type that boxes up a **wstring**.

Similarly, Java supports a pointer model for arrays. So arrays are mapped to a CORBA value type that boxes up an IDL sequence. The boxed types provide full compatibility with Java semantics.

From a programmer's perspective, the two things that really matter in the Java-to-IDL mapping are: 1) how you describe your remote interfaces in Java, and 2) how you pass parameters in a remote invocation—including object types. As you can see from the table, you define your remote CORBA interfaces in Java using RMI semantics. And you can pass parameters that contain local objects by value in a remote invocation. In the next sections, we cover these two topics in more detail.

RMI/IDL Remote Interfaces

The Java-to-IDL mapping uses RMI semantics to define a Java interface that can be invoked remotely. A Java interface is a conforming RMI/IDL remote interface if:

✔ The interface inherits from **java.rmi.Remote** either directly or indirectly.

✔ Any other interface that it extends (either directly or indirectly) is also a conforming RMI/IDL remote interface.

✔ All methods in the interface must throw **java.rmi.RemoteException.**

✔ All the method parameters and result types must be conforming RMI/IDL types. A conforming RMI/IDL type is a Java type whose values may be transmitted across an RMI/IDL remote interface at run time. This includes: 1) the Java primitive types, 2) a reference to a remote object, 3) conforming value types (see next section), 4) an array of conforming RMI/IDL types, 5) an exception type, and 6) a **java.lang.Object** type.

In short, this covers almost the entire RMI interface semantics. The one exception is that the overloading of similarly-named methods can only be within a single interface. This is the overloading constraint we told you about earlier.

Here's an example of a simple RMI/IDL remote interface:

```
interface Dog extends java.rmi.Remote
{
  // Methods
  void bark(int how_long) throws RemoteException;
  void sit(String  where);

  // Properties Using JavaBeans Design Patterns
  void getName() throws RemoteException;
  void setName(int x) throws RemoteException;
  String getURL() throws RemoteException;
}
```

This code gets automatically mapped to the following CORBA IDL:

```
interface Dog
{
  // Methods
  void bark(in long how_long);
  void sit(in WstringValue where);
```

```
// CORBA attributes
attribute long Name;
readonly attribute WstringValue URL;
};
```

RMI/IDL Value Types

An RMI/IDL *value type* represents a class whose state you can move between systems. Instead of passing a reference to a remote object, you pass the actual state of the object. The receiving system must have an analogous class that can hold the received value. You can pass value types as parameters (or results) of a remote method invocation. You can also pass them as fields within other objects that you pass remotely.

A Java class is a conforming RMI/IDL value type if it implements the **java.io.Serializable** interface either directly or indirectly. The class may also implement **java.io.Externalizable** and provide its own serialization (we cover Java serialization in Part 7).

The Java-to-IDL mapping does not place any restrictions on the method signatures, static fields, or transient fields of a value type. The only restriction is that a value type cannot—either directly or indirectly—implement the **java.rmi.Remote** interface. Remember, both RMI and CORBA pass remote objects by reference only. There are no other restrictions on the kind of interfaces you can implement with a value type.

Here is an example of a conforming RMI/IDL value type:

```
public class Point implements java.io.Serializable
{
  private int x;
  private int y;
  public Point(int x, int y){ ... }
  public int getX() { ... }
  public int getY() { ... }
}
```

Note that most of the core Java classes are now serializable. This means that you can use them as value objects with RMI/IDL. The list includes classes such as **java.util.Hashtable**, **java.util.Vector**, **java.util.Date**, and **java.lang.Number**.

As we go to press, it's still not clear if you can use RMI over IIOP to pass object behavior as well as state. As we explained earlier, CORBA's *Objects-by-Value* does not preclude you from doing both. However, it's not clear that *Java-to-IDL* will let you pass the bytecodes if the class is not on the target machine.

CONCLUSION

The CORBA *Java-to-IDL* and *Objects-by-Value* specifications have gone a long way toward unifying the CORBA and RMI distributed object camps. In our book, this is very good news for Java programmers. It means we won't have to choose between *Java RMI* and *Java IDL*.

Enterprise JavaBeans (EJB) is a good example of this new unification in action. As you will see in Part 7, an EJB-compliant bean must declare its remote interfaces using the RMI/IDL subset we described in this chapter. This means that CORBA IDL can be automatically generated for any EJB. So an EJB is a CORBA server object that you define using Java RMI semantics. The IDL allows clients—written in any CORBA-supported languages—to access EJB servers over an IIOP ORB. At the risk of sounding too soapy, this is really a marriage made in heaven.

Chapter 22

The Introspective CORBA/Java Object

CORBA/Java objects are derived from both the CORBA and Java **Object** classes. As a result, they are supersmart objects that can tell you quite a lot about themselves. An object is *introspective* if it can describe its behavior at run time. These introspective properties make objects very attractive to client/server tool vendors, Trader Services, and dynamic clients. Introspection lets you discover at run time the stuff that only compilers previously recognized.

A CORBA/Java object is doubly introspective. It combines the introspection properties of the CORBA and Java object models. CORBA introspection includes a wealth of information that is contained in Interface Repositories; it provides enough detail to let you dynamically construct and invoke a method at run time. Java's introspection is currently more limited than CORBA's; it consists of local information you can obtain from the *java.language* **Class** and **Object** classes as well as the new JDK 1.1 reflection classes. In contrast, CORBA supports distributed introspection via the Interface Repository. JavaBeans extends the Java introspection model to include the description of methods, events, and properties a component supports (we cover Java reflection as well as JavaBeans introspection in Part 7).

In this chapter, we start out by reviewing the CORBA and Java object models. You may recall from Part 2 that a CORBA skeleton object extends both the Java and

CORBA object models. So when you extend your server objects from a skeleton you automatically get both object models. We will develop a simple program called *AskMe* that demonstrates the introspective powers of a CORBA/Java object. We then develop a useful program called *WalkIR*. This program walks the Interface Repository and then writes out its contents. These two programs will help bring together many of the concepts we introduced in this Part.

CORBA INTROSPECTION

A CORBA object derives its introspective powers from **CORBA::Object**. In Java, the root **org.omg.CORBA.portable.ObjectImpl** class implements both **CORBA:: Object** and **java.lang.Object**. The **_XXXImplBase** classes—meaning the interface-specific skeletons—are all derived from this class. Your servant classes inherit all this functionality by extending **_XXXImplBase**. In addition, **CORBA::ORB** provides two useful helper functions: *object_to_string* and *string_to_object* (see the light methods in Figure 22-1). Here's a quick description of CORBA introspection:

- **CORBA::Object** defines operations that are supported by every CORBA object reference. It's the root interface of all CORBA objects. The ORB provides these operations for free. You simply inherit them when you create your object. Seven of these methods deal with introspection. You already saw *get_interface* in Chapter 8; it returns a reference to an **InterfaceDef**, which is an object inside an Interface Repository that describes this interface. You invoke *get_implementation* on an object reference to obtain an **ImplementationDef** object. This is an Implementation Repository object that describes the implementation of your object.

  You invoke *is_nil* to determine if the object exists. You can also invoke *non_existent* to determine if the object has been destroyed. You invoke *is_equivalent* to determine if two object references are equivalent; the ORB returns TRUE if your object reference is equivalent to the object reference you pass as a parameter. If two object references are identical, they are equivalent. Two different object references that refer to the same object are also equivalent. To improve the performance of object searches, the ORB may maintain an internal hash value for an object reference. If two object references *hash* differently, they are not identical. However, the reverse is not always true. Finally, you invoke *is_a* to determine if an object is really an instance of the Repository Type you specify.

- **CORBA::ORB** is a pseudo-object interface that defines general-purpose ORB methods. You can invoke these methods on an ORB pseudo-object from either a client or server implementation. Two of these methods are introspection-related. You invoke *object_to_string* to create a "stringified" version of the

get_implementation	CORBA::Object	non_existent
get_interface		is_equivalent
is_nil		hash
duplicate		create_request
release		_request
is_a		

object_to_string	CORBA::ORB	BOA_init
string_to_object		list_initial_services
create_list		resolve_initial_references
create_operation_list		send_multiple_requests_oneway
get_default_context		send_multiple_requests_deferred
create_environment		poll_next_response
		get_next_response

Figure 22-1. The CORBA Object Introspection Methods.

object that you can then pass around. You invoke *string_to_object* to convert a string representation to an object reference on which you can invoke methods.

In summary, every CORBA object is introspective. You can invoke ORB-implemented methods on every object reference to obtain information about this object. Your implementation never receives these calls. Note that the actual metadata is stored in the Interface Repository. The introspection methods simply return object references to Interface Repository objects.

JAVA REFLECTION

Java objects are by definition reflective. The reflection APIs are automatically built into the Java VM. At run time, you can get class information for any running instance by interfacing with its **Class** object. For example, the following code fragment returns the run-time Class descriptor for the class named **java.net.Socket**:

```
Class mysocket = Class.forName("java.net.Socket");
```

You can obtain an object's class by invoking its *getClass* method. All Java objects inherit this method from **java.lang.Object**—the root class of all Java objects. For example, here's how you obtain an object's **Class**:

```
Class myClass  = myObject.getClass();
```

The Java VM directly instantiates **Class** objects to represent the various classes and interfaces in a running Java application. A **Class** object provides class-related metadata; it gives you access to a universe of lower-level reflection classes that describe every language-aspect of this object—you'll know as much about this class as the compiler. The JavaBeans introspection APIs describe the component aspects of a bean—for example, its icons, events, properties, property editors, and customizer. Think of it as a higher-form of metadata (we cover both Java reflection and JavaBeans introspection in Part 7).

THE ASK ME PROGRAM

The best way to demonstrate CORBA/Java introspection at work is to write a small code example. In this section we develop a small standalone Java program called *AskMe*. You pass AskMe an *Interoperable Object Reference (IOR)* for a CORBA/Java object. AskMe will then do the following: 1) convert the IOR string to a live CORBA object reference, 2) invoke both CORBA and Java introspection methods to obtain metadata about this object, and 3) print the results.

The AskMe Code

The AskMe program consists of two Java classes: **AskMe** and **PrintIDL**. Here's what these two classes do:

- **AskMe** provides a *main* method that does the following: 1) obtains an IOR from the Naming Service, 2) prints the IOR, 3) invokes *ORB::string_to_object* to convert the IOR to a live object reference, 4) invokes *get_interface* on the object reference to obtain its **InterfaceDef**, 5) creates a new **PrintIDL** object, 6) tells the **PrintIDL** object to print the signature of each method that is defined by this interface, 7) invokes *getClass* on the object and its parent to obtain their Java class objects, 8) invokes *getName* on the class objects to obtain their class names, and 9) invokes *getInterfaces* on the class object to obtain the list of interfaces this object implements.

- **PrintIDL** is a helper class that prints out the contents of an IR container object. For example, if you pass it a **ModuleDef,** it will print all the interfaces and attributes that are contained in this module. If you pass it a **Repository** object, it will walk the IR and print its entire contents. In this case, we pass it an **InterfaceDef** object. Consequently, it will print all the methods, attributes, and typedefs that this interface defines. We will continue our explanation of **PrintIDL** after you glance at the code.[1]

---

[1] We adapted the PrintIDL class from a IR walker utility that was originally developed by Jonathan Weedon of Visigenic.

Here is the code that implements these two classes:

Listing 22-1. The AskMe Class.

```
// AskMe.java
import java.io.*;

import org.omg.CosNaming.*;

class AskMe
{ public static void main(String args[])
  { try
    { // Initialize the ORB
      org.omg.CORBA.ORB orb = org.omg.CORBA.ORB.init(args, null);

      System.out.println("From CORBA Introspection:");
      System.out.println("------------------------");


      // Get a reference to the Naming service
      org.omg.CORBA.Object nameServiceObj =
              orb.resolve_initial_references ("NameService");
      if (nameServiceObj == null)
      {
        System.out.println("nameServiceObj = null");
        return;
      }

      org.omg.CosNaming.NamingContext nameService =
              org.omg.CosNaming.NamingContextHelper.narrow (nameServiceObj);
      if (nameService == null)
      {
        System.out.println("nameService = null");
        return;
      }

      // Use the Naming Service to get an IOR to the Count object
      NameComponent[] countName = {new NameComponent("countName", "")};
      org.omg.CORBA.Object myObject = nameService.resolve(countName);
      CounterPortable.Count counter =
        CounterPortable.CountHelper.narrow(myObject);

      // print out stringified IOR
      String IOR = orb.object_to_string(myObject);
      System.out.println("My IOR string is: \n" + IOR + "\n");
```

```
      // print interface IDL using PrintIDL class
      System.out.println("I implement the following CORBA interface:");
      org.omg.CORBA.InterfaceDef myInterface = myObject._get_interface();
      PrintIDL print = new PrintIDL();
      print.printInterface(myInterface);

      System.out.println("\n\nFrom Java Introspection:");
      System.out.println("------------------------");

      // print Java class information

      Class parentClass = myObject.getClass();
      Class myClass = counter.getClass();
      System.out.println("My parent class is called: " +
                         parentClass.getName());
      System.out.println("I belong to a class called: " +
                         myClass.getName());
      System.out.println("I implement the following interfaces:");
      Class[] myInterfaces = myClass.getInterfaces();
      for (int i=0; i < myInterfaces.length; i++)
          System.out.println(myInterfaces[i]);

   } catch(Exception e)
   { System.err.println("System Exception");
     System.err.println(e);
   }
  }
}
```

Listing 22-2. The PrintIDL Class.

```
// PrintIDL.java

import java.io.PrintStream;

public class PrintIDL extends Thread {

  private PrintStream out = System.out;
  private int indent;

  public void print(org.omg.CORBA.Container container)
  {
    org.omg.CORBA.Contained[] contained =
      container.contents(org.omg.CORBA.DefinitionKind.dk_all, true);
```

```
    for(int i = 0; i < contained.length; i++)
    {
      switch(contained[i].def_kind().value())
      {
        case org.omg.CORBA.DefinitionKind._dk_Module:
          printModule(org.omg.CORBA.ModuleDefHelper.narrow(contained[i]));
          break;
        case org.omg.CORBA.DefinitionKind._dk_Interface:

printInterface(org.omg.CORBA.InterfaceDefHelper.narrow(contained[i]));
          break;
        case org.omg.CORBA.DefinitionKind._dk_Attribute:

printAttribute(org.omg.CORBA.AttributeDefHelper.narrow(contained[i]));
          break;
        case org.omg.CORBA.DefinitionKind._dk_Constant:

printConstant(org.omg.CORBA.ConstantDefHelper.narrow(contained[i]));
          break;
        case org.omg.CORBA.DefinitionKind._dk_Exception:

printException(org.omg.CORBA.ExceptionDefHelper.narrow(contained[i]));
          break;
        case org.omg.CORBA.DefinitionKind._dk_Operation:

printOperation(org.omg.CORBA.OperationDefHelper.narrow(contained[i]));
          break;
        case org.omg.CORBA.DefinitionKind._dk_Alias:
          printAlias(org.omg.CORBA.AliasDefHelper.narrow(contained[i]));
          break;
        case org.omg.CORBA.DefinitionKind._dk_Struct:
          printStruct(org.omg.CORBA.StructDefHelper.narrow(contained[i]));
          break;
        case org.omg.CORBA.DefinitionKind._dk_Union:
          printUnion(org.omg.CORBA.UnionDefHelper.narrow(contained[i]));
          break;
        case org.omg.CORBA.DefinitionKind._dk_Enum:
          printEnum(org.omg.CORBA.EnumDefHelper.narrow(contained[i]));
          break;
        case org.omg.CORBA.DefinitionKind._dk_none:
        case org.omg.CORBA.DefinitionKind._dk_all:
        case org.omg.CORBA.DefinitionKind._dk_Typedef:
        case org.omg.CORBA.DefinitionKind._dk_Primitive:
        case org.omg.CORBA.DefinitionKind._dk_String:
        case org.omg.CORBA.DefinitionKind._dk_Sequence:
```

```java
      case org.omg.CORBA.DefinitionKind._dk_Array:
      default:
        break;
    }
  }
}

private void printModule(org.omg.CORBA.ModuleDef def)
{
  println("module " + def.name() + " {");
  indent++;
  print(def);
  indent--;
  println("};");
}


public  void printInterface(org.omg.CORBA.InterfaceDef idef)
{
  String superList = "";
  {
    org.omg.CORBA.InterfaceDef[] base_interfaces =
                                 idef.base_interfaces();
    if (base_interfaces.length > 0) {
      superList += " :";
      for(int j = 0; j < base_interfaces.length; j++) {
        String comma = j == base_interfaces.length - 1 ? "" : ",";
        superList += " " + base_interfaces[j].absolute_name() +
                     comma;
      }
    }
  }
  println("interface " + idef.name() + superList + " {");
  indent++;
  print(idef);
  indent--;
  println("};");
}


private void printAttribute(org.omg.CORBA.AttributeDef def)
{
  String readonly =
      def.mode() == org.omg.CORBA.AttributeMode.ATTR_READONLY ?
    "readonly " : "";
```

```
    println(readonly + "attribute " + toIdl(def.type_def()) +
            " " + def.name() + ";");
}


private void printConstant(org.omg.CORBA.ConstantDef def)
{
    println("const " + toIdl(def.type_def()) +
            " " + def.name() + " = " + def.value() + ";");
}


private void printException(org.omg.CORBA.ExceptionDef def)
{
    println("exception " + def.name() + " {");
    indent++;
    org.omg.CORBA.StructMember[] members = def.members();
    for(int j = 0; j < members.length; j++)
    {
        println(toIdl(members[j].type_def) + " " +
                    members[j].name + ";");
    }
    indent--;
    println("};");
}


private void printOperation(org.omg.CORBA.OperationDef def)
{
    String oneway = def.mode() ==
            org.omg.CORBA.OperationMode.OP_ONEWAY ?
            "oneway " : "";
    println(oneway + toIdl(def.result_def()) + " " + def.name() + "(");
    indent++;
    org.omg.CORBA.ParameterDescription[] parameters = def.params();
    for(int k = 0; k < parameters.length; k++)
    {
        String[] mode = { "in", "out", "inout" };
        String comma = k == parameters.length - 1 ? "" : ",";
        println(mode[parameters[k].mode.value()] + " " +
                toIdl(parameters[k].type_def) + " " +
                parameters[k].name + comma);
    }
    indent--;
    org.omg.CORBA.ExceptionDef[] exceptions = def.exceptions();
```

```
    if (exceptions.length > 0)
    {
      println(") raises (");
      indent++;
      for(int k = 0; k < exceptions.length; k++) {
        String comma = k == exceptions.length - 1 ? "" : ",";
        println(exceptions[k].absolute_name() + comma);
      }
      indent--;
    }
    println(");");
  }

  private void printAlias(org.omg.CORBA.AliasDef def)
  {
    org.omg.CORBA.IDLType idlType = def.original_type_def();
    String arrayBounds = "";
    while(true)
    {
      org.omg.CORBA.ArrayDef arrayDef =
            org.omg.CORBA.ArrayDefHelper.narrow(idlType);
      if (arrayDef == null)
      {
        break;
      }
      arrayBounds += "[" + arrayDef.length() + "]";
      idlType = arrayDef.element_type_def();
    }
    println("typedef " + toIdl(idlType) +
            " " + def.name() + arrayBounds + ";");
  }

  private void printStruct(org.omg.CORBA.StructDef def)
  {
    println("struct " + def.name() + " {");
    indent++;
    org.omg.CORBA.StructMember[] members = def.members();
    for(int j = 0; j < members.length; j++)
    {
      println(toIdl(members[j].type_def) + " " +
              members[j].name + ";");
    }
    indent--;
    println("};");
  }
```

```
private void printUnion(org.omg.CORBA.UnionDef def)
{
  try
  {
    println("union " + def.name() + " switch(" +
            toIdl(def.discriminator_type_def()) + ") {");
    org.omg.CORBA.UnionMember[] members = def.members();
    int default_index = def.type().default_index();
    indent++;
    for(int j = 0; j < members.length; j++)
    {
      if (j == default_index) {
        println("default:");
      }
      else {
        println("case " + members[j].label + ":");
      }
      indent++;
      println(toIdl(members[j].type_def) + " " +
                    members[j].name + ";");
      indent--;
    }
    indent--;
    println("};");
  } catch (Exception e)
  { System.err.println("System Exception");
    System.err.println(e);
  }
}


private void printEnum(org.omg.CORBA.EnumDef def)
{
  try
  {
    org.omg.CORBA.TypeCode type = def.type();
    println("enum " + type.name() + " {");
    indent++;
    int count = type.member_count();
    for(int j = 0; j < count; j++)
    {
      println(type.member_name(j) + ((j == count - 1) ? "" : ","));
    }
    indent--;
    println("};");
```

```
    } catch (Exception e)
    { System.err.println("System Exception");
      System.err.println(e);
    }
  }


  private void println(Object o)
  {
    for(int i = 0; i < indent; i++) {
      out.print("  ");
    }
    out.println(o);
  }


  private String toIdl(org.omg.CORBA.IDLType idlType)

  {
    org.omg.CORBA.Contained contained =
          org.omg.CORBA.ContainedHelper.narrow(idlType);
    if (contained == null)
      return idlType.type().toString();
    else
      return contained.absolute_name();
  }


}
```

If this program appears strange, you should review Chapters 19 and 20. The **PrintStream** class consists of the top-level *print* method and a variety of helper methods. You pass *print* an IR container object, and it will print its contained objects. The key statement in this code is:

```
CORBA.Contained[] contained =
      container.contents(org.omg.CORBA.DefinitionKind.dk_all, true);
```

All IR container objects inherit the *contents* method from the **Container** interface. The first parameter in this method is *dk_all*, which means return all the types—or what the IR calls *definition kinds*—contained in this container. You could have narrowed the returns by specifying a particular definition kind. For example, *dk_Interface* would only return the contained interfaces. The second parameter is set to true, which means don't return the parent types. The method returns an array of contained objects. Next, the code looks at the def_kind of each contained object, and then it invokes the appropriate helper function to print its contents. This is all there is to it.

Compile AskMe

We're now ready to compile the AskMe program. Make sure you've installed VisiBroker for Java and Symantec Visual Café. Then go to the appropriate subdirectory and enter the following commands at the prompt:

```
prompt> javac -d \CorbaJavaBook.2e\classes AskMe.java
prompt> javac -d \CorbaJavaBook.2e\classes PrintStream.java
```

The -d option tells the compiler to put the (.class) files it creates into the directory we specify. In this case, it's the *\CorbaJavaBook.2e\classes* subdirectory.

If all goes well, you should have some compiled Java code that you can now run.

Run AskMe

Here are the steps you follow to run AskMe:

1. First, you need to generate an IOR. Start the CountPortableServer (from Chapter 7). This creates a Count object, and then registers its IOR in the Naming Service.

2. Next, you must start an Interface Repository. Enter the following command:

   ```
   prompt> start irep myIR myIR.dat
   ```

3. Then, add some IDL to the Interface Repository. Enter the following commands:

   ```
   prompt>IDL2IR Count.idl
   prompt>IDL2IR Coordinator.idl
         .
         .
         .
   ```

4. You can now run AskMe. Enter the following command at the prompt:

   ```
   prompt> java AskMe
   ```

You should see the following output:

```
From CORBA Introspection:
--------------------------
My IOR string is:
IOR:000000000000001e49444c3a436f756e746572506f727461626c652f436f756e6e7
43a312e30000000000000020000000000000005000010000000000c392e3131332e32
352e35330043700000000003400504d43000000010000001e49444c3a436f756e746
572506f727461626c652f436f756e743a312e300000000000000130966d2e00000001
000000240000000000000001000000010000001400000000000000000000000000010
10900000000


I implement the following CORBA interface:
interface Count {
  attribute long sum;
  long increment(
  );
};


From Java Introspection:
-------------------------
My parent class is called: com.visigenic.vbroker.orb.ObjectImpl
I belong to a class called: CounterPortable._st_Count
I implement the following interfaces:
interface CounterPortable.Count
```

As you can see, an IOR is a monster string—that's what it takes to interoperate at the intergalactic level. CORBA introspection was able to determine at run time the interface and its method signatures. Java introspection was able to determine the parent class and the interface this object implements. Notice that Java only recognizes the object's stub class, not the server implementation. This is what we would expect because the introspection is being done on the client side. Remember, the client is discovering its server objects.

This program demonstrates that CORBA's object introspection complements Java's. You should feed AskMe some IORs and let it introspect them for you. Give it a try.

THE WALK IR PROGRAM

The WalkIR program prints the entire contents of an Interface Repository. You can pass it the name of an IR as a parameter or you can let it discover its own IR. In either case, it will output a nicely formatted listing of the contents of this IR. It's quite a useful program.

The WalkIR Code

The WalkIR program consists of two Java classes: **WalkIR** and **PrintIDL**. We're simply reusing as is **PrintIDL** from the last section, so we won't repeat it here. But, here's what **WalkIR** does: 1) initializes the ORB, 2) binds to an Interface Repository—either the one you pass it or the one it uses, 3) creates a new **PrintIDL** object, and 4) invokes the *print* method on the **PrintIDL** object and passes it the object reference of the IR you want to print.

The **PrintIDL** treats the IR like any other container object. It prints all its contained objects, which means that you'll get to see all the contents of this IR.

Here's the code that implements the **WalkIR** class:

Listing 22-3. The WalkIR Class.

```
public class WalkIR
{
  public static void main(String[] args)
  {
    try
    { org.omg.CORBA.ORB orb = org.omg.CORBA.ORB.init(args, null);
      org.omg.CORBA.Repository rep;
      if (args.length == 1)
      { rep = org.omg.CORBA.RepositoryHelper.bind(orb, args[0]);
      }
      else
      { rep = org.omg.CORBA.RepositoryHelper.bind(orb);
      }

      new PrintIDL().print(rep);

    } catch(Exception e)
    {
      e.printStackTrace();
    }
  }
}
```

Warning: This program is not portable. It uses the Visigenic *bind* to locate the IR. Instead, we should have used of the standard CORBA bootstrap mechanism—*resolve_initial_references*. The problem is that VisiBroker does not automatically register the IR as a bootstrap service.

Compile WalkIR

We're now ready to compile the WalkIR program. Make sure you've installed VisiBroker for Java and Symantec Visual Café. Then go to the appropriate subdirectory and enter the following commands at the prompt:

```
prompt> javac -d \CorbaJavaBook.2e\classes WalkIR.java
prompt> javac -d \CorbaJavaBook.2e\classes PrintStream.java
```

The -d option tells the compiler to put the (.class) files it creates into the directory we specify. In this case, it's the *\CorbaJavaBook.2e\classes* subdirectory.

If all goes well, you should have some compiled Java code that you can now run.

Run WalkIR

Here are the steps you follow to run WalkIR:

1. First, start an Interface Repository. Enter the following command at the prompt:

   ```
   prompt> start irep myIR myIR.dat
   ```

2. Next, add some IDL to the Interface Repository. Enter the following commands:

   ```
   prompt> IDL2IR Count.idl
   prompt> IDL2IR Coordinator.idl
              .
              .
              .
   ```

3. You can now run WalkIR. Enter the following command at the prompt:

   ```
   prompt> java WalkIR
   ```

You should see the following output:

```
module CounterPortable {
  interface Count {
    attribute long sum;
    long increment(
    );
  };
};
```

```
module Client {
  interface ClientControl {
    boolean start(
    );
    string stop(
    );
  };
};

module MultiCoordinator {
  interface Coordinator {
    boolean register(
      in string clientNumber,
      in ::Client::ClientControl clientObjRef
    );
    boolean start(
    );
    string stop(
    );
  };
};


module Bank {
  exception BankException {
    string reason;
  };
  interface DebitCredit {
    void debitCreditTransaction(
      in double random1,
      in double random2,
      in boolean staticTxn
    ) raises (
      ::Bank::BankException
    );
  };

  interface Dispenser {
    ::Bank::DebitCredit reserveDebitCreditObject(
    ) raises (
      ::Bank::BankException
    );
```

```
    void releaseDebitCreditObject(
      in ::Bank::DebitCredit debitCreditObject
    ) raises (
      ::Bank::BankException
    );
  };
};
```

Again, this program demonstrates the power of CORBA's object introspection. You now have an IR Walker that you can use to discover the contents of any Interface Repository. Give it a try.

CONCLUSION

This concludes Part 5, the "existential" CORBA. You should now have a better understanding of how an ORB really works. You got a healthy dose of the core functions every ORB must provide—including initialization, activation, metadata, and introspection. Are you ready to take on some mission-critical client/server applications using CORBA and Java? This is what we will be doing in Part 6. So let's go on with the show.

Part 6
JDBC 2-Tier
Versus 3-Tier

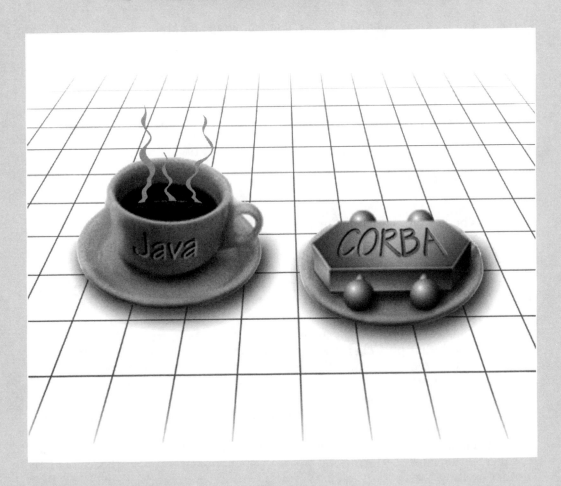

An Introduction to Part 6

In some circles, client/server is synonymous with SQL databases. This is not too surprising, considering that SQL database is the most prevalent application model for client/server today. So one way to determine if CORBA and Java are ready for client/server prime time is to see how well they handle databases. The *Java Database Connectivity (JDBC)* defines Java class-wrappers for SQL database access. It's the Java object version of Microsoft's very popular ODBC—a procedural call-level interface for SQL access.

The plan for Part 6 is to first give you a complete tutorial of JDBC and SQL CLIs. It's so thorough that we call it "the world's longest tutorial chapter." If you survive this tutorial and are still interested in SQL and JDBC, we have a great treat for you. We provide a three-chapter Debit-Credit benchmark series that compares the performance of 2-tier versus 3-tier client/server systems using CORBA, Java, and JDBC. We will also compare the performance of static SQL versus Dynamic SQL, JDBC-style.

At the end of this three-chapter series, you will have acquired the following JDBC and CORBA skills:

- How to design and develop working models of 2-tier and 3-tier client/server systems using Java, CORBA, and JDBC.

- How to create a complete JDBC database system from the ground up.

- How to build a scalable CORBA middle-tier application server.

- How to measure the performance of *Online Transaction Processing (OLTP)* systems.

- How to build from the ground up a benchmarking system for JDBC/CORBA Java client/server applications.

Most importantly, you will learn—in a fun way—some of the architectural trade-offs of the client/server discipline. You will then be able to apply these trade-offs in the design of distributed object systems—using Java, CORBA, and JDBC.

A lot of this material is previously uncharted territory. As far as we know, this is the first benchmark that puts client/server systems that use CORBA, Java, and JDBC through the wringer. Consequently, we will develop from scratch complete 2-tier and 3-tier client/server frameworks for these technologies. In the 3-tier case, we even end up building a poor man's TP Monitor to load-balance and manage the CORBA server-side objects. Our Monitor prestarts a pool of JDBC-oriented server objects, it preconnects the server objects to the database, and then it manages incoming client requests. You will learn all about OLTP etiquette and how it's used to squeeze the most performance out of system resources. So this should be another exciting Part.

Chapter 23

JDBC Primer

The *Java Database Connectivity (JDBC)* is a set of Java classes that provide an ODBC-like interface to SQL databases. You can use JDBC from within your Java programs to access almost every SQL database on the planet—including Oracle, Sybase, DB2, SQL Server, Access, FoxBase, Paradox, Progress, SQLBase, and XDB. JDBC drivers are available from Symantec, Intersolv, IBM, JavaSoft, Connect Software, I-Kinetics, Borland/Visigenic, IDS Software, KonaSoft, OpenLink, SAS Institute, NetAway, SCO, Sybase, Oracle, and WebLogic. JDBC is a key piece of the Java client/server arsenal. It lets you SQL-enable your Java applications with very little effort.

JDBC—now part of the Java JDK core—is more than just a rewrite of ODBC in Java. The JDBC protocol was jointly developed by JavaSoft, Sybase, Informix, IBM and others to provide an object interface to relational databases. In contrast, ODBC is a procedural API. ODBC deals with handles and API calls; JDBC deals with objects, interfaces, and methods. Unlike ODBC, JDBC must pay close attention to mobile code issues. In a sense, JDBC is ODBC done right. To be fair, the designers of JDBC were unburdened by a debt to history. They were given *carte blanche* to create the "latest and greatest" interface to SQL. Consequently, JDBC is by far the best interface to SQL on any platform. We expect that JDBC might eventually become an even more important database API standard than ODBC or OLE/DB. But don't take our word for it—read this chapter and be the judge.

This chapter is a fast-paced, in-depth introduction to JDBC. We assume that you're already familiar with SQL. Ideally, you are also familiar with a SQL *Call Level Interface (CLI)* like ODBC, SAG, or X/Open. If you're not, you may want to look at the SQL references at the back of this book. The plan for this chapter is to give you all the JDBC background you will need to understand the programming chapters that follow. The JDBC classes and interfaces are part of the *java.sql* package. We first give you the bird's-eye view of *java.sql*. Then we zoom-in on the individual classes and methods. In between, we throw in some object interaction scenarios that show how the different pieces play together. You may want to do a quick reading of this chapter just to get the JDBC gestalt. You can come back later for the details when you get into the programming chapters.

THE ORIGINS OF JDBC

JDBC is not a new query language. It is simply a Java object interface to SQL. Your applications use JDBC to submit SQL statements to a DBMS. You must still write SQL to perform database queries and updates. So you can think of JDBC as just a Java SQL wrapper. JDBC neither adds nor subtracts from the power of SQL. It's simply a mechanism for submitting SQL statements. JDBC handles details such as connecting to a database, fetching query results, committing or rolling back transactions, and converting SQL types to and from Java program variables.

As we mentioned earlier, JDBC is based on the X/Open SQL CLI, which is also the basis for Microsoft's ODBC interface. ODBC is a C interface; it cannot be used "as is" in Java. Calls from Java to native C code have many drawbacks—including security, robustness, and lack of portability. Consequently, JDBC is a native Java implementation of the SQL CLI. It uses Java classes and interfaces to represent the basic abstractions and concepts defined in the SQL X/Open CLI and ODBC—including drivers, connections, SQL statements, cursors, transactions, result sets, stored procedures, BLOBs, and exceptions. This section gives you some background on the JDBC's origins. It will help you understand where JDBC fits as well as its strengths and limitations.

The X/Open SAG CLI

The SQL *Call Level Interface (CLI)* was originally defined by the *SQL Access Group (SAG)*—a multivendor consortium—to provide a unified standard for remote data access. The CLI requires the use of intelligent database drivers that accept a CLI call and translate it into the native database server's access language. With the proper driver, any data source application can function as a CLI-server and can be accessed by the front-end tools and client programs that use the CLI. The CLI requires a driver for each database to which it connects. Each driver must be written for a specific server using the server's access methods and network transport stack. The CLI provides a *driver manager* that talks to a driver through a *Service Provider Interface (SPI)*.

The SAG APIs are based on dynamic SQL. They allow you to connect to a database through a local *driver* (3 calls), prepare SQL requests (5 calls), execute the requests (2 calls), terminate a statement (3 calls), and terminate a connection (3 calls). In December 1994, SAG turned over this simple API to X/Open; it is now called the *X/Open CLI* to differentiate it from Microsoft's ODBC and other SAG imitations. In early 1996, the X/Open CLI became an international standard—it's now the ISO 9075-3 "Call Level Interface." The forthcoming SQL3 CLI is based on the X/Open CLI, with some extensions.

You should note that a CLI is not a new query language. It is simply a procedural interface to SQL. Your applications use the CLI to submit SQL statements to a DBMS. You must write SQL to perform database queries and updates. So you can think of CLI as just a SQL wrapper. Like JDBC, the CLI neither adds nor subtracts from the power of SQL. It's simply a mechanism for submitting SQL statements.

The Microsoft ODBC CLI

Microsoft's *Open Database Connectivity (ODBC)* Windows API standard for SQL is an extended version of the SAG CLI. In August 1992, Microsoft released the ODBC 1.0 SDK; it was to be the shrink-wrapped answer for database access under Windows. Since then, ODBC has gone cross-platform. Visigenic received an exclusive license from Microsoft to provide ODBC SDKs on non-Windows platforms. In addition to Visigenic, third parties—such as Intersolv (*Q+E Software*) and OpenLink—are offering ODBC driver suites on Windows, Windows 95, Windows NT, OS/2, Mac, and Unixes that run against a variety of database servers.

ODBC 1.0 was slow and buggy; it was limited to the Windows platform and lacked the documentation and code examples necessary to educate developers. In April 1994, Microsoft shipped the ODBC 2.0 SDK, which fixed many of the problems with the previous driver manager. In December 1994, the first 32-bit drivers were shipped. ODBC 2.0 defines about 61 API calls that fall into three conformance levels:

- *Core* provides 23 base calls that let you connect to a database, execute SQL statements, fetch results, commit and rollback transactions, handle exceptions, and terminate the connection.

- *Level 1* provides an additional 19 calls that let you retrieve information from a database catalog, fetch large objects (BLOBs), and deal with driver-specific functions.

- *Level 2* provides yet another additional 19 calls that let you retrieve data using cursors; it supports both forward and backward scrolling.

Applications are responsible for making sure that an ODBC driver supports a conformance level. Note that the X/Open CLI includes ODBC's Core as well as some of the Level 1 and Level 2 functions. It also includes SQL descriptors that are not in ODBC. The X/Open CLI does not include the ODBC functions that support Microsoft applications—such as SQL Server, Access, and Excel.

Most database server vendors—including Microsoft, IBM, Oracle, Sybase, Tandem, CA/Ingres, and Informix—now support the ODBC API in addition to their native SQL APIs. They also include ODBC drivers for their respective servers (see Figure 23-1). The problem is that ODBC always seems to play second fiddle to the native interfaces on the client and server sides. For example, Oracle supports ODBC as an optional API, but its native CLI is the *Oracle Call-Level Interface (OCI)*. IBM's DB2 family supports ODBC (with extensions) and the X/Open CLI (with extensions), but its native protocol is *ESQL/DRDA*. Sybase supports ODBC as an optional API, but its native CLI is the *Sybase Open Client*. Informix has no native CLI; it plans to support an extension of ODBC. Microsoft's SQL Server 6.5 is, of course, the exception; it uses ODBC as its native protocol.

The other problem is that server vendors add their own proprietary extensions to the server driver and to the ODBC CLI (for example, most vendors extend ODBC to support stored procedures). If you really must have a portable ODBC solution, your best bet is to require CLIs and drivers from a third party that specializes in ODBC middleware—for example, Intersolv, OpenLink, and Visigenic (see the next Soapbox).

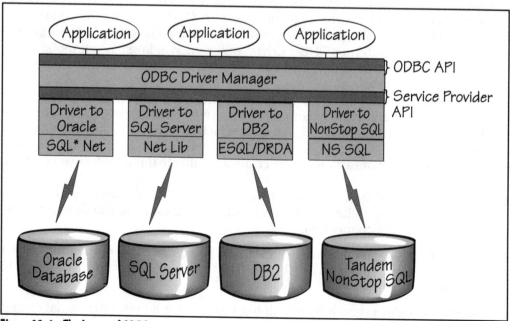

Figure 23-1. The Layers of ODBC.

In November 1996, Microsoft shipped ODBC 3.0, which introduces 20 new function calls and supports Unicode. ODBC 3.0 also returns more information on approximately 40 new items. You should note that Microsoft fully controls the ODBC standard. So the million-dollar question is: Will the future ODBC align itself with the SQL3/CLI, or will it become a proprietary OLE-based standard? According to Microsoft, the answer is all of the above. Microsoft promises SQL3 support, yet it announced OLE/DB as the future ODBC replacement.

ODBC has many drawbacks. The most serious one is that the specification is controlled by Microsoft, and it is constantly evolving. Its future is also uncertain, given Microsoft's current commitment to OLE/DB, which introduces a different programming paradigm—it is object-based rather than procedural. ODBC drivers are also difficult to build and maintain. The current drivers have different ODBC conformance levels, which are not well documented. The ODBC layers introduce a lot of overhead (especially for SQL updates and inserts), and they are never as fast as the native APIs. Note that for simple read-only functions, the ODBC drivers are now within 10% of native driver performance.

Is CLI Always the Least Common Denominator?

Soapbox

The average corporation has eight databases today, and I'd rather have one common client/server language everyone can speak.

— David Waller, Director
Intersolv

Use native (direct) APIs whenever possible. Standard APIs like ODBC should be considered as a last resort...not the first.

— Richard Finkelstein, President
Performance Computing

The reason Finkelstein doesn't like "standard" CLIs is that they require too many levels of translations before they reach the native APIs. Any type of layering scheme requires release-level synchronizations between the different components, which all come from different vendors. As can be expected, vendors will first support their native API sets and then worry about the "standard CLIs." This means the CLIs will not be synchronized with the latest releases of the database engines and drivers. In addition, the CLI approach on top of database drivers adds layers of complexity. For example, debug is far more complicated. You can expect a lot more fingerpointing between vendors when the protocol stacks, API libraries, database drivers, native OSs, and database engines all have to be in sync for things to work.

But the million-dollar question is: Why can't vendors—like Oracle, Informix Sybase, and IBM—make the X/Open CLI the "native API" of their respective databases? The answer is that each database engine offers a unique set of extensions to native SQL; these extensions require a different set of APIs to invoke their services. Will vendors ever offer a non-extended version of SQL? Of course not—they're out there trying to differentiate their product! So by definition, the common CLI will always be a "least common denominator" approach that is not optimized for a particular database. Database vendors are not likely to reveal their future "extended plans" to standards bodies, so common CLIs will always trail behind the SQL engine's native API capabilities. And forget portability because even the "standard CLIs" have escape clauses (or pass-throughs) that defeat that goal. The bottom line is that any program that takes advantage of the advanced capabilities of a database engine will not be database-neutral. So much for standards! ❑

CLI Versus Embedded SQL

The alternative to CLI is *Embedded SQL (ESQL)*, which is the ISO SQL-92 defined standard for embedding SQL statements "as is" within ordinary programming languages. The SQL-92 standard specifies the syntax for embedding SQL within C, C++, COBOL, FORTRAN, PL/I, Pascal, MUMPS, and Ada. Each SQL statement is flagged with language-specific identifiers that mark the beginning and end of the SQL statement. This approach requires running the SQL source through a *precompiler* to generate a source code file that the language compiler understands. As an example, for C, an embedded SQL statement must start with the *EXEC SQL* keyword pair and end with a semicolon (;). These bracketed statements will be processed by the precompiler, and anything else in your source code will be passed through unchanged.

From a client/server packaging perspective, the biggest hurdle with ESQL is that the target database must be known (and available) when the program is being developed. This makes it hard to target a client program to a database at run time. In addition, the installation process involves binding applications to each server database they connect to—a process that may be too complicated for the "shrink-wrapped" client/server software market. Finally, precompilers have traditionally been tied to a particular database product; you must recompile your embedded SQL code for each vendor's database server. The same features that make precompilers so popular with IS shops and corporate developers have turned into liabilities for the providers of shrink-wrapped client/server software.

In April 1997, Oracle, Tandem, and IBM announced that they were working on an ESQL implementation for Java called *JSQL*. Like all ESQLs, JSQL lets you directly insert SQL statements inside your Java programs. It promises to be more concise than JDBC, and more amenable to compiler-time type checking. JSQL will have an all-Java precompiler.

In December 1997, Oracle posted a downloadable reference implementation of JSQL on its Web site. It also renamed JSQL to *SQLJ* to avoid a trademark infringement. If you look at the source code of the reference implementation you'll see that it's just a thin layer on top of JDBC. IBM is working on a more optimized version that uses static SQL.

Table 23-1 compares the CLI with the more traditional ESQL style of programming.

Table 23-1. The X/Open CLI Versus ISO ESQL.

Feature	X/Open SQL Call-Level Interface (CLI)	ISO SQL-92 Embedded SQL (ESQL)
Requires target database to be known ahead of time	No	Yes
Supports static SQL	No (future)	Yes
Supports dynamic SQL	Yes	Yes
Compile-time type checking	No	Yes
Uses the SQL declarative model	No	Yes
Applications must be precompiled and bound to database server	No	Yes
Easy to program	No	Yes
Tool-friendly	Yes	No
Easy to debug	Yes	No
Easy to package	Yes	No
Supports database-independent catalog tables	Yes	No
Supports database-independent metadata	Yes	No
Supports database-independent BLOB fetches	Yes	No

THE JDBC ARCHITECTURE

JDBC is a portable SQL CLI written entirely in Java. It lets you write DBMS-independent Java code. Like ODBC and X/Open, JDBC provides two major sets of interfaces: 1) an *application interface* that lets you access SQL services in a DBMS-independent manner, and 2) a *driver interface* that DBMS vendors must adapt to their particular databases. Like the other CLIs, JDBC uses a driver manager to automatically load the right JDBC driver to talk to a given database (see Figure 23-2).

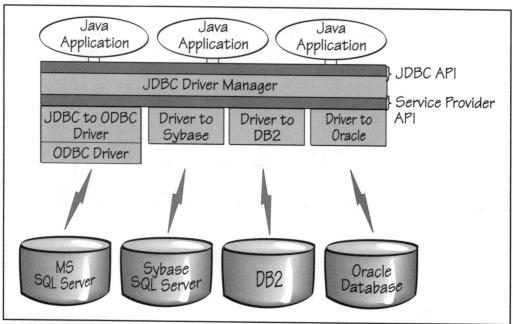

Figure 23-2. The Layers of JDBC.

JDBC Drivers

JDBC drivers are either *direct* or *ODBC-bridged*. A direct driver sits on top of the DBMS's native interface. For example, Symantec provides direct drivers for *Oracle 7.X* using *OCI*, *Sybase 10* using *DB-Lib*, and Microsoft *SQL Server 6.5* and *Access 7.0* using ODBC. IBM also provides a native JDBC driver for its DB2 product line. In contrast to direct drivers, bridged drivers are built on top of existing ODBC drivers. JDBC is patterned after ODBC. Consequently, the translation between these two protocols should be minimal. JavaSoft and Intersolv provide a reference *JDBC-to-ODBC* bridge implementation that makes it easier to translate between JDBC and the various ODBC drivers.

To pass the JDBC compliance tests, a driver must provide at least ANSI SQL92 Entry Level functionality. This is currently the least common denominator among the SQL DBMSs on the market. As a result, the JDBC applications you write are guaranteed to be portable across multivendor DBMSs. Portability is a Java credo. JDBC reinforces this credo and extends the portable Java core to include multivendor SQL database access.

More specifically, JDBC drivers must provide implementations of the abstract classes and interfaces defined in the *java.sql* package. At a minimum, a JDBC driver must implement the core *java.sql* interfaces and classes. We cover these interfaces in later sections. In addition, JDBC requires that all operations on *java.sql* objects be thread-safe. This means that the drivers must provide the required synchronization protection; multiple threads must be able to safely call the same object.

The JDBC URL Naming Conventions

So how does an application find its database? It does this using the following URL-based naming scheme:

```
jdbc:<subprotocol><domain name>
```

For example, the URL to access "MyJavaDB" via a JDBC-to-ODBC bridge might look like this:

```
jdbc:odbc://www.bob.com/MyJavaDB
```

In this example, the subprotocol is "odbc" and the hostname is "www.bob.com." You can also use this scheme to provide a level of indirection in database names. You do this by specifying a naming service as the subprotocol. Here's an example of a URL that does this:

```
jdbc:dcenaming:MyJavaDB
```

In this example, the URL specifies that the DCE naming service is used to resolve the database name "MyJavaDB" into a global name that connects to the database. JDBC recommends that you provide a pseudo-driver that looks up names via a networked name server. It then uses the information to locate the real driver and pass it the connection information.

The JDBC naming scheme makes it easy for different drivers to use a naming syntax that matches their needs. Each driver need only understand a single URL naming syntax; it can then reject any other URLs it encounters. JavaSoft is acting as an informal registry for JDBC subprotocol names.

Registering Drivers

The JDBC **DriverManager** class needs to know which drivers are available. JDBC gives you two ways to do this:

- *Using a system property.* The **DriverManager** class will look for a *jdbc.drivers* property when it initializes. If the property exists, it should contain a list of colon-separated driver class names. Each named class should implement a JDBC-specified **Driver** interface. The **DriverManager** will load each named **Driver** class.

- *Using an explicit method invocation.* You can invoke the standard Java *Class.forName* method to load a **Driver** class. For example, to load the **my.db.Mydriver** class you invoke: *Class.forName("my.db.MyDriver")*.

In both cases, the newly loaded **Driver** class must register itself with the **Driver-Manager** by invoking the *DriverManager.registerDriver* method. We describe these classes in great detail in the later sections.

JDBC Security

As we mentioned earlier, JDBC must pay close attention to mobile code issues. For example, a JDBC driver must prevent an untrusted applet from accessing databases outside its home machine—meaning the machine from which the applet originates. Likewise, a driver that is downloaded as an applet can only be allowed to access its home database. Of course, applets and drivers can get around these limitations by convincing the Java loader that they are trustworthy—for example, by presenting certificates that authenticate them.

For regular Java applications, JDBC will happily load drivers from the local *CLASS-PATH* and allow the application free access to remote servers. A single application can maintain multiple database connections to one or more databases using one or more drivers. The JDBC management layer keeps track of which class loader provided which driver. It only uses drivers from the local file system or from the same class loader as the application making the connection requests.

Mapping SQL Data Types to Java

JDBC defines Java mappings for the common SQL data types, and vice versa. The mappings provide the type information you need to correctly store and retrieve parameters and to recover results from SQL statements. Table 23-2 shows the default Java mappings for common SQL data types.

Table 23-2. Standard SQL/Java Mappings.

SQL Type	Java Type	Notes
CHAR	String	
VARCHAR	String	Typically, up to 32K characters.
LONGVARCHAR	String	Multimegabytes. Can be retrieved using Java streams.
NUMERIC	java.math.BigDecimal	Fixed point. Used for currency.
DECIMAL	java.math.BigDecimal	Fixed point. Requires absolute precision. Can be used for currency.
BIT	boolean	
TINYINT	byte	8-bit values.
SMALLINT	short	16-bit values.
INTEGER	int	32-bit values.
BIGINT	long	64-bit values.
REAL	float	7 digits of mantissa precision.
DOUBLE	double	15 digits of mantissa precision.
FLOAT	double	15 digits of mantissa precision.
BINARY	byte[]	
VARBINARY	byte[]	Typically, up to 32 KBytes.
LONGVARBINARY	byte[]	Multimegabytes. Can be retrieved using Java streams.
DATE	java.sql.Date	Uses ISO "yyyy-mm-dd"
TIME	java.sql.Time	Uses ISO "hh-mm-ss"
TIMESTAMP	java.sql.Time-stamp	Provides nanosecond precision.

JDBC Transactions

Like ODBC, JDBC provides a transaction control model. New JDBC connections are initially in *autocommit* mode. This means that JDBC implicitly issues a commit after each statement it executes. To execute several statements within a single transaction, you must first disable autocommit, issue your statements, and then issue either *commit* or *rollback* at the end of the transaction. The *commit* or *rollback* will also implicitly start a new transaction. When a transaction commits or aborts, JDBC by default releases all resources associated with the connection—including prepared statements, cursors, locks, and result sets. You should note that JDBC does not let you commit transactions across different connections.

JDBC Stored Procedures

The syntax for invoking a stored procedure in JDBC is:

```
{call procedure_name[(argument1, argument2, ...)]}
```

The syntax for a procedure that returns a parameter is:

```
{?= call procedure_name[(argument1, argument2, ...)]}
```

An input argument can either be a literal or a variable that you bind at run time. A stored procedure can return multiple result sets. JDBC also provides methods for passing *out* parameters within a stored procedure. We will tell you more about stored procedures later in this chapter.

JDBC INTERFACES: AN OVERVIEW

The JDBC specification includes eight new Java interfaces and ten new classes. We can divide these interfaces into the following groups: 1) *JDBC Core* interfaces are the interfaces and classes every JDBC driver must implement; 2) *Java language extensions* are Java language extensions for SQL; 3) *Java utility extensions* are extensions of **java.util.Date**; and 4) *SQL metadata* interfaces let you dynamically discover what SQL databases and JDBC drivers can do.

In the spirit of Java, JDBC uses different methods to express different functions. This is both good news and bad news. The good news is that it's easy to understand what each method does. The bad news is that SQL databases are very function-rich. Consequently, there is an explosion of JDBC methods. The *java.sql* package contains some of the largest Java classes in existence. For example, the **Database-**

MetaData interface has a grand total of 133 methods. Yes, it's a new "Guiness World Record" for methods-per-class.

So how do we introduce these giant classes without writing an entire new book on JDBC? We will divide and conquer. This section contains a high-level overview of the JDBC classes and interfaces; you get to see the big picture. In the next section, we dive deeper and look at all the methods these interfaces provide. Finally, we end the chapter with three object interaction scenarios that demonstrate how these classes and interfaces play together.

The JDBC Core

The JDBC core consists of seven interfaces and two classes (see Figure 23-3). These are the interfaces and abstract classes all JDBC drivers must implement. You use these classes to locate DBMS drivers, establish connections to remote databases, submit SQL statements, and process the result sets. These core functions account for over 90 percent of what you do with a database.

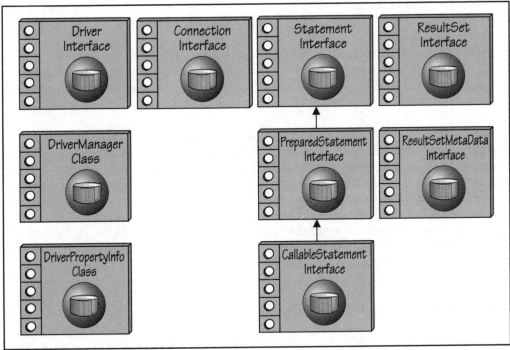

Figure 23-3. The JDBC Core Classes and Interfaces.

Each JDBC driver must provide a class that implements the **Driver** interface. This is the class the generic **DriverManager** uses when it needs to locate a driver for the database URL you specify. The **DriverManager** class is part of the JDBC run time; it loads **Driver** objects and creates new database **Connection** objects when you request it. Only specialized clients use the **DriverPropertyInfo** class. Typically, these clients need to interact with a **Driver** via the *getPropertyInfo* method; you use this class to discover and supply properties for connections.

You use **Connection** objects to represent a connection of your application to a particular database. You can connect to multiple databases or to the same database multiple times using different **Connection** objects. You also use the connection to commit or rollback a transaction and to control its lock *isolation level*. The connection is your session with the remote database.

Statement objects are containers for executing SQL statements on a given connection. They represent the execution state of your SQL statement. You can allocate multiple **Statement** objects and reuse each one repeatedly to process many SQL statements. The **Statement** interface has two important extensions: **Prepared-Statement** and **CallableStatement**.

You use a **PreparedStatement** object to precompile and then execute a statement multiple times. The object provides a series of *setXXX* methods to pass Java variables to the parameter fields in a SQL statement. To fill in the parameter fields, you can invoke these methods before each statement execution.

You use a **CallableStatement** object to represent and execute a stored procedure. JDBC defines a SQL escape that lets you call stored procedures in a consistent manner across DBMSs. The **CallableStatement** object provides methods for passing Java parameters to stored procedures and obtaining the results.

A **ResultSet** object encapsulates the rows returned by the database when you execute a query **Statement**. The object maintains a *cursor* that points to a current row of data. You can use the *next* method to move the cursor to the next row. You can access column values within a row in any order. The object provides *getXXX* methods that let you retrieve column values using either the index number of the column or its name. The *getXXX* also converts the SQL data to the specified Java type. Each method returns a suitable Java value. You can invoke the *getMetaData* method to obtain a **ResultSetMetaData** object. You can use this object to retrieve the types and properties of a result set.

The JDBC Java Language Extensions

JDBC requires new numeric Java data types to meet the precision requirements of SQL. These high-precision data types are mostly used to store and process data

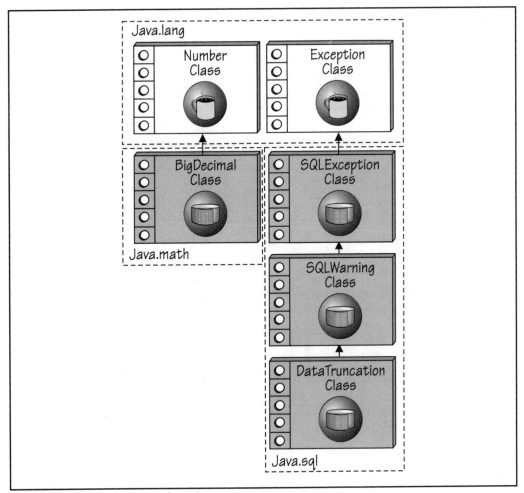

Figure 23-4. Java.sql Extensions of Java.lang.

representations of money. Yes, Java now plays in the big leagues. JDBC also introduces new exception handling requirements. SQL defines its own exception and warning types that must, somehow, be grafted into Java.

To meet these SQL requirements, JDBC depends on the floating-point capability of the **BigDecimal** class introduced in the JDK 1.1 *java.math* package. It also defines three new classes in *java.sql* (see Figure 23-4). The new exception classes—**SQLException**, **SQLWarning**, and **DataTruncation**—extend *java.lang*'s **Exception** class.

The JDBC Java Utilities

SQL also has requirements for very fine-grained time and date utilities that let you measure time in nanosecond precision. To meet these requirements, *java.sql* defines three new classes—**Date**, **Time**, and **Timestamp**. Each of these classes extends *java.util's* **Date** class (see Figure 23-5).

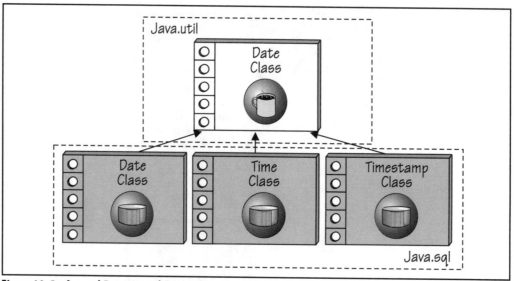

Figure 23-5. Java.sql Extensions of Java.util.

JDBC Metadata

SQL was designed from day one as a self-describing system. All the commercial databases provide information about themselves—or *metadata*—that you can discover at run time. Each database maintains a dynamic catalog that describes the objects it stores—including tables, views, privileges, indexes, stored procedures, and triggers. In addition, you can query the database to discover its limits, capabilities, configuration, and state.

To standardize access to metadata across multivendor DBMSs, *java.sql* defines the **DatabaseMetaData** interface (see Figure 23-6). This is the infamous interface with 133 methods. Your JDBC vendor should provide a class that implements all these methods. In addition, *java.sql* defines a public class called **Types** that defines constants you use to identify the X/Open SQL types. This class is just a placeholder for constants; it does not support any methods.

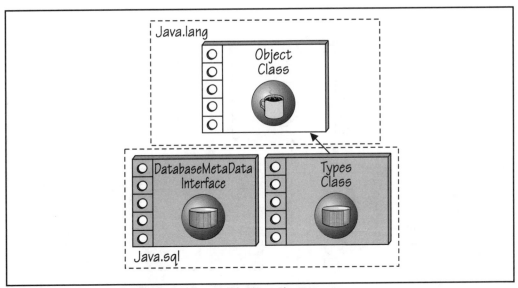

Figure 23-6. The Java.sql Metadata Interface and the Types Class.

JDBC INTERFACES: IN-DEPTH

This section provides the next level of detail on the workings of JDBC. These are the details you'll need to understand the programming chapters. You can skip over this section and return to it later when you're ready to walk through the code. The plan is to go over the different JDBC classes and interfaces at the method level.

JDBC Core: The Driver Interfaces

Figure 23-7 shows the details of the interface and two classes that provide the JDBC core driver management facilities. Here's a description of what these classes and interface do:

■ The **DriverManager** class manages JDBC drivers and dispenses **Connection** objects. As part of its initialization, the class will load and locate the JDBC device drivers you specify in the *jdbc.drivers* property. A newly loaded driver class should call *registerDriver* to make itself known to the **DriverManager**. The driver calls *deregisterDriver* to remove itself from the driver list; *getDrivers* returns an **Enumeration** of all the currently loaded JDBC drivers that the caller can access. You invoke *getConnection* to establish a connection to the given database URL. The driver manager will then pick an appropriate driver from the set of registered JDBC drivers. You can also invoke *getDriver* to locate a

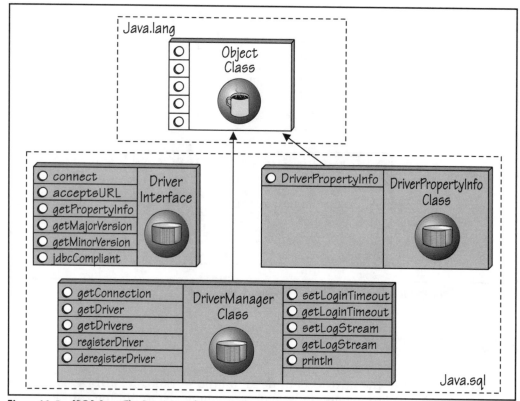

Figure 23-7. JDBC Core: The Driver Interfaces and Classes.

driver that understands the given URL. The class also provides some administrative functions. For example, you invoke *setLoginTimeout* to set the maximum time in seconds that all drivers can wait when attempting to log into a database.

■ The **Driver** interface specifies the methods every JDBC driver must implement. When a driver is loaded, it creates an instance of itself and then registers it with the **DriverManager**. If you know your driver, you can directly invoke its *connect* method to make a database connection to the given URL. You can use the **java.util.Properties** object to pass arbitrary string tag/value pairs as connection arguments. For example, you may use the tag/value pairs to provide *user* and *password* properties. You can invoke *acceptsURL* to find out if a driver can connect to a URL. The *getPropertyInfo* method is used by GUI tools to discover what properties it should request from a user to connect to a database. The *jdbcCompliant* method returns true if a driver fully supports the SQL 92 Entry Level specification.

■ The **DriverPropertyInfo** class is primarily of interest to GUI tool vendors. It provides public variables that let you dynamically discover the properties that a connection requires. The variables provide descriptions of the required properties, their current values, and the choice of acceptable values for a given property. You can also obtain the driver-supplied default values.

The class descriptions that follow give the next level of detail on how to use these methods.

Listing 23-1. The Java.sql DriverManager Class.

```
public class DriverManager extends Object
{
     // Methods
  public static synchronized Connection getConnection(String url)
                                            throws SQLException;
  public static synchronized Connection getConnection(String url,
                                            Properties info)
                                            throws SQLException;
  public static synchronized Connection getConnection(String url,
                                            String user,
                                            String password)
                                            throws SQLException;
  public static Driver getDriver(String url) throws SQLException;
  public static Enumeration getDrivers();
  public static synchronized void registerDriver(Driver driver)
                                            throws SQLException;
  public static void deregisterDriver(Driver driver) throws SQLException;
  public static void setLoginTimeout(int seconds);
  public static int getLoginTimeout();
  public static void setLogStream(PrintStream out);
  public static PrintStream getLogStream();
  public static void println(String message);
}
```

Listing 23-2. The Java.sql Driver Interface.

```
public interface Driver
{
     // Methods
  public abstract Connection connect(String url, Properties info)
                             throws SQLException;
  public abstract boolean acceptsURL(String url) throws SQLException;
```

```
public abstract DriverPropertyInfo[] getPropertyInfo(String url,
                                                     Properties info)
                                         throws SQLException;

public abstract int getMajorVersion();
public abstract int getMinorVersion();
public abstract boolean jdbcCompliant();
}
```

Listing 23-3. The Java.sql DriverPropertyInfo Class.

```
public class DriverPropertyInfo extends Object
{
    // Fields
  public String name;
  public String description;
  public boolean required;
  public String value;
  public String choices[];

    // Constructors
  public DriverPropertyInfo(String name, String value);
}
```

JDBC Core: The Connection Interface

A **Connection** object represents a session with a specific database; it provides you with a context for executing SQL statements and processing their results. Figure 23-8 shows the details of the **Connection** interface that is implemented by your JDBC driver vendor. You use a **Connection** to obtain statement objects that you then use to execute SQL commands. You invoke *createStatement* to obtain a **Statement** object. You invoke *prepareStatement* to obtain a **PreparedStatement** object. You invoke *prepareCall* to obtain a **CallableStatement** object. Finally, you invoke *close* to release a connection's resources.

If a connection is in *autocommit* mode, then all its SQL statements will be executed and committed as individual transactions. You can explicitly control the transaction state of a connection by invoking *setAutoCommit(false)*. You invoke *commit* to make all changes permanent since the previous commit/rollback. You invoke *rollback* to drop all changes made since the previous commit/rollback; the call also releases any database locks the **Connection** object currently holds. You invoke *setReadOnly* to put a connection in read-only mode—it's a hint to enable database optimizations. You invoke *setTransactionIsolation* to change the transaction's isolation level on a newly opened connection.

The **Connection** object returns tons of information about the state of the database. For example, you can invoke *getMetaData* to obtain the infamous **DatabaseMeta-Data** object with its 133 methods worth of information. In addition, you can directly obtain information on the state of the connection by invoking *getAutoCommit*, *getTransactionIsolation*, *isReadOnly*, *isClosed*, *getCatalog*, and *getWarnings*.

Figure 23-8. JDBC Core: The Connection Interface.

The class description that follows provides the next level of detail on how to use these methods:

Listing 23-4. The Java.sql Connection Interface.

```java
public interface Connection
{
      // Constants
   public final static int TRANSACTION_NONE;
   public final static int TRANSACTION_READ_UNCOMMITTED;
   public final static int TRANSACTION_READ_COMMITTED;
   public final static int TRANSACTION_REPEATABLE_READ;
   public final static int TRANSACTION_SERIALIZABLE;

      // Instance Methods
   public abstract Statement createStatement() throws SQLException;
   public abstract PreparedStatement prepareStatement(String sql)
                  throws SQLException;
```

```
public abstract CallableStatement prepareCall(String sql)
                 throws SQLException;
public abstract String nativeSQL(String sql) throws SQLException;
public abstract void setAutoCommit(boolean autoCommit)
                 throws SQLException;
public abstract boolean getAutoCommit() throws SQLException;
public abstract void commit() throws SQLException;
public abstract void rollback() throws SQLException;
public abstract void close() throws SQLException;
public abstract boolean isClosed() throws SQLException;
public abstract DatabaseMetaData getMetaData() throws SQLException;
public abstract void setReadOnly(boolean readOnly)
                 throws SQLException;
public abstract boolean isReadOnly() throws SQLException;
public abstract void setCatalog(String catalog) throws SQLException;
public abstract String getCatalog() throws SQLException;
public abstract void setTransactionIsolation(int level)
                 throws SQLException;
public abstract int getTransactionIsolation() throws SQLException;
public abstract SQLWarning getWarnings() throws SQLException;
public abstract void clearWarnings() throws SQLException;
}
```

JDBC Core: The Statement Interfaces

Figure 23-9 shows the details of the **Statement** interface and its two derived interfaces: **PreparedStatement** and **CallableStatement**. Here's a brief description of what these interfaces provide:

■ A **Statement** object lets you execute a static SQL statement and obtain its results. You typically invoke *execute* to submit a SQL statement that may return multiple results. You use *getMoreResults* to obtain the next result. You invoke *executeQuery* to submit a SQL SELECT; you invoke *getResultSet* to obtain the **ResultSet** object the query returns. You invoke *setCursorname* to create a SQL cursor name. Cursors are used by positional UPDATE or DELETE commands to point to the current row within a result set. You must execute the positioned commands on a separate **Statement** object than the one that generated the result set.

You invoke *executeUpdate* to submit a SQL INSERT, UPDATE, DELETE or DDL statement. You invoke *cancel* to abort a statement that executes on another thread. You invoke *close* to immediately release a statement's resources. Finally, you invoke *getWarnings* to obtain the first **SQLWarning** object attached to this statement.

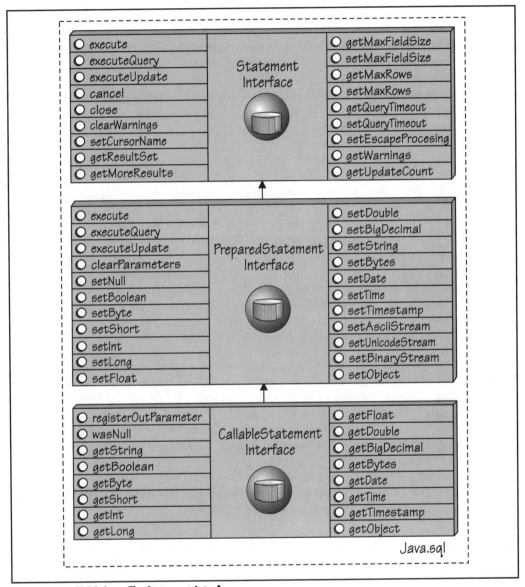

Figure 23-9. JDBC Core: The Statement Interfaces.

The **Statement** object also lets you get and set the following statement-related limits: *setQueryTimeout* defines the number of seconds the driver will wait for a statement to execute; *setMaxFieldSize* defines the maximum number of bytes returned for any column value—it only applies to BINARY, VARBINARY, LONG-VARBINARY, CHAR, VARCHAR, and LONGVARCHAR columns; and *setMaxRows* defines the maximum number of rows that any **ResultSet** can contain.

- A **PreparedStatement** object lets you submit precompiled SQL commands; it serves as a container for SQL statements that you execute multiple times. You typically invoke *execute* to submit a prepared SQL statement that may return multiple results. You invoke *executeQuery* to submit a SQL SELECT. You invoke *executeUpdate* to invoke a SQL INSERT, UPDATE, or DELETE statement. Finally, you invoke *clearParameters* to clear the previous values of a prepared statement before you reinvoke it with new values; it will clear any resources associated with the previous values.

  You use the *setXXX* methods to set the statement's IN parameter values; you must specify types that are compatible with the defined SQL type of the input parameter. For example, you invoke the *setInt* method to set an IN parameter of SQL type Integer. For each *setXXX* method, you must specify the parameter index—the first parameter is 1, the second is 2, and so on. You must also specify the Java value that needs to be converted to the corresponding SQL type. You use the *setObject* method to perform an arbitrary parameter type conversion. You use the *setAsciiStream* and *setBinaryStream* methods to pass large objects via a **java.io.InputStream**; JDBC will read the data from the stream as needed until it reaches end-of-file. The JDBC driver will do any necessary conversion from ASCII to the database char format. The stream object can either be a standard Java stream object or a subclass.

- A **CallableStatement** object lets you submit stored procedures using JDBC's calling syntax. If the procedure returns a result, you must register it as an OUT parameter. The procedure's other parameters can be IN or OUT, or both. You sequentially refer to parameters within a stored procedure by number. The first parameter is 1. You set the IN parameter values using the *setXXX* methods inherited from **PreparedStatement**. You must invoke *registerOutParameter* for each OUT parameter before executing the stored procedure. You must pass it the **java.sql.Type** that corresponds to the parameter's SQL type. When you read the value of an OUT parameter, you must use the *getXXX* method whose Java type corresponds to the parameter's registered SQL type.

The class descriptions that follow give the next level of detail on how to use these interfaces in your programs.

Listing 23-5. The Java.sql Statement Interface.

```
public interface Statement
{
        // Methods
    public abstract boolean execute(String sql) throws SQLException;
    public abstract ResultSet executeQuery(String sql) throws SQLException;
    public abstract int executeUpdate(String sql) throws SQLException;
    public abstract void cancel() throws SQLException;
```

```
public abstract void close() throws SQLException;
public abstract void clearWarnings() throws SQLException;
public abstract void setCursorName(String name) throws SQLException;
public abstract ResultSet getResultSet() throws SQLException;
public abstract boolean getMoreResults() throws SQLException;
public abstract int getMaxFieldSize() throws SQLException;
public abstract void setMaxFieldSize(int max) throws SQLException;
public abstract int getMaxRows() throws SQLException;
public abstract void setMaxRows(int max) throws SQLException;
public abstract int getQueryTimeout() throws SQLException;
public abstract void setQueryTimeout(int seconds) throws SQLException;
public abstract void setEscapeProcessing(boolean enable)
                    throws SQLException;
public abstract SQLWarning getWarnings() throws SQLException;
public abstract int getUpdateCount() throws SQLException;
}
```

Listing 23-6. The Java.sql PreparedStatement Interface.

```
public interface PreparedStatement extends Statement
{
      // Methods
public abstract boolean execute() throws SQLException;
public abstract ResultSet executeQuery() throws SQLException;
public abstract int executeUpdate() throws SQLException;
public abstract void clearParameters() throws SQLException;
public abstract void setNull(int parameterIndex, int sqlType)
                    throws SQLException;
public abstract void setBoolean(int parameterIndex, boolean x)
                    throws SQLException;
public abstract void setByte(int parameterIndex, byte x)
                    throws SQLException;
public abstract void setShort(int parameterIndex, short x)
                    throws SQLException;
public abstract void setInt(int parameterIndex, int x)
                    throws SQLException;
public abstract void setLong(int parameterIndex, long x)
                    throws SQLException;
public abstract void setFloat(int parameterIndex, float x)
                    throws SQLException;
public abstract void setDouble(int parameterIndex, double x)
                    throws SQLException;
public abstract void setBigDecimal(int parameterIndex, BigDecimal x)
                    throws SQLException;
```

```
public abstract void setString(int parameterIndex, String x)
                    throws SQLException;
public abstract void setBytes(int parameterIndex, byte x[])
                    throws SQLException;
public abstract void setDate(int parameterIndex, Date x)
                    throws SQLException;
public abstract void setTime(int parameterIndex, Time x)
                    throws SQLException;
public abstract void setTimestamp(int parameterIndex, Timestamp x)
                    throws SQLException;
public abstract void setAsciiStream(int parameterIndex,
                                    InputStream x,
                                    int length)
                                    throws SQLException;
public abstract void setUnicodeStream(int parameterIndex,
                                    InputStream x,
                                    int length)
                                    throws SQLException;

public abstract void setBinaryStream(int parameterIndex,
                                    InputStream x,
                                    int length)
                                    throws SQLException;
public abstract void setObject(int parameterIndex,
                               Object x,
                               int targetSqlType,
                               int scale)
                               throws SQLException;
public abstract void setObject(int parameterIndex,
                               Object x,
                               int targetSqlType)
                               throws SQLException;
public abstract void setObject(int parameterIndex,
                               Object x) throws SQLException;
}
```

Listing 23-7. The Java.sql CallableStatement Interface.

```
public interface CallableStatement extends PreparedStatement
{
      // Instance Methods
    public abstract void registerOutParameter(int parameterIndex,
                                              int sqlType)
                                              throws SQLException;
```

```
public abstract void registerOutParameter(int parameterIndex,
                                           int sqlType,
                                           int scale)
                                     throws SQLException;
public abstract boolean wasNull() throws SQLException;
public abstract String getString(int parameterIndex)
                                       throws SQLException;
public abstract boolean getBoolean(int parameterIndex)
                    throws SQLException;
public abstract byte getByte(int parameterIndex) throws SQLException;
public abstract short getShort(int parameterIndex)
                   throws SQLException;
public abstract int getInt(int parameterIndex) throws SQLException;
public abstract long getLong(int parameterIndex) throws SQLException;
public abstract float getFloat(int parameterIndex)
                   throws SQLException;
public abstract double getDouble(int parameterIndex)
                   throws SQLException;
public abstract BigDecimal getBigDecimal(int parameterIndex, int scale)
                       throws SQLException;
public abstract byte[] getBytes(int parameterIndex)
                   throws SQLException;
public abstract Date getDate(int parameterIndex) throws SQLException;
public abstract Time getTime(int parameterIndex) throws SQLException;
public abstract Timestamp getTimestamp(int parameterIndex)
                       throws SQLException;
public abstract Object getObject(int parameterIndex) throws SQLException;
}
```

JDBC Core: The ResultSet Interfaces

Figure 23-10 shows the details of the two interfaces that let you manipulate **ResultSet** objects and dynamically discover their metadata. Here's a brief description of what these two interfaces do:

■   The **ResultSet** object provides methods that let you access the results of a query. The object maintains a cursor that points to its current row of data. You can obtain the name of this cursor by invoking *getCursorName*. The cursor is initially positioned before the first row. You call *next* to make the first row the current row. You then call *next* repeatedly to sequentially move the cursor from one row to the next. You can access column values within a row in any order using the *getXXX* methods. You can retrieve values either using the index number of the column or by using the name of the column. In general, using

ResultSet Interface	
○ next	○ getLong
○ close	○ getFloat
○ getWarnings	○ getDouble
○ clearWarnings	○ getBigDecimal
○ getCursorName	○ getBytes
○ getMetaData	○ getDate
○ findColumn	○ getTime
○ wasNull	○ getTimestamp
○ getString	○ getAsciiStream
○ getBoolean	○ getUnicodeStream
○ getByte	○ getBinaryStream
○ getShort	○ getObject
○ getInt	

ResultSetMetaData Interface	
○ isAutoIncrement	○ getColumnCount
○ isCaseSensitive	○ getColumnDisplaySize
○ isSearchable	○ getColumnLabel
○ isCurrency	○ getColumnName
○ isNullable	○ getColumnType
○ isSigned	○ getColumnTypeName
○ isReadOnly	○ getSchemaName
○ isWritable	○ getPrecision
○ isDefinitelyWritable	○ getScale
	○ getTableName
	○ getCatalogName

Figure 23-10. The JDBC Core: The ResultSet Interfaces.

the column index will be more efficient. Columns are numbered starting from 1. To ensure maximum portability, you should read the columns within each row in left-to-right order. The *getXXX* methods convert the SQL data in the column you specify to its corresponding Java type. Table 23-3 shows the *getXXX* methods JDBC recommends for performing the different SQL-to-Java type conversions.

A column may have the value of SQL NULL; you invoke *wasNull* to discover if the value read by a *getXXX* call is SQL NULL. You invoke *findColumn* to obtain the column number that corresponds to a column name you provide. Note that the *getXXX* methods are overloaded; you can specify the column by providing either its case-insensitive column name or a column number. You invoke the *getMetaData* method to obtain a **ResultSetMetaData** object that provides information on the types and properties of a **ResultSet**'s columns. JDBC automatically deletes a **ResultSet** object when you close the statement that generated it. You can also invoke *close* to immediately release a **ResultSet**'s resources.

■ The **ResultSetMetaData** object provides metadata information on the column numbers, types, and properties of a **ResultSet**. Some of these methods are more useful than others. You invoke *isCaseSensitive* to find out if a column's case matters. You invoke *isCurrency* to find out if the column contains a cash value. You invoke *isSigned* to find out if a column contains signed numbers. The *getColumnCount* method returns the number of columns in the **ResultSet**. The *getColumnDisplaySize* method returns the column's normal maximum width in characters. The *getColumnLabel* method returns the suggested column title that you can use in printouts and displays. The *getColumnType* method returns a column's SQL type. The *getPrecision* method returns a column's number of decimal digits. The *getScale* method returns a column's number of digits to the right of the decimal. The *getTableName* method returns a column's table name.

Table 23-3. Recommended Methods for SQL-to-Java Conversions.

SQL Type	Java Type	Recommended getXXX Conversion Method
CHAR	String	getString()
VARCHAR	String	getString()
LONGVARCHAR	String	getAsciiStream(), getUnicodeStream()
NUMERIC	java.math.BigDecimal	getBigDecimal()
DECIMAL	java.math.BigDecimal	getBigDecimal()
BIT	boolean	getBoolean()
TINYINT	byte	getByte()
SMALLINT	short	getShort()
INTEGER	int	getInt()
BIGINT	long	getLong()
REAL	float	getFloat()
DOUBLE	double	getDouble()
FLOAT	double	getDouble()
BINARY	byte[]	getBytes()
VARBINARY	byte[]	getBytes()

Table 23-3. Recommended Methods for SQL-to-Java Conversions. (Continued)

SQL Type	Java Type	Recommended getXXX Conversion Method
LONGVARBINARY	byte[]	getBinaryStream()
DATE	java.sql.Date	getDate()
TIME	java.sql.Time	getTime()
TIMESTAMP	java.sql.Timestamp	getTimestamp()

The class descriptions that follow give the next level of detail on how to use these methods.

Listing 23-8. The Java.sql ResultSet Interface.

```java
public interface ResultSet
{
      // Methods
   public abstract boolean next() throws SQLException;
   public abstract void close() throws SQLException;
   public abstract SQLWarning getWarnings() throws SQLException;
   public abstract void clearWarnings() throws SQLException;
   public abstract String getCursorName() throws SQLException;
   public abstract ResultSetMetaData getMetaData() throws SQLException;
   public abstract int findColumn(String columnName) throws SQLException;
   public abstract boolean wasNull() throws SQLException;
   public abstract String getString(int columnIndex)
               throws SQLException;
   public abstract String getString(String columnName)
                  throws SQLException;
   public abstract boolean getBoolean(int columnIndex)
                  throws SQLException;
   public abstract boolean getBoolean(String columnName)
                  throws SQLException;
   public abstract byte getByte(int columnIndex) throws SQLException;
   public abstract byte getByte(String columnName) throws SQLException;
   public abstract short getShort(int columnIndex) throws SQLException;
   public abstract short getShort(String columnName)
                  throws SQLException;
   public abstract int getInt(int columnIndex) throws SQLException;
   public abstract int getInt(String columnName) throws SQLException;
   public abstract long getLong(int columnIndex) throws SQLException;
   public abstract long getLong(String columnName) throws SQLException;
```

```
public abstract float getFloat(int columnIndex) throws SQLException;
public abstract float getFloat(String columnName)
                    throws SQLException;
public abstract double getDouble(int columnIndex)
                    throws SQLException;
public abstract double getDouble(String columnName)
                    throws SQLException;
public abstract BigDecimal getBigDecimal(int columnIndex, int scale)
                    throws SQLException;
public abstract BigDecimal getBigDecimal(String columnName, int scale)
                    throws SQLException;
public abstract byte[] getBytes(int columnIndex) throws SQLException;
public abstract byte[] getBytes(String columnName)
                    throws SQLException;
public abstract Date getDate(int columnIndex) throws SQLException;
public abstract Date getDate(String columnName) throws SQLException;
public abstract Time getTime(int columnIndex) throws SQLException;
public abstract Time getTime(String columnName) throws SQLException;
public abstract Timestamp getTimestamp(int columnIndex)
                    throws SQLException;
public abstract Timestamp getTimestamp(String columnName)
                    throws SQLException;
public abstract InputStream getAsciiStream(int columnIndex)
                        throws SQLException;
public abstract InputStream getAsciiStream(String columnName)
                        throws SQLException;
public abstract InputStream getUnicodeStream(int columnIndex)
                        throws SQLException;
public abstract InputStream getUnicodeStream(String columnName)
                        throws SQLException;
public abstract InputStream getBinaryStream(int columnIndex)
                        throws SQLException;
public abstract InputStream getBinaryStream(String columnName)
                        throws SQLException;
public abstract Object getObject(int columnIndex)
                        throws SQLException;
public abstract Object getObject(String columnName)
                        throws SQLException;
}
```

Listing 23-9. The Java.sql ResultSetMetaData Interface.

```
public interface ResultSetMetaData
{
```

```
    // Fields
public final static int columnNoNulls;
public final static int columnNullable;
public final static int columnNullableUnknown;

    // Methods
public abstract boolean isAutoIncrement(int column)
                        throws SQLException;
public abstract boolean isCaseSensitive(int column)
                        throws SQLException;
public abstract boolean isSearchable(int column) throws SQLException;
public abstract boolean isCurrency(int column) throws SQLException;
public abstract int isNullable(int column) throws SQLException;
public abstract boolean isSigned(int column) throws SQLException;
public abstract boolean isReadOnly(int column) throws SQLException;
public abstract boolean isWritable(int column) throws SQLException;
public abstract boolean isDefinitelyWritable(int column)
                        throws SQLException;
public abstract int getColumnCount() throws SQLException;
public abstract int getColumnDisplaySize(int column)
                        throws SQLException;
public abstract String getColumnLabel(int column)
                        throws SQLException;
public abstract String getColumnName(int column) throws SQLException;
public abstract int getColumnType(int column) throws SQLException;
public abstract String getColumnTypeName(int column)
                        throws SQLException;
public abstract String getSchemaName(int column) throws SQLException;
public abstract int getPrecision(int column) throws SQLException;
public abstract int getScale(int column) throws SQLException;
public abstract String getTableName(int column) throws SQLException;
public abstract String getCatalogName(int column) throws SQLException;
}
```

JDBC Java Language Extensions: The Exception Classes

Figure 23-11 shows the details of the three *java.sql* exception classes. Here's a
description of what these classes do:

■ The **SQLException** class provides information on a database access error. Each
SQLException object provides the following information: 1) a string describing
the error that you can access by invoking the *java.lang.Throwable.getMessage*
method, 2) the X/Open SQLstate error string that you can access by invoking

getSQLState, 3) a vendor-specific integer error code that you can access by invoking *getErrorCode*, and 4) a chain to a next **Exception** that provides additional error information. You obtain the next exception by invoking *getNextException*. You create a **SQLException** object by invoking its class constructor; you must pass it the appropriate information. You can add an **SQLException** to the end of the exception chain by invoking *setNext-Exception*.

■   The **SQLWarning** class provides information on a database access warning. Warnings are silently chained to the object (such as **ResultSet**, **Statement**, or **Connection**) that caused it to be reported. You obtain the first **SQLWarning**

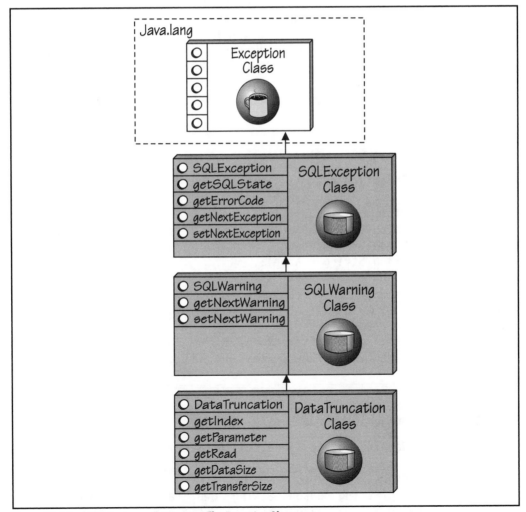

Figure 23-11. JDBC Language Extensions: The Exception Classes.

object by invoking the *getWarnings* method on the object. You then invoke *getNextWarning* on the returned **SQLWarning** object to obtain a warning chained to this one. You create a **SQLWarning** object by invoking its class constructor; you must pass it the appropriate information. You can add an **SQLWarning** to the end of the warning chain by invoking *setNextWarning*.

■ The **DataTruncation** class reports a **DataTruncation** warning on reads. It is also used to throw a **DataTruncation** exception on writes. The SQLState for a **DataTruncation** is set to "01004". You invoke *getIndex* to get the index of the column or parameter that was truncated. You invoke *getParameter* to determine if the value was a parameter. You invoke *getRead* to check if the value was truncated when read from the database. You invoke *getDataSize* to obtain the number of bytes that should have been transferred—it returns a "-1" if the size is unknown. You invoke *getTransferSize* to obtain the number of bytes that actually transferred—it returns a "-1" if the size is unknown. You can create a **DataTruncation** object by invoking its class constructor. But most typically, these objects are created by JDBC when something goes wrong.

The class descriptions that follow give the next level of detail on how to use these methods.

Listing 23-10. The Java.sql SQLException Class.

```
public class SQLException extends java.lang.Exception
{
    // Constructors
  public SQLException(String reason, String SQLState, int vendorCode);
  public SQLException(String reason, String SQLState);
  public SQLException(String reason);
  public SQLException();
    // Methods
  public String getSQLState();
  public int getErrorCode();
  public SQLException getNextException();
  public synchronized void setNextException(SQLException ex);
}
```

Listing 23-11. The Java.sql SQLWarning Class.

```
public class SQLWarning extends java.sql.SQLException
{
    // Constructors
  public SQLWarning(String reason, String SQLstate, int vendorCode);
  public SQLWarning(String reason, String SQLstate);
  public SQLWarning(String reason);
```

```
  public SQLWarning();

    // Methods
  public SQLWarning getNextWarning();
  public void setNextWarning(SQLWarning w);
}
```

Listing 23-12. The Java.sql DataTruncation Class.

```
public class DataTruncation extends java.sql.SQLWarning
{
    // Constructors
  public DataTruncation(int index,
                        boolean parameter,
                        boolean read,
                        int dataSize,
                        int transferSize);

    // Methods
  public int getIndex();
  public boolean getParameter();
  public boolean getRead();
  public int getDataSize();
  public int getTransferSize();
}
```

JDBC Date and Time Classes

Figure 23-12 shows the details of the three classes that provide the JDBC date and time services. Here's a description of what these classes do:

■ The **Date** class represents SQL DATE information; it deals with years, months, and days. You invoke the class constructor to create a new **Date** object; you must pass it the year, month, and day. JDBC uses the ISO "yyyy-mm-dd" date format. Drivers must translate the ISO date representation into something the underlying DBMS understands. Months are represented by numbers between 0 and 11; days are represented by numbers between 1 and 31. You invoke *valueOf* to convert a "yyyy-mm-dd" string to a **Date** object. You invoke *toString* to return a "yyyy-mm-dd" string representation of a **Date** object. The class also provides *getXXX* and *setXXX* methods to let you manipulate the date's years, months, and days.

■ The **Time** class represents SQL TIME information; it deals with hours, minutes, and seconds. You invoke the class constructor to create a new **Time** object; you must pass it the hour, minute, and second. JDBC uses the ISO "hh-mm-ss" time format. Drivers must translate the ISO time representation into something the underlying DBMS understands. Hours are represented by numbers between 0 and 23; minutes and seconds are represented by numbers between 0 and 59. You invoke *valueOf* to convert an "hh-mm-ss" string to a **Time** object. You invoke *toString* to return an "hh-mm-ss" string representation of a **Time** object. The class also provides *getXXX* and *setXXX* methods to let you manipulate the time's hours, minutes, and seconds.

■ The **Timestamp** class represents SQL TIMESTAMP information; it deals with years, months, days, hours, minutes, seconds, and nanoseconds. You invoke the class constructor to create a new **Timestamp** object; you must pass it the year, month, day, hour, minute, second, and nanosecond. JDBC uses the ISO "yyyy-mm-dd hh:mm:ss.f" time format. The "f" in the string represents nanoseconds; it is represented by a number between 0 and 999,999,999. Drivers must translate the ISO timestamp representation into something the underlying DBMS understands. You should note that the granularity of subsecond timestamp precision may vary among DBMSs. The stored value is rounded to the DBMS's internal precision for this field.

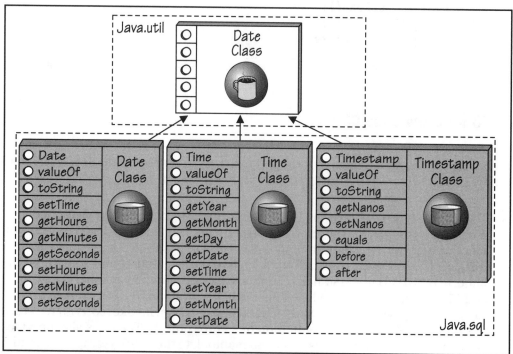

Figure 23-12. The JDBC Date, Time, and TimeStamp Classes.

You invoke *valueOf* to convert a "yyyy-mm-dd hh:mm:ss.f" string to a **Time-stamp** object. You invoke *toString* to return a "yyyy-mm-dd hh:mm:ss.f" string representation of a **Timestamp** object. You invoke *getNanos* to obtain the **Timestamp** object's nanosecond value. You invoke *setNanos* to set the **Time-stamp** object's nanosecond value. You invoke *equals* to test two **Timestamp** values for equality.

The class descriptions that follow give the next level of detail on how to use these methods.

Listing 23-13. The Java.sql Date Class.

```
public class Date extends java.util.Date
{
  // Constructors
 public Date(int year, int month, int day);
 public Date(long date);

  // Methods
 public static Date valueOf(String s);
 public String toString();
 public void setTime(long date);
 public int getHours();
 public int getMinutes();
 public int getSeconds();
 public void setHours(int i);
 public void setMinutes(int i);
 public void setSeconds(int i);
}
```

Listing 23-14. The Java.sql Time Class.

```
public class Time extends java.util.Date
{
  // Constructors
 public Time(int hour, int minute, int second);
 public Time(long time);

  // Methods
 public static Time valueOf(String s);
 public String toString();
 public int getYear();
 public int getMonth();
 public int getDay();
```

```
public int getDate();
public void setTime(long time);
public void setYear(int i);
public void setMonth(int i);
public void setDate(int i); }
}
```

Listing 23-15. The Java.sql Timestamp Class.

```
public class Timestamp extends java.util.Date
{
      // Constructors
  public Timestamp(int year,   int month,  int date, int hour,
                   int minute, int second, int nano);
  public Timestamp(long time);

      // Methods
  public static Timestamp valueOf(String s);
  public String toString();
  public int getNanos();
  public void setNanos(int n);
  public boolean equals(Timestamp ts) ;
  public boolean before(Timestamp ts) ;
  public boolean after(Timestamp ts) ;
}
```

JDBC DatabaseMetaData Interface

Figure 23-13 shows 60 of the **DatabaseMetadata** interface's 133 methods. The listing at the end of this section describes all 133 methods. The figure represents our "Top 60." We just wanted you to get a feel for the richness of information you can obtain from the objects that implement this interface. For the most part, these methods are self-explanatory. They follow the Java tradition of providing one function per method. In the rest of this section, we explain the more cryptic functions.

The *getSQLKeywords* method returns a comma-separated list of all the database's SQL keywords that are not SQL92 keywords. The *getNumericFunctions* method returns a comma-separated list of math functions the DBMS supports. The *getProcedures* returns a description of all the stored procedures that are registered in the DBMS's catalog. You can then invoke *getProcedureColumns* to obtain a stored procedure's parameters and result columns. The *getTableTypes* call returns the table types this DBMS supports. Examples of types are TABLE, VIEW, SYSTEM TABLE, TEMPORARY, and ALIAS.

○ getURL	○ getColumnPrivileges
○ getDatabaseProductName	○ getTablePrivileges
○ getDatabaseProductVersion	○ getVersionColumns
○ getDriverName	○ getPrimaryKeys
○ getDriverVersion	○ getCrossReference
○ getSQLKeywords	○ getTypeInfo
○ getNumericFunctions	○ getIndexInfo
○ getStringFunctions	○ getDefaultTransactionIsolation
○ getSystemFunctions	○ supportsMixedCaseIdentifiers
○ getTimeDateFunctions	○ supportsColumnAliasing
○ getMaxColumnNameLength	○ supportsMultipleResultSets
○ getMaxColumnsInGroupBy	○ supportsNonNullableColumns
○ getMaxColumnsInIndex	○ supportsANSI92EntryLevelSQL
○ getMaxColumnsInOrderBy	○ supportsANSI92IntermediateSQL
○ getMaxColumnsInSelect	○ supportsANSI92FullSQL
○ getMaxConnections	○ supportsPositionedDelete
○ getMaxIndexLength	○ supportsPositionedUpdate
○ getMaxRowSize	○ supportsSelectForUpdate
○ doesMaxRowSizeIncludeBlobs	○ supportsStoredProcedures
○ getMaxStatementLength	○ supportsTransactions
○ getMaxStatements	○ supportsOpenCursorsAcrossCommit
○ getMaxTableNameLength	○ supportsOpenCursorsAcrossRollback
○ getMaxTablesInSelect	○ supportsOpenStatementsAcrossCommit
○ getProcedures	○ supportsOpenStatementsAcrossRollback
○ getProcedureColumns	○ supportsTransactionIsolationLevel
○ getTables	○ dataDefinitionCausesTransactionCommit
○ getSchemas	○ dataDefinitionIgnoredInTransactions
○ getCatalogs	○ nullsAreSortedHigh
○ getTableTypes	○ usesLocalFiles
○ getColumns	○ usesLocalFilePerTable

DatabaseMetaData Interface

Figure 23-13. JDBC DatabaseMetaData Interface: The Top 60 Methods.

The *getVersionColumns* method returns a description of a table's columns that are automatically updated when you update any value in a row. The *getCrossReference* method returns a description of the foreign key columns in a secondary table—they reference the primary key columns in the primary table. The *getTypeInfo* method returns a description of all the standard SQL types supported by this DBMS. The *dataDefinitionCausesTransactionCommit* method returns true if a CREATE statement within a transaction forces a commit. The *usesLocalFiles* method returns true if the database stores its tables in local files.

The class descriptions that follow give the next level of detail on how to use these methods. We also throw in the definition of the **java.sql.Types** class. This is the class that defines the SQL types; it does not support any methods.

Listing 23-16. The Java.sql DatabaseMetaData Interface.

```java
public interface DatabaseMetaData extends Object;
{
      // Constants
  public final static int procedureResultUnknown;
  public final static int procedureNoResult;
  public final static int procedureReturnsResult;
  public final static int procedureColumnUnknown;
  public final static int procedureColumnIn;
  public final static int procedureColumnInOut;
  public final static int procedureColumnOut;
  public final static int procedureColumnReturn;
  public final static int procedureColumnResult;
  public final static int procedureNoNulls;
  public final static int procedureNullable;
  public final static int procedureNullableUnknown;
  public final static int columnNoNulls;
  public final static int columnNullable;
  public final static int columnNullableUnknown;
  public final static int bestRowTemporary;
  public final static int bestRowTransaction;
  public final static int bestRowSession;
  public final static int bestRowUnknown;
  public final static int bestRowNotPseudo;
  public final static int bestRowPseudo;

  public final static int versionColumnUnknown;
  public final static int versionColumnNotPseudo;
  public final static int versionColumnPseudo;
  public final static int importedKeyCascade;
  public final static int importedKeyRestrict;
  public static final int importedKeyNoAction;
  public static final int importedKeySetDefault;
  public static final int importedKeyInitiallyDeferred;
  public static final int importedKeyInitiallyImmediate;
  public static final int importedKeyNotDeferrable;
  public final static int importedKeySetNull;
  public final static int typeNoNulls;
  public final static int typeNullable;
```

```
public final static int typeNullableUnknown;
public final static int typePredNone;
public final static int typePredChar;
public final static int typePredBasic;
public final static int typeSearchable;
public final static short tableIndexStatistic;
public final static short tableIndexClustered;
public final static short tableIndexHashed;
public final static short tableIndexOther;

    // Methods
public abstract boolean allProceduresAreCallable()
                                throws SQLException;
public abstract boolean allTablesAreSelectable() throws SQLException;
public abstract String getURL() throws SQLException;
public abstract String getUserName() throws SQLException;
public abstract boolean isReadOnly() throws SQLException;
public abstract boolean nullsAreSortedHigh() throws SQLException;
public abstract boolean nullsAreSortedLow() throws SQLException;
public abstract boolean nullsAreSortedAtStart() throws SQLException;
public abstract boolean nullsAreSortedAtEnd() throws SQLException;
public abstract String getDatabaseProductName() throws SQLException;
public abstract String getDatabaseProductVersion()
                                throws SQLException;
public abstract String getDriverName() throws SQLException;
public abstract String getDriverVersion() throws SQLException;
public abstract int getDriverMajorVersion();
public abstract int getDriverMinorVersion();
public abstract boolean usesLocalFiles() throws SQLException;
public abstract boolean usesLocalFilePerTable() throws SQLException;
public abstract boolean supportsMixedCaseIdentifiers()
                                throws SQLException;
public abstract boolean storesUpperCaseIdentifiers()
                                throws SQLException;
public abstract boolean storesLowerCaseIdentifiers()
                                throws SQLException;
public abstract boolean storesMixedCaseIdentifiers()
                                throws SQLException;
public abstract boolean supportsMixedCaseQuotedIdentifiers()
                                throws SQLException;
public abstract boolean storesUpperCaseQuotedIdentifiers()
                                throws SQLException;
public abstract boolean storesLowerCaseQuotedIdentifiers()
                                throws SQLException;
```

```java
public abstract boolean storesMixedCaseQuotedIdentifiers()
                              throws SQLException;
public abstract String getIdentifierQuoteString()
                              throws SQLException;
public abstract String getSQLKeywords() throws SQLException;
public abstract String getNumericFunctions() throws SQLException;
public abstract String getStringFunctions() throws SQLException;
public abstract String getSystemFunctions() throws SQLException;
public abstract String getTimeDateFunctions() throws SQLException;
public abstract String getSearchStringEscape() throws SQLException;
public abstract String getExtraNameCharacters() throws SQLException;
public abstract boolean supportsAlterTableWithAddColumn()
                              throws SQLException;
public abstract boolean supportsAlterTableWithDropColumn()
                              throws SQLException;
public abstract boolean supportsColumnAliasing() throws SQLException;
public abstract boolean nullPlusNonNullIsNull() throws SQLException;
public abstract boolean supportsConvert() throws SQLException;
public abstract boolean supportsConvert(int fromType, int toType)
                              throws SQLException;
public abstract boolean supportsTableCorrelationNames()
                              throws SQLException;
public abstract boolean supportsDifferentTableCorrelationNames()
                              throws SQLException;
public abstract boolean supportsExpressionsInOrderBy()
                              throws SQLException;
public abstract boolean supportsOrderByUnrelated()
                              throws SQLException;
public abstract boolean supportsGroupBy() throws SQLException;
public abstract boolean supportsGroupByUnrelated()
                              throws SQLException;
public abstract boolean supportsGroupByBeyondSelect()
                              throws SQLException;
public abstract boolean supportsLikeEscapeClause()
                              throws SQLException;
public abstract boolean supportsMultipleResultSets()
                              throws SQLException;
public abstract boolean supportsMultipleTransactions()
                              throws SQLException;
public abstract boolean supportsNonNullableColumns()
                              throws SQLException;
public abstract boolean supportsMinimumSQLGrammar()
                              throws SQLException;
public abstract boolean supportsCoreSQLGrammar() throws SQLException;
```

```
public abstract boolean supportsExtendedSQLGrammar()
                              throws SQLException;
public abstract boolean supportsANSI92EntryLevelSQL()
                              throws SQLException;
public abstract boolean supportsANSI92IntermediateSQL()
                              throws SQLException;
public abstract boolean supportsANSI92FullSQL() throws SQLException;
public abstract boolean supportsIntegrityEnhancementFacility()
                              throws SQLException;
public abstract boolean supportsOuterJoins() throws SQLException;
public abstract boolean supportsFullOuterJoins() throws SQLException;
public abstract boolean supportsLimitedOuterJoins()
                              throws SQLException;
public abstract String  getSchemaTerm() throws SQLException;
public abstract String  getProcedureTerm() throws SQLException;
public abstract String  getCatalogTerm() throws SQLException;
public abstract boolean isCatalogAtStart() throws SQLException;
public abstract String  getCatalogSeparator() throws SQLException;
public abstract boolean supportsSchemasInDataManipulation()
                              throws SQLException;
public abstract boolean supportsSchemasInProcedureCalls()
                              throws SQLException;
public abstract boolean supportsSchemasInTableDefinitions()
                              throws SQLException;
public abstract boolean supportsSchemasInIndexDefinitions()
                              throws SQLException;
public abstract boolean supportsSchemasInPrivilegeDefinitions()
                              throws SQLException;
public abstract boolean supportsCatalogsInDataManipulation()
                              throws SQLException;
public abstract boolean supportsCatalogsInProcedureCalls()
                              throws SQLException;
public abstract boolean supportsCatalogsInTableDefinitions()
                              throws SQLException;
public abstract boolean supportsCatalogsInIndexDefinitions()
                              throws SQLException;
public abstract boolean supportsCatalogsInPrivilegeDefinitions()
                              throws SQLException;
public abstract boolean supportsPositionedDelete()
                              throws SQLException;
public abstract boolean supportsPositionedUpdate()
                              throws SQLException;
public abstract boolean supportsSelectForUpdate()
                              throws SQLException;
```

```java
public abstract boolean supportsStoredProcedures()
                                throws SQLException;
public abstract boolean supportsSubqueriesInComparisons()
                                throws SQLException;
public abstract boolean supportsSubqueriesInExists()
                                throws SQLException;
public abstract boolean supportsSubqueriesInIns()
                                throws SQLException;
public abstract boolean supportsSubqueriesInQuantifieds()
                                throws SQLException;
public abstract boolean supportsCorrelatedSubqueries()
                                throws SQLException;
public abstract boolean supportsUnion() throws SQLException;
public abstract boolean supportsUnionAll() throws SQLException;
public abstract boolean supportsOpenCursorsAcrossCommit()
                                throws SQLException;
public abstract boolean supportsOpenCursorsAcrossRollback()
                                throws SQLException;
public abstract boolean supportsOpenStatementsAcrossCommit()
                                throws SQLException;
public abstract boolean supportsOpenStatementsAcrossRollback()
                                throws SQLException;
public abstract int getMaxBinaryLiteralLength() throws SQLException;
public abstract int getMaxCharLiteralLength() throws SQLException;
public abstract int getMaxColumnNameLength() throws SQLException;
public abstract int getMaxColumnsInGroupBy() throws SQLException;
public abstract int getMaxColumnsInIndex() throws SQLException;
public abstract int getMaxColumnsInOrderBy() throws SQLException;
public abstract int getMaxColumnsInSelect() throws SQLException;
public abstract int getMaxColumnsInTable() throws SQLException;
public abstract int getMaxConnections() throws SQLException;
public abstract int getMaxCursorNameLength() throws SQLException;
public abstract int getMaxIndexLength() throws SQLException;
public abstract int getMaxSchemaNameLength() throws SQLException;
public abstract int getMaxProcedureNameLength() throws SQLException;
public abstract int getMaxCatalogNameLength() throws SQLException;
public abstract int getMaxRowSize() throws SQLException;
public abstract boolean doesMaxRowSizeIncludeBlobs()
                                throws SQLException;
public abstract int getMaxStatementLength() throws SQLException;
public abstract int getMaxStatements() throws SQLException;
public abstract int getMaxTableNameLength() throws SQLException;
public abstract int getMaxTablesInSelect() throws SQLException;
public abstract int getMaxUserNameLength() throws SQLException;
```

```
public abstract int getDefaultTransactionIsolation()
                              throws SQLException;
public abstract boolean supportsTransactions() throws SQLException;
public abstract boolean supportsTransactionIsolationLevel(int level)
                              throws SQLException;
public abstract boolean
          supportsDataDefinitionAndDataManipulationTransactions()
                              throws SQLException;
public abstract boolean supportsDataManipulationTransactionsOnly()
                              throws SQLException;
public abstract boolean dataDefinitionCausesTransactionCommit()
                              throws SQLException;
public abstract boolean dataDefinitionIgnoredInTransactions()
                              throws SQLException;
public abstract ResultSet getProcedures(String catalog,
                              String schemaPattern,
                              String procedureNamePattern)
                              throws SQLException;
public abstract ResultSet getProcedureColumns(String catalog,
                              String schemaPattern,
                              String procedureNamePattern,
                              String columnNamePattern)
                              throws SQLException;
public abstract ResultSet getTables(String catalog,
                              String schemaPattern,
                              String tableNamePattern,
                              String types[])
                              throws SQLException;
public abstract ResultSet getSchemas() throws SQLException;
public abstract ResultSet getCatalogs() throws SQLException;
public abstract ResultSet getTableTypes() throws SQLException;
public abstract ResultSet getColumns(String catalog,
                              String schemaPattern,
                              String tableNamePattern,
                              String columnNamePattern)
                              throws SQLException;
public abstract ResultSet getColumnPrivileges(String catalog,
                              String schema,
                              String table,
                              String columnNamePattern)
                              throws SQLException;
public abstract ResultSet getTablePrivileges(String catalog,
                              String schemaPattern,
                              String tableNamePattern)
                              throws SQLException;
```

```
public abstract ResultSet getBestRowIdentifier(String catalog,
                                               String schema,
                                               String table,
                                               int scope,
                                               boolean nullable)
                           throws SQLException;
public abstract ResultSet getVersionColumns(String catalog,
                                            String schema,
                                            String table)
                           throws SQLException;
public abstract ResultSet getPrimaryKeys(String catalog,
                                         String schema,
                                         String table)
                           throws SQLException;
public abstract ResultSet getImportedKeys(String catalog,
                                          String schema,
                                          String table)
                           throws SQLException;
public abstract ResultSet getExportedKeys(String catalog,
                                          String schema,
                                          String table)
                           throws SQLException;
public abstract ResultSet getCrossReference(String primaryCatalog,
                                            String primarySchema,
                                            String primaryTable,
                                            String foreignCatalog,
                                            String foreignSchema,
                                            String foreignTable)
                           throws SQLException;
public abstract ResultSet getTypeInfo() throws SQLException;
public abstract ResultSet getIndexInfo(String catalog,
                                       String schema,
                                       String table,
                                       boolean unique,
                                       boolean approximate)
                           throws SQLException;
}
```

Listing 23-17. The Java.sql Types Class.

```
public class Types extends Object
{
    // Constants
```

```
public final static int BIT;
public final static int TINYINT;
public final static int SMALLINT;
public final static int INTEGER;
public final static int BIGINT;
public final static int FLOAT;
public final static int REAL;
public final static int DOUBLE;
public final static int NUMERIC;
public final static int DECIMAL;
public final static int CHAR;
public final static int VARCHAR;
public final static int LONGVARCHAR;
public final static int DATE;
public final static int TIME;
public final static int TIMESTAMP;
public final static int BINARY;
public final static int VARBINARY;
public final static int LONGVARBINARY;
public final static int NULL;
public final static int OTHER;

    // Constructors
public Types();
}
```

JDBC SCENARIOS

It's time for a few scenarios that show how these JDBC classes play together. In the first scenario, we submit a simple SQL query using a **Statement** object. In the second scenario, we repeatedly submit a SQL UPDATE using a **Prepared-Statement** object. In the last scenario, we show how to submit a stored procedure using a **CallableStatement** object.

JDBC Scenario 1: Invoking a SQL Query

Figure 23-14 shows how you use JDBC's **Statement** object to submit a SQL query. Let's walk through the steps:

1. ***Connect to the database.*** A JDBC database is identified by its URL. You first invoke the *getConnection* method on the **DriverManager** and pass it the URL for the database. The **DriverManager** will locate a **Driver** object that can handle the URL; it then returns a **Connection** object that uses this driver.

2. ***Obtain a Statement object.*** You invoke *createStatement* on the **Connection** object; it will return a **Statement** object.

3. ***Execute the query.*** Invoke the *executeQuery* method on the **Statement** object and pass it the SQL SELECT in a string; it will execute the query and return the results in a **ResultSet** object.

4. ***Position the cursor to the next row.*** You invoke *next* to point the cursor to

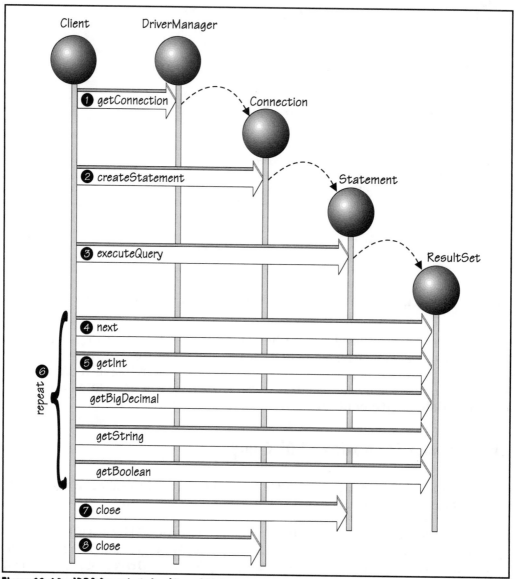

Figure 23-14. JDBC Scenario 1: Invoking a SQL Query.

the next row in the **ResultSet** object. The cursor will point to the first row after you invoke *next* for the first time.

5. ***Retrieve the row values one column at a time.*** You must invoke a *getXXX* call for each column value that you need to retrieve. The exact function you invoke depends on the column's SQL type. In this scenario, we invoke *getInt*, *getBigDecimal*, *getString*, and *getBoolean* to retrieve four column values of SQL type INTEGER, DECIMAL, VARCHAR, and BIT.

6. ***Repeat while there are rows to be processed.*** Repeat the last two steps as long as *next* returns true; it returns false if there are no more rows.

7. ***Release the Statement object***. Invoke *close* to free the resources associated with the **Statement** object.

8. ***Release the Connection object***. Invoke *close* to free the resources associated with the **Connection** object.

JDBC Scenario 2: Invoking a Prepared Command

Figure 23-15 shows how you use JDBC's **PreparedStatement** object to submit a precompiled command. You simply prepare the command once and you then execute it multiple times. JDBC lets you specify placeholders for the command variables. You use the *setXXX* commands to set the values in these placeholders every time you re-execute the command. In this scenario, we will repeatedly execute the following SQL command: *UPDATE TELLER SET BALANCE = BALANCE + ? WHERE TELLER_ID = ?.* The question marks (?) are placeholders for IN parameters; we must set the values of these placeholders every time we execute the SQL command. Here's a step-by-step walk through this scenario:

1. ***Connect to the database.*** A JDBC database is identified by its URL. You invoke the *getConnection* method on the **DriverManager** and pass it the URL for the database. The **DriverManager** will locate a **Driver** object that can handle the URL and then return a **Connection** object that uses this driver.

2. ***Compile the command.*** You invoke *prepareStatement* on the **Connection** object and pass it the SQL UPDATE string; it will compile the command and return a **PreparedStatement** object. You can precompile and store any SQL statement in a **PreparedStatement** object—with or without IN parameters. You can then use this object to efficiently execute this statement multiple times. Note that some drivers may not support precompilation. In this case, the statement may not be sent to the database until the **PreparedStatement** is executed. This does not affect how you use this command.

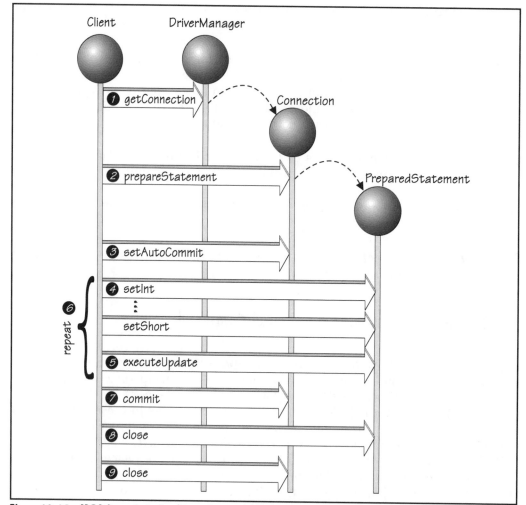

Figure 23-15. JDBC Scenario 2: Invoking a Prepared SQL Statement Multiple Times.

3. ***Disable autocommit***. In our scenario, a transaction only succeeds if the entire command loop executes successfully. Otherwise, we rollback the entire transaction and undo any command that executed since the last commit. The JDBC default is to automatically commit each SQL command. We disable this default by invoking *setAutoCommit* and passing it a parameter of false.

4. ***Provide values for the placeholders***. We invoke a *setXXX* method for each placeholder parameter in the **PreparedStatement** object. The parameters are identified by their position in the statement. For example, the first parameter is 1, the next parameter is 2, and so on. The *setXXX* method you invoke will depend on the parameter's SQL type. In our example, the first parameter has a SQL type of INTEGER; the second parameter is of SQL type SMALLINT.

Consequently, we invoke the methods *setInt* and *setShort*. These methods set the parameter values using the appropriate Java-to-SQL type conversions.

5. ***Execute the command.*** Invoke the *executeUpdate* method on the **PreparedStatement** object; it executes the SQL UPDATE statement. The command returns the row count for INSERT, UPDATE or DELETE—or it returns 0 for SQL statements that return nothing.

6. ***Resubmit the command with new values.*** Repeat the last two steps for as many UPDATEs as you need to submit. Use the *setXXX* methods to pass different parameter values to the SQL UPDATE.

7. ***Commit your work.*** Invoke *commit* on the **Connection** object to make your updates permanent in the database. The commit also releases any database locks you currently hold on this **Connection**. If you change your mind, you can always invoke *rollback*; it will drop all the changes you made since the previous commit/rollback.

8. ***Release the PreparedStatement object.*** Invoke *close* to free the resources associated with the **PreparedStatement** object.

9. ***Release the Connection object.*** Invoke *close* to free the resources associated with the **Connection** object.

JDBC Scenario 3: Invoking a Stored Procedure

Figure 23-16 shows how you use JDBC's **CallableStatement** object to submit a stored procedure. Here's a step-by-step walk through this scenario:

1. ***Connect to the database.*** A JDBC database is identified by its URL. You invoke the *getConnection* method on the **DriverManager** and pass it the URL for the database. The **DriverManager** will locate a **Driver** object that can handle the URL and then return a **Connection** object that uses this driver.

2. ***Precompile the stored procedure.*** Invoke *prepareCall* and pass it the string for the stored procedure; it may contain one or more (?) parameter placeholders. JDBC will return a **CallableStatement** object that serves as a wrapper object for the precompiled stored procedure. The object provides methods that let you set its IN and OUT parameters and then execute the procedure. Note that some drivers may send the call statement to the database when the *prepareCall* is done; others may wait until you invoke *execute*. In either case, this should not directly affect your programs.

3. ***Register the output parameters.*** Before you execute the stored procedure, you must explicitly call *registerOutParameter* to register the SQL type of each

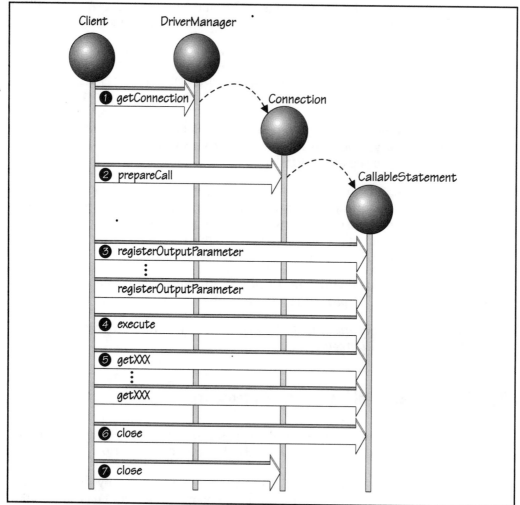

Figure 23-16. JDBC Scenario 3: Invoking a Stored Procedure.

OUT parameter. The SQL type codes are defined in **java.sql.Types**. How do you identify the parameters? You identify them by their position inside the stored procedure—the first parameter is 1, the second is 2, and so on.

4. ***Execute the stored procedure***. You can now invoke the *execute* method on the **CallableStatement** object. The object inherits this method from its parent—the **PreparedStatement** interface.

5. ***Retrieve the results one parameter at a time***. You must invoke a *getXXX* call for each parameter value that the stored procedure returns. The *getXXX* method must correspond to the SQL type you previously registered for that parameter.

6. ***Release the PreparedStatement object***. Invoke *close* to free the resources associated with the **CallableStatement** object.

7. ***Release the Connection object***. Invoke *close* to free the resources associated with the **Connection** object.

CONCLUSION

This concludes the longest tutorial we've ever written. SQL and relational databases have been around for at least 20 years. During this time, they accumulated a ton of functionality. JDBC makes all this functionality readily available to your Java programs. With very minor changes, your JDBC programs should be able to work with the more than 100 SQL database products—from entry-level Access databases to DB2 databases on the largest mainframes.

In addition to JDBC, JavaSoft is working with the object database vendors to create ODMG-compliant Java bindings for ODBMSs. These bindings should give you the most direct path to store your Java objects; you will be able to totally bypass SQL. However, you will still need JDBC to access the huge amounts of data that are currently stored in RDBMSs.

Chapter 24

The JDBC Debit-Credit Benchmark

This chapter is the first of a three-chapter series on the performance trade-offs of 2-tier versus 3-tier client/server architectures that use CORBA, Java, and JDBC. We will create a benchmarking toolkit that simulates a small bank. We call it Bob's Bank. Bob's Bank has a server that also runs a JDBC database; it contains customers, accounts, and the like. Of course, one of the things you do in Bob's Bank is debit and credit your account.

The plan for this series is to use our favorite CORBA/Java technologies to create two versions of a Debit-Credit program for Bob's Bank. The first Debit-Credit program is a 2-tier client/server solution; Java clients talk directly to JDBC servers. The second Debit-Credit program is a 3-tier client/server solution; Java clients talk to middle-tier server objects using a CORBA ORB. The server objects then talk to the JDBC bank. In this implementation, the clients never deal directly with the bank's database. Of course, we need to understand which solution is best for Bob's Bank. So we create a benchmarking testbed around the Debit-Credit client/server programs so that Bob can measure their relative performance. It's quite an undertaking.

This chapter starts the series by explaining the rules of the benchmark we will create. Next, we tell you something about the Debit-Credit program. Then, we design the JDBC database for Bob's Bank. But this chapter is not all talk. We will also be writing a small JDBC program that creates the bank's database and fills it with data.

In the next chapter, we create the 2-tier client/server version of Debit-Credit. In the last chapter of this series, we create the CORBA 3-tier client/server version of Debit-Credit. You will then be able to run the two programs and compare the 2-tier versus 3-tier results. We will then declare the winner. Note that this is purely a contest between client/server architectures. For once, it's not about Microsoft versus the rest of the world.

DESIGNING THE BENCHMARK

This section gives you a quick overview of the performance issues that we must address in the design of the Debit-Credit benchmark. Bob's Bank is really a mission-critical OLTP application. This is the most demanding type of client/server application. An OLTP client/server application must be able to support multiple users submitting their transactions against one or more large databases. In this section, we first tell you how to measure the performance of OLTP-style client/server applications. Then we define the Debit-Credit benchmark.

What to Look for in an OLTP Benchmark

An OLTP application repeatedly and simultaneously executes a set of predefined SQL statements. Clients must come in, do their thing, and then leave. The mantra of OLTP is resource reuse. No one is allowed to monopolize scarce resources. Everyone must learn how to share. Over the last three decades, OLTP designers have mastered the art of squeezing the maximum performance out of their systems. They know how to write applications that scale. The important metrics for designers of OLTP applications are throughput, response time, and number of concurrent users.

The following is a list of what we will be measuring in the Debit-Credit benchmark:

- **Throughput:** This is the rate at which the OLTP system can process transactions. We measure throughput in *transactions per second (tps)*. As we add users, the system reaches a maximum throughput and then starts to drop as more users join the system. A good OLTP system must be able to maintain a stable throughput as we add more users.

- **Response time:** This is the elapsed time you experience from the time you submit a transaction until you receive a response. The response time should grow linearly—not exponentially—as we add more users to the system.

- **_Concurrent users:_** The number of concurrent users is an important factor in OLTP systems. Throughput and response times are meaningful when we measure them as a function of number of users. We should also measure the performance of the system at peak times. Bob's Bank will certainly be interested in peak performance numbers.

- **_The exact definition of a transaction:_** For a *tps* to be meaningful it is important that we all agree on what exactly is a transaction. A *transaction*, of course, varies from application to application. A transaction that reserves an airline seat is obviously different from a manufacturing shop floor transaction. Our benchmark must be able to specify exactly what is a transaction. For example, we must describe both the actual SQL commands and how we apply commits, logs, and locks.

- **_System steady-state verification:_** A system reaches "steady state" when its performance remains constant from that point on. The system performance may vary by 20% or more before it reaches a steady state. We can attribute this variance to many factors—including buffers that fill up and the swapping of pages from memory to disk as the system load increases. We must report the benchmark results at the steady-state condition.

- **_Cost per transaction:_** The system cost must be used to normalize *tps* test results across widely differing systems—for example, a $1000 PC versus a mainframe. This means that we must measure the cost per *tps*.

- **_The test environment:_** Our benchmark must specify the system's hardware and software configurations. The hardware configuration must include the speed of the processor, the amount of memory, the size of the buffer pool, and the speed of the disks. We must also specify the communications environment between the client and the server.

- **_Full disclosure:_** We must provide enough information to allow an auditor to replicate our test results.

Whew! That is clearly a long list of requirements. Let's go to work.

The Debit-Credit Benchmark

Luckily for Bob's Bank, Jim Gray (and friends) defined in 1985 a standard Debit-Credit benchmark that is also known as TP1, ET1, or TPC-A. The benchmark was first specified in *Datamation* in an article submitted by 24 computer professionals active in transaction processing.[1] The purpose of the article was "to record the

---

[1] Anon et al., "A Measure of Transaction Processing Power," **Datamation** (April 1, 1985).

folklore we use to measure system performance." The benchmark was further refined and clarified over the years.

The Debit-Credit benchmark models a hypothetical banking application. It defines a standard transaction called *DebitCredit*, a standard database, a scaling method for larger systems, and a measure of throughput and price performance.

The Debit-Credit Database

The Debit-Credit database consists of four tables and a set of rules that define their contents and sizes. The four tables are: ACCOUNTS, TELLERS, BRANCHES, and HISTORY. This last table records every transaction that is submitted to this bank. The Debit-Credit benchmark specifies an automatic scaling factor of the first three tables. A *1-tps* system supports a database with 100,000 accounts, 100 tellers, and 10 branches. A system that runs at a higher *tps* rate is required to scale its database linearly. For example, a *100-tps* system has a database that is 100 times larger than that of a *1-tps* system.

For a *100-tps* system, the ACCOUNTS table should use 10 million account records, which translates into at least 1 GByte of disk space. The HISTORY table should be able to hold 90 days of transaction history. This innocent-looking provision may turn out to be a tough requirement to meet.

The Debit-Credit Transaction

The Debit-Credit transaction is deceptively simple and also quite general. The transaction simulates an online teller who enters a debit/credit transaction. This is how the transaction executes (see Figure 24-1):

1. The client—a teller—generates a deposit/withdrawal transaction and sends it to the server. The client starts the timer before it invokes the transaction.

2. The server randomly selects and updates a record in the ACCOUNT table to reflect the transaction.

3. The server updates a record in the TELLER table.

4. The server updates a branch totals record in BRANCH table.

5. The server inserts a record in the HISTORY table to record the transaction.

6. The server commits the transaction.

7. The server returns a response. The client receives the message and then stops the timer. The transaction response time is the elapsed time between the send and the completion of the receive.

Each client must generate a transaction every 100 seconds, which requires 100 clients for each reported *tps*. The more popular alternative is to let a transaction driver simulate the client message load. Typically, the transaction driver performs back-to-back invocations.

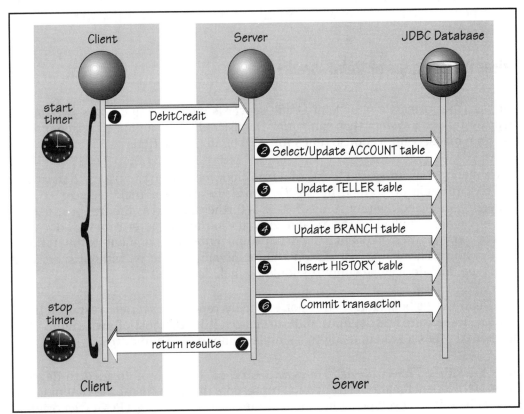

Figure 24-1. The Debit-Credit Transaction.

The Debit-Credit Constraints

Here's a list of the constraints that must be met by the system:

■ Each Debit-Credit transaction must randomly generate the account branch and teller numbers, and at least 15% of the transactions must be inter-branch. The random generation of numbers is usually sufficient to meet this requirement (especially with a large database).

- All the tables must be protected by a fine granularity of *locking* and *logging*.

- The OLTP system under test must be observed over 10-minute windows.

- 95% of the transactions must provide a response time of less than one second. A system that can run 1 transaction-per-second with less than one second response time for 95% of all transactions is classified as a *1-tps* system.

Price/Performance of Debit-Credit

The price/performance of a Debit-Credit server is measured in *dollars-per-tps*. A *1-tps* system is a system that can run 1 Debit-Credit transaction per second with less than one-second response times for 95% of all transactions.

As we mentioned earlier, the "cost" of a transaction can be quite tricky to measure. The cost formula prescribed by the *Datamation* article is the "five-year cost of ownership of the computing facility." This is further defined as the five-year capital cost of vendor-supplied hardware and software in the computer room. It does not include expenditures on client PCs, LANs, application development, or operations. It does, however, include installation and maintenance charges without specifying what type of maintenance support should be included.

The Debit-Credit benchmark does not explicitly report an average response time. Instead, it measures throughput and normalizes it by the cost-of-ownership. The benchmark rates a system using two simple numbers: *tps* and *$/tps*.

In late 1988, a *Transaction Processing Council (TPC)* was formed to develop formal OLTP benchmarks. The council represents the major database vendors. The council has since developed a number of standards—including TPC-A (the original Debit-Credit), TPC-B, TPC-C, TPC-D, and so on.

THE JDBC DEBIT-CREDIT BENCHMARK FACILITY

Debit-Credit can be a difficult and demanding benchmark to install and run. Depending on the available tools, it can take anywhere from a day to several months to install, configure, and build a test system. We will develop a Java-based JDBC Debit-Credit toolkit that you can use in all kinds of flexible configurations. It is powerful, flexible, and a pleasure to experiment with.

Build Your Java Debit-Credit Benchmark in One Afternoon

You should be able to put together a custom Debit-Credit test system in less than half a day. Once you've got a system up and running, you'll find yourself running all kinds of tests. We will provide an applet-based control panel that puts you at the controls. Just play with the knobs. But, we're getting ahead of our story. Let's first describe our benchmarking toolkit.

We've put together a flexible toolkit that lets you mix-and-match to your heart's content. And if that's not enough, you can always modify and recompile the source code to create any variation you may fancy. The toolkit builds on the MultiCount benchmarking foundation we developed in Chapter 9. We will graft into this foundation the JDBC Debit-Credit programs we develop in this three-chapter series.

Figure 24-2 shows the various components we will use in the Debit-Credit benchmark. Some of these names should be very familiar. If not, please review Chapter 9. Here's a description of the players:

- **CreateBank** is a new Java application that uses JDBC to create a *Bank* database. It then creates the Bank tables and their indexes. Finally it loads Bank data into each table. We will develop this program later in the chapter. It will be our first JDBC program.

- **Coordinator** is our old friend from Chapter 9. Remember, this is the server that brokers races. As usual, clients register their callback objects with the Coordinator when they first come up. The Coordinator receives its start/stop instructions from the MultiConsole control applet. It then broadcasts the start/stop commands to all the clients that have registered their callback objects with it. The Coordinator collects the results from each client and returns them to the MultiConsole. It's just like before. And like before, the Coordinator uses CORBA to communicate with its clients as well as with MultiConsole. CORBA provides the race-control infrastructure.

- **MultiConsole** is our other old friend from Chapter 9. It's the applet that serves as the control panel for our races. You use it to start and stop a race and to display the results. In this case, MultiConsole will display the Debit-Credit results.

- **DebitCreditMultiClient** is a new Java application. It's a Debit-Credit client simulator. You can start as many of these clients as you want. Each client will register its callback interface with the Coordinator so that you can control it remotely. It's the old CORBA callback trick from Chapter 9. Notice that the dotted lines represent JDBC invocations. They are used in 2-tier JDBC client/server configurations; the clients directly communicate with the DBMS server using JDBC. In the 3-tier case, the clients invoke the CORBA DebitCreditServer instead of JDBC. So, the dotted lines go away. In the 3-tier case, only CORBA server objects can talk to JDBC.

■ ***DebitCreditServer*** is a new Java application. It's a poor man's *TP Monitor* for CORBA server objects. We prestart a pool of objects and run them each within their own thread. Each server object maintains an active JDBC connection to the database. We also implement an object dispenser; it manages the pool of prestarted objects. A 3-tier client uses the dispenser to obtain an object reference to a prestarted server object. It's an exciting application; it shows you how to create scalable, multithreaded CORBA/Java servers. The DebitCredit-Server application is only used in the 3-tier Debit-Credit benchmark. In the 2-tier case, the clients bypass the middle-tier server and go directly to the DBMS (see dotted lines).

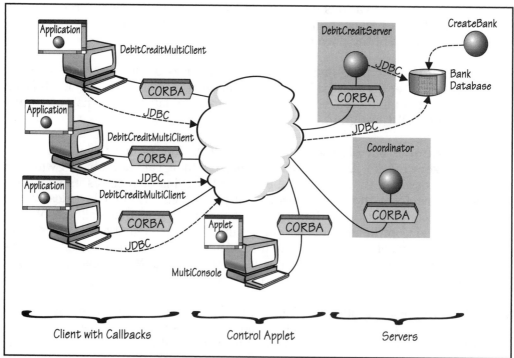

Figure 24-2. The Debit-Credit Benchmarking Infrastructure.

2-Tier Versus 3-Tier

You can use the Debit-Credit benchmarking toolkit to measure almost anything that has do with Java databases. For example, you can use it to conduct a bake-off between vendor SQL database engines or between vendor JDBC drivers. If you have enough hardware, you can use the toolkit to stress system limits—it can help you decide if Java is ready for client/server prime time.

In this book, we use the Debit-Credit toolkit to understand the architectural trade-offs of 2-tier versus 3-tier client/server systems. We also use it to compare the performance of static versus dynamic SQL. The toolkit also demonstrates how to write client/server applications using CORBA, Java, and JDBC.

So what is all this 2-tier versus 3-tier fuss about? It's about how you split client/server applications into functional units that you can then assign to either the client or to one or more servers. The most typical functional units are the user interface, the business logic, and shared data. There are many possible variations of multi-tier architectures. It all depends on how you split the application and on the middleware you use to communicate between tiers.

In 2-tier client/server systems, the application logic is buried either inside the user interface on the client or within the database on the server (or both). In 3-tier client/server systems, the application logic (or process) lives in the middle-tier; it is separated from the data and the user interface. Processes become first-class citizens; they can be managed and deployed separately from the GUI and database.

In theory, 3-tier client/server systems are more scalable, robust, and flexible. In addition, they can integrate data from multiple sources. Examples of 3-tier client/server systems are TP Monitors, distributed objects, and the Web. Examples of 2-tier client/server systems are file servers and database servers with stored procedures. According to Gartner Group, 3-tier will grow to 33% of all client/server applications in 1998.

JDBC 2-Tier

Figure 24-3 shows a 2-tier JDBC client/server split. In this "fat client" approach, the client maintains JDBC drivers for every database engine it needs. In the pure 2-tier approach, the application logic runs on the client. In a less-pure 2-tier approach, you can offload some of the application logic to stored procedures on the database engine. You should note that stored procedures are extremely non-standard. They lock you into a proprietary vendor implementation. For example, you write Oracle stored procedures in PL/SQL; you write Microsoft stored procedures in Transact-SQL. You should not use stored procedures if you want your JDBC applications to be portable across mulivendor DBMSs.

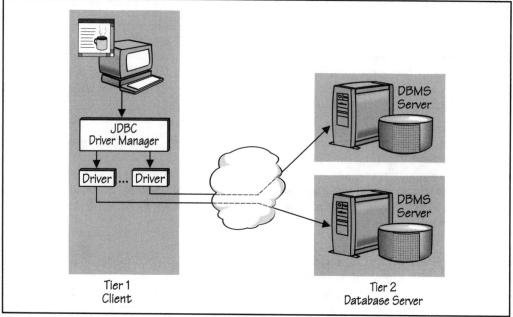

Figure 24-3. JDBC 2-Tier.

JDBC 2-Tier Plus

Figure 24-4 shows an innovative twist of the 2-tier architecture model; we'll call it *2-tier Plus*. The 2-tier Plus approach introduces a middle-tier "JDBC driver server" that sits between the client and the DBMS engines. Clients invoke normal JDBC calls that are then transmitted—via ORB or RPC—to the JDBC driver manager on the server. The driver manager hands the call to the appropriate JDBC driver. In 2-tier Plus, all the JDBC drivers reside on the server side. Examples of 2-tier Plus products include Symantec's *dbANYWHERE*, Visigenic's *VisiChannel*, and I-Kinetics' *OPENjdbc*. Symantec uses a sockets-based RPC to communicate calls between the client and the driver server; Visigenic and I-Kinetics use CORBA. In both cases, the underlying ORB is totally transparent to your clients; you simply invoke JDBC calls.

The 2-tier Plus approach is a major improvement over simple 2-tier. Here are some of the benefits:

■ *A simpler client environment.* You have less software to install and maintain on the client. You don't need to be constantly deploying the "latest and greatest" JDBC drivers to each client. In addition, you don't have to deal with conflicting JDBC drivers on the client and their CLASSPATH requirements. In general,

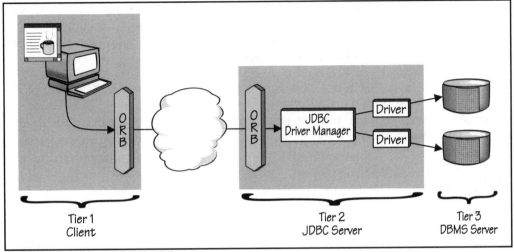

Figure 24-4. JDBC 2-Tier Plus.

2-tier Plus removes some of the administrative burdens associated with managing the 2-tier client.

- ■ *A mixed client environment.* For example, I-Kinetics provides CORBA IDL definitions of the JDBC interface. This allows clients written in any CORBA-compliant language (such as C++ and Smalltalk) to invoke its JDBC middle-tier server.

- ■ *Standard client/server middleware.* Both I-Kinetics and Visigenic use CORBA IIOP as a standard client/server middleware for JDBC. The I-Kinetics middle-tier server—called *DataBroker*—supports any IIOP-compliant CORBA ORB—including VisiBroker and Orbix.

- ■ *A managed server environment.* All the drivers are on the server. This makes it easier to upgrade, maintain, and control the JDBC environment. It lets you easily add or replace third-party JDBC drivers. And, it also reduces your administrative overhead.

- ■ *A more secure environment.* You can centralize all data access controls on the server. You're also dealing with a single point of management for security.

- ■ *A better performing client/server environment.* The 2-tier Plus architecture could potentially improve the performance of a system by caching data on the server. For example, *dbANYWHERE* allows a server to satisfy requests for recently accessed data directly from its cache; it doesn't need to access the DBMS for every request. In addition, *dbANYWHERE* can cache the results of a large query; it then returns, on demand, subsets of the query results. In theory, caching can dramatically reduce bandwidth requirements. Consequently, it can improve performance. You should run the JDBC benchmarking toolkit and find out for yourself if practice matches theory.

You must remember that 2-tier Plus is still a fat client approach. The bulk of the application logic still runs on the client. So your nightmares may not be over. On the plus side, the client can be a lot slimmer than its 2-tier counterpart; the drivers are now on the server.

JDBC 3-Tier

Figure 24-5 shows a 3-tier JDBC split using distributed objects. In this next step up in the evolutionary scale, a significant part of the application is offloaded from the client to server-side objects. Any function that deals with JDBC data should be on the server side. The idea is to make the application that handles the data reside on the server with the JDBC drivers and possibly the DBMS engine. You can always offload some of the processing by running the DBMS engines on their own server machines. It's all one big trade-off. Again, the JDBC toolkit should help you understand what partitioning scheme can best meet your needs.

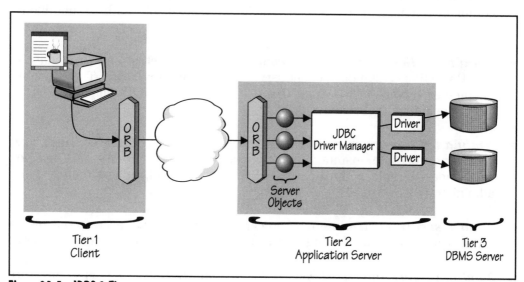

Figure 24-5. JDBC 3-Tier.

LET'S CREATE A BANK

In the next two chapters, we will create the 2-tier and 3-tier versions of the Debit-Credit application. The 2-tier version will work with either the 2-tier or 2-tier Plus drivers. The 3-tier Debit-Credit is a pure CORBA/Java solution. But first, let's create the Bank database that we will use in the next two chapters.

We will develop a small JDBC program that consists of two Java classes: **Create-Bank** and **BankAdmin**. The **CreateBank** simply provides a *main* method that creates a **BankAdmin** object. The **BankAdmin** does all the work. We broke it down into classes to make it easier for you to include **BankAdmin** with your programs; it doesn't have a *main*.

The CreateBank Class

CreateBank simply provides a *main* method and creates a **BankAdmin**. Here's the code:

Listing 24-1. The CreateBank Class.

```java
// CreateBank.java

class CreateBank {

  public static void main(String args[])
  {
    try
    {
      BankAdmin myBank = new BankAdmin();
      if (args.length == 1)
        myBank.createDB(Integer.parseInt(args[0]));
      else
        myBank.createDB(1);
      System.out.println("Database bank created");
    } catch( Exception e )
    {
      System.out.println("Creation of database bank failed");
      e.printStackTrace();
      System.exit(1);
    }
    System.exit(0);
  }
}
```

The BankAdmin Class

The **BankAdmin** class is the worker object that creates the database and populates it with data. It provides the following methods: *createDB, connect, closeConnection, createBank, createBankTables, createBankProcedures, loadBankData, createBankIndexes,* and *dropBank.* The *createBank* method is the top-level function; it calls all the other methods in sequence. Here are the steps it follows: 1) loads a JDBC driver, 2) connects to a DBMS server via a JDBC URL, 3) deletes an existing bank database, 4) creates a new database called bank, 5) reconnects to the bank database, 6) creates the four Debit-Credit tables, 7) adds a stored procedure that lets us do an update-in-place of an account balance, 8) loads the tables with bank data, and 9) creates indexes on these tables. Here's the code:

Listing 24-2. The BankAdmin Class.

```
// BankAdmin.java   JDBC Bank Class
package DCBank;
import java.net.URL;
import java.sql.*;

class BankAdmin
{
  Connection con;
  Statement stmt;
  PreparedStatement pstmt;

  public void createDB(int tps) throws Exception
  {
    connect("LocalServer", "master", "sa", "");
    dropBank();
    createBank();
    closeConnection();
    connect("LocalServer", "bank", "sa", "");
    createBankTables();
    createBankProcedures();
    loadBankData(tps);
    createBankIndexes();
  }

  public void connect(String datasource, String db,
                      String id, String pw)
                      throws Exception
  {
    try
```

```
  {
    // Load the jdbc-odbc bridge driver
    // Class.forName ("sun.jdbc.odbc.JdbcOdbcDriver");
    // String url   = "jdbc:odbc:" + datasource + ";database=" + db;

    // Load Connect Software's FastForward JDBC driver
    Class.forName ("connect.microsoft.MicrosoftDriver");
    String url = "jdbc:ff-microsoft://" + datasource + ":1433/" + db;

    System.out.println("Connecting to " + url);
    con = DriverManager.getConnection(url, id, pw);
  } catch(Exception e)
  { System.err.println("System Exception in connect");
    System.err.println(e);
    throw e;
  }
}
public void closeConnection() throws Exception
{
  try
  {
    System.out.println("Closing connection");
    con.close();
  } catch (Exception e)
  { System.err.println("System Exception in closeConnection");
    System.err.println(e);
    throw e;
  }
}


private void dropBank() throws Exception
{
  try
  {
    System.out.println("Dropping database bank");
    stmt = con.createStatement();
    stmt.execute("DROP DATABASE bank");
    stmt.close();
  } catch(Exception e)
  { System.err.println("System Exception in dropBank");
    System.err.println(e);
  }
}
```

```java
private void createBank() throws Exception
{
  try
  {
    System.out.println("Creating database bank");
    stmt = con.createStatement();
    stmt.execute("CREATE DATABASE bank ON bank = 30");
    stmt.close();
  } catch(Exception e)
  { System.err.println("System Exception in createDBbank");
    System.err.println(e);
    throw e;
  }
}


private void createBankTables() throws Exception
{
  try
  {
    System.out.println("Creating bank tables");
    stmt = con.createStatement();
    stmt.execute("CREATE TABLE ACCOUNT(" +
                 "ACCT_NUM INT NOT NULL, " +
                 "NAME CHAR(20) NOT NULL, " +
                 "BRANCH_ID SMALLINT NOT NULL, " +
                 "BALANCE INT NOT NULL, " +
                 "ADDRESS CHAR(30) NOT NULL, " +
                 "TEMP1 CHAR(40) NOT NULL)");

    stmt.execute("CREATE TABLE BRANCH(" +
                 "BRANCH_ID SMALLINT NOT NULL, " +
                 "BRANCH_NAME CHAR(20) NOT NULL, " +
                 "BALANCE INT NOT NULL, " +
                 "AREA_CODE CHAR(4) NOT NULL, " +
                 "ADDRESS CHAR(30) NOT NULL, " +
                 "TEMP1 CHAR(40) NOT NULL)");

    stmt.execute("CREATE TABLE TELLER(" +
                 "TELLER_ID   SMALLINT NOT NULL, " +
                 "TELLER_NAME CHAR(20) NOT NULL, " +
                 "BRANCH_ID SMALLINT NOT NULL, " +
                 "BALANCE INTEGER  NOT NULL, " +
                 "TELLER_CODE CHAR(2)  NOT NULL, " +
```

```
                "ADDRESS CHAR(30) NOT NULL, " +
                "TEMP1 CHAR(40) NOT NULL)");

    stmt.execute("CREATE TABLE HISTORY( " +
                "ACCT_NUM INTEGER NOT NULL, " +
                "TELLER_ID SMALLINT NOT NULL, " +
                "BRANCH_ID SMALLINT NOT NULL, " +
                "BALANCE INTEGER NOT NULL, " +
                "DELTA INTEGER NOT NULL, " +
                "PID INTEGER NOT NULL, " +
                "TRANSID INTEGER NOT NULL, " +
                "ACCTNAME CHAR(20) NOT NULL, " +
                "TEMP1 CHAR(6) NOT NULL)");

    con.commit();
    stmt.close();
  } catch(Exception e)
  { System.err.println("System Exception in createBankTables");
    System.err.println(e);
    throw e;
  }
}


private void createBankProcedures() throws Exception
{
  try
  {
    System.out.println("Creating bank Stored Procedures");
    stmt = con.createStatement();
    stmt.execute("CREATE PROCEDURE " +
                "UpdateAcctBalance(@acct_num INT, @delta INT) AS \n"+
                "DECLARE c1 CURSOR FOR " +
                "SELECT BALANCE FROM ACCOUNT WHERE " +
                "ACCT_NUM = @acct_num FOR UPDATE\n" +
                "OPEN c1 \n" +
                "FETCH NEXT FROM c1 \n" +
                "UPDATE ACCOUNT SET BALANCE = BALANCE + @delta " +
                        "WHERE CURRENT OF c1 \n" +
                "CLOSE c1 \n" +
                "DEALLOCATE c1 \n"
                );
    con.commit();
    stmt.close();
  } catch(Exception e)
```

```java
    { System.err.println("System Exception in createBankTables");
      System.err.println(e);
      throw e;
    }



}
private void loadBankData(int tps) throws Exception
{
   String   name     = "<--20 BYTE STRING-->";
   String   address  = "<------ 30 BYTE STRING ------>";
   String   temp1    = "<----------- 40 BYTE STRING ----------->";
   int      balance = 1000;
   int      acctNum = 0;
   short    branchID = 0;
   short    tellerID = 0;
   String   tellerCode = "ab";
   String   areaCode = "abcd";
   try
   {
     System.out.println("Inserting bank data");
     con.setAutoCommit(false);

     // Calculate Start time
     System.out.println("Starting data insertion into ACCOUNT table..");
     long startTime = System.currentTimeMillis();

     pstmt = con.prepareStatement(
     "INSERT INTO ACCOUNT (ACCT_NUM, NAME, BRANCH_ID, " +
     "BALANCE, ADDRESS, TEMP1) VALUES ( ?, ?, ?, ?, ?, ? )");

     // Insert accounts in ACCOUNT table, commit every 10,000 rows
     for (int i=0; i < tps; i++)
     {
       for (int j=0; j < 10; j++)
       {
         pstmt.setString(2, name);
         pstmt.setInt(4, balance);
         pstmt.setString(5, address);
         pstmt.setString(6, temp1);
         for (int k=1; k <= 10000; k++)
         {
           acctNum = i*100000 + j*10000 + k;
           branchID = (short)(Math.random() * 10 + 1);
```

```java
            pstmt.setInt(1, acctNum);
            pstmt.setShort(3, branchID);
            pstmt.executeUpdate();
        }

        con.commit();
        System.out.println(acctNum + " accounts created.");
    }
}

pstmt.close();
long stopTime = System.currentTimeMillis();
System.out.println("Account table load complete.");
System.out.println("Load time = " +
                    ((stopTime - startTime)/(1000f)) +
                    " seconds");

// Insert 100 tellers into TELLER table
pstmt = con.prepareStatement(
            "INSERT INTO TELLER (TELLER_ID, TELLER_NAME, " +
            "BRANCH_ID, BALANCE, TELLER_CODE, ADDRESS, TEMP1) " +
            "VALUES ( ?, ?, ?, ?, ?, ?, ?)");
pstmt.setString(2, name);
pstmt.setInt(4, balance);
pstmt.setString(5, tellerCode);
pstmt.setString(6, address);
pstmt.setString(7, temp1);

for (tellerID = 1; tellerID <= 100; tellerID++)
{ branchID = (short)(Math.random() * 10 + 1);
  pstmt.setShort(1, tellerID);
  pstmt.setShort(3, branchID);
  pstmt.executeUpdate();
}

con.commit();
pstmt.close();
System.out.println("Teller Insert succeeded.");

// Insert 10 Branches into BRANCH table
pstmt = con.prepareStatement(
            "INSERT INTO BRANCH (BRANCH_ID, BRANCH_NAME, " +
            "BALANCE, AREA_CODE, ADDRESS, TEMP1) " +
            "VALUES ( ?, ?, ?, ?, ?, ?)");
```

```java
      pstmt.setString(2, name);
      pstmt.setInt(3, balance);
      pstmt.setString(4, areaCode);
      pstmt.setString(5, address);
      pstmt.setString(6, temp1);

      for (branchID = 1; branchID  <= 10; branchID++)
      {
        pstmt.setShort(1, branchID);
        pstmt.executeUpdate();
      }

      con.commit();
      pstmt.close();
      System.out.println("Branch Insert succeeded.");
      System.out.println("Bank data insertion complete");
    } catch(Exception e)
    { System.err.println("System Exception in loadBankData");
      System.err.println(e);
      throw e;
    }
  }


  private void createBankIndexes() throws Exception
  {
    try
    {
      System.out.println("Creating bank indexes");

      stmt = con.createStatement();
      stmt.execute("CREATE INDEX ACCTINDX ON ACCOUNT(ACCT_NUM)");
      stmt.execute("CREATE INDEX BRANINDX ON BRANCH(BRANCH_ID)");
      stmt.execute("CREATE INDEX TELLINDX ON TELLER(TELLER_ID)");

      con.commit();
      stmt.close();
    } catch(Exception e)
    { System.err.println("System Exception in createBankIndexes");
      System.err.println(e);
      throw e;
    }
  }
}
```

Most of this code is straight JDBC. It should be understandable if you read the "world's longest tutorial." However, the *loadBankData* method really requires further explanation. What we're doing is following the rules specified by the Debit-Credit benchmark for loading data in the tables. The benchmark specifies rules for scaling the database size and for randomizing the data that appears in some of the tables. Here's how we implement these rules.

First, note that we pass to *main* a *tps* argument that represents a scaling factor for the size of the database to be built. The database of a 1-tps system is defined as:

```
100,000 Accounts
100 Tellers
10 Branches
```

The *loadBankData* method creates a database whose size is a multiple of the 1-tps numbers shown above. The scaling factor is provided by the tps parameter that you pass to the program. If you do not pass an argument, the default is to create a 1-tps database. Make sure you have enough disk space to accommodate the tps number you provide.

Next, here's a description of what data goes into each table:

- The **ACCOUNTS** table contains an entry for each customer account record. We generate this data one row at a time using host variables. Here are the rules we follow:

  - This table contains tps*100,000 rows; each row is 100 bytes long—it represents a customer's bank account.

  - A row contains the account number, the account balance, the customer's name and address, and the branch_id. The account records have account numbers from 1 to (tps*100,000).

  - The branch_id is a random number from 1 to (tps*10). The Debit-Credit benchmark requires that the accounts you use for a given transaction be truly random. To accomplish this effect, we generate the branch_id field as a pseudo-random number using Java's *Math.random* function.

  - We commit to the database after every 10,000 inserts to prevent our logs from overflowing.

- The **TELLER** table contains an entry for each teller in all of the branch offices. We generate this data one row at a time using host variables. Here are the rules we follow:

- This table contains (tps*100) rows. Each row is 100 bytes long; it represents a bank teller in a branch office.

- A row contains the teller_id, the teller name, the branch_id, the teller balance, a teller code of "ab", and the address strings.

- The branch_id is a random number from 1 to (tps*10).

- The teller_id's are generated sequentially and range from 1 to (tps*100).

■ The **BRANCH** table contains an entry for each branch office. We generate this data one row at a time using host variables. Here are the rules we follow:

- This table contains (tps*10) rows. Each row is 100 bytes long; it represents a bank branch office.

- A row contains the branch_id, the branch name and address strings, and the branch balance.

- The branch numbers are generated sequentially and range from 1 to (tps*10).

■ The **HISTORY** table contains an entry for each Debit-Credit transaction executed against the database. This table gets populated when you execute the benchmark.

We've completed our first JDBC program. Most SQL programmers will find it quite familiar. The complications were mostly inflicted by the rules of the benchmark.

COMPILE THE CREATE BANK PROGRAM

We're now ready to compile our first JDBC program. Make sure you've installed Symantec Visual Café. To compile, go to the appropriate directory and enter the following commands at the prompt:

```
prompt> javac -d \CorbaJavaBook.2e\classes BankAdmin.java
prompt> javac -d \CorbaJavaBook.2e\classes CreateBank.java
```

The -d option tells the compiler to put the (.class) files it creates into the directory we specify—in this case, the *\CorbaJavaBook.2e\classes* subdirectory.

If all goes well, you should have some compiled Java code that you can now run.

RUN THE CREATE BANK PROGRAM

We're now ready to create a bank database. Note that the *CreateBank* program uses Connect Software's *FastForward* native JDBC driver. To run the program, you must first install Microsoft *SQL Server 6.5*. To install SQL Server, follow the instructions on the CD-ROM.

You can now create a bank database and load it with data. At the prompt, enter the following command:

prompt> java CreateBank 1

Notice that we're using a 1-tps database. However, you can load as much data as you want by simply changing the tps number. Be careful though; it can fill up your disk very fast.

Debit-Credit: To Cheat or Not To Cheat?

To produce correct results, you must strictly follow the Debit-Credit benchmark specification. The toolkit lets you control the benchmark environment at a very granular level. You can decide on a level of adherence that works for you. In this book, we chose to follow a very lax interpretation. This is another way of saying *we will do a little bit of cheating*. Why?

Remember, our focus is on the relative performance measurements of client/server architectures. We are *purposely not measuring maximum raw performance* so as not to get embroiled in the controversial benchmarking wars. This difference leads us to purposely run our tests on ordinary PCs, not superservers. We also use a lax interpretation of Debit-Credit when loading our data. So, please don't quote any numbers in this book as absolute. But you can quote the relative results—for example, 2-tier vs. 3-tier or static vs. dynamic SQL.

Having made this disclaimer, we still want to point out that the toolkit provides a very credible set of tools for doing some useful benchmark work, if you can afford the right hardware platform. This means lots of memory, many client machines on a network, a heavy-duty "superserver" machine with disk arrays, and lots of disk space for the 60-day history table.

For your information, we've included a list of *common shortcuts*—this is another polite word for cheating. This is what people in the business warn you to look for when evaluating *other* people's benchmark results (see Table 24-1).

Table 24-1. Debit-Credit: To Cheat or Not To Cheat.

Debit-Credit Requirements	Common "Shortcuts"	What You Can Do With the Toolkit
Database scaling	None	Yes. Specify the required tps level.
Some user interface	None	Yes. We have an AWT panel.
Open benchmark code	Not available	Source and executable code is available and fully documented in this book.
Network support	None	2 versions of networked Debit-Credit: - 2-Tier using JDBC remote driver - 3-Tier using CORBA
Single History table	Multiple tables	Single table.
1-second response time	Not measured	Returns the average transaction time.
95 percent of transactions under 1 second	Not measured	Returns the average transaction time.
Random account numbers	Not provided	Yes.
90-day history	No provisions	Yes, if you provide enough disk space.
Error-checking	None	SQL return codes. Will check if account is non-existent.
Frequent checkpoints	Not activated	Under your control.
Steady state response	Not measured	Under your control using MultiConsole.

CONCLUSION

We now have a database full of data. So, where do we go from here? The next step is to create our two flavors of Debit-Credit transactions—2-tier and 3-tier—and measure their performance.

Chapter 25

2-Tier Debit-Credit with JDBC

This is the second chapter of a three-chapter series where we develop a Debit-Credit benchmark for JDBC. In this chapter, we create the 2-tier, client/server version of the Debit-Credit transaction. As you will see, it's relatively easy—and tempting—to add JDBC data access to an applet or client application. But, this is also an open invitation for disaster down the road. In our view, you should not use JDBC 2-tier in intergalactic environments.

JDBC itself is a tier-neutral protocol. You can use it in 2-tier as well as 3-tier configurations; JDBC doesn't care. In this sense, JDBC gives you the rope to hang yourself. The verdict is still out on JDBC 2-tier Plus. You can use the client program we develop in this chapter to evaluate it. Our bias is toward 3-tier JDBC—the topic of the next chapter. We believe that 3-tier is the better architecture for the Object Web.

This is going to be a relatively short chapter. We will first develop the 2-tier JDBC Debit-Credit. The good news is that in "pure" 2-tier database applications you must only write code for the client; the server is a shrink-wrapped DBMS engine. We will run our client against the bank database we created in the last chapter. If you haven't done so yet, please review the "world's longest tutorial" (the JDBC tutorial). You'll need it to breeze through this chapter's code.

THE DEBIT-CREDIT 2-TIER ENVIRONMENT

Figure 25-1 shows the Debit-Credit 2-tier testbed. We show two protocols flowing on the network: CORBA and JDBC/SQL. In this 2-tier application, we only use CORBA to organize the benchmark. The **MultiConsole** controls the **Coordinator** via CORBA exchanges. And the clients use CORBA to register their callback interfaces with the **Coordinator**. Finally, the **Coordinator** uses CORBA callbacks to control the races; it tells the clients when to start and stop. This should all be very familiar. We're just reusing code from Chapter 9. So what's new and exciting? The **DebitCredit2TClient** JDBC code is (see dotted lines)! This is the code that executes the DebitCredit transaction.

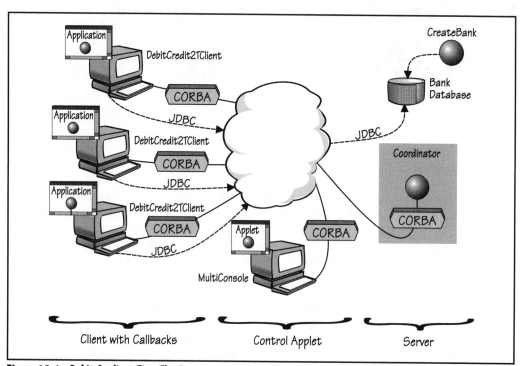

Figure 25-1. Debit-Credit 2-Tier: The Environment.

Figures 25-2 and 25-3 show the 2-tier JDBC setup in more detail. You can run the **DebitCredit2TClient** Java client in either JDBC 2-tier or 2-tier Plus modes. But you must make sure you have the right drivers in place. In this chapter, we use Connect Software's *FastForward* native JDBC driver; it does not provide 2-tier Plus functionality. You can easily modify this program to run with 2-tier Plus products. Note that you can run all the programs on a single machine; it helps during debug.

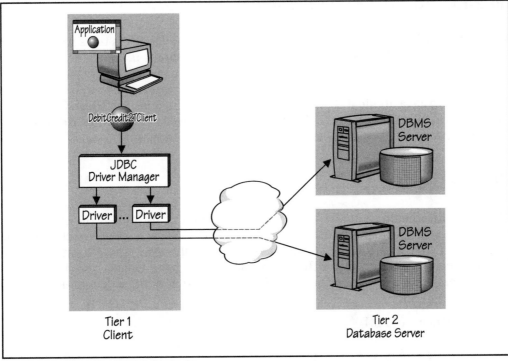

Figure 25-2. The 2-Tier JDBC Debit-Credit.

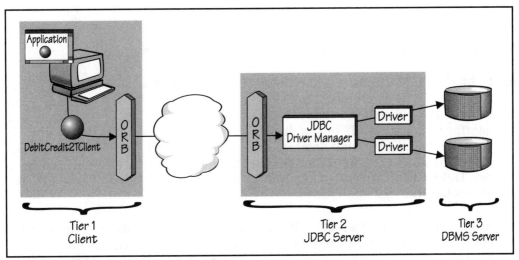

Figure 25-3. The 2-Tier Plus JDBC Debit-Credit.

THE 2-TIER CLIENT/SERVER CODE STRUCTURE

As we said earlier, there is no server code to write—the DBMS is the server. We're also reusing the CORBA server **Coordinator** from Chapter 9. So we're done with the server.

The client is a Java application that includes the following classes: **DebitCredit2T-Client**, **BankDB**, **ClientControlImpl**, **ClientControlThread**, and **ClientDebit-CreditThread**. The last two classes run in their own separate threads.

Meet the Players

We use multithreading to allow the client to walk and chew gum at the same time. It can receive callbacks from the server, respond to local user interactions, and pound the JDBC DBMS server with back-to-back SQL calls. The **ClientControl-Thread** and the **ClientControlImpl** are old friends from Chapter 9; they implement the callback interface. Here's the CORBA IDL that defines this interface:

```
// ClientControl.idl
module Client
{ interface ClientControl
  { // start and stop operations for controlling client counting
    boolean start();
    string  stop();
  };
};
```

Let's take a look at what's new and exciting—the JDBC-related classes:

- **DebitCredit2TClient** provides the *main* method for the client program. This method calls the class constructor. It then resizes the window frame and displays its contents. The class constructor performs the following: 1) creates a user interface consisting of four widgets, 2) creates a new **BankDB** object, 3) connects to a JDBC bank database, 4) creates a new **ClientControlThread** object, 5) starts the **ClientControlThread** in high-priority mode, 6) creates a new **DebitCreditThread** object, and 7) starts the **DebitCreditThread** thread at regular priority.

  In addition to *main*, **DebitCredit2TClient** provides the following three methods: *action*, *startCounting*, and *stopCounting*. The frame invokes the *actionPerformed* method when the user clicks on the "Run" or "Stop" buttons. When this happens, the method simply turns around and invokes its helper functions: *startCounting* and *stopCounting*. The *startCounting* method does the following: 1) resets the transaction count field, 2) calculates the start time, and 3) invokes *resume* on the **DebitCreditThread** object.

The *stopCounting* method does the following: 1) sets the *runTest* flag to false, 2) calculates the stop time, 3) formats the statistics, 4) displays the client's statistics in the status field (see Figure 25-4), and 5) returns the formatted statistics.

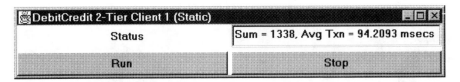

Figure 25-4. The Debit-Credit Client Display.

- **ClientDebitCreditThread** extends the Java **Thread** class. It implements a *run* method that gets invoked when you *start* or *resume* the thread. The *run* method implements a continuous loop that: 1) generates two random number arguments—one for the teller ID and one for the branch ID, 2) invokes the *debitCreditTransaction* method on a **BankDB** object, and 3) increments the local statistics. You control the do-forever loop by suspending and resuming this thread.

- **BankDB** is a worker class; it handles all the interactions with JDBC. We tried to keep this class as general as possible; we will be reusing it in the next chapter. The class provides three public methods: *connect*, *closeConnection*, and *debitCreditTransaction*. This last method does all the Debit-Credit work. It implements two flavors of Debit-Credit: static and dynamic. The static flavor prepares the SQL statements once per benchmark run; it simulates the performance of static SQL. The dynamic flavor prepares the SQL statements every time it is invoked; it simulates dynamic SQL performance. We will look at this method in more detail after you see its code.

It's definitely time for a scenario that shows how all these classes work together. So we'll provide a quick scenario and then jump into the code.

A Multithreaded Scenario

Figure 25-5 shows how the different classes and threads within the client interact with each other and with their servers. In this scenario, a single client is remotely controlled by a **Coordinator** server. Here's a step-by-step explanation of what takes place within a client to make this happen:

1. *Create the callback thread*. The **DebitCredit2TClient** constructor creates a new **ClientControlThread** object and then runs it in a high-priority thread. This object creates a **ClientControlImpl** object that implements the IDL-defined callback interface the client exposes to its servers.

2. *Create the Debit-Credit client thread*. The **DebitCredit2TClient** constructor also creates a new **ClientDebitCreditThread** object and then runs it in a regular-priority thread.

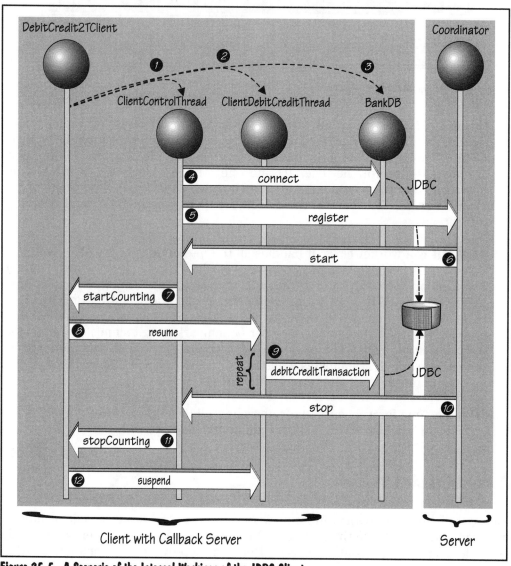

Figure 25-5. A Scenario of the Internal Workings of the JDBC Client.

3. ***Create the JDBC helper object***. The **DebitCredit2TClient** constructor creates a new **BankDB** object. This is the worker object that interacts with JDBC. This object runs within the same thread as its creator—in this case, *main*.

4. ***Connect to a database***. The **DebitCredit2TClient** constructor invokes the *connect* method on **BankDB** and passes it a database name, password, and user ID. The method will load a JDBC driver, which it uses to connect to the database.

5. ***Register the callback with the Coordinator***. The **ClientControlThread** object invokes the *register* method on the **Coordinator**; it passes it the object reference to its callback interface.

6. ***The Coordinator tells everyone to start***. You click on the MultiConsole applet's "Run" button to start the benchmark. The **Coordinator** will relay your command to all the clients that have registered with it by invoking their *start* method via a callback.

7. ***Pass the command to the main thread***. The **ClientControlThread** invokes the *startCounting* method on the **DebitCredit2TClient** object.

8. ***Activate the ClientDebitCreditThread object***. The main thread invokes the *resume* method on the **ClientDebitCreditThread** object to activate its thread. Note that the *start*, *suspend*, and *resume* methods are inherited from the parent **Thread** class.

9. ***Invoke Debit-Credit transactions***. The active **ClientDebitCreditThread** spins in a do-forever loop continuously invoking the *debitCreditTransaction* method on the **BankDB** object. The **BankDB** uses JDBC to submit the Debit-Credit SQL statements to the remote database server.

10. ***The Coordinator tells everyone to stop***. Eventually, you will click on the MultiConsole applet's "Stop" button. The **Coordinator** will then relay your command to all the clients that have registered with it by invoking their *stop* methods. It's a callback.

11. ***Pass the command to the main thread***. The **ClientControlThread** invokes the *stopCounting* method on the **DebitCredit2TClient** object.

12. ***Suspend the ClientDebitCreditThread***. The main thread invokes the *suspend* method on the **ClientDebitCreditThread** object to suspend its thread. This stops the client. The main thread also returns the client's local statistics to the **Coordinator**.

This scenario is very similar to the MultiCount of Chapter 9. One big difference is that we're invoking Debit-Credit transactions instead of Pings. The other big difference is that there's no server-side code to write. The JDBC 2-tier is a fat client.

This means that all the application code runs on the client. The server can be any off-the-shelf SQL database engine that supports JDBC.

THE DEBIT-CREDIT 2-TIER CODE

After this long scenario, you should be ready for some code. So here it is without further ado:

Listing 25-1. 2-Tier Client Code: The DebitCredit2TClient Class.

```java
// DebitCredit2TClient.java

package TwoTier;
import java.awt.*;
import java.awt.event.*;

import org.omg.CosNaming.*;

public class DebitCredit2TClient extends Frame
              implements ActionListener, WindowListener
{ public  TextField statusField;
  private Button run, stop;
  private org.omg.CosNaming.NamingContext nameService;
  public  DCBank.BankDB myBankDB;
  public  long clientSum;
  private long startTime, stopTime;
  private Thread debitCreditThread;
  private Thread controlThread;
  public  String clientNumber;
  boolean runTest = false;
  public  boolean staticTxn = false;

  public DebitCredit2TClient(String[] args)
  {
    if ((args.length == 3) && args[2].equals("static"))
    { staticTxn = true;
      setTitle("DebitCredit 2-Tier Client " + args[0] + " (Static)");
    }
    else
    { staticTxn = false;
      setTitle("DebitCredit 2-Tier Client " + args[0] + " (Dynamic)");
    }

    // Create a 2 by 2 grid of widgets.
    setLayout(new GridLayout(2, 2, 5, 5));
```

```java
// Add the four widgets, initialize where necessary
add(new Label("Status", Label.CENTER));
add(statusField = new TextField());
statusField.setEditable(false);
statusField.setText("ready");
add(run = new Button("Run"));
run.addActionListener(this);
add(stop = new Button("Stop"));
stop.addActionListener(this);
addWindowListener(this);

try
{
  org.omg.CORBA.ORB orb = org.omg.CORBA.ORB.init(args, null);

  // Get a reference to the Naming service
  org.omg.CORBA.Object nameServiceObj =
              orb.resolve_initial_references ("NameService");
  if (nameServiceObj == null)
  {
    statusField.setText("nameServiceObj = null");
    return;
  }

  nameService =
          org.omg.CosNaming.NamingContextHelper.narrow (nameServiceObj);
  if (nameService == null)
  {
    statusField.setText("nameService = null");
    return;
  }

  clientNumber = args[0];
  controlThread = new ClientControlThread(this, args, nameService);
  controlThread.start();
  controlThread.setPriority(Thread.NORM_PRIORITY + 1);

  myBankDB = new DCBank.BankDB();
  myBankDB.connect(args[1], "bank", "sa", "");
  System.out.println("BankDB Object Created");

} catch(Exception e)
{ statusField.setText("Exception" + e);
  System.err.println(e);
}
```

```java
    debitCreditThread = new ClientDebitCreditThread(this);
    debitCreditThread.start();

}


public void windowClosing(WindowEvent event)
{ System.exit(0);
}

public void windowClosed(WindowEvent event) {}
public void windowDeiconified(WindowEvent event) {}
public void windowIconified(WindowEvent event) {}
public void windowActivated(WindowEvent event) {}
public void windowDeactivated(WindowEvent event) {}
public void windowOpened(WindowEvent event) {}


public void actionPerformed(ActionEvent ev)
{
  String arg = ev.getActionCommand();
  if ("Run".equals(arg))
     startCounting();
  if ("Stop".equals(arg))
     stopCounting();
}


public boolean startCounting()
{ // initialize client sum, update status
  clientSum = 0;
  statusField.setText("Running");

  // Calculate Start time
  startTime = System.currentTimeMillis();

  // start test
  runTest = true;
  debitCreditThread.resume();
  return true;
}


public String stopCounting()
```

```
  {
    runTest = false;

    // Calculate stop time; show statistics
    long stopTime = System.currentTimeMillis();
    String statistics = "Sum = " + clientSum + ", Avg Txn = " +
         Float.toString((float)(stopTime - startTime)/(float)clientSum) +
         " msecs";
    statusField.setText(statistics);
    return "Client " + clientNumber + ": " + statistics;
  }


  public static void main(String[] args)
  {
    DebitCredit2TClient f = new DebitCredit2TClient(args);
    f.setSize(480, 90);
    f.show();
  }
}
```

Listing 25-2. 2-Tier Client Code: The ClientControlThread Class.

```
class ClientControlThread extends Thread
{
  private DebitCredit2TClient thisClient;
  private MultiCoordinator.Coordinator myCoordinator;
  private String[] args;
  private org.omg.CosNaming.NamingContext nameService;

  ClientControlThread(DebitCredit2TClient client, String[] myargs,
                      org.omg.CosNaming.NamingContext naming)
  { thisClient = client;
    myargs = args;
    nameService = naming;
  }

  public void run()
  { try
      { // Initialize the ORB
        org.omg.CORBA.ORB orb = org.omg.CORBA.ORB.init(args, null);

        // Create the ClientControl object
        ClientControlImpl control =
```

```
        new ClientControlImpl(thisClient);

    // Export the newly created object
    orb.connect(control);

    // resolve the Coordinator object reference
    NameComponent[] coordName =
              {new NameComponent("Coordinator", "Multi")};
    myCoordinator = MultiCoordinator.CoordinatorHelper.narrow(
                              nameService.resolve(coordName));

    // Register with Coordinator
    if (myCoordinator.register(thisClient.clientNumber,
                        (Client.ClientControl)control))
      {
       System.out.println("Registration Succeeded");
       thisClient.statusField.setText("Ready");
      }
    else
      {
       System.out.println("Registration Failed");
       thisClient.statusField.setText("Registration Failed");
      }

    // Ready to service requests
    System.out.println("Control: Waiting for requests");
    Thread.currentThread().join();
    }
  catch(Exception e)
  { System.err.println(e);
  }
  }
}
```

Listing 25-3. 2-Tier Client Code: The ClientControlImpl Class.

```
class ClientControlImpl extends Client._ClientControlImplBase
                        implements Client.ClientControl
{
  private DebitCredit2TClient thisClient;

  ClientControlImpl(Object client)
  {
    super();
```

```
    thisClient = (DebitCredit2TClient)client;
    System.out.println("Client Control Object Created as client"
                        + thisClient.clientNumber);
  }

  public  boolean start()
  { return thisClient.startCounting();
  }

  public  String stop()
  { return thisClient.stopCounting();
  }

}
```

Listing 25-4. 2-Tier Client Code: The ClientDebitCreditThread Class.

```
class ClientDebitCreditThread extends Thread
{ DebitCredit2TClient myClient;

  ClientDebitCreditThread(DebitCredit2TClient client)
  { myClient = client;
  }

  public void run()
  { // run debit/credit transactions
    while (true)
    { try
      {
        if (!myClient.runTest) this.suspend();
        myClient.myBankDB.debitCreditTransaction(
                                Math.random(),
                                Math.random(),
                                myClient.staticTxn);
        myClient.clientSum++;
      } catch(Exception e)
      { myClient.statusField.setText("System Exception" + e);
        this.suspend();
      }
    }
  }
}
```

Listing 25-5. 2-Tier Client Code: The BankDB Class.

```java
// BankDB.java   JDBC BankDB Class

package DCBank;
import java.net.URL;
import java.sql.*;

public class BankDB
{
  Connection con;
  Driver driver = null;
  ResultSet rs;
  CallableStatement pstmt;
  PreparedStatement pstmt1;
  PreparedStatement pstmt2;
  PreparedStatement pstmt3;
  boolean prepared = false;

  public void connect(String datasource, String db,
                      String id, String pw) throws Exception
  {
    try
    {
      // Load the jdbc-odbc bridge driver
      // Class.forName ("sun.jdbc.odbc.JdbcOdbcDriver");
      // String url   = "jdbc:odbc:" + datasource + ";database=" + db;

      // Load Connect Software's FastForward JDBC driver
      Class.forName ("connect.microsoft.MicrosoftDriver");
      String url = "jdbc:ff-microsoft://" + datasource + ":1433/" + db;

      System.out.println("Connecting to " + url);
      con = DriverManager.getConnection(url, id, pw);

    } catch(Exception e)
    { System.err.println("System Exception in connect");
      System.err.println(e);
      throw e;
    }
  }

  public void closeConnection() throws Exception
  {
    try
```

```
  {
    System.out.println("Closing connection");
    con.close();
  } catch (Exception e)
  { System.err.println("System Exception in closeConnection");
    System.err.println(e);
    throw e;
  }
}

public void debitCreditTransaction(double random1, double random2,
                                   boolean staticTxn)
                                   throws Exception
{
  int     balance = 1000;
  int     delta   = 100;
  int     acctNum = 0;
  short   branchID = 0;
  short   tellerID = 0;
  String  tellerCode = "ab";
  String  areaCode = "abcd";

  try
  {
    // randomly select account, teller, branch
    acctNum  = (int)((random1 * random2 * 100000) + 1);
    tellerID = (short)((random1 * 100) + 1);
    branchID = (short)((random2 *  10) + 1);

    if ((staticTxn && !prepared) || !staticTxn)
    {
      pstmt   = con.prepareCall("{?= call UpdateAcctBalance(?,?)}");
      pstmt1 = con.prepareStatement(
           "UPDATE TELLER SET BALANCE = BALANCE + ? WHERE TELLER_ID = ?");
      pstmt2 = con.prepareStatement(
           "UPDATE BRANCH SET BALANCE = BALANCE + ? WHERE BRANCH_ID = ?");
      pstmt3 = con.prepareStatement(
           "INSERT INTO HISTORY(ACCT_NUM, TELLER_ID, BRANCH_ID, BALANCE, " +
           "DELTA, PID, TRANSID, ACCTNAME, TEMP1) " +
           "VALUES(?, ?, ?, ?, ?, 1, 3, ?, 'hist  ')");
      prepared = true;
    }
    pstmt.registerOutParameter(1,Types.INTEGER);
    pstmt.setInt(2, acctNum);
    pstmt.setInt(3, delta);
```

```java
        pstmt.execute();
        ResultSet rs1 = pstmt.getResultSet();
        rs1.next();
        balance = rs1.getInt(1);
        rs1.close();

        // Update the TELLER table's balance
        pstmt1.setInt(1, delta);
        pstmt1.setShort(2, tellerID);
        pstmt1.executeUpdate();

        // Update the Branch balance
        pstmt2.setInt(1, delta);
        pstmt2.setShort(2, branchID);
        pstmt2.executeUpdate();

        //Update the history
        pstmt3.setInt(1, acctNum);
        pstmt3.setShort(2, tellerID);
        pstmt3.setShort(3, branchID);
        pstmt3.setInt(4, balance);
        pstmt3.setInt(5, delta);
        pstmt3.setString(6, "Account Name, len=20");
        pstmt3.executeUpdate();

        if ((staticTxn && !prepared) || !staticTxn)
        {
          pstmt.close();
          pstmt1.close();
          pstmt2.close();
          pstmt3.close();
        }

        //Commit the Transaction
        con.commit();
      }
    catch( Exception e )
    { System.err.println("System Exception in debitCreditTransaction");
      System.err.println(e);
      con.rollback();
      throw e;
    }
  }
}
}
```

If you read the JDBC tutorial, you'll find that there are no surprises in this code. However, we should really walk you through the *debitCreditTransaction* method of the class **BankDB**. This is the method that does the "real Debit-Credit work." Here's a step-by-step description of what it does:

1. ***Simulate a random event.*** The method uses the two random numbers that are passed to it to generate an account number, teller ID, and branch ID. This simulates a real-world random event as required by the Debit-Credit specification.

2. ***Select an account and update its value.*** We execute this step through the stored procedure patch we told you about earlier (see Listing 24-2 on page 588). The SQL SELECT statement retrieves the balance for that random account from the ACCOUNT table. It then does an UPDATE to add some money to it. We're going to be very generous with everybody! This operation also demonstrates how to use a SQL cursor. You associate the cursor with a SELECT. You can then use the cursor to navigate the results. In this case, we only retrieve a single account (all accounts are unique). The NEXT command causes the cursor to point to the first and only row. We use the cursor to retrieve the balance from this row and then put it into the host variable *balance*. The UPDATE SQL command with the keyword CURRENT updates the row on which the cursor is currently positioned. So your account just got credited with a delta sum.

3. ***Update the teller's balance.*** The code does a non-cursored SQL UPDATE for a random teller in the TELLER table.

4. ***Update the branch's balance.*** The code does a non-cursored SQL UPDATE for a random branch in the BRANCH table.

5. ***Record the transaction in history.*** The code does a SQL INSERT to record the transaction in the HISTORY table. Again, this is straightforward; we just have to make sure that the host variables map to the numbered columns.

6. ***Commit.*** This Debit-Credit transaction is committed for posterity in the database. It makes us all slightly richer. It's a bit like printing money, isn't it?

Notice that this method implements both static and dynamic flavors of SQL, depending on a parameter you pass to *debitCreditTransaction*. The static flavor prepares the SQL statements once per benchmark run. The dynamic flavor prepares each SQL statement every time it is invoked. This simulates dynamic SQL performance. We will run a Debit-Credit 2-tier benchmark that compares the performance of static versus dynamic SQL. This completes the code for 2-tier. Let's compile it and run some benchmarks.

COMPILE DEBIT-CREDIT 2-TIER

We're now ready to compile the Debit-Credit program. First, we must create the skeletons and stubs. Make sure you've installed VisiBroker for Java and OSAgent.

Then go to the appropriate subdirectory and enter the following command at the prompt:

```
prompt> idl2java ClientControl.idl -no_comments
```

To compile the code, make sure you've installed Symantec Visual Café and the Connect Software *FastForward* JDBC driver. Then go to the appropriate directory and run the make file. Or, you can enter the following commands at the prompt:

```
prompt> javac -d \CorbaJavaBook.2e\classes DebitCredit2TClient.java
prompt> javac -d \CorbaJavaBook.2e\classes BankDB.java
```

The -d option tells the compiler to put the (.class) files it creates into the directory we specify, in this case, the *\CorbaJavaBook.2e\classes* subdirectory.

If all goes well, you should have some compiled Java code—including a stub and skeleton—that you can now run.

RUN THE DEBIT-CREDIT 2-TIER BENCHMARK

We will run a simple benchmark with 3 clients. The client machine is a 120 MHz Pentium with 40 MBytes of memory and the server machine is a 233 MHz Pentium with 96 MBytes of memory. The client and server are connected via a 10 Mbit/s Ethernet (see Figure 25-6).

To create the server, you must first install a database that supports JDBC. In this test, we will use Microsoft SQL Server 6.5. To install SQL Server, follow the

Figure 25-6. The Debit-Credit 2-Tier Benchmark Configuration.

instructions on the CD-ROM. Next, you must create a bank database and fill it with data. We will use the **CreateBank** program from the last chapter to do this. At the prompt, enter the following command:

prompt> java CreateBank 1

We're using a 1-tps database. So we're obviously not interested in absolute numbers. However, you should be. You can load as much data as you want by simply changing the tps number. Be careful though—it's the fastest way to fill up a disk drive.

First start the Naming Service as we described in Chapter 7.

Next you must install the **Coordinator**. Let's put it on the server machine. Then enter the following command at the prompt:

prompt> start java -DORBservices=CosNaming
                    -DSVCnameroot=JavaCorba CoordinatorServer

You're now ready to run as many client programs as you require for this benchmark. You can run multiple client programs from the same machine. Or, you can give each client its own machine. In this low-cost benchmark, we will run our three clients from a single machine. To run the clients, you must first install a JDBC driver. We used Connect Software's *FastForward* driver. Next, you must run the client software we developed in this chapter.

To start a dynamic SQL client program, enter the following command at the prompt:

prompt> java -DORBservices=CosNaming -DSVCnameroot=JavaCorba
              TwoTier.DebitCredit2TClient 1 myDBServer

You must give each client a number. The MultiConsole applet uses this number to display the client's statistics. You also pass the name of the database server to the client program. If all goes well, you should see the client's panel on the screen. You can ignore it for now. You'll be running the benchmarks using the MultiConsole panel.

To start a static SQL client program, enter the following command at the prompt:

prompt> java -DORBservices=CosNaming -DSVCnameroot=JavaCorba
              TwoTier.DebitCredit2TClient 1 myDBServer static

Notice that if you don't enter the *static* parameter, the program automatically defaults to dynamic SQL.

Finally, you'll also need to run the **MultiConsole** from Chapter 9. This is the applet that controls the races. You can run it from anywhere. In this low-cost benchmark,

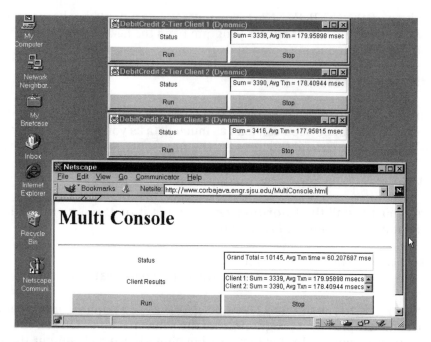

Figure 25-7. A Debit-Credit 2-Tier Dynamic SQL Run With 3 Clients.

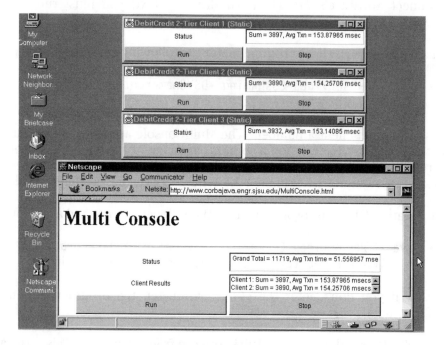

Figure 25-8. A Debit-Credit 2-Tier Static SQL Run With 3 Clients.

we'll run it on the same machine as our three clients—this should save you some walking. To do this, install Netscape Communicator on the client. Then point to an HTML page that contains the applet; you can use the HTML file from Chapter 9.

The MultiConsole applet should appear within the browser. At this point, you're ready to run the benchmark. So click on the "Run" button. Let the benchmark run for least ten minutes (look at your watch). Finally, click on the "Stop" button to see the results. Figure 25-7 shows the screen capture of a dynamic SQL run. Figure 25-8 shows the screen capture of a static SQL run.

The results show that static (or precompiled) SQL is about 15% faster than dynamic SQL (19.4 tps versus 16.6 tps). So it helps to precompile your SQL statements if you're going to repeatedly use them.

CONCLUSION

The results from this chapter are what you would expect: the Debit-Credit static SQL is faster than its dynamic counterpart. Most importantly this chapter demonstrates a realistic JDBC application in action using the 2-tier model. This application can serve as a model for writing 2-tier client/server applications using JDBC. Finally, this chapter demonstrates the flexibility of our benchmarking architecture. We were able to reuse most of the code from Chapter 9 without change.

Chapter 26

3-Tier Debit-Credit with JDBC and CORBA

This is the last chapter of a three-chapter series in which we develop a Debit-Credit benchmark for JDBC. In this chapter, we develop the 3-tier client/server version of the Debit-Credit transaction. As you already know, JDBC is a tier-neutral protocol. You can use it in 2-tier as well as 3-tier configurations; JDBC doesn't care.

One of the recurring themes in this book is that the Web is a 3-tier client/server architecture in transition. It is transitioning from HTTP/CGI to distributed objects. The two competing platforms for distributed objects on the Web are CORBA/Java and DCOM/ActiveX (with some Java). They are both inherently 3-tier.

In comparison, the 2-tier JDBC approach is a throwback to the past. It lets client applications and applets directly manipulate the database. This may be OK in certain controlled situations, but it's not a good solution for the intergalactic Web. We believe that 3-tier is the better architecture for the Object Web. We will make our case later in this chapter.

But before we can run benchmarks, we must develop a working 3-tier application framework that uses CORBA, Java, and JDBC. As you may have guessed, there isn't one that you can just get off-the-shelf. So, we must develop it from scratch. This chapter will create a rudimentary server-side framework for 3-tier solutions that uses JDBC, CORBA, and Java. We will use this framework to develop the 3-tier version of Debit-Credit. Finally, we will run the 3-tier benchmark. You will then be able to do an apple-to-apple comparison of JDBC 2-tier versus 3-tier.

THE 3-TIER DEBIT-CREDIT ENVIRONMENT

Figure 26-1 shows the 3-tier JDBC Debit-Credit testbed. The middleware is all CORBA. There are no JDBC/SQL message exchanges on this network. We use CORBA for client/server exchanges as well as for controlling the benchmark.

The 3-tier benchmark introduces two new Java programs. The first is **DebitCredit-MultiClient**—a "thin" client that invokes CORBA servers. It replaces the **DebitCredit2TClient**—a "fat" client that directly invokes JDBC. The second program is **DebitCreditServer**. This is a new middle-tier CORBA/Java server application. It's a poor man's TP Monitor for server objects.

In the 3-tier Debit-Credit, CORBA clients talk to CORBA server objects. The server objects in turn talk to one or more DBMSs via JDBC. In the 2-tier case, the clients bypass the middle-tier server and go directly to the DBMS.

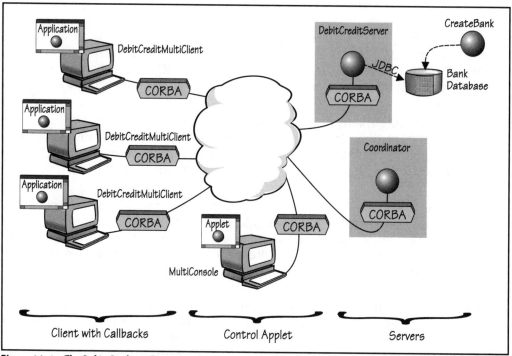

Figure 26-1. The Debit-Credit 3-Tier Environment.

Figure 26-2 shows the 3-tier JDBC setup in more detail. You will need VisiBroker for Java to provide the ORB services. You must make sure you have the right JDBC drivers in place on the server side. There are no drivers on the client.

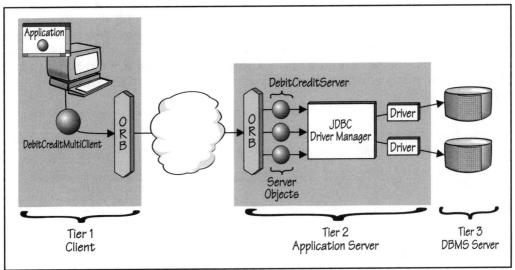

Figure 26-2. The 3-Tier JDBC Debit-Credit.

THE DEBIT-CREDIT 3-TIER CODE STRUCTURE

The 3-tier Debit-Credit requires that we write both client and server code. The multithreaded client is an application that consists of the following Java classes: **DebitCreditMultiClient**, **ClientControlImpl**, **ClientControlThread**, and **ClientDebitCreditThread**. You already saw these last three in the 2-tier Debit-Credit. They provide the same function within a 3-tier client/server configuration.

The server-side consists of the following classes: **DebitCreditServer**, **DispenserImpl**, **DebitCreditStatus**, **DebitCreditImpl**, and **BankDB**. This is the same **BankDB** worker class that you encountered in the last chapter. We moved it to the server side, as is. That should tell you something about the new division of labor. In a 3-tier thin client implementation, the work is done on the server side. The idea is that only the server should deal with the database. So this is why we moved **BankDB** to the server.

We're also using the CORBA server **Coordinator** from Chapter 9. You can run it on a separate server machine or on the same server as Debit-Credit. You can decide where to run it when you execute the benchmark.

Meet the Client Players

The multithreaded design lets the client walk and chew gum at the same time. The client's structure is very similar to the one from the last chapter, except that the Debit-Credit logic is now on the server. Instead of invoking *debitCredit-Transaction* on a local **BankDB** object, the client must now invoke it on a server object across a CORBA ORB. Consequently, the client must now obtain a reference to a remote server object, and then issue back-to-back remote invocations against it. The **ClientControlThread** and the **ClientControlImpl** are old friends from Chapter 9; they implement the callback interface. Here's the CORBA IDL that defines the interface:

```
interface ClientControl
  { // start and stop operations for controlling client counting
    boolean start();
    string  stop();
  };
```

Let's take a look at our only new client class:

■ **DebitCreditMultiClient** provides the *main* method for the client program. This method calls the class constructor. It then resizes the window frame and displays its contents. The class constructor performs the following: 1) creates a user interface consisting of four widgets, 2) initializes the ORB, 3) locates a **Dispenser** server (more on this later), 4) creates a new **ClientControlThread** object, 5) starts the **ClientControlThread** in high-priority mode, 6) creates a new **DebitCreditThread** object, and 7) starts the **DebitCreditThread**.

In addition to *main*, **DebitCreditMultiClient** provides the following three methods: *actionPerformed*, *startCounting*, and *stopCounting*. These methods behave like their counterparts from the last chapter. The one exception is that *startCounting* must first obtain a reference to a remote Debit-Credit server object. It does this by invoking *reserveDebitCreditObject* on the **Dispenser**. When the benchmark terminates, the *stopCounting* method must release the remote object. It does this by invoking *releaseDebitCreditObject* on the **Dispenser**.

The rest of the classes are unchanged from the last chapter. Even the invocation of the remote server is transparent to the **ClientDebitCreditThread** class. One of the great benefits of reuse is that we don't have to explain this code again.

The Server: What the Client Sees

To participate in the benchmark, clients must interact with our old friend the **Coordinator**. We will reuse it as is, which means there's no new code to explain. So what's new? Figure 26-3 shows the two CORBA interfaces a Debit-Credit server exposes to its clients: **DebitCredit** and **Dispenser**. A client obtains a **DebitCredit** object by invoking the *reserveDebitCreditObject* method on a **Dispenser** object. The client can then invoke the object's *debitCreditTransaction* method as many times as the benchmark requires it. At the end of a benchmark run, the client must release the remote object by invoking *releaseDebitCreditObject*. If the client wants to be a good OLTP citizen, it could even release the server object after each invocation (see the next Briefing box).

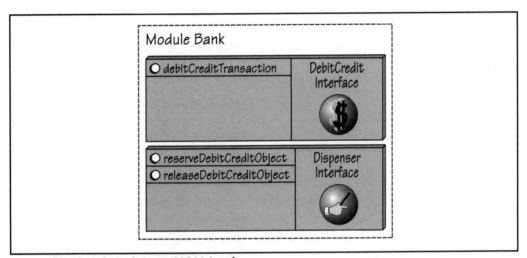

Figure 26-3. The DebitCreditServer CORBA Interfaces.

Why can't the client simply find its own server object using the Naming Service? Why are we putting the **Dispenser** in the middle? What does the added overhead buy us? As you will see in the next section, the **Dispenser** is a broker of server objects. It prestarts and manages a pool of server objects, which it then allocates to clients on demand. Each server object runs in its own thread and maintains a permanent connection to a JDBC database. But we're getting ahead of our story.

Meet the New Server Players

The good news is that the 3-tier Debit-Credit server does not introduce any new JDBC code. We simply reuse **BankDB**. The bad news is that we must create from scratch a CORBA object framework for JDBC. We couldn't find one off the shelf—even though we know of 10 vendors that are working on CORBA Object Transaction

Monitors (see the Enterprise JavaBeans chapter). So we will create a middle-tier framework for SQL databases that provides a poor man's CORBA/Java environment for enforcing the OLTP rules of etiquette (see the next Briefing box).

OLTP Etiquette: The Five Commandments

Briefing

OLTP systems have a 30-year tradition of squeezing every ounce of performance out of system resources. They're the masters of scale. Most of the world's largest client/server systems follow the OLTP discipline. They are typically synchronized by a TP Monitor. To play in an OLTP system, your programs must abide by these commandments:

- ***Thou shalt not covet a system resource for too long***. You must never hog a system resource—including database connections, locks, communication sessions, server objects, and file handles. Clients should never hold state on the server for too long.

- ***Thou shalt use transactions to clean up your messes***. You must use transactions to let the outside world know when you're committing your work. TP Monitors, SQL Databases, and ODBMSs use transaction boundaries to schedule and release the resources you use. Transactions are also used to synchronize the actions of OLTP server-side objects. Finally, transactions provide ACID properties that are used to clean up messes. For example, a resource manager can undo the effects of a failed transaction.

- ***Thou shalt reuse resources across clients***. Servers must prestart pools of resources and allocate them to a client on an as-needed basis. When the client commits (or releases a resource), the server can assign it to another client. System resources are scarce; they must be recycled and shared.

- ***Thou shalt come in, do your work, and get out***. Pat Helland—the MTS architect from Microsoft—calls it the "surgical strike approach." Servers must provide granular services; clients must come in, use the service, and get out.

- ***Thou shalt deal with large numbers of small things***. This typically means that you must componentize your software. TP Monitors were the first to introduce a server component discipline. However, the components were procedural. ORBs and a new generation of Object Transaction Monitors—*Component Broker* from IBM, *MTS* from Microsoft, and *Iceberg* from BEA Systems—will be used to orchestrate server objects.

These five deceptively simple rules capture the folklore OLTP architects have successfully used to create some of the world's most complex distributed systems. Most of these rules apply to server-side CORBA objects. Our object dispenser provides a poor man's framework for applying these rules. The good news is that OLTP only uses five commandments. This could mean that distributed systems are less complicated than their Biblical counterparts. ☐

In addition to **BankDB**, here are the Java classes a 3-tier server supports:

- **DebitCreditServer** provides the *main* method for the server. It provides the following functions: 1) initializes the ORB, 2) creates a new **DispenserImpl** object and passes it the size of the server pool—this is a parameter that you pass to *main*, 3) invokes *orb.connect* to register the newly created **DispenserImpl** object, 4) registers the dispenser with the Naming Service, and 5) waits for incoming requests.

- **DispenserImpl** implements the IDL-defined **Dispenser** interface. The class constructor creates a pool of **DebitCreditImpl** objects and stores their references in an array of **DebitCreditStatus** objects. Finally, it invokes *orb.connect* to register each newly created **DebitCreditImpl** object with the ORB. The class implements two IDL-defined methods: *reserveDebitCreditObject* and *releaseDebitCreditObject*.

```
interface Dispenser
{
  DebitCredit reserveDebitCreditObject() raises (BankException);
  void releaseDebitCreditObject(in DebitCredit debitCreditObject)
                               raises (BankException);
};
```

The *reserveDebitCreditObject* method finds an available **DebitCredit** object and returns its reference to the client. It then marks the object as busy. The *releaseDebitCreditObject* method returns an object reference that you pass to the pool of available server objects.

- **DebitCreditImpl** implements the IDL-defined **DebitCredit** interface. The class constructor creates a new **BankDB** object and then connects to it. The object is preconnected to the database. The class implements the IDL-defined method *debitCreditTransaction*.

```
interface DebitCredit
{
  void debitCreditTransaction(in double random1,
                             in double random2, boolean staticTxn)
                             raises (BankException);
};
```

The *debitCreditTransaction* method is where you would put the non-data part of the logic in a more general application. In this case, it simply delegates the *debitCreditTransaction* invocation to **BankDB**. This is what helpers are for! We already crawled through the **BankDB** implementation of this method in the last chapter. Remember, this is the method that actually performs the Debit-Credit transaction. It's where the buck stops.

■ **DebitCreditStatus** implements a structure with two fields: *reference* and *inUse*. The first field stores the reference to a server object. The second field contains its current status. The **DispenserImpl** maintains an array of these field-pairs to keep track of the pool of objects that it controls.

The bottom line is that the **Dispenser** maintains a pool of server objects. Each object has its own **BankDB** object. Each server object maintains a live JDBC connection to an SQL database via its **BankDB** object (see Figure 26-4). The **Dispenser** assigns these objects to clients on a first-come basis.

You can easily extend this simple-minded scheduler to provide more exciting functions. For example, you can schedule objects based on client priority, load-balancing conditions, table routing, and so on. You should also be able to prestart objects dynamically based on the load conditions. But, we'll leave these add-ons as an exercise for the reader. We must first get our "simple-minded" scheduler to work as advertised.

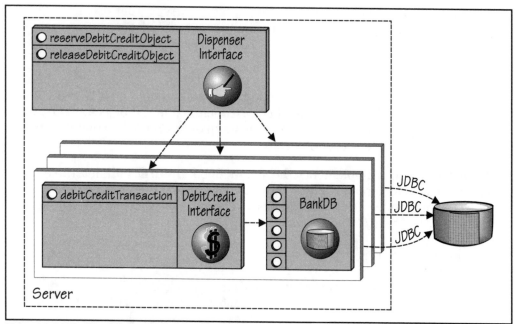

Figure 26-4. The Dispenser as a Scheduler of Server Objects.

It's time for a scenario. But before we do this, we have a quiz: Where are the threads in this multithreaded server? Who creates and starts the threads? And, what code runs inside a thread? These are all very legitimate questions. Without multithreading, the concept of a server pool is totally meaningless. But as you will soon see in our server code, there is no mention of threads anywhere. Do you know the answer?

OK, let's put an end to the suspense. The threads are created and run by the ORB. All we have to do is create multiple instances of our server objects. The ORB will then run each object in its own thread. In this case, VisiBroker for Java will run each instance of **DebitCreditImpl** in its own thread.

A 3-Tier Client/Server Scenario

Figure 26-5 shows how the 3-tier client and server classes interact with each other. In this scenario, a single client is invoking back-to-back Debit-Credit calls on the server. Let's walk through this scenario:

1. ***The client creates the Debit-Credit client thread***. The **DebitCreditMulti-Client** constructor creates a new **ClientDebitCreditThread** object and then runs it as a thread.

2. ***The server creates a dispenser object***. The **DebitCreditServer** creates a **DispenserImpl** object and passes it the size of the server pool. Note that the **DispenserImpl** class implements the IDL-defined **Dispenser** interface.

3. ***The dispenser prestarts a pool of server objects***. The **DispenserImpl** creates a pool of **DebitCreditImpl** objects and stores their references in an array of **DebitCreditStatus** objects. It also invokes *orb.connect* to register each newly created **DebitCreditImpl** object with the ORB.

4. ***The server object creates its JDBC helper***. Each **DebitCreditImpl** object creates a **BankDB** helper. This is the worker object that will interact with JDBC. Note that this object runs within the same thread as its creator.

5. ***The server object connects to the database.*** Each **DebitCreditImpl** object invokes *connect* on its **BankDB** helper to open a JDBC connection with a SQL database. Here's another quiz: Why is it so important to prestart these database connections? The answer is that a database connect is typically very slow—it can take many seconds to execute. It's a logon. So you don't want to connect to a database every time a client requests a service. To get around this problem, TP Monitors have traditionally maintained pools of prestarted processes that are already connected to a database. This is an example of how TP Monitors have learned how to squeeze the most performance out of system resources over the years.

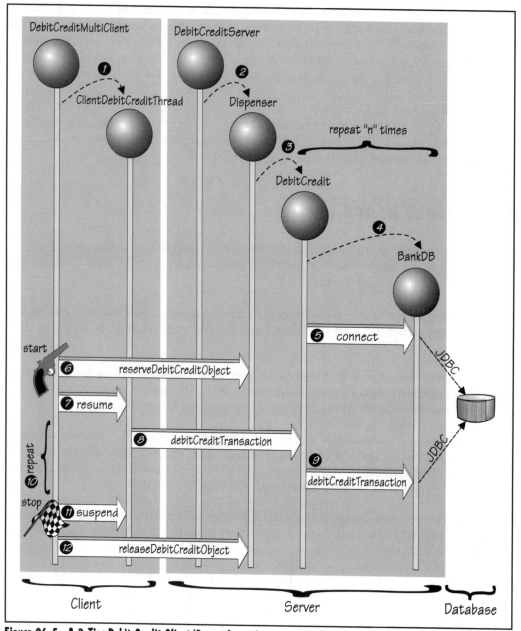

Figure 26-5. A 3-Tier Debit-Credit Client/Server Scenario.

6. **_The client requests a server object._** The client invokes _reserveDebitCredit-Object_ on the **Dispenser** to obtain a server object.

7. **_The client activates the ClientDebitCreditThread object_**. The main thread

invokes the *resume* method on the **ClientDebitCreditThread** object to activate its thread. Note that the *start, suspend,* and *resume* methods are inherited from the parent **Thread** class.

8. ***The client invokes Debit-Credit transactions.*** The **ClientDebitCredit-Thread** spins in a do-forever loop continuously invoking the *debitCredit-Transaction* method on the remote CORBA server object.

9. ***The server object delegates to the helper.*** The **DebitCreditImpl** invokes the *debitCreditTransaction* method of its **BankDB** helper object. The **BankDB** issues SQL calls via JDBC to the database engine.

10. ***Repeat the invocations.*** The client looping will continue until the **Coordinator** tells everyone to stop.

11. ***Suspend the ClientDebitCreditThread.*** The main thread invokes the *suspend* method on the **ClientDebitCreditThread** object to suspend its thread. This stops the client invocations. The main thread also returns the client's local statistics to the **Coordinator**.

12. ***Release the server object.*** The client invokes *releaseDebitCreditObject* on the **Dispenser** to return the server object to the pool; it must pass the object reference as a parameter.

THE 3-TIER DEBIT-CREDIT CODE

After this long scenario, you should be ready for some code. We hope all the mysteries have been unraveled. Consequently, it should read like a novel. So here's the straight code.

The Debit-Credit 3-Tier Client Code

Listing 26-1. 3-Tier Client Code: The DebitCreditMultiClient Class.

```java
// DebitCreditMultiClient.java

package ThreeTier;
import java.awt.*;
import java.awt.event.*;
import org.omg.CosNaming.*;

public class DebitCreditMultiClient extends Frame
          implements ActionListener, WindowListener
```

```java
{ public  TextField statusField;
  private Button run, stop;
  private org.omg.CosNaming.NamingContext nameService;
  public  Bank.DebitCredit myDebitCredit;
  public  Bank.Dispenser   myDispenser;
  public  long clientSum;
  private long startTime, stopTime;
  private Thread debitCreditThread;
  private Thread controlThread;
  public  String clientNumber;
  boolean runTest = false;
  public  boolean staticTxn = false;

  public DebitCreditMultiClient(String[] args)
  {
    if ((args.length == 2) && args[1].equals("static"))
    { staticTxn = true;
      setTitle("DebitCredit Client Number " + args[0] + " (Static)");
    }
    else
    { staticTxn = false;
      setTitle("DebitCredit Client Number " + args[0] + " (dynamic)");
    }

    // Create a 2 by 2 grid of widgets.
    setLayout(new GridLayout(2, 2, 5, 5));

    // Add the four widgets, initialize where necessary
    add(new Label("Status", Label.CENTER));
    add(statusField = new TextField());
    statusField.setEditable(false);
    statusField.setText("ready");
    add(run = new Button("Run"));
    run.addActionListener(this);
    add(stop = new Button("Stop"));
    stop.addActionListener(this);
    addWindowListener(this);

    try
    { // Initialize the ORB
      org.omg.CORBA.ORB orb = org.omg.CORBA.ORB.init(args, null);

      // Get a reference to the Naming Service
      org.omg.CORBA.Object nameServiceObj =
                orb.resolve_initial_references ("NameService");
```

```java
    if (nameServiceObj == null)
    {
      statusField.setText("nameServiceObj = null");
      return;
    }

    nameService =
          org.omg.CosNaming.NamingContextHelper.narrow (nameServiceObj);
    if (nameService == null)
    {
      statusField.setText("nameService = null");
      return;
    }

    // resolve the Dispenser object reference
    NameComponent[] countName =
          {new NameComponent("DebitCredit", "Bank")};
    myDispenser   =
          Bank.DispenserHelper.narrow(nameService.resolve(countName));
    if (myDispenser == null)
    {
      statusField.setText("Failed to resolve DebitCredit");
      return;
    }

    clientNumber = args[0];
    controlThread = new ClientControlThread(this, args, nameService);
    controlThread.start();
    controlThread.setPriority(Thread.NORM_PRIORITY + 1);

  } catch(Exception e)
  { statusField.setText("Exception" + e);
    System.err.println(e);
  }

  debitCreditThread = new ClientDebitCreditThread(this);
  debitCreditThread.start();

}


public void windowClosing(WindowEvent event)
{ System.exit(0);
}
```

```java
public void windowClosed(WindowEvent event) {}
public void windowDeiconified(WindowEvent event) {}
public void windowIconified(WindowEvent event) {}
public void windowActivated(WindowEvent event) {}
public void windowDeactivated(WindowEvent event) {}
public void windowOpened(WindowEvent event) {}
public void actionPerformed(ActionEvent ev)
{
  String arg = ev.getActionCommand();
  if ("Run".equals(arg))
     startCounting();
  if ("Stop".equals(arg))
     stopCounting();
}


public boolean startCounting()
{ // initialize client sum, update status
  clientSum = 0;
  statusField.setText("Running");

  // Calculate Start time
  startTime = System.currentTimeMillis();

  try
  {
    myDebitCredit = myDispenser.reserveDebitCreditObject();
  } catch(Exception e)
  { System.out.println(e);
  }

  // start test
  runTest = true;
  debitCreditThread.resume();
  return true;
}


public String stopCounting()
{
  runTest = false;

  try
  {
    myDispenser.releaseDebitCreditObject(myDebitCredit);
```

```
  } catch(Exception e)
  { System.out.println(e);
  }

  // Calculate stop time; show statistics
  long stopTime = System.currentTimeMillis();
  String statistics =  "Sum = " + clientSum + ", Avg Txn = " +
       Float.toString((float)(stopTime - startTime)/(float)clientSum) +
       " msecs";
  statusField.setText(statistics);
  return "Client " + clientNumber + ": " + statistics;
}

public static void main(String[] args)
{
  DebitCreditMultiClient f = new DebitCreditMultiClient(args);
  f.setSize(480, 90);
  f.show();
}
}
```

Listing 26-2. 3-Tier Client Code: The ClientControlThread Class.

```
class ClientControlThread extends Thread
{
  private DebitCreditMultiClient thisClient;
  private MultiCoordinator.Coordinator myCoordinator;
  private String[] args;
  private org.omg.CosNaming.NamingContext nameService;

  ClientControlThread(DebitCreditMultiClient client, String[] myargs,
                      org.omg.CosNaming.NamingContext naming)
  { thisClient = client;
    args = myargs;
    nameService = naming;
  }

  public void run()
  { try
    { // Initialize the ORB
      org.omg.CORBA.ORB orb = org.omg.CORBA.ORB.init(args, null);

      // Create the ClientControl object
      ClientControlImpl control =
```

```
                        new ClientControlImpl(thisClient);

        // Export the newly created object
        orb.connect(control);

        // resolve the Coordinator object reference
        NameComponent[] coordName =
                        {new NameComponent("Coordinator", "Multi")};
        myCoordinator = MultiCoordinator.CoordinatorHelper.narrow(
                                nameService.resolve(coordName));

        // Register with Coordinator
        if (myCoordinator.register(thisClient.clientNumber,
                                (Client.ClientControl)control))
           {
            System.out.println("Registration Succeeded");
            thisClient.statusField.setText("Ready");
           }
        else
           {
            System.out.println("Registration Failed");
            thisClient.statusField.setText("Registration Failed");
           }

        // Ready to service requests
        System.out.println("Control: Waiting for requests");
        Thread.currentThread().join();
       }
    catch(Exception e)
    { System.err.println("Exception in ClientControl: " + e);
    }
   }
 }
}
```

Listing 26-3. 3-Tier Client Code: The ClientControlImpl Class.

```
class ClientControlImpl extends Client._ClientControlImplBase
                        implements Client.ClientControl
{
  private DebitCreditMultiClient thisClient;

  ClientControlImpl(Object client)
  {
    super();
```

```
    thisClient = (DebitCreditMultiClient)client;
    System.out.println("Client Control Object Created as client"
                       + thisClient.clientNumber);
  }

  public  boolean start()
  { return thisClient.startCounting();
  }

  public  String stop()
  { return thisClient.stopCounting();
  }
}
```

Listing 26-4. 3-Tier Client Code: The ClientDebitCreditThread Class.

```
class ClientDebitCreditThread extends Thread
{ DebitCreditMultiClient myClient;

  ClientDebitCreditThread(DebitCreditMultiClient client)
  { myClient = client;
  }

  public void run()
  { // run debit/credit transactions
    while (true)
    { try
      {
        if (!myClient.runTest) this.suspend();
        myClient.myDebitCredit.debitCreditTransaction(
                  Math.random(), Math.random(), myClient.staticTxn);
        myClient.clientSum++;
      } catch(org.omg.CORBA.SystemException e)
      { myClient.statusField.setText("System Exception" + e);
        this.suspend();
      } catch(org.omg.CORBA.UserException e)
      { myClient.statusField.setText("User Exception" + e);
        this.suspend();
      }
    }
  }
}
```

The 3-Tier Debit-Credit Server Code

This section presents the 3-tier server code. We do not include the code for the **Coordinator**—we use it "as is" from Chapter 9.

Listing 26-5. 3-Tier Server: The CORBA IDL.

```
// Bank.idl

module Bank
{
  exception BankException
  { string reason;
  };

  interface DebitCredit
  {
    void debitCreditTransaction(in double random1,
                                in double random2,
                                in boolean staticTxn)
                raises (BankException);
  };

  interface Dispenser
  {
    DebitCredit reserveDebitCreditObject() raises (BankException);
    void        releaseDebitCreditObject(in DebitCredit debitCreditObject)
                          raises (BankException);
  };

};
```

Listing 26-6. 3-Tier Server Code: The DebitCreditServer Class.

```
// DebitCreditServer.java

import org.omg.CosNaming.*;

class DebitCreditServer
{ static public void main(String[] args)
  {
    int      numberInstances = 3;

    try
```

```
    {
      // Initialize the ORB.
      org.omg.CORBA.ORB orb = org.omg.CORBA.ORB.init(args, null);

      // Create the BankDispenser object
      DispenserImpl dispenser =
              new DispenserImpl(args[0], "My Dispenser", numberInstances);

      // Export the newly create object
      orb.connect(dispenser);

      // Get a reference to the Naming service
      org.omg.CORBA.Object nameServiceObj =
              orb.resolve_initial_references ("NameService");
      if (nameServiceObj == null)
      {
        System.out.println("nameServiceObj = null");
        return;
      }

      org.omg.CosNaming.NamingContext nameService =
              org.omg.CosNaming.NamingContextHelper.narrow (nameServiceObj);
      if (nameService == null)
      {
        System.out.println("nameService = null");
        return;
      }

      // bind the dispenser object in the Naming service
      NameComponent[] dispenserName =
              {new NameComponent("DebitCredit", "Bank")};
      nameService.rebind(dispenserName, dispenser);

      // wait forever for current thread to die
      Thread.currentThread().join();

    } catch(Exception e)
    { System.err.println(e);
    }
  }
}
```

Listing 26-7. 3-Tier Server Code: The DispenserImpl Class.

```java
public class DispenserImpl extends Bank._DispenserImplBase
{
  private int maxObjects = 10;
  private int numObjects = 0;
  private DebitCreditStatus[] debitCredit =
                    new DebitCreditStatus[maxObjects];

  public DispenserImpl(java.lang.String args,
                    java.lang.String name, int num)
  {
    super(name);

    try
    {
      // get reference to orb
      org.omg.CORBA.ORB orb = org.omg.CORBA.ORB.init(args, null);

      // prestart n DebitCredit Objects
      numObjects = num;
      for (int i=0; i < numObjects; i++)
      {
        debitCredit[i] = new DebitCreditStatus();
        debitCredit[i].ref =
                  new DebitCreditImpl(args[0], "DebitCredit" + (i+1));
        orb.connect(debitCredit[i].ref);
      }
    } catch(org.omg.CORBA.SystemException e)
    { System.err.println(e);
    }

  }


  public Bank.DebitCredit reserveDebitCreditObject( )
                  throws Bank.BankException
  {
    for (int i=0; i < numObjects; i++)
    {
      if (!debitCredit[i].inUse)
          { debitCredit[i].inUse = true;
            System.out.println("DebitCredit" + (i+1) + " reserved.");
            return debitCredit[i].ref;
          }
```

```
    }
    return null;
  }

  public void releaseDebitCreditObject(
                    Bank.DebitCredit debitCreditObject)
                    throws Bank.BankException
  {
    for (int i=0; i < numObjects; i++)
    {
      if (debitCredit[i].ref == debitCreditObject)
        { debitCredit[i].inUse = false;
          System.out.println("DebitCredit" + (i+1) + " released.");
          return;
        }
    }
    System.out.println("Reserved Object not found");
    return;
  }
}
```

Listing 26-8. 3-Tier Server Code: The DebitCreditStatus Class.

```
class DebitCreditStatus
{
  DebitCreditImpl ref;
  boolean          inUse;

  DebitCreditStatus()
  { ref = null;
    inUse = false;
  }
}
```

Listing 26-9. 3-Tier Server Code: The DebitCreditImpl Class.

```
// DebitCreditImpl.java

public class DebitCreditImpl extends Bank._DebitCreditImplBase
{
  private DCBank.BankDB myBankDB;
  private String instanceName;

  public DebitCreditImpl(java.lang.String args, java.lang.String iName)
```

```java
  {
    super(iName);
    try
    {
      myBankDB = new DCBank.BankDB();
      myBankDB.connect(args[0], "bank", "sa", "");
      System.out.println("BankDB Object " + iName + " Created");
      instanceName = iName;
    } catch (Exception e)
    { System.out.println("System Exception ");
    }
  }


  public void debitCreditTransaction(double random1,
                                     double random2, boolean staticTxn)
             throws Bank.BankException,org.omg.CORBA.SystemException
  {
    try
    {
      myBankDB.debitCreditTransaction(random1, random2, staticTxn);
    } catch (Exception e)
    { System.out.println("System Exception during debitCreditTransaction");
      throw new Bank.BankException("debitCredit Error");
    }
  }
}
```

Listing 26-10. 3-Tier Server Code: The BankDB Class.

```java
// BankDB.java   JDBC BankDB Class

package DCBank;
import java.net.URL;
import java.sql.*;

public class BankDB
{
  Connection con;
  Driver driver = null;
  ResultSet rs;
  CallableStatement pstmt;
  PreparedStatement pstmt1;
  PreparedStatement pstmt2;
```

```java
PreparedStatement pstmt3;
boolean prepared = false;

public void connect(String datasource, String db,
                    String id, String pw)
                    throws Exception
{
  try
  {
    // Load the jdbc-odbc bridge driver
    // Class.forName ("sun.jdbc.odbc.JdbcOdbcDriver");
    // String url    = "jdbc:odbc:" + datasource + ";database=" + db;

    // Load Connect Software's FastForward JDBC driver
    Class.forName ("connect.microsoft.MicrosoftDriver");
    String url = "jdbc:ff-microsoft://" + datasource + ":1433/" + db;

    System.out.println("Connecting to " + url);
    con = DriverManager.getConnection(url, id, pw);

  } catch(Exception e)
  { System.err.println("System Exception in connect");
    System.err.println(e);
    throw e;
  }
}


public void closeConnection() throws Exception
{
  try
  {
    System.out.println("Closing connection");
    con.close();
  } catch (Exception e)
  { System.err.println("System Exception in closeConnection");
    System.err.println(e);
    throw e;
  }
}

public void debitCreditTransaction(double random1,
                                   double random2,
                                   boolean staticTxn)
                                   throws Exception
```

```java
{
  int     balance = 1000;
  int     delta   = 100;
  int     acctNum = 0;
  short   branchID = 0;
  short   tellerID = 0;
  String  tellerCode = "ab";
  String  areaCode = "abcd";

  try
  {
    // randomly select account, teller, branch
    acctNum  = (int)((random1 * random2 * 100000) + 1);
    tellerID = (short)((random1 * 100) + 1);
    branchID = (short)((random2 *  10) + 1);

    if ((staticTxn && !prepared) || !staticTxn)
    {
      pstmt  = con.prepareCall("{?= call UpdateAcctBalance(?,?)}");
      pstmt1 = con.prepareStatement(
           "UPDATE TELLER SET BALANCE = BALANCE + ? WHERE TELLER_ID = ?");
      pstmt2 = con.prepareStatement(
           "UPDATE BRANCH SET BALANCE = BALANCE + ? WHERE BRANCH_ID = ?");
      pstmt3 = con.prepareStatement(
           "INSERT INTO HISTORY(ACCT_NUM, TELLER_ID, BRANCH_ID, BALANCE, " +
           "DELTA, PID, TRANSID, ACCTNAME, TEMP1) " +
           "VALUES(?, ?, ?, ?, ?, 1, 3, ?, 'hist  ')");
      prepared = true;
    }
    pstmt.registerOutParameter(1,Types.INTEGER);
    pstmt.setInt(2, acctNum);
    pstmt.setInt(3, delta);
    pstmt.execute();
    ResultSet rs1 = pstmt.getResultSet();
    rs1.next();
    balance = rs1.getInt(1);
    rs1.close();

    // Update the TELLER table's balance
    pstmt1.setInt(1, delta);
    pstmt1.setShort(2, tellerID);
    pstmt1.executeUpdate();

    // Update the Branch balance
    pstmt2.setInt(1, delta);
```

```
      pstmt2.setShort(2, branchID);
      pstmt2.executeUpdate();

      //Update the history
      pstmt3.setInt(1, acctNum);
      pstmt3.setShort(2, tellerID);
      pstmt3.setShort(3, branchID);
      pstmt3.setInt(4, balance);
      pstmt3.setInt(5, delta);
      pstmt3.setString(6, "Account Name, len=20");
      pstmt3.executeUpdate();

      if ((staticTxn && !prepared) || !staticTxn)
      {
        pstmt.close();
        pstmt1.close();
        pstmt2.close();
        pstmt3.close();
      }

      //Commit the Transaction
      con.commit();
    }
    catch( Exception e )
    { System.err.println("System Exception in debitCreditTransaction");
      System.err.println(e);
      con.rollback();
      throw e;
    }
  }
}
```

This completes the 3-tier code. Let's compile it and run some benchmarks.

COMPILE THE 3-TIER DEBIT-CREDIT

We're now ready to compile the Debit-Credit program. First, we must create the skeletons and stubs. Make sure you've installed VisiBroker for Java. Then go to the appropriate subdirectory and enter the following commands at the prompt:

```
prompt> call idl2java DebitCredit.idl -no_comments
prompt> call idl2java ClientControl.idl -no_comments
```

To compile the client and server code, make sure you've installed Symantec Visual Café. Then go to the appropriate directory and run the make file. Or, you can enter the following commands at the prompt:

```
prompt> javac -d \CorbaJavaBook.2e\classes DebitCreditServer.java
prompt> javac -d \CorbaJavaBook.2e\classes DebitCreditImpl.java
prompt> javac -d \CorbaJavaBook.2e\classes DispenserImpl.java
prompt> javac -d \CorbaJavaBook.2e\classes BankDB.java
prompt> javac -d \CorbaJavaBook.2e\classes DebitCreditMultiClient.java
```

The -d option tells the compiler to put the (.class) files it creates into the directory we specify—in this case, the \CorbaJavaBook.2e\classes subdirectory.

If all goes well, you should have some compiled Java code—including stubs and skeletons—that you can now run.

RUN THE DEBIT-CREDIT 3-TIER BENCHMARK

We will run a simple benchmark with three clients. The client machine is a 120 MHz Pentium with 40 MBytes of memory and the server machine is a 233 MHz Pentium with 96 MBytes of memory. The client and server are connected via a 10 Mbit/s Ethernet (see Figure 26-6).

Figure 26-6. The 3-Tier Debit-Credit Benchmark Configuration.

To create the server, you must first install a database that supports JDBC. In this test, we will use Microsoft SQL Server 6.5. To install SQL Server, follow the instructions on the CD-ROM. Next, you must create a bank database and fill it with data. We will use the **CreateBank** program from the last chapter to do this. At the prompt, enter the following command:

prompt> `java CreateBank 1`

Notice that we're using a 1-tps database. We're obviously not interested in absolute numbers. However, you can load the database with as much data as you please. You do this by simply changing the tps number.

First start the Naming Service as we described in Chapter 7.

You can now start the server program. Enter the following command:

prompt> `start java DebitCreditServer 3`

We're telling the **Dispenser** to create a pool of three server objects.

Next, you must install the **Coordinator**. Let's put it on the server machine. Enter the following command at the prompt:

prompt> `start java -DORBservices=CosNaming`
`                -DSVCnameroot=JavaCorba CoordinatorServer`

You're now ready to run as many client programs as you require for this benchmark. You can run multiple client programs from the same machine. Or, you can give each client its own machine. In this low-cost benchmark, we will run three client programs from one client machine. To run each client, enter the following command at the prompt:

prompt> `java -DORBservices=CosNaming -DSVCnameroot=JavaCorba`
`                ThreeTier.DebitCreditMultiClient 1 static`

You must give each client a number. The MultiConsole applet uses this number to display the client's statistics. If all goes well, you should see the client's panel on the screen. You can ignore it for now. You'll be running the benchmarks using the MultiConsole panel.

Finally, you'll also need the **MultiConsole** applet from Chapter 9. This is the applet that controls the races. You can run it from anywhere. In this low-cost benchmark, we'll run it on the same machine as our three clients—that should save you some walking. To do this, install Netscape Communicator on the client. Then point to an HTML page that contains the applet; you can use the HTML file from Chapter 9.

A MultiConsole should appear inside the browser. At this point, you're ready to run the benchmark. So click on the "Run" button. Let the benchmark run for at least ten minutes (look at your watch). Finally, click on the "Stop" button to see the results. Figure 26-7 shows the screen capture for a 3-tier Debit-Credit run.

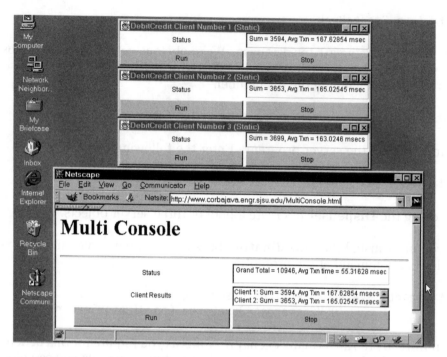

Figure 26-7. A Debit-Credit 3-Tier Run with 3 Clients.

2-TIER VERSUS 3-TIER

The results show the 3-tier JDBC to be slightly slower than its 2-tier counterpart (18.1 tps versus 19.4 tps). This is both good news and bad news. The bad news is that you would expect 3-tier to be considerably faster than 2-tier—in a similar C benchmarking environment we found 3-tier to be over twice as fast as 2-tier. So what's the good news? The good news is that the results are much better than we anticipated. Why?

In general, here's what makes 3-tier faster than 2-tier: 1) fewer network exchanges—one remote method invocation versus multiple remote SQL calls, 2) a chunk of client logic is offloaded to a faster server machine, and 3) superior load-balancing, scheduling, and process management (especially if you use a commercial TP Monitor).

In the JDBC Debit-Credit environment, here's what we think makes 2-tier faster than 3-tier: 1) a fast network that makes up for the larger number of network exchanges—10 Mbit/s Ethernet is much faster than your average Internet connection, 2) a slow server—we're using an ordinary PC, 3) the Java VM—it's very CPU-intensive, and 4) the JDBC driver may be serializing all DBMS accesses—if this is the case, it defeats all our multithreaded scheduling.

Given all these factors, we were pleasantly surprised that 3-tier did not do worse. If you think about it, the JDBC 3-tier performance is almost equal to that of remote SQL against a seasoned DBMS—SQL Server 6.5. The DBMS server does not run a single line of Java code. In contrast, our 3-tier server framework is completely written in Java. We believe that 1086 Debit-Credit transactions per minute on an ordinary Pentium PC is not too shabby. Perhaps it's safe to say that Java is almost ready for client/server prime time. You should seriously consider writing your 3-tier client/server applications using CORBA, Java, and JDBC.

Before we close this discussion, we must tell you why 3-tier is better than 2-tier. Table 26-1 compares the two approaches.

Table 26-1. Client/Server: 2-Tier Versus 3-Tier.

	2-Tier	3-Tier
Applet downloading	Slow (fat client)	Fast (thin client)
System administration	Complex (more logic on the client to manage)	Less complex (application can be centrally managed on the server)
Security	Low (data-level security)	High (fine-tuned at the method level)
Encapsulation of data	Low (data tables are exposed)	High (methods are exposed)
Performance	Poor (except for Java JDBC)	Good (except for Java JDBC)
Scale	Poor	Excellent (can load-balance across multiple systems)
Application reuse	Poor (monolithic application on client)	Excellent (can reuse server objects)
Ease of development	High	Getting better (starting to use the same tools)
Server-to-Server infrastructure	No	Yes—via server-side CORBA bus

CONCLUSION

This series clearly demonstrates that you can develop serious 3-tier client/server systems today using Java, JDBC, and CORBA. We showed that these *avant-garde* systems can perform almost as well as their seasoned 2-tier counterparts. We also expect that some of the performance bottlenecks we encountered in this chapter will soon be fixed. Remember, we're working with beta code. In any case, the toolkit we developed in this 3-chapter series should help you conduct your own benchmarks. You can then decide for yourself.

Part 7
From JavaBeans To
Enterprise JavaBeans

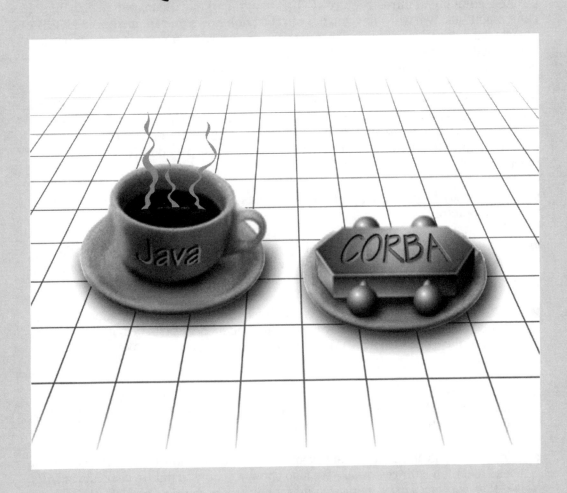

An Introduction to Part 7

When we talk about distributed objects, we're really talking about independent software *components*. These are smart pieces of software that can play in different networks, operating systems, and tool palettes. A component is an object that's not bound to a particular program or application. Objects built as components provide the right "shapes" for distributed applications. They are the optimal building blocks for creating the next generation of distributed systems, which we call the *Object Web*.

CORBA objects are, by definition, components because of the way they are packaged. In distributed object systems, the unit of work and distribution is a component. The distributed object infrastructure makes it easier for components to be more autonomous, self-managing, and collaborative.

JavaBeans are also components. They augment CORBA with a toolable and portable component infrastructure. CORBA augments JavaBeans with a distributed component bus. We will show you later in the book how you can make your CORBA objects into JavaBeans, and vice versa. And we will show you how to create Web-based, client/server applications with CORBA and JavaBeans. But before we do this, we must we must first tell you all about vanilla JavaBeans.

In Part 7, we cover the JavaBeans component model. We also tell you a little bit about Enterprise JavaBeans and CORBA beans. This entire Part is one giant tutorial on JavaBeans. If you are already familiar with JavaBeans, then you can safely skip over to Chapter 33. Otherwise, brace yourself for a fast-paced introduction. Here's what we will be covering in Part 7:

- ■ *Chapter 27* is an overview of the JavaBeans component model. You get to see the big picture.

- ■ *Chapter 28* is about the world's happiest bean. We called it *Smiley*. We use this minimalist bean to show you how to create a bean as well as a container application that runs the bean.

- ■ *Chapter 29* introduces the JavaBean publish-and-subscribe event model. Beans simply use (and extend) the new Java event model. Beans can be both consumers and producers of events. We will use this chapter to make Smiley more event-driven.

- ■ *Chapter 30* is about propertied beans. In the world of JavaBeans, a property can be simple, bound, or constrained. We will introduce these features by adding active properties to our Smiley bean.

- ■ *Chapter 31* is about persistent beans. We show you how to save the state of a bean and then later restore it. We also show you how to put these beans in JARs so that you can carry them around or ship them across the Net. JARs have

An Introduction to Part 7

manifests, digests, certificates, and a lot of the paraphernalia that comes with a component packaging technology. We will use this technology to save Smiley, package it, and safely transport it in a signed JAR.

■ *Chapter 32* is about introspection and toolability, JavaBean-style. JavaBeans were born to be toolable. We'll look at the two technologies that make beans supertoolable: *introspection* and *customization*. We will demonstrate all the things Smiley can tell you about itself. And we will describe all the support classes JavaBeans provides to make your beans tool-friendly.

■ *Chapter 33* is about CORBA beans. Yes, CORBA and JavaBeans are coming together in a big way. This chapter tells you how. We will look at the OMG's new *CORBA Component Initiative*; it appears to be JavaBeans++. We will explain the pluses.

■ *Chapter 34* is about *Enterprise JavaBeans (EJBs)*. The EJB specification defines a contract between a server-side JavaBean and a new breed of *component coordinator*, which Gartner calls an *Object Transaction Monitor (OTM)*. The OTM manages server-side beans in a scalable way using transactions, state management, and automatic activation and deactivation. EJB was designed from ground zero to be 100% CORBA-compatible. It augments CORBA by defining the interfaces between a server-side component (or bean) and its *container*. The beauty of the EJB framework is that it lets you declaratively define most of your server-side, run-time attributes. So you can use visual tools to administer, package, and set the properties of your server-side components—including their transactional, security, and state management policies.

So without further ado, let's jump into this world of beans.

Chapter 27

The JavaBean Component Model

In this chapter, we describe the JavaBean component model. A *component* is an identifiable piece of software with well-defined boundaries. Think of it as a lego-like software building block. The component model defines the shapes and boundaries of these legos. For example, it specifies how components expose their properties, methods, and events to the outside world. The model also defines how components interact with their *containers*. A container—which can also be a component—provides a context within which components can play together. Yes, it's very recursive. Component models are the next step in the evolution of objects.

The JavaBeans specification describes a component architecture for Java. It addresses the needs of two sets of programmers: 1) *component developers* who write code at the source level, and 2) *component assemblers* who create large applications by combining beans together either visually or by writing some glue code (or both).

If you are reading this book, you are already a 90% bona fide bean component developer. As you will see, the JavaBeans component model is based on Java classes. The model simply adds a few rules that you must follow to make your classes toolable and reusable. Beans are architected to support visual assembly tools. A bean may be *visible*—for example, a JFC widget. Or it may be *invisible*—for example, a CORBA server bean. In both cases, the bean will be visible within a tool.

JavaBeans are *black-box components*, which means that you can't extend them (unless you have the source code). In addition, JavaBeans do not derive from some universal base class that gives them bean-like properties. Your beans are regular Java classes. In general, you will find the bean model to be non-intrusive; it is even less demanding than programming an applet.

THE BEAN COMPONENT MODEL

Does this excessive "laissez-faire" make the bean component model lightweight? Paradoxically, the JavaBeans model is both lightweight and heavyweight. The beans you build are lightweight in terms of code; they build on the existing JDK run time—including AWT/JFC, persistence, and ORB facilities. But, they're also heavyweight in terms of function—they let you seamlessly use any of the JDK facilities.

Beans Versus Applets

To many people, Java already has a component model—it's called *applets*. So, why does Java need beans when it has applets? As it turns out, an applet can be a bean, and vice versa. The beauty of JavaBeans is that almost anything written in Java can be made into a bean. As you will see later, an applet augmented with bean-like characteristics is a lot more toolable and composable than a regular applet. Most builder tools let you manipulate beans to create both applets and applications.

Like applets, beans can be embedded inside an HTML page. Unlike applets, you can easily assemble and compose beans to create very interactive visual ensembles. Beans can also be invisible components that live on servers. In contrast, applets tend to live within browsers. Beans know how to interact with each other as well with their containers. Applets tend to be more container-centric. Finally, a bean can be an applet, application, or simply a set of Java classes. You should think of a bean as a reusable component that you can use to create applets, applications, or even HTML pages. The same bean should be able to play in any of these containers.

JavaBeans: The Black-Box View

Figure 27-1 shows a programmer's view of a bean (also see the next Soapbox). As you can see, a bean exposes to the world its methods, properties, and the events it emits. Another bean or tool can dynamically discover this information. The bean saves its state in a (.ser) file that you can package inside a JAR. A bean is introspective; it can tell you quite a bit about itself via the **BeanInfo** class. A bean may provide a **Customizer** class to help you customize its behavior at design time—this is a custom wizard that you invoke from within a tool. In most cases, you will be able to customize a bean by setting its properties via property editors.

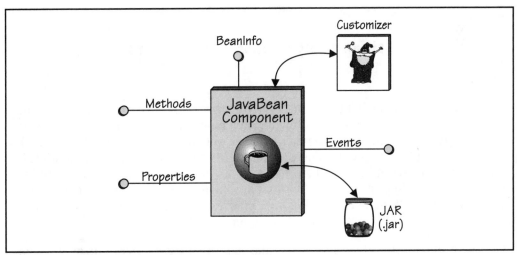

Figure 27-1. The Black-Box View of a JavaBean Component.

There is no IDL—or component definition language—that describes a bean. So how does a bean reveal its interfaces to the outside world? The JavaBean specification defines a set of naming conventions (JavaBeans calls them *design patterns*) that you use to identify the methods, events, and properties of your bean.

A visual assembly tool can pass your bean to an **Introspector** class to generate the **BeanInfo** metadata. The **Introspector** is part of the JavaBeans runtime; it knows exactly how to interpret the naming conventions. So it's important that you follow these naming rules. Alternatively, you can explicitly specify a bean's metadata by providing your own **BeanInfo** class; it lets you define—via descriptors—all (or parts of) the introspection information for your bean.

JavaBeans: The JDK as a Component Framework

So where is the component infrastructure for running these beans? If you come from the world of ActiveX or OpenDoc development, you may be expecting us to shortly dump a truckload of new classes on you. You can relax. The JavaBeans run time introduces at most 20 new classes and interfaces. On the other hand, the JDK itself is now a giant framework for running your JavaBeans.

In this JDK-as-a-framework view, beans are the end product of all Java development—this means that almost everything in Java is there only to support your components. Your job as a developer is to either: 1) create new beans from scratch, or 2) customize and assemble applications as well as bean subassemblies from existing beans. This is the software version of an assembly line.

Getting a Grip on Those Elusive Beans

Soapbox

Notice that we still haven't told you exactly what a bean is. We're taking our time because it is very difficult to pin down a Java bean. We could take the easy way out and say, "You'll know a bean when you see one in your tool's palette or HTML page." But that's a cop out. The problem is that the JavaBean specification is totally non-constraining; it introduces tons of conventions, which are all optional. According to the specification, any Java class is a bean. Of course, we could simply declare beans to be Java classes, and then move on to Part 8. However, this would not make you a very happy reader.

One way out of this dilemma is to take a more prescriptive approach. For example, we could insist that you follow these JavaBeans-defined conventions to the teeth to create useful beans. If you don't follow these conventions, then you won't be getting the full benefits of beans. Introspection is really what differentiates beans from ordinary Java classes. Tools that recognize the JavaBeans naming conventions can look inside a bean to discover its properties and behavior. So, let's agree that these conventions are rules that we will all follow. This way we won't have to preface each statement with, "You don't have to do this, but..." ❑

JavaSoft designed the JavaBeans framework from day one to satisfy two groups of customers: bean developers and bean visual assembly tool vendors. It's very important that you note this distinction because there are different classes in the JDK to satisfy each of these two constituencies. Figure 27-2 shows the JDK as a framework for running beans. In this view, the JDK is simply a giant set of component services to satisfy the needs of JavaBeans.

The JDK provides the following infrastructure-type services to JavaBeans:

■ *Visual layout and presentation*. A component infrastructure must support the visual layout of components in containers—for example, a form or an HTML page. It must also provide services that let components visually interact with each other and with their containers. In the case of JavaBeans, these services are provided by the *Java Foundation Classes (JFC)*, which include AWT, the 2-D graphics, and the new Swing components.

A visible JavaBean inherits its visual behavior from the AWT **Component** class (see Figure 27-3). A containing bean (or application) also inherits from the AWT **Container** class. The new, all-Java, lightweight Swing components inherit from the **JComponent** class.

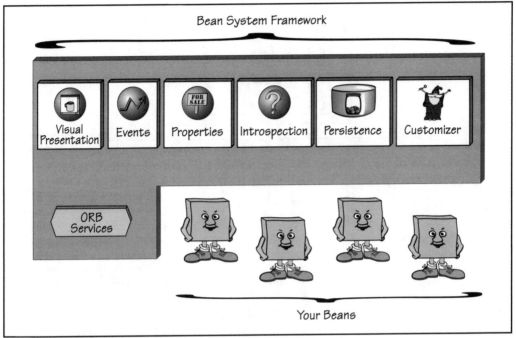

Figure 27-2. The JDK as a Framework View of JavaBeans.

JFC also provides bean-to-bean run-time interaction services—for example, drag-and-drop, clipboard support, and data transfer. A containing bean (or application) inherits from the AWT **Container** class.

JDK 1.2 introduces a **BeanContext** interface; it lets a bean exchange information with its container, discover other beans, and access common services. This new context interface can be used by both visible and invisible beans. Think of it as a *relationship service* that you can use to describe relationships between beans and their containers; it also provides a focal point for beans to discover the services that are available to them.

■ *Events*. A component must be able to tell the world at large when something of interest happens to it. A component does this by posting an event. Other components that have an interest in this event can subscribe to it. They will be notified when the event "fires." This loosely-coupled arrangement is ideal for wiring components together using a visual tool. The JavaBeans event model—also known as the *event-delegation* model—is the same one JDK 1.1 introduced for AWT. It requires that interested beans explicitly register for events in which they have an interest. This model works well for beans; it lets you create general-purpose event connections outside the GUI hierarchy. In the previous JDK, events were tied to the GUI hierarchy.

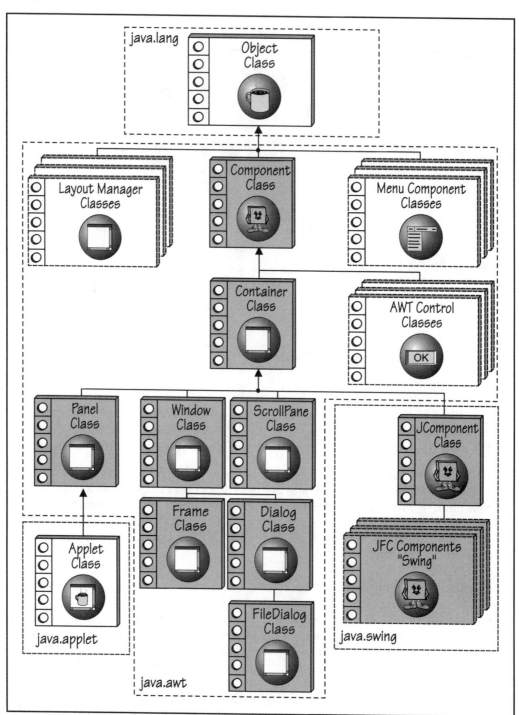

Figure 27-3. JFC/AWT: The Visual Framework for JavaBeans.

- **_Properties_**. Components have state. Properties can identify and surface this state information; they define the characteristics of a bean. A _property_ is a discrete named attribute that you can use to read and modify the state of a bean—typically using a property editor within a visual tool. JavaBeans abide by object encapsulation principles. Consequently, a bean does not let outsiders directly manipulate its properties. Instead, you must invoke get/set accessor (and mutator) methods for each variable.

  The JavaBeans API supports both _single-value_ and _indexed_ properties. In addition, properties can be _bound_ and _constrained_. There's nothing sinister going on here. A bound property will notify interested parties—via events—when its value changes. A constrained property allows the interested parties to veto the modification. Of course, the bean is responsible for specifying the behavior of its properties and for posting the events they generate.

- **_Introspection_**. A component infrastructure must define the mechanisms by which components make their services available to the outside world. JavaBeans provides a higher-level _introspector_ facility that makes it easy for a visual tool to discover a bean's incoming and outgoing interfaces. This facility is built on top of the JDK's lower-level _reflection_ classes. Developers can define the behavior of their beans by either using the JavaBeans naming conventions or by providing an explicit **BeanInfo** class.

- **_Persistence_**. You should be able to store away a component instance and then recreate it at a later time. In addition, visual tools require components that support some form of persistence. For example, a tool lets you customize a component by changing its properties; it must then be able to tell the component to save its newly modified state. Beans take advantage of the JDK serialization service to automatically save and restore their states. Your beans can be made to be implicitly persistent—you don't have to do any extra work unless you want to customize how a bean is stored. The serialization service also supports a simple form of _versioning_, which is an important requirement in component environments. It enforces simple rules that let newer beans load state written by their older versions; it also lets newer beans store state in a format that's consistent with older versions. Finally, beans can be packaged and distributed using JAR files, another built-in facility of the JDK.

- **_Customization_**. A component must be toolable to encourage its widespread reuse. Of course, toolability is an important part of the JavaBeans component model. This is the area where you will find most of the new JavaBeans classes. They encourage you to provide as many hooks as possible to allow your beans to be used by non-programmers (and also programmers, but we won't admit it). _Property editor_ classes provide the first level of support for tools. They let you visually edit a particular type of property—for example, a font, color, or integer.

Property sheets are visual interfaces that group all the property editors you need to edit a bean (see Figure 27-4).

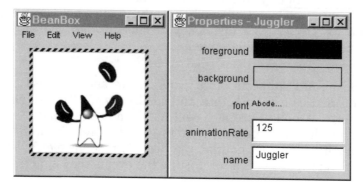

Figure 27-4. A Property Sheet.

Finally, bean *customizers* provide wizard-like dialogs that let you edit a bean as a whole. In this case, JavaBeans only specifies a **Customizer** interface and leaves the implementation of the wizard as an exercise for the programmer. In most situations, property sheets provide all the customization your users will ever need.

■ ***ORB services***. You should be able to invoke a component's services across languages, operating systems, and networks. CORBA ORBs let you invoke methods on beans across all these boundaries. We will show you how CORBA and JavaBeans play together in Part 8. Note that you can also use RMI for Java-to-Java bean communications. The JavaBeans component model simply builds on the JDK's distributed object facilities. The *Enterprise JavaBeans* specification further extends this model to support distributed transactions.

The story here is that the *java.beans* package is only the icing on the JavaBeans cake. This package provides bean-specific classes—including customizers, introspectors, property editors, and specialized event managers. However, you'll find that the JavaBeans cake consists of the familiar JDK services—including Java AWT, events, serialization, security, multithreading, JARs, reflection, CORBA, and RMI. In this tutorial, we will only look at these packages from the perspective of JavaBeans. We're obviously not going to cover all of Java.

JavaBeans: Design-Time Versus Run-Time

Beans must be able to operate in a running application as well as inside a builder. So the next piece of the bean puzzle is to understand the difference between design-time versus run-time beans. Figure 27-5 says it all. To be toolable, the bean

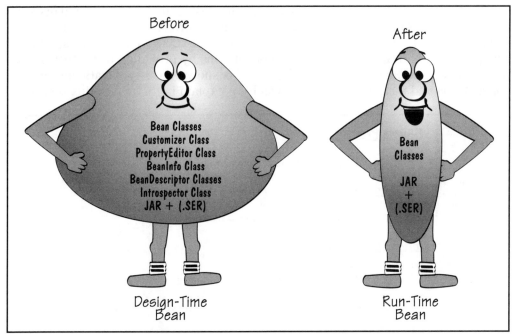

Figure 27-5. Design-Time Versus Run-Time Beans.

must carry a lot of extra baggage. Your bean must provide the design information necessary to edit its properties and customize its behavior. This includes metadata, property editors, customizers, icons, and any other paraphernalia a builder tool requires.

However, this is precisely the type of baggage you don't want your bean to carry around at run time—especially over low-bandwidth networks. The run-time beans must be compact. You can create compact beans by packaging the customization support classes separately. You typically include these classes in a helper package. So you should ship your beans in design-time or run-time JARs, depending on how they will be used.

You can invoke the *Beans.isDesignTime* method to determine the current mode of a bean. In JDK 1.1, the mode was a VM-global attribute. With JDK 1.2, you can use the **BeanContext** to better scope this mode. A container can now delegate its mode to its descendant beans; it can also inform them via a property change event when the mode changes value.

THE SO-CALLED DESIGN PATTERNS

The JavaBeans architecture specifies standard naming and type signature conventions for methods that a bean uses to expose its properties, events, and methods.

Visual development tools use these naming "patterns" to analyze a bean and discover what it does. An intended side effect of this approach to introspection is to encourage you to use standard naming conventions. Like we said earlier, you can always get around these rigid naming conventions by providing a **BeanInfo** class that contains explicit metadata. Figure 27-6 shows the key JavaBeans naming conventions and method signatures, which we explain in the rest of this section.

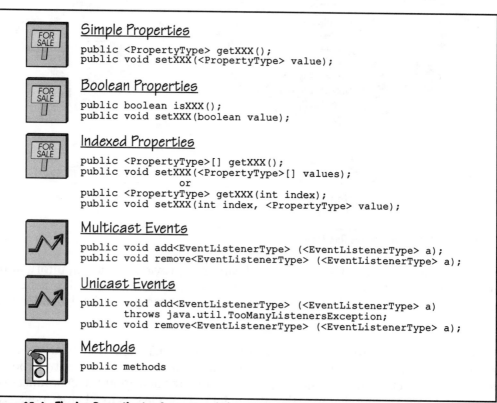

Figure 27-6. The JavaBeans Naming Conventions (a.k.a., Design Patterns).

Simple Property Naming Patterns

An introspector discovers a bean's properties by looking for accessor methods that begin with *get* and *set* followed by the name of the property. For example, if your bean had a property called age, its getter method would be called *getAge* and its setter method would be called *setAge*. You can make a property read-only by not providing a setter method.

You can optionally use an *isXXX* getter method to flag to the introspector a single-valued *boolean* property; it has a value of either true or false. For example, if your bean had a boolean property called married, its getter method would be called *isMarried* and its setter method would be called *setMarried.*

Indexed Properties Naming Patterns

An *indexed property* contains a collection of values that are of the same type. You use the standard getter and setter accessor methods to retrieve or set an entire array of properties. JavaBeans also lets you retrieve and set individual elements within a property array. To do this, you must provide an additional index argument in your getter and setter methods. In either case, an introspector can discover your bean's indexed properties. Note that indexed properties are primarily used by scripting languages.

Event Naming Patterns

Beans send event notifications to *listeners* that register an interest in being notified when the event fires. Listener beans receive notification of events by having the source call the appropriate method. An event-source bean provides a pair of methods that allow listeners to be added or removed from an event notification list. The introspector uses these method pairs to discover the events that a bean emits. *EventListenerType* refers to the object type of the listener interface that is registered with the bean. A listener object must implement this interface; its name must also end with *Listener.* Here is an example for **LotteryWinner** events:

```
public void addLotteryWinnerListener (LotteryWinnerListener a);
public void removeLotteryWinnerListener (LotteryWinnerListener a);
```

Most beans will emit *multicast events*, which means that they will allow more than one event listener to register. The **LotteryWinner** event is of the multicast variety.

You can also define an event source as *unicast.* In this case, the bean only accepts one listener at any one time. Any attempt to register a second listener will fail. The idea is to make sure the bean sends the event to a single listener. You indicate an event source to be unicast by simply adding a throws clause with the exception **java.util.TooManyListenersException**. Here is an example for **OnDuty** events:

```
public void addOnDutyListener (OnDutyListener a)
              throws java.util.TooManyListenersException;
public void removeOnDutyListener (OnDutyListener a);
```

Method Naming Patterns

Your bean can export any method by simply declaring it *public*. In addition, as we described earlier, your bean must also provide public methods to expose its properties and events. An introspector knows the difference between an accessor public method and a regular method. As usual, you can restrict and control what an introspector sees by providing an explicit **BeanInfo** class. Visual tools will typically display whatever the introspector discovers.

THE JAVABEANS CLASSES: AN OVERVIEW

As we explained earlier, the entire Java core—including JFC/AWT, JARs, serialization, RMI, CORBA, events, security, and threads—provides run-time services for beans. So is there such a thing as a JavaBeans API? The answer is that there are some bean-specific classes in the *java.beans* package; they provide introspection, property editors, and design-time services for beans. In addition, JDK 1.2 adds new classes and interfaces to support bean containment and related run-time services.

JDK 1.1 JavaBeans Classes

The JavaBeans JDK 1.1 *java.beans* package contains about 20 interfaces and classes. We can break them down into three groups:

■ *Bean run-time support*—these interfaces and classes let you create beans and obtain information about the bean's run-time environment (see Figure 27-7). As you can see, JDK 1.1 is very skimpy in its run-time support for beans; it relies on the Java core for most of its run-time services.

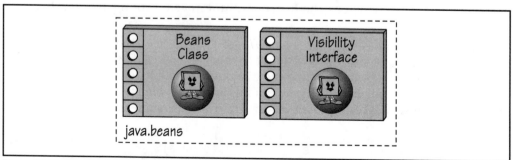

Figure 27-7. The JavaBeans Runtime-Support Classes and Interfaces.

■ ***Bean introspection support***—these interfaces and classes support design-time introspection (see Figure 27-8). They are mostly used by tools to discover a bean's icon, methods, properties, and events.

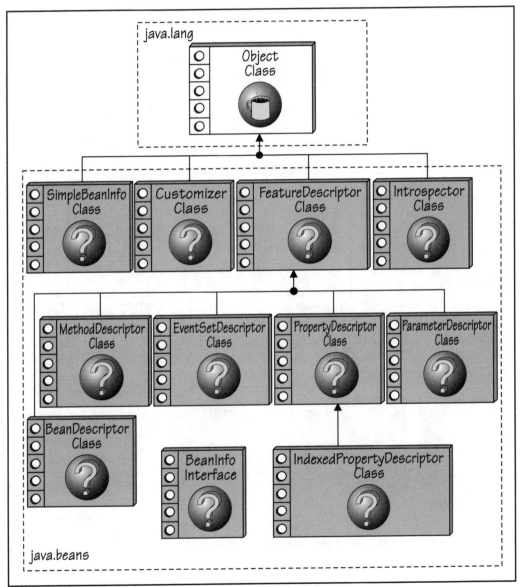

Figure 27-8. The JavaBeans Introspection-Support Classes and Interfaces.

■ ***Bean property support***—these interfaces and classes help you manage a bean's properties (see Figure 27-9). The property editors are exclusively used at design time. The property change and support classes are used during both run time and design time. They propagate events that are triggered when the value of a property (either bound or constrained) changes. It's classical publish-and-subscribe using the new event-delegation model.

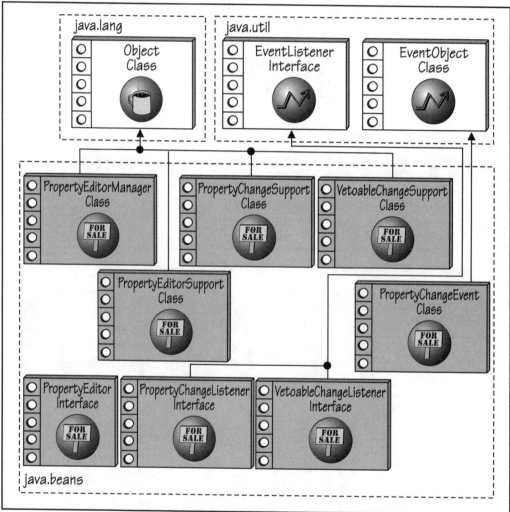

Figure 27-9. The JavaBeans Property-Support Classes and Interfaces.

JDK 1.2 JavaBeans Enhancements

JDK 1.2 introduces the so-called Glasgow improvements to JavaBeans. These improvements give more attention to the visual integration of JavaBeans. They also deal with bean containment semantics. JDK 1.2 adds about six new interfaces and classes to the existing *java.beans* package (see Figure 27-10); it also introduces a new package called *java.beans.beancontext* (see Figure 27-11). Here's a list of the major enhancements to the JavaBeans component model that JDK 1.2 introduces:

■ *Better support for Applet semantics*. JDK 1.2 makes it easier to implement objects that are both Java beans and applets. The JDK 1.2 version of the *java.beans* package defines a new interface called **AppletInitializer** (see Figure 27-10); it works with the *java.beans.Beans.instantiate* method to

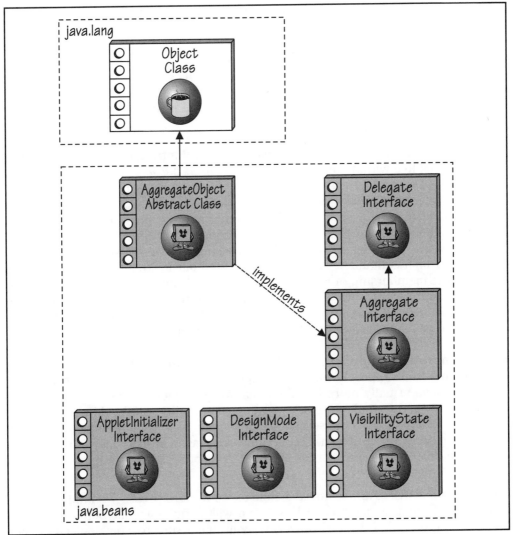

Figure 27-10. The JDK 1.2 Additions to Java.beans.

properly initialize beans that are also applets. The *initialize* method is called to associate a newly instantiated JavaBean/Applet with its **AppletContext**, **AppletStub**, and **Container**. The *activate* method can mark a newly instantiated JavaBean/Applet as active, and optionally invoke its *start* method.

- *Object aggregation/delegation support.* Java is based on a single implementation-inheritance model. However, there are times when you need the equivalent of multiple inheritance. Instead of changing the semantics of the language to support multiple inheritance, JavaBeans simulates multiple inheritance using an *aggregate/delegate* object model. An aggregate object delegates work to other object instances. The JDK 1.2 version of the *java.beans* package includes an **AggregateObject** base class that helps you derive the semantics of the new aggregation mechanisms (see Figure 27-10).

- *Better design-time support.* The JDK 1.2 version of *java.beans* specifies a new **DesignMode** interface (see Figure 27-10). It is used by beans to determine their current *designTime* property. In addition, a *VisibilityState* interface defines a single method called *isOkToUseGui* that beans can invoke to discover their context.

- *Bean container protocol and service.* JDK 1.2 introduces a new protocol to help beans live within containers. The new *java.beans.beancontext* package defines three new interfaces and six new classes that a bean can use to get information about the services available to it from the container (see Figure 27-11). It also allows beans to better integrate and operate within different containers—for example, a browser, Webtop, or custom AWT window frame. The new interfaces let you add and remove single beans or collections of beans to and from a container. They allow interested parties to be notified via events when the membership of a container changes. Beans can query a container to discover its membership. The **BeanContextSupport** class is a helper class that implements the **BeanContext** interface; it implements more than sixty methods that you can subclass to create your own containers.

- *Drag-and-drop support.* JDK 1.2—or more precisely, JFC—finally introduces drag-and-drop support in Java. This important facility will help you create beans that behave visually more like their real-world objects. A visual container of beans can start to look more like a place that contains people, things, and other places. You can move these beans across places via drag and drop. You can also use drag and drop to trigger actions in beans. For example, you should be able to drop a generic business card bean on top of a form to populate it with personal data.

The first beta of JDK 1.2 became available as we went to press. We implement the bean examples in this book using JDK 1.1; it will be quite a while before tools and browsers support JDK 1.2. However, we will make sure to point out any major changes JDK 1.2 introduces.

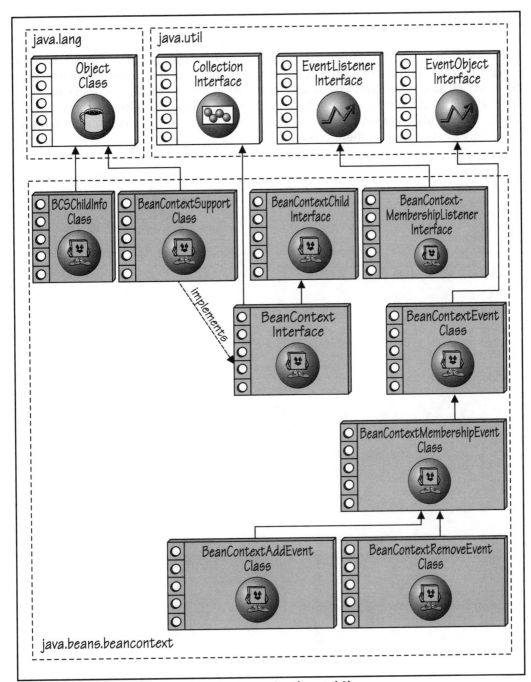

Figure 27-11. The New JDK 1.2 Java.beans.beancontext Interfaces and Classes.

CONCLUSION

The bottom line here is that JavaBeans are transforming Java into a rapid application development environment. Beans let you create reusable objects that can then be visually manipulated and assembled from within builder tools. You can use beans to represent both client and server objects. From a bean developer's perspective, the JDK is simply a giant framework for running beans; it provides the foundation for a truly portable component model.

Chapter 28

The
Smiley
JavaBean

In this chapter, we develop a very simple bean—*Smiley.* We then run Smiley within an application that serves as a container. In subsequent chapters, we add properties, events, and persistence to Smiley. Then we wire it with other beans—both visually and via hand-coded applications.

In the Smiley series, we will focus on the bean-specific aspects of the code. We will develop beans at the source level, and we will later use visual tools to customize these beans, test them, and wire them with other beans. We will also emphasize the interbean dynamics at both the tool and application levels.

THE MINIMALIST SMILEY BEAN

In this first pass, Smiley provides a default no-arg constructor and two public methods: *paint* and *toggleSmile* (see Figure 28-1). You invoke *toggleSmile* to put a frown on that happy face (and later to restore the beautiful smile). This method lets you toggle between smiles and frowns, depending on your mood.

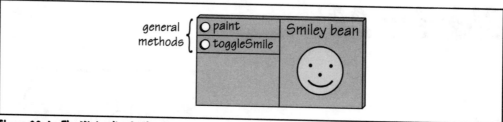

Figure 28-1. The Minimalist Smiley Bean.

The Minimalist Smiley Bean

The **SmileyBean** is a visual component. Consequently, it must derive from the AWT **Component** class. In this case, it inherits from **Canvas**, which itself is derived from the **Component** class. **Canvas** provides both a rectangular paint area and a *paint* method that you override to draw something useful—for example, a smiling face. Here's the code for this simplest of beans:

Listing 28-1. SmileyBean: The Minimalist Smiley Bean.

```java
// SmileyBean.java - a simple SmileyBean

import java.awt.*;
import java.beans.*;

public class SmileyBean extends Canvas
{
  // Private data fields

  private Color ourColor = Color.yellow;
  private boolean smile = true;

  // Construct a Smiley

  public SmileyBean()
  {
    setSize(250,250);
  }


  // public methods

  public synchronized void toggleSmile()
  {
```

```
    smile = !smile;
    repaint();
}


// paint the Smiley face

public void paint(Graphics g)
{
    int cx = getSize().width/2; // center x
    int cy = getSize().height/2; // center y
    double r = Math.min(cx,cy)*0.97; // find smallest radius
    int r007 = (int)(r*0.07); int r007x2 = r007*2; // precompute
    int r020 = (int)(r*0.20); int r020x2 = r020*2; // misc.
    int r030 = (int)(r*0.30); int r030x2 = r030*2; // radius
    int r060 = (int)(r*0.60); int r060x2 = r060*2; // values
    int r100 = (int)(r*1.00); int r100x2 = r100*2;

    g.setColor(ourColor);
    g.fillOval(cx-r100,cy-r100,r100x2,r100x2); // face background

    g.setColor(Color.black); // black
    g.drawOval(cx-r100,cy-r100,r100x2,r100x2); // outline

    if (smile) g.drawArc(cx-r060,cy-r060,r060x2,r060x2,200,140); //smile
    else g.drawArc(cx-r060,cy+r030,r060x2,r060x2,020,140); // frown

    g.fillOval(cx-r030-r007,cy-r030-r007,r007x2,r007x2); // left eye
    g.fillOval(cx+r030-r007,cy-r030-r007,r007x2,r007x2); // right eye
    g.fillOval(cx-r007,cy+r020-r007,r007x2,r007x2); // nose
  }
}
```

SmileyPlace: A Rudimentary Bean Container

Now that we have a bean, we must create a container that can run it. You can run beans from within tools, applications, applets, or HTML pages. In this section, we write a simple application for displaying our happy bean (see Figure 28-2). Components are typically instantiated inside containers. In subsequent chapters, we will evolve our containers to become places where beans can be assembled, connected via events, and stored in JARs.

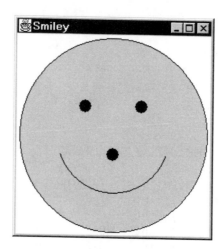

Figure 28-2. Smiley Bean Running in a SmileyPlace Window Container.

The application's single class—**SmileyPlace**—provides a *main* method that invokes a constructor to instantiate a Smiley bean and then display it within a window frame. Here's the code:

Listing 28-2. The SmileyPlace Application.

```
// SmileyPlace.java - Application for a simple Smiley

import java.awt.*;
import java.awt.event.*;
import java.beans.*;

public class SmileyPlace extends Frame implements WindowListener
{
  SmileyPlace()
  {
    SmileyBean smiley = null;

    try
    {
      smiley = (SmileyBean)Beans.instantiate(null, "SmileyBean");

    } catch (Exception e)
    { System.err.println("Exception:");
      System.err.println(e);
    }
```

```java
    add(smiley);
    addWindowListener(this);
  }

static public void main(String args[])
{
  SmileyPlace smileyPlace = new SmileyPlace();
  smileyPlace.setSize(400,400);
  smileyPlace.setTitle("Smiley");
  smileyPlace.pack();
  smileyPlace.setVisible(true);
}


// The following methods implement the
// Window Listener interface

public void windowClosing(WindowEvent event)
{
 System.exit(0);
}

public void windowClosed(WindowEvent event) {}
public void windowDeiconified(WindowEvent event) {}
public void windowIconified(WindowEvent event) {}
public void windowActivated(WindowEvent event) {}
public void windowDeactivated(WindowEvent event) {}
public void windowOpened(WindowEvent event) {}
}
```

The shaded sections of the code are bean-related. The only new element in this code is the **Beans** class. No, this is not the "mother of all Java bean classes." It's simply a global class that provides some useful services for beans. We explain this class in the next section. The important point here is that you never "new" a bean. Instead, you always create beans by invoking the *java.beans.Beans.instantiate* method. You must do this to maintain compatibility with future versions of JavaBeans.

The first parameter of the *instantiate* method is the name of the class loader that will create your bean; you'll typically specify *null* to use the system class loader. The second parameter specifies the name of the bean. You can either provide a fully-qualified class name or the name of a (.ser) file that contains a serialized version of the bean. This method first tries to load a serialized object with that name. If it fails, it looks for a class with the same name and then uses it to create an instance of the bean.

Notice that you simply *add* a bean to a container—in this case, an AWT **Frame**—like any ordinary JWT component. The code also implements the **WindowListener** interface. We do this to trap a window close event. Without this code, you would have to kill the Java VM to get rid of the window. We explain event listeners in the next chapter.

The Beans Class

The **Beans** class contains global methods that are used by applications or tools to create a bean; it is also used to obtain bean-related "environmental" information. The class provides a constructor and seven methods (see Figure 28-3). You already saw the *instantiate* method in action. We'll briefly cover the remaining six methods.

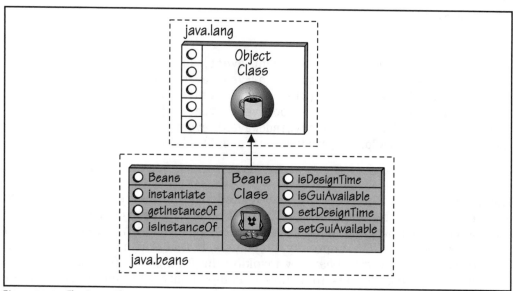

Figure 28-3. The Beans Class.

You pass a bean to the *getInstanceOf* method, and it returns an object representing a type view that you specify. You invoke the *isInstanceOf* method to determine if a bean can be viewed as a given target type. According to the JavaBeans architecture, you should never use Java casts or the Java *instanceof* operator to convert a bean between different types. Instead, you must use the *Beans.isInstanceOf* and *Beans.getInstanceOf* methods to obtain different type views of a bean. Why? Again, this makes your code compatible with future versions of JavaBeans.

You invoke *isDesignTime* to determine if the bean is running within a builder tool. A tool—or trusted application—invokes *setDesignTime* to indicate that the Java VM is running within an application builder environment. This method is security checked and is not available to untrusted applets.

You invoke *isGuiAvailable* to determine if your bean is running in a GUI environment. For example, you could invoke this method before popping up a visual dialog element. A trusted application invokes *setGuiAvailable* to indicate whether a GUI environment is available or not. For example, server beans typically do not run in GUI environments.

If you need more details, here is the class description:

Listing 28-3. The Java.beans Beans Class.

```
public class Beans extends Object
{
   // Constructor
   public Beans();

   // Class Methods
   public static Object instantiate(ClassLoader cls,
                                    String beanName)
                                    throws IOException,
                                    ClassNotFoundException;
   public static Object getInstanceOf(Object bean,
                                      Class targetType);
   public static boolean isInstanceOf(Object bean,
                                      Class targetType);
   public static boolean isDesignTime();
   public static boolean isGuiAvailable();
   public static void setDesignTime(boolean isDesignTime)
                                    throws SecurityException;
   public static void setGuiAvailable(boolean isGuiAvailable)
                                      throws SecurityException;
}
```

FIRST GUIDELINES FOR WRITING PORTABLE BEANS

This concludes our first bean. As you can see, the bean component model is built on familiar Java constructs. This is a common theme in the architecture of JavaBeans. However, there are some rules you must follow to create a well-behaved bean. Here are the rules we uncovered in this chapter:

✔ ***Never new a bean***. Instead, create your beans using the *Beans.instantiate* method.

✔ ***Always provide a zero-argument constructor***. Your bean must provide a zero-argument default constructor so that it can be correctly instantiated by *Beans.instantiate*. You can optionally provide a detailed constructor—with args—that gets invoked by the default constructor.

✔ ***Derive your visible beans from java.awt.Component***. This class—or, preferably, its **Canvas** subclasses—provides most of the basic functionality that visual beans require. This functionality includes rendering support, component event management, language locale, font type, and background and foreground colors. All you must do is trap events from the user and implement the *paint* function for your bean. Note that some beans may support other toolkit interfaces in addition to **java.awt.Component**; you can use *Beans.getInstanceOf* to convert these beans to AWT components.

✔ ***Use AWT containers to hold beans***. The container itself can be a bean. The pattern for populating containers with beans is to: 1) optionally instantiate a class loader or use the default class loader, 2) invoke *instantiate* to create a bean, and 3) invoke the standard AWT *add* call to add the bean to the container (see Figure 28-4). You repeatedly invoke steps 2 and 3 to assemble and layout an agglomerate of beans. In the next chapters, we will show you how the container sets up the event network that connects its beans.

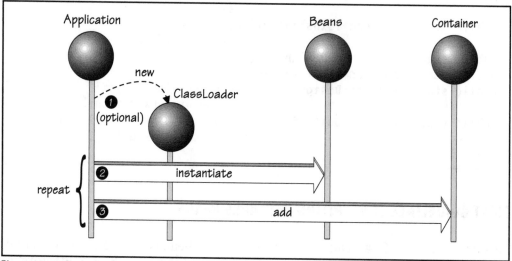

Figure 28-4. Beans Inside Containers.

✔ ***Don't use casts or instanceof.*** Instead, use the *Beans.isInstanceOf* and *Beans.getInstanceOf* methods to convert a bean between different types. These methods allow JavaBeans to provide more flexible mechanisms in the future. For example, beans that don't directly inherit from **Component** will still be able to return a **java.awt.Component** view of themselves.

CONCLUSION

In this chapter, we developed a simple Java bean and its container. The code should be familiar to Java programmers. This is not a coincidence. As we said earlier, the central idea behind JavaBeans is to provide a component model within Java itself. In a sense, Java simply becomes a giant framework for running the components you write. This is both good news bad news. It is good news if you're planning to write all your components in Java. It is bad news if you need to include components written in other languages. Of course, this is where CORBA beans come into the picture. But first let's continue with our JavaBeans story. In the next chapter, we cover events and beans.

Chapter 29

The Event-Driven JavaBean

Components must be able to communicate with other components. JavaBeans lets you do this using either events or via general-purpose method invocations. Events provide a more loosely-coupled form of communications. Consequently, they are used by most visual Java tools to "wire" together beans. As you'll see later in this chapter, events also result in method invocations. However, they do this via a protocol that introduces a level of indirection. It's this level of indirection that makes it possible for tools to get in the middle.

An *event* usually signals a state change in a bean; it can also signal an unpredictable occurrence—for example, "the house is on fire." It's a way for a bean to tell interested parties that something is happening. Of course, if no one is listening, it's a "non-event." Listeners are the consumers of events. They provide the event-handling logic.

Beans use the AWT *delegation event* model introduced in JDK 1.1. This model follows a publish-and-subscribe metaphor—events are received by subscription only. This is a good thing because it cuts down on the event traffic. In the pre-Java 1.1 days, you received your events by subclassing from a GUI container class. This resulted in the propagation of a lot of unwanted events up and down the class hierarchy. In addition, the old event model was tied to a GUI hierarchy, which made it unsuitable for generic components.

The new event model is ideal for visual tools. It lets them dynamically discover the events a bean emits and then match them with interested subscribes (or listeners). These relationships between event sources and subscribers are the wires that you use to connect your beans.

In this chapter, we provide a very quick introduction to the new event model and how it applies to beans. We will use events to wire *Smiley* with other components. We also show you how to create event adapters using Java's new *inner classes*. Finally, we will develop a CORBA event adapter that keeps track of Smiley's mood changes. An adapter is an intermediary piece of software that catches events before they arrive at the listener. It gives you a chance to control the propagation of events before they are delivered to their final destinations.

THE DELEGATION EVENT MODEL IN A NUTSHELL

The event model in AWT 1.0 was quite simple. All events were passed via the inheritance hierarchy, thus forcing objects to catch and process events by subclassing and overriding either the *handleEvent* or *action* methods. You had to write switch statements to determine which object triggered an event. This shotgun approach to the propagation of events was not scalable. It also tied the event model to the GUI hierarchy, which is not suitable for general-purpose components.

Sources and Listeners

With the new *delegation model* you identify events by their class instead of their ID. The events are propagated—or "delegated"—from an event *source* to a set of *listeners*. So there are three players in an event interaction:

■ *Event objects* encapsulate the change in state at the source. All event objects are derived from the class **java.util.EventObject**. JDK 1.1 introduced 12 AWT-specific event object types defined in *java.awt.events*. If none of these objects do the job for you, then you should create your own event type. The name of your event objects must end with Event. For example, here's how you create your own **BangEvent**:

```
// Your very own BangEvent class
public class BangEvent extends EventObject
  private long bangtime;
  public BangEvent (Object source, long time)
  {
    super (source);
```

```
      bangtime = time;
   }
   public long getBangTime ()
   {
      return bangtime;
   }
}
```

- **Event listeners** are the sinks that receive event notifications. All event listeners must implement an interface derived from **java.util.EventListener**—an empty interface that tags a listener class. You must extend this interface with your own notification methods. Each method gets invoked when an event fires. An interface can represent a single event or a group of closely-related events. All the notification methods are passed a single event object. To abide by the JavaBeans naming patterns, your new interface name must end with Listener. For example, the listener for a **BangEvent** would be called **BangListener**. The methods within the interface do not follow specific naming patterns. However, you should use names that describe the event that is firing. Here's an example of a listener interface that supports two related events:

```
// A BangListener with two methods--onbang and obbangbang
public interface BangListener extends EventListener
{
   public abstract void onbang(BangEvent e);
   public abstract void onbangbang(BangEvent e);
}
```

- **Event Sources** are beans that emit events. The source makes its events available to subscribers by providing an *addListenerType* and *removeListenerType* method pair for each listener type. For example, the **BangEvent** would support its subscribers via the *addBangListener* and *removeBangListener* methods. Note that these methods follow the JavaBeans-specified naming patterns:

```
// Snippet of code for adding and removing BangEvent listeners
private Vector bangListeners = new Vector();
public synchronized void addBangListener (BangListener 1)
{
   bangListeners.addElement (1);
}
```

```
public synchronized void removeBangListener (BangListener 1)
{

  bangListeners.removeElement (1);

}
```

Note that the source bean must keep track of all its subscribers. In this example, we do this using a **Vector**. As you will see in the next chapter, JavaBeans provides helper classes to which you can delegate this kind of work. These helpers even notify all the individual subscribers when the event fires. Here's how you would do it yourself for the **BangEvent**:

```
// Snippet of code for notifying listeners that a bang took place

protected void notifyBang ()
{
  // Create a Bang Event
  BangEvent e = new BangEvent (this, System.currentTimeMillis());

  // Now, notify all your listeners
  for (int i=0; i < bangListeners.size(); i++)
  {
    BangListener bl = (BangListener)bangListeners.elementAt (i);
    bl.onbang(e);
  }
}
```

Notice that you send events by invoking the *onbang* method on each of the subscribe objects. The event state is actually passed as the argument of the method.

This simple example introduces the different players that are involved in the delegation event model. In the next section, we walk through a scenario that shows how these players interact.

The Big Bang Scenario

Figure 29-1 demonstrates a "big bang" object interaction diagram. We have two subscriber beans that implement the **BangListener** interface. These two beans register their listeners with a bang-producing bean. The source bean emits two related bang events—*bang* and *bangbang*. They both pass a **BangEvent** as a parameter. Let's walk through the steps:

1. ***Bean listener 1 subscribes for bangs.*** The listener bean invokes *addBangListener* on the source and passes it a listener interface callback object.

2. ***Bean listener 2 subscribes for bangs.*** The second listener goes through the same steps; it passes a listener interface to its own callback object.

3. ***A bang occurs***. The source bean generates a **BangEvent** object and then sends

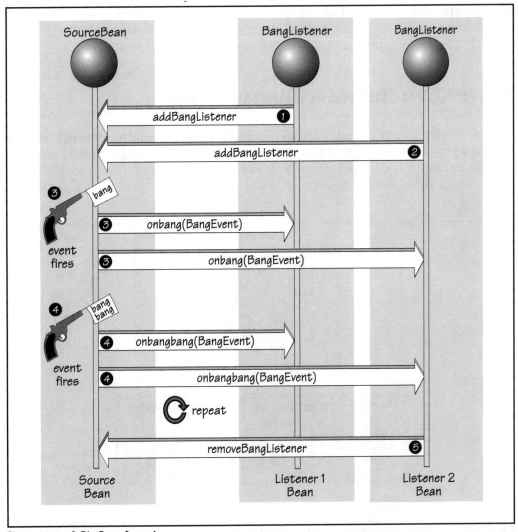

Figure 29-1. A Big Bang Scenario.

it to all its subscribers. It does this by invoking the *onbang* method on each listener and passing it the **BangEvent** as a parameter.

4. ***A bangbang occurs***. The source generates a **BangEvent** object and then sends it to all its subscribers. It does this by invoking the *onbangbang* method on each listener and passing it the **BangEvent** as a parameter.

5. ***Bean listener 2 has had enough bangs.*** The bean invokes *removeBang-Listener* on the source to unsubscribe.

This loosely-coupled protocol between event sources and subscribers makes it possible for tools to get into the middle of the act and provide wiring. More on this later. The scenario also shows that an event is really a combination of an event object and a method invocation on the listener. The event object encapsulates information that uniquely describes a specific event occurrence—including its source.

The EventObject Class and EventListener Interface

The *java.util* package defines both the **EventObject** class and the **EventListener** interface (see Figure 29-2). As we mentioned earlier, **EventListener** is simply a tagging interface; it does not define any methods. Introspectors and tools use the tag at design time to discover listener beans.

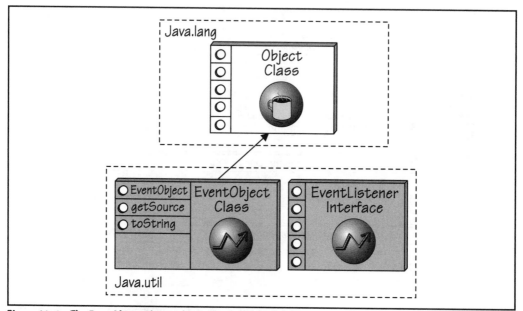

Figure 29-2. The EventObject Class and EventListener Interface.

The **EventObject** class is the mother of all Java delegation events. This class supports a constructor that lets you create new event instances. You must pass to the constructor the source of the event. An event object encapsulates all the information that is specific to an event's state; it is passed as a parameter in a method invocation on the listener. A listener can determine the source of an event by invoking *getSource*; it returns the object that generated the event. Finally, the *toString* method returns a human-readable string that describes the event. Here are the detailed class descriptions:

Listing 29-1. The Java.util EventListener Interface.

```
public interface EventListener
{
   // A tagging interface that your event listener interfaces must extend
}
```

Listing 29-2. The Java.util EventObject Class.

```
public Class EventObject extends Object implements Serializable
{
   // Variables
   protected transient Object source;

   // Constructors
   public EventObject(Object source);

   // Methods
   public Object getSource();
   public String toString();
}
```

Note that **EventObject** implements the **Serializable** interface, which means that all Java events can be stored persistently. The *source* field is declared *transient*, which means that it is not persistent. We cover Java persistence in a later chapter.

SMILEY BEAN DOES EVENTS

In this example, we will create a container that connects together two beans: Smiley and an ordinary AWT **Button**. We will extend Smiley for the occasion to become a listener of action events. **ActionEvent** is a general-purpose type of event that is emitted by many AWT components—including **Button**. You will be able to change Smiley's mood by simply clicking on the toggle button (see Figure 29-3). Each click triggers an action event that gets sent to the Smiley action listener.

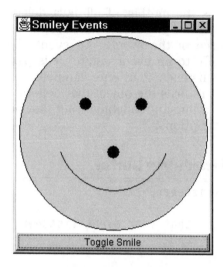

Figure 29-3. Smiley Bean Connected via Events With a Button Bean.

In this section, we first tell you something about the AWT **ActionListener** and **ActionEvent** classes. Then we extend Smiley to implement the **ActionListener** interface. Finally, we create a container application that uses events to connect the Smiley bean with an off-the-shelf **Button** bean. As you will see, we don't have to write any code for the **Button**. We must simply figure out how to subscribe to the **ActionEvent** it generates.

The ActionEvent and ActionListener Classes

Figure 29-4 shows where the **ActionListener**, **ActionEvent**, and **Button** classes sit in the AWT 1.1 hierarchy. **Button** is an AWT control that is also a JavaBean; it sources the AWT-defined **ActionEvent**. The **Button** class provides *addActionListener* and *removeActionListener* methods to let interested components subscribe to its events.

The **ActionListener** interface is directly derived from **java.util.EventListener**. It supports a single method—*actionPerformed*—which is invoked when an action fires. Interested beans must implement this interface:

Listing 29-3. The Java.awt.event ActionListener Interface.

```
public interface ActionListener extends EventListener
{
  public abstract void actionPerformed(ActionEvent e);
}
```

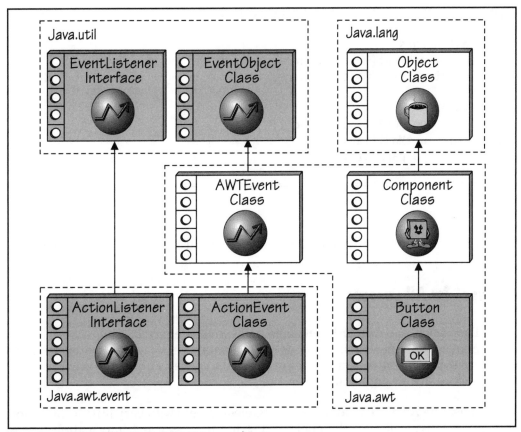

Figure 29-4. AWT's ActionEvent, ActionListener, and Button.

The **ActionEvent** class is derived from **java.awt.AWTEvent**. Here is the class
definition:

Listing 29-4. The Java.awt.event ActionEvent Class.

```
public class ActionEvent extends AWTEvent
{
  // Variables
  public static final int SHIFT_MASK;
  public static final int CTRL_MASK;
  public static final int META_MASK;
  public static final int ALT_MASK;
  public static final int ACTION_FIRST;
  public static final int ACTION_LAST;
```

```
    public static final int ACTION_PERFORMED;

    // Constructors
    public ActionEvent(Object source, int id, String command);
    public ActionEvent(Object source, int id, String command, int modifiers);

    // Methods
    public String getActionCommand();
    public int getModifiers();
    public String paramString();
}
```

The action command is represented by a string. The id represents an event subtype.

An Event for All Seasons

In AWT parlance, the **ActionEvent** falls under the category of *semantic event*; it corresponds to a high-level user action. A semantic event can be used by a variety of different beans. In contrast, *low-level* events convey information that is more GUI-specific—for example, mouse events.

You can use the **ActionEvent** to signal stateless events with very little information content. You typically use the command string to pass event information that is relevant to your bean or application. For example, you can specify a set of semantic commands for a suite of beans. The **ActionEvent** is the closest thing to a generic JavaBean event that you can reuse in multiple situations. You should use standard events whenever possible. It makes your beans more wireable.

The Event-Savvy Smiley

Figure 29-5 shows our new additions to the Smiley bean. In addition to *paint* and *toggleSmile*, the new Smiley implements the **ActionListener** interface. Consequently, it must provide an *actionPerformed* method. The container will connect a Smiley bean with a **Button** bean via an **ActionEvent**. Notice that the AWT **Button** provides the tell-tale *addActionListener* and *removeActionListener* methods. This is how it tells the world at large that it is a source of action events.

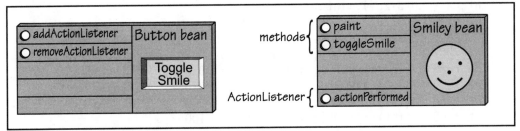

Figure 29-5. The Event-Savvy Smiley Bean.

The code for this simplest of event-listening beans follows. After this long introduction, there should be no surprises. We shaded the new event-related code.

Listing 29-5. SmileyBean: The Eventful Smiley Bean.

```java
// SmileyBean.java - a SmileyBean that reacts to a Button event

import java.awt.*;
import java.awt.event.*;
import java.beans.*;

public class SmileyBean extends Canvas implements ActionListener
{
  // Private data fields:
  private Color ourColor = Color.yellow;
  private boolean smile = true;

  // Construct a Smiley
  public SmileyBean()
  {
    setSize(250,250);
  }

  // public methods
  public synchronized void toggleSmile()
  {
    smile = !smile;
    repaint();
  }

  // Paint the Smiley face
  public void paint(Graphics g)
  {
```

```
    int cx = getSize().width/2; // center x
    int cy = getSize().height/2; // center y
    double r = Math.min(cx,cy)*0.97; // find smallest radius
    int r007 = (int)(r*0.07); int r007x2 = r007*2; // precompute
    int r020 = (int)(r*0.20); int r020x2 = r020*2; // misc.
    int r030 = (int)(r*0.30); int r030x2 = r030*2; // radius
    int r060 = (int)(r*0.60); int r060x2 = r060*2; // values
    int r100 = (int)(r*1.00); int r100x2 = r100*2;

    g.setColor(ourColor);
    g.fillOval(cx-r100,cy-r100,r100x2,r100x2); // face background

    g.setColor(Color.black); // black
    g.drawOval(cx-r100,cy-r100,r100x2,r100x2); // outline

    if (smile) g.drawArc(cx-r060,cy-r060,r060x2,r060x2,200,140); //smile
    else g.drawArc(cx-r060,cy+r030,r060x2,r060x2,020,140); // frown

    g.fillOval(cx-r030-r007,cy-r030-r007,r007x2,r007x2); // left eye
    g.fillOval(cx+r030-r007,cy-r030-r007,r007x2,r007x2); // right eye
    g.fillOval(cx-r007,cy+r020-r007,r007x2,r007x2); // nose
  }

  // called by event source
  public void actionPerformed(ActionEvent e)
  {
    toggleSmile();
  }

}
```

SmileyPlace: A Hard-Wired Bean Container

Now that we have some event-savvy beans, let's connect them together in a container. The scenario in Figure 29-6 shows how a containing application connects its beans via events. In this case, it's a hard-wired situation. Here are the steps:

1. **Create the Smiley bean**. The application invokes *instantiate* to create an instance of **SmileyBean**.

2. **Create a button bean**. The application invokes *instantiate* to create an instance of **Button**.

3. **Write the label on the button**. In non-bean situations, the application would invoke the *new* constructor on a **Button** and pass it an initial label. However, in a bean environment, you must invoke *instantiate*, which in turn calls a no-arg constructor. So you must explicitly invoke *setLabel* on an instance of the button. Yes, it's inconvenient.

4. **Add the beans to the visual container**. The application first selects a layout manager and then invokes *add* for each bean that goes into the visual container.

5. **Connect the beans**. The application invokes *addActionListener* on the button bean passing it a reference to the Smiley bean—the event listener. Smiley is now subscribed to action events fired by the button. The two beans are now connected (or wired).

6. **Click on the button**. The button bean fires an **ActionEvent**. The bean then invokes *actionPerformed* on each of its subscribers and passes them the **ActionEvent** as a parameter. In this case, there is only one subscriber—the Smiley bean.

We now present the code behind this scenario.

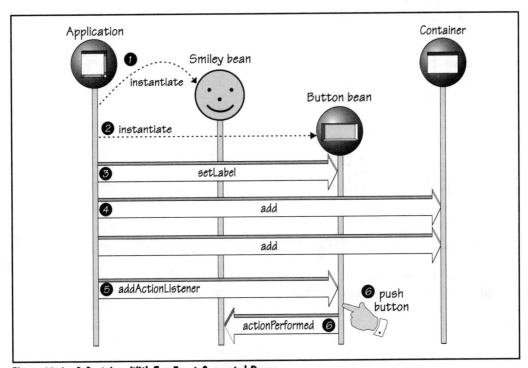

Figure 29-6. A Container With Two Event-Connected Beans.

Listing 29-6. The SmileyPlace Application.

```java
// SmileyPlace.java - Application for a Smiley with events

import java.awt.*;
import java.awt.event.*;
import java.beans.*;

public class SmileyPlace extends Frame implements WindowListener
{
  SmileyPlace()
  {
    SmileyBean smiley = null;
    Button button = null;

    // instantiate beans in container
    try
    {
      smiley = (SmileyBean)Beans.instantiate(null, "SmileyBean");
      button = (Button)Beans.instantiate(null, "java.awt.Button");
    } catch (Exception e)
    { System.err.println("Exception:");
      System.err.println(e);
    }

    // give the button a label

    button.setLabel("Toggle Smile");

    // place the beans

    setLayout(new BorderLayout());
    add(smiley, "North");
    add(button, "South");

    // connect the beans
    button.addActionListener(smiley);

    // trap the window exit
    addWindowListener(this);

  }
```

```
static public void main(String args[])
{
  SmileyPlace smileyPlace = new SmileyPlace();
  smileyPlace.setSize(200,200);
  smileyPlace.setTitle("Smiley Events");
  smileyPlace.pack();
  smileyPlace.setVisible(true);
}
```

```
  // The following implement methods in the
  // Window Listener interface

  public void windowClosing(WindowEvent event)
  {
   System.exit(0);
  }

  public void windowClosed(WindowEvent event) {}
  public void windowDeiconified(WindowEvent event) {}
  public void windowIconified(WindowEvent event) {}
  public void windowActivated(WindowEvent event) {}
  public void windowDeactivated(WindowEvent event) {}
  public void windowOpened(WindowEvent event) {}
```

```
}
```

The application's single class—**SmileyPlace**—provides a *main* method that invokes a constructor to instantiate the two beans and then add them to the window frame. This application creates an event connection between Smiley and the **Button** bean (see shaded lines). The code simply implements the scenario we described earlier. So there should be no surprises.

We now finally have the know-how to unravel the mysterious *WindowListener* code (see shaded area). This code is a simple application of the delegation-event model. In this case, the **SmileyPlace** object registers itself as a listener of window events that it also generates. It does this by calling *addWindowListener* on itself; it inherits this method from its **java.awt.Window** ancestor. So, in essence, the object is subscribing to events that it also sources. Also notice that we're only interested in *windowClosing* events (we simply want to know when the user terminates the application). However, Java doesn't allow us to selectively implement a method within an interface, which is why you see all these empty methods. In the next section, we show you how to use an anonymous *inner class* to get around specifying all these empty methods.

Anonymous Inner Class Adapters

An *anonymous class* is an inner Java class that lets you combine in a single expression the instantiation and definition of a new *inner class*. This lets you create very concise adapter classes. To do this, you combine *new* with a class body. The class (or interface) named after the new token is subclassed by the body of code you write. The resulting *anonymous inner class* has the same meaning as if you had defined it locally, with a name, in the current block of statements. Here's a snippet of code that shows a very concise implementation of the **WindowListener** interface we described in the previous section:

```
WindowListener 1 = new WindowAdapter()
{  public void windowClosing(WindowEvent e) {System.exit(0);}
};
addWindowListener(1);
```

In this snippet, we define and instantiate an anonymous inner class that overrides the **WindowAdapter** class—this is an AWT class that provides empty method implementations of the **WindowListener** interface. The body of code defines an inner class that extends **WindowAdapter** by overriding the *windowClosing* method. Finally, we register an instance of this new inner class as a listener for window events. In general, you must keep anonymous constructs very simple to avoid deeply nested code.

EVENT ADAPTERS

In the code we just created, the firing bean was directly connected to the target bean. *Adapters* are go-between objects. In this case, we use them to mediate between event sources and their targets. Instead of passing the destination bean directly to the source, you pass it an adapter that acts as its proxy. The adapter listens on behalf of the destination and calls it when some event occurs.

Why Adapters?

At a first glance, the advantages of adapters are not immediately obvious—all they seem to do is provide a level of indirection between event sources and their final destinations. The JavaBeans specification does not provide too much help in this area; it only mentions adapters, but does not specify a generic architecture for implementing them.[1] In general, the decoupling of an event source from a target

---

[1] Note that a good example of a generic event adapter architecture is the *CORBA Event Channel*.

is beneficial when you need to filter events, queue them, and send them to remote destinations. It is also the primary mechanism visual tools use to wire disparate beans. In addition, you can use adapters to make existing code play in the world of beans. In the following sections, we provide a taxonomy of adapter types. Then we develop some code that shows you how to use these adapters.

Event Adapters: A Taxonomy

In this section, we provide a taxonomy of event adapters. The primary idea here is to get you to think about how you can use event adapters in your code. The taxonomy is by no means exhaustive. Here's a quick list of the types of adapters you can create:

- ■ ***Demultiplexing adapters*** let you invoke different handlers for identical events received from multiple sources (see Figure 29-7). You must create an adapter for each source bean that requires specific handling. You can implement the different adapters via Java *inner classes*. The advantage of inner classes is that they share the scope of the encapsulating class, which means they have access to its variables; it also reduces the proliferation of public classes.

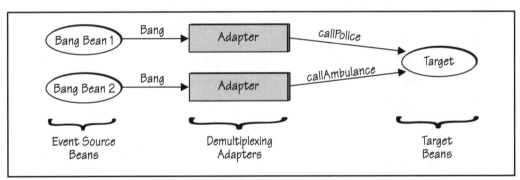

Figure 29-7. Demultiplexing Adapters.

The scenario in Figure 29-8 shows how you would use demultiplexing adapters to funnel requests to the appropriate methods on the target. Here are the steps: 1) the destination bean instantiates a different adapter object for each event source, 2) each adapter registers itself with a source, 3) a **BangEvent** from the first bean causes the *callPolice* method to be invoked on the target, and 4) a **BangEvent** from second bean causes the *callAmbulance* method to be invoked on the target.

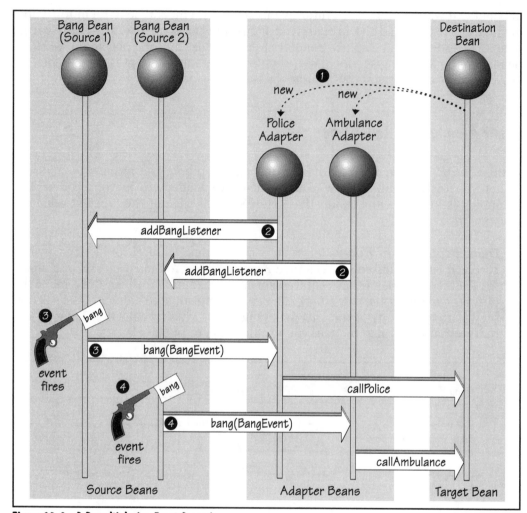

Figure 29-8. A Demultiplexing Event Scenario.

■ *Generic adapters* map incoming events from different sources into specific method invocations on one or more target beans (see Figure 29-9). You must provide a map of events to target methods. The adapter then uses Java introspection to discover the methods a target object supports. Finally, it uses *invoke* on a **java.lang.reflect.Method** object to dynamically invoke the method. Note that if the target is remote, you can use the CORBA DII to dynamically invoke the method.[2]

---

[2] Two of our graduate students developed for a class project a generic adapter, which they called *CorbaBean*. At build time, this adapter does an IR introspection on any CORBA object that you specify via an IOR or name. It then dynamically generates DII code to invoke methods on that object's interface.

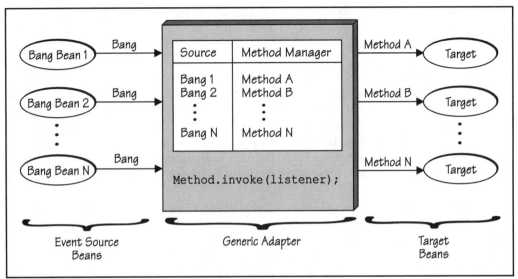

Figure 29-9. A Generic Demultiplexing Adapter.

■ **Wiring adapters** are used by visual tools to connect disparate beans. The tool dynamically discovers—via introspection—the events a source bean fires and the methods a target bean supports. It then lets you visually connect the source with the target method that you pick. Under the cover, the builder creates an adapter class that listens to the event and calls the target method when it fires. One way to rank bean assembly tools is by the power of their adapters. The best tools will let you wire any bean to any other bean without requiring that you write a line of code.

■ **Wrappering adapters** are used to connect beans to existing code. These adapters are useful when you cannot modify the target code. In this case, the adapter provides the listener code and registers itself with event sources. When an event fires the adapter will invoke the target method on the existing code.

■ **Distributed event adapters** are used to invoke remote CORBA or RMI methods. You can also use adapters to map between the CORBA and JavaBean event models.[3]

■ **Queuing adapters** place the fired events in a queue and then deliver them to the targets. This arrangement allows the source bean to resume execution

---

[3] Another one of our graduate students developed a two-way gateway between CORBA typed-event channels and bean events. This lets CORBA server objects register their interest in GUI events on the client; it also allows client beans to be notified when something of interest happens on the server.

without blocking until the event is consumed by the target. Queuing adapters make it possible to support target beans that are either busy or not available when the event fires.

■ *Filtering adapters* apply rules to the delivery of events. In this case, you use the adapter to filter events before they arrive at the listener. This lets you control the propagation of events to the destination beans. By interjecting itself between the source and destination, the adapter can then log events, route them to multiple recipients, sort them by priority, and apply all kinds of business rules. For example, the adapter could look for a combination of events that is of interest to the destination. The sky is the limit with what you can do in this area.

This list was just a teaser to get you to think about the fun things you can do with event adapters. In the next two sections, we provide two very simple adapter code examples. The first example is a wrappering adapter; it lets us use the event-unaware Smiley from the previous chapter as is. In other words, Smiley does not have to implement the listener interface to receive event notifications. The second adapter invokes the infamous CORBA **Count** object every time Smiley receives an event notification; it lets a server keep track of Smiley's mood changes. We're sure that you'll come up with more imaginative uses for your adapters.

The Smiley Event Adapter

The **SmileyEventAdapter** class implements the **ActionListener** interface on behalf of the original Smiley from the last chapter. You don't touch the original Smiley code. When the event fires, the adapter invokes Smiley's *toggleSmile* method. Here's the code:

Listing 29-7. The SmileyEventAdapter.

```
// SmileyEventAdapter.java - Event adapter

import java.awt.*;
import java.awt.event.*;

public class SmileyEventAdapter implements java.awt.event.ActionListener
{
  private SmileyBean target;

  SmileyEventAdapter(SmileyBean t)
  {
      target = t;
  }
```

```java
    public void actionPerformed(ActionEvent arg0) {
        target.toggleSmile();
    }
}
```

Now we need a container application to wire the Smiley and Button beans via this adapter.

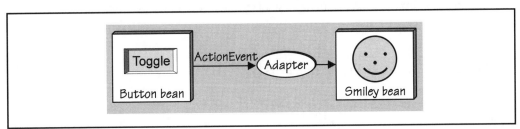

Figure 29-10. A Wrappering Adapter for Smiley.

Here's the code:

Listing 29-8. The SmileyPlace Application.

```java
// SmileyPlace.java - Application for a Smiley with an event adapter

import java.awt.*;
import java.awt.event.*;
import java.beans.*;

public class SmileyPlace extends Frame
{
  SmileyPlace()
  {
    SmileyBean smiley = null;
    Button button = null;

    // instantiate beans in container
    try
    {
      smiley = (SmileyBean)Beans.instantiate(null, "SmileyBean");
      button = (Button)Beans.instantiate(null, "java.awt.Button");
    } catch (Exception e)
    { System.err.println("Exception:");
      System.err.println(e);
    }
```

```
    // give the button a label
    button.setLabel("Toggle Smile");

    // place the beans
    setLayout(new BorderLayout());
    add(smiley, "North");
    add(button, "South");

    // connect the beans
    button.addActionListener(new SmileyEventAdapter (smiley));

}

static public void main(String args[])
{
  SmileyPlace smileyPlace = new SmileyPlace();
  smileyPlace.setSize(100,100);
  smileyPlace.setTitle("Smiley Adapter Events");
  smileyPlace.pack();
  smileyPlace.setVisible(true);
  // trap window exit event with anonymous inner class
  WindowListener l = new WindowAdapter()
    {
      public void windowClosing(WindowEvent e) {System.exit(0);}
    };
  smileyPlace.addWindowListener(l);

}
}
```

The shaded areas highlight the new code in this container. As you can see, we now pass to the button a reference to the **SmileyEventAdapter** instead of to the Smiley bean itself. The adapter is invoked when the button event fires; it then invokes the Smiley *toggleSmile* method. The code also demonstrates our new anonymous inner class in action.

The CORBA Count Event Adapter

In this section, we develop a CORBA event adapter for the Count server from Chapter 7. The CORBA adapter will register itself as an **ActionEvent** listener. This way it will track the changes in the mood of the Smiley bean. So every time you press the button, two things happen: 1) Smiley toggles its facial expression, and 2) the CORBA adapter invokes the *increment* method on the Count server object (see

Figure 29-11). This allows the server to keep a running count of Smiley's mood changes. How exciting!

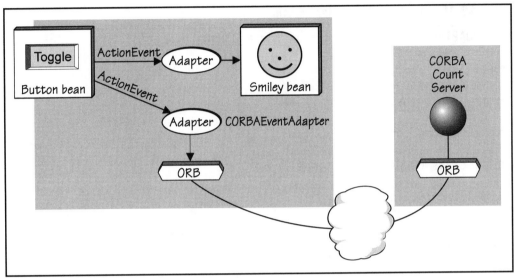

Figure 29-11. A CORBA JavaBean Event Adapter.

Here's the code for the **CORBAEventAdapter** class:

Listing 29-9. The CORBAEventAdapter.

```
// CORBAEventAdapter.java - Event Adapter

import java.awt.*;
import java.awt.event.*;

public class CORBAEventAdapter implements java.awt.event.ActionListener
{
  private CounterPortable.Count target;

  CORBAEventAdapter(CounterPortable.Count t)
  {
    target = t;
  }

  public void actionPerformed(ActionEvent arg0)
  {
    int sum = target.increment();
  }
}
```

Of course, we now need a container to run this new set of beans. Here's the code for a **CORBAPlace** container class:

Listing 29-10. The CORBAPlace Application.

```java
// CORBAPlace.java - Application for a CORBA invocation

import java.awt.*;
import java.awt.event.*;
import java.beans.*;

import org.omg.CosNaming.*;

public class CORBAPlace extends Frame
{
  CORBAPlace(String[] args)
  {

    SmileyBean smiley = null;
    Button     button = null;
    CounterPortable.Count counter = null;

    try
    {
      // instantiate beans in container
      smiley = (SmileyBean)Beans.instantiate(null, "SmileyBean");
      button = (Button)Beans.instantiate(null, "java.awt.Button");


      // Initialize the ORB
      org.omg.CORBA.ORB orb = org.omg.CORBA.ORB.init(args, null);

      // Get a reference to the Naming service
      org.omg.CORBA.Object nameServiceObj =
              orb.resolve_initial_references ("NameService");
      if (nameServiceObj == null)
      {
        System.out.println("nameServiceObj = null");
        return;
      }
      // Locate the Naming Service
      org.omg.CosNaming.NamingContext nameService =
          org.omg.CosNaming.NamingContextHelper.narrow(nameServiceObj);
```

```
      if (nameService == null)
      {
        System.out.println("nameService = null");
        return;
      }


      // Locate an object called countName
      // relative to initial namecontext
      NameComponent[] countName = {new NameComponent("countName", "")};
      counter = CounterPortable.CountHelper.narrow(
                                      nameService.resolve(countName));


      // Set sum to initial value of 0
      counter.sum((int)0);

    } catch (Exception e)
    { System.err.println("Exception:");
      System.err.println(e);
    }

    // give the button a label
    button.setLabel("Toggle Smile");

    // place the beans
    setLayout(new BorderLayout());
    add(smiley, "North");
    add(button, "South");

    // connect the beans
    button.addActionListener(new SmileyEventAdapter (smiley));
    button.addActionListener(new CORBAEventAdapter(counter));

  }

  static public void main(String args[])
  {
    CORBAPlace corbaPlace = new CORBAPlace(args);
    corbaPlace.setSize(200,200);
    corbaPlace.setTitle("CORBA Adapter Events");
    corbaPlace.pack();
    corbaPlace.setVisible(true);


    // trap window exit event with anonymous inner class
```

```
    WindowListener l = new WindowAdapter()
      {
        public void windowClosing(WindowEvent e) {System.exit(0);}
      };
    corbaPlace.addWindowListener(l);
  }
}
```

As you can see, our bean containers are acquiring smarts as this book progresses. In addition to providing regular bean wiring and placement, the **CORBAPlace** initializes the ORB and instantiates CORBA objects (see shaded areas). It is also responsible for managing the event adapters, which are used to wire beans together.

MORE GUIDELINES FOR WRITING PORTABLE BEANS

Here are some of the guidelines we uncovered in this chapter for writing portable beans:

✔ *Use standard naming patterns to surface events.* Beans that fire events must provide *addListenerType* and *removeListenerType* methods. Subscribers must implement listener interfaces ending in the word *Listener*. Event object classes must end in the word *Event*.

✔ *Fully describe an event's state.* Create event objects that capture all the information that describes an event. You should always subclass **java.util.Event-Object** to create a meaningful event—even if you don't add any new function or information.

✔ *Create a hierarchy of event listeners.* Subscribers must only implement the interfaces that they find "interesting." Use a hierarchy of listeners to give them exactly what they want. The source bean must refine its support for listeners to make its subscribers happy.

✔ *Group closely-related event notifications into a single listener.* If you do this, you must then use descriptive method names in your listener interface to differentiate the different handlers in the set.

✔ *Use standard AWT events where it makes sense.* Reuse is generally a good thing. You should reuse or extend an existing event/listener combination instead of creating new ones at a whim. For example, in this chapter, we reused the **ActionEvent** instead of creating a new class of event. Note that ease-of-use may win over reuse; it's a delicate balancing act.

✔ ***Use adapters to wire beans.*** Adapters provide the glue for assembling disparate beans. You can think of them as providing the bean plumbing. They compensate for impedance mismatches among beans in a container. Adapters also help beans play in client/server networks. In general, the adapters are something the container must provide and manage—they are container artifacts.

✔ ***Use smart bean containers.*** The containers we saw in this chapter provided the following services: 1) instantiation and customization of beans, 2) display of beans in windows, 3) wiring of beans via adapters and events, and 4) setting up the CORBA environment for remote bean invocations.

✔ ***Use tools wherever possible.*** Wiring beans together using events is something a tool can easily automate. So look for a good tool to do your wiring. You may also want to look at the adapter code the tool creates. Make sure it's good code.

CONCLUSION

In this chapter, we looked at how Java's new delegation event model applies to JavaBeans. Instead of creating a separate event model for beans, the Java designers chose to entirely recreate the Java event model into something that could support the generic needs of beans. The result is a well-designed event model that follows the publish-and-subscribe metaphor.

The Java event model is designed to be simple. You are encouraged to extend this model with your own custom adapters whenever you need to do something more esoteric. In this chapter, we developed a taxonomy to describe the different ways you can extend bean events with adapters. For example, the Java event model is not distributed. So we used a CORBA adapter to extend the reach of a Java event across an IIOP network. We anticipate that JavaBeans will eventually incorporate some of the more generic adapters.

Finally, we continued to evolve our bean containers. Some of the new smarts our containers acquired in this chapter include the wiring of beans via adapters and connecting them to a distributed CORBA environment. As you can imagine, our containers will only get smarter as the book progresses. The next chapter looks at how containers and their beans deal with bound and constrained properties.

Chapter 30

The Propertied JavaBean

Properties are a very versatile piece of the component arsenal—they make it possible for end-users to customize beans without writing a line of code. Most visual builder tools for beans provide *property editors* that you can use to modify and customize an individual bean. In general, you should be able to modify at least one bean property to create a unique instance of a component. It's a key requirement for reusing beans. In GUI environments, properties typically let you control the visual appearance of your beans. In server environments, properties let you control the behavior of a bean—for example, you should be able to specify the transactional awareness of a bean by simply setting one of its properties.

A *property* is a public attribute of a bean that you can manipulate via getter and setter methods. Properties typically correspond to fields (or instance data) that define the internal state of an object. Like a CORBA attribute, a JavaBean property can be read-write, read-only, or write-only. In addition, a JavaBean property can be simple, indexed, bound, or constrained. You can use all these mechanisms to manipulate the internal state of a bean via getter and setter methods. As we explained in Chapter 27, you make these properties known to introspectors by following the JavaBeans naming patterns.

In JavaBeans, the changing of a property can result in the firing of an event. We call these *active properties*. For example, both the bound and constrained properties use events to notify interested beans when a property changes. You can use these events to connect the value of a property in one bean to the value of the property in another bean.

In this chapter, we tell you all about how to use properties with your beans. We explain the naming patterns that you must use to surface a bean's properties. As usual, we use our Smiley beans to demonstrate the workings of the various JavaBeans property mechanisms.

STANDALONE PROPERTIES

This section covers the basic property types. A basic property can be *single-valued* or *multi-valued*. It is standalone (or inactive), which in this case means that it is not connected via events to listeners. The property's state change is only of interest to the bean that initiates the update and to the target bean that performs the update. The rest of the world couldn't care less.

Simple Properties

A bean property is typically an internal variable that you can access via an accessor method that begins with *get* followed by the name of the property. You can change the property via a mutator method that begins with *set* followed by the name of the property. You can make a property read-only by not providing a mutator. Optionally, you can use an *isXXX* accessor method to flag to the introspector a single-valued *boolean* property; it has a value of either true or false.

Here's a snippet of code for a **Person** bean with two properties *age* and *single*:

```
public class Person
{
  private int age;
  private boolean single;

  Person(int newage)
  {
    age = newage;
  }

  // Read-Only age property
  public int getAge ()
  {
    return age;
  }
```

```
// Read-Write single boolean property
public void setSingle (boolean status)
{
  single = status;
}
public boolean isSingle ()
{
  return single;
}
}
```

The getter and setter methods in this code define the properties. They are used to access internal variables that contain the state of the properties. It's a one-to-one mapping. Of course, you can also calculate the value of a property "on-the-fly."

Multi-Valued Indexed Properties

An *indexed* property contains a collection of values that are of the same type. You use the standard getter and setter methods to retrieve or set an entire array of properties. JavaBeans also lets you retrieve and set individual elements within a property array. To do this, you must provide an additional index argument in your getter and setter methods.

Here's a snippet of code for a **MyFriends** bean with a read-only *friends* indexed property:

```
public class MyFriends
{
  private String friends[];

  MyFriends(String[] friendList)
  {
    friends = friendList;
  }

  // return a friend
  public String getFriends (int index)
  {
    return friends[index];
  }
  // return all friends
  public String[] getFriends ()
```

```
  {
    return friends;
  }
}
```

ACTIVE PROPERTIES

In this section, we explain how simple properties can be extended to notify interested parties when they are modified. The bean with the property will inform all the interested parties of any changes in its state. A mechanism also exists to allow interested parties to veto any changes. Any listener with veto power can refuse changes and thus prevent the source bean from changing its inner state.

The technology for doing these notifications combines simple properties with an event broadcast system. The events connect the properties to listeners. A connected property (or *active property*) is either *bound* or *constrained*. This may sound like a sinister, sado-masochistic ritual for beans. It really isn't. We're talking about the "bonding" of property changes in beans with anonymous event listeners. So we will first cover the property-related classes and interfaces defined in the *java.beans* package. Then we will use Smiley programming examples to illustrate how events and properties play together to create these new bonds.

Bound Properties

A *bound property* fires an event when its value changes. The firing of the event notifies listener beans that the property has changed its state. You may remember from the last chapter that the event mechanism consists of event objects, event sources, and event listeners. You will see instances of all three in this section.

To support bound properties, JavaBeans defines a new event type called the **PropertyChangeEvent** class (see Figure 30-1). The listener interface that supports this new event is called the **PropertyChangeListener**. Finally, JavaBeans provides a support class—called **PropertyChangeSupport**—to help source beans notify subscribers when an event fires.

A bean that supports bound properties must provide the following design pattern:

```
void addPropertyChangeListener(PropertyChangeListener l);
void removePropertyChangeListener(PropertyChangeListener l);
```

You invoke the *addPropertyChangeListener* to add a subscriber on a per-bean basis. You invoke *removePropertyChangeListener* to remove a subscriber also on

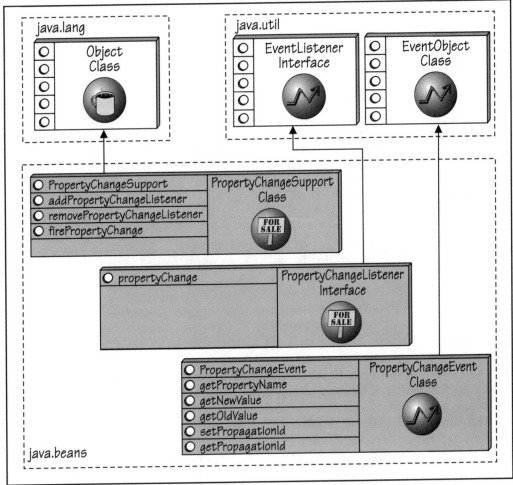

Figure 30-1. Bound Properties: Interfaces and Classes.

a per-bean basis. You should note that a bean can support more than one bound property. These two methods service all the bound properties within a bean.

The JavaBeans 1.01 update (July, 1997) specifies that you can now add (or remove) a listener for a named property that you specify using the following design pattern:

```
void addPropertyChangeListener(String name, PropertyChangeListener 1);
void removePropertyChangeListener(String name, PropertyChangeListener 1);
```

The source bean will associate the listener with the given property name; it only invokes the listener's *propertyChange* method when the named property changes.

The Bound Property Classes and Interfaces

Here's a brief description of the single interface and two classes the *java.beans* package provides in support of bound properties:

- The **PropertyChangeEvent** class contains all the information about a changed property. The source bean creates an object of this class when any of its bound or constrained properties change. The object contains the name of the property as well as its old and new values. The source passes this object in an argument when it invokes its listeners. The listeners obtain the old and new values of a changed property by invoking *getOldValue* and *getNewValue*. A source bean may provide null values for the old and the new values if it does not know their values. The target bean invokes *getPropertyName* to obtain the string name of the changed property; the source may send a null object as the name to indicate that an arbitrary set of its properties have changed. In this case, the old and new values must also be null. *A propagation Id* is reserved for future beans.

- The **PropertyChangeListener** interface defines a single method called *propertyChange*. Beans that register for property value changes must implement this interface.

- The **PropertyChangeSupport** is a helper class. Source beans use it to manage events that are fired by their bound properties. You can either derive your bean from this class or you can use an instance of this class as a member field of your bean and then delegate work to it. The *addPropertyChangeListener* and *removePropertyChangeListener* methods handle the registration and unregistration of property change listeners. The *firePropertyChange* method notifies any registered listeners when a bound property changes; it will not fire if the old and new values are equal and also not null.

The following class descriptions provide more detail:

Listing 30-1. The Java.beans PropertyChangeEvent Class.

```
public class PropertyChangeEvent extends EventObject
{
  // Constructor
  public PropertyChangeEvent(Object source,
                             String propertyName,
                             Object oldValue,
                             Object newValue);
```

```
// Methods
public String getPropertyName();
public Object getNewValue();
public Object getOldValue();
public void setPropagationId(Object propagationId);
public Object getPropagationId();
}
```

Listing 30-2. The Java.beans PropertyChangeListener Interface.

```
public interface PropertyChangeListener extends EventListener
{
  // Methods
  public abstract void propertyChange(PropertyChangeEvent evt);
}
```

Listing 30-3. The Java.beans PropertyChangeSupport Class.

```
public class PropertyChangeSupport
          extends Object implements Serializable
{
  // Constructor
  public PropertyChangeSupport(Object sourceBean);

  // Methods
  public synchronized void addPropertyChangeListener(
                          PropertyChangeListener listener);
  public synchronized void removePropertyChangeListener(
                          PropertyChangeListener listener);
  public void firePropertyChange(String propertyName, Object oldValue,
                          Object newValue);
}
```

A Bound Property Scenario

It's time for a scenario that shows how these classes play together. Figure 30-2 shows a bean with a bound property called *price*. In this scenario, the bean communicates a price change to its bound subscribers. Here are the steps:

1. ***The bean creates a helper object***. This is a smart bean that knows how to delegate work. So it creates a **PropertyChangeSupport** helper object.

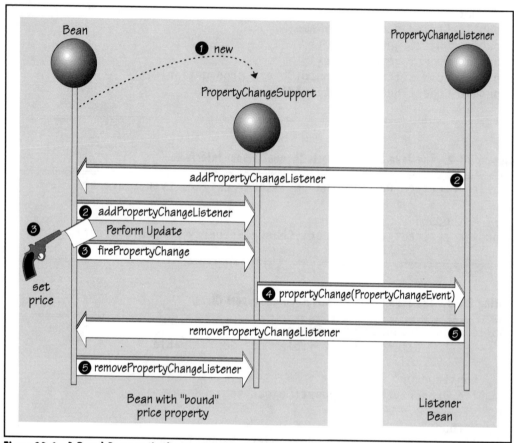

Figure 30-2. A Bound-Property Notification Scenario.

2. *A subscriber bean wants to track price changes*. The subscriber invokes *addPropertyChangeListener* on the source bean and passes it a reference to its listener interface. Note that the source bean simply turns around and invokes *addPropertyChangeListener* on its helper. The helper adds the subscriber to its list.

3. *The price changes*. The source bean invokes its helper's *firePropertyChange* method and passes it the name of the property as well as its old and new values.

4. *The helper notifies all its subscribers*. The helper first constructs an instance of **PropertyChangeEvent** with the new information. Then it invokes the *propertyChange* method on all its registered subscribers; it passes a **PropertyChangeEvent** object as a parameter.

5. *The listener bean has had enough*. The listener bean unsubscribes by invoking *removePropertyChangeListener* on the source bean. The source

again turns around and invokes *removePropertyChangeListener* on its helper. Then the helper removes the subscriber from the list it maintains.

This scenario shows how beans use events to be notified when properties change. It's also a classical example of delegation at work. The source bean delegates all the work to its helper. Life is sweet.

The Bound-Propertied Smiley

It's time to add a few properties to our Smiley bean. Figure 30-3 shows an incarnation of the Smiley one with two new properties: *color* and *smile*. Smile demonstrates the naming pattern for a boolean property. It is also a bound property that lets you directly manipulate the beautiful smile. The new Smiley also provides a pair of methods that let other beans subscribe (and unsubscribe) to the bound property. Smiley—the Mona Lisa of beans—will notify all its subscribers of any changes in the state of its enigmatic smile.

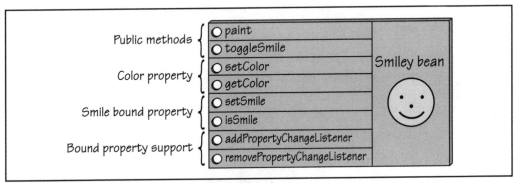

Figure 30-3. A Smiley With Two Properties: Bound and Boolean.

The code for this bound-propertied Smiley bean follows:

Listing 30-4. SmileyBean: The Bound-Propertied Smiley Bean.

```java
// SmileyBean.java - a SmileyBean with a bound property

import java.awt.*;
import java.awt.event.*;
import java.beans.*;

public class SmileyBean extends Canvas
{
```

```java
// Private data fields:
private Color ourColor = Color.yellow;
private boolean smile = true;

// create a helper object
private PropertyChangeSupport changes =
                new PropertyChangeSupport(this);

// Construct a Smiley
public SmileyBean()
{
  setSize(250,250);
}

// public methods
public synchronized void toggleSmile()
{
  setSmile(!isSmile());
}

// property methods

// Smiley color
public synchronized Color getColor()
{
  return ourColor;
}

public void setColor(Color newColor)
{
  ourColor = newColor;
  repaint();
}

// Smiley smile state
public synchronized boolean isSmile()
{
  return smile;
}

public void setSmile(boolean newSmile)
{
  boolean oldSmile = smile;
  smile = newSmile;
  repaint();
```

```
      changes.firePropertyChange("smile", new Boolean(oldSmile),
                                          new Boolean(newSmile));
   }

   // property change listener methods
   public void addPropertyChangeListener(PropertyChangeListener l)
   {
      changes.addPropertyChangeListener(l);

   }

   public void removePropertyChangeListener(PropertyChangeListener l)
   {
      changes.removePropertyChangeListener(l);

   }

   // methods that implement SmileyBean function
   public void paint(Graphics g)
   {
      // Code from last chapter not repeated here to save a few trees
   }
}
```

The *setSmile* mutator is the most interesting part of this code (see shaded area). It shows that a bound property must first update its internal state before invoking its subscribers. Also note that the bean lets its **PropertyChangeSupport** helper object take care of all the notifications. So there isn't much to write about.

The Event Adapters

The container we develop in the next section needs two adapters to wire its beans:

■ The **SmileyEventAdapter** class from the last chapter implements the **Action-Listener** interface on behalf of Smiley. We will not repeat the code here.

■ The **SmileyBoundAdapter** class implements the **PropertyChangeListener** interface on behalf of beans that need to be synchronized with Smiley's smile. In our examples, the subscribers are other Smiley beans.

Here's the code for the **SmileyBoundAdapter** class:

Listing 30-5. The SmileyBoundAdapter Class.

```
import java.awt.*;
import java.beans.*;
public class SmileyBoundAdapter implements PropertyChangeListener
{ private SmileyBean target;

  SmileyBoundAdapter(SmileyBean t)
  { target = t;
  }

  public void propertyChange(PropertyChangeEvent arg0)
  { target.toggleSmile();
  }
}
```

SmileyPlace: A Container for Bound Beans

We now have a Smiley bean that knows how to do bound properties, so let's put it to some good use. We are going to build a container for the Smiley twins. The container will wire the twin to the original Smiley's smile property. So every time you click on the button bean to toggle the smile on the original Smiley, the twin will follow suit. The container only wires the button to the first Smiley. So how do the twins synchronize their beautiful smiles? They are wired together using property change events. Figure 30-4 shows how the container wires its beans. The screen shot in Figure 30-5 shows how it all visually comes together.

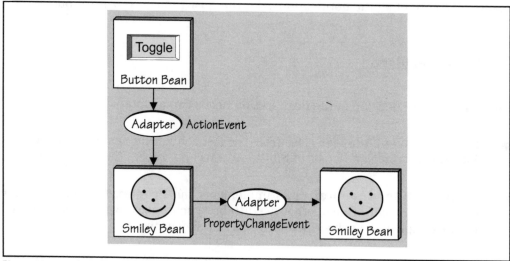

Figure 30-4. A Container With Bound Smiley Twins.

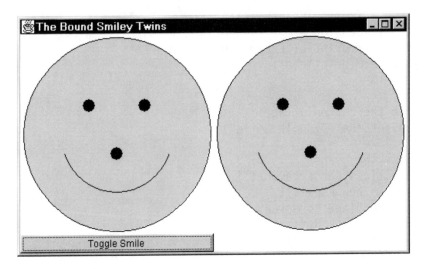

Figure 30-5. A Screen Shot of the Bound Smiley Twins.

The code for the container follows. By now, it should be easy to grasp. The container first instantiates the beans—two Smileys and a button. Next, it adds the beans to a visual container. Finally, it wires the beans via its adapters. It's all the usual stuff. Here's the code:

Listing 30-6. The SmileyPlace Application.

```
// SmileyPlace.java - Application for a Smiley with a bound property

import java.awt.*;
import java.awt.event.*;
import java.beans.*;

public class SmileyPlace extends Frame
{
  SmileyPlace()
  {
    SmileyBean smiley1 = null;
    SmileyBean smiley2 = null;
    Button button = null;

    // instantiate beans in container
    try
    {
      smiley1 = (SmileyBean)Beans.instantiate(null, "SmileyBean");
      smiley2 = (SmileyBean)Beans.instantiate(null, "SmileyBean");
```

```java
        button = (Button)Beans.instantiate(null, "java.awt.Button");
    } catch (Exception e)
    { System.err.println("Exception:");
      System.err.println(e);
    }

    // give the button a label
    button.setLabel("Toggle Smile");

    // place the beans
    setLayout(new BorderLayout());
    Panel p1 = new Panel();
    p1.setLayout(new BorderLayout());
    p1.add(smiley1, "North");
    p1.add(button,"South");
    add(p1,"West");

    Panel p2 = new Panel();
    p2.setLayout(new BorderLayout());
    p2.add(smiley2, "North");
    add(p2,"East");


    // connect the beans

    // connect the Smiley1 to the button
    button.addActionListener(new SmileyEventAdapter (smiley1));

    // connect the Smiley2 to Smiley1 via a bound property
    smiley1.addPropertyChangeListener(
        (PropertyChangeListener) new SmileyBoundAdapter(smiley2));

  }

static public void main(String args[])
{
  SmileyPlace smileyPlace = new SmileyPlace();
  smileyPlace.setSize(100,100);
  smileyPlace.setTitle("The Bound Smiley Twins");
  smileyPlace.pack();
  smileyPlace.setVisible(true);

  // trap window exit event with anonymous inner class
  WindowListener l = new WindowAdapter()
    {
```

```
        public void windowClosing(WindowEvent e) {System.exit(0);}
    };
    smileyPlace.addWindowListener(l);
  }
}
```

The shaded areas highlight the code in this container that is relevant to bound beans. As you can see, a bound property is a simple application of the delegation event model. It's just a matter of wiring beans via adapters.

Constrained Properties

Like a bound property, a *constrained property* informs its subscribers of any changes in a property. But, unlike a bound property, a *constrained property* must first validate the change with all its subscribers before it performs the update. Any vetoable subscriber can stop the change. In case of a veto, the bean must revert the property to its previous value on all the subscribers.

A constrained bean maintains a list of subscribers that implement the **VetoableChangeListener** interface. Before the bean changes a property value, it tries to update all its vetoable subscribers. Any subscriber can refuse the change by throwing a **PropertyVetoException**. If this happens, the source must revert all the listeners to their previous value.

The 1.01 update to the JavaBeans specification recommends that all your constrained properties also be bound. In addition, a **VetoableChangeListener** bean must also implement **PropertyChangeListener**. The source bean must first determine if the change is OK with all the vetoable listeners. If it's OK, it updates the property and then notifies all the bound listeners.

If you think about it, we are implementing a "two-phase commit" for constrained property updates. In the first phase, a dual-listener bean makes sure the proposed value is acceptable; it can veto unacceptable changes. In the second phase, the *propertyChange* method is invoked on the target bean to indicate that the change is now effective. The target bean can then act on the new value.

Constrained Properties: Classes and Interfaces

To support constrained properties, JavaBeans defines the **VetoableChange-Listener** interface (see Figure 30-6). This new interface works with the same **PropertyChangeEvent** we used for bound properties. The listener throws a

PropertyVetoException. To help you track the listeners, the JavaBeans run time provides a support class called **VetoableChangeSupport**. If it encounters a veto, this class will revert all listeners to their previous value.

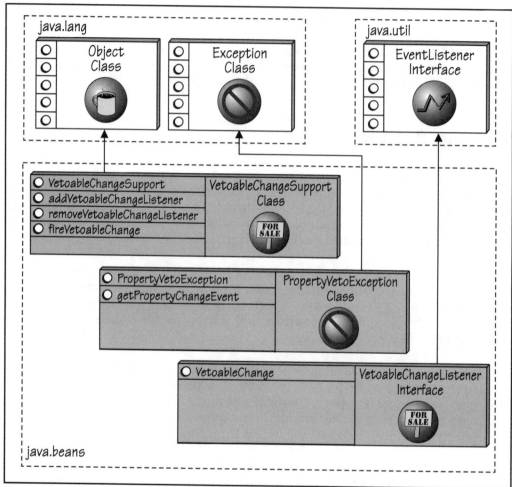

Figure 30-6. The Constrained Property Interfaces and Classes.

A bean that supports constrained properties must provide the following design pattern:

```
void addVetoableChangeListener(VetoableChangeListener l);
void removeVetoableChangeListener(VetoableChangeListener l);
```

You invoke the *addPropertyChangeListener/removePropertyChangeListener* method pair to add and remove subscribers to all the constrained properties on a bean. You should note that a bean can support more than one constrained property. These two methods service all the constrained properties on a per-bean basis.

Starting with JDK 1.01, you can now add (or remove) a constrained listener on a per-property basis using the following design pattern:

```
void addVetoableChangeListener(String name, VetoableChangeListener 1);
void removeVetoableChangeListener(String name, VetoableChangeListener 1);
```

The source bean will associate the listener with the given property name; it will only invoke the listener's *vetoableChange* method when the named property changes.

Here's a brief description of the single interface and two classes the *java.beans* package provides in support of bound properties:

- The **VetoableChangeListener** interface defines a single method named *vetoableChange*. This method receives a **PropertyChangeEvent** as a parameter; it throws a **PropertyVetoException** if it doesn't like what it sees. Beans that register for vetoable property changes must implement this interface.

- The **PropertyVetoException** extends the **Exception** class to convey veto information. A listener registers a veto by constructing an object of this class. The constructor takes two arguments. The first argument is a string that indicates the reason for the veto. The second argument is the **PropertyChangeEvent** object that caused the veto. The class also supports a *getPropertyChangeEvent* that returns the event that caused the veto.

- The **VetoableChangeSupport** is a helper class. Source beans use it to manage events that are fired by their constrained properties. You can either derive your bean from this class or you can use an instance of this class as a member field of your bean and then delegate work to it. The *addVetoableChangeListener* and *removeVetoableChangeListener* methods handle the registration and unregistration of constrained property listeners. The bean invokes *fireVetoableChange* to notify any registered listeners when a constrained property changes; it will not fire if the old and new values are equal and not null. The helper class performs the following steps if it encounters a veto: 1) breaks out of the sending loop, 2) creates a new event with the new and old values reversed, 3) goes back to the start of the list and reinvokes the *vetoableChange* method with the new event on all the listeners, and 4) returns to the source a **PropertyVetoException**. Yes, this helper does quite a bit of work.

The following class descriptions provide more detail:

Listing 30-7. The Java.beans VetoableChangeListener Interface.

```
public interface VetoableChangeListener extends EventListener
{
  // Methods
  public abstract void vetoableChange(PropertyChangeEvent evt);
}
```

Listing 30-8. The Java.beans VetoableChangeSupport Class.

```
public class VetoableChangeSupport extends Object
                                   implements Serializable
{
  // Constructor
  public VetoableChangeSupport(Object sourceBean);

  // Methods
  public synchronized void addVetoableChangeListener(
                              VetoableChangeListener listener);
  public synchronized void removeVetoableChangeListener(
                              VetoableChangeListener listener);
  public void fireVetoableChange(String propertyName,
                            Object oldValue,
                            Object newValue)
                            throws PropertyVetoException;
}
```

Listing 30-9. The Java.beans PropertyVetoException Class.

```
public class PropertyVetoException extends Exception
{
  // Constructor
  public PropertyVetoException(String mess, PropertyChangeEvent evt);

  // Methods
  public PropertyChangeEvent getPropertyChangeEvent();
}
```

A Constrained Property Scenario

It's time for a scenario that shows constrained properties at work. Figure 30-7 shows a bean with a constrained property called *price*. In this scenario, the bean communicates a price change to its constrained subscribers without encountering a veto. Here are the steps:

1. *The bean creates a helper object*. This is another smart bean that knows how to delegate work. So it creates a **VetoableChangeSupport** helper object.

2. *A subscriber demands veto rights*. The subscriber invokes *addVetoableChangeListener* on the source bean and passes it a reference to its listener interface. Note that the source bean simply turns around and invokes *addVetoableChangeListener* on its helper. The helper adds the subscriber to its list.

3. *The source bean proposes a price change*. The source bean invokes its

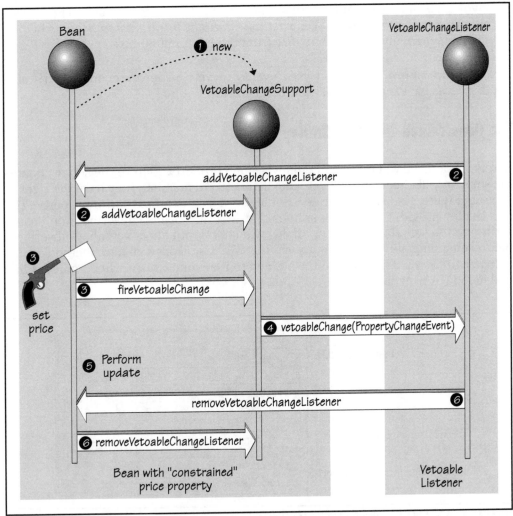

Figure 30-7. A Constrained-Property Notification Scenario.

helper's *fireVetoableChange* method and passes it the name of the property as well as its old and new values.

4. ***The helper notifies all its subscribers.*** The helper first constructs an instance of **PropertyChangeEvent** with the new information. Next, it invokes the *vetoableChange* method on all its registered subscribers with the **PropertyChangeEvent** object as a parameter.

5. ***No veto is received.*** The method returns without throwing an exception. The source bean can now apply the change. If this were part of a two-phase commit, the source would send *propertyChange* invocations to all its subscribers. We don't show this step in this single-subscriber scenario.

6. ***The listener bean has had enough.*** The listener bean unsubscribes by invoking *removeVetoableChangeListener* on the source bean. The source again turns around and invokes *removeVetoableChangeListener* on its helper. The helper removes the subscriber from the list it maintains.

This scenario shows how beans use events to veto property changes. It's also another classical example of delegation at work.

The Constrained-Property Smiley

In this section, we will constrain Smiley's smile property. Before the setter updates the smile, it will check with its vetoable listeners. Remember, they have the right of refusal. Figure 30-8 shows our new Smiley with a constrained *smile* property. The new Smiley provides a pair of methods that let other beans subscribe (and unsubscribe) to the vetoable property. Smiley will check with all its vetoable subscribers before changing its world-famous smile. We also added a new method called *vetoableChange*. This method throws a veto if anyone calls it when Smiley is in a bad mood (or frowning).

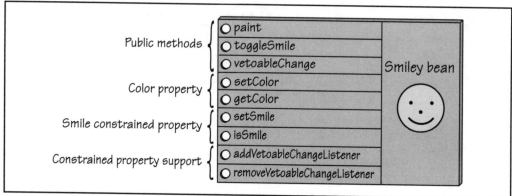

Figure 30-8. A Smiley With a Constrained Smile Property.

The code for constrained Smiley bean follows:

Listing 30-10. SmileyBean: The Constrained-Propertied Smiley Bean.

```java
// SmileyBean.java - a SmileyBean with a bound property

import java.awt.*;
import java.awt.event.*;
import java.beans.*;

public class SmileyBean extends Canvas
{
  // Private data fields:
  private Color ourColor = Color.yellow;
  private boolean smile = true;

  // create a helper object
  private VetoableChangeSupport vetos = new VetoableChangeSupport(this);

  // Construct a Smiley
  public SmileyBean()
  {
    setSize(250,250);
  }

  // public methods
  public synchronized void toggleSmile()
  {
    setSmile(!isSmile());
  }

  // property methods

  // Smiley color
  public synchronized Color getColor()
  {
    return ourColor;
  }

  public void setColor(Color newColor)
  {
    ourColor = newColor;
    repaint();
  }
```

```
// Smiley smile state
public synchronized boolean isSmile()
{
  return smile;
}
```

```
public void setSmile(boolean newSmile)
{
  boolean oldSmile = smile;
  try
  {
  vetos.fireVetoableChange("smile", new Boolean(oldSmile),
                                     new Boolean(newSmile));
  smile = newSmile;
  repaint();
  } catch (Exception e)
  { System.out.println("Change vetoed!");
  }
}
```

```
// vetoable property listener methods
public void addVetoableChangeListener(VetoableChangeListener l)
{
  vetos.addVetoableChangeListener(l);
}
```

```
public void removeVetoableChangeListener(VetoableChangeListener l)
{
  vetos.removeVetoableChangeListener(l);
}

public void vetoableChange(PropertyChangeEvent x)
                       throws PropertyVetoException
{
  if (!smile)
    throw new PropertyVetoException("No!", x);
}
```

```
// methods that implement SmileyBean function
public void paint(Graphics g)
{
  // Code from last chapter not repeated here to save a few trees
}
}
```

The shaded areas show some of the more interesting parts of this code. Here are the three things you should notice in this code:

- The *setSmile* mutator must first get the OK from its listeners before it updates the property.

- This bean is also a vetoer. The *vetoableChange* method returns an exception if Smiley is unhappy (or frowning). This method does not affect Smiley's own mood (i.e., it does not result in a property update).

- The bean lets its **VetoableChangeSupport** helper object take care of all the notifications.

So, as you can see, Smiley plays a dual role. It is both an exporter of a constrained property and a vetoer. The bean will veto change requests based on its own state. If Smiley is in a good mood (or smiling), it will then allow others to do their own thing. How nice!

The Event Adapters

The container we develop in the next section needs two adapters to wire its beans:

- The **SmileyEventAdapter** class from last chapter implements the **ActionListener** interface on behalf of Smiley. We will not repeat the code here.

- The **SmileyVetoAdapter** class implements the **VetoableChangeListener** interface on behalf of beans that need veto power over Smiley's mood changes. In the example, the subscribers are other Smiley beans. So it will be fun.

Here's the code for **SmileyVetoAdapter** class:

Listing 30-11. The SmileyVetoAdapter Class.

```
import java.awt.*;
import java.beans.*;

public class SmileyVetoAdapter implements VetoableChangeListener
{
  private SmileyBean target;

  SmileyVetoAdapter(SmileyBean t)
  {
      target = t;
  }
```

```
public void vetoableChange(PropertyChangeEvent arg0)
                            throws PropertyVetoException
{
    target.vetoableChange(arg0);
}
}
```

SmileyPlace: A Container for Constrained Beans

We now have a Smiley bean that knows how to do constrained properties. To show you how beans exercise their veto power, we will create a container with four beans: two Smileys and two buttons. We will wire these beans using the adapters from the previous section. Smiley2 will have veto power over changes to Smiley1's smile property. Like before, you click on button1 to change Smiley1's property. However, this time Smiley2—the vetoer—must approve all the mood changes. So when does Smiley2 approve these changes? It only does this when it's smiling. A happy Smiley2 does not exercise its right to veto. So only then can you apply property changes on Smiley1.

Figure 30-9 shows how the container wires its beans. The screen shot in Figure 30-10 shows how it all visually comes together.

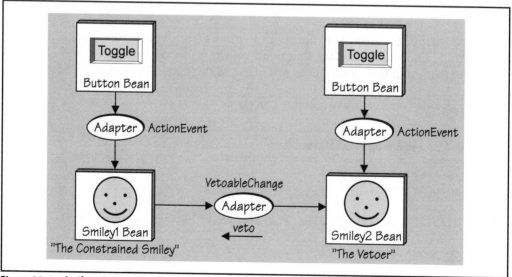

Figure 30-9. Smiley1 Is Constrained by Smiley2, "The Vetoer."

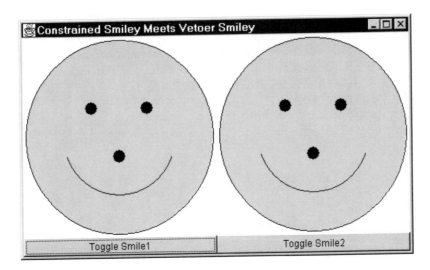

Figure 30-10. A Screen Shot of the Two Smileys: Constrained and Vetoer.

The code for the container follows. By now, it should be perfectly clear. The container first instantiates the beans—two Smileys and two buttons. Next, it adds the beans to a visual container. Finally, it uses the adapters to wire the beans together. It uses an event adapter to wire each Smiley to a button. In addition, it uses a vetoable adapter to connect the two Smileys to each other, which creates the vetoable relationship. Here's the code:

Listing 30-12. The SmileyPlace Application.

```java
// SmileyPlace.java - Application for a Smiley with a bound property

import java.awt.*;
import java.awt.event.*;
import java.beans.*;

public class SmileyPlace extends Frame
{
  SmileyPlace()
  {
    SmileyBean smiley1 = null;
    SmileyBean smiley2 = null;
    Button button1 = null;
    Button button2 = null;

    // instantiate beans in container
    try
```

```
  {
    smiley1 = (SmileyBean)Beans.instantiate(null, "SmileyBean");
    smiley2 = (SmileyBean)Beans.instantiate(null, "SmileyBean");
    button1 = (Button)Beans.instantiate(null, "java.awt.Button");
    button2 = (Button)Beans.instantiate(null, "java.awt.Button");
  } catch (Exception e)
  { System.err.println("Exception:");
    System.err.println(e);
  }

  // give the button a label

  button1.setLabel("Toggle Smile1");
  button2.setLabel("Toggle Smile2");

  // place the beans

  setLayout(new BorderLayout());

  Panel p1 = new Panel();
  p1.setLayout(new BorderLayout());
  p1.add(smiley1, "North");
  p1.add(button1, "South");
  add(p1, "West");

  Panel p2 = new Panel();
  p2.setLayout(new BorderLayout());
  p2.add(smiley2, "North");
  p2.add(button2, "South");
  add(p2, "East");

  // connect the beans

  // connect the Smiley1 to button1
  button1.addActionListener(new SmileyEventAdapter (smiley1));

  // connect the Smiley2 to button2
  button2.addActionListener(new SmileyEventAdapter (smiley2));

  // connect the Smileys via the constrained property relation
  smiley1.addVetoableChangeListener(
    (VetoableChangeListener) new SmileyVetoAdapter(smiley2));

}
```

```
static public void main(String args[])
{
  SmileyPlace smileyPlace = new SmileyPlace();
  smileyPlace.setSize(200,200);
  smileyPlace.setTitle("Constrained Smiley Meets Vetoer Smiley");
  smileyPlace.pack();
  smileyPlace.setVisible(true);

  // trap window exit event with anonymous inner class
  WindowListener l = new WindowAdapter()
    {
      public void windowClosing(WindowEvent e) {System.exit(0);}
    };
  smileyPlace.addWindowListener(l);
}
}
```

The shaded areas highlight the code in this container that is relevant to constrained beans. As you can see, it's purely an exercise in wiring beans via adapters.

MORE GUIDELINES FOR WRITING PORTABLE BEANS

Here are some more guidelines we uncovered in this chapter for writing portable beans:

✔ *Use standard naming patterns to surface your properties.* A bean's properties are defined by the presence of getter and setter methods that adhere to the JavaBeans naming conventions. You must also follow these conventions to surface bound and constrained properties.

✔ *Reserve the get/set method names for properties.* Do not use names that start with *get* or *set* for general-purpose methods. It will only confuse the bean introspector.

✔ *Use a 2-phase commit to update constrained properties.* You must implement both the bound and vetoable listeners for beans that need to mirror property updates but still have the right of refusal. In the first phase, a dual-listener bean determines if the change is acceptable. If everything is OK, the change is applied during the second phase via a bound property update. Note that if you're simply a vetoer on a constrained property, then you don't have to implement the bound property listener.

CONCLUSION

This concludes our overview of the JavaBeans property model. Properties are very visible to both users and tools. Consequently, you can assume that most beans will be manipulated via their properties. As you saw in this chapter, properties are easy to implement. So we encourage you to lavishly adorn your beans with specialized properties—for example, *transactional, SQL-aware*, or *secure*. These properties can then be easily personalized by an end-user, administrator, or system integrator. They will encourage the users of your beans to practice *attribute-based programming*—which means programming by visually manipulating properties instead of writing code.

For some important properties, you may find it useful to define events that are fired when a property changes in some specific way. In some cases, interested beans may even want to veto changes they do not like. As you saw in this chapter, JavaBeans can accommodate these needs with its bound and constrained properties. Both are examples of design patterns that combine properties with events. You can define your own events that are fired when a property changes. Yes, the mixing of properties with events can be a lot of fun. But we must move on to persistence and JARs—the next stop in our JavaBeans tour.

Chapter 31

The Persistent JavaBean

A *persistent* component knows how to store its state—or instance data—at shutdown and then later reactivate it. Persistence is a fundamental part of the embedding contract between a container and its components. A uniform persistence model makes it easier to reuse a component in multiple containers (or applications). In addition, a uniform persistence model is an absolute requirement for the packaging and exchanging of components between applications on the Web.

The default persistence mechanism for JavaBeans is the *Java Serialization* service; it provides a lightweight persistence service that lets you easily store away the state of a bean (or pickle it) and then later resurrect it in the same state. For scalable server applications, you will want to couple this simple persistence mechanism with an ORB's transaction service (more on this when we cover *Enterprise JavaBeans*). In addition, you may want to store the persistent state of your bean in a scalable ODBMS or RDBMS instead of in a flat file.

A component infrastructure must also provide services that let you package, transport, and distribute the beans you create (or purchase). JavaBeans lets you package components via JARs. With the *jar* utility, you can compress a set of beans and their related resources into a single container (or file) for storage and distribution. You can then use JAR files to transport beans across machines, download them over the Internet, and store them in persistent stores—like ODBMSs, RDBMSs, or the local file system.

In this chapter, we first show you how to store one or more beans inside a (.ser) file and then later bring them back to life. Next, we cover the *jar* utility. We explain the structure of a JAR file and the *manifest* we use to describe its contents. Finally, we create persistent Smiley beans that we store in (.ser) files and deploy in JARs. In real life, you will be able to use this persistent bean technology (and JARs) to create Shippable Places and to package and transport mobile agents. Persistence is also a key technology for visual tools; it lets you customize a bean and then later run it in a container (or application).

BEAN PERSISTENCE

The simplest way to make your beans persistent is to use the core Java serialization facilities. For most beans, persistence will be almost automatic—you will just flag the bean as persistent and then let Java serialization take care of everything else. The serialization service also provides framework-like hooks to let you add special persistence functions that your bean may require. For example, you could restore a transient data field from a DBMS and then let the default Java persistence mechanism handle the rest. Finally, the persistence service is flexible enough to let more complex beans handle their own serialization; it will just get out of the way and let you do it all yourself.

Making your beans persistent is only half of the story. The other half is to provide the containers (or applications) that know when and where to serialize the beans they contain. So it takes two to do this tango: the persistent beans and the containers that know when and where to put them away. The Java serialization service provides a set of support classes that let you serialize a group of beans to an output stream and then later deserialize them back into memory using an input stream.

The Bean-Related Persistence Interfaces

In this section, we look at the *java.io* interfaces you must implement to make your beans persistent. In the simplest case, you implement the **Serializable** interface to let the Java VM know that your bean is persistent. **Serializable** has no methods or fields (see Figure 31-1). So you have nothing to implement. Is it really this simple? Yes, you simply tag your bean as serializable to indicate that it wants to be serialized. A container application can then rely on the Java VM to automatically save your bean's internal data fields along with the state of any other objects that your bean may refer to; it also saves the state of all the parent classes.

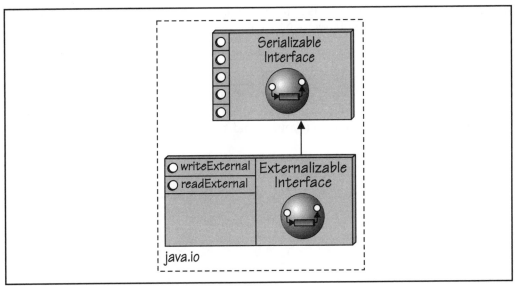

Figure 31-1. The Serializable and Externalizable Interfaces.

These are the rules the serialization process follows:

■ The data fields of a bean that implements **Serializable** must also be serializable. If the serialization mechanism encounters a non-serializable object, it will throw a **NotSerializableException**.

■ The *static variables* are not serialized. The serialization mechanism only deals with instance data; it does not serialize class variables.

■ Any data fields you mark as *transient* will not be serialized. You can also use the transient modifier to mark data members that point to non-serializable classes.

■ The highest serializable class in your bean's hierarchy is serialized first. The serialization process walks down the hierarchy to serialize data from each subclass in turn.

■ The subclasses of objects that are not serializable can be serializable. In this case, the non-serializable class must have a no-arg constructor to allow its fields to be initialized.

■ The serialization process maintains information about the class type of a serialized object, but it does not store the class implementation. The class description information is stored before the instance data.

■ The serialization process maintains a single copy of an object even if it is referenced by multiple objects. In this way, it is quite efficient and avoids circular references.

If your bean can live with this default serialization behavior, then you're all set. You don't have to do anything else. However, if your bean requires special handling during the serialization, then you must do some extra work. The next step in do-it-yourself complexity is to let your serializable bean implement the following two *private* methods:

```
private void writeObject(java.io.ObjectOutputStream out)
        throws IOException;
private void readObject(java.io.ObjectInputStream in)
        throws IOException, ClassNotFoundException;
```

These two methods allow your bean to write and restore its own instance data. If you provide a *writeObject* method, it will be invoked when your object is serialized. Your method must then store away the state of its instance data so that *readObject* can later restore it. Typically, you first invoke the *out.defaultWriteObject* method to save the object's data fields. You will then execute whatever extra code you need to store additional information inside the **ObjectOutputStream** (more on this in the next section).

Your *readObject* method is invoked during the deserialization process. It is responsible for restoring the object's state from the input stream. You may choose to first invoke *in.defaultReadObject* to let the default mechanism restore your object's non-static and non-transient fields. This method uses information in the stream to load the state of the object saved in the stream. It uses named fields to restore the object. Consequently, it can handle situations where the class has evolved to add new fields.

Your methods don't need to handle the state of their superclasses or subclasses. This is automatically handled by the default serialization mechanism. If your bean needs to control the serialization of its parents, then it must implement the **Externalizable** interface. This interface lets you control all aspects of the serialization process.

The **Externalizable** interface defines two public methods—*writeExternal* and *readExternal*—that you must implement. These methods give you total control over the format and contents of the stream you use to store your beans. They also let you explicitly control the coordination with the parent classes of your bean to save their state. If your bean implements the **Externalizable** interface, then *writeExternal* is invoked when the bean is being saved; *readExternal* is invoked when it's being restored (see the next Warning box).

Protect Your Externalizable Information

Warning

The **Externalizable** *writeExternal* method is public, which means that a malicious program can invoke it to copy your bean's state information to a stream (in-memory or in-file). In addition, any outsider can invoke *readExternal* to force a new state on your object. In contrast, the **Serializable** *writeObject* is private, so it provides better protection for sensitive information. So the rule here is not to place sensitive information in an externalizable bean. Instead, make your bean serializable and then use the private *writeObject* and *readObject* methods to control its state. ❏

The following interface descriptions provide more details:

Listing 31-1. The Java.io Serializable Interface.

```
public interface Serializable
{
}
```

Listing 31-2. The Java.io Externalizable Interface.

```
public interface Externalizable extends Serializable
{
  // Methods
  public abstract void writeExternal(ObjectOutput out)
                  throws IOException;
  public abstract void readExternal(ObjectInput in)
                  throws IOException,
                  ClassNotFoundException;
}
```

The Container-Related Persistence Classes

So far we've explained how you make your beans persistent but we haven't talked about where this persistent information is streamed. This is where the *java.io* **ObjectOutputStream** and **ObjectInputStream** classes come into the picture (see Figure 31-2). These streams are very similar to the **DataOutputStream** and **DataInputStream** classes we encountered in Part 4. Like their familiar counterparts, the new streams let you efficiently store primitive data types in a portable binary format. However, the new streams also let you store objects. Note that the new binary streams are not compatible with those produced by the older classes.

Here's a brief description of the three new serialization classes that deal with object streams:

■ **ObjectOutputStream** class is used to write primitive data types and graphs of Java objects to a portable binary stream. You can persistently store these objects by using a file for the stream. If the stream is a network socket stream, the objects can be reconstituted on another host or in another process. You write serializable objects to the stream by invoking *writeObject* and passing it the object as an argument (see the next Warning Box). It will encode and store the class of each serializable object in a hierarchy tree—including the class name and signature of the class, the values of the object's fields and arrays, and any other objects referenced from the initial objects. Note that if you provide a private *writeObject* it will be called instead with the stream passed as a parameter. You can call *defaultWriteObject* from within the private method.

Which WriteObject/ReadObject Methods?

Warning

Notice that there are two uses of the *writeObject* and *readObject* methods. In the first flavor, *writeObject* and *readObject* are private methods that you must implement. The serialization mechanism passes you a stream; you must then serialize your object to the stream or read it from the stream. In the second flavor, *writeObject* and *readObject* are implemented for you by **ObjectOutputStream** and **ObjectInputStream** respectively. You pass an object to *writeObject* to write it to the stream; you invoke *readObject* on the stream to read an object. Yes, this choice of names is confusing. ❑

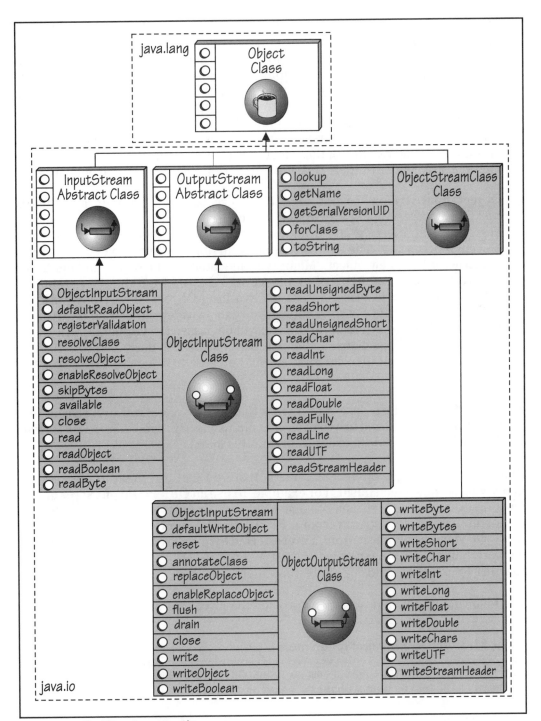

Figure 31-2. The Object Streaming Classes.

The *annotateClass* method currently does nothing. A subclass can implement this method to store class data. The corresponding method in the **ObjectInput-Stream** is *resolveClass*. The *replaceObject* method also does nothing. A subclass can implement it to substitute one object for another during serialization. The *enableReplaceObject* must first be called to enable the replacement; it checks that the stream requesting to do the replacement can be trusted. The *writeStreamHeader* also does nothing. You can subclass it to add your own header information to the stream—for example, a version number. Note that JDK 1.2 implements most of these methods (more on this later). The rest of the methods are similar to their **DataOutputStream** counterparts from Part 4.

■ **ObjectInputStream** class is used to deserialize primitive data and objects previously written using an **ObjectOutputStream**. The *readObject* method deserializes an object graph from the stream; it will load the classes for these objects if necessary. The reconstruction of an object is analogous to invoking a constructor for a new object. Memory is allocated for the object and initialized to zero (NULL). The fields of an object are restored from the stream starting with the serializable class closest to **java.lang.Object** and ending with the object's most specific class. Of course, you can provide your private *readObject* method to do your own restoration; you will be passed the **ObjectInputStream** as a parameter. Objects that implement **Externalizable** must restore their state via a *readExternal* invocation; they will be passed **ObjectInputStream** as a parameter.

■ **ObjectStreamClass** describes a class that can be serialized to a stream or a class that was serialized to a stream. It contains the name and the *stream unique identifier (SUID)* of the class (more on this later).

One of the advantages of Java streams is that you can use them to abstract the underlying storage mechanism. For example, to use an **ObjectOutputStream,** you must first obtain a base stream of some kind and then create a filter on it. So you can obtain your object stream from a **FileOutputStream** to store your beans in files. Or you can obtain it from a **ByteArrayOutputStream** to store them in a memory buffer. As we explained in Part 4, *java.io* lets you chain these streams together to create all kinds of interesting filters.

The following interface descriptions provide the next level of detail:

Listing 31-3. The Java.io ObjectOutputStream Class.

```
public class ObjectOutputStream extends OutputStream
implements ObjectOutput, ObjectStreamConstants
{
  // Constructor
  public ObjectOutputStream(OutputStream out) throws IOException;
```

```
// Methods
public final void defaultWriteObject() throws IOException;
public void reset() throws IOException;
protected void annotateClass(Class cl) throws IOException;
protected Object replaceObject(Object obj) throws IOException;
protected final boolean enableReplaceObject(boolean enable)
                            throws SecurityException;
public void flush() throws IOException;
protected void drain() throws IOException;
public void close() throws IOException;
public void write(int data) throws IOException;
public void write(byte b**) throws IOException;
public void write(byte b**, int off, int len)throws IOException;
public final void writeObject(Object obj) throws IOException;
public void writeBoolean(boolean data) throws IOException;
public void writeByte(int data) throws IOException;
public void writeBytes(String data) throws IOException;
public void writeShort(int data) throws IOException;
public void writeChar(int data) throws IOException;
public void writeInt(int data) throws IOException;
public void writeLong(long data) throws IOException;
public void writeFloat(float data) throws IOException;
public void writeDouble(double data) throws IOException;
public void writeChars(String data) throws IOException;
public void writeUTF(String data) throws IOException;
protected void writeStreamHeader() throws IOException;
}
```

Listing 31-4. The Java.io ObjectInputStream Class.

```
public class ObjectInputStream extends InputStream
implements ObjectInput, ObjectStreamConstants
{
  // Constructor
  public ObjectInputStream(InputStream in) throws IOException,
                    StreamCorruptedException;
  // Methods
  public final void defaultReadObject()
                        throws IOException,
                        ClassNotFoundException,
                        NotActiveException;
  public synchronized void registerValidation(
                        ObjectInputValidation obj, int prio)
                        throws NotActiveException,
```

```
                                 InvalidObjectException;
    protected Class resolveClass(ObjectStreamClass v)
                               throws IOException,
                               ClassNotFoundException;
    protected Object resolveObject(Object obj) throws IOException;
    protected final boolean enableResolveObject(boolean enable)
                               throws SecurityException;
    public int skipBytes(int len) throws IOException;
    public int available() throws IOException;
    public void close() throws IOException;
    public int read() throws IOException;
    public int read(byte data**, int offset, int length)
                               throws IOException;
    public final Object readObject()
                               throws OptionalDataException,
                               ClassNotFoundException,
                               IOException;
    public boolean readBoolean() throws IOException;
    public byte readByte() throws IOException;
    public int readUnsignedByte() throws IOException;
    public short readShort() throws IOException;
    public int readUnsignedShort() throws IOException;
    public char readChar() throws IOException;
    public int readInt() throws IOException;
    public long readLong() throws IOException;
    public float readFloat() throws IOException;
    public double readDouble() throws IOException;
    public void readFully(byte data**) throws IOException;
    public void readFully(byte data**, int offset, int size)
                               throws IOException;
    public String readLine() throws IOException;
    public String readUTF() throws IOException;
    protected void readStreamHeader() throws IOException,
                               StreamCorruptedException;
}
```

Listing 31-5. The Java.io ObjectStreamClass Class.

```
public class ObjectStreamClass extends Object
implements Serializable
{
  // Class Methods
  public static ObjectStreamClass lookup(Class cl);
```

```
// Methods
public String getName();
public long getSerialVersionUID();
public Class forClass();
public String toString();
}
```

A Serialization Scenario

As a bean creator, you must make sure your beans are serializable by using one of the methods we just described. As a bean application developer, you must determine when and where to save and restore the beans inside your container. Typically, you will store your beans in one or more (.ser) files. Perhaps you will place these (.ser) files in a JAR to distribute them. In any case, you must serialize your beans in a (.ser) file by first creating a stream and then invoking *writeObject* for every bean you may want to store.

In this section, we go over a scenario that demonstrates how a container application could save its beans (see Figure 31-3). Here are the steps:

1. ***Create a file-based object output stream***. We first create a file-based stream by invoking the **FileOutputStream** constructor and passing it the name of a (.ser) file. Then we create an **ObjectOutputStream** filter on top of this file stream. Here's a code snippet that shows this:

   ```
   FileOutputStream fos = new FileOutputStream("mybeans.ser");
   ObjectOutputStream oos = new ObjectOutputStream(fos);
   ```

2. ***Get a bean count***. We invoke *getComponentCount* on a visual **Container** object to determine the number of beans it contains.

3. ***Write the count to the object stream***. We invoke *writeInt* to record the number of beans we will store in this stream. This step is optional. It helps the reader determine the number of beans that are stored in the stream. Alternatively, the reader can go into a loop reading objects until it encounters a null (or empty object).

4. ***Write all your beans to the stream***. We read a component from the visual container by invoking *getComponent*. Then we write the bean to the stream by invoking *writeObject* and passing it the bean as a parameter. We repeat these two steps for each bean in the visual container.

5. ***Flush the contents of the stream***. We invoke *flush* on the object stream to write all its beans to the (.ser) file.

6. **Release the object stream**. We invoke *close* to free this object stream resource.

As you can see, our container has acquired a new skill. It now knows how to store away a collection of beans.

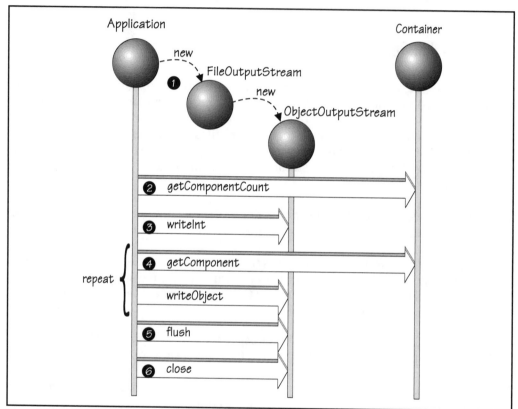

Figure 31-3. Scenario: How a Container Stores Its Beans.

A Deserialization Scenario

So how does a container reconstruct a collection of beans? In Figure 31-4, we show a possible deserialization scenario for the beans that we packaged in the previous scenario. Somehow, this container application received a *mybeans.ser* file. Here are the steps it follows to unravel the contents:

1. **Create a file-based object input stream**. We first create a file-based stream by invoking the **FileInputStream** constructor and passing it the name of a (.ser) file. Then we create an **ObjectInputStream** filter on top of this file stream.

Here's a code snippet that shows this:

```
FileInputStream fis = new FileInputStream("mybeans.ser");
ObjectInputStream ois = new ObjectInputStream(fis);
```

2. ***Read the bean count from the stream***. We invoke *readInt* on the stream to read the number of objects it contains.

3. ***Load the beans into the visual container***. We instantiate each bean in the stream by invoking *readObject*; it returns an object that we must cast to the appropriate bean type. We then *add* the bean to the visual container. The following code snippet shows how we load a **Button** bean:

```
Button mybutton (Button)ois.readObject();
add(mybutton);
```

4. ***Release the object stream***. We invoke *close* to free this object stream resource.

This container is getting smarter by the minute. It's time to apply these persistent skills to our Smiley containers.

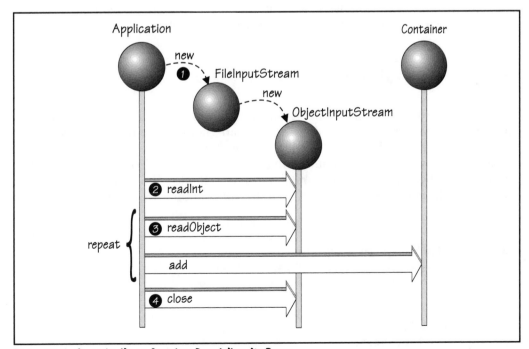

Figure 31-4. Scenario: How a Container Deserializes Its Beans.

The Persistent Smiley

It may come as a pleasant surprise that our Smiley one is already persistent. This is because **Smiley** extends the AWT **Canvas**—a persistent class. So if a bean has persistent parents, then it's automatically made persistent. So what does it mean for Smiley to be persistent? It means that its instance data will be automatically stored when a *writeObject* is invoked on a stream passing it Smiley as a parameter. The Smiley instance data consists of the following fields:

```
// Private data fields:
private Color ourColor = Color.yellow;
private boolean smile = true;
private transient PropertyChangeSupport changes =
                    new PropertyChangeSupport(this);
```

Notice that only the first two properties are persistent. Their contents are saved when you pass a Smiley bean to a *writeObject*. So both the smile and the color of your bean will be captured for posterity. Later you will be able to bring your Smiley back to life in the same state in which you left it. Also notice that we made the *changes* field *transient*; it contains a reference to the helper object. We'll obtain a new reference the next time we instantiate the bean. Finally, you should also note that the persistent information overrides any default values.

SmileyPlace: A Container for Persistent Beans

In this section, we extend our SmileyBean container to work with persistent Smileys. The container will restore the Smileys to the state they were in when you closed the window. You will see the original Smiley and its twin with their smiles intact. The container then wires the twin to its sibling's *smile* property. So every time you click on the button bean to toggle the smile on the first Smiley, the twin will follow suit. This part of the code is similar to the bound-bean container we developed in the last chapter.

Listing 31-6. The SmileyPlace Application.

```
// SmileyPlace.java - Application for a Smiley with a bound property

import java.awt.*;
import java.io.*;
import java.awt.event.*;
import java.beans.*;
```

```java
public class SmileyPlace extends Frame
{
  SmileyBean smiley1 = null;
  SmileyBean smiley2 = null;
  Button button = null;

  SmileyPlace()
  {
    // instantiate beans from (.ser) file
    try
    {
      smiley1 = (SmileyBean)Beans.instantiate(null, "Smiley1");
      smiley2 = (SmileyBean)Beans.instantiate(null, "Smiley2");

    } catch (Exception e)
    {
      try
      {
        // instantiate beans from class file
        smiley1 = (SmileyBean)Beans.instantiate(null, "SmileyBean");
        smiley2 = (SmileyBean)Beans.instantiate(null, "SmileyBean");

      } catch (Exception ex)
      { System.err.println("Exception:");
        System.err.println(ex);
      }
    }

    // instantiate button
    try
    {
      button = (Button)Beans.instantiate(null, "java.awt.Button");
    } catch (Exception e)
    { System.err.println("Exception:");
      System.err.println(e);
    }

    // give the button a label
    button.setLabel("Toggle Smile");

    // place the beans
    setLayout(new BorderLayout());
    Panel p1 = new Panel();
    p1.setLayout(new BorderLayout());
```

```
      p1.add((Component)smiley1, "North");
      p1.add(button,"South");
      add(p1,"West");

      Panel p2 = new Panel();
      p2.setLayout(new BorderLayout());
      p2.add((Component)smiley2, "North");
      add(p2,"East");

      // connect the beans

      // connect the Smiley1 to the button
      button.addActionListener(new SmileyEventAdapter (smiley1));

      // connect the Smiley2 to Smiley1 via a bound property
      smiley1.addPropertyChangeListener(
          (PropertyChangeListener) new SmileyBoundAdapter(smiley2));
  }

static public void main(String[] args)
{
    final SmileyPlace smileyPlace = new SmileyPlace();
    smileyPlace.setSize(200,200);
    smileyPlace.setTitle("The Bound Smiley Twins");
    smileyPlace.pack();
    smileyPlace.setVisible(true);

    // trap window exit event with anonymous inner class
    WindowListener l = new WindowAdapter()
      {
        public void windowClosing(WindowEvent e)
        {

            try
            {
              // save the smiley1

              FileOutputStream fos = new FileOutputStream("smiley1.ser");
              ObjectOutputStream oos = new ObjectOutputStream(fos);
              oos.writeObject(smileyPlace.smiley1);
              oos.flush();
              oos.close();
```

```
            // save the smiley2
            fos = new FileOutputStream("smiley2.ser");
            oos = new ObjectOutputStream(fos);
            oos.writeObject(smileyPlace.smiley2);
            oos.flush();
            oos.close();
        } catch (Exception ex)
        { System.err.println("Exception:");
          System.err.println(ex);
        }


    // exit

    System.exit(0);
      }
    };
    smileyPlace.addWindowListener(1);
  }
}
```

The shaded areas highlight code that is relevant to the serialization of Smiley beans. In this incarnation, the container serializes its stateful beans when you close the window. We chose to serialize each Smiley in its own (.ser) file. We did this to show you how *instantiate* works with (.ser) files. This method first appends a (.ser) to the name string and then attempts to load the bean from the serialized file; it expects the (.ser) file to contain a single bean. If this fails, it will treat the string as a class name and use it to create a fresh bean. In our example, if the (.ser) load fails because there are no serialized files named *Smiley1* or *Smiley2*, we catch the error and instantiate a couple of fresh Smiley beans using the **SmileyBean** class name. The code also demonstrates that you don't have to give the (.ser) file the same name as the (.class) file.

If you prefer, you can store all your serialized beans into a single file using the techniques we described in the scenarios. The following snippet of code shows how you would serialize multiple Smileys into a single (.ser) file:

```
// Serializing two Smileys in one (.ser) file
FileOutputStream fos = new FileOutputStream("smiley.ser");
ObjectOutputStream oos = new ObjectOutputStream(fos);
oos.writeObject(smiley1);
oos.writeObject(smiley2);
oos.flush();
oos.close();
```

Here's how you would then deserialize the Smileys:

```
// Instantiating the two Smileys from one (.ser) file
FileInputStream fis = new FileInputStream("smiley.ser");
ObjectInputStream ois = new ObjectInputStream(fis);
smiley1 = (SmileyBean)ois.readObject();
smiley2 = (SmileyBean)ois.readObject();
ois.close();
```

Notice that *readObject* returns a Smiley typed as **Object**. So we need to cast the returned object to a **SmileyBean**.

The Versioning of a Bean's State

As your beans evolve over time, you may be adding new functions and capabilities. At a functional level, the general rule is that you can evolve the function of your beans as long as you honor their contractual interfaces with clients—for example, you can't change the signatures of public methods. With non-persistent objects, it's OK to change the internal representation of your objects. However, if your objects are persistent, you must be very careful. The problem is that old (.ser) files never die. So you may always encounter situations where someone hands your glitzy new bean an old (.ser) file from prehistoric times.

The good news is that Java will protect your new bean from getting clobbered by an old (.ser) file. Before loading the state, the deserializer verifies that the new version of a class is compatible with the original class type stored in the (.ser) file. Here's how it works. When you serialize a bean, its class type signature is saved along with the instance data. This signature is a 64-bit identifier; it is a hash of the class structure—including the class name, non-static fields, and methods. Java calls this identifier the *stream unique identifier (SUID)*. So if you change your class structure, you will end up with a new SUID. If the new SUID does not match the SUID in the (.ser) file, the persistence mechanism will give you an exception.

You can discover your bean's SUID by running the JDK's *serialver* utility from the command line. It's best to run it with the *-show* argument to get a graphical interface from which you can copy and paste. We ran serialver as follows:

```
prompt> serialver -show
```

We then entered the **SmileyBean** class name in the graphical window shown in Figure 31-5 to obtain its version.

Serial Version Inspector

Full Class Name: SmileyBean   [Show]

Serial Version: static final long serialVersionUID = -4675992995001629966L;

Figure 31-5. The GUI-Based Serialver Output.

You can now mark this SUID and paste it into your code. Why would you ever do this? Here's why. Let's assume that you've made some serialization-compatible class changes in a new version of Smiley. Even if your changes are totally compatible, it is very likely that the SUID for the new class will change. So the deserializer will throw an error if you attempt to load an old state into a new class (or new state into an old class). You can get around this problem by giving the new Smiley the original SUID value. You do this by adding the following line to the new Smiley class:

```
static final long serialVersionUID = -4675992995001629966L;
```

Note that this line is identical to the output *serialver* generated for the old Smiley. So copy it and paste it into the new Smiley code to tell the serializer that the new class is compatible with the previous version. However, now you are responsible for making sure this is true.

So the million-dollar question is: What constitutes a serialization-compatible class change? Here are the key rules you must follow:

✔ It's OK to add/remove classes from the hierarchy. However, it's not OK to move classes up or down the hierarchy.

✔ It's OK to add or remove *writeObject* and *readObject* methods.

✔ It's OK to add fields to a class. However, it's not OK to delete existing non-static fields. You can change a field from static to non-static and from transient to non-transient because it's equivalent to adding a field. Of course, the reverse is not OK because it's equivalent to deleting a field. Finally, you can't change the data type of a primitive field. Note that it's OK to change the access to a field—for example, from private to public.

In general, you must do whatever it takes to make sure that: 1) older versions of you bean can accept (.ser) data from newer beans, and 2) newer versions of the bean can accept (.ser) data from older versions. Finally, note that you can invoke the *getSerialVersionUID* on an **ObjectStreamClass** to determine your bean's SUID at run time. An instance of this object is stored in the (.ser) file along with the state of your bean. This object contains your bean's SUID and class name.

JDK 1.2 Serialization Enhancements

JDK 1.2 introduces the following two enhancements to Java Serialization:

■ *Explicit specification of the persistent state.* By default, the serializable fields of a class are non-transient and non-static. JDK 1.2 lets you override these defaults by declaring a *serialPersistentFields* field inside your class. You use this field to specify your bean's serializable fields. The serialization mechanism will first look for the presence of this field when it serializes your object. If it doesn't find one, it uses the default mechanism instead. JDK 1.2 also provides an API to let you write and read these persistent data fields to and from a stream using the existing protocol. This ensures compatibility with the default writing and reading mechanisms.

■ *Replaceable interfaces*. JDK 1.2 introduces a **Replaceable** interface that allows a serialized class to nominate its own replacement in the stream before the object is written. It also lets you replace the object read from the stream before it is returned to the caller. The interface defines two methods: *writeReplace* and *readResolve*. By implementing these two methods, your class can directly control the types of its own instances being deserialized. Java serialization will call your methods at the appropriate times to give you a chance to do the replacement.

These JDK 1.2 add-ons appear to fall in the esoteric category. We do not recommend that you use them. Instead, we recommend that you use the automatic default serialization for simple bean persistence. If you need more scalable persistence, then use an ODBMS or RDBMS with Object-to-Relational mapping. Preferably, they will both run under the control of an *Object Transaction Monitor* (more on this in the Enterprise JavaBeans chapter).

BEANS IN JARS

JDK 1.1 introduced the *Java Archiver (JAR)*—a utility that lets you compress and store a set of related files. You can then transport these files across machines. In some ways, JARs are similar to familiar archiving tools such as ZIP and TAR. Like these tools, JARs let you compress and store multiple files into a single file. In addition, JARs provide the following benefits:

- **An all-Java archiving solution**. JARs can work on any platform that supports the Java VM. In contrast, ZIP and TAR are platform-specific. Note that JARs use the ZIP format for archiving and inflating files.

- **Self-describing contents**. You can describe the contents of your JARs—including the beans they contain—using a *manifest*.

- **Security and authentication**. You can protect the contents of your JARs via message digests, electronic signatures, and signed digital certificates. This means that you can verify that the JARs were delivered from a trusted source and were not tampered with in-flight.

- **HTML and browser support**. You can use standard HTML tags to tell a browser to download a JAR instead of individual Java classes. JARs let you package for delivery a set of related Java classes. This lets the browser download a group of compressed Java files over a single TCP/IP session instead of one connection for each Java class you download.

We cover all these features later in this section. But first let's go over the JAR fundamentals.

A Manifest for JARs

The bean classes you store in a JAR must include the main bean class and the other (.class) files it needs. A bean's resources may also include help files, icons, images, and configuration files. You can also use JARs to package the design-time classes that represent a bean to a visual tool. These classes may include a **BeanInfo** for introspection, a GIF icon to represent the bean in the tool palette, and whatever customizer or property editors this bean requires. You can discover the contents of a JAR by reading its *manifest*.

A *manifest* is a plain text file that describes the contents of a JAR. It is the first file you must place inside a JAR. A manifest identifies the beans in a JAR and provides a ton of other useful information. For example, the manifest tells you whether these are design-time or run-time beans. It also tells you something about the security mechanism that was used to JAR the beans. Finally, a manifest can optionally specify the names of related (or dependent) JAR files.

Figure 31-6 shows the deflated contents of a JAR archive's directory tree. The manifest—it always goes by the name *MANIFEST.MF*—is stored in a directory called *META-INF*. This directory also contains two signature-related files. The first is a plain-text security *signature directive* file (.sf); it describes the elements in a certificate. The second is an encrypted version of the (.sf) signature. In this case,

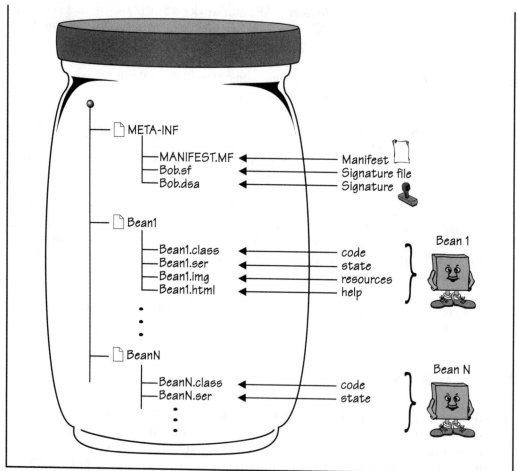

Figure 31-6. A JAR File Filled With Beans.

we used the *Digital Signature Algorithm (DSA)* to create a (.dsa) hash file. You typically sign your JARs using the JDK-supplied *javakey* utility. This utility includes the freely available DSA hash algorithm. Future versions of the JDK may also support RSA encryption.

Back to our JAR. Notice that there is a directory entry for each bean. Each directory contains the bean's (.class) files, the (.ser) file, and other bean-related resources—including image files (.img) and help files (.html). So who keeps track of the beans in a JAR? The manifest of course. It contains an entry for each bean stored in the JAR.

The JAR Utility

You create and manipulate jars using the JDK-provided *jar* utility. The general usage for this utility is:

```
prompt> jar [options] [manifest] destination input-file [input-files]
```

Table 31-1 shows the three command options. Note that you cannot combine the *c*, *t*, and *x* command options. You can only issue one of these commands at a time; the additional options are shown in Table 31-2.

Table 31-1. JAR Utility: The Command Options.

Command Options	Description
c	Create a new or empty JAR file. You must also use the f option to specify an archive file; otherwise, it will go to the standard output.
t	List the table of contents of this JAR.
x file	Extract all files in JAR, or just the named files.

Table 31-2. JAR Utility: Additional Command Options.

Additional Command Options	Description
v	Generate verbose output on stderr.
f	Specify the JAR file name following the options.
m	Include manifest information from the manifest file you provide.
M	Do not create a manifest file. The default is for the utility to automatically generate a manifest.
0	Do not use ZIP compression.

We'll create our first JAR file by entering the following command at the prompt:

```
prompt> jar cvf smiley.jar Smiley*.class
```

This command uses the *create*, *verbose*, and *file* options. The utility will create a new JAR called *smiley.jar*; it contains all the bean classes we developed for this chapter. We explicitly specified this (.jar) using the *file* option. Note that you must always use the Unix-like forward slash "/" separator, regardless of your OS. We enabled the verbose feature so you will see the following output:

```
adding: SmileyBean.class (in=2132) (out=1186) (deflated 44%)
adding: SmileyBoundAdapter.class (in=515) (out=337) (deflated 34%)
adding: SmileyEventAdapter.class (in=508) (out=340) (deflated 33%)
adding: SmileyPlace$1.class (in=1151) (out=684) (deflated 40%)
adding: SmileyPlace.class (in=2143) (out=1210) (deflated 43%)
```

As you can see, the code was deflated (or shrunk) by an average of 38.8% because of compression. This should make it considerably faster to download over the Internet. Note that you can also jar multiple subdirectories into a single (.jar) file.

After you create the JAR, you can list its contents by entering the following command:

```
prompt> jar tvf smiley.jar
```

You will then see the following output:

```
 795 Sun Oct 26 10:23:22 PST 1997 META-INF/MANIFEST.MF
2132 Sun Oct 26 10:10:32 PST 1997 SmileyBean.class
 515 Sun Oct 26 10:10:40 PST 1997 SmileyBoundAdapter.class
 508 Sun Oct 26 10:10:36 PST 1997 SmileyEventAdapter.class
1151 Sun Oct 26 10:10:46 PST 1997 SmileyPlace$1.class
2143 Sun Oct 26 10:10:46 PST 1997 SmileyPlace.class
```

You can see from this verbose output that the (.jar) contains a manifest as well as all our classes. It also shows the original size of each file (in bytes) as well as its timestamp. In case you're wondering, *SmileyPlace$1* is our anonymous inner class.

You can selectively extract files from a (.jar) file and recreate the subdirectory structure. For example, you can extract the META-INF directory from *smiley.jar* by entering the following command:

```
prompt> jar xf smiley.jar META-INF
```

This command creates a META-INF directory on your drive, if one does not already exist. The command then extracts all the files from the JAR's META-INF directory and copies them to your directory. One of the inflated files is *MANIFEST.MF*.

In our example, a manifest was automatically created by the jar utility when we jarred the Smiley classes. Let's take a quick look at the contents of this automatic *MANIFEST.MF*:

```
Manifest-Version: 1.0
Name: SmileyBean.class
Digest-Algorithms: SHA MD5
SHA-Digest: T1D6Rj1YfF1VXnIkOPoizZVBUcY=
MD5-Digest: x9nBQ8gKZINybHOO4q3NuA==

Name: SmileyBoundAdapter.class
Digest-Algorithms: SHA MD5
SHA-Digest: 4pvhBJG749JFmXaQC1Uj3sOKud8=
MD5-Digest: m4kZTYQwXq8rh9b8uX9/OA==

Name: SmileyEventAdapter.class
Digest-Algorithms: SHA MD5
SHA-Digest: 6BviA2z+fDCGVyzWfqWeDPoy/FM=
MD5-Digest: l/jiDfLU1X69KOWOtZboNQ==

Name: SmileyPlace$1.class
Digest-Algorithms: SHA MD5
SHA-Digest: YBQhE1qrCOljpCuqwLaneOVBpJA=
MD5-Digest: 1Tlx52rGMPdh1ojBl+3QzA==

Name: SmileyPlace.class
Digest-Algorithms: SHA MD5
SHA-Digest: 6hzgG1tJx27QIBQk/ugA8XWp6CA=
MD5-Digest: SIp/8MXtUiQRpsGlhCnD5A==
```

Notice that this manifest does not contain anything that is bean-specific. It simply lists a version number and a list of classes. For each class, it lists the two digest algorithms that *jar* used to create the hash values for this class entry. It also lists the actual hash values computed by each algorithm. We cover the details of the manifest structure in the next section.

The Structure of a Manifest

As you just saw, the *jar* utility does not produce any bean-related information. Consequently, you must create your own manifest to identify the beans that you store in a JAR. Every manifest must start with a line that specifies its version number. Following this are entries for each file the manifest tracks. The entries are separated by blank lines and have the following format:

```
Name: <name>
<attribute> : <value>
<attribute> : <value>
        .
        .
<attribute> : <value>
```

Each entry consists of a name followed by a list of attributes and their values. You must always provide a file name for each entry. Most of the information contained within a manifest file consists of *attribute: value* pairs (inspired by the RFC 822 standard). Most of these attributes are optional. So, an *entry* (or section) is a group of attribute-value pairs. Entries are separated from each other by empty lines. You cannot have two entries for the same file in the manifest. If duplicate entries are found, only the first is recognized.

Figure 31-7 shows the structure of a manifest file. It consists of two entries: *Bean1.class* and *Bean1.ser*. The *Java-Bean* attribute identifies a bean's main class to the visual tool or application container that receives the JAR. In this example, we tagged both the main class and the (.ser) file with *Java-Bean: True* (case is not important).

The *Digest-Algorithm* attribute identifies the algorithm we use to hash this file. In our example, we use the JDK-provided SHA algorithm; it's also a NIST-anointed standard. Digests are used to ensure that the file in this entry has not been corrupted. The actual value of the digest is stored in the *SHA-Digest* attribute. It's a binary value represented in *base 64*.

You can choose to list multiple digest algorithms. If you do so, a corresponding *xxx-Digest* attribute value will be created by the *jar* tool for each algorithm you list. For example, you can specify both the MD5 (RFC 1321) and SHA-1 (NIST) hash algorithms. In this case, the *jar* tool will create the following two digests: *MD5-Digest* and *SHA-Digest*.

The JavaBeans specification recently defined two new attributes: *Depends-On* and *Design-Time-Only*. *Depends-On* lets you specify a list of space-separated JAR entry names that are associated with a particular bean. *Design-Time-Only* lets you

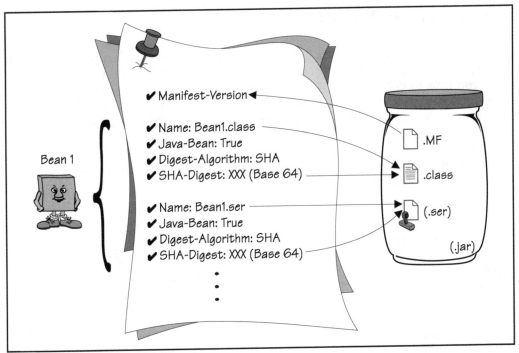

Figure 31-7. The Structure of a Manifest File.

specify whether the given entry is only needed at design time; you must specify a value of either true or false (case doesn't matter). The idea here is to allow builder tools to exclude these type of entries when they package your beans as part of a constructed application.

The following entry uses all the bean-related manifest attributes:

```
Name: smileypersist/SmileyBean.class
Java-Bean: True
Design-Time-Only: False
Depends-On: SmileyEventAdapter.class SmileyPlace.class
Depends-On: SmileyPlace$1.class
Depends-On: Smiley1.ser
```

You can list more than one file in a *Depends-On* attribute, or you can have more than one *Depends-On* line (as we just showed). You can also reference a file in your JAR that is not listed in the manifest.

Creating Your Own Manifest

Every Java class is potentially a bean. So you must create the proper entries in a manifest to identify the classes in a JAR that are also beans. In this section, we will show you how to create your own manifest. Creating your own manifest is useful if you have beans to declare or if you want to provide attribute values other than the default name and hash attributes. To play it safe, you should list all your class files and their resources in the manifest.

So let's create a *smiley.mf* manifest to describe the persistent Smiley classes. Here's what this file should contain:

```
Manifest-Version: 1.0

Name: SmileyBean.class
Java-Bean: True
Design-Time-Only: False

Name: Smiley1.ser
Java-Bean: True
Design-Time-Only: False

Name: Smiley2.ser
Java-Bean: True
Design-Time-Only: False

Name: SmileyEventAdapter.class
Java-Bean: False
Design-Time-Only: False

Name: SmileyPlace.class
Java-Bean: False
Design-Time-Only: False

Name: SmileyPlace$1.class
Java-Bean: False
Design-Time-Only: False

Name: SmileyBoundAdapter.class
Java-Bean: False
Design-Time-Only: False
```

Now let's create a new JAR called *smileys.jar*. At the prompt, enter the following command:

```
prompt> jar cfm smileys.jar smiley.mf Smiley*.class
```

This command tells the *jar* utility to use the manifest file we specify.

Let's take a look at the manifest that the *jar* utility created. At the prompt, enter the following command:

```
prompt> jar xf smileys.jar META-INF
```

Here's the manifest *jar* created with the input we gave it:

```
Manifest-Version: 1.0

Name: SmileyBean.class
Java-Bean: True
Design-Time-Only: False
Digest-Algorithms: SHA MD5
SHA-Digest: T1D6RjlYfFlVXnIkOPoizZVBUcY=
MD5-Digest: x9nBQ8gKZINybHOO4q3NuA==

Name: Smiley1.ser
Java-Bean: True
Design-Time-Only: False
Digest-Algorithms: SHA MD5
SHA-Digest: 48sokweb7kooPe4E6L3+Qyz45wO=
MD5-Digest: on3BztciVDwSS9TJmT+vnA==

Name: Smiley2.ser
Java-Bean: True
Design-Time-Only: False
Digest-Algorithms: SHA MD5
SHA-Digest: b491YjU7rzJjl+jVyFTURWjVjYQ=
MD5-Digest: 33Gbabfaj+CXgb6RLPBn+g==

Name: SmileyEventAdapter.class
Java-Bean: False
Design-Time-Only: False
Digest-Algorithms: SHA MD5
SHA-Digest: 6BviA2z+fDCGVyzWfqWeDPoy/FM=
```

```
MD5-Digest: 1/jiDfLU1X69KOWOtZboNQ==

Name: SmileyPlace.class
Java-Bean: False
Design-Time-Only: False
Digest-Algorithms: SHA MD5
SHA-Digest: 6hzgG1tJx27QIBQk/ugA8XWp6CA=
MD5-Digest: SIp/8MXtUiQRpsGlhCnD5A==

Name: SmileyPlace$1.class
Java-Bean: False
Design-Time-Only: False
Digest-Algorithms: SHA MD5
SHA-Digest: YBQhE1qrCOljpCuqwLaneOVBpJA=
MD5-Digest: 1Tlx52rGMPdh1ojB1+3QzA==

Name: SmileyBoundAdapter.class
Java-Bean: False
Design-Time-Only: False
Digest-Algorithms: SHA MD5
SHA-Digest: 4pvhBJG749JFmXaQC1Uj3sOKud8=
MD5-Digest: m4kZTYQwXq8rh9b8uX9/0A==
```

As you can see, the *jar* utility added the hash attributes on its own.

Signing a JAR

JDK 1.1 provides a tool called *javakey* that lets you sign the contents of your JARs. A *signature* verifies that the JAR came from a "trusted" signer. To generate a signature, the signer must have a public/private key pair. The public key must be authenticated by one or more certificates. The *javakey* utility maintains a persistent database of *entities*. This includes their keys and certificates, as well as information about each entity's trustworthiness.

Javakey manages two types of entities: identities and signers. *Identities* are people, companies, or organizations that have public keys. *Signers* have both public keys and their associated private keys, which are used for signing. In addition, each entity must have at least one certificate authenticating its public key. A *certificate* is a digitally signed statement from one entity guaranteeing the authenticity of the public key of some other entity.

Javakey lets you either import existing keys and certificates or generate new ones. All entities have a *username* managed by *javakey*. You create a new signer using the *create signer (cs)* option. For example, here's how you create a new signer identity called Jeri.

```
prompt> javakey -cs Jeri true
```

The true indicates that Jeri is to be trusted. You can now generate a DSA public/private key pair for Jeri with the following command:

```
prompt> javakey -gk Jeri DSA 512
```

Jeri is now the proud owner of a 512-bit signing key. To generate a X509 certificate for Jeri, we must first create a *certificate directive* file with the following information: 1) the issuer (or signer of the certificate), 2) the owner (or subject) of the certificate, 3) the type of certificate, 4) the signature algorithm, and 5) the name of a file in which to store a copy of the certificate.

Here is an example of a certificate directive file called *jeri.cert_dir*:

```
# issuer information
issuer.name=Jeri
issuer.cert=1

# subject information
subject.name=Jeri
subject.real.name=Jeri Edwards
subject.org=BEA Systems
subject.org.unit=Corporate
subject.country=US

# certificate information
start.date=1 Feb 1998
end.date=15 Feb 1998
serial.number=1001

# certificate algorithm if not DSA
signature.algorithm=MD5/RSA

# name of generated certificate file
out.file=jeri.cer
```

We can now generate the certificate using the *generate certificate (gc)* option. At the prompt, enter the following command:

```
prompt> javakey -gc jeri.cert_dir
```

Javakey will create a x509 certificate using the information we supplied in the directive file. It also uses information stored in its database, such as Jeri's public key and the private key of the issuer (required to sign the certificate). Typically, the issuer of the certificate will be a trusted third party—for example, Verisign. It doesn't make too much sense to issue a certificate that you sign yourself.

You can import, export, and display certificates stored as files. For example, to display Jeri's certificate via the *display certificate (dc)* directive, enter the following command:

```
prompt> javakey -dc jeri.cer
```

Now Jeri can use *javakey* to sign JAR files. To sign a JAR, she must first generate a *signature directive* file, which she calls *jeri.sf*. Javakey uses this directive file to sign the JAR file. Here's an example of a signature directive:

```
# Which signer to use. This signer must be in the database.

signer=Jeri

# Certificate number to use for this signer. This is the number
# javkey previously assigned to the signer's certificate when it
# generated it (or imported it).

cert=1

# Certificate chain depth of a chain of certificates to include. This
# is currently not supported.

chain=0

# The name to give to the generated signature file and associated
# signature block. This must be 8 characters or less. It will be
# given an extension based on the signature algorithm javakey uses.
# For example, jeri.dsa or jeri.rsa.

signature.file=Jeri
```

```
# (Optional) The name to give to the signed JAR file.

out.file=signedSmiley.jar
```

Now, you can finally use the *javakey* command to sign the JAR file. At the prompt, enter the following command:

```
prompt> javakey -gs jeri.sf signedSmiley.jar
```

The output of this command is a signed JAR file called *signedSmiley.jar*. Javakey automatically adds *jeri.sf* and *jeri.dsa* to the JAR's META-INF directory. Note that a JAR signed by Jeri will not exactly open the gates of the Internet. Typically, Jeri's signature must be guaranteed by some well-known trusted signer, which is why we have *certificate authorities* like Verisign. A *certificate chain* contains the signatures of a chain of signers. The receiver of the JAR traverses the signature chain looking for a signer she trusts.

JARs and Browsers

You can also use JARs to optimize the download of related Java classes in applets and beans. You do this using the new HTML *archives* tag. Here's how you would add a JAR to your HTML:

```
<APPLET>
  CODE="MySmiley.class" ARCHIVES="MySmiley.jar"
  WIDTH=150 HEIGHT=150>
</APPLET>
```

The *archives* tag tells the browser to download *MySmiley.jar*. This lets the browser download all the bean-related files over a single TCP/IP session (instead of a session per file). This will improve your download time. In addition, the contents of a JAR are zipped, which should further reduce the download time. Note that the class loader first searches for your (.class) files in the JAR. If it doesn't find them, it will then search the server and the local file system.

You can specify multiple comma-separated (.jar) files in a single *archives* tag. For example:

```
ARCHIVES="MySmiley.jar, MyContainer.jar"
```

Placing JARs in Your CLASSPATH

You can also use JARs to bundle your Java (.class) files. A group of such files could constitute a Java package or library. For example, you could add the following JARs to your CLASSPATH:

```
CLASSPATH="SmileyPersist.jar;SmileyEvents.jar;SmileyProperty.jar;"
```

JDK 1.2 JAR Enhancements

JDK 1.2 introduces some minor JAR enhancements, including: 1) minor improvement to the *jar* command-line tool, 2) new APIs for reading and writing JAR files from within your programs, and 3) a policy and mechanism for handling dependencies on standard extensions and other third-party libraries packaged as JAR files.

THE JAVA SECURITY APIS

In this chapter, we showed you how to work with Java security using the *javakey* tool. As you may already know, this tool is built on top of lower-level APIs that let you directly create and manipulate the security constructs we covered in the last section—including signatures, certificates, identities, and digests.

In this security API section, we give you a very high-level overview of what's available today. However, we strongly recommend that you avoid writing code to these APIs, if you can get away with it. They're far too unstable (see the next Warning box). Instead, you should use a tool like *javakey* to insulate you from the underlying APIs—until they become more stable. So you won't find any programming examples that use Java Security in this edition of the book; they should be in the next one.

The Security Classes and Interfaces

Figures 31-8 and 31-9 show the interface and class hierarchy for Java Security. These classes first appeared in JDK 1.1 as part of the *java.security* package. They provide the following security functions: 1) create and manage private and public keys, 2) encapsulate security algorithms such as digests and signatures, and 3) provide interfaces and classes for principals, signers, certificates, security providers, and keys.

773

Java Security: Hard Hat Area

Warning

As we go to press, the security APIs are still under construction. Amazingly, many of the Security APIs introduced in JDK 1.1 are already being deprecated in JDK 1.2. It's a new Guiness World Record for short-lived APIs. In general, the new JDK 1.2 security features—including roles, credentials, and access control lists—make Java Security more compatible with distributed security models such as CORBA Security. So it's a move in the right direction. We cover the JDK 1.2 security enhancements later in this chapter. ❑

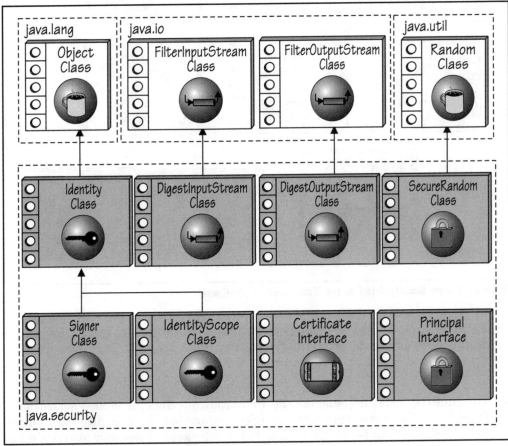

Figure 31-8. Java Security: Interface and Class Hierarchy.

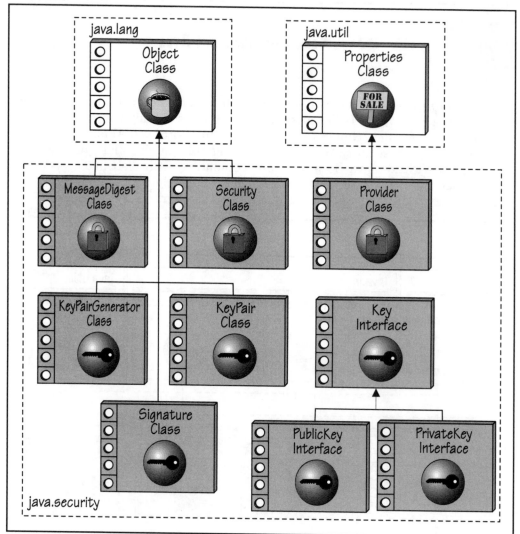

Figure 31-9. Java Security: Interface and Class Hierarchy (Continued).

Figures 31-10 and 31-11 show the methods that the security classes and interfaces support. Here's a brief description of what they do:

■ The **Identity** class implements the **Principal** interface; it is also serializable. Objects of this class represent people, companies, or organizations whose identities can be authenticated using their public keys. They may also represent constructs, such as daemon threads or smart cards. Every **Identity** object has a name and a public key; it also has a set of certificates (all certifying the identity's

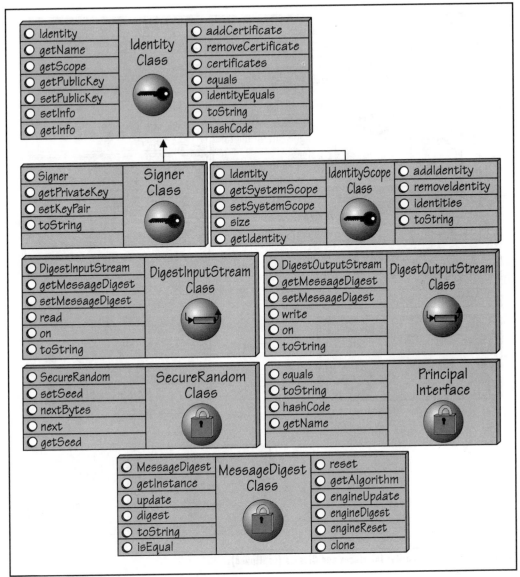

Figure 31-10. Java Security: Interfaces and Classes.

public key). You can subclass an identity to include postal and email addresses, telephone numbers, images of faces and logos, and so on.

You invoke the *Identity* constructor to create an identity object with the name you specify; you can optionally specify an **IdentityScope** object. You invoke *addCertificate* and *removeCertificate* to add or remove a certificate. The *certificates* method returns a copy of all the certificates for this identity. You

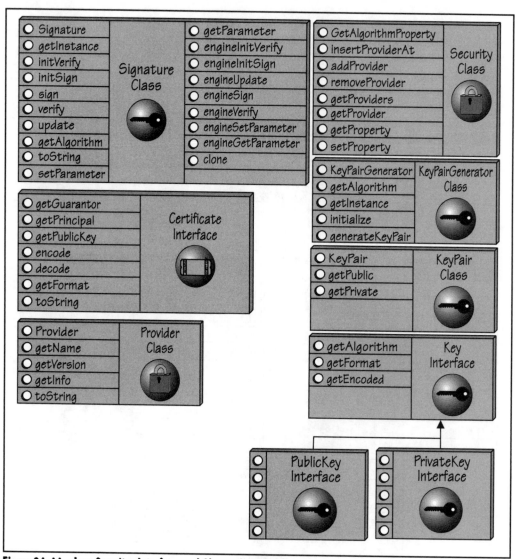

Figure 31-11. Java Security: Interfaces and Classes (continued).

invoke *setPublicKey* to set this identity's public key; it will also remove the old key and all of its certificates. You invoke *setInfo* to pass a string with some general information for this identity. You can obtain the public key information and scope of an identity by invoking the corresponding *getXXX* method. The *hashcode* method returns a hashcode for this identity. Finally, you invoke *equals* or *identityEquals* to test for equality between this identity and the object or identity you specify.

- The **IdentityScope** class represents a scope for identities. It's an **Identity** itself. Consequently, it has a name and can optionally have a scope as well as a public key and associated certificates. You invoke the *IdentityScope* constructor to create a new identity scope object with the specified name and scope. You invoke *addIdentity* to add an identity to the scope. You invoke *getIdentity* to retrieve the identity associated with the name or public key you specify. The *identities* method returns an enumeration of all the identities within this identity scope. The *size* method returns the number of identities within this identity scope. You can always invoke *removeIdentity* to remove an identity from this identity scope. Finally, you invoke *setSystemScope* to set the system's identity scope.

- The **Signer** class represents an identity that can also digitally sign data. You invoke the constructor *Signer* to create a signer with the specified identity name. You provide a **KeyPair** object for this signer by invoking *setKeyPair*. You can then obtain the signer's private key by invoking *getPrivateKey*.

- The **DigestInputStream** class lets you compute a digest on bits you read from a stream. You can turn the digest on or off using the *on* method (the default is on). You invoke the *DigestInputStream* constructor to create a digest filter on the input stream you specify. You then invoke *setMessageDigest* to associate a **MessageDigest** object with this stream. You invoke *read* to read a byte (or an array of bytes) from the input stream. If the digest is on, this method will then call *update* on the **MessageDigest** object and pass it the bytes read. Finally, you invoke *getMessageDigest* to retrieve the message digest object associated with this stream. To complete the message digest computation you must call one of the digest methods on the associated **MessageDigest**.

- The **DigestOutputStream** class lets you compute a digest on bits you write to a stream. It provides functions similar to **DigestOutputStream,** but for writing to a stream. To complete the message digest computation, you must call one of the digest methods on the associated **MessageDigest** object after you're done with your *write* calls to the output stream.

- The **MessageDigest** class encapsulates a hash algorithm, such as MD5 or SHA. Message digests are functions that take arbitrary-sized data and return a fixed-length hash value. This class provides a *Service Provider Interface (SPI)* that is implemented by providers that supply specific algorithms; it consists of all the *engineXXX* methods. Each engine method is called by a correspondingly-named public API method.

You invoke *getInstance* to obtain a **MessageDigest** object that implements the algorithm you specify. You then generate the digest hash by successively invoking *update* with the data to be processed. At any point, you can call *reset* to reset the digest. After all the data is processed, you must call the *digest* method to complete the hash and obtain the final digest value; it's returned in an array of bytes. Finally, you can invoke *isEqual* to compare two digests for equality.

■ The **SecureRandom** class provides a crytpographically strong pseudo-random number generator based on the SHA-1 hash algorithm; it implements strengthened versions of the calls it inherits from **java.util.Random**. You can either invoke an empty constructor to use the class's self-seeding algorithm, or provide your own seed. You can obtain the seed by invoking *getSeed*. You invoke *setSeed* to reseed the object. Finally, you can generate random bytes and bits by invoking *nextBytes* and *next*.

■ The **Principal** interface represents a secure identity—for example, an individual. The *getName* method returns the name of this principal; you can get the hashcode version by invoking *hashcode* instead. You invoke *equals* to compare this principal to a specified object; it returns true if there's a match.

■ The **Certificate** interface provides a common abstraction to access different types of certificates—for example, X.509 or PGP. The *encode* and *decode* methods let you encode and decode certificates to and from streams. The *getFormat* method returns the format of the encoded keys—for example, X.509 or PGP. You invoke *getGuarantor* to obtain the **Principal** of the Certificate Authority vouching for this certificate—for example, the U.S. Postal Service or Verisign. You invoke *getPrincipal* to obtain the **Principal** that owns the certificate. Finally, *getPublicKey* returns the certificate's public key, which is an object that implements the **PublicKey** interface.

■ The **Key** interface is the top-level interface for all keys. You can obtain the algorithm for that key—for example, DSA, RSA, MD-5, or SHA-1—by invoking the *getAlgorithm* method. You obtain the format used to encode this key externally—for example, X.509 or PKCS#8—by invoking *getFormat*. Finally, *getEncoded* returns the encoded version of the key in X.509 or PKCS. You use this encoded version to present the key to outside parties.

■ The **PublicKey** and **PrivateKey** interfaces extend **Key**. They do not provide any new methods or constants of their own. They're simply used to group keys for security purposes.

■ The **KeyPair** class is a simple holder for a public/private key pair. You invoke the constructor *KeyPair* to construct an object with the public and private keys you specify. The *getPublic* method returns the public key from this key pair. The *getPrivate* method returns the private key. Warning: The class does not enforce security, consequently, you must treat it like a private Key.

■ The **KeyPairGenerator** class generates pairs of public and private keys. You invoke the constructor *KeyPairGenerator* to specify the generator algorithm. Then you invoke the *getInstance* static method to create a **KeyPairGenerator** object for the specified algorithm. You invoke *initialize* to specify the key strength and randomness source for the keys. Finally, you invoke *generate-KeyPair* to obtain a **KeyPair** object.

■ The **Provider** class represents a security provider that may implement some or all parts of Java Security. Each **Provider** object has a name and a version number. The default provider is SUN. You invoke the constructor *Provider* to create a provider object with the specified name, version number, and information. You can then invoke the appropriate *getXXX* method to retrieve these values.

■ The **Security** class manages security providers. You invoke *addProvider* to add a provider in the next available position. You can add a provider in a specified position by invoking *insertProviderAt*. You can delete a provider from the list of providers by invoking *removeProvider*. You can find a provider or all providers installed in a location by invoking *getProvider* or *getProviders*. You can add a property by invoking *setProperty*. You can later read the property by invoking *getProperty* or *getAlgorithmProperty*.

■ The **Signature** class encapsulates the function of a digital signature algorithm—for example, RSA with MD5 or DSA. A **Signature** object is used to generate and verify digital signatures. Like Java Security's other algorithm-based classes, the **Signature** class provides *engineXXX* methods that are implemented by service providers. You can request via the constructor an algorithm name. You then invoke *getInstance* to generate a **Signature** object that implements the algorithm.

A signature object goes through three phases (or states): 1) *Initialization*—you either initialize the object for signing by invoking *initSign* with a private key or for verification by invoking *initVerify* with a public key, 2) *Updating*—depending on the type of initialization, you invoke *update* to either sign or verify the bytes you pass, and 3) *Signing or Verifying*—you invoke *sign* to return an X.509-encoded signature of all the updated data, or *verify* to compare the X.509-encoded passed-in signature.

A couple of scenarios should help us make some sense of how these security objects play together.

A Security Signing Scenario

Our first scenario shows how a signing application uses the Java Security classes to generate a digital signature (see Figure 31-12). Let's walk through the steps:

1. ***Create a DSA KeyPairGenerator object.*** You first invoke the constructor *KeyPairGenerator* to specify the generator algorithm, which in our scenario is

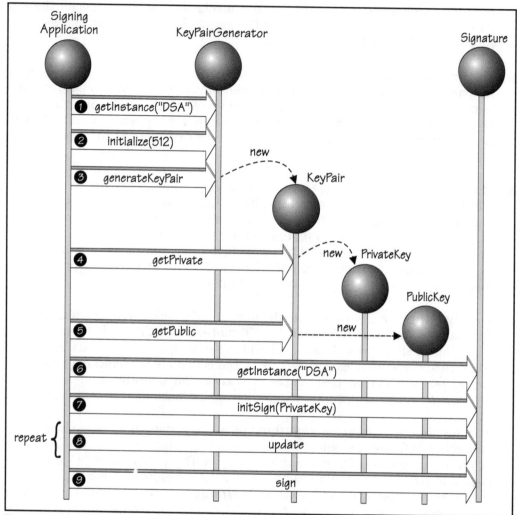

Figure 31-12. Java Security: An Electronic Signing Scenario.

DSA. Then you invoke the *getInstance* static method on this class to create a **KeyPairGenerator** object for the specified algorithm.

2. ***Specify the key strength.*** Invoke *initialize* to specify a key strength of 512 bits.

3. ***Generate a KeyPair.*** Invoke the *generateKeyPair* method to obtain a **KeyPair** object.

4. ***Generate a private key.*** Invoke the *getPrivate* method on the **KeyPair** object to obtain a **PrivateKey** object.

5. ***Generate a public key.*** Invoke the *getPublic* method on the **KeyPair** object to obtain a **PublicKey** object.

6. ***Request a DSA Signature object***. Invoke *getInstance* to generate a **Signature** object that implements the DSA algorithm.

7. ***Initialize the Signature object for signing***. Invoke the *initSign* method on the **Signature** object and then pass it your **PrivateKey**.

8. ***Feed the Signature object the signature bytes to be signed***. Invoke the *update* method on the **Signature** object and then pass it the bytes you want signed. The bytes are signed using the private key.

9. ***Obtain the X.509-encoded signature***. Invoke the *sign* method on the **Signature** object to obtain the X.509-encoded signature/certificate for the data you just processed.

A Security Signature Verification Scenario

Our second scenario shows how a receiving application would verify the signature we generated in the last scenario (see Figure 31-13). Let's walk through the steps:

1. ***Get the Certificate Authority***. Invoke *getGuarantor* to obtain the principal of the Certificate Authority that vouches for this certificate—for example, the U.S. Postal Service or Verisign.

2. ***Get the Principal***. Invoke *getPrincipal* to obtain the **Principal** that owns the certificate. Access rights are typically assigned to a **Principal**.

3. ***Get the public key of the Principal***. Invoke the *getPublicKey* method to obtain the signer's **PublicKey** object.

4. ***Determine the signing algorithm.*** Invoke the *getAlgorithm* method to obtain the algorithm for that key. In our scenario, it's DSA. Note that this method is inherited from the **Key** interface.

5. ***Request a DSA Signature object***. Invoke *getInstance* to generate a **Signature** object that implements the DSA algorithm.

6. ***Initialize the Signature object for verifying***. Invoke *initVerify* with the **PublicKey** of the sender.

7. ***Feed the Signature object some bytes to be verified***. Invoke the *update* method on the **Signature** object and then pass it the bytes you want verified. The *update* method uses the **PublicKey** to unravel the signed bytes.

8. ***Verify the results.*** Invoke *verify* to compare the X.509-encoded, passed-in signature with the results of the *update* method. It returns true or false.

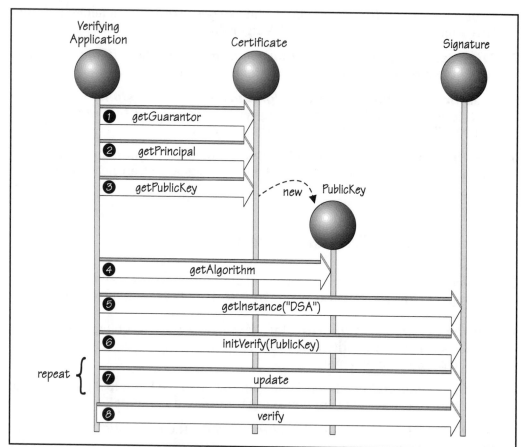

Figure 31-13. Java Security: A Signature Verification Scenario.

JDK 1.2 SECURITY ENHANCEMENTS

JDK 1.2 introduces a new permissions-based security model that builds on many of the security features of JDK 1.1 (such as digitally signed code). The new security model—with its policy-based, configurable access controls—creates a more permeable version of the Java sandbox.

The New JDK 1.2 Security Model

The key idea behind the original Java *sandbox* model is that local code is to be trusted; it has full access to vital system resources such as the file system. In contrast, downloaded remote code is not to be trusted; it can only access the limited resources inside the sandbox (or the penalty box).

JDK 1.1 extends the sandbox by introducing *signed applets*. A correctly digitally signed applet is treated the same as trusted local code. Of course, the signature key must be recognized as trusted by the system that receives the applet. Signed applets, together with their signatures, are delivered in JARs.

JDK 1.2 completely removes the separation between applets and applications. Now all Java code must be granted permission to access resources—including applets, applications, beans, EJBs, and servlets. JDK 1.2 offers fine-grained access controls to all these codebases. If you have the right permissions, you can do almost anything. If you don't have permissions, you live inside the sandbox. Gone is the old idea that only local code and digitally signed code can be trusted.

The JDK 1.2 Security Enhancements: A Summary

Here are some of the major security enhancements JDK 1.2 introduces:

- *Fine-grained access controls*. JDK 1.2 introduces two new concepts: *permissions* and *policies*. These concepts apply to Java applets, beans, EJBs, applications, and servlets. When the VM loads any of these pieces of code, it assigns them permissions based on the security policy currently in effect. Each permission specifies a permitted access to a particular resource—including *read* and *write* access to a specified file or directory; *connect* access to a given host and port; and *destroy, invoke, invoke:method_name*, and *manage* access to an Enterprise JavaBean. You can provide a *configurable policy file* that specifies the permissions available for code from various signers. Unless a permission is explicitly granted to code, it cannot access the resource that is guarded by that permission.

- *X.509 v3 implementation of new certificate interfaces*. JDK 1.2 introduces new certificate interfaces that make it easier for tool vendors to build tools that parse certificates, enforce site-specific certificate policies, revoke certificates, and manage secure local databases of certificates. The JDK includes an X.509 v3 implementation of the new certificate interfaces.

- *New and improved security tools*. JDK 1.2 replaces *javakey* with three new tools: *keytool, jarsigner*, and the *policytool*. Like *javakey*, the *keytool* lets you create key pairs and self-signed X.509 v1 certificates. However, it also manages a keystore, which is a protected database of keys and certificates. Like *javakey*, the new *jarsigner* tool signs JAR files. Unlike *javakey*, the new tool also verifies the signature(s) of signed JAR files by accessing the keystore. Finally, the new *policytool* lets you create and modify external policy configuration files that define your installation's Java security policy.

■ **Domain-based security.** A security *domain* is an environment that has its own set of security policies. A domain is scoped by the set of objects that are directly accessible by a *principal*, which is an entity in the computer system to which permissions are granted. Many security holes develop at the intersection of two security domains. For example, a user-level application can exploit a bug in an operating system routine to gain additional permissions. JDK 1.2 introduces mechanisms that automatically examine the intersection of permissions granted by different domains; it ensures that a less-privileged process does not gain additional permissions by calling more privileged code in a different domain. The Java VM will automatically check the permissions of all of the processes in the call stack to ensure that an application doesn't violate the currently active security policy by calling more privileged code.

JDK 1.2 deprecates a few of the JDK 1.1 security APIs—for example, the service provider *enginexxx* methods. They've been replaced by separate service provider classes—including **SignatureSpi**, **MessageDigestSpi**, and **KeyPairGenerator-Spi**. JDK 1.2 also introduces a number of cosmetic changes to the APIs—for example, the method *Identity.certificates* is now *Identity.getCertificates*. However, all this pales in comparison to the dozens of new security interfaces and classes JDK 1.2 introduces to overhaul the Java security model.

JDK 1.2 New Security Classes

In this section, we give you a quick sampling of JDK 1.2's most important new security classes. We start with the policy classes and their related features such as permissions. Then we cover access control and guarded objects. We conclude with secure class loading. So without further ado, here's our list of JDK 1.2's most interesting new security classes:

■ The **java.security.CodeSource** class extends the concept of a codebase within HTML to encapsulate not only the location (URL) but also the set of public keys that are used to verify signed code originating from that location. The public key is of type **java.security.PublicKey**. Note that this is not the equivalent of the *CodeBase* tag in HTML files.

■ The **java.security.Permission** class abstracts access to system resources. You typically subclass it to represent specific accesses. These subclassed permissions generally belong to their own packages. For example, **FilePermission** is located in the *java.io* package, **BeanPermission** is in *java.ejb*, **SocketPermission** is in *java.net*, and **PropertyPermission** is in *java.util*.

You create a new permission instance by passing one or more string parameters to the class constructor. In the most common case, you pass two parameters: the name of the target resource (for example, a bean or a file name) and the action allowed (for example, *read* on a file, *invoke_method* on a bean). You can also specify a set of actions by separating them with commas.

- The **java.security.PermissionCollection** class represents a homogeneous collection of **Permission** objects.

- The **java.security.Permissions** class represents a heterogeneous collection of **Permission** objects.

- The **java.security.Policy** class contains the overall system security policy being enforced for this Java VM's run time. The policy is evaluated for a given **CodeSource** to produce a set of permissions appropriate for this code in this domain. There can be multiple instances of the **Policy** object, but only one is in effect at any time; it is instantiated and initialized when the Java VM starts. You specify the policy using a text configuration file; it contains a list of entries, each consisting of a **CodeSource**, its permissions, and the signer names. Here's the format for an entry:

```
grant [SignedBy "signer_names"] [, CodeBase "URL"]
{
    permission permission_class_name [ "target_name" ]
    [, "action"] [, SignedBy "signer_names"];
};
```

In this example, four permissions are granted to code that resides at **http://engr.sjsu.edu**, it is signed by Bob.

```
grant codeBase "http://engr.sjsu.edu/", signedBy "Bob"
{
  permission java.io.FilePermission "/tmp", "read";
  permission java.io.SocketPermission "*", "connect";
  permission java.util.PropertyPermission "user.*";
  permission java.ejb.BeanPermission "*", "invoke";
};
```

- The **java.security.AccessController** class is used to make access control decisions. You invoke the method *checkPermission* to determine whether a particular action is allowed. This method is typically invoked by code that needs to control access to system resources. The **AccessController** examines the current execution context and makes the right decision. If the requested access is not allowed, it throws an **AccessControlException**.

- The **java.security.SecureClassLoader** class is an implementation of **java.lang.Classloader** that also handles remote class loading. All applets and applications (except for system classes) are loaded by a **SecureClassLoader**—either directly or indirectly. JDK 1.2 introduces a new classpath that can enforce the secure loading of local classes.

- The **java.security.GuardedObject** and **java.security.Guard** classes allow the supplier of a resource to create a **GuardedObject** guarded by a **Guard** object. You can only access the resource if certain security checks inside the **Guard** are satisfied. Note that **Guard** is an interface. Consequently, any object can implement it to become a **Guard**. The interface supports a single method called *checkGuard*. The **Permission** class in *java.security* implements the **Guard** interface. You can use the basic pattern of **GuardedObject** and **Guard** in many situations—for example, a **Guard** can check for the time of the day, signer, or other relevant information.

- The **java.security.SignedObject** class contains a copy of a serialized signed object and a valid signature. You cannot tamper with the signed object without invalidating the signature. In the future, JavaSoft may provide a **SealedObject** that uses encryption to hide the content of an object.

As you can see, Java security is still a moving target. If you can, use one of the JDK tools to meet your current security needs. You should code to the APIs as a last resort.

GUIDELINES FOR WRITING PERSISTENT BEANS

According to the JavaBeans specification, all beans must be persistent. A bean must either implement the **Serialization** or **Externalization** interfaces. Bean containers are in charge of storing and reactivating the beans they contain. So here are some persistence-related guidelines that your beans and their containers may want to follow:

✔ *Make your beans thoughtfully persistent*. Is it OK to save everything? Consider security issues. You may want to encrypt some of the information.

✔ *Use a DBMS or ODBMS when you need scale*. Consider storing some of your transient fields in ODBMSs or RDBMSs under the control of custom *writeObject* and *readObject* methods. For example, server beans will rarely store their entire state in (.ser) files. Instead, they will save their data in more efficient (and reliable) persistent stores. Typically, a server bean's state will be managed within the confines of a transaction. You should very carefully design the persistent structure of your server beans. Client beans are less demanding.

✔ **Use the manifest to specify your beans**. As a general rule, you must provide a manifest entry for each bean you package in a JAR. You must also include any file that you sign in the manifest.

✔ **Make sure all your non-transient instance variables are serializable**. The primitive Java datatypes are serializable by default. You must carefully check all non-primitive types by reading the documentation. When in doubt, declare your fields *transient*. You may also want to initialize transient and static variables when you deserialize your bean.

✔ **Handle default values with care**. In non-transient fields, the deserialized values override any default values. However, non-persistent variables are initialized with their default values. If this is not OK, you may want to provide a custom *readObject* method.

✔ **Do not maintain persistent references to other beans**. Remember, the containers are responsible for serializing and deserializing beans as well as recreating their interconnections.

✔ **Use JARs to store and distribute your beans**. Use JARs to package all the resources associated with a bean. Use different JARs for design-time beans versus run-time beans. Use manifest entries to fully describe the classes in a bean package. Use the HTML *archives* tag to download your JARs. Finally, record your JARs with CLASSPATH.

✔ **Evolve the state of your beans gracefully.** Don't forget that the persistent state is a key part of a bean. If possible, you must be able to load old states in new beans and new states in old beans.

✔ **If you can, use one of the JDK tools to sign and verify your JARs**. Avoid coding directly to the Java security APIs. They're still under construction. Of course, they're also getting better with every new JDK release.

CONCLUSION

Java persistence helps you store your beans; JARs make it possible to transfer your beans across applications. The persistence mechanism is an essential part of the contract between a bean and its container. This long chapter shows that your beans are in good hands when it comes to both persistence and JAR-based packaging. Together, these two mechanisms provide most of the services you need to not only package your beans but also to store them.

Server-side beans will need to store some of their state in a scalable, multiuser ODBMS or RDBMS. They must do this under transaction control, which is where *Enterprise JavaBeans (EJBs)* come into the picture. We cover EJB in a later chapter. But before we go into these advanced topics, we must still cover the mechanisms JavaBeans provide for introspection and tool support.

Chapter 32

The Introspective and Toolable JavaBean

JavaBeans were born to be toolable. This is not surprising given that visual application tool vendors—including Symantec, IBM/Lotus, Borland, Penumbra, and Sybase—played a big part in the original specification of JavaBeans. So from day one, the design point of the bean component model was toolability. To borrow a line from the movie *Field of Dreams*: "If you build it, they will come." In this case, JavaSoft built a toolable component model and the tool vendors did indeed come—and in record numbers!

As we go to press, over 22 visual builder tools for JavaBeans are shipping. It's an all-time record for tool support—especially for a component model that is still in its first release. These tools are being offered by both established vendors and innovative start-ups.

Examples of tools for JavaBeans from established vendors include: Borland's *JBuilder*, Sybase's *PowerJ*, IBM's *VisualAge for Java*, Symantec's *Visual Café*, Lotus Development's *BeanMachine*, Taligent's *VisualAge WebRunner*, Unify's *Vision*, Netscape's *Visual JavaScript*, ObjectShare's *Parts for Java*, Silicon Graphics' *Cosmo Code*, Informix's *Data Director for Java*, and SunSoft's *Java Workshop* and *Java Studio*.

Examples of tools for JavaBeans from start-ups include: Penumbra's *Super Mojo*, BulletProof's *JDesignerPro*, KonaSoft's *Packajar*, Lighthouse Design's *JavaPlan*, Asymetrix's *SuperCede*, Tek-Tools' *Kawa*, Vision Software's *Vision JADE*, Applicom Software's *RadJa*, Imperial Software's *Visaj*, Visix Software's *Vibe*, JRad Technologies' *j.rad*, OMNIS Software's *OMNIS Studio*, and Pierian Spring Software's *Digital Chisel 3*.

Most of these tools come with rich palettes filled with core JavaBeans that you can reuse to assemble new components. These bootstrapping components could help create a self-feeding loop that could result in an explosion of JavaBeans written by medium-skilled programmers. In any case, JavaBeans have become synonymous with visual tools.

In this chapter, we will look at the two technologies that make beans supertoolable: *introspection* and *customization*. The JavaBeans component model provides an introspective layer on top of the core Java *reflection* APIs; it consists of helper classes that make the introspection of beans uniform across tools. The customization classes let you visually configure and manipulate beans from within a tool environment. Collectively, these classes give you total control over the appearance and ease-of-customization of your beans within a tool environment.

WHICH TOOL?

A visual builder tool uses the introspection (and reflection) APIs to learn about your beans. The tool lets you visually connect beans (or wire them) using the methods, events, and properties that it discovered via introspection. You should be able to customize any bean by using its visual property editors and customizers. Finally, the tool lets you package a set of related beans inside a JAR for delivery to other container applications—including other tools, browsers, and Java applications.

After playing with the current crop of JavaBeans tools, we concluded that there's currently no "one size fits all" tool on the market. Instead, we found that each tool does one or two things very well. In our book, the ideal JavaBeans tool combines the best features in all these tools. Until we get this perfect tool, we will assemble our beans using a variety of vendor tools.

In theory, you should be able to export a JAR full of assembled beans from one tool and then import it into a different tool to provide value-added services. For example, here's an inter-tool scenario that would have made us very happy if it had worked:

1. Start assembling your beans using Symantec's *Visual Café* to take advantage of its rich palette of visual components, IDE-support, wiring services, and JIT compiler. It also has powerful visual layout capabilities that let you create a gridbag with simple drag-and-drop.

2. Import the assembly of beans into Borland's *JBuilder* to take advantage of its built-in CORBA IDE facilities and wizards.

3. Import the resulting bean assembly into IBM's *VisualAge for Java* to graphically create the client/server connections.

As we explain in later chapters, this scenario doesn't quite work. But we're getting ahead of our story.

THE INTROSPECTIVE JAVABEAN

Introspection is the ability to dynamically discover a component's features at run time—including its properties, methods, and the events it emits. Introspection is really what differentiates beans from ordinary Java classes. Tools that recognize the JavaBeans naming conventions (or design patterns) can look inside a bean to discover its properties and behavior. The Java *reflection* APIs provide a lower-level form of introspection. You can use reflection to discover the members of any Java class—including its constructors, methods, fields, and modifiers.

In this section, we briefly introduce the reflection APIs, but we don't dig into the details. Instead, we will look in more detail at the JavaBeans introspection APIs. The idea is that you will specify the behavior of your beans via naming patterns so that an *introspector* can automatically discover them at run time. In many cases, you may have to directly get involved with the introspection APIs—for example, to provide a **BeanInfo** class that explicitly defines your bean. But only in the rarest cases will you ever have to deal with a reflection API.

The Core Reflection Classes

Figure 32-1 shows the different packages that are involved with either Java reflection or introspection. Under-the-covers bean introspection uses the **Class** class and its helper classes in the *java.lang.reflect* package to discover and use bean information. You already got a taste of **Class** in Part 5.

The **Class** class is the mother of all reflection classes. Every instance of a Java class has a **Class** object associated with it. This object can tell you everything you need to know about a Java class—for example, its name, superclass, loader, signers, and the interfaces it supports. You can invoke the *getClass* method on any Java object to obtain its **Class** object. This method is implemented by **java.lang.Object**. As a result, every Java object supports it. Note that the Java VM automatically creates these **Class** objects when it loads a class. There is no way for you to directly create one of these objects—there are no public constructors for **Class**.

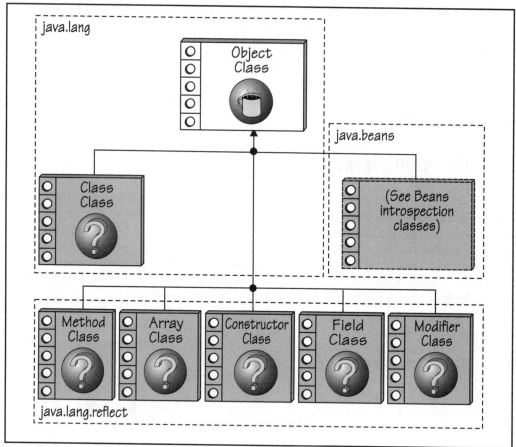

Figure 32-1. The Reflection Classes.

Once you have a **Class** object, you can then discover its fields, methods, constructors, and other pieces of information. JDK 1.1 added several new methods to **Class** to support reflection (see light methods in Figure 32-2). Most of these methods return instances of classes defined in the *java.lang.reflect* package—including **Method**, **Constructor**, **Field**, **Modifier**, and **Array**.

For example, *getConstructors* returns an array of **Constructor** objects this class supports; *getMethods* returns an array of **Method** objects reflecting all the public methods this class supports, including those declared by the class as well as those inherited from superclasses, while *getDeclaredMethods* returns an array of **Method** objects reflecting all the methods declared in this class. The *getMethod* returns a **Method** object that reflects the stringified name of the method you pass to it as a parameter.

● toString	○ getClasses
● forName	○ getFields
● newInstance	○ getMethods
○ isInstance	○ getConstructors
○ isAssignableFrom	○ getField
● isInterface	○ getMethod
○ isArray	○ getConstructor
○ isPrimitive	○ getDeclaredClasses
● getName	○ getDeclaredFields
● getClassLoader	○ getDeclaredMethods
● getSuperClass	○ getDeclaredConstructors
● getInterfaces	○ getDeclaredField
○ getComponentType	○ getDeclaredMethod
○ getModifiers	○ getDeclaredConstructor
○ getSigners	○ getResourceAsStream
○ getDeclaringClass	

Class
Class

Figure 32-2. The Enhanced Class Class.

The returned reflection objects provide methods that let you drill down to the next level of reflective detail. For example, the **Method** class returns information about, and access to, a single reflected method on a class or interface. The reflected method may be a class method or an instance method.

You can then invoke the methods of a reflected **Method** object to obtain its name, declaring class, modifiers, return type, parameter types, and exception types (see Figure 32-3). The *invoke* method even lets you invoke this method on an object you specify, passing it a matching parameter list; it also returns anything it receives from the target object.

○ getDeclaringClass	Method	○ getExceptionTypes
○ getName	Class	○ equals
○ getModifiers		○ hashCode
○ getReturnType		○ toString
○ getParameterTypes		○ invoke

Figure 32-3. The Reflective Method Class.

In summary, the Java VM provides a considerable amount of run time information about ordinary Java classes. In the next sections, we go over the additional features that the JavaBeans run time provides to discover implicit and explicit information about a bean.

JavaBeans Introspection: An Overview

The *java.beans* package provides a set of classes (and interfaces) that directly support the introspection of beans (see Figure 32-4). Many of these classes use the lower-level reflection APIs. They are there to help a visual tool discover a bean's icon, methods, properties, and events.

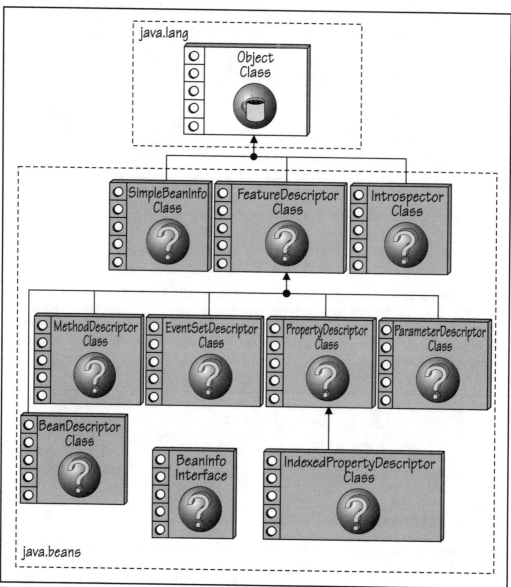

Figure 32-4. The JavaBeans Introspection-Support Classes and Interfaces.

Instead of using the low-level methods in *java.lang.reflect*, a tool asks the JavaBeans **Introspector** class for the information associated with a bean. The tool then works with **BeanInfo** to discover the properties, methods, and events a bean supports. Bean creators can optionally restrict what the tool sees by providing an explicit class that implements the **BeanInfo** interface. You typically do this by extending the **SimpleBeanInfo** class.

Your **BeanInfo** can optionally describe the *features* of your bean—including its properties, events, methods, and the parameters of each method. The JavaBeans *descriptor* classes describe these features. The descriptors contain metadata that describe each feature. A bean relies on these separate metadata objects to provide information on its behalf. Why are these objects not implemented within the bean itself? The idea is that there is no reason for each bean to carry this extra baggage around all the time. You should be able to discover and then access the descriptor objects using the **BeanInfo** for this bean.

The **FeatureDescriptor** class is the root class of all the descriptor metadata objects; it defines accessor methods to set and get attributes that are common to all the descriptor classes. The descriptor metadata classes describe the different features of a bean, including the bean itself. You provide the metadata that goes into these descriptor objects via constructors and setter methods. You invoke various getter methods to retrieve this information.

JavaBeans Introspection: The Metadata Descriptor Classes

Figure 32-5 shows the JavaBeans descriptor classes and their methods. These are the classes that describe all the metadata elements associated with a bean. Instances of these classes provide metadata for a particular bean in the form of run-time objects. The **BeanInfo** serves as the collection point for the metadata objects that are associated with a given bean type. Let's quickly go over the main functions these metadata classes provide:

■ The **FeatureDescriptor** class is the root class of all bean descriptors. It provides methods to get and set a feature's display name, programmatic name, and short textual description. You can set (and get) a *hidden* flag to mark the features that should not be exposed to humans (i.e., it's only intended for tool use). You can set (and get) an *expert* flag to distinguish between features that are intended for expert users from those intended for normal users. You can associate an arbitrary attribute/value pair with a bean using *setValue*; it creates a name/value pair. You can read a named attribute using *getValue*. You invoke *attributeNames* to obtain an enumeration of all the attributes you registered with *setValue*.

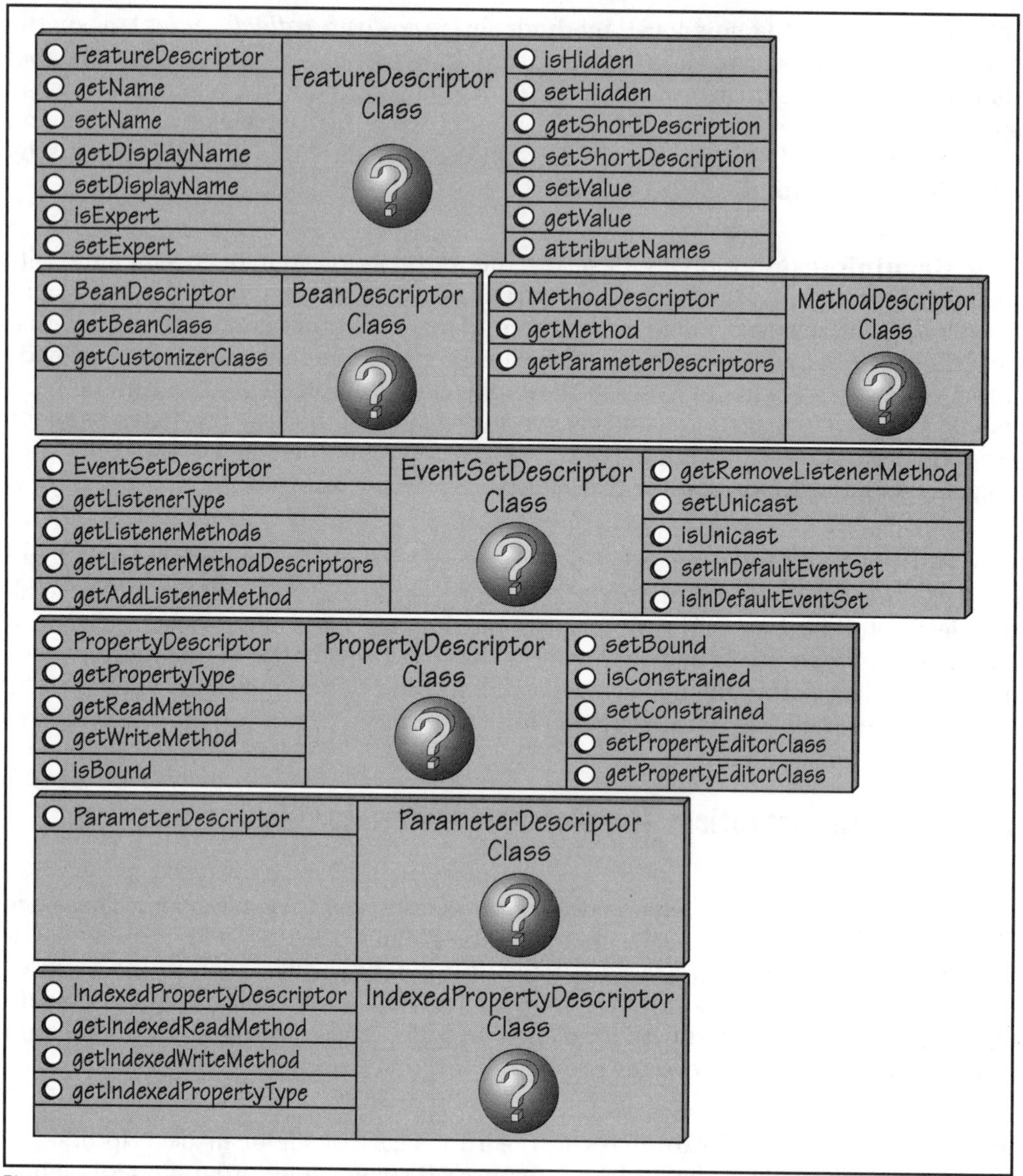

Figure 32-5. JavaBeans Introspection: The Descriptor Classes.

■ The **BeanDescriptor** class provides additional information about a bean beyond its properties, events, and methods. The constructor lets you pass both the class of a bean and optionally its customizer class. You can invoke *getBeanClass* to obtain the bean's **Class** object. You invoke *getCustomizerClass* to obtain the customizer's **Class** object.

- The **MethodDescriptor** class describes the metadata for a particular method a JavaBean supports. The constructor lets you pass a **Method** object and an optional array of **ParameterDescriptor** objects. You can invoke *getMethod* to retrieve the **Method** object. You invoke *getParameterDescriptors* to return an array of **ParameterDescriptor** objects—one for each parameter in the method signature.

- The **EventSetDescriptor** class describes a group of events a bean fires. The group consists of the event method calls associated with a single event listener interface. The class provides four constructors. Which constructor you use depends on how well your bean conforms to the default naming patterns for events. The less the conformance, the more parameters you must specify. The *getListenerType* method returns the **Class** of the event listener interface. The *getListenerMethods* returns an array of **Method** objects that describe the methods of the listener interface. The *getListenerMethodDescriptors* returns an array of **MethodDescriptor** objects for that listener interface.

  The methods *getAddListenerMethod* and *getRemoveListenerMethod* return **Method** objects that describe the methods used to register and unregister a listener. You invoke *setUnicast* to mark an event set as unicast; event sources are normally multicast. You invoke *isUnicast* to determine if an event source is unicast. Your bean may define a *default event set* that serves as the default event group. You invoke *setInDefaultEventSet* with a boolean value of true to mark an event set as default. You can determine if an event set is a default by invoking *isInDefaultEventSet*; it will return true if it is.

- The **ParameterDescriptor** class lets you specify additional information for each of a method's parameters beyond what the **Method** class provides. This class does not provide any new methods. However, it derives quite a bit of functionality from its base class. For example, it lets you invoke *getDisplayName* to obtain a display name for a parameter inside a method.

- The **PropertyDescriptor** class describes a single property exported by a JavaBean via a pair of accessor methods. You can set and get the editor for this property via the *setPropertyEditorClass* and *getPropertyEditorClass* methods. Normally, property editors are found using the **PropertyEditorManager** class. You invoke *getPropertyType* to obtain a **Class** object that describes the built-in type for this property—for example, *int*. You can obtain the getter and setter methods of this property by invoking *getReadMethod* and *getWriteMethod*—they both return **Method** objects. You can set your property to bound by invoking *setBound* and passing it a boolean true. You can determine if a property is bound by invoking *isBound*. Similarly, you can set a property to constrained by invoking *setConstrained*; you can determine if a property is constrained by invoking *isConstrained*.

■ The **IndexedPropertyDescriptor** class describes an indexed property. This class extends the **PropertyDescriptor** class with three new methods. You invoke *getIndexedReadMethod* to obtain the getter for this indexed property. You invoke *getIndexedWriteMethod* to obtain its setter. Finally, you invoke *getIndexedPropertyType* to obtain the type that will be returned by the indexed getter.

As you can see, the descriptor classes are run-time constructs that reflect the bean features we described in the previous chapters. They are holders of metadata that describe a bean. So how is all this introspective information presented on a per-bean basis? This is where the **BeanInfo** comes into the picture; it's the class that brings all this information together. The **BeanInfo** represents all your bean's metadata to the outside world.

We cover **BeanInfo** in the next section, but first here are the detailed class descriptions for the descriptors we just covered:

Listing 32-1. The java.beans.FeatureDescriptor Class.

```
public class FeatureDescriptor extends Object
{
  // Constructor
  public FeatureDescriptor();

  // Methods
  public String getName();
  public void setName(String name);
  public String getDisplayName();
  public void setDisplayName(String displayName);
  public boolean isExpert();
  public void setExpert(boolean expert);
  public boolean isHidden();
  public void setHidden(boolean hidden);
  public String getShortDescription();
  public void setShortDescription(String text);
  public void setValue(String attributeName, Object value);
  public Object getValue(String attributeName);
  public Enumeration attributeNames();
}
```

Listing 32-2. The java.beans.BeanDescriptor Class.

```
public class BeanDescriptor extends FeatureDescriptor
{
  // Constructors
  public BeanDescriptor(Class beanClass);
```

```
  public BeanDescriptor(Class beanClass, Class customizerClass);

  // Methods
  public Class getBeanClass();
  public Class getCustomizerClass();
}
```

Listing 32-3. The java.beans.MethodDescriptor Class.

```
public class MethodDescriptor extends FeatureDescriptor
{
  // Constructors
  public MethodDescriptor(Method method);
  public MethodDescriptor(Method method,
                          ParameterDescriptor parameterDescriptors[]);

  // Methods
  public Method getMethod();
  public ParameterDescriptor[] getParameterDescriptors();
}
```

Listing 32-4. The java.beans.EventSetDescriptor Class.

```
public class EventSetDescriptor extends FeatureDescriptor
{
  // Constructors
  public EventSetDescriptor(Class sourceClass,
                            String eventSetName,
                            Class listenerType,
                            String listenerMethodName)
                            throws IntrospectionException;
  public EventSetDescriptor(Class sourceClass,
                            String eventSetName,
                            Class listenerType,
                            String listenerMethodNames[],
                            String addListenerMethodName,
                            String removeListenerMethodName)
                            throws IntrospectionException;
  public EventSetDescriptor(String eventSetName,
                            Class listenerType,
                            Method listenerMethods[],
                            Method addListenerMethod,
                            Method removeListenerMethod)
                            throws IntrospectionException;
  public EventSetDescriptor(String eventSetName,
```

```
                             Class listenerType,
                             MethodDescriptor listenerMethodDescriptors[],
                             Method addListenerMethod,
                             Method removeListenerMethod)
                             throws IntrospectionException;

  // Methods
  public Class getListenerType();
  public Method[] getListenerMethods();
  public MethodDescriptor[] getListenerMethodDescriptors();
  public Method getAddListenerMethod();
  public Method getRemoveListenerMethod();
  public void setUnicast(boolean unicast);
  public boolean isUnicast();
  public void setInDefaultEventSet(boolean inDefaultEventSet);
  public boolean isInDefaultEventSet();
}
```

Listing 32-5. The java.beans.ParameterDescriptor Class.

```
public class ParameterDescriptor extends FeatureDescriptor
{
  // Constructor
  public ParameterDescriptor();
}
```

Listing 32-6. The java.beans.PropertyDescriptor Class.

```
public class PropertyDescriptor extends FeatureDescriptor
{
  // Constructors
  public PropertyDescriptor(String propertyName,
                            Class beanClass)
                            throws IntrospectionException;
  public PropertyDescriptor(String propertyName,
                            Class beanClass,
                            String getterName,
                            String setterName)
                            throws IntrospectionException;
  public PropertyDescriptor(String propertyName,
                            Method getter,
                            Method setter)
                            throws IntrospectionException;

  // Methods
```

```
  public Class getPropertyType();
  public Method getReadMethod();
  public Method getWriteMethod();
  public boolean isBound();
  public void setBound(boolean bound);
  public boolean isConstrained();
  public void setConstrained(boolean constrained);
  public void setPropertyEditorClass(Class propertyEditorClass);
  public Class getPropertyEditorClass();
}
```

Listing 32-7. The java.beans.IndexedPropertyDescriptor Class.

```
public class IndexedPropertyDescriptor extends PropertyDescriptor
{
  // Constructors
  public IndexedPropertyDescriptor(String propertyName,
                                   Class beanClass)
                                   throws IntrospectionException;
  public IndexedPropertyDescriptor(String propertyName,
                                   Class beanClass,
                                   String getterName,
                                   String setterName,
                                   String indexedGetterName,
                                   String indexedSetterName)
                                   throws IntrospectionException;
  public IndexedPropertyDescriptor(String propertyName,
                                   Method getter,
                                   Method setter,
                                   Method indexedGetter,
                                   Method indexedSetter)
                                   throws IntrospectionException;

  // Methods
  public Method getIndexedReadMethod();
  public Method getIndexedWriteMethod();
  public Class getIndexedPropertyType();
}
```

Introspecting with BeanInfo

The **BeanInfo** is a one-stop shop for obtaining all the metadata information for your bean. Objects that implement this interface must provide the bean metadata that

goes into the various descriptor objects we described in the last section. Obviously, it takes quite a bit of programming effort to provide this metadata descriptor information. In some cases, it may even require more effort than writing the bean itself. The good news is that the JavaBeans run time can automatically generate most of this metadata by analyzing your beans. In some cases, you won't have to write a single line of additional code.

The JavaBeans run time provides an **Introspector** class that knows how to automatically generate a **BeanInfo**—including its associated metadata objects—using the low-level reflection APIs. Of course, the **Introspector** can only accomplish this feat on beans that adhere to the JavaBeans design patterns we described in the previous chapters. The **Introspector** uses these design patterns to discover the metadata information that goes into the descriptor classes—including your bean's properties, events, and methods. In a sense, the **Introspector** is the codification of the JavaBeans design patterns; it has the final word on how to interpret these patterns, which it uses to automatically construct the descriptors.

JavaBeans gives you the choice of overruling the **Introspector** by providing explicit bean metadata yourself. In this case, you must provide your own **BeanInfo** class. Typically, you will derive this class from the **SimpleBeanInfo** that comes with the run time. Your **BeanInfo** class must follow a design pattern of its own. It consists of appending the string *BeanInfo* to the name of your bean class—for example, **SmileyBeanBeanInfo**.

The **Introspector** first looks for an explicit **BeanInfo** class by taking the full package-qualified name of the target bean class and appending "BeanInfo" to form a new class name. If this fails, then it takes the classname component of this name (without the package name), appends "BeanInfo" to it, and then looks for that class in each of the packages you specify in the *BeanInfo search path*. If this also fails, the **Introspector** creates its own **BeanInfo** with the information it discovers using the reflection APIs and your naming patterns. Note that the **Introspector** also looks at all of your bean's superclasses for either explicit or implicit information it can use to build the **BeanInfo**.

JavaBeans also provides a collaborative approach to introspection. In this approach, you provide an explicit **BeanInfo,** but you can return nulls for the methods you do not want to implement yourself. The **Introspector** will then implement the null methods on your behalf. Note that any metadata you provide in the non-null methods is definitive. The **Introspector** will not probe any further. This means that the information you provide must be complete. For example, if you implement the *BeanInfo.getPropertyDescriptors*, then you must provide descriptors for all the bean properties you want to expose.

The Introspector and BeanInfo Interfaces

Figure 32-6 shows the classes and interfaces that are at the top of the JavaBeans introspection food chain. These are the objects that tool vendors and bean providers will typically handle. Here's a description of what this interface and two classes do:

■ The **BeanInfo** interface defines getter methods for obtaining metadata descriptors that describe the various features of your beans: *getBeanDescriptor* returns a **BeanDescriptor**; *getEventSetDescriptors* returns an array of **EventSetDescriptor** objects; *getPropertyDescriptors* returns an array of **PropertyDescriptor** objects; and *getMethodDescriptors* returns an array of **MethodDescriptor** objects. Note that any of these methods may return null to indicate that the information is to be obtained by automatic analysis.

The *getIcon* method returns an **Image** object that can represent your bean inside tool palettes. The image is a GIF that comes in one of four flavors: 16x16 color, 32x32 color, 16x16 mono, and 32x32 mono. If your bean only offers a single icon, JavaBeans recommends that you provide 16x16 color; the icons must also have a "transparent" background so that they can be rendered on an existing background. The *getAdditionalBeanInfo* method returns other **BeanInfo** objects that provide additional information on the current bean. If there are conflicts, the current **BeanInfo** takes precedence over the additional objects.

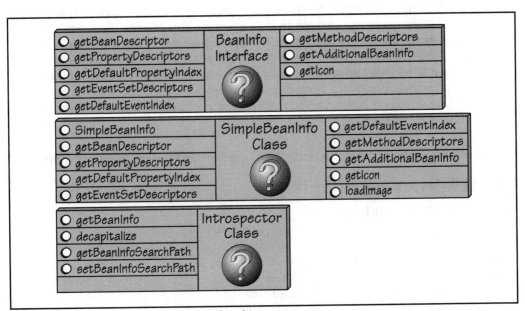

Figure 32-6. JavaBeans Introspection: BeanInfo and Introspector.

The *getDefaultEventIndex* returns an index to the event that a human will most commonly use on this bean; it returns -1 if there is no default event. The *getDefaultPropertyIndex* returns an index to the property that a human will most commonly pick when customizing this bean.

■ The **SimpleBeanInfo** is a support class that you can extend when implementing your **xxxBeanInfo** class. It returns nulls for each of the methods defined by **BeanInfo**. You can selectively override any of these methods to provide explicit metadata. When the **Introspector** encounters a null, it will automatically construct the information using your design patterns and the lower-level reflection APIs. In addition, the class includes a nice little utility called *loadImage*. You invoke this method to load the icons; it takes as its single input parameter the name of a GIF file relative to the directory holding your bean's (.class) file. The method returns a null if the load fails.

■ The **Introspector** class provides a standard way for tools to learn about the properties, events, and methods supported by a target Java bean. It also knows how to consistently interpret the latest and greatest JavaBeans design patterns. When in doubt, the **Introspector** has the final word. To obtain a **BeanInfo,** you invoke the *getBeanInfo* method and pass it the bean class and optionally a "stop" ancestor class. The **Introspector** either finds the **BeanInfo** object that comes with this bean or it creates a new one "on-the-fly." In the latter case, it will learn about the properties, events, and methods your bean exposes below the stop class.

The *getBeanInfoSearchPath* returns an array of package names that will be searched in that order to find **BeanInfo** classes. You can set the search path by invoking *setBeanInfoSearchPath* and then passing it an array of package names. The *decapitalize* method is a helper function; it takes a string and converts it to the normal Java variable name capitalization. The helper normally converts the first character from uppercase to lowercase. However, it leaves the string unchanged if both the first and second characters are uppercase—for example, URL stays URL.

For our readers who are writing code, here are the detailed class descriptions:

Listing 32-8. The java.beans.BeanInfo Interface.

```
public interface BeanInfo
{
  // Variables
  public final static int ICON_COLOR_16x16;
  public final static int ICON_COLOR_32x32;
  public final static int ICON_MONO_16x16;
  public final static int ICON_MONO_32x32;
```

```
// Methods
public abstract BeanDescriptor getBeanDescriptor();
public abstract PropertyDescriptor[] getPropertyDescriptors();
public abstract int getDefaultPropertyIndex();
public abstract getEventSetDescriptors();
public abstract int getDefaultEventIndex();
public abstract MethodDescriptor[] getMethodDescriptors();
public abstract BeanInfo[] getAdditionalBeanInfo();
public abstract Image getIcon(int iconKind);
}
```

Listing 32-9. The java.beans.SimpleBeanInfo Class.

```
public class SimpleBeanInfo extends Object implements BeanInfo
{
  // Constructor
  public SimpleBeanInfo();

  // Methods
  public BeanDescriptor getBeanDescriptor();
  public PropertyDescriptor[] getPropertyDescriptors();
  public int getDefaultPropertyIndex();
  public EventSetDescriptor[] getEventSetDescriptors();
  public int getDefaultEventIndex();
  public MethodDescriptor[] getMethodDescriptors();
  public BeanInfo[] getAdditionalBeanInfo();
  public Image getIcon(int iconKind);
  public Image loadImage(String resourceName);
}
```

Listing 32-10. The java.beans.Introspector Class.

```
public class Introspector extends Object
{
  // Class Methods
  public static BeanInfo getBeanInfo(Class beanClass)
                                throws IntrospectionException;
  public static BeanInfo getBeanInfo(Class beanClass,
                                Class stopClass)
                                throws IntrospectionException;
  public static String decapitalize(String name);
  public static String[] getBeanInfoSearchPath();
  public static void setBeanInfoSearchPath(String path[]);
}
```

SCENARIO TIME

It's time for two very short scenarios that show how these introspection objects play together. In both scenarios, we assume that we're dealing with beans that fully adhere to the JavaBeans design patterns. The first scenario only deals with the introspection classes. The second scenario starts out with introspection, but then adds a bit of reflection to the mix.

Scenario 1: Discovering a Bean's Events

The scenario in Figure 32-7 shows how an application dynamically discovers the events a bean emits; it's Bean Analysis 101. Let's walk through the steps:

1. ***Obtain the BeanInfo for MyBean.*** Invoke the *getBeanInfo* method on the **Introspector** to obtain an object that implements the **BeanInfo** interface for **MyBean**. Since this is a well-behaved bean, we will let the **Introspector** build this object on-the-fly, which means we do not provide a **MyBeanBeanInfo.class**

2. ***Ask for the bean's EventSetDescriptors.*** Invoke *getEventSetDescriptors* on the **BeanInfo** object to obtain an array of **EventSetDescriptor** objects. Each of these objects contains metadata that describes a single event set.

3. ***Ask for the bean's default event.*** Invoke *getDefaultEventIndex* on the **BeanInfo** object to obtain an index to the event that will most commonly be invoked by a user of the bean.

4. ***Discover the default event's listener type.*** Use the index to de-reference the **EventSetDescriptor** object for the default event. Then invoke the *getListenerType* method on this object to obtain the **Class** of this event's listener interface.

5. ***Discover the listener's methods.*** Invoke *getListenerMethods* on the default **EventSetDescriptor** to obtain an array of **Method** objects. Each object describes a method supported by the listener interface.

6. ***Discover the AddListener method for this event.*** Invoke the *getAddListenerMethod* on the default **EventSetDescriptor** to obtain a **Method** object that describes the subscribe method for this event. This is the method a listener bean invokes to subscribe to the event.

7. ***Discover the RemoveListener method for this event.*** Invoke the *getRemoveListenerMethod* on the default **EventSetDescriptor** to obtain a **Method** object that describes the unsubscribe method for this event. This is the method a listener bean invokes to unsubscribe to the event.

8. ***Discover if the event is unicast.*** Invoke the *isUnicast* method on the default **EventSetDescriptor** to discover if this event is unicast. It will return true if it is. Note that most bean events are multicast.

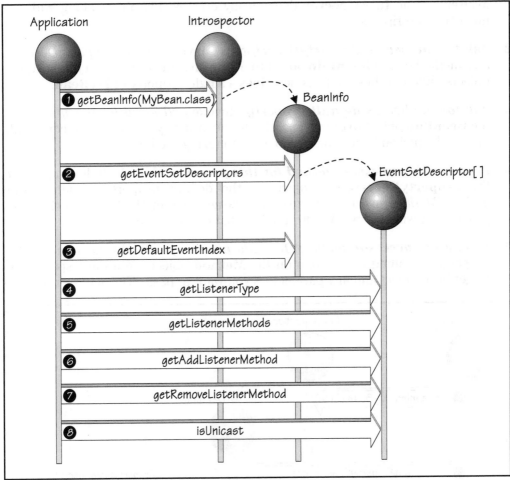

Figure 32-7. Introspection Scenario: Discovering a Bean's Events.

There's a lot more discovery we can do with this scenario. The key idea here is that you must first find the **BeanInfo** for your bean. You then use the **BeanInfo** to navigate through the various metadata objects. The information you want is found in these metadata objects.

Scenario 2: Reading a Property Value "On-the-Fly"

The scenario in Figure 32-8 shows how you would dynamically discover a bean's property and then invoke its accessor method to read the property's value on-the-fly. Let's walk through the steps:

1. ***Obtain the BeanInfo for MyBean***. Invoke the *getBeanInfo* method on the **Introspector** to obtain an object that implements the **BeanInfo** interface for

MyBean. The **Introspector** dynamically creates this object along with the metadata descriptors.

2. *Ask for the bean's PropertyDescriptors*. Invoke the *getPropertyDescriptors* method on the **BeanInfo** object to obtain an array of **PropertyDescriptor** objects. Each of these objects describes a single property of **MyBean**.

3. *Ask for the bean's default property*. Invoke *getDefaultPropertyIndex* on the **BeanInfo** object to obtain an index to the property that will most commonly be initially picked by a human who is customizing the bean.

4. *Discover the accessor method for this property*. Use the index to point to the **PropertyDescriptor** object for the default property. Then invoke *getReadMethod* on this object to obtain the accessor method (or getter) for this property; it will return a **Method** object that describes this method.

5. *Invoke the accessor method for this property*. Obtain the value of this property by calling the *invoke* on the **Method** object. You must specify the target bean object and any parameters you want to pass. The accessor method

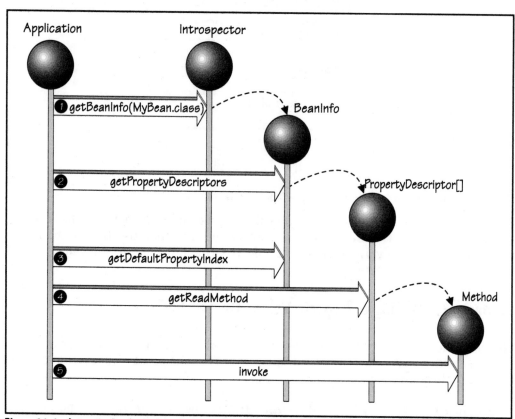

Figure 32-8. Introspection Scenario 2: Dynamically Invoking a Property.

does not take any input parameters, but it returns the value of the property. The **Method** object is part of the reflection API. Here's the signature for its *invoke* method:

```
public Object invoke(Object obj, Object args[])
                        throws IllegalAccessException,
                        IllegalArgumentException,
                        InvocationTargetException;
```

If the method completes normally, it will return the value of the parameter in an **Object** wrapper for the primitive Java type.

This scenario shows that you can indirectly read and write any bean property at run time by invoking the discovered accessor methods. This technique is mostly used by tools to customize the beans they discover at build time without having access to their source code.

The Introspective Smiley

As you know from previous chapters, our **SmileyBean** follows all the JavaBeans design patterns to the letter. Consequently, we don't have to do anything special to make it introspective. The metadata is in the design patterns. Visual tools can simply invoke the **Introspector** to discover Smiley's lovely features on-the-fly. However, if we're going to display Smiley within tool palettes, then we should give it a recognizable icon.

To make Smiley icons available via introspection, we first create two color GIF icons: *smiley16.gif* and *smiley32.gif*. We put these two files in the same directory as the rest of the Smiley code. Next, we create a **BeanInfo** for our Smiley to load the new icons. We will also use it to provide a display name for our Smiley one. Here's the code:

Listing 32-11. The SmileyBeanBeanInfo.class

```
package smileyi;

import java.beans.*;
import java.awt.*;

public class SmileyBeanBeanInfo extends SimpleBeanInfo
{
    // Smiley's icon
    public Image getIcon(int iconKind)
```

```
    {
      if (iconKind == ICON_COLOR_16x16)
      {  Image icon = loadImage("smiley16.gif");
         return icon;
      }
      if (iconKind == ICON_COLOR_32x32)
      {  Image icon = loadImage("smiley32.gif");
         return icon;
      }
      return null;
    }


    // Smiley's tool name
    public BeanDescriptor getBeanDescriptor()
    {
       BeanDescriptor bdesc = new BeanDescriptor
                                   (smileyi.SmileyBean.class);
       bdesc.setDisplayName ("Smiley Bean");
       return bdesc;
    }
}
```

Notice that we used the *loadImage* utility that comes with the **SimpleBeanInfo**. It takes the name of a GIF file as an input parameter relative to the directory holding the class file. The method returns a null if the load fails.

The Bean Analyst

Our implementation of **BeanInfo** is as minimalist as it gets. Of course, we're depending on the **Introspector** to automatically discover the features of our Smiley one. To demonstrate the type of information that is "discoverable," we wrote a program called the **BeanAnalyst**; it's a shrink for beans. We will use this program to put our Smiley one on a psychiatrist's couch. But first, here's the code that performs the analysis:

Listing 32-12. BeanAnalyst.java

```
import java.beans.*;
import java.awt.*;
import java.lang.reflect.*;

public class BeanAnalyst
```

```
{
 static public void main(String args[])
 {
   try
   {
    // Instantiate a bean
    Object s = Beans.instantiate(null, args[0]);

    // Introspect on class and stop after direct parent class
    BeanInfo bi  = Introspector.getBeanInfo(s.getClass(),
                                   s.getClass().getSuperclass());

    // Discover the display name
    BeanDescriptor bdsc = bi.getBeanDescriptor();
    System.out.println("Hi! Your display name is = "
                              + bdsc.getDisplayName());

    // Get the bean's properties
    PropertyDescriptor[] pd = bi.getPropertyDescriptors();

    System.out.println("\n\nYour properties are: \n");
    for (int i = 0; i < pd.length; i++)
    { System.out.println("property = " + pd[i].getName() +
          " (write method = " + pd[i].getWriteMethod().getName() +
          ", read method = " + pd[i].getReadMethod().getName() + ")");
    }

    // Get the bean's methods
    MethodDescriptor[]  md = bi.getMethodDescriptors();

    System.out.println("\n\nYour methods are: \n");
    for (int i = 0; i < md.length; i++)
    { System.out.println("" + md[i].getMethod() );
    }

    // Get the bean's events
    EventSetDescriptor[] evsd = bi.getEventSetDescriptors();
    Method[]  evm = evsd[0].getListenerMethods();
    System.out.println("\n\nYou emit the following Events: \n");
    for (int i = 0; i < evm.length; i++)
    {
       System.out.println("" + evm[i].getName() );
    }

    //Get the bean's icon types
```

```java
System.out.println("\n\nYou provide the following icon types: \n");
if (bi.getIcon(BeanInfo.ICON_COLOR_32x32) != null)
  System.out.println("32x32 color");
if (bi.getIcon(BeanInfo.ICON_COLOR_16x16) != null)
  System.out.println("16x16 color");
if (bi.getIcon(BeanInfo.ICON_MONO_32x32) != null)
  System.out.println("32x32 mono");
if (bi.getIcon(BeanInfo.ICON_MONO_16x16) != null)
  System.out.println("16x16 mono");

//Discover the bean's environment
if (Beans.isDesignTime())
  System.out.println("\n\nYour bean is in design-time mode.");
else
  System.out.println("\n\nYour bean is in run-time mode.");

if (Beans.isGuiAvailable())
  System.out.println("A GUI is available to your bean.");
else
  System.out.println("A GUI is not available to your bean.");

// Are you a persistent bean?
Class myClass = s.getClass();
boolean serializable = false;
boolean externalizable = false;

while (!myClass.getName().equals("java.lang.Object"))
{
  Class[] interfaces = myClass.getInterfaces();
  for (int i = 0; i < interfaces.length; i++)
  {
    if (interfaces[i].getName().equals("java.io.Serializable"))
      serializable = true;

    if (interfaces[i].getName().equals("java.io.Externalizable"))
      externalizable = true;
  }
  myClass = myClass.getSuperclass();
}
if (serializable)
  System.out.println("You are a serializable persistent bean.");
if (externalizable)
  System.out.println("You are an externalizable persistent bean.");

System.exit(0);
```

```
    } catch (Exception e)
    { System.out.println("Exception: " + e);
    }
 }
}
```

Here's the output we get when we run the **BeanAnalyst** on Smiley:

```
Hi! Your display name is = SmileyBean

Your properties are:

property = color  (write method = setColor, read method = getColor)
property = smile  (write method = setSmile, read method = isSmile)

Your methods are:

public void smileys.SmileyBean.removePropertyChangeListener
                            (java.beans.PropertyChangeListener)
public void smileys.SmileyBean.setColor(java.awt.Color)
public void smileys.SmileyBean.setSmile(boolean)
public synchronized java.awt.Color smileys.SmileyBean.getColor()
public synchronized boolean smileys.SmileyBean.isSmile()
public void smileys.SmileyBean.addPropertyChangeListener
                            (java.beans.PropertyChangeListener)
public void smileys.SmileyBean.paint(java.awt.Graphics)
public synchronized void smileys.SmileyBean.toggleSmile()

You emit the following Events:
propertyChange

You provide the following icon types:
32x32 color
16x16 color

Your bean is in run-time mode.
A GUI is available to your bean.
You are a serializable persistent bean.
```

Tools Discover Smiley

So, is Smiley toolable? We'll soon find out. In this section, we import our Smiley one into two very popular bean tools: Symantec *Visual Café* and Borland *JBuilder*.

We will then discover what they can tell us about our Smiley one. We assume they will have introspective capabilities that are at least on par with the **BeanAnalyst** we developed in the last section.

To import a new bean into a tool's palette, you must first package it in a JAR. This is a good time to add the two icon files and the **SmileyBeanBeanInfo** to our *smiley.jar*. We will first mark them both as design-time artifacts. To do this, we append the following three entries to the *smiley.mf* manifest file from the last chapter:

```
Name: smileypersist/smiley16.gif
Java-Bean: False
Design-Time-Only: True

Name: smileypersist/smiley32.gif
Java-Bean: False
Design-Time-Only: True

Name: smileypersist/SmileyBeanBeanInfo.class
Java-Bean: False
Design-Time-Only: False
```

Now let's recreate the *smiley.jar*. At the prompt, enter the following command:

prompt> jar cfm smiley.jar smiley.mf /smileypersist/Smiley*.*

To import the *smiley.jar* into *Visual Café*, first insert Smiley into the component library. Once Smiley is in the component library, you can drag Smiley from the component library window and drop it on the palette.

To import the *smiley.jar* into *JBuilder*, right-button click on the palette and use the *palette properties* wizard to place Smiley on the palette using import from archive option.

The screen captures in Figures 32-9 and 32-10 show that both *Visual Café* and *JBuilder* were able to discover our two Smileys and also the SmileyPlace. Both tools prominently display the Smiley icon in their palettes. And, they both discovered Smiley's various properties and events—including the ones that are inherited from parent classes.

The properties appear inside a *property sheet* in both tools. Note that Symantec calls it a *property list* while Borland calls it an *inspector*. A property sheet displays a list of bean properties along with their current values. You can click on any property to activate its type-specific property editor; it lets you alter the displayed

Chapter 32. The Introspective and Toolable JavaBean

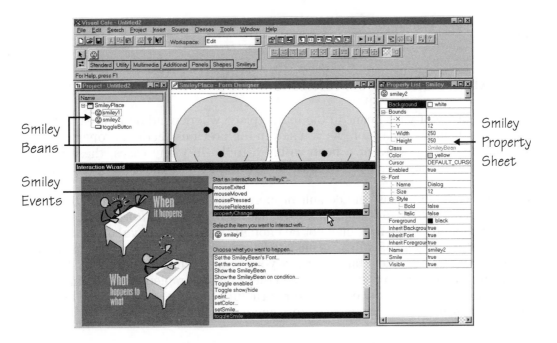

Figure 32-9. Symantec Visual Café's Introspection of Smiley.

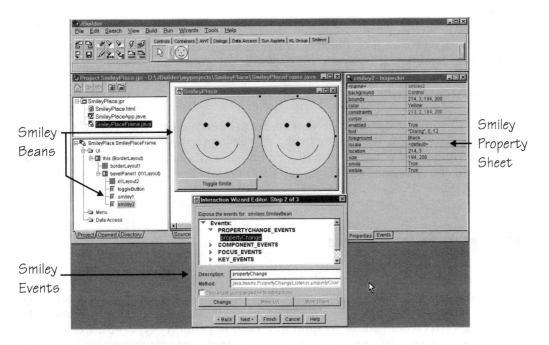

Figure 32-10. Borland's JBuilder Introspection of Smiley.

value. You use these property editors to customize the behavior and appearance of a bean.

PROPERTY EDITORS AND CUSTOMIZERS

The acceptance of your beans in the marketplace will depend on how easy it is to customize them within a tool. As you saw in the previous section, property sheets let you control the state of a bean within a tool. In many cases, these default property sheets may be all you need to visually manipulate the state of a bean.

For more complex beans, the default property editors may not be enough. They may also require that you supply a set of *custom property editors*. And, in some cases, even a property sheet may not be enough. Your bean may require a custom expert system or what JavaBeans calls a *customizer* to do the job. You must plan on writing whatever code it takes to make your beans highly customizable. In some cases, the customization code may exceed the code that implements the function of a bean. In this section, we cover the infrastructure JavaBeans provides to help you create and manage your property editors and customizers.

Built-In Property Editors

The property sheets we encountered in the last section use *built-in property editors* that are provided by the tool (via the JDK). They include property editors for the basic Java types: *boolean, byte, short, int, float,* and *double*. The JDK—and most tools—also provide property editors for the following three classes: **java.lang.String, java.awt.Font,** and **java.awt.Color.**

Figure 32-11 shows a side-by-side view of the property sheets that *Visual Café* and *JBuilder* generated for the Smiley bean. All these properties have built-in editors. Consequently, we did not have to write a single line of code to help generate these property sheets. They are gifts from the tool vendor (and JavaSoft). Yes, Virginia, there is a Santa.

The Property Editor Interfaces

As we said earlier, the more complex beans may require that you provide a set of custom editors. For example, you must provide a *custom editor* if your property isn't one of the supported types. In some cases, you may even find it necessary to create your own custom editor to support a built-in property type—for example, to provide a specialized editing function or to create a more intuitive user interface. A custom property editor is a class you must provide to let a user edit a property of

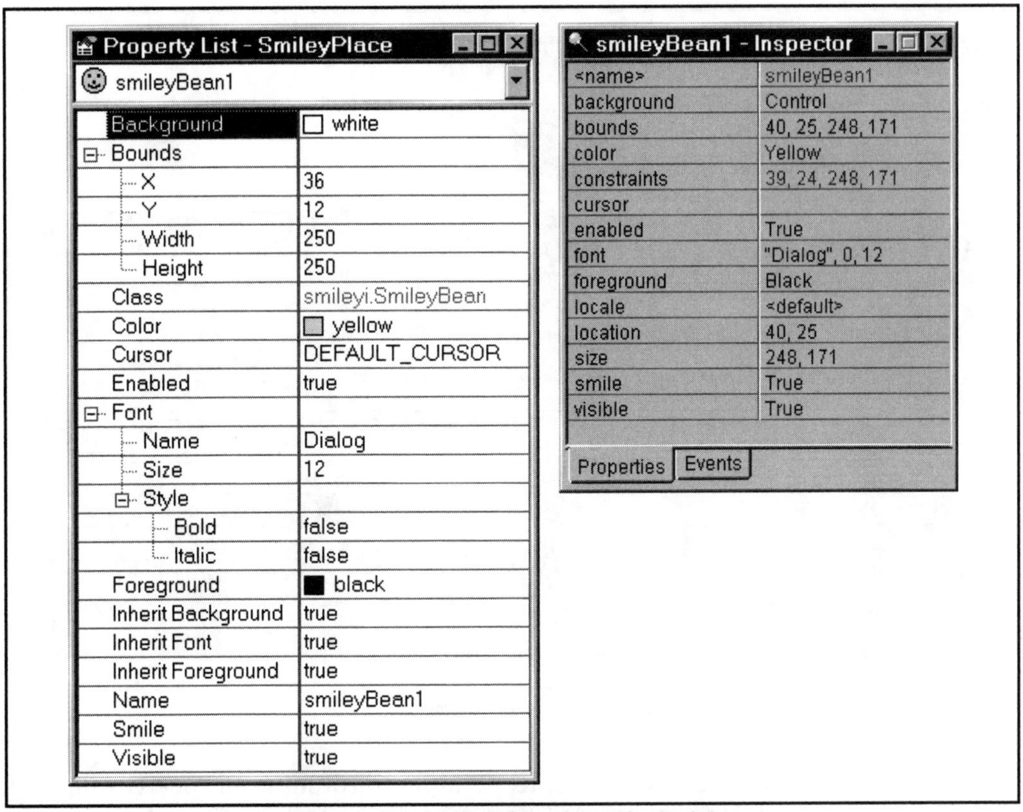

Property List - SmileyPlace

smileyBean1

Background	□ white
⊟ Bounds	
— X	36
— Y	12
— Width	250
— Height	250
Class	smileyi.SmileyBean
Color	□ yellow
Cursor	DEFAULT_CURSOR
Enabled	true
⊟ Font	
— Name	Dialog
— Size	12
⊟ Style	
— Bold	false
— Italic	false
Foreground	■ black
Inherit Background	true
Inherit Font	true
Inherit Foreground	true
Name	smileyBean1
Smile	true
Visible	true

smileyBean1 - Inspector

<name>	smileyBean1
background	Control
bounds	40, 25, 248, 171
color	Yellow
constraints	39, 24, 248, 171
cursor	
enabled	True
font	"Dialog", 0, 12
foreground	Black
locale	<default>
location	40, 25
size	248, 171
smile	True
visible	True

Properties | Events

Figure 32-11. Smiley Property Sheets in Visual Café (left) and JBuilder (right).

a specific type. The property editor displays its contents within a property sheet under the control of a visual tool.

To help you create custom property editors, JavaBeans defines a new interface and two new classes (see Figure 32-12). Each property editor must implement a relatively convoluted interface called the **PropertyEditor**. The **PropertyEditor-Support** is a helper class that implements this interface; it makes it a bit easier to implement a property editor. We recommend that you develop your property editors by extending this helper class. You should use its default method implementations and only override the functions you really need to implement. Finally, the **PropertyEditorManager** class lets you register a new editor type.

Here's a quick description of property editor interface and classes:

■ A **PropertyEditor** interface defines the methods your property editor classes must implement. This interface defines a variety of methods for displaying and updating property values. Most property editors will only need to support a

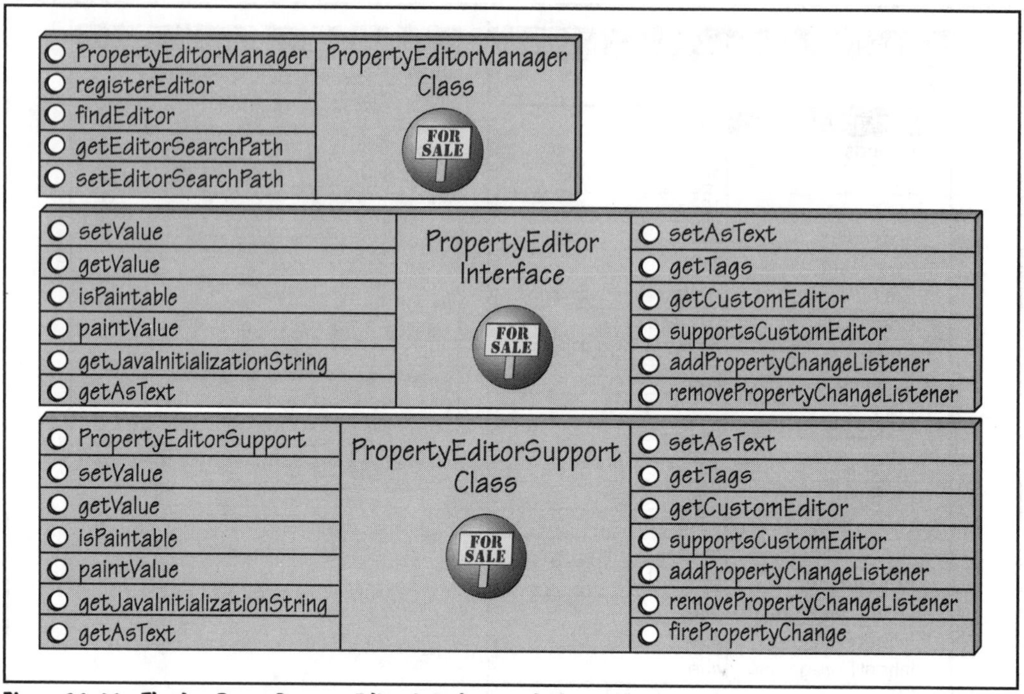

Figure 32-12. The JavaBeans Property Editor Interfaces and Classes.

subset of these methods. For example, a simple editor may only need to support the *getAsText*, *getTags*, and *setAsText* methods. Complex editors may need to provide their own GUIs. So instead, they will support *isPaintable*, *paintValue* and *getCustomEditor*. In addition, every property editor must support *setValue*, which passes as its argument an object of the property type (or, the value of the property that you are currently editing). Every property editor must also provide a null constructor so that a tool can instantiate it via *Class.newInstance*.

Note that the methods in this interface are typically called by a visual tool that manages a property sheet. Your property editor does not interact directly with either the user or the bean. The tool calls *setValue* to set the value of the property. It then calls *getValue* to obtain the updated value. It calls *getAsText* to obtain the property value as a human editable string. It calls *setAsText* to set the property value passed as a string. It calls *getTags* to obtain an array of strings that represent the acceptable values of a property.

The method *isPaintable* returns true if the editor supports its own GUI—for example, you may want to paint a gauge to represent a *meter* property. The tool invokes *paintValue* to paint a representation of the value into a given area of the screen. The *addPropertyChangeListener* allows listeners to register for **PropertyChange** events. The editor fires these events when it changes the property value. Of course, there must be *removePropertyChangeListener* to allow the listeners to unsubscribe.

■ The **PropertyEditorSupport** is a helper class; it implements all the methods defined by the **PropertyEditor** interface. In addition, the helper class implements two constructors and a *firePropertyChange* method. The first constructor is a no-arg default constructor; you use it when your property editor inherits this helper class. The second constructor takes as its single argument the source object of the events fired; you use this constructor when your editor delegates to a helper object (i.e., when it does not inherit the function). The *firePropertyChange* method is a helper function; it fires events to all interested listeners when you modify the property.

■ The **PropertyEditorManager** class is used to locate a property editor for any given type name. The class provides three techniques for locating an editor. First, it provides a *registerEditor* method that lets you explicitly register an editor for a particular type. Second, it tries to locate a suitable editor by adding "Editor" to the fully qualified classname of the given type—for example, **mypackage.TemperatureEditor**. Finally, it takes the simple classname (without the package name), adds "Editor" to it, and looks in a search-path of packages for a matching class.

The *findEditor* method is used to locate a property editor for a given property type. The *setEditorSearchPath* method lets you specify a list of package names that are used to find property editors. The initial path is set to *sun.beans.editors*. Finally, you invoke *getEditorSearchPath* to obtain the array of package names that are searched to find property editors.

You shouldn't worry if things aren't perfectly clear. We will present a scenario that shows how all these pieces work together. But first, here are the detailed class descriptions for our readers that need to look at the code:

Listing 32-13. The java.beans.PropertyEditor Interface.

```
public interface PropertyEditor
{
  // Methods
  public abstract void setValue(Object value);
  public abstract Object getValue();
  public abstract boolean isPaintable();
  public abstract void paintValue(Graphics gfx, Rectangle box);
  public abstract String getJavaInitializationString();
  public abstract String getAsText();
  public abstract void setAsText(String text)
                          throws IllegalArgumentException;
```

```java
  public abstract String[] getTags();
  public abstract Component getCustomEditor();
  public abstract boolean supportsCustomEditor();
  public abstract void addPropertyChangeListener(
                    PropertyChangeListener listener);
  public abstract void removePropertyChangeListener(
                    PropertyChangeListener listener);
}
```

Listing 32-14. The java.beans.PropertyEditorSupport Class.

```java
public class PropertyEditorSupport
            extends Object implements PropertyEditor
{
  // Constructors
  protected PropertyEditorSupport();
  protected PropertyEditorSupport(Object source);

  // Methods
  public void setValue(Object value);
  public Object getValue();
  public boolean isPaintable();
  public void paintValue(Graphics gfx, Rectangle box);
  public String getJavaInitializationString();
  public String getAsText();
  public void setAsText(String text) throws IllegalArgumentException;
  public String[] getTags();
  public Component getCustomEditor();
  public boolean supportsCustomEditor();
  public synchronized void addPropertyChangeListener(
                                PropertyChangeListener listener);
  public synchronized void removePropertyChangeListener(
                                PropertyChangeListener listener);
  public void firePropertyChange();
}
```

Listing 32-15. The java.beans.PropertyEditorManager Class.

```java
public class PropertyEditorManager extends Object
{
  // Constructor
  public PropertyEditorManager()

  // Class Methods
```

```
    public static void registerEditor(Class targetType,
                                      Class editorClass);
    public static PropertyEditor findEditor(Class targetType);
    public static String[] getEditorSearchPath();
    public static void setEditorSearchPath(String path[]);
}
```

A Property Editing Scenario

The best way to untangle this story is to describe the interactions between a bean, its property editor, and the tool that displays a property sheet. Figure 32-13 shows how a tool collaborates with a **SmileEditor** to allow a user to change a property of our Smiley bean. In the next section, we will develop the code for this editor. First, let's go over this scenario:

1. ***The tool discovers Smiley's properties via introspection.*** It uses this information to create a property sheet for Smiley.

2. ***The tool launches the Smile property editor.*** This scenario only shows the instantiation of a single property editor. Typically, the tool launches a property editor for each type it finds in the property sheet.

3. ***The tool registers itself as a property change listener.*** The tool invokes the editor's *addPropertyChangeListener* method to register its interest in the property changes.

4. ***The tool reads the current value of the smile property.*** It does this by invoking the bean's *getSmile* accessor.

5. ***The tool passes the smile value to the property editor.*** It invokes the editor's *setValue* method and passes it a boolean value. The property editor saves the value in an instance variable of type boolean.

6. ***The tool requests a text version of the smile.*** It invokes the editor's *getAsText* method to obtain the string version of the smile property. Note that the editor simply converts the local boolean value to a string. The tool displays this text in the property sheet.

7. ***The tool requests an array of valid values.*** It invokes *getTags* to obtain an array of strings that represent permissible values for this property. Our smile property can have only two string values: "happy" and "sad." The property sheet presents these values to the user in a choice listbox. By providing this list of available choices, we made the interface more user-friendly and less error-prone.

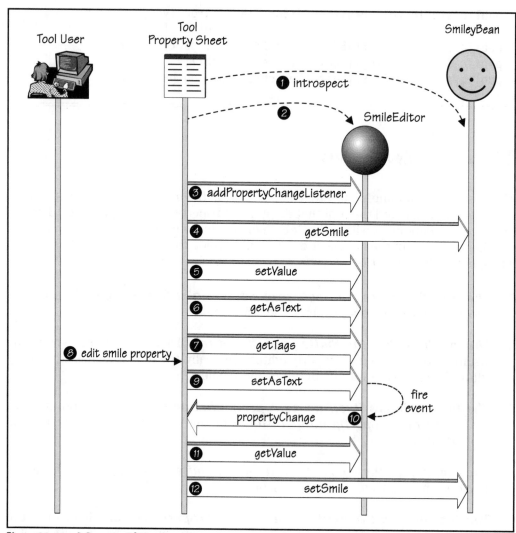

Figure 32-13. A Property-Editing Scenario.

8. **The user edits the property value.** The user updates the smile property by selecting a choice from the listbox. Of course, the listbox is displayed within the property sheet.

9. **The tool passes the new value of the property to the editor.** The tool invokes the *setAsText* method of the property editor and passes it the new string value of the property. The editor converts the updated string value to a boolean and then stores it in its local instance variable. The editor then invokes its inherited *firePropertyChange* method. This method creates a **PropertyChangeEvent** and fires it to all the subscribers; it invokes their listener's *propertyChange* method.

10. ***The tool receives a propertyChange event notification.*** The tool is a subscriber to property change events, so it receives a notification that the property changed; it also contains the source of the event.

11. ***The tool obtains the boolean value of the property.*** The tool invokes the property editor's *getValue* method to obtain the new boolean value of this property. Note that the value of the property was not used in the event model.

12. ***The tool updates the Smiley bean with the new value***. The tool invokes Smiley's *setSmile* method to set the new value of this property.

As you can see from this scenario, editing a property can be a convoluted affair. The trick is to understand that the property editor does not directly interact with a bean. The tool's property sheet mediates the entire exchange; it acts as a broker between the property editor and the target bean's property.

The Smile Editor

In this section, we write the code that implements this scenario. As you know, Smiley's beautiful *smile* is of type boolean, so it already has a built-in property editor. In this code example, we will create a custom editor class for the smile, which we call **SmileEditor**. Instead of displaying true and false, this new editor will display a listbox with two string choices that represent Smiley's mood: "happy" and "sad." Figure 32-14 shows the new-look smile as it appears in the property sheets of *Visual Café* and *JBuilder*. Notice that we've also cropped out some of the parent properties to make the property sheets easier to read.

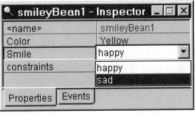

Figure 32-14. New-Look Smiley Property Sheets In Visual Café and JBuilder.

First, here's the **SmileEditor** class that implements the scenario from the previous section:

Listing 32-16. The SmileEditor Class.

```java
package smileyp;
import java.beans.*;

public class SmileEditor extends PropertyEditorSupport
{
  // current state of smile property
  protected boolean smile;

  // set the object value of smile
  public void setValue (Object obj)
  {
    // cast the object version to boolean
    smile = ((Boolean)obj).booleanValue();
  }

  // return current object value of smile
  public Object getValue()
  {
    // return the object version of the boolean type
    return new Boolean(smile);
  }


  // return text value of smile
  public String getAsText()
  {
    if (smile)
    {
      return "happy";
    }
    else
    {
      return "sad";
    }
  }

  // return acceptable choices
  public String[] getTags()
  {
    String [] str = { "happy", "sad" };
```

```
      return str;
   }

   // set property from text value of smile
   public void setAsText (String str)
   {
      if (str.equals("happy"))
      {
         smile = true;
      }
      else
      {
         smile = false;
      }

      // call inherited method to fire event

      firePropertyChange();
   }
}
```

After going through the scenario, the code for this simple property editor should now appear trivial. Next, we must inform the tool that we have a new editor for this smile property. There are two approaches for doing this:

1. Update the Smiley bean code to introduce a new object type called *smile*. Then change the getters and setters to pass this new property type instead of a boolean. Finally, register the **SmileEditor** with the **PropertyEditorManager** by invoking the *registerEditor* method.

2. Update the Smiley **BeanInfo** to explicitly associate our new **SmileEditor** with this particular property. The new editor will then replace the built-in boolean-type editor for this particular property. Notice that in this case, we're specifying a property editor for a particular property on a particular bean.

We don't want to change our Smiley bean. Consequently, we're going to implement the second approach. Here's the code for our new **BeanInfo**:

Listing 32-17. The SmileyBeanBeanInfo.class

```
package smileyp;

import java.beans.*;
import java.awt.*;
import java.lang.reflect.*;
```

```java
public class SmileyBeanBeanInfo extends SimpleBeanInfo
{
    // Smiley's icon
    public Image getIcon(int iconKind)
    {
      if (iconKind == ICON_COLOR_16x16)
      {
         Image icon = loadImage("smiley16.gif");
         return icon;
      }
      if (iconKind == ICON_COLOR_32x32)
      {
         Image icon = loadImage("smiley32.gif");
         return icon;
      }
      return null;
    }

    // Smiley's tool name
    public BeanDescriptor getBeanDescriptor()
    {
       BeanDescriptor bdesc = new BeanDescriptor (smileyp.SmileyBean.class);
       bdesc.setDisplayName ("Smiley Bean");
       return bdesc;
    }
```

```java
    // Return an explicit array of property descriptors
    public PropertyDescriptor[] getPropertyDescriptors()
    {
       try
       {
       // create a descriptor for the Color property
       PropertyDescriptor pdesc1 = new PropertyDescriptor ( "Color",
                                smileyp.SmileyBean.class);

       // create a descriptor for the Smile property
       PropertyDescriptor pdesc2 = new PropertyDescriptor ( "Smile",
                                smileyp.SmileyBean.class);

       // specify a specific property editor
       pdesc2.setPropertyEditorClass(smileyp.SmileEditor.class);
```

```
        // create an array of descriptors
        PropertyDescriptor[] pdesc = { pdesc1, pdesc2};

        // return the array of descriptors
        return pdesc;
        } catch (Exception e)
        {return null;
        }
    }
}
```

As you can see, we added explicit metadata information in the **BeanInfo** to describe the Smiley properties (see shaded area). This metadata has the final word. Note that in the smile property descriptor, we explicitly associated a property editor with the smile.

This is a good time to add the new **SmileEditor** to our *smiley.jar*. We will flag it as a design-time artifact by appending the following entry to the *smiley.mf* manifest file:

```
        .
        .
Name: SmileEditor.class
Java-Bean: False
Design-Time-Only: True
```

Now let's rebuild the *smiley.jar* with the new files. At the prompt, enter the following command:

prompt> jar cfm smiley.jar smiley.mf /smileypersist/Smiley*.*

You can now import *smiley.jar* into *Visual Café* and *JBuilder*. If everything goes well, you should be able to see the new property sheet editors (see Figure 32-14 on page 823).

BEAN CUSTOMIZERS

A *customizer* class provides the next-level of assistance to a design-time user that needs to configure a bean. It's a wizard for beans. Unlike a property editor, a customizer communicates directly with its bean. The customizer can do anything it pleases on the bean that's handed to it. Typically, a customizer provides an AWT user interface that allows a designer to visually customize a bean. It handles an entire bean, as opposed to a single property. It can also customize behavior that is not property-related—for example, you could use a customizer to specify SQL statements a bean will execute.

Instead of relying on a builder tool's standard property sheets, a customizer gives you complete control over how your bean will present itself to a tool user. As a result, it provides a less general approach to customization than a property sheet; it's a custom approach to configuration that can be different for each bean.

So what exactly is a customizer? It turns out that the only feature customizers have in common is that they must all implement the JavaBeans-defined **Customizer** interface. In addition, a customizer must extend **Component**—or one of its subclasses—so that it can be displayed inside a builder tool. The customizer must also provide a no-arg constructor that will be called by the tool via *Class.newInstance*; you can use it to set up the GUI. Finally, you must provide a **BeanInfo** that returns a customizer class for your bean. Note that there are no standard naming patterns for a customizer. There is also no customizer manager class.

The Customizer Interface

A customizer class provides a complete GUI for customizing a target bean; it must also implement the three methods defined in the **Customizer** interface (see Figure 32-15). The first two methods—*addPropertyChangeListener* and *removePropertyChangeListener*—support property change listeners. The customizer can alter any of the target bean's properties by simply calling property getters and setters. The customizer must fire **PropertyChange** events whenever it updates a target bean's properties. Tools invoke the third method—*setObject*—to pass the target bean to the customizer. Note that this last method is called only once—before the tool adds the customizer to a parent AWT container.

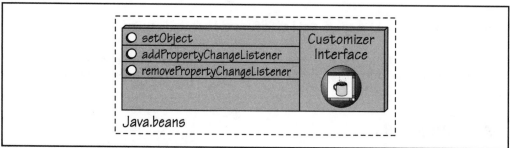

Figure 32-15. The Java.beans.Customizer Interface.

Here's the code that specifies this interface:

Listing 32-18. The java.beans.Customizer Interface.

```
public interface Customizer
```

```
{ // Methods
  public abstract void setObject(Object bean);
  public abstract void addPropertyChangeListener(
                            PropertyChangeListener listener);
  public abstract void removePropertyChangeListener(
                            PropertyChangeListener listener);
}
```

GUIDELINES FOR WRITING TOOLABLE BEANS

Components will be reused based on how easily they can be customized to fit different application-level requirements. Here are some guidelines that should help make your beans more toolable and consequently more reusable:

✔ *Follow the JavaBeans design patterns to the letter.* These patterns free you from providing explicit metadata about your beans. We also recommend that you follow the JavaBeans design patterns, even if you plan to provide explicit bean metadata.[1]

✔ *Provide a BeanInfo with selective metadata information.* You must always provide an icon and a tool-friendly name for your bean. If you can avoid it, don't provide explicit metadata in your **BeanInfo**; let the **Introspector** earn its keep (also see the next bullet).

✔ *Provide explicit metadata when there's lots of inheritance.* For beans that make a heavy use of inheritance, the **Introspector** may generate tons of potentially confusing metadata; it will discover all the properties, methods, and events of all the classes in the hierarchy. Most of these ancestor classes may not even be beans, and they may not follow bean design patterns and naming conventions. So you can imagine the confusion this could generate. Consequently, we recommend that you provide explicit metadata in the **BeanInfo** whenever you suspect that a user of your bean may get overwhelmed with too much metadata (see the next Warning Box). This lets you control the exact set of properties, events, and methods your bean will present to the outside world.

✔ *Use the manifest to specify your design-time classes.* Describe everything you provide in the manifest. You may also want to consider creating design-time specific JARs.

✔ *Design for customization and toolability.* As you saw in this chapter, it takes a lot of code to customize your beans. Plan ahead. You must allocate time to

---

[1] Note that some developers recommend that you use explicit metadata and non-standard names to force customers to pay for the build-time versions of your beans. We think this approach is brain-dead. Consistent naming patterns are essential to the success of beans. If we want to get paid for the use of our beans inside tools, then it makes much more sense for us to lobby JavaSoft to come up a bean-licensing scheme that really works.

develop icons, BeanInfos, property editors, customizers, manifests, and JARs. These are the things that will improve the packaging of your beans and make them more competitive on the market. So plan on writing whatever code it takes to make your beans highly customizable.

Metadata Overload Versus Error-Prone Maintenance

Warning

Maintaining metadata code in the form of a **BeanInfo** and the various feature descriptor classes is a painful and potentially error-prone process. It requires that we discipline ourselves to update metadata classes that are not part of our core implementation. Consequently, we must keep in sync two sets of classes: our bean implementations and the corresponding metadata. Unlike CORBA, the JavaBeans run time does not provide an IDL compiler or Interface Repository to help you generate the metadata and then manage it. You must do it all manually. So is this a case of the cure being worse than the disease? Perhaps. But without turning this into a Soapbox, we believe that the convenience of the human users of our beans must come first. ❑

CONCLUSION

This brings us to the end of our coverage of the core JavaBeans component model. In the next two chapters, we explain how *CORBA Components* and *Enterprise JavaBeans (EJBs)* extend this basic model to play on servers and over networks. You can think of these last six chapters as describing the core JavaBeans foundation on which everything else builds. It's prerequisite reading for understanding CORBA beans and EJB.

So there is really only one JavaBeans model. The CORBA Component Initiative extends this model with a distributed object foundation; it also allows objects written in other languages to access beans and to even look like beans. EJB builds on CORBA and JavaBeans; it extends them both by defining a set of framework-like interfaces between a server-side component and a server *component coordinator*, also known as an *Object Transaction Monitor (OTM)*. By building on this common core, all these beans become toolable from day one. So you will be able to use the same off-the-shelf bean tools to visually assemble, package, and deploy applications that consist of client and server beans.

Chapter 33

CORBA Beans

> A component is a piece of software small enough to create and maintain, big enough to deploy and support, and with standard interfaces for interoperability.
>
> — Jed Harris

Component technology promises to radically alter the way software systems are developed. The promise is compelling: We will be able to put together complex client/server information systems by simply assembling and extending reusable software components. You can modify or replace any of the objects without affecting the rest of the components in the system or how they interact. The components may be shipped in preassembled containers, where all the pieces are known to work together to perform a specific task. Components will revolutionize the way we create client/server systems; they are an essential element of the *Object Web*. Distributed components promise to provide the ultimate in mix-and-match capabilities.

So how does reality stack up against this vision? You may have gathered from the last six chapters that JavaBeans are extremely toolable. However, they are by no means a server-side component technology. In their current incarnation, JavaBeans don't even extend beyond the boundaries of a single Virtual Machine. This is where

CORBA Components and *Enterprise JavaBeans* come into the picture. They both extend the JavaBeans component model to play in distributed systems. In this chapter, we will look at CORBA beans.

Today, a CORBA bean is simply a CORBA object that you can invoke via IIOP from within your client beans. In Part 8, we will show you how to do this using off-the-shelf JavaBeans tools. We will also show you how to make a CORBA server object look like an invisible bean. We will even use a visual assembly tool to connect—via method invocations—ordinary beans to these CORBA beans. However, this is only a beginning. As you will soon discover—in both this chapter and the next one—there is a lot more that CORBA can do for JavaBeans, and vice versa.

In this chapter, we will look at the OMG's new architecture for *CORBA components*; it appears to be a direct map to JavaBeans. In the next chapter, we will look at Enterprise JavaBeans; it should not come as a surprise that Enterprise JavaBeans are also tightly-mapped to CORBA.

CORBA AND JAVABEANS

In a CORBA system, the unit of work and distribution is an IDL-defined object. A CORBA object provides standard interfaces for interoperability across languages and networks. This makes CORBA objects, by definition, components—even in their current incarnation. JavaBeans are also components. They augment CORBA with a toolable and portable component infrastructure. CORBA augments Java-Beans with a distributed multi-lingual component infrastructure. Before jumping into the new CORBA components model, we will first look at what CORBA and JavaBeans can do for each other.

What CORBA Can Do for JavaBeans

Without bringing Enterprise JavaBeans into the picture, here's a quick list of how CORBA augments the core JavaBeans component model:

- **Provides a language-neutral component infrastructure.** Ideally, components must be able to interoperate across languages, tools, operating systems, and networks. CORBA augments JavaBeans with a language-neutral component infrastructure. For example, today you can use CORBA/Java client-side stubs inside a JavaBeans visual assembly tool to represent server objects written in C++, COBOL, or Smalltalk; it makes these objects look like ordinary JavaBeans.

- **Provides a component object bus for beans.** A component is what Brad Cox calls a *software IC*. *Containers* are the boards into which we plug these components; families of software ICs that play together are called *suites*. The CORBA ORB provides the distributed bus—or component backplane—into which you can plug boards made of beans.

■ ***Provides a distributed services infrastructure***. Today's JavaBeans live within the confines of a single Java VM. CORBA provides the fastest way to extend the reach of JavaBeans to the intergalactic network. For example, ORB vendors should be able to provide CORBA event channels to distribute bean events across a network. They could make bean metadata available on the ORB via CORBA Interface Repositories. They should also be able to dynamically generate **BeanInfo** classes from metadata inside these repositories. The list of CORBA distributed services that beans can use is long. It includes CORBA traders, naming services, transactions, security, dynamic invocations, and IIOP firewall support. We will resume this discussion in the next chapter after we cover Enterprise JavaBeans.

The bottom line is that CORBA augments JavaBeans with a distributed component infrastructure; it also augments it with cross-language distributed method invocations.

What JavaBeans Can Do for CORBA

JavaBeans can potentially bring CORBA components to the masses. The mantra of JavaBeans is toolability and ease-of-use. Here's how the JavaBeans component model can augment CORBA's:

■ ***Automatic discovery of metadata from design patterns***. By adopting the JavaBeans naming patterns, CORBA components can benefit from automatic introspection by tools. It also lets you populate CORBA Interface Repositories without writing IDL.

■ ***Explicit event metadata***. A CORBA component today does not explicitly describe the events it generates in its IDL. Consequently, a tool cannot use events to visually wire together CORBA objects at design time. Note that the CORBA *Event Service* lets you publish and subscribe events at run time. However, you do this without the help of visual tools. As we explained in the last chapters, events provide a powerful visual metaphor for connecting loosely-coupled components. So CORBA can benefit from JavaBeans-style event metadata at design time.

■ ***Active properties—or properties that fire events***. CORBA can benefit from JavaBeans-style bound and constrained properties. Remember, these are properties that fire events when their state changes. Active properties can be quite useful in middle-tier server environments. For example, you can use them to propagate changes in bound data components to interested business-logic listeners without writing code.

- **Component packaging.** As you saw in the previous chapters, JavaBeans JARs let you package all the resources that a component needs. The *manifest* describes the contents of the JARs and contains deployment information. JARs and manifests are welcome additions to the CORBA component arsenal. You can use them to package CORBA client stubs with applets or to deploy CORBA objects on servers. And, just as importantly, you can use these JARs to import CORBA objects into standard bean tools.

- **Design-time support for tools.** In the last chapter, we mentioned that beans gave the tool vendors the hooks they wanted and consequently they came to JavaBeans in droves. Tool vendors require the standard interfaces JavaBeans defines for customizers, property editors, icons, and introspectors. CORBA components can become instantly toolable by simply tapping into this standard infrastructure. Consequently, you should be able to use the same JavaBeans tools to also customize CORBA components, program them by setting their properties, and then visually connect them.

The bottom line is that JavaBeans augments the CORBA component model by making it more toolable. As a result, you will be able to use visual assembly tools to easily customize CORBA beans. You will be able to create n-tier client/server applications by simply wiring together client and server beans.

THE NEW CORBA COMPONENT MODEL

The synergy between CORBA and JavaBeans was recognized by major players in the software industry. In May 1997, the *Gang of Four (G4)*—Netscape, Oracle, IBM, and Sun—published a white paper called the *CORBA Component Imperatives*.[1] This influential paper was a call for action to marry the CORBA and JavaBeans component models. It caused the OMG to issue an RFP one month later to solicit technology for a CORBA/JavaBeans component model.[2] In November 1997, the OMG received a joint submission from the G4 and others.[3] The CORBA Component Model should be finalized by mid-1998. The speed at which this standard is being adopted is an all-time record for OMG.

In this section, we first present a short excerpt from the G4 white paper; it should give you a feel for the sense of urgency that's driving the CORBA component

---

[1] See OMG Document *orbos/97-05-25*.
[2] See OMG Document *orbos/97-06-12*.
[3] See OMG Document *orbos/97-11-24*.

initiative. Then we cover the initial G4 submission and compare it to JavaBeans. The strong similarities between the two component models are, of course, not coincidental. Be warned that a lot of the material covered in this section is still under construction.

The CORBA/JavaBeans Call for Action

The following is an excerpt from the G4's *CORBA Component Imperatives* white paper:

Now is the time to move CORBA from the current domain, which delivers excellent results for expert programmers creating distributed systems, to the ubiquity of business applications, developed by unsophisticated programmers using visual development tools and scripting languages. CORBA has the potential to dominate business application building, but will only realize that potential if the OMG defines a standard component infrastructure to support these sorts of tools. This document outlines the standards that must exist to create such an infrastructure...

CORBA components must fit seamlessly into the standard infrastructure provided by the Web. This means that it must be possible to name objects using URLs and LDAP directory services. Furthermore, it must be possible to support object security based on SSL-3, using the already-adopted OMG SSL security specification. Above all, it must be easy to access distributed objects (implemented in any language, residing on any host) from Java, and control their operation using a scripting language such as Javascript...Only by this measure can CORBA drive the mass market for distributed multi-tier computing...

JavaBeans has rapidly emerged as an important standard for component objects...The existing synergy between CORBA and Java would be greatly enhanced by defining a CORBA component model compatible with JavaBeans. This means that the information required by the JavaBeans introspection interface must be available from the CORBA component in a form that the JavaBeans environment can access...

All major software vendors are building visual development tools, logically the successors to Visual Basic and PowerBuilder...All these tools have similar paradigms for the development process. The application canvas presents a WYSIWYG view of the application under development. Components residing in a palette may be dropped on the canvas, looking just as they will when the application is run. Property sheet editors may be invoked for each component to adjust the design-time and run-time parameters of the component. The tools provide a connection paradigm for specifying how components in the application interact. All this is familiar from earlier generations of tools; what must be added to create web-enabled applications revolving around CORBA objects?

For visual development tools to make use of CORBA objects, there must be some mechanism to find out at design time the properties of arbitrary objects. IDL specifies operations and attributes, but says nothing about design time known dependencies and component connections. What is needed is something like the JavaBeans notion of events. Properties, in the JavaBeans sense, are part of the externally-accessible view of the object, and are accessed by get- and set-methods. JavaBeans properties also encompass the notion of generating change events on modification of particular properties—termed bound and constrained properties. We need to supplement CORBA to support a similar notion...

One of the main motivations to define a standard CORBA component model is to enable powerful distributed applications to be constructed with minimal expertise required of the application builder. This includes the development and use of components for all three (logical) tiers of the application model:

1. ***End-user**—presentation views.*
2. ***Business objects**—logical views, entities, tasks, and so on.*
3. ***Back-end**—databases, TP Monitors, wrapped legacy applications, and so on.*

While all components will likely have a visual representation during development time, only those seen by the end-user will have a run-time visual representation. Middle-tier components, for example, are typically accessed via components in the end-user tier...

The white paper goes on to describe the technologies necessary to support this universal use of CORBA objects as toolable components. Many of these technologies are represented in RFPs and submissions already before the OMG—for example, *Objects By Value* and *CORBA Multiple Interfaces*. In the next section, we describe the proposed G4 *CORBA Components* submission in detail. As you will see, it creates a coherent framework for all these technologies based on the JavaBeans model.

The end goal of all this effort is to bring CORBA to the programming masses. The idea is that a small number of "elite" programmers will continue to read books like the one you're reading to develop CORBA components. You will then JAR your CORBA server objects (or beans) and release them to the visual-programming masses. The hope is that these masses will be able to find thousands of ways to reuse your objects. They will visually connect and reconnect them into client/server ensembles (or bean subassemblies) in combinations you never even dreamed of. So

welcome to the brave new world of n-tier client/server visual assembly with components.

CORBA Components: JavaBeans++

This section contains preliminary information. It is based on the component model jointly submitted to the OMG by the following companies: Netscape, Oracle, IBM, Sun, Iona, Visigenic, BEA, Unisys, and ICL.[4] The final standard may be out by the time you read this book; it should be very close to the material we present in this section.

In a nutshell, CORBA components are JavaBeans++ (see Figure 33-1). You should be able to write your CORBA components using any of the OMG-supported languages. To a visual tool, these CORBA objects will be represented by Java proxies that look like ordinary JavaBeans. The tool will be able to import these CORBA objects—they are packaged in CORBA JARs called CARs—and display them in its palette. You will then be able to drag a CORBA object from the palette to a container,

---

[4] See OMG Document *orbos/97-11-24*.

introspect on it, customize it using property sheets, and then connect it visually to other beans. Unlike ordinary JavaBeans, the CORBA visual proxies can be wired to invoke remote methods, properties, and events.

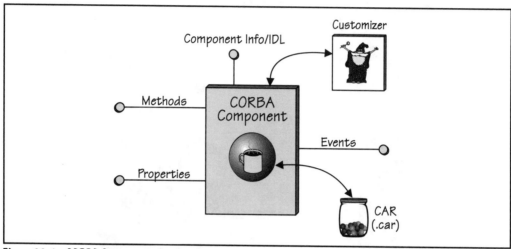

Figure 33-1. CORBA Components Are JavaBeans++.

Table 33-1 compares the CORBA component model with JavaBeans. As you can see, CORBA components support all the elements of the JavaBeans model we described in the last six chapters. This includes the JavaBeans design patterns, events, properties, packaging, metadata, and tool support. In addition, the CORBA component model defines explicit interfaces for a bean to interact with its container, and vice versa. CORBA also adds server-side component *deployment descriptor* information to the manifest (à la Enterprise JavaBeans).

Of course, we will not repeat here the last six chapters (on JavaBeans) to describe each element of the CORBA component model. Instead, we will focus on what is different or new—including CORBA remote events, the server-side packaging, and the container/containee interfaces.

Table 33-1. CORBA Components Versus JavaBeans.

Feature	CORBA Component	JavaBean
Events		
add/remove event listeners	Yes	Yes
EventObject	Yes	Yes
EventListener	Yes	Yes
TooManyListeners (multicast/unicast)	Yes	Yes

Table 33-1. CORBA Components Versus JavaBeans. (Continued)

Feature	CORBA Component	JavaBean
Simple Properties		
get/set single-value	Yes	Yes
get/set indexed	Yes	Yes
is/set boolean	Yes	Yes
Bound Properties		
PropertyChangeEvent	Yes	Yes
PropertyChangeListener	Yes	Yes
PropertyChangeSupport	Yes	Yes
Constrained Properties		
PropertyChangeEvent	Yes	Yes
VetoableChangeListener	Yes	Yes
VetoableChangeSupport	Yes	Yes
PropertyVetoException	Yes	Yes
Asynchronous veto notification	Yes	No
Customization		
PropertyEditor	Yes	Yes
Customizer	Yes	Yes
HTML Help	Yes	Yes
MetaData		
Interface Repository/IDL	Yes	No
Introspector	Yes	Yes
BeanInfo	Yes, ComponentInfo	Yes
FeatureDescriptor	Yes	Yes
PropertyDescriptor	Yes	Yes
MethodDescriptor	Yes (derived from the CORBA IR's OperationDef)	Yes

Table 33-1. CORBA Components Versus JavaBeans. (Continued)

Feature	CORBA Component	JavaBean
EventSetDescriptor	Yes	Yes
VersionDescriptor	Yes	No
Packaging		
Serialization	Yes	Yes
JARs	Yes (called Component Archive or CAR)	Yes
Manifest	Yes	Yes
Deployment Descriptor	Yes	Yes, with EJB
Installation script	Yes	No
Composition and Containment		
Container	Yes	Yes, JDK 1.2 BeanContext
Containee	Yes	Yes, with JDK 1.2
ContainerListener	Yes	Yes, with JDK 1.2
Multiple interfaces	Yes, aggregation	Yes, Beans.getInstanceOf
Component LifeCycle		
Factories	Yes	Yes, with EJB
Activate/deactivate	Yes	Yes, with EJB
Persistent object refs	Yes	Yes, with EJB
Move	Yes	No
Remove	Yes	No

CORBA Remote Events

Like JavaBeans, CORBA components can be producers or consumers of events. Like their JavaBeans counterparts, CORBA listeners must implement an **EventXXXListener** that extends the **EventListener** interface. And like their JavaBeans counterparts, CORBA event producers must provide *addXXXListener* and *removeXXXListener* method pairs for each event type they support. The event itself is an object derived from **EventObject**; it describes the state changes that took place in the component. In CORBA, the **EventObject** base interface is a *value* object that looks like this:

```
value EventObject
{
  state
  {
    public Object src;
  }
};
```

As in JavaBeans, you must define an event interface (derived from the base **EventObject**) for each type of event. For example, here's how the CORBA component model defines a **PropertyChangeEvent** object:

```
value PropertyChangeEvent : EventObject
{
  state
  {
    public string name;
    public long PropogationId;
    public any oldVal;
    public any newVal;
  }
};
```

Unlike JavaBeans, your CORBA event objects can also be transmitted over the network. Note that the event is passed over the network using the new CORBA object pass-by-value semantics. The target machine must have a **PropertyChangeEvent** class (i.e., an implementation) that can receive this state; it also provides the methods that let you access it.

You should also be able to use the standard CORBA *Event Service* to augment this model with a distributed *event channel*. This is a well-known object on the network that serves as a broker (or intermediary) between producers and consumers of events.[5]

---

[5] Most CORBA vendors—including Iona, Borland/Visigenic, and IBM—provide standard implementations of the CORBA Event Service. We describe the Event Service in our book, **Instant CORBA** (Wiley, 1997).

CORBA Containers

In CORBA, a component can be composed of other components to form a hierarchy. The **Container** interface embodies the notion of a component hierarchy (see Figure 33-2). It defines methods that let you: 1) add/remove components to and from a container, 2) navigate the containment hierarchy, and 3) enumerate the component objects (or containees) that exist in the container. The **Containee** interface represents one or more containers in which a component may live. The component can receive container events by implementing the **ContainerListener** interface.

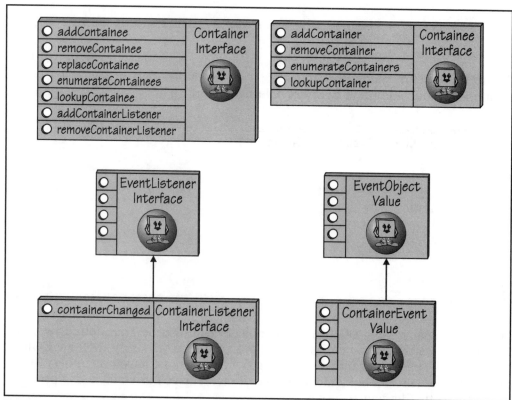

Figure 33-2. The CORBA Container/Containee Interfaces and Values.

The idea here is that you will be able to assemble components inside a container. The container itself is a component; it represents a subassembly of connected components. The container must be able to: 1) create instances of all its containees (recursively if needed), 2) internalize their state or invoke their initialization operations, 3) add the containees to the container causing event notifications to be executed, and 4) recreate the event source to listener connections (i.e., the wiring).

If you followed the SmileyPlaces code in the previous chapters, you will find this container/containee stuff to be second nature. However, our SmileyPlaces were quite ad hoc. There was very little to guide us in the JavaBeans specification when it came to containers. The CORBA container/containee interfaces are a welcome addition to this space.

Here's the early IDL definitions for the new container-related CORBA interfaces:

Listing 33-1. CORBA Components: The Container Interface.

```
interface Container
{
  //type defintions
  typedef struct
  {
    Object obj;
    String usename;
  } Member;
  typedef sequence<Member> contents;

  //methods
  void addContainee(in Member memb) raises (MemberDuplication);
  void removeContainee(in string usename) raises (MemberNotFound);
  void replaceContainee(in Member memb) raises (MemberNotFound);
  contents enumerateContainees();
  Member lookupContainee(in string usename);
  void addContainerListener(in ContainerListener lst);
  void removeContainerListener(in ContainerListener lst);
};
```

Listing 33-2. CORBA Components: The Containee Interface.

```
interface Containee
{

  // type definitions
  typedef sequence<Container> Containers;

  // Methods
  void addContainer(in Member mbr) raises (MemberDuplication);
  void removeContainer(in string useName) raises (MemberNotFound);
  Containers enumerateContainers();
  Container lookupContainer(in string useName);
};
```

Listing 33-3. CORBA Components: The EventListener Interface.

```
interface EventListener
{
  // empty flag
};
```

Listing 33-4. CORBA Components: The ContainerListener Interface.

```
interface ContainerListener : EventListener
{
  void ContainerChanged(in ContainerEvent evt);
};
```

Listing 33-5. CORBA Components: The EventObject Value.

```
value EventObject
{
  state
  {
    public Object src;
  }
};
```

Listing 33-6. CORBA Components: The ContainerEvent Interface.

```
value ContainerEvent : EventObject
{
  attributebool isContaineeAdded; // false if member deleted event
};
```

Component Packaging

The CORBA packaging scheme defines how a component is delivered, distributed, and then installed by a customer. In general, you will be able to install an Enterprise JavaBean JAR file as if it were a CORBA component package (more on this in the next chapter). Unlike JavaBeans, CORBA components may require additional information to support multiple platforms in a single package.

The CORBA version of a JAR is called the *Component ARchive (CAR)*. Like a JAR, a CAR is simply a ZIP file with a manifest that explains the contents. Each (.car) package may also include the IDL interface for the component. If it's a Java package, the IDL can be inferred by using the Java-to-IDL mapping.

The CORBA version of the **BeanInfo** is called **ComponentInfo**. It supports the JavaBeans metadata classes we described in the last chapter. Like its JavaBeans counterpart, the CORBA **Introspector** will be able to automatically generate metadata by analyzing the design patterns of CORBA components. Note that the CORBA design patterns are identical to the ones that are defined by JavaBeans (see previous chapters). So we won't repeat them here. Unlike its JavaBeans counterpart, the CORBA **Introspector** can also create a **ComponentInfo** from IDL descriptions or from the Interface Repository; it also uses the design patterns to automatically analyze a Java component.

Like Enterprise JavaBeans, CORBA manifests and CARs must include a *deployment descriptor*. This is a file that contains a textual description of the deployment properties for a component type—for example, it can include a target database, connections to legacy applications, and declarative information on the transaction and security policies. The deployment descriptor is typically created by the developer of the component. In some cases, it may be modified by an administrator via a tool. We explain the deployment descriptor in more detail when we cover Enterprise JavaBeans in the next chapter.

Like a JAR, a CAR has a hierarchical structure with the manifest at the root. The next levels contain individual components, or component groups. At the component level, the CAR contains information that is platform independent—for example, the IDL file. Below this are branches that contain language-dependent and platform-dependent entries.

An *installation script* is used to parse the CAR file, extract the manifest, and install the various components. The CAR must contain *factories* for the different components. A container uses these factories to create its subcomponents based on a *customization template* that a tool generates. For example, you can use a visual tool to customize the component's security and transactional attributes. The factory will then initialize the component's instance properties appropriately.

How It All Comes Together

You will use a visual tool to assemble CORBA components by dragging and dropping components into a *container*. Once in the container, you assign the CORBA components names and they become *containees*. You can connect containees together via events, method invocations, or scripts. To customize a container's behavior, you can attach scripts you write to events a container emits—for example, you can provide an initialize script that connects to databases when the container is first started.

At this point, you've created an instance of a component assembly. This instance will serve as the *prototype* (or *customization template*) that a run-time application uses to create new instances of the assembly. You now use the tool to define a factory that will take this prototype and other initialization parameters and then create new instances of the container and containees. The *prototype* can be in one of two forms: 1) the tool can generate code to implement the factory and initialization operations, or 2) the tool can generate a string of data (or data structure) that is interpreted by a generic factory. In addition, the prototype may specify the state to be loaded at initialization.

When all is said and done, a CORBA component assembly will consist of:

- ***A container implementation.*** A typical container will extend or specialize the standard CORBA container. It will expose a set of event sources to its listeners using the JavaBeans design patterns. A container must also implement the CORBA navigation interfaces to provide access to its subcomponents (the containees) by name.

- ***A set of factories.*** First there must be a factory for the container itself. This factory knows how to reproduce the customized prototype and construct the internal wiring. Each containee may also have a factory and prototype. The container uses them to create and personalize the subcomponent.

- ***The supporting artifacts.*** This is the list we described in the previous section—including **ComponentInfo**, IDL, component descriptors, deployment descriptors, and so on.

At run time, a CORBA component is identified by its object reference. A CORBA component can also support multiple interfaces, each of which has a separate object reference. The component will return the object reference for the interface you request.

CONCLUSION

This chapter shows how the CORBA and JavaBeans component models are starting to morph together. From a tool perspective, a CORBA object is like any other JavaBean. The OMG architects seem to have adopted the entire JavaBeans component model—including its design patterns, events, properties, metadata classes, customizers, property editors, and manifest-based packaging. However, the end result is more than just a JavaBean. A CORBA bean is a JavaBean++. It's a language-independent bean that you can also invoke and introspect across a network.

In addition, the CORBA component architects have addressed one of the major shortcomings of JavaBeans—the lack of a container/containee protocol.[6] And they've put a lot more thought into what it means to customize, package, and deploy a server-side component. We will have more to say on server-side component packaging in the next chapter when we go over Enterprise JavaBeans.

---

[6] Note that one of the designers of CORBA Components is Larry Cable of JavaSoft, who is also the JavaBeans lead architect. Also, the JDK 1.2 version of JavaBeans now includes a rudimentary container model.

Chapter 34

Enterprise JavaBeans and CORBA

What is particularly exciting about Enterprise JavaBeans for Oracle is that it provides a standardized way to build manageable Java business components. Enterprise JavaBeans will take full advantage of Oracle's Network Computing Architecture's Cartridge infrastructure for manageability, IIOP connectivity, and CORBA services.

— Beatriz Infante
Senior VP, Oracle

Iona Technologies welcomes the release of the Enterprise JavaBeans specification. It leverages related OMG and CORBA standards and clearly shows JavaSoft's commitment to using open standards where possible. We look forward to supporting Enterprise JavaBeans in the Orbix family of products.

— Annrai O'Toole
CTO, IONA Technologies

After more than a year in the making, JavaSoft released—in December, 1997—a public draft of its *Enterprise JavaBeans (EJB)* specification. The EJB specification defines a server component model for JavaBeans. An EJB is a specialized, non-visual JavaBean that runs on a server. Like JavaBeans, EJBs can be assembled via tools to create new applications.

The EJB server-side component architecture brings together most of the CORBA/Java concepts we cover in this book (and some more). As you can deduce from the above endorsements, EJBs were a big hit with the CORBA camp. Perhaps it's because they were designed from ground zero to be 100% CORBA-compatible. The designers seem to have met their target—the document that describes the EJB-to-CORBA mapping is a mere 20 pages.[1]

We can attribute this lack of "impedance mismatch" to the fact that EJBs use the RMI/IDL CORBA subset for their distributed object model (see Chapter 21). In addition, they use the *Java Transaction Service (JTS)*—a Java implementation of the CORBA *Object Transaction Service*—for their distributed transaction model. EJB also requires CORBA IIOP to: 1) interoperate across multivendor servers, 2) propagate transaction and security contexts, 3) service multilingual clients, and 4) support ActiveX clients via DCOM-to-CORBA bridges.

EJB augments CORBA by defining the interfaces between a server-side component (or bean) and its container. Server components are managed beans that run on a server. The *container* acts as a component coordinator. It uses a standard JAR package to import EJBs from tools and other containers. Once an EJB is inside its container, it can then be managed in a scalable way using transactions, state management, and automatic activation and deactivation.

The beauty of the EJB framework is that it lets you declaratively define most of your server-side run-time attributes. So you can use visual tools to administer and set the properties of your server-side components—including their transactional, security, and state management policies.

In this chapter, we first introduce a new breed of CORBA server-side component coordinators called OTMs. Then we explain what EJBs do for these OTMs, and vice versa. Finally, we go over the details of the EJB component model. Be warned that this chapter deals with bleeding-edge technology, much of which is still under construction.

EJBS AND CORBA OBJECT TRANSACTION MONITORS

EJB is primarily a contract between a server-side JavaBean and a new breed of component coordinator. The Gartner Group calls this new breed of middleware an *Object Transaction Monitor (OTM)*; EJB calls it a server-side *Container*. An OTM is a morph of a TP Monitor with an ORB. Or, if you prefer, it's a TP Monitor built

---

[1] See JavaSoft's *Enterprise JavaBeans to CORBA Mapping* (December, 1997).

on top of an ORB. In this section, we explain what is an OTM. We then tell you something about CORBA OTM products. Finally, we explain what EJB does for CORBA OTMs.

So, What Exactly Is an OTM?

An OTM is like an iceberg. Your application only sees the visible 10%. The other 90% provides functions that are beneath the water-line. OTMs imbue your applications with these invisible functions.

— *Jeri Edwards*
VP of Strategy, BEA Systems

An ORB is simply an object bus. With an object bus, anything goes. In contrast, an OTM provides a *framework*—or organized environment—for running server-side components (see Figure 34-1). With an OTM, you get organized anarchy: Everything goes as long as you play by the framework's rules.

Like all good frameworks, OTMs follow the *Hollywood Principle*: "Don't call us; we'll call you." The OTM framework is the primary orchestrator of your server-side components. It calls your components at the right time, and in the right sequence. If you play by the OTM's rules, your objects become managed, transactional, robust, persistent, and high-performing.

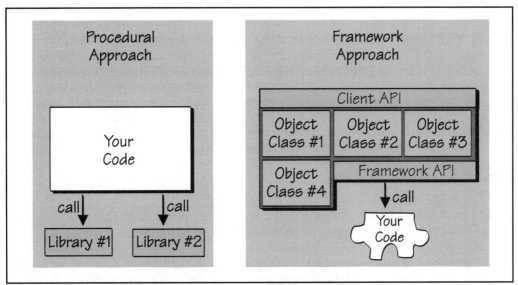

Figure 34-1. Procedural Versus Framework Approaches to Developing Code.

An OTM maximizes the reuse of scarce system resources by your components. It prestarts pools of objects, distributes their loads, provides fault-tolerance, and coordinates multi-component transactions. Without this new breed of component coordinators, you cannot manage millions of server-side objects—a key requirement of the Object Web.

In Part 6, we had to develop an object dispenser from scratch to get our application to scale. This was our "poor man's" version of a server-side framework. In contrast, with commercial OTMs, you will be able to get off-the-shelf frameworks that embody the best server-side programming practices. Your components will inherit these "best practices" from your OTM. The OTM becomes the central figure in the life of your components. Here are some of the activities an OTM orchestrates on behalf of your components:

- *Activates and deactivates your components.* In the CORBA world, the OTM works with the POA to activate and deactivate objects when requests arrive and when they complete.

- *Coordinates distributed transactions.* The OTM lets you declaratively define your transactional objects. It starts transactions if none exist. It will then manage the completion of a transaction using the underlying CORBA *Object Transaction Service (OTS)*.

- *Notifies your component of key events during its life cycle.* The OTM notifies a component when it is created, activated, deactivated, and destroyed. Your component can then use these calls to explicitly manage its state, and to grab or release system resources.

- *Automatically manages the state of your persistent component.* The more advanced OTMs can automatically load the state of a component from a persistent store and then later save it on transactional boundaries.

In summary, OTMs have what it takes to fulfill the promise of scalable server-side objects.

CORBA OTMs

A number of CORBA-based component coordinators are currently under construction. They come from four groups of vendors (see Figure 34-2):

1. *TP Monitor vendors moving to ORB-based middleware*. The two examples from this camp are IBM's *Component Broker* and BEA System's *Tuxedo/ Iceberg*. Both of these products are currently in beta. The IBM *Component*

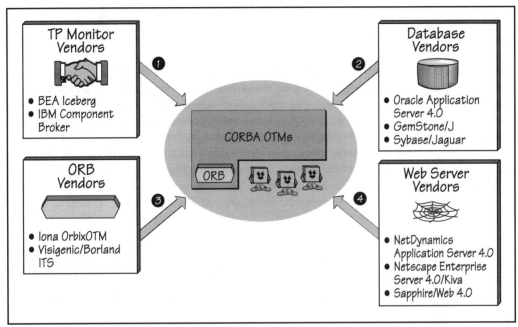

Figure 34-2. CORBA Object Transaction Monitors (OTMs)

Broker builds on the SOM CORBA ORB and borrows elements from the Encina and CICS TP Monitors. The result is a framework for managed components that lets you mix in over nine CORBA services. In addition, Component Broker provides *instance managers* that let you automatically manage an object's state and map it to data in an RDBMS. BEA *Iceberg* combines the scalable *Tuxedo* TP Monitor infrastructure with the BEA *Object Broker* CORBA ORB; it also provides a higher-level framework for managed components.

2. ***DBMS vendors moving from 2-tier to 3-tier.*** The textbook example of a CORBA OTM from this camp is Oracle's *Application Server 4.0*; it provides an application server for CORBA/Java components on top of the Borland/Visigenic ORB (and an Oracle server-side IIOP ORB). *Gemstone/J* is an application server that uses an ODBMS-enabled Java VM to manage a component's state. And, there's always a chance that Sybase may adapt its *Jaguar* application server to CORBA.

3. ***ORB vendors moving from pipes to TP-based application servers.*** The two examples of CORBA OTMs from this camp are Iona's *OrbixOTM* and Borland/Visigenic's *Integrated Transaction Service (ITS)*.

4. ***Web server vendors moving to TP-based application servers.*** The two examples of CORBA OTMs from this camp are NetDynamics' *Application Server 4.0* and Netscape/Kiva's forthcoming *Enterprise Server 4.0*. In addi-

tion, BlueStone is also starting to move in this space; its *Sapphire/Web 4.0* application server now supports IIOP. Finally, Lotus' forthcoming IIOP-based *Domino 5.0* may also be included in this category.

All these OTMs support the CORBA object model with extensions. And, they all strive to provide robust object application platforms that can scale to support millions of server-side objects. The more advanced OTMs build on the CORBA *Object Transaction Service (OTS)*. Some even provide transaction connectivity to existing products such as *CICS*, *IMS*, *Tuxedo*, and *MQSeries*. In addition, they can coordinate CORBA transactions with RDBMSs (and other resource managers) via the X/Open DTP standard and its XA interfaces. This means that an advanced OTM can coordinate—as part of a single transaction—CORBA objects, TP Monitor applications, and resource managers such as RDBMSs, ODBMSs, and Message Queues.

In parallel, Microsoft is building its own server-side component infrastructure; it is based on DCOM and ActiveX. The *Microsoft Transaction Server* (née Viper) is the DCOM OTM, and it is tightly integrated with the Microsoft IIS Web Server. Microsoft's transaction model is called the *Distributed Transaction Coordinator (DTC)*—previously known as OLE/TP.

Enterprise JavaBeans and CORBA OTMs

So, what does all this have to do with EJB? This may come as a surprise: CORBA does not define a server-side component coordinator framework. The CORBA POA is a framework for managing persistent or transient objects. However, it does not deal with issues such as transactions, component packaging, or automatic state management. The integration of these pieces is left as an exercise for the vendors.

In addition, CORBA does not have a fully completed server-side component model. In the past five years, ORB vendors have concentrated on the interoperable aspects of CORBA. The CORBA services were defined using the Bauhaus Principle—every service does one thing well. However, there was no notion of a server-side component that could be used to represent a *managed object*—meaning a toolable object that also incorporates a variety of CORBA services—such as transactions, externalization, events, and licensing. The CORBA beans we described in the last chapter simply make regular CORBA objects more toolable. They are not managed server-side objects.

Consequently, the server-side components that are now being defined by the various CORBA OTM vendors will probably not be interchangeable (even if they are all CORBA-based). This is exactly where Enterprise JavaBeans come to the rescue. EJB defines a server-side component model as well as a component coordinator framework that is totally compatible with CORBA. If the CORBA OTM vendors all decide to implement the EJB specification, then we may get this totally portable server-side component infrastructure (at least for Java components).

As it turns out, all the major CORBA OTM vendors were heavily involved in the development of the EJB specification, which is probably why it took so long to develop. So now we have a JavaBeans-based component model that covers both the client and server sides of the equation. Informally, we were told that G4 plans to extend its CORBA Component Specification to include EJB when it is completed. In other words, the CORBA component model may include both JavaBeans and EJB. JavaBeans will represent simple CORBA objects; EJBs will represent managed CORBA objects that are also OTM-aware. To become a CORBA standard, EJBs must first be extended to support more than just Java on the server. Most of the CORBA OTMs support multilingual components. So there's still work to be done in this area.

The EJB Container Framework

In a multitier application architecture, most of an application's logic is moved from the client to one or more servers. A server component model simplifies the process of moving the logic to the server. The component model implements a set of automatic services to manage the component.

> — **Ann Thomas**
> **Seybold Group Analyst**

EJB provides the first formalized component-to-OTM contract for the CORBA world; it starts out where CORBA/POA leaves off. EJB defines the callback interfaces a JavaBean must expose to its OTM, and vice versa. In addition, EJB specifies a packaging mechanism for server-side components. Figure 34-3 shows the major functions a server-side container (or OTM) provides to the EJBs that run within it. Let's go over the pieces:

■ *Distributed object infrastructure*—EJB does not concern itself with the distributed object infrastructure; it assumes an underlying ORB that understands the CORBA RMI/IDL semantics. The ORB transport must also be able to propagate CORBA OTS transactions; IIOP ORBs are designed to provide this type of service.

■ *Component packaging and deployment*—EJB defines a packaging mechanism for server-side components based on JARs, manifests, and deployment descriptors. The container un-JARs the EJB and then runs it based on the instructions it gets from the manifest and the deployment descriptors.

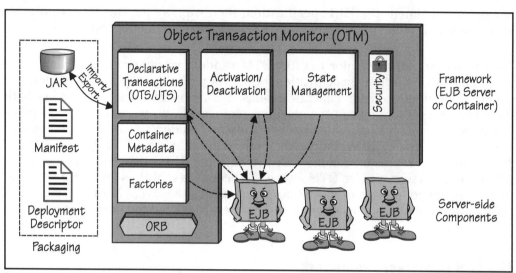

Figure 34-3. What EJBs Can Expect From Their Containers.

■ *Declarative transaction management*—EJB supports implicit transactions built on the CORBA OTS/JTS service. Your bean does not need to make explicit calls to OTS/JTS to participate in a distributed transaction. The EJB container automatically manages the start, commit, and rollback of a transaction. You define the transactional attributes of a bean at design time (or during deployment) using declarative statements in the deployment descriptor. Optionally, a bean can explicitly control the boundaries of a transaction using explicit CORBA OTS/JTS semantics.[2]

■ *Factory support*—EJB containers manage the entire life cycle of an enterprise bean. As a bean provider, you are responsible for defining a remote factory interface for your bean. You must define a factory interface that extends **Factory** and defines one or more *create* methods, one for each way you create an EJB object. The container provider will automatically generate the factory implementation. However, your bean must implement an *ejbCreate* method for each *create* method you defined in the factory interface. As a last step, you must register your factories with the container so that clients can create new beans. The container also provides a **Finder** interface to help clients locate existing entity beans.

■ *Bean activation and passivation*—as part of managing the life cycle of an enterprise bean, the container calls your bean when it is loaded into memory (or *activated*); it also calls it when it is *deactivated* from memory (or *passivated*).

---

[2] For an introduction to CORBA OTS see our book, **Instant CORBA** (Wiley, 1997).

■ **Bean state management**—EJB containers can manage both transient and persistent beans. Persistent (or *entity*) beans encapsulate in their object reference a unique ID that points to their state. An entity bean manages its own persistence by implementing the persistence operations directly. The container simply hands it a unique key and tells it to load its state. In a future release of EJB, the entity bean will be able to delegate the management of its persistence to its container. In the simplest case, the container will serialize the bean's state and store it in some persistent store. The more sophisticated containers will be able to map the bean's persistent fields to columns in an RDBMS. Finally, the container may choose to implement persistence using an embedded ODBMS.

■ **Container metadata**—EJB containers can provide metadata about the beans they contain. For example, the container can return the class name of the enterprise bean that this factory interface is associated with.

■ **Security**—EJB containers automate the management of some of the security aspects of your beans. You get to declaratively define the security rules for your enterprise bean in a **SecurityDescriptor** object; you must then serialize this object and put it in your bean's JAR. The EJB container uses this object to perform all security checks on behalf of your bean.

This short list should give you a good idea of what an EJB container does for its beans.

Session and Entity Beans

Like CORBA objects, an enterprise bean can either be transient or persistent. The EJB specification calls them *session* and *entity* beans. A session bean is a transient object that will not outlive the VM in which it is created. In contrast, the lifetime of an entity bean is not limited by the lifetime of the Java VM process in which it executes; a crash of the Java VM may result in a rollback of current transaction, but it neither destroys the EJB entity object nor invalidates a reference to it held by clients. You can later reconnect to this same bean using its object reference. Like its CORBA counterpart, this persistent object reference encapsulates a unique primary key; it allows the bean (or its container) to reload the state of that object.

According to the EJB specification, a typical *session bean* has the following characteristics:

✔ Executes on behalf of a single client. By definition, a session bean instance is an extension of the client that creates it.
✔ Can be transaction-aware.
✔ Updates data in an underlying database.

✔ Is relatively short-lived. Its lifetime is typically that of its client.

✔ Is destroyed when the EJB server crashes. The client has to re-establish a new session object to continue a computation.

✔ Does not represent data that should be stored in a database.

A session bean typically reads and updates data in a database on behalf of its client. Its fields may contain conversational state on behalf of the client. This state describes the conversation represented by a specific client/instance pair. Within a transaction, some of this data may be cached in the bean.

Session beans are intended to be private resources used only by the client that creates them. For this reason, a session EJB is anonymous; it hides its identity. In contrast, an entity EJB exposes its identity as a primary key. According to the EJB specification, a typical *entity bean* has the following characteristics:

✔ Supports shared access from multiple users.

✔ Participates in transactions.

✔ Represents data in the database.

✔ Can be long-lived (lives as long as the data in the database).

✔ Survives crashes of the EJB server. A crash is transparent to the client.

✔ Has a persistent object reference. The object reference encapsulates the Object Id (or persistent key) for this bean.

The support for session objects is mandatory for an EJB 1.0 compliant container. The support for entity objects is optional, but it becomes mandatory for EJB 2.0 compliant containers.

The EJB Client/Server Development Process

Today, for all practical purposes, EJB is a CORBA++ system. In fact, the only mapping EJB defines is for CORBA. You define your EJB server objects using the OMG's new RMI/IDL reverse-language mapping (see Chapter 21). Figure 34-4 shows the steps:

1. *Define your EJB's remote interface.* Your EJB must declare its remote services via a Java interface. You do this by extending the **java.ejb.EJBObject** interface, which in turn extends the **java.rmi.Remote** interface. Each method in a remote interface must throw a **java.rmi.RemoteException**. If your EJB is transactional, then you must extend the CORBA **TransactionalObject** interface. It's just an empty flag that tells the ORB to propagate the transaction context over IIOP. Finally, you must define a factory interface for your EJB.

2. *Optionally, generate CORBA IDL.* Run your interfaces through an *RMI2IDL* translator to generate CORBA IDL. You will need CORBA IDL to support

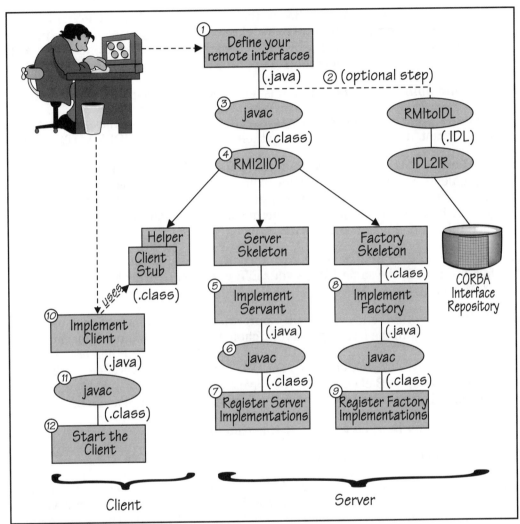

Figure 34-4. The EJB Client/Server Development Process.

non-Java clients and to populate an Interface Repository.

3. ***Compile your interface***. You must compile your interface using *javac*.

4. ***Create the IIOP stubs and skeletons***. Run an *RMI2IIOP* postprocessor against the (.class) files to generate client stubs and server skeletons for your remote classes. The postprocessor will also generate the necessary helper classes as well as stubs and skeletons for your remote factory interface.

5. ***Implement the servant***. You must provide a Java server class that implements

the remote interface you published to the outside world. You can either directly derive this class from an **ImplBase** class or you may use the CORBA Tie mechanism to delegate the calls to a separate implementation class. EJB recommends that you follow the Tie approach (we cover Tie in Chapter 20).

6. *Compile your EJB class.* You must compile your servant class using *javac*.

7. *Register your EJB implementation with the server.* You must package your EJB servant object in an EJB JAR and then register it with a CORBA OTM server.

8. *Implement the Factory object for this EJB.* Typically, the code that implements your factory interface will automatically be generated for you. Remember that you must still: 1) define the factory interface for your EJB type, and 2) implement an *ejbCreate* method in your bean class for each *create* method you define in the factory interface.

9. *Register your Factory with the server.* Typically, you will package your factory class in the same JAR as your EJB and then register it with the CORBA OTM server.

10. *Write your client code.* With the appropriate CORBA bindings, you can write the EJB client in the language of your choice. You can obtain a reference to an EJB either via a Naming Service or by finding a **Factory** and then creating one. You can always ask your container (or OTM) to provide a reference to a **Factory** for a particular EJB class. Once you have a reference to the remote object, you then simply invoke its methods via the IIOP stubs that serve as its proxy.

11. *Compile the client code.* You do this using *javac*.

12. *Start the client.* You must load the client classes and their stubs.

As we go to press, there are no *RMI2IIOP* compilers on the market. There are also no CORBA OTMs that currently support EJBs. Consequently, we cannot validate the development steps we just showed you. We warned you that this was bleeding-edge stuff.

The Client's View of an EJB

To a client, an EJB is simply a remote CORBA object. You must first obtain an object reference for an EJB. Then you invoke the EJB like any local language object. It's just plain old CORBA. In addition, EJB specifies three new CORBA objects on the server that a client can use to find an existing enterprise bean or to create a new one from scratch (see Figure 34-5).

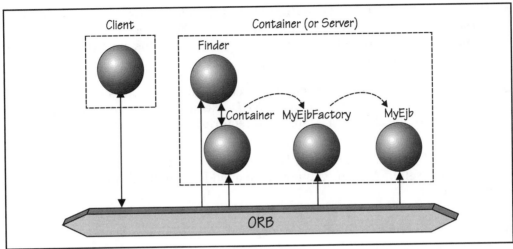

Figure 34-5. The Client's View of an EJB.

An EJB **Container** is a named object that represents the server where an enterprise bean lives. A client can find a **Container** object by name using a directory service. Once the client has a reference to a **Container** object, it can do the following:

- ***Obtain a factory object.*** The client invokes the *getFactory* method to obtain a factory; it then uses the factory to create new EJB objects in the container.

- ***Destroy an EJB object.*** Typically, a client will explicitly destroy a session EJB object. In contrast, the life cycle of an entity EJB is usually controlled by its OTM. However, the client can hint that the object should be destroyed.

- ***Obtain a Finder object.*** This allows a client to find existing entity beans in this container. Note that session objects are not tracked via a **Finder**; they're disposable objects.

- ***Get metadata describing the container.*** The container maintains all sorts of information on the EJBs that run within it. Authorized clients can access some of this information.

In Figure 34-5, the client invokes the *getFactory* method on the **Container** object to obtain **MyEjbFactory**. Then it invokes *create* on **MyEjbFactory** to create **MyEjb**.

In addition, a client can obtain a reference to an existing EJB entity object in any of the following ways:

- Receive a reference as a parameter in a method call (input parameter or result).

- Invoke the **Finder** to locate objects that already exist in a given container.

■ Obtain a reference from a bean **Handle**. Note that a **Handle** contains a serialized version of an object reference inside a stream. You invoke *getEJBObject* on a **Handle** to obtain a live object reference for this bean. This function is equivalent to CORBA's *string-to-object*.

■ Invoke a CORBA Trader or Naming service. In addition, EJB supports the *Java Naming and Directory Interface (JNDI)*. Netscape also intends to let you find CORBA/EJB objects via LDAP-based directories using URLs.

The CORBA object reference to an EJB contains additional Helper functions that you may find useful. A client can now invoke added functions on a CORBA object reference to:

■ Obtain a reference to the object's container.

■ Obtain the name of the enterprise bean class that provides the implementation of the business methods.

■ Obtain the EJB object's primary key. Every entity EJB object has a unique identity within its container. A client that holds a reference to an EJB object can determine the object's identity by invoking the *getPrimaryKey* method on the reference.

■ Obtain the EJB object's **Handle**.

■ Destroy the EJB object.

Note that these additional Helper functions are defined by the **java.ejb.EJBObject** interface. They are implemented by the container on behalf of your EJB. A CORBA container can easily implement these functions on top of the POA.

The Remote EJB Interfaces

Figure 34-6 shows the remote EJB interfaces. These are the same interfaces we covered in the last section. They are implemented as CORBA (or RMI) objects that are accessible to remote clients. Remember, the new Java-to-IDL reverse-language mapping uses **java.rmi.Remote** to flag a remote CORBA interface.

We also include the more detailed interface definitions. Be warned that these interfaces were still under construction as we go to press.[3]

---

[3] This chapter is based on JavaSoft's Version 0.8 of the *Enterprise JavaBeans* and *Enterprise JavaBeans to CORBA Mapping*. They were both published in December, 1997.

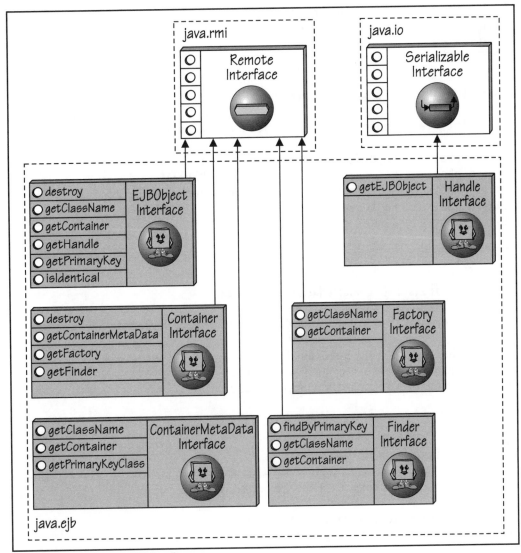

Figure 34-6. The Remote EJB Interfaces.

Listing 34-1. The java.ejb.EJBObject Interface.

```
public interface EJBObject extends java.rmi.Remote
{
 public abstract void destroy();
 public abstract String getClassName();
 public abstract Container getContainer();
 public abstract Handle getHandle();
```

```
 public abstract Object getPrimaryKey();
 public abstract boolean isIdentical(EJBObject bean);
}
```

Listing 34-2. The java.ejb.Container Interface.

```
public interface Container extends java.rmi.Remote
{
 public abstract void destroy(Handle handle);
 public abstract void destroy(Object primaryKey);
 public abstract ContainerMetaData getContainerMetaData();
 public abstract Factory getFactory();
 public abstract Finder getFinder();
}
```

Listing 34-3. The java.ejb.ContainerMetaData Interface.

```
public interface ContainerMetaData extends java.rmi.Remote
{
 public abstract String getClassName();
 public abstract Container getContainer();
 public abstract Class getPrimaryKeyClass();
}
```

Listing 34-4. The java.ejb.Factory Interface.

```
public interface Factory extends java.rmi.Remote
{
 public abstract String getClassName();
 public abstract Container getContainer();
}
```

Listing 34-5. The java.ejb.Finder Interface.

```
public interface Finder extends java.rmi.Remote
{
 public abstract EJBObject findByPrimaryKey(Object primaryKey);
 public abstract String getClassName();
 public abstract Container getContainer();
}
```

Listing 34-6. The java.ejb.Handle Interface.

```
public interface Handle extends java.io.Serializable
{
 public abstract EJBObject getEJBObject();
}
```

An EJB Client/Server Scenario

Figure 34-7 shows an EJB client/server interaction scenario; it assumes an IIOP ORB. The client creates a new EJB instance and then invokes its methods. Here are the steps:

1. ***Find a container by name***. The client invokes the CORBA **ORB** pseudo-object's *resolve_initial_references* to obtain an object reference to a Naming Service. It then uses it to obtain a reference to the named container.

2. ***Get a Factory for this class of bean***. The client invokes *getFactory* on the **Container** to obtain a reference to the **MyEjbFactory** object.

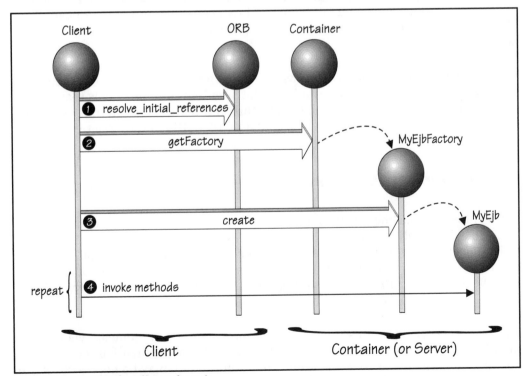

Figure 34-7. An EJB Client/Server Scenario.

3. ***Create and initialize a new bean***. The client invokes *create* on **MyEjbFactory** and passes it initialization information. If this is an entity bean, the factory object works with the POA to generate an object reference with a unique key.

4. ***Invoke the methods on this enterprise bean***. The client can now invoke the CORBA methods that implement the business function on **MyEJB**. Note that the call may first go to a Tie object servant, which then delegates it to a separate implementation object. EJB requires this level of indirection to allow a container to interject its value-added functions.

As you can see, there's nothing too earth-shattering in the way a client interacts with its EJB. Most of the EJB magic is totally invisible to clients.

THE EJB/CONTAINER PROTOCOL

At the heart of the EJB architecture is the managed object framework a container (or OTM) provides to its beans. From the time it is created until it is destroyed, an enterprise bean lives inside a container. The container provides security, concurrency, transactions, persistence, and other services to the EJB object. Even though much of this magic is totally transparent to remote clients, it requires a tight level of synchronization between a container and its beans. Of course, the beans must play by the rules of their framework—the container (or OTM)—to reap all these benefits.

We already gave you the 50,000 foot view of what a container does for its beans. In the next few sections, we will zoom-in on the interfaces and protocols that the two sides require of each other. Remember, this is a server-side affair—the clients remain totally oblivious to the protocols that tie the EJBs to their containers.

The Container/Bean Callbacks

EJB is mostly about the interfaces a managed object exposes to its container, and vice versa. The only purpose of these interfaces is to help the container manage all of its objects in the most scalable way. The container can activate and deactivate any object it wants whenever it finds it necessary. In addition, the container can help the object participate in transactions; it can also synchronize the active lifetime of an object with the boundaries of a transaction.

To synchronize their actions, the container and its EJBs communicate via callback interfaces. Containers make no actual service demands on their beans. The container calls its beans to notify them when some action may be necessary; it also passes them object references to the container's context-based services.

Figure 34-8 shows the key callback interfaces a container exposes to its beans, and vice versa. From a container/bean viewpoint, session and entity beans are not alike—they each have their own interfaces. A container maintains a **SessionContext** object for each session bean that runs within it. Likewise, it maintains an **EntityContext** object for each entity bean. The container first creates a bean and then passes it a context object; the bean is associated with its context for the duration of its lifetime.

The container communicates with a session bean by invoking the methods defined in the **SessionBean** interface. A transactional session bean may also choose to implement the optional **SessionSynchronization** interface. To communicate with an entity bean, the container invokes the methods defined in the **EntityBean** interface. The bottom line is that to be called EJBs, your CORBA servants must also implement either the **SessionBean** or **EntityBean** interfaces.

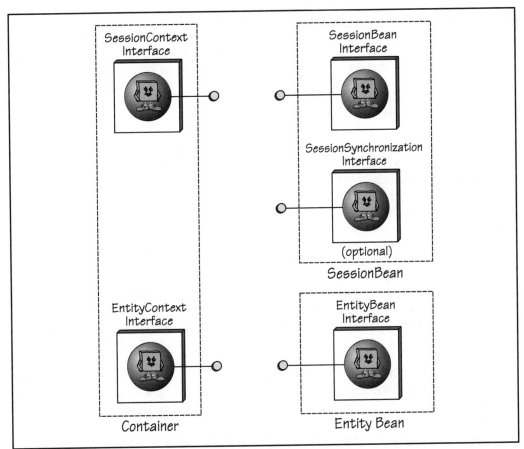

Figure 34-8. The Key EJB Container/Bean Callback Interfaces.

The Container/Bean Interfaces

Figure 34-9 shows the hierarchy structure of the *java.ejb* callback interfaces. The left side shows the container interfaces; the right side shows the interfaces for both session and entity beans. Notice that all EJBs are serializable. The **Enterprise-Bean** interface is just a flag; every EJB class must implement it. Session beans must implement the **SessionBean** interface; entity beans must implement the **Entity-Bean** interface. These are the two callback interfaces that allow a container to manage the life cycle of its beans.

The best way to understand these interfaces is to walk through the major transitions in the life of an EJB instance:

- ***Creation.*** An EJB instance's life starts when a container creates a new instance of a bean and then invokes either *setSessionContext* or *setEntityContext* to pass the bean a reference to its context object—which is the object the bean uses to callback the container. Your EJB implementation can take advantage of this call to allocate the resources it will need during its lifetime—for example, a DBMS connection. Note that an instance can be reused during its lifetime to serve multiple EJB objects. Consequently, the resources cannot be specific to an EJB object reference.

- ***Life by the pool.*** EJB instances will live happily inside pools of available instances until a client request arrives. If there is no EJB instance in the ready state to service this request, the container picks an instance off the pool. All instances in the pool are identical—they are not associated with the identity of a specific EJB object.

- ***From pool to active state.*** There are two possible transitions from the pool to the ready state: 1) via the *ejbCreate* method, and 2) via the *ejbActivate* method. The container invokes the *ejbCreate* method when a client invokes the corresponding *create* method on the EJB factory. If the client invokes a request for an object that already exists, the container will instead invoke *ejbActivate*. In both cases, the instance is now active and associated with an EJB object reference.

  The *ejbCreate* method gives your instance a chance to validate the client-supplied arguments and initialize the instance variables from the input arguments. An entity instance must invoke the *setPrimaryKey* method on its **EntityContext** to provide the container with a primary key that it can then embed into the EJB object reference. This is also the reference the factory returns to the client. Typically, your entity instance will also insert a record into a database to represent this EJB object reference; it will copy or compute the initial values from the input arguments of the *ejbCreate*.

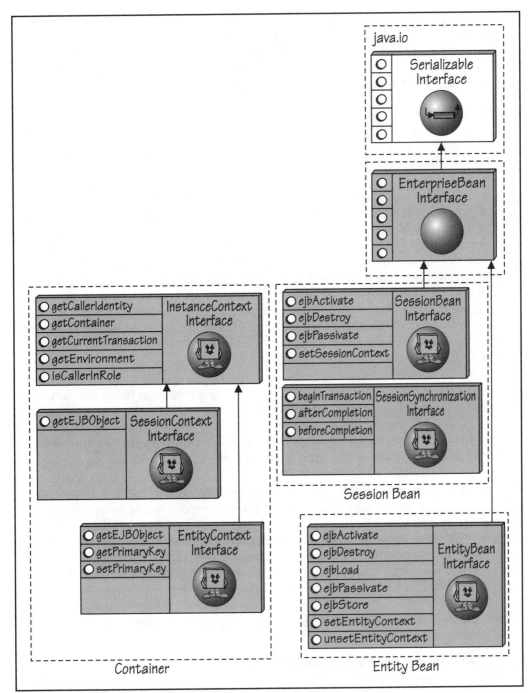

Figure 34-9. The EJB Container/Bean Interfaces.

The *ejbActivate* method gives your instance a chance to acquire additional resources that it needs while it is in the active state. An entity instance uses this call to obtain the identity of the EJB object by invoking either the *getPrimary-Key* or *getEJBObject* methods on its **EntityContext** object. It can then use this primary key to load its state from a database.

■ *The active state.* The EJB can receive any number of method invocations from its clients. In addition, the container invokes the *ejbLoad* and *ejbStore* methods whenever it needs to notify an entity bean instance to synchronize (or refresh) its state with a persistent store.

■ *Back to the pool.* There are two ways for a bean to transition back to the pooled state: 1) when the container calls *ejbPassivate*, and 2) when it calls *ejbDestroy*. The container invokes the *ejbPassivate* method to disassociate the instance from the EJB object reference; the instance uses this method to deallocate resources it obtained during the *ejbActivate*. The container invokes the *ejbDestroy* method to destroy the EJB object (when the client invokes the *destroy* method on the EJB object or one of the *destroy* methods on the container). The entity bean uses *ejbDestroy* to delete its entity state from the database. In all cases, the instance returns to the pool; it is no longer associated with the identity of the EJB object. The container can then reassign the instance to any EJB object of the same enterprise bean class.

■ *Destruction.* An entity instance in the pool is terminated when the container calls its *unsetEntityContext* method. Your instance can take advantage of this call to free any resources it holds. Because the container does not reference this instance, the Java garbage collector will eventually invoke the *finalize* method on the instance and then garbage collect it.

This short explanation should help you understand almost all the interfaces in Figure 34-9. You should note that some of the callbacks provide return values that an EJB can use to vote on the outcome of a transaction (more on this in the next section). The optional **SessionSynchronization** interface allows a session bean to be notified by its container of transaction boundaries. In general, we recommend that you only use explicit DBMS transactions with a session bean. We believe that using JTS/OTS with a session bean is overkill.

In case you're interested, here are the detailed interface descriptions:

Listing 34-7. The java.ejb.EnterpriseBean Interface.

```
public interface EnterpriseBean extends java.io.Serializable
{
}
```

Listing 34-8. The java.ejb.SessionBean Interface.

```java
public interface SessionBean extends EnterpriseBean
{
 public abstract void ejbActivate();
 public abstract void ejbDestroy();
 public abstract void ejbPassivate();
 public abstract void setSessionContext(SessionContext ctx);
}
```

Listing 34-9. The java.ejb.EntityBean Interface.

```java
public interface EntityBean extends EnterpriseBean
{
 public abstract void ejbActivate();
 public abstract void ejbDestroy();
 public abstract void ejbLoad();
 public abstract void ejbPassivate();
 public abstract void ejbStore();
 public abstract void setEntityContext(EntityContext ctx);
 public abstract void unsetEntityContext();
}
```

Listing 34-10. The java.ejb.InstanceContext Interface.

```java
public interface InstanceContext
{
 public abstract Identity getCallerIdentity();
 public abstract Container getContainer();
 public abstract CurrentTransaction getCurrentTransaction();
 public abstract Properties getEnvironment();
 public abstract boolean isCallerInRole(Identity role);
}
```

Listing 34-11. The java.ejb.SessionContext Interface.

```java
public interface SessionContext extends InstanceContext
{
 public abstract EJBObject getEJBObject();
}
```

Listing 34-12. The java.ejb.EntityContext Interface.

```java
public interface EntityContext extends InstanceContext
{
```

```
public abstract EJBObject getEJBObject();
public abstract EJBObject getEJBObject(Object primaryKey);
public abstract Object getPrimaryKey();
public abstract void setPrimaryKey(Object primaryKey);
}
```

Listing 34-13. The java.ejb.SessionSynchronization Interface.

```
public interface SessionSynchronization
{
public abstract void beginTransaction();
public abstract void afterCompletion(boolean committed);
public abstract void beforeCompletion();
}
```

SUPPORT FOR TRANSACTIONS

One of the key features of EJB is its support for distributed transactions. EJB lets you write an application that atomically updates data that is distributed across multiple DBMSs and sites. The sites may use EJB servers from different vendors. EJB insulates you from dealing with the complexity of distributed transactions. It shifts the burden of managing transactions to the OTM providers. You simply declare the transaction scope of your bean and then let the OTM implement the necessary low-level, two-phase commit protocols between a transaction manager and a database system. IIOP—augmented with OTS—can transparently handle the propagation of the transaction context across the network.

The EJB Transaction Model

Enterprise JavaBeans supports flat transactions, modeled after the OMG *Object Transaction action Service (OTS)*. An enterprise bean object that is transaction-enabled corresponds to a CORBA *Transactional Server* object. A future release may allow an enterprise bean to act as a CORBA *Recoverable Server* object. The framework hides most of the CORBA OTS details from the application developer. Consequently, most enterprise beans will not directly access the CORBA OTS APIs (or the Java version called JTS). However, the OTM must implement OTS (or JTS) for EJB to work.[4]

---

[4] Note that in EJB Release 1.0, an enterprise bean does not use the JTS/OTS interfaces directly. There is one exception to this rule. An enterprise bean with the BEAN_MANAGED transaction attribute is allowed to use the **java.jts.CurrentTransaction** interface to demarcate transaction boundaries.

EJB Transaction Usage

EJB allows an application program to update data in multiple databases in a single transaction. In Figure 34-10, a client invokes EJB1 in Server 1 to update data inside Oracle and DB2 DBMSs. Then, EJB1 calls EJB2 in Server 2 to update data inside a Sybase DBMS and to invoke a mainframe transaction via CICS. We use IIOP/OTS to implicitly propagate the transaction across the wire.

When the transaction commits (or aborts), the EJB servers use the OTS distributed two-phase commit protocol (as well as XA) to ensure that the database updates are atomic. In other words, all the updates to all the resource managers are either all committed or all rolled back; it's all-or-nothing. CORBA OTS gateways to CICS, IMS, Tuxedo, and MQSeries are available from InSession, BEA, Visigenic/Borland, and IBM. Gateways make it possible for existing resource managers to transparently participate in EJB transactions.

As an EJB application programmer, you do not have to write any special code to make all this happen. You invoke standard JDBC calls (without any commits or rollbacks). Behind the scenes, the EJB servers enlist all the DBMS managers that are part of the transaction. They take care of issuing the commit on behalf of your beans. They will also represent your beans in the two-phase commit negotiation.

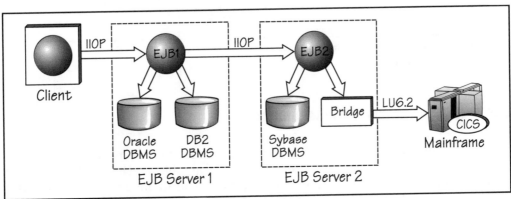

Figure 34-10. The Transparent Propagation of an EJB Transaction.

Figure 34-11 shows how a client uses the **java.jts.CurrentTransaction** interface to explicitly demarcate transaction boundaries. In this case, the client: 1) invokes *begin* on the CORBA **CurrentTransaction** object to start the transaction, 2) invokes EJB1 on Server 1 to update data inside Oracle and DB2 DBMSs, 3) invokes EJB2 on Server 2 to update data inside a Sybase DBMS and to invoke a mainframe transaction via CICS, and 4) completes the transaction by invoking *commit* on its **CurrentTransaction** object.

Under-the-cover IIOP automatically propagates the transaction context to all the EJB servers. When the client calls *commit*, the two servers use CORBA OTS to automatically perform the two-phase commit protocol. Again, if all this sounds a bit strange, you may want to read our introduction to CORBA OTS in **Instant CORBA**.

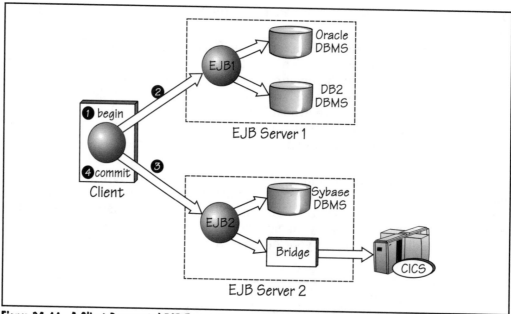

Figure 34-11. A Client-Demarcated EJB Transaction.

Declarative Transaction Management

One of the key concepts in EJB is that the container can interpose itself between every client method invocation on an enterprise bean object. This is why they want your servant to delegate the implementation to a separate instance via the CORBA Tie mechanism. This interposition makes it possible for an EJB container to take over the transaction management responsibilities. Your job is then to use simple declarative attributes to inform the container of the transactional needs of your beans. You specify these *transaction attributes* in your enterprise bean's deployment descriptor. A transaction attribute can be on a per-method basis or for an entire bean.

Table 34-1 explains the actions a container takes when it receives a call for a transactional bean. Each value of that attribute results in a different action on the part of the container.

Table 34-1. EJB's Declarative Transaction Attributes.

Transaction Attribute Value	Container Action
Not_Supported	The container invokes the bean's method outside the scope of a transaction. If the client calls within a transaction scope, the container suspends the transaction scope within the current thread before delegating the method call to the enterprise bean. The container resumes the suspended transaction when the bean completes the method call.
Bean_Managed	An enterprise bean with this attribute can issue explicit transaction calls using the **java.jts.CurrentTransaction** interface.
Requires	The container invokes the bean's method within the client's transaction. If the client is not part of a transaction, the container automatically starts a new transaction before delegating the call to the enterprise bean object. The container attempts to commit the transaction when the bean completes the call. The container performs the commit protocol before sending the method results back to the client.
Supports	The container invokes an enterprise bean with this attribute in the client's transaction. If the client is not part of a transaction, then the container invokes the method outside of a transaction; it does not start a new transaction.
Requires_New	The container always invokes a bean with this attribute inside a new transaction. The container will automatically start the new transaction before calling the bean; it then attempts to commit the transaction when the method completes. The container performs the commit protocol before it returns the method result to the client. Note that if a client request is associated with a transaction, the container suspends the incoming transaction; it resumes it when the new transaction completes.
Mandatory	The container always invokes a bean with this attribute inside the client's transaction. If the client is not part of a transaction, the container throws a **TransactionRequired** exception to the client.

Figure 34-12 shows how you would use declarative transaction attributes to let an EJB container automatically manage the propagation of transactions on your behalf. In this case, a non-transactional client invokes EJB1, which has a *Requires_new* value on its transactional attribute. So, the container starts a T1 transaction before passing the method call to EJB1. EJB1 then calls EJB2, which has a *Supports* value on its transactional attribute. So, the container will pass it the T1 transaction context. Finally, EJB2 calls EJB3, which has a *Mandatory* value in its transaction attribute. The container is very happy to oblige and also passes it the T1 transaction context. As a result, all the beans execute as part of the T1 transaction. The good news is that you don't have to write a single line of code to make all this happen.

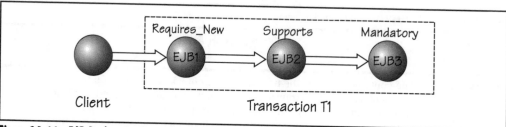

Figure 34-12. EJB Declarative Transactions: Scenario 1.

Figure 34-13 is another example of how you would use declarative transaction attributes with your beans. In this case, we're dealing with a transaction-savvy client. The client invokes *begin* on the CORBA **CurrentTransaction** object to start transaction T1; it then invokes EJB1, which has a *Supports* value on its transactional attribute. EJB1—now part of T1—first invokes EJB2 and then EJB3. EJB2 has a *Supports* value, so it happily joins the T1 transaction. However, EJB3 is marked as *Requires_New*. So the container automatically starts a new transaction on its behalf called T2, and then hands it the call. EJB3 in turn calls EJB4 and infects it with the T2 transaction. In this scenario, we end up with two independent transactions T1 and T2. Each transaction will enlist new supporters as it propagates its merry way.

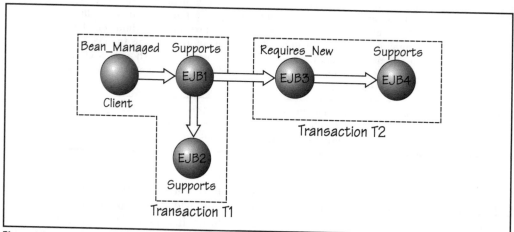

Figure 34-13. EJB Declarative Transactions: Scenario 2.

EJB PACKAGING

One of the great strengths of EJB is that it extends the existing JavaBeans packaging technology to take care of the needs of server-side beans. You can use EJB packaging to distribute a single enterprise bean or to distribute an entire server-side application built of multiple enterprise beans.

EJB-JAR and Manifest

Enterprise beans are packaged for deployment in a standard JAR called an *ejb-jar* file. An ejb-jar file contains: 1) the EJB's class files, 2) its *deployment descriptor*, and 3) a manifest that identifies the enterprise beans included in the JAR.

As usual, the manifest is named META-INF/MANIFEST.MF. The sections that provide information on enterprise beans use the following format:

```
Name = name of serialized (.ser) deployment descriptor file
Enterprise-Bean = True
```

For example:

```
Name: book/SmileyEJBDeployment.ser
Enterprise-Bean: True
```

Deployment Descriptor

You must include a *deployment descriptor* for each enterprise bean in your JAR. A deployment descriptor is a serialized instance of a **java.ejb.deployment.Entity-Descriptor** or **java.ejb.deployment.SessionDescriptor** object.

Security Descriptor

The EJB architecture also allows a container to perform declarative security management. Again, this means that you don't have to write code to protect your bean. However, this requires that you provide a *security descriptor*, which is a serialized instance of **java.ejb.deployment.SecurityDescriptor**.

The EJB Deployment Classes

Figure 34-14 shows the key classes in the *java.ejb.deployment* package. These classes describe the deployment and security properties of a bean. Think of them as glorified data structures. You include serialized versions of these classes in an ejb-jar to specify your bean's deployment and security attributes. The idea is to use an EJB deployment tool to set the values of these attributes for your bean; you then package the (.ser) files as part of an ejb-jar file. The container uses the getter functions to read the deployment descriptor from the ejb-jar file when it imports your bean.

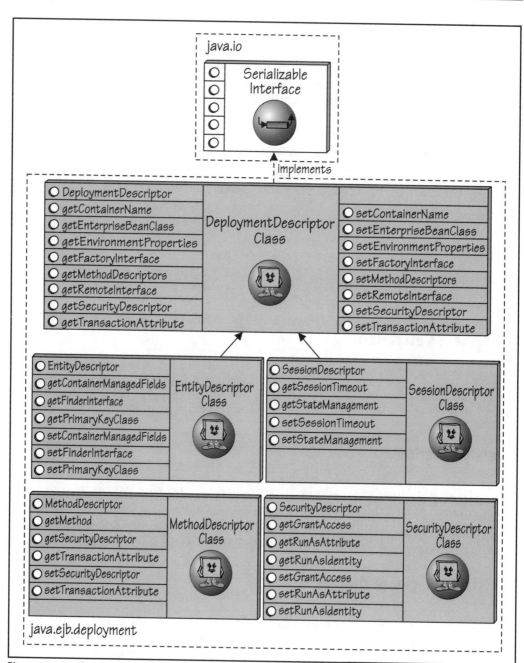

Figure 34-14. The EJB Deployment Classes.

Here's a quick description of these classes:

- The **DeploymentDescriptor** class is the common base class for the **Session-Descriptor** and **EntityDescriptor** classes. The *setSecurityDescriptor* method associates a **SecurityDescriptor** with this bean. It causes the container to apply the **SecurityDescriptor** to all the methods of your enterprise bean. You can override the per-bean security with a per-method security by using a **MethodDescriptor** object. The *setTransactionAttribute* method sets the enterprise bean's transaction attribute; the acceptable values of the transaction attribute are defined in the class **TransactionAttribute**. The transaction attribute applies to all the methods of the enterprise bean, unless you override it with a per-method **MethodDescriptor** object.

- The **EntityDescriptor** class defines the deployment descriptor for an entity enterprise bean. You use a serialized instance of this class as the standard format for passing an entity EJB's declarative attributes in the ejb-jar file.

- The **SessionDescriptor** class defines the deployment descriptor for a session enterprise bean. You use a serialized instance of this class as the standard format for passing a session EJB's declarative attributes in the ejb-jar file. You can declare the state management of a session bean to be *pinned*, which means a container can never deactivate it. You can declare it to be *stateful*, which means a container can deactivate it between transactions. Finally, you can declare it to be *stateless*, which means a container can use multiple instances of it.

- The **MethodDescriptor** class defines deployment information for a single method. This per-method information overrides any information you set at a per-bean level. You can provide a **MethodDescriptor** object for any remote method—including the EJB's remote interface, factory, and finder.

- The **SecurityDescriptor** class describes the security-related attributes of an EJB. You can use a **SecurityDescriptor** to cover an entire bean or on a per-method basis. The descriptor lets you specify the **Identity** that will be used to run this bean. It can be a client's identity, a specified user account, or a privileged account. It also lets you grant access to a bean and its methods—for example, you can grant an array of identities access to a specific method.

Again, you may find the actual class definitions to be helpful. So here they are:

Listing 34-14. The java.ejb.deployment.DeploymentDescriptor Class.

```
public class DeploymentDescriptor
extends java.lang.Object implements java.io.Serializable
{
  // Constructor
```

```
    public DeploymentDescriptor();

    // Methods
    public Name getContainerName();
    public Class getEnterpriseBeanClass();
    public Properties getEnvironmentProperties();
    public Class getFactoryInterface();
    public MethodDescriptor[] getMethodDescriptors();
    public MethodDescriptor getMethodDescriptors(int index);
    public Class getRemoteInterface();
    public SecurityDescriptor getSecurityDescriptor();
    public int getTransactionAttribute();
    public void setContainerName(Name value);
    public void setEnterpriseBeanClass(Class value);
    public void setEnvironmentProperties(Properties value);
    public void setFactoryInterface(Class value);
    public void setMethodDescriptors(int index, MethodDescriptor value);
    public void setMethodDescriptors(MethodDescriptor value[]);
    public void setRemoteInterface(Class value);
    public void setSecurityDescriptor(SecurityDescriptor value);
    public void setTransactionAttribute(int value);
}
```

Listing 34-15. The java.ejb.deployment.EntityDescriptor Class.

```
public class EntityDescriptor extends DeploymentDescriptor
{
  // Constructor
  public EntityDescriptor();

  // Methods
  public Field[] getContainerManagedFields();
  public Field getContainerManagedFields(int index);
  public Class getFinderInterface();
  public Class getPrimaryKeyClass();
  public void setContainerManagedFields(Field values[]);
  public void setContainerManagedFields(int index, Field value);
  public void setFinderInterface(Class value);
  public void setPrimaryKeyClass(Class value);
}
```

Listing 34-16. The java.ejb.deployment.SessionDescriptor Class.

```
public class SessionDescriptor extends DeploymentDescriptor
```

```
{
 // Constants
 public final static int PINNED;
 public final static int stateful;
 public final static int STATELESS;

 // Constructor
 public SessionDescriptor();

 // Methods
 public int getSessionTimeout();
 public int getStateManagement();
 public void setSessionTimeout(int value);
 public void setStateManagement();
}
```

Listing 34-17. The java.ejb.deployment.MethodDescriptor Class.

```
public class MethodDescriptor extends java.lang.Object
{
 // Constructor
 public MethodDescriptor(Method method);

 // Methods
 public Method getMethod();
 public SecurityDescriptor getSecurityDescriptor();
 public int getTransactionAttribute();
 public void setSecurityDescriptor(SecurityDescriptor value);
 public void setTransactionAttribute(int value);
}
```

Listing 34-18. The java.ejb.deployment.SecurityDescriptor Class.

```
public class SecurityDescriptor extends java.lang.Object
{
 // Constants
 public final static int Client;
 public final static int SpecifiedUser;
 public final static int System;


 // Constructor
 public SecurityDescriptor();
```

```
// Methods
public Identity[] getGrantAccess();
public Identity getGrantAccess(int index);
public int getRunAsAttribute();
public Identity getRunAsIdentity();
public void setGrantAccess(Identity values[]);
public void setGrantAccess(int index, Identity value);
public void setRunAsAttribute(int value);
public void setRunAsIdentity(Identity value);
}
```

Listing 34-19. The java.ejb.deployment.TransactionAttribute Class.

```
public class TransactionAttribute extends java.lang.Object
{
// Constants
public final static int BEAN_MANAGED;
public final static int MANDATORY;
public final static int NOT_SUPPORTED;
public final static int REQUIRED;
public final static int REQUIRES_NEW;
public final static int SUPPORTS;
}
```

EJB DESIGN GUIDELINES

This is a very preliminary set of design guidelines for CORBA EJB programmers:

✔ *Your remote interface must follow the CORBA RMI/IDL subset.* Remember the RMI/IDL subset we describe in Chapter 21? Your EJB interfaces must adhere to this subset.

✔ *Define a remote factory interface.* The factory interface must follow the RMI/IDL subset rules. The signature of the *create* methods you define must match your bean's **ejbCreate** methods.

✔ *Don't mess around with threads.* You must not start new threads in your code. Also, don't attempt to terminate the running thread. Finally, don't use thread synchronization primitives or class variables. The idea is that OTMs will provide the multithreading and load-balancing. So don't get in their way.

✔ ***Don't issue commits or rollbacks.*** A transaction-enabled EJB that uses JDBC is not allowed to invoke commit or rollback methods. If your EJB is not transaction-enabled, then it's OK to issue commits or rollbacks.

✔ ***Give your containers a full ejb-jar package.*** The more EJB-relelated information you give to a container, the better it can manage your beans. So make sure to provide a full ejb-jar that includes the following classes: all the EJB bean implementation classes, the EJB servant Tie class, EJB factory, EJB Finder, the deployment and security descriptors, any classes the EJB depends on, and a manifest that identifies the EJBs in the ejb-jar file. You may also want to package in the same JAR CORBA client stubs for your EJBs, factories, and finders.

Currently, we don't have any experience with EJB systems. We're sure this list will grow as we start to experiment with these new types of systems. We also expect that tools will automate a lot of this work.

CONCLUSION

EJB augments CORBA with declarative transactions, a server-side component framework, and tool-oriented deployment and security descriptors. CORBA augments EJB with a distributed object framework, multilingual client support, a world-class *Object Transaction Service (OTS)*, IIOP interoperability, and transaction propagation. If you add CORBA and EJB, you get both a scalable and toolable server-side component story. It's the basic foundation technology for the Object Web.

We delayed the publication of this book to include this chapter on EJB; it was well worth the wait. For us, even this pre-Beta version of EJB is a dream come true. Our regret is that we don't have working code examples to show you. Oh well. It's something we can leave for a Third Edition. In any case, we've seen enough to believe that the marriage of EJB and CORBA/OTS will change the way we develop the server side of our distributed systems. We also understand that there's room for improvement. The specification we reviewed in this chapter still has a few holes.

Part 8
The Grand Finale: Club Med
with CORBA/JavaBeans

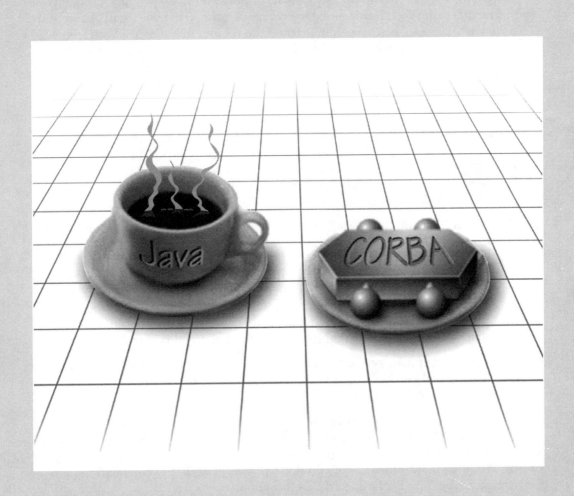

An Introduction to Part 8

Part 8 is the grand finale that brings together all the elements of this book—including CORBA, JDBC, Java applets, and JavaBeans. The idea is to create a complete 3-tier client/server application for the Web using CORBA and JavaBeans. To pick on a fun topic, we will develop a fictitious Web-based reservation system for Club Med.

In this 3-tier client/server application, Club Med client beans invoke operations on CORBA middle-tier server objects via an IIOP ORB. The server objects provide the business logic, and they store their persistent data in a JDBC-compliant SQL database. This representative application should help us determine if the Object Web is ready to take on the lucrative OLTP market.

Here's what we will be covering in Part 8:

- *Chapter 35* is an overview of the Club Med application. We provide a framework for documenting Web-based client/server applications that use CORBA. We start with what the user sees. We then go over the remote methods that are triggered by users interacting with their GUI beans. We publish the IDL for the CORBA interfaces the server exports to its clients. We then go over the structure of the Club Med SQL database. We also write a small JDBC program that creates the Club Med database.

- *Chapter 36* presents the code for the Club Med client beans—**BargainHunter-Bean** and **ClubMedBean**. We will develop these beans using three popular visual builder tools for beans: Symantec's *Visual Café*, Borland's *JBuilder*, and IBM's *VisualAge for Java*. We will briefly compare these tools and show you how they handle the invocation of CORBA server-side objects. In one case, we will even make the CORBA server-side objects look like invisible JavaBeans to the tool.

- *Chapter 37* is about the server side of Club Med. As you would expect, we use CORBA server objects to provide the middle tier. These objects interact with client beans on the front-end and SQL databases on the back-end. The interfaces to the server objects are defined in CORBA IDL; they provide a binding contract between the server and its clients. We chose to implement stateless server objects. So we maintain all the persistent information in the Club Med SQL database, and then we access it using JDBC wrapper objects. Once again, we reuse the object Dispenser—our poor man's TP Monitor. Club Med couldn't scale without it.

- *Chapter 38* summarizes our client/server experience with CORBA/Java. We look at the good, the bad, and the ugly. We also explain what remains to be done and where we go from here.

So, are you ready for another programming trilogy? The good news is that a lot of the material will feel familiar. By the time you finish reading Part 8, all the pieces should finally snap together. Yes, you will experience the inner beauty of CORBA/Java Nirvana! However, if you don't reach Nirvana, the consolation prize is that you will have finally completed this long book.

Chapter 35

The Club Med 3-Tier Client/Server

We will end this book with a grand finale program that brings together CORBA, JDBC, and JavaBeans. The idea is to create a complete 3-tier client/server application for the Web using CORBA and JavaBeans. To pick a fun topic, we will develop a fictitious Web-based reservation system for Club Med.

In this 3-tier client/server application, Club Med client beans invoke operations on CORBA middle-tier server objects via an IIOP ORB. The server objects provide the business logic and store their persistent data in a JDBC-compliant SQL database. This representative application should help us determine if the Object Web is ready to take on the lucrative OLTP market.

In general, the best way to understand a client/server application is to: 1) develop some client-driven scenarios, 2) go over the published list of interfaces a server exports to its clients—preferably in IDL, and 3) go over the database structure. In a CORBA system, the IDL is the published contract between the server and its clients.

We will develop the Club Med client/server program in a three-chapter series. In this first chapter of the trilogy, we explain the Club Med application. We start with what the user sees. We then describe the remote methods triggered by users interacting with their GUI beans. We publish the IDL for the CORBA interfaces the server exports to its clients. We then describe the structure of the Club Med SQL database. We also write a small JDBC program that creates the Club Med database. At the end of this chapter, you should have a good feeling for what the Club Med application does and how the pieces come together.

In the next chapter, we present the code for the Club Med client beans. In the final chapter of the series, we present the code for the server side of Club Med. We will then have all the pieces to run this application.

THE CLUB MED CLIENT

A client/server application is by its very nature *client-driven*. A Java-driven applet places the controls of the client in the hands of a user manipulating form-like visual beans. Whatever the user does to these beans becomes the source of CORBA method invocations. Meanwhile, the server objects passively wait on requests from clients to trigger the execution of their methods.

In this section, we show how a user interacts with a **ClubMedBean** within an applet front-end. As we walk through the scenario, we will point out the bean events that trigger method invocations on the server. You'll find that this scenario does more to explain the Club Med application than a hundred pages of non-visual specifications. We're only sorry that you can't see the application live on the pages of your book. But we'll substitute a live demo of Club Med with "not so live" screen captures. We will also annotate the scenario with some juicy tidbits on what goes on behind the scenes or, to be more exact, "behind the glass" of the screen. We will also introduce our second bean, the **BargainHunterBean**.

Ten Minutes in the Life of a Club Med Bean

In this section, we give you a snapshot of ten minutes in the life of a **ClubMedBean**. We present a scenario in which Lucky Bob first books a trip to paradise. Later, reality catches up with Bob. So he cancels his trip. Yes, it's now Unlucky Bob. Let's go over this roller-coaster scenario (see Figure 35-1):

1. *Point to the Club Med HTTP server.* Start a Java-enabled browser—for example, Netscape Communicator—and then point to your Club Med server's Web page. You will see a tabbed panel with a list of clubs (see Figure 35-2). *Behind the scenes:* The browser downloads an applet that contains the **ClubMedBean**. As part of its initialization, the bean invokes the *getClubs* method on the CORBA server object to populate the list of clubs.

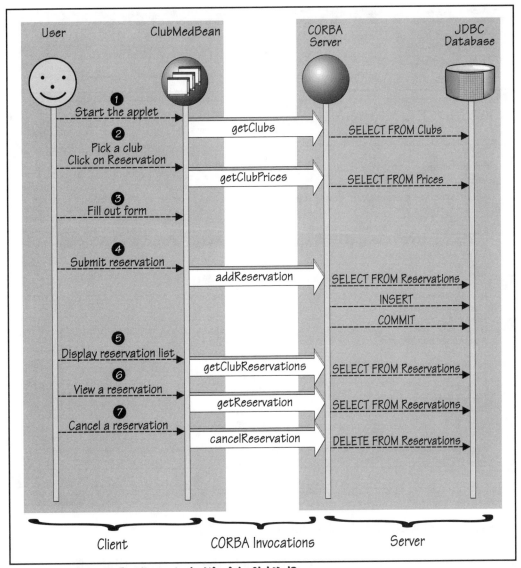

Figure 35-1. Scenario: Ten Minutes in the Life of the ClubMedBean.

2. **Select a club.** Select a club from the list and then click on the Make Reservation tab. **Behind the scenes:** The bean first obtains the selection. It then invokes the *getClubPrices* method on the CORBA server object. Finally, it displays a reservation panel with the weekly prices for the club.

3. **Fill the reservation panel.** In this scenario, Lucky Bob makes a reservation for two in Club Med Playa Blanca, Mexico (see Figure 35-3). Notice that the

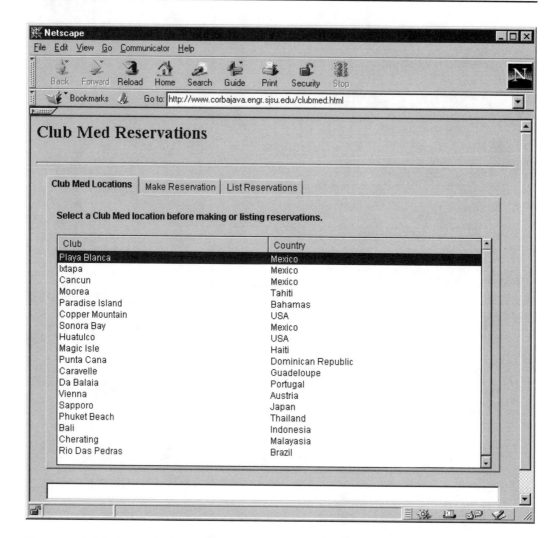

Figure 35-2. ClubMedBean: The Club Med Locations Panel.

fares are different for each week. Bob picks the first week of July. Then he tabs from field to field to fill-in the required information. The data must match the mask type for each field. ***Behind the scenes:*** Each field is an individual bean. The entire multi-paneled application is a bean—we call it the **ClubMedBean**. The embedded beans interact with each other to calculate the total fare for this escapade (see Figure 35-3). They validate the data you enter and perform the calculations without getting the server involved.

4. ***Submit the reservation.*** Bob clicks on the Submit button to make the reservation. ***Behind the scenes:*** The **ClubMedBean** gathers all the data for this transaction and invokes the *addReservation* method on the CORBA server

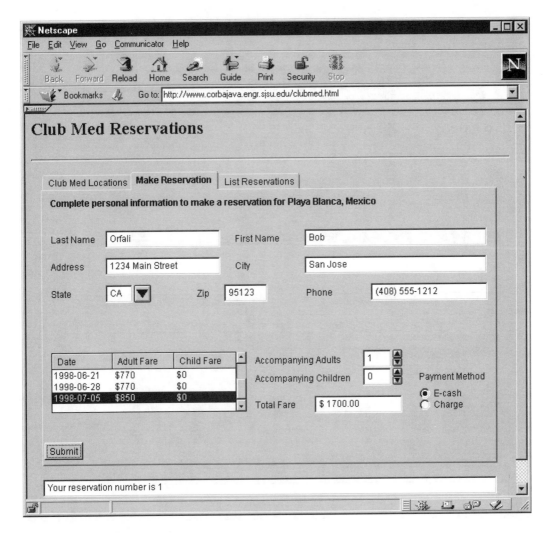

Figure 35-3. ClubMedBean: The ClubMedBean Make Reservation Panel.

object. If the transaction succeeds, the CORBA server returns a confirmation number. This number is displayed in the status field at the bottom of the panel.

5. ***Display the reservation list.*** Later, Bob clicks on the List Reservations tab to obtain a list of reservations. ***Behind the scenes:*** The bean first obtains the Club selection. It then invokes the *getClubReservations* method on the CORBA server object. The server returns a guest list for this club. The bean displays the list in a listbox (see Figure 35-4).

6. ***View the reservation.*** Bob clicks on his name. In this scenario, we assume that he has the proper authorization credentials. ***Behind the scenes:*** The bean

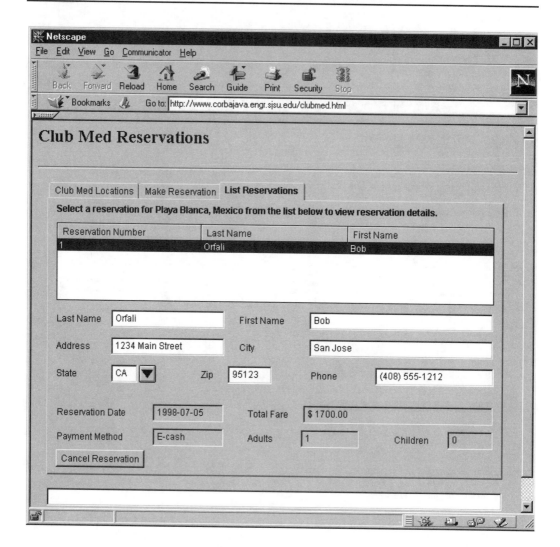

Figure 35-4. ClubMedBean List Reservations Panel.

first obtains the name you select. It then invokes the *getReservation* method on the CORBA server object. The server returns the reservation details. The bean displays these details in the bottom half of the panel (see Figure 35-4).

7. ***Cancel the reservation***. Bob clicks on the Cancel Reservation button to cancel his trip to paradise. ***Behind the scenes:*** The bean first obtains the selection data. It then invokes the *cancelReservation* method on the CORBA server object. The server returns a cancellation number. This number is displayed in the status field. Bob will not be going to Playa Blanca.

Notice that the bean within the applet can do quite a bit of local interaction with the user before invoking the remote CORBA methods. So there's a good balance between the client and the server sides.

The Bargain Hunter Bean

Figure 35-5 shows a screen capture of our second bean called the **BargainHunter-Bean**. Again, this bean runs inside an applet. You can use it to find the best Club Med bargains for a particular week. When you click on a week, the bean invokes the *getBargainInfo* method on the CORBA server and returns the Club with the lowest prices for this week. It then displays the name of the Club and the adult fare.

Figure 35-6 shows two minutes in the life of a **BargainHunterBean**. Lets go over the client/server interactions:

1. ***Point to the Bargain Hunter's Web page***. Start a Java-enabled browser—for example, Netscape—and then point to the Bargain Hunter's Web page. You will see a bean that displays a list of weeks within an applet. ***Behind the scenes:***

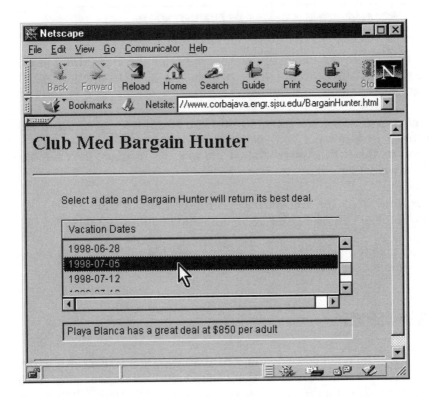

Figure 35-5. The BargainHunterBean.

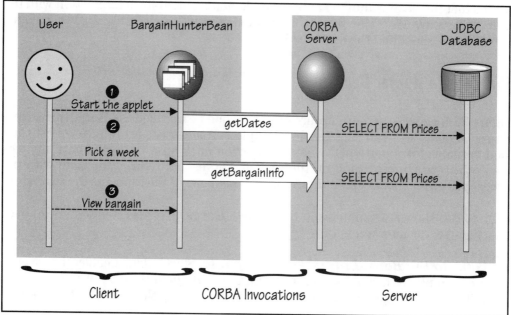

Figure 35-6. Scenario: Two Minutes in the Life of the BargainHunterBean.

The browser downloads an applet that contains the **BargainHunterBean**. As part of its initialization, the bean invokes the *getDates* method on the CORBA server object to populate the list of dates.

2. ***Select a date***. Pick a week for your Club Med vacation. ***Behind the scenes:*** The bean first obtains your selection. It then invokes the *getBargainInfo* method on the CORBA server object. Finally, it displays the Club Med bargain for this week (see Figure 35-5).

3. ***Plan your vacation accordingly***. You can now decide if this is the bargain that will make you pack your swimsuits and head for paradise.

In the next chapter, we will try to visually assemble the client and server sides of this very simple bean (without writing any code).

CLUB MED SERVER

Club Med is a 3-tier client/server solution. In the spirit of reuse, we borrow elements of the server-side framework from the 3-tier Debit-Credit (see Chapter 26). In this section, we first explain the elements of the 3-tier Club Med. Then we go over the IDL-defined interfaces a server exports to its clients.

The 3-Tier Club Med

In the 3-tier Club Med, CORBA client beans talk to CORBA server objects. The server objects in turn talk to one or more DBMSs via JDBC (see Figure 35-7). The Club Med client is provided by two beans: **ClubMedBean** and **BargainHunter-Bean**. The middle-tier server consists of three main classes: 1) a **ClubMedDispenser** that manages a pool of server objects, 2) a pool of server objects of the class **ClubMed**, and 3) a pool of helper objects of the class **ClubMedDB**—these are worker objects with persistent JDBC connections. The third tier of Club Med consists of the JDBC database—this is where the persistent state is stored. Notice that the Club Med also has its own **ClubMedAdmin** utility. This is a standalone Java JDBC program that you use to create a *ClubMed* database as well as its tables.

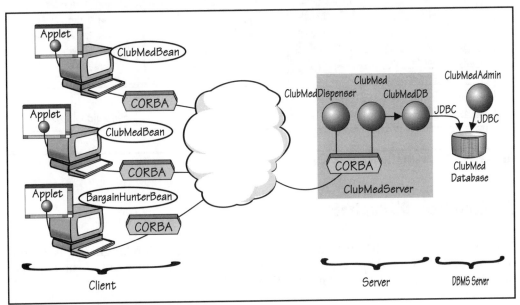

Figure 35-7. The 3-Tier Club Med.

Like its Debit-Credit counterpart, the **ClubMedDispenser** maintains a pool of server objects that it assigns to clients on a first-come basis. Instead of dispensing **DebitCredit** objects, it dispenses **ClubMed** objects. Each **ClubMed** object starts its own **ClubMedDB** JDBC helper object. It should all be very familiar. Of course, the idea here is that we're creating a poor man's scheduler that manages a pool of prestarted multithreaded server objects. The **ClubMedDispenser** allocates these objects on demand. A client must release its checked-out object when it completes its work. It's all part of the OLTP sharing etiquette that we described in Chapter 26.

The Club Med Server: What the Client Sees

Figure 35-8 shows the two CORBA interfaces a Club Med server exposes to its clients: **ClubMed** and **ClubMedDispenser**. A client obtains a **ClubMed** object by invoking the *reserveClubMedObject* method on a **ClubMedDispenser** object. The client can then invoke the **ClubMed** object's interfaces. When it completes its work, the client must release the remote object by invoking *releaseClubMed-Object*.

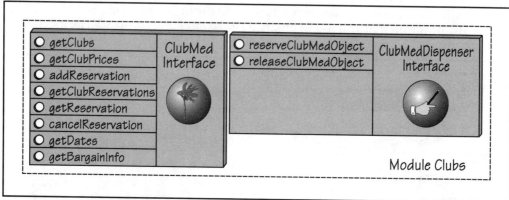

Figure 35-8. The ClubMedServer CORBA Interfaces.

The Club Med IDL Contract

The beauty of CORBA IDL is that it makes a great specification language. It defines the contract between the server and its clients. Here's the fine print of the contract between the Club Med server and its clients:

Listing 35-1. The Club Med CORBA Contract: Clubmed.idl.

```
// ClubMed.idl
module Clubs
{
  exception ClubException
  { string reason;
  };

  struct clubStruct
  {
    string name;
    string country;
```

```
};
typedef sequence<clubStruct> clubSeq;

struct pricesStruct
{
  string date;
  short  adultFare;
  short  childFare;
};
typedef sequence<pricesStruct> pricesSeq;

typedef long resvNo;

struct resvStruct
{
  string club;
  string fname;
  string lname;
  string weekDate;
  string address;
  string city;
  string state;
  string zip;
  string phone;
  string totalFare;
  short  partyAdults;
  short  partyChildren;
  string payment;
};
typedef sequence<resvStruct> resvSeq;

struct resvSummaryStruct
{
  resvNo resv;
  string fname;
  string lname;
};
typedef sequence<resvSummaryStruct> resvSumSeq;

typedef sequence<string> dates;

struct bargainStruct
{
  string club;
  short  adultFare;
```

```
   };

   interface ClubMed
   {
     clubSeq       getClubs();
     pricesSeq     getClubPrices(in string club);
     resvNo        addReservation(in string club, in resvStruct resvData);
     resvSumSeq    getClubReservations(in string club);
     resvStruct    getReservation(in resvNo resv);
     boolean       cancelReservation(in resvNo resv);
     dates         getDates();
     bargainStruct getBargainInfo(in string date);
   };

   interface ClubMedDispenser
   {
     ClubMed reserveClubMedObject() raises (ClubException);
     void    releaseClubMedObject(in ClubMed clubMedObject)
                             raises (ClubException);
   };

};
```

This IDL defines two interfaces: **ClubMed** and **ClubMedDispenser**. Notice that in addition to the method signatures, we also use the IDL to define the data structures that we pass in the parameters. IDL is a comprehensive client/server specification language. And it's also very readable. You don't need a law degree to read all the fine print.

CLUB MED DATABASE

The ClubMed database consists of three tables: **Clubs**, **Prices**, and **Reservations**. Here are the SQL DDL statements that create these tables:

```
CREATE TABLE Clubs(  Club        CHAR(32) NOT NULL,
                     Country     CHAR(32) NOT NULL);
CREATE TABLE Prices( Club        CHAR(32) NOT NULL,
                     WeekDate    CHAR(12) NOT NULL,
                     AdultPrice  SMALLINT NOT NULL,
```

```
                              ChildPrice     SMALLINT NOT NULL );

CREATE TABLE Reservations( ResvNo          INT NOT NULL,
                           Club            CHAR(32) NOT NULL,
                           WeekDate        CHAR(12) NOT NULL,
                           LastName        CHAR(32) NOT NULL,
                           FirstName       CHAR(32) NOT NULL,
                           PartyAdults     SMALLINT NOT NULL,
                           PartyChildren   SMALLINT NOT NULL,
                           TotalFare       CHAR(12),
                           PaymentMethod   CHAR(9),
                           PhoneNo         CHAR(20),
                           ADDRESS         CHAR(32),
                           City            CHAR(32),
                           State           CHAR(2),
                            Zip             CHAR(10));
```

We will now write a small JDBC program called CreateClubMed that creates a Club Med database and its tables.

The CreateClubMed Program

The CreateClubMed program consists of two Java classes: **CreateClubMed** and **ClubMedAdmin**. Here's a description of what these classes do:

- **CreateClubMed** provides a *main* method that: 1) creates a **ClubMedAdmin** object, and 2) invokes the *createDB* method on this new object.

- **ClubMedAdmin** is a helper class that creates a ClubMed database and its tables. You invoke *createDB* to create a new database. This method will then: 1) connect to a database server, 2) delete an existing ClubMed database, 3) create a new ClubMed database, 4) connect to the new ClubMed database, 5) create the ClubMed tables, and 6) add indexes to the tables. The rest of the methods in this class are helper functions. They help *createDB* accomplish its task.

There are no surprises in this program. The code follows.

Listing 35-2. The CreateClubMed Class

```
// CreateClubMed.java

class CreateClubMed {
```

```java
public static void main(String argv[])
{
  try
  {
    ClubMedAdmin myClubMed = new ClubMedAdmin();
    myClubMed.createDB();
    System.out.println("Database ClubMed created");

  } catch( Exception e )
  {
    System.out.println("Creation of database ClubMed failed");
    e.printStackTrace();
    System.exit(1);
  }
  System.exit(0);
}
}
```

Listing 35-3. The ClubMedAdmin Class.

```java
// ClubMedAdmin.java
import java.net.URL;
import java.sql.*;


class ClubMedAdmin
{
  Connection con;
  Statement stmt;
  PreparedStatement pstmt;

  public void createDB() throws Exception
  {
    connect("LocalServer", "master", "sa", "");
    dropClubMed();
    createClubMed();
    closeConnection();
    connect("LocalServer", "ClubMed", "sa", "");
    createClubMedTables();
    createClubMedIndexes();
  }
```

```java
public void connect(String datasource, String db,
                    String id, String pw)
                    throws Exception
{
  try
  {
    // Load the jdbc-odbc bridge driver
    Class.forName ("sun.jdbc.odbc.JdbcOdbcDriver");

    String url   = "jdbc:odbc:" + datasource + ";database=" + db;
    System.out.println("Connecting to " + url);
    con = DriverManager.getConnection(url, id, pw);
  } catch(Exception e)
  { System.err.println("System Exception in connect");
    System.err.println(e);
    throw e;
  }
}


public void closeConnection() throws Exception
{
  try
  {
    System.out.println("Closing connection");
    con.close();
  } catch (Exception e)
  { System.err.println("System Exception in closeConnection");
    System.err.println(e);
    throw e;
  }
}


private void dropClubMed() throws Exception
{
  try
  {
    System.out.println("Dropping database ClubMed");
    stmt = con.createStatement();
    stmt.execute("DROP DATABASE ClubMed");
    stmt.close();
  } catch(Exception e)
  { System.err.println("System Exception in dropClubMed");
    System.err.println(e);
```

```java
    }
}


private void createClubMed() throws Exception
{
  try
  {
    System.out.println("Creating database ClubMed");
    stmt = con.createStatement();
    stmt.execute("CREATE DATABASE ClubMed on clubs = 5");
    stmt.close();
  } catch(Exception e)
  { System.err.println("System Exception in createClubMed");
    System.err.println(e);
    throw e;
  }
}


private void createClubMedTables() throws Exception
{
  try
  {
    System.out.println("Creating ClubMed tables");
    stmt = con.createStatement();
    stmt.execute("CREATE TABLE Clubs( " +
                "Club           CHAR(32) NOT NULL, " +
                "Country        CHAR(32) NOT NULL) ");

    stmt.execute("CREATE TABLE Prices(" +
                "Club           CHAR(32) NOT NULL, " +
                "WeekDate       CHAR(12) NOT NULL, " +
                "AdultPrice     SMALLINT NOT NULL, " +
                "ChildPrice     SMALLINT NOT NULL )");

    stmt.execute("CREATE TABLE RESERVATIONS(" +
                "ResvNo         INT NOT NULL, " +
                "Club           CHAR(32) NOT NULL, " +
                "WeekDate       CHAR(12) NOT NULL, " +
                "LastName       CHAR(32) NOT NULL, " +
                "FirstName      CHAR(32) NOT NULL, " +
                "PartyAdults    SMALLINT NOT NULL, " +
                "PartyChildren  SMALLINT NOT NULL, " +
                "TotalFare      CHAR(12), "  +
```

```
                    "PaymentMethod  CHAR(9),  "  +
                    "PhoneNo        CHAR(20), "  +
                    "ADDRESS        CHAR(32), "  +
                    "City           CHAR(32), "  +
                    "State          CHAR(2),  "  +
                    "Zip            CHAR(10))");

        con.commit();
        stmt.close();
      } catch(Exception e)
      { System.err.println("System Exception in createClubMedTables");
        System.err.println(e);
        throw e;
      }
  }


  private void createClubMedIndexes() throws Exception
  {
    try
    {
      System.out.println("Creating ClubMed indexes");

      stmt = con.createStatement();
      stmt.execute("CREATE UNIQUE INDEX CLUBSX1 ON CLUBS(Club)");
       stmt.execute("CREATE UNIQUE INDEX PRICESX1 ON Prices(Club, WeekDate
)");
      stmt.execute("CREATE INDEX RESERVX1 ON RESERVATIONS(Club, WeekDate)");

      con.commit();
      stmt.close();
    } catch(Exception e)
    { System.err.println("System Exception in createClubMedIndexes");
      System.err.println(e);
      throw e;
    }
  }
}
```

Compile the CreateClubMed Program

We're now ready to compile the CreateClubMed JDBC program. Make sure you've
installed Symantec Visual Café (which includes the JDBC packages that are part of

JavaSoft's JDK 1.1). To compile, go to the appropriate directory and type the following commands at the prompt:

```
prompt> javac -d \CorbaJavaBook.2e\classes CreateClubMed
prompt> javac -d \CorbaJavaBook.2e\classes ClubMedAdmin
```

The -d option tells the compiler to put the (.class) files it creates into the directory we specify—in this case, the *\CorbaJavaBook.2e\classes* subdirectory.

If all goes well, you should have some compiled Java code that you can now run.

Run the CreateClubMed Program

We're now ready to create a ClubMed database. But first, you must install your favorite ODBC-compliant DBMS. Note that the *CreateBank* program uses the *Intersolv* JDBC-to-ODBC driver that is part of JDK 1.1. Consequently, the program should work with any ODBC-compliant DBMS.

To run the program, you must first install a database that supports JDBC and ODBC. In this test, we will use Microsoft *SQL Server 6.5*. To install SQL Server, follow the instructions on the CD-ROM.

You can now create a ClubMed database and load it with data. At the prompt, enter the following command:

```
prompt> java CreateClubMed
```

We now have a database with some tables and indexes. But we still need to load it with some data. To load the database, execute the *loaddata.bat* file that we provide with the CD-ROM. At the prompt, enter the following command:

```
prompt> loaddata
```

This batch file uses the SQL Server *bcp* utility to load ASCII-delimited data from two files we provide: *prices.del* and *clubs.del*.

CONCLUSION

We now have a ClubMed database full of data. So, where do we go from here? The next step is to create the Club Med client beans and their applet containers. We must also create the CORBA server objects. This is exactly what we will do in the next two chapters. We will first start with the client side of the application.

Chapter 36

The Club Med Client Beans

Club Med is a new-breed of 3-tier client/server application for the Web. It is a new breed because it uses CORBA and JavaBeans instead of HTTP/CGI for its client/server interactions. In this chapter, we create two client beans—**ClubMed-Bean** and **BargainHunterBean**—that we package inside applet containers. The first bean is really an entire client application inside a bean. It consists of a tabbed folder with multiple panels. You may have noticed from the last chapter that our panels look a little more polished than your everyday Java applet. This is because we created them using AWT's powerful *gridbag layout* (see the next Briefing Box). The second bean is the minimalist **BargainHunterBean** that we also described in the last chapter.

In the last edition of this book, we had to manually code our Club Med client application. It was not a pretty sight. The code went on for over 20 pages. We discovered the hard way that gridbag was really meant for tools, not humans. The good news is that there are now over 20 tools that can help us create bean-based front-ends. Two of the tools we cover in this chapter—Symantec *Visual Café* and Borland *JBuilder*—let you create gridbag layouts by directly placing components on a canvas. Of course, they still require that you fine-tune the last 10% of a visual placement to make it look right.

The plan for this chapter is to create the same **ClubMedBean** using *Visual Café* and *JBuilder*. Both of these tools come with very rich palettes of third-party beans. They both make it very easy to visually assemble and layout beans via drag-and-drop. Furthermore, they both let you assemble beans into a variety of containers—including applets and applications. Finally, they both let you package beans inside JARs. Visual Café provides a powerful visual programming metaphor for connecting beans; it also provides an excellent bean wizard that helps you create your bean metadata. *JBuilder* has its share of excellent features; it also includes a built-in ORB—*VisiBroker for Java*. So we show you how to create the same bean using both tools. Then you get to decide which one you like more.

In this chapter, we also use IBM's *VisualAge for Java* to create the **BargainHunterBean**. This tool is a dog when it comes to visual layout. It has neither the gridbag layout capabilities of its rivals nor the rich set of bundled components. We also found it to be overly clumsy to use—for example, it requires that you explicitly import every bean and Java class into its environment. However, when it comes to wiring client/server beans—or visual programming—*VisualAge for Java* has no rival. This product has the best visual programming environment in the industry.

The **BargainHunterBean** has a very simple GUI. Consequently, it lets us show-off VisualAge's client/server prowess without getting entangled in the layout. In particular, we're interested in the visual wiring of CORBA beans. We also introduce a CORBA bean delegate that lets you visually program CORBA components today. So, you don't have to wait for CORBA beans to get started.

FYI

What Is Gridbag Layout?

Briefing

The **GridBagLayout** class is a flexible layout manager. It aligns components horizontally and vertically inside a grid without requiring that the components be of the same size. Each component occupies one or more cells—or a *display area*. Each component in a gridbag uses a different set of constraints as defined by the component's **GridBagConstraints** object. This object specifies how the component is to be laid out within its display area. These constraint objects let you use the screen real estate more effectively. Note that **GridBagLayout** is the most powerful layout manager that AWT provides; it is also the most complicated. Remember that the idea behind these AWT layout managers is to provide geometry-independent placement so that your visual objects can be ported to the maximum number of platforms. You do not hard code the positional layout of your components. Instead, you provide hints that help the layout manager determine the most optimal arrangement. ❑

THE VISUAL CAFÉ CLUB MED BEAN

Symantec *Visual Café 2.1*—released in December 1997—is a second-generation JavaBeans tool from Symantec. The *Professional Development Edition (PDE)* version of this tool includes over 100+ JavaBeans, the JIT compiler 3.0, and a visual development environment for beans. This latest release also adds a bean wizard, automatic gridbag layout, and improved JAR packaging, and it fixes a ton of bugs.

In this section, we first tell you a little bit about bean development, *Visual Café* style. Then we walk you through the **ClubMedBean**. Finally, we explain how this client bean invokes CORBA middle-tier server objects.

Developing JavaBeans with Visual Café 2.1

Here are the steps you follow to create and package a bean using Visual Café:

1. ***Start a new project using the bean wizard***. You start the Visual Café development by selecting from a number of default project templates and wizards. In this case, pick the *bean wizard* (see Figure 36-1). The wizard lets you create the following types of beans: *singular, composite, container, non-visual,* and *custom*. Click on composite to create a bean that can contain other beans inside a static container—meaning that the end-user can't add beans to it at run time. Give your bean a name and package name. Your bean will be derived from **Panel**. You can override the parent methods and add new properties using property wizard.

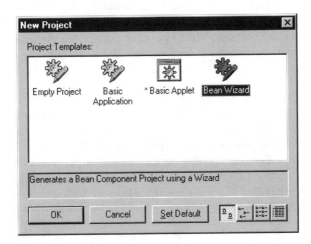

Figure 36-1. Create a New Project Using the Bean Wizard.

2. *Define the properties and methods for your bean.* Your composite bean is derived from **Panel**. You can override the parent methods and add new properties using the property wizard (see Figure 36-2). Finally, the bean wizard will display a dialog that lets you specify one or more icons for your bean. When you're done, click on finish.

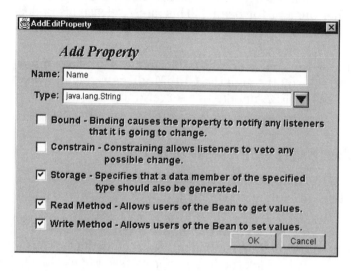

Figure 36-2. Define the Properties of Your Bean.

3. *Drag-and-drop beans into a visual form.* To create a composite visual bean, drag-and-drop components from the palette into a form. Visual Café automatically adds Java source code to your bean class for each bean that you drop into the form. Right-button click on your class file to view your code using the *Source Editor*. The Visual Café palette includes a rich selection of beans—including JFC components, KL Group widgets, and composite beans such as calendar, tabbed panel, tree, and grid. It also comes with invisible beans such as a timer control.

4. *Customize each bean using its property list.* Click on any bean to display its property sheet—Symantec calls it a *property list*. You can then change the embedded bean's properties. Visual Café will automatically reflect your property changes in the form and source editor. Figure 36-3 shows a form with four embedded beans. On the right, you can see the property list for the selected bean. On the left, the project window's class browser displays your **NewBean** class and its **BeanInfo**. Notice that the class includes the components we just added to the form. You can click on the class to open the source editor.

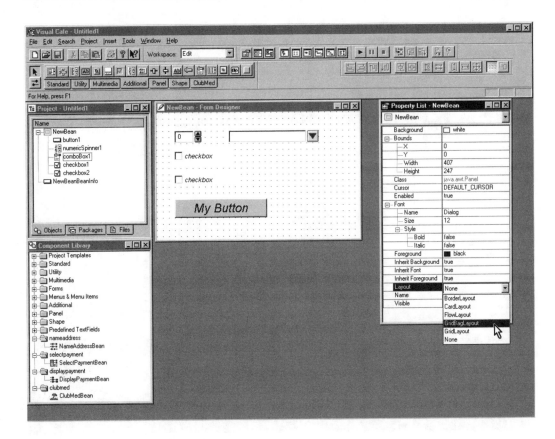

Figure 36-3. Customize Each Bean in the Form.

5. ***Convert to gridbag layout***. Visual Café's default mode for laying out components is *exact positioning* or (*null layout*). Click on the form to display its
property list (see Figure 36-3). Then select gridbag layout. Visual Café will
capture most of your intended layout in gridbag layout form. You may have to
set a few of the gridbag constraint properties to fine-tune your placement.
Remember, this is the 10% manual effort we told you about. The good news is
that this release of Visual Café gets you 90% there (it's miles ahead of the
previous release). At the end of this process, you'll have a platform-neutral
gridbag layout.

6. ***Wire your embedded beans using the Interaction Wizard***. To add
interactions between components, first click on the interaction wizard icon (see
annotation on Figure 36-4). Then simply click on any component (the source)
and wire it to a target. The Interaction Wizard will show you the events the
source generates and the methods that the target accepts (see Figure 36-5).
Pick a source/target combination to make the connection. The wizard will

Interaction Wizard

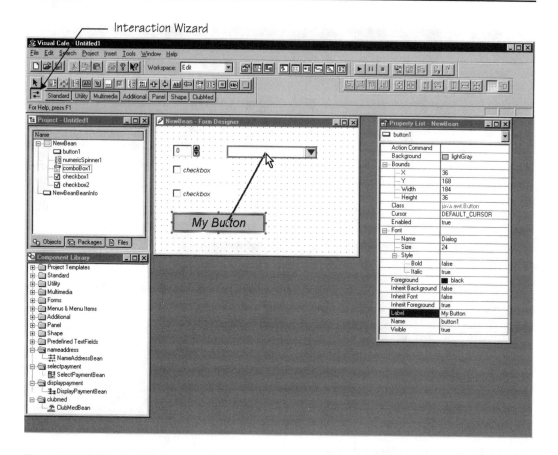

Figure 36-4. Rubber Banding: Source to Target.

prompt you for the parameters of a method. It will automatically generate the code for this interaction—including the event adapters and method invocations. The new code will automatically appear in the source editor.

7. **Compile your bean.** Click on the *project* menu and select the *build* option. You can also click on *execute* to test your bean live. This is where you get to debug your bean using the IDE facilities.

8. **JAR your bean.** Click on the *project* menu and select *Auto JAR*. Or, you can use the JAR option to finely control what goes into your JAR. It will list your bean classes and their dependent classes (see Figure 36-6). You can then choose the ones you want to exclude from the JAR; you can also add resource files the tool does not know about.

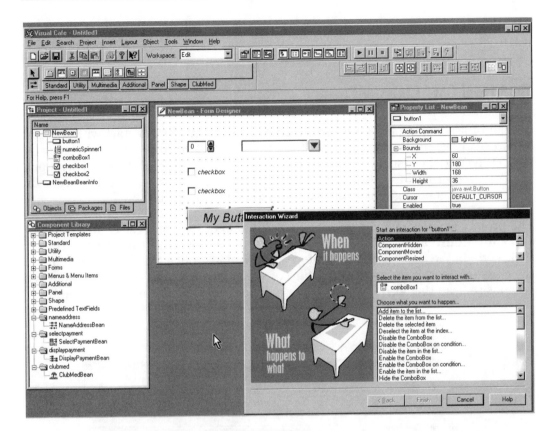

Figure 36-5. Connect the Source Event to the Target Method.

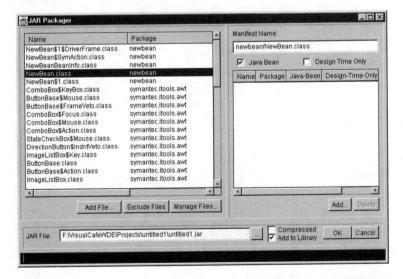

Figure 36-6. JAR Your Bean.

With this tutorial behind us, we can now look at how Visual Café handles **ClubMed-Bean**.

The Visual Café ClubMedBean

Instead of assembling the **ClubMedBean** from scratch, we will start with the one we already created. So copy the files from the *VisualCaféProjects* subdirectory on the CD-ROM to the Visual Café *projects* subdirectory on your local disk. Then open the *ClubMed* project from the Visual Café *projects* subdirectory. You should see on your screen something that looks like the screen shot in Figure 36-7.

The project window shows that our bean consists of two classes: **ClubMedBean** and **ClubMedBeanBeanInfo**. You can click on any of these two classes to view their code in the Source Editor. Before you do this, notice the panel hierarchy in the class outliner; it shows the structure of the embedded beans. So Club Med is a composite bean that also contains other composite beans. It's all very recursive.

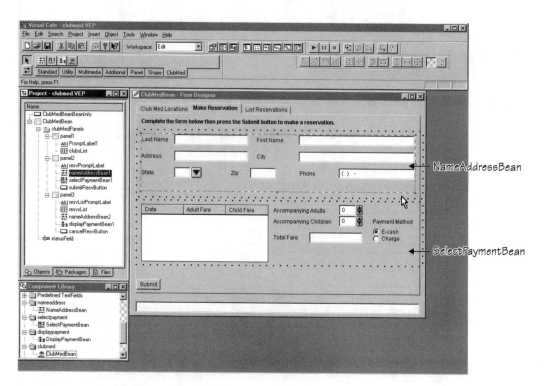

Figure 36-7. The ClubMedBean Within Visual Café.

In the middle is the form designer. Visual Café lets you directly navigate the tabs from within the designer. So click on any tab to view the underlying form. Remember that everything you see in the form is a bean. We show two composite beans—**NameAddressBean** and **SelectPaymentBean**—that you can reuse in other situations. For example, we reused one of them in two of our panels. We even added these two beans to both the palette and the component library (see the lower-left window). Almost everyone has name/address fields in their forms. So you can reuse our **NameAddressBean** whenever you need this function. You can customize the bean's behavior to fit your needs by setting its properties. It's business as usual.

How Visual Café Does CORBA

Our original plan was to use the Visual Café Interaction Wizard to wire our CORBA server objects. We were planning to provide an invisible bean that served as a proxy to the CORBA server objects (more on this in the VisualAge Section). Unfortunately, the Interaction Wizard only supports methods with *in* parameters and *void* return values. This limitation means that the server can't return anything to the client. So it's not very useful in client/server situations.

Our revised plan was to use Visual Café to do the visual layout and VisualAge for the server wiring. However, this plan didn't work either. We had trouble importing the Visual Café beans into VisualAge because it currently doesn't support inner classes (we were told VisualAge will support inner classes in the next release). We finally downsized our expectations. In the current plan, we invoke CORBA objects directly from within the **ClubMedBean** class (see Figure 36-8). There's no visual programming here.

In the code snippet shown in Figure 36-8, we invoke the *getClubs* CORBA method to populate a multi-column listbox bean. The method returns an array of structures that we then convert to an array of semicolon (;) delimited strings. This is how you pass result sets to this multi-column listbox bean. In the future, we expect the **InfoBus** to define standard structures for exchanging data between beans. Much of our client code is spent converting between the dissimilar data structures that different beans support.

So how does this bean initially connect to the CORBA object? In this example, we embed the **ClubMedBean** inside an applet called **ClubMedApplet** (see Listing 36-1). The applet serves as a container for the bean. Note that Visual Café adds special comments to the code to mark where the form designer generates code for the visual elements added to the applet, in this case our **ClubMedBean**.

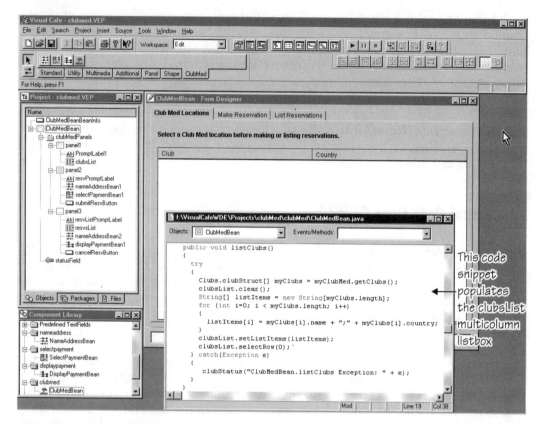

Figure 36-8. How Visual Café Does CORBA.

Listing 36-1. The ClubMedApplet Class.

```java
import java.awt.*;
import java.applet.*;
import clubmed.ClubMedBean;
public class ClubMedApplet extends Applet
{
    public void init()
    {
        //{{INIT_CONTROLS
        setLayout(new BorderLayout(0,0));
        setSize(635,505);
        clubMedBean1 = new clubmed.ClubMedBean();
        GridBagLayout gridBagLayout;
        gridBagLayout = new GridBagLayout();
        clubMedBean1.setLayout(gridBagLayout);
        clubMedBean1.setBounds(0,0,635,505);
```

```
        clubMedBean1.setBackground(java.awt.Color.lightGray);
        add("Center", clubMedBean1);
        //}}

        clubMedBean1.initializeORB(this);
        clubMedBean1.listClubs();

    }
    //{{DECLARE_CONTROLS
    clubmed.ClubMedBean clubMedBean1;
    //}}

    public void destroy()
    {
        clubMedBean1.releaseClubMed();
    }

}
```

As part of *init*, the applet instantiates a **ClubMedBean**. Then it calls the bean's
initializeORB method, which executes the following code:

```
public void initializeORB(Applet applet)
{
  try
  { // Initialize the ORB.
    System.out.println("Initializing the ORB");
    org.omg.CORBA.ORB orb = org.omg.CORBA.ORB.init(applet, null);

    // Get a reference to the Naming service
    org.omg.CORBA.Object nameServiceObj =
               orb.resolve_initial_references ("NameService");
    if (nameServiceObj == null)
    {
      System.out.println("nameServiceObj = null");
      return;
    }

    org.omg.CosNaming.NamingContext nameService =
               org.omg.CosNaming.NamingContextHelper.narrow
                                           (nameServiceObj);
```

```
    if (nameService == null)
    {
      System.out.println("nameService = null");
      return;
    }

    // resolve the Count object in the Naming service
    NameComponent[] clubMedName = {new NameComponent("ClubMed", "")};
    Clubs.ClubMedDispenser myClubMedDispenser =
      Clubs.ClubMedDispenserHelper.narrow(
                   nameService.resolve(clubMedName));

    myClubMed = myClubMedDispenser.reserveClubMedObject();

  } catch(Exception e)
  {
    clubStatus("ClubMedBean.initializeORB Exception: " + e);
  }
}
```

As part of *destroy* the applet invokes the **ClubMedBean** *releaseClubMed* method.
It executes the following code:

```
public void releaseClubMed()
{
  try
  {
    myClubMedDispenser.releaseClubMedObject(myClubMed);
  } catch(Exception e)
  { clubStatus("Applet Exception: " + e);
  }
}
```

You can use the following HTML to run this applet:

```
<h2>Club Med Reservations</h2>
<hr>
<center>
<applet code=ClubMedApplet.class width=640 height=440
        CODEBASE=classes ARCHIVE="clubmed.jar">
```

```
            <param name=org.omg.CORBA.ORBClass
                  value=com.visigenic.vbroker.orb.ORB>
            <param name=ORBservices value=CosNaming>
            <param name=SVCnameroot value=JavaCorba>
</applet>
</center>
<hr>
```

In the HTML we specified the JAR file for our **ClubMedBean** using the ARCHIVE option. We then passed parameters to our applet so it can find the Naming Service.

This concludes our **ClubMedBean** using Visual Café. In the next section, we recreate this bean using *JBuilder*.

THE JBUILDER CLUB MED BEAN

JBuilder from Borland brings a Delphi-like environment to the development of JavaBeans. Like Delphi, you interact with concurrent views of an application inside a code window and a visual design window. Any changes you make in one window are reflected immediately in the other. Like *Visual Café, JBuilder* comes with 100+ JavaBeans (with source). It also includes a bean wizard called *BeansExpress*. Finally, JBuilder provides easy access to databases through JDBC.

Like Visual Café, JBuilder comes in three versions: *Standard Edition, Development Edition*, and *Client/Server Edition*. Borland first shipped the *Client/Server Edition* in November, 1997. It includes an optimized compiler, wizards, database connectivity, InterSolv's PVCS software for team development, and built-in CORBA support. In this section, we first tell you a little bit about bean development, *JBuilder* style. Next, we tell you about its support for CORBA. Finally, we tell you how it does the **ClubMedBean**.

JBuilder 101

The JBuilder bean development process is very similar to Visual Café's. You interact with JBuilder via its main window and the *browser window* (see Figure 36-9). The main window contains the menus, a tool bar, and a tabbed component palette. The browser is your work area. It is split vertically. The two panes on the left provide a tree view of your project. With JBuilder, you can click on any element of the tree to see the related code. The pane on the right is a viewer.

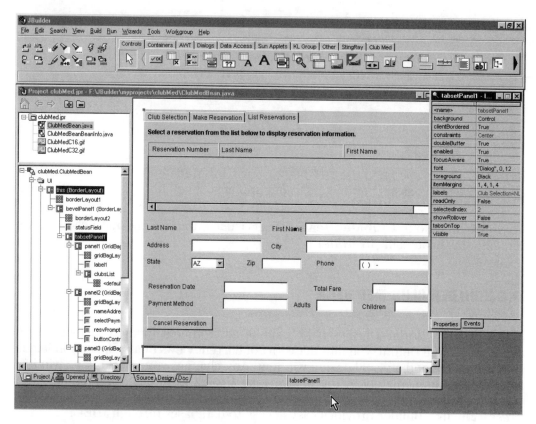

Figure 36-9. JBuilder Client/Server: The Design Viewer.

You can control what gets displayed inside the viewer by clicking on one of three tabs:

- **Design** displays the visual elements of your bean (see Figure 36-9). You drag-and-drop components from the palette into this area to visually compose your bean. Like Visual Café, JBuilder automatically adds Java source code to your bean class for each bean that you drop into the form.

- **Source** displays the source code for your bean class. You can directly edit the source code using a syntax-directed editor (see Figure 36-10).

- **Doc** displays an HTML document that is generated from the comments in the source code.

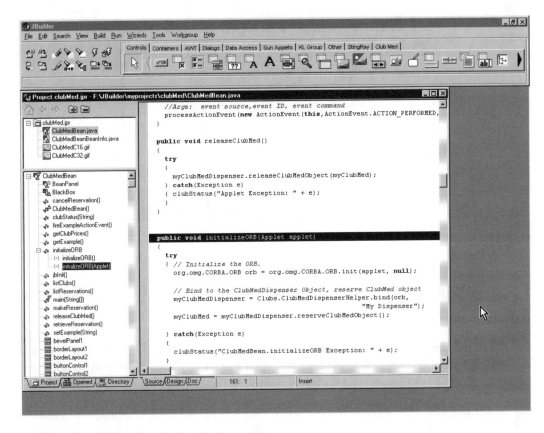

Figure 36-10. JBuilder Client/Server: The Source Viewer.

Developing JavaBeans with JBuilder

Like Visual Café, JBuilder provides a variety of wizards to guide you through the bean development process. Here are the steps you follow in JBuilder to create and package a bean:

1. ***Start a new project***. Create a new project for your bean using the *Project Wizard*. Go to the *File* menu and click on *New Project*. Then follow the steps.

2. ***Create a Java class for your bean***. Here's the fastest way to create a new bean that extends **Panel**. Go to the *File* menu. Select *New*. Click on the *BeansExpress* tab (see Figure 36-11). Then double-click on the *New Bean* icon. The wizard will generate a source code template for your new bean.

3. ***Drag-and-drop beans into a visual form***. You visually create a composite bean by dragging beans off the palette and dropping them into the design area.

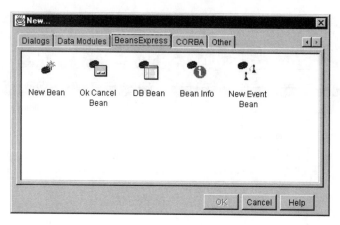

Figure 36-11. JBuilder's BeansExpress.

4. ***Customize each bean.*** Click on a bean to set its properties using the *Inspector* (see Figure 36-12).

5. ***Convert the form to gridbag layout***. JBuilder's default mode for laying out components is called the *XYLayout*. Like Visual Café, it lets you position components on a form. You can then switch to a gridbag layout and still preserve about 90% of your placement. Like Visual Café, you must do a bit of tweaking to get the last 10% right.

6. ***Wire your embedded beans using the Interaction Wizard.*** Like Visual Café, JBuilder provides an *Interaction Wizard* to help you wire your components.

7. ***Compile and run your bean.*** Go to the *Build* menu and select *Make Project*. JBuilder displays compile errors and warnings in an error pane. Click on the error and it will take you right to the source.

8. ***Create a BeanInfo***. Go to *BeansExpress* and click on the *BeanInfo* icon. You will be presented with a template **BeanInfo** class for your bean. Edit this code to fit your needs.

9. ***JAR your bean.*** Go to the *Wizards* menu and select the *Deployment Wizard*. Use it to select the files to include in your JAR. You must also provide a name for your JAR.

As you can see, the JBuilder bean development process is very similar to Visual Café.

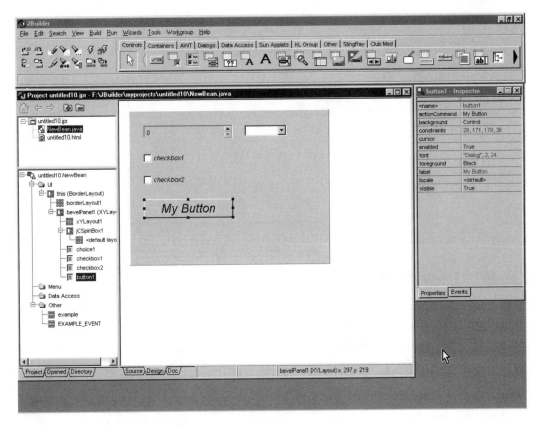

Figure 36-12. Customize Your Beans Using the JBuilder Inspector.

JBuilder's CORBA Support

JBuilder Client/Server includes a full CORBA development environment based on *VisiBroker for Java*. As you know, Borland acquired Visigenic. So we expect to see a tremendous amount of visual integration between JBuilder and VisiBroker. In the current release, the tool simply provides an IDE for CORBA, which includes five wizards. Here's how you create CORBA applications, JBuilder-style:

1. ***Define the interface to the CORBA object.*** You can do this with either an *IDL Wizard* or a *Java IIOP Wizard* that uses Caffeine. To use the IDL Wizard, go to the *File* menu and select *New*. Select the CORBA tab. Then double-click on the IDL icon (see Figure 36-13). To use the IIOP Wizard, double-click the Java IIOP icon instead.

2. ***Compile the IDL or Remote Java Interface***. Use the *CORBA Settings Wizard* to compile the IDL. To open this wizard, go to the *Tools* menu and select *CORBA Settings*.

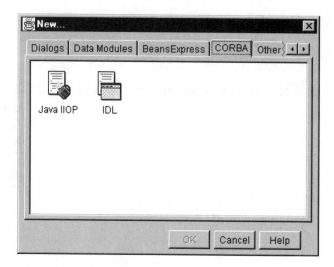

Figure 36-13. The JBuilder CORBA Interface Wizards.

3. ***Implement the CORBA interface***. You must provide an implementation for your CORBA servant. JBuilder provides the VisiBroker-generated *_example* files to help you get started.

4. ***Create a CORBA server***. You must create the CORBA server program. JBuilder helps you create a simple server using the *Generate CORBA Server Wizard*. To activate this wizard, go to the *Wizards* menu and select *Generate CORBA Server*.

5. ***Create the client***. There is no help here. Your must provide a Java client class (see examples in this book).

6. ***Compile the Java files***. Click on the *Run* menu and select *Run*.

7. ***Deploy the application***. Use the *Deployment Wizard*. Click on the *Wizards* menu and select *Deployment*.

8. ***Run the CORBA application***. You can run and debug your CORBA application from within JBuilder. The ORB is embedded inside the tool.

As you can see, we're just dealing with an IDE here. The current product does not support visual assembly with CORBA beans. We expect that you'll get tons of this in later releases of the product.

The JBuilder ClubMedBean

Instead of assembling the **ClubMedBean** from scratch, we will start with the one we already created. So copy the files from the *JBuilderProjects* subdirectory on

the CD-ROM to the JBuilder *myprojects* subdirectory on your local disk. Open the *clubMed* project from the JBuilder *myprojects* subdirectory. You should see on your screen something that looks like Figure 36-9 (on page 918).

The project upper-left pane shows that our bean consists of two classes: **ClubMed-Bean** and **ClubMedBeanBeanInfo**. You can click on either of these two classes to view the structure of the code (see lower-left pane). The code itself appears in the right pane. You can click on the design tab to see the visual elements. So now you have everything you need to navigate the code for this bean. The CORBA code is embedded in the bean. It's almost identical to the code we use with Visual Café. There are some minor differences that have to do with data translations. Remember, we use beans that come with JBuilder in this version.

THE VISUALAGE BARGAIN HUNTER BEAN

It should not come as a surprise that IBM's *VisualAge for Java* also comes in three editions: *Entry, Professional*, and *Enterprise*. In this book, we use the *Professional* edition. The *Enterprise* edition adds access to DBMSs, CICS, and C++. But it's also a lot more expensive—$1780 versus $99 for the *Professional* edition. In both cases, you must have at least 64 MBytes of memory on your system to get acceptable performance.

In this section, we use VisualAge to visually assemble a client/server CORBA application. We will introduce you to the tool as we build the **BargainHunterBean**. We will visually wire the client to a CORBA proxy bean, which we call the **ClubMedCorbaBean**. This is an invisible bean that represents Club Med server objects inside a visual tool.

The ClubMedCorbaBean

We must first design a server proxy bean. This is a bean you can use within assembly tools to visually represent a CORBA server interface. In our first attempt, we tried to use a CORBA stub to represent the server object. After all, this is what stubs are for. However, we discovered that visual tools—like VisualAge—create a private instance of the bean when you drop it on a form. Of course, stubs were not designed to be used on a per-object basis. You use one stub for all the objects that need to connect with a server interface.

In our second attempt, we designed a delegate bean. This is a class that implements the server interface. It then invokes the methods on the actual server by invoking the object reference. We discovered that we were creating a Tie class for clients (we explain Tie in Part 5).

In our third—and last—attempt, we decided to use for our proxy a modified version of the standard Tie class. Remember, this is one of the classes that a CORBA-compliant IDL-to-Java compiler generates for your interface. Here's the code for a **ClubMedCorbaBean** that implements a client-side delegate for the **ClubMed** server interface:

Listing 36-2. The Client-Side ClubMedCorbaBean Class.

```
package Clubs;
import org.omg.CosNaming.*;

public class ClubMedCorbaBean
{
  // Fields
  Clubs.ClubMedDispenser   myClubMedDispenser;
  private Clubs.ClubMed _delegate;

  // Constructor
  public ClubMedCorbaBean(java.applet.Applet applet)
  {
    try
    {
      System.out.println("Initializing the ORB");
      org.omg.CORBA.ORB orb = org.omg.CORBA.ORB.init(applet, null);

      // Get a reference to the Naming service
      org.omg.CORBA.Object nameServiceObj =
                orb.resolve_initial_references ("NameService");
      if (nameServiceObj == null)
      {
        System.out.println("nameServiceObj = null");
        return;
      }

      org.omg.CosNaming.NamingContext nameService =
                org.omg.CosNaming.NamingContextHelper.narrow (nameServiceObj);
      if (nameService == null)
      {
        System.out.println("nameService = null");
        return;
      }

      // resolve the Count object in the Naming service
      NameComponent[] clubMedName = {new NameComponent("ClubMed", "")};
      Clubs.ClubMedDispenser myClubMedDispenser =
```

```
        Clubs.ClubMedDispenserHelper.narrow(
                        nameService.resolve(clubMedName));
        _delegate = myClubMedDispenser.reserveClubMedObject();
  } catch(Exception e)
  { System.out.println("Applet Exception: " + e);
  }
}

// Delegate method for ClubMedDispenser
public void releaseClubMedObject()
{
  try
  {
    myClubMedDispenser.releaseClubMedObject(_delegate);
  } catch(Exception e)
  { System.out.println("Applet Exception: " + e);
  }
}


// Delegate methods for ClubMed
public Clubs.clubStruct[] getClubs()
{
  return this._delegate.getClubs();
}

public Clubs.pricesStruct[] getClubPrices(java.lang.String club)
{
  return this._delegate.getClubPrices(club);
}

public int addReservation(java.lang.String club,
                            Clubs.resvStruct resvData)
{
  return this._delegate.addReservation(club, resvData);
}
public Clubs.resvSummaryStruct[] getClubReservations(
                                            java.lang.String club)
{
  return this._delegate.getClubReservations(club);
}
public Clubs.resvStruct getReservation(int resv)
{
  return this._delegate.getReservation(resv);
}
```

```java
public boolean cancelReservation(int resv)
{
  return this._delegate.cancelReservation(resv);
}

public String[] getDates()
{
  return this._delegate.getDates();
}

public Clubs.bargainStruct getBargainInfo(String date)
{
  return this._delegate.getBargainInfo(date);
}

 // accessor for delegate
public Clubs.ClubMed _delegate()
{
  return this._delegate;
}

}
```

The shaded area is Tie code that *IDL2Java* automatically generates for our **ClubMed** server-side interface. We added to this code a constructor that: 1) initializes the ORB, 2) locates a Name Server, 3) finds a **ClubMedDispenser**, and 4) invokes *reserveClubMedObject* to obtain an object reference to a **ClubMed** object, and 5) assigns this reference to the *_delegate* variable. We also added the *releaseClubMedObject* method to release the server object when the applet terminates.

So this proxy does two things: 1) it represents the server-side object within a visual tool, and 2) it locates an object reference at run time that it invokes on behalf of the client. As you can see, we're only one step away from having the IDL-to-Java compiler automatically generate a proxy bean for each of our CORBA interfaces. Let's go back to VisualAge for Java to see what we can do with this proxy.

VisualAge 101

The first thing you see when you start VisualAge is the *Workbench*. The icons at the top let you access the main functions—including Editing tools, Run, Debug, Search, and New program elements. The program elements include project, package, class, applet, method, and field.

Right below the icons are a number of tabs that let you view and access the programming elements in your workspace—including projects, packages, classes, interfaces, and unresolved problems.

Creating the BargainHunterBean with VisualAge

In this section, we use VisualAge to create the **BargainHunterBean**. We connect it to a server object via the proxy bean. Let's walk through the steps:

1. *Import the VisiBroker classes*. Everything you do in VisualAge is repository-based. Consequently, you must explicitly tell VisualAge about all the objects you will be importing into its environment. Yes, it's painful. The VisualAge *Workbench* maintains a hierarchy of projects, packages, and classes for all the objects it knows about. Click on the *Import SmartGuide* to create a VisiBroker project and import its JAR (see Figure 36-14). This step takes about 15 minutes, so you may want to go and get a cup of coffee.

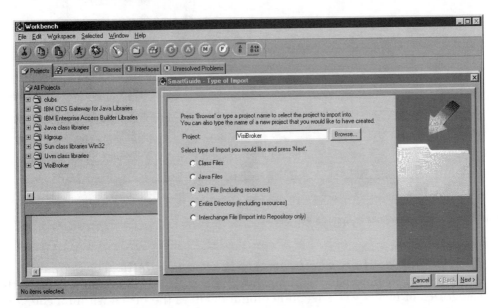

Figure 36-14. Use SmartGuide To Import All Your Classes into VisualAge.

2. *Import the KL Group beans*. VisualAge is pretty stingy when it comes to bundled beans. So we will create a project for *KL Group* beans and import them into the VisualAge repository. Note that these are the same KL Group beans that are bundled with both JBuilder and Visual Café. Point to the JAR that comes with Visual Café.

3. *Import the Club Med objects*. Create a project called *Clubs*. Use SmartGuide

to import the Club Med classes—including the stubs, skeletons, helpers, holders, and the **ClubMedCorbaBean**.

4. ***Create a project called Bargain Hunter***. Use SmartGuide to import the **ConverterUtil** class. This is a class we wrote to translate an array of strings into a format that the listbox bean we used could understand.

5. ***Create a new Java class for your bean***. Click on *Quick Start*. Select *new applet*. The system will then display a *SmartGuide* window. Fill in the applet name—we call it **BargainHunterBean** (see Figure 36-15). You must also tell it that you want to develop this applet visually (as opposed to writing the source code yourself). VisualAge will then take you to the *Visual Composition Editor*.

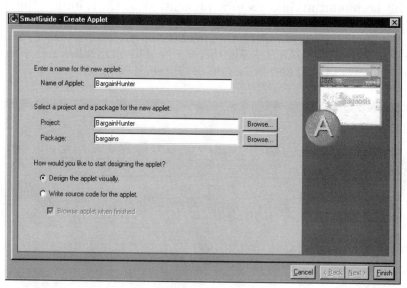

Figure 36-15. Use SmartGuide To Create a New Bean.

6. ***Add the ClubMedCorbaBean bean to the beans palette***. The *Beans Palette* is on the left of the Visual Composition Editor. The first column displays the categories of beans. The second column displays the beans within a category. To add a new bean to the palette go to the *Options* menu. Then select *modify palette*. Click on the *AddNewBean* option (see Figure 36-16). We add both the **ClubMedCorbaBean** and the **ConverterUtil** to the palette.

7. ***Drag-and-drop beans into the visual composition form***. We start creating the **BargainHunterBean** by selecting beans from the palette and dropping them into the visual form (see Figure 36-17). Notice that we have some GUI controls on the left. On the right are two *invisible beans* that are instances of **ClubMedCorbaBean** and **ConverterUtil**.

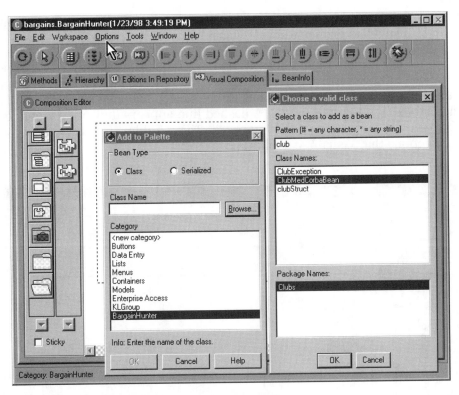

Figure 36-16. Adding Embedded Beans to the Visual Composition Form.

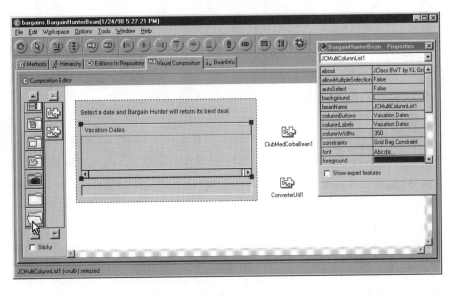

Figure 36-17. Adding Beans to the VisualAge Palette.

8. *Customize each bean using its property sheet*. You can left-click on any bean to display its property sheet (VisualAge calls it *Properties*).

9. *Wire your beans*. Right-click on the source bean. A pop-up menu appears; now select *Connect*. Then pick an event. This causes a rubber band to appear. Connect it to the target. Next, click on the target bean and pick a method from the listbox (see Figure 36-18). A dashed line appears indicating a connection between the two beans (see Figure 36-19). Table 36-1 lists the types of connections that VisualAge supports.

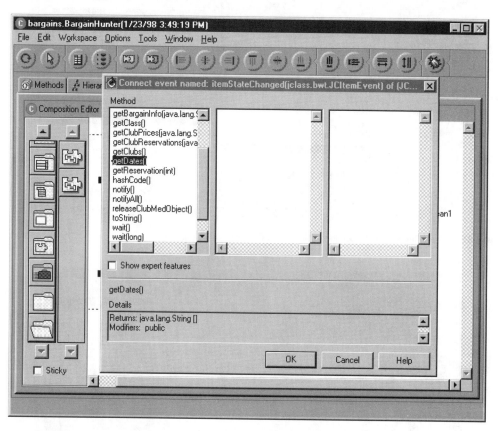

Figure 36-18. Pick a Target Bean Method.

We must create a number of connections (see wires in Figure 36-19). The first connection wires the listbox to the *getDates* method of the **ClubMedCorba-Bean**. Next, we wire the result of this method—an array of strings—to the listbox. The next connection wires the listbox *itemStateChanged* event to the *getBargainInfo* method of the **ClubMedCorbaBean**. The parameter for this method comes from the *getSelectedItem* property of the listbox (another wire).

We wire the result of this method invocation to the *toBargainString* method on **ConverterUtil** Finally, we wire the output of *toBargainString* to the display field at the bottom. So welcome to CORBA visual programming with wires.

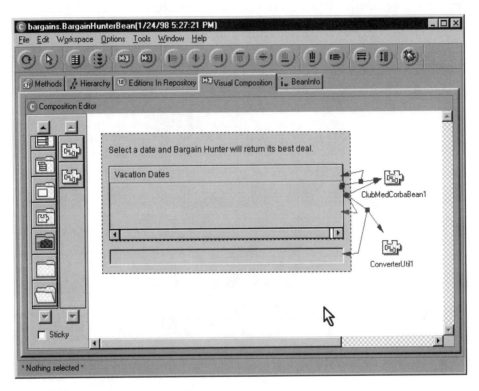

Figure 36-19. The Embedded Bean Connections.

Table 36-1. VisualAge Connection Types.

VisualAge Connection Type	What Happens
Property-to-Property	Links two properties. When one property changes, the other changes too.
Event-to-Method	The firing of the event results in the invocation of a method.
Event-to-Script	The firing of the event causes some Java code to execute.
Parameter-from-Property	The method parameter obtains its value from this property.
Parameter-from-Script	The method parameter obtains its value by running some Java code.
Parameter-from-Method	The method parameter obtains its value from the result of this method.

10. ***Compile and run your bean.*** Go to the *File* menu and select *Save Bean.* VisualAge will then generate and compile the code for the **BargainHunterBean**;

it also saves everything inside its repository. You can now run the bean by clicking on the *Test* icon at the top left of the Visual Composition editor.

11. ***Create a BeanInfo***. Click on the *BeanInfo* tab to generate a **BeanInfo** class (see Figure 36-20).

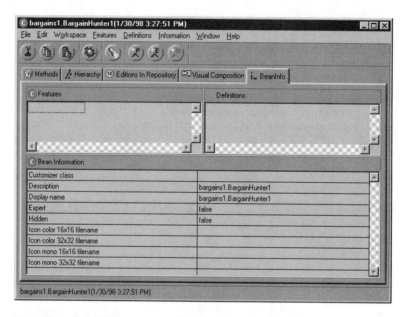

Figure 36-20. Generating the BeanInfo.

12. ***JAR your bean***. Go to the *File* menu on the Workbench and select *Export*. It will put you in the *SmartGuide for Export*. Select JAR file. Then select the classes to be marked as beans and pick a name for your JAR. Finally, click on *Finish*. We're done.

CONCLUSION

This long chapter should give you an idea of where things stand in the area of client/server assembly with CORBA and JavaBeans. The good news is that there are some very good visual assembly tools for JavaBeans. In this chapter, we showed what you can do with three of these tools. The other good news is that tools like JBuilder now include CORBA in their IDE. The wizards make it much easier to develop CORBA code. However, visual assembly with CORBA and JavaBeans is still in its infancy. The **ClubMedCorbaBean** proxy we developed in this chapter demonstrates how easy it is to create a more bean-friendly CORBA. This is the area where we expect to see a ton of new innovation over the next year. In any case, we now have two CORBA-enabled client beans. The final step is to create the ClubMed server, which is the topic of the next chapter.

Chapter 37

The Club Med CORBA Server

Club Med is a 3-tier client/server application for the Web. In this 3-tier rendition, CORBA server objects provide the middle tier. The server objects interact with client beans on the front-end and the SQL databases on the back-end. The interfaces to the server objects are defined in CORBA IDL; they provide a binding contract between the server and its clients. You already saw what the Club Med IDL looks like in Chapter 35.

The Club Med server architecture is identical to the one we used in the 3-tier Debit-Credit. Again, we chose to implement stateless server objects. They're much easier to program.[1] We maintain all the persistent information in the Club Med's SQL database, and then access it using JDBC-wrapper objects. And, once again, we reuse the object Dispenser—our poor man's TP Monitor. The Club Med couldn't scale without it.

The good news is that there is very little new material to explain in this chapter. We're just reusing a server design pattern that works. You will see first-hand how easy it is to adapt this design pattern to a new server application—in this case, Club

---

[1] We recommend that you use stateless objects until the Object Transaction Monitor vendors start providing *OTMs* that automatically manage the state of the object (i.e., POAs that also handle object persistence). We covered OTMs in the Enterprise JavaBeans Chapter.

Med. So, the plan for this chapter is to first give you a quick overview of the Club Med server architecture. Then we introduce the Club Med server classes—they should be very familiar by now. Finally, we jump into the server code. There should be no major surprises in this chapter. It's just a matter of seeing how the different pieces come together. After all, this is a grand finale. By the end of the chapter, we'll be able to run the Club Med client/server application. Yes, we will have fireworks—there is much to celebrate.

CLUB MED SERVER: THE CODE STRUCTURE

In this section, we first explain the Club Med middle-tier application server. Then we show how the **ClubMedDispenser** works—this should be old news if you read the 3-tier Debit-Credit chapter. Finally, we go over the Club Med server classes.

The 3-Tier Club Med

Figure 37-1 shows the three tiers of the Club Med application. The first tier belongs to the client applet and beans that we developed in the last chapter. The third tier belongs to the SQL database (it could have just as easily been IMS transactions, Lotus Notes, or any other source of data). The middle tier belongs to a pool of server *object-pairs*. You tell the **ClubMedDispenser** how many object-pairs are in the pool. It will then prestart these objects and allocate them to clients when they request it. Why object-pairs? It's really a matter of taste. We like the idea of dividing

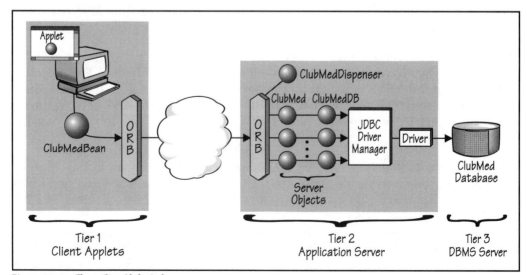

Figure 37-1. The 3-Tier Club Med.

the work between 1) *data objects* that encapsulate the JDBC database, and 2) *application server objects* that encapsulate interactions with clients—they also implement the business logic.

The ClubMedDispenser

Figure 37-2 shows the next level of detail in the operation of the middle-tier server. In our implementation, both the **ClubMedDispenser** and **ClubMed** are IDL-defined CORBA objects. A Club Med server exposes both of these interfaces to its clients.

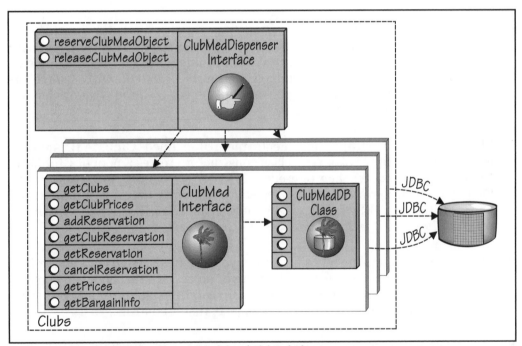

Figure 37-2. The ClubMedDispenser as a Scheduler of ClubMed Objects.

A **ClubMedDispenser** is a broker of server objects. It prestarts and manages a pool of server object-pairs, which it then allocates to clients on demand. Each server object runs in its own thread and maintains a permanent connection to a JDBC database. Note that **ClubMedDB** is a Java-only object; it is not a remote object.

A client obtains a **ClubMed** object by invoking the *reserveClubMedObject* method on a **ClubMedDispenser** object. The client can then invoke any of the object's methods. In reality, the client obtains the services of an object-pair. However, it never sees the **ClubMedDB** object; it's all done under-the-covers. At the end of a client/server interaction, the client must release the remote object by invoking *releaseClubMedObject*. This returns the object-pair to the pool. One of the design tradeoffs we must wrestle with is: How long do we cling to this object? OLTP etiquette requires that you release any shared resource as soon as possible (see Chapter 26). So, you make the judgement call—after all, it's your application.

Meet the Server Players

Here are the Java classes a 3-tier Club Med server supports:

■ **ClubMedServer** provides the *main* method for the server. It provides the following functions: 1) initializes the ORB, 2) creates a new **ClubMedDispenser** object and passes it the size of the server pool—this is a parameter that you pass to *main*, 3) invokes *orb.connect* to register the object with the ORB, 4) registers the newly created **ClubMedDispenserImpl** object with the Naming Service, and 5) waits for incoming requests.

■ **ClubMedDispenserImpl** implements the IDL-defined **ClubMedDispenser** interface (see Chapter 35). The class constructor creates a pool of **ClubMedImpl** objects and stores their references in an array of **ClubMedStatus** objects. Finally, it invokes *orb.connect* to register each newly created **ClubMedImpl** object with the ORB. The class implements two IDL-defined methods: *reserveClubMedObject* and *releaseClubMedObject*.

■ **ClubMedStatus** implements a structure with two fields: *reference* and *inUse*. The first field stores the reference to a server object. The second field contains its current status. The **ClubMedDispenserImpl** maintains an array of these field-pairs to keep track of the pool of objects that it controls.

■ **ClubMedImpl** implements the IDL-defined **ClubMed** interface (see Chapter 35). The class constructor creates a new **ClubMedDB** object and then connects to it. The object is preconnected to the database. The class implements the following IDL-defined methods:

```
interface ClubMed
{
  clubSeq    getClubs();
  pricesSeq  getClubPrices(in string club);
  resvNo     addReservation(in string club, in resvStruct resvData);
  resvSumSeq getClubReservations(in string club);
```

```
resvStruct      getReservation(in resvNo resv);
boolean         cancelReservation(in resvNo resv);
dates           getDates();
bargainStruct   getBargainInfo(in string date);
};
```

Each of these methods services a client request with a corresponding helper method on the **ClubMedDB** object.

■ **ClubMedDB** is a database-encapsulator class; it handles all the interactions with JDBC. The class provides ten methods: *connect, closeConnection, getClubs, getClubPrices, addReservation, getClubReservations, getReservation, cancelReservation, getDates,* and *getBargainInfo*. Notice that the last eight methods have a one-to-one correspondence to their **ClubMedImpl** counterparts. That's what helpers are for!

The bottom line is that the **ClubMedDispenserImpl** maintains a pool of server objects. Each server object maintains a live JDBC connection to an SQL database via its **ClubMedDB** object.

A Club Med Client/Server Scenario

Figure 37-3 shows how the 3-tier Club Med client and server classes interact with each other. In this scenario, a client bean will complete a reservation. Let's walk through the steps:

1. ***The server creates a dispenser object.*** The **ClubMedServer** creates a **ClubMedDispenserImpl** object and passes it the size of the server pool. Note that the **ClubMedDispenserImpl** class implements the IDL-defined **ClubMed-Dispenser** interface.

2. ***The dispenser prestarts a pool of server objects.*** The **ClubMedDispenser-Impl** creates a pool of **ClubMedImpl** objects and stores their references in an array of **ClubMedStatus** objects. It also invokes *orb.connect* to register each newly created **ClubMedImpl** object with the ORB.

3. ***The server object creates its JDBC helper.*** Each **ClubMedImpl** object creates a **ClubMedDB** helper. This is the worker object that encapsulates JDBC. Note that this object runs within the same thread as its creator.

4. ***The server object connects to the database.*** Each **ClubMedImpl** object invokes *connect* on its **ClubMedDB** helper to open a JDBC connection with a SQL database.

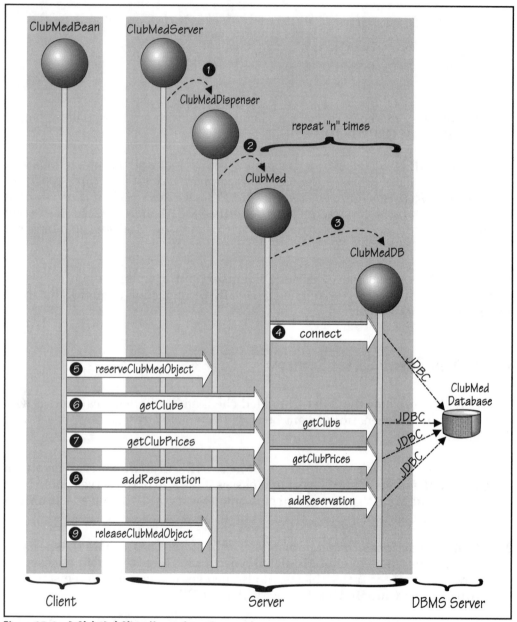

Figure 37-3. A Club Med Client/Server Scenario.

5. ***The client requests a server object.*** The client invokes *reserveClubMed-Object* on the **ClubMedDispenser** to obtain a server object.

6. ***The client bean invokes the getClubs method.*** When the applet first starts, it invokes *getClubs* on the **ClubMedImpl** object to obtain a list of Clubs. The

object obtains the data from the JDBC database by invoking *getClubs* on its **ClubMedDB** helper.

7. **The client bean invokes the getClubPrices method.** The bean must obtain the latest pricing information from the server. It then displays it in a reservation form. The bean does this by invoking *getClubPrices* on the **ClubMedImpl** object. This object in turn obtains the data from the JDBC database by invoking *getClubPrices* on its **ClubMedDB** helper.

8. **The client makes the reservation.** The bean invokes *addReservation* on the **ClubMedImpl** object to make the reservation. The object invokes *addReservation* on its **ClubMedDB** helper to commit the information to the JDBC database. You can now spend your week in paradise.

9. **Release the server object.** The client invokes *releaseClubMedObject* on the **ClubMedDispenser** to return the server object to the pool; it must pass the object reference as a parameter.

THE CLUB MED SERVER CODE

We're now ready to present the Club Med server code. This code demonstrates how to use CORBA's rich data types from within your Java code. Many of the remote methods pass and return CORBA sequences of structures. These are variable-sized arrays of structures that you can pass back and forth between the client and the server. It's extremely powerful stuff!

The code also demonstrates a useful design pattern for returning a variable number of rows. Here's how it works: 1) the JDBC helper does a SQL SELECT to obtain data; 2) it then copies the data from the result set into a Java **Vector** object one row at a time; 3) it returns this vector to the **ClubMed** server object; 4) the server object invokes the *copyInto* method on the **Vector** to copy its results to an array of structures (its length was previously unassigned); and 5) the server then returns the array to the client via a CORBA sequence. The client sees the sequence as an array; it can then determine the number of items returned from the array length. Here's the code that does all this.

Listing 37-1. Club Med Server: ClubMedServer Class.

```
// ClubMedServer.java

import org.omg.CosNaming.*;

class ClubMedServer
{ static public void main(String[] args)
  {
```

```java
int numberInstances;

try
{
  if (args.length == 0)
    numberInstances = 4;
  else
    numberInstances = Integer.parseInt(args[0]);

  // Initialize the ORB
  org.omg.CORBA.ORB orb = org.omg.CORBA.ORB.init(args, null);

  // Create the ClubMedDispenser object
  ClubMedDispenserImpl dispenser =
          new ClubMedDispenserImpl(args,
                                   "My Dispenser", numberInstances);

  // Export the newly create object
  orb.connect(dispenser);

  // Get a reference to the Naming service
  org.omg.CORBA.Object nameServiceObj =
          orb.resolve_initial_references ("NameService");
  if (nameServiceObj == null)
  {
    System.out.println("nameServiceObj = null");
    return;
  }

  org.omg.CosNaming.NamingContext nameService =
      org.omg.CosNaming.NamingContextHelper.narrow(nameServiceObj);
  if (nameService == null)
  {
    System.out.println("nameService = null");
    return;
  }

  // bind the Count object in the Naming service
  NameComponent[] clubMedName = {new NameComponent("ClubMed", "")};
  nameService.rebind(clubMedName, dispenser);

  // wait forever for current thread to die
  Thread.currentThread().join();

} catch(Exception e)
```

```
      { System.err.println(e);
      }
    }
}
```

Listing 37-2. Club Med Server: ClubMedImpl Class.

```java
// ClubMedImpl.java

import java.util.*;
public class ClubMedImpl extends Clubs._ClubMedImplBase
{
  private ClubMedDB myClubMedDB;
  private String instanceName;

  public ClubMedImpl(java.lang.String name) {
    super(name);
    try
    {
      myClubMedDB = new ClubMedDB();
      myClubMedDB.connect("LocalServer", "ClubMed", "sa", "");
      System.out.println("ClubMedDB Object " + name + " Created");
      instanceName = name;
    } catch (Exception e)
    { System.out.println("System Exception ");
    }
  }


  public ClubMedImpl()
  {
    super();
  }


  public Clubs.clubStruct[] getClubs()
  {
    try
    {
      Clubs.clubStruct[] clubData;
      Vector clubs = myClubMedDB.getClubs();
      clubData = new Clubs.clubStruct[clubs.size()];
      clubs.copyInto(clubData);
      return(clubData);
```

```java
      } catch (Exception e)
      { System.out.println("System Exception in getClubs");
        return null;
      }
}


public Clubs.pricesStruct[] getClubPrices( java.lang.String club )

{
   try
   {
      Clubs.pricesStruct[] priceData;
      Vector prices = myClubMedDB.getClubPrices(club);
      priceData = new Clubs.pricesStruct[prices.size()];
      prices.copyInto(priceData);
      return(priceData);
   } catch (Exception e)
   { System.out.println("System Exception in getClubPrices");
     return null;
   }
}


public int addReservation( java.lang.String club,
                           Clubs.resvStruct resvData )

{
   try
   {
      return myClubMedDB.addReservation(club, resvData);
   } catch (Exception e)
   { System.out.println("System Exception in getClubPrices");
     return 0;
   }
}


public Clubs.resvSummaryStruct[] getClubReservations(
                                   java.lang.String club )

{
   try
   {
      Clubs.resvSummaryStruct[] resvData;
```

```java
      Vector resvs = myClubMedDB.getClubReservations(club);
      resvData = new Clubs.resvSummaryStruct[resvs.size()];
      resvs.copyInto(resvData);
      return(resvData);
   } catch (Exception e)
   { System.out.println("System Exception in getClubReservations");
      return null;
   }
}


public Clubs.resvStruct getReservation( int resv )

{
   try
   {
      return myClubMedDB.getReservation(resv);
   } catch (Exception e)
   { System.out.println("System Exception in getReservation");
      return null;
   }
}


public boolean cancelReservation( int resv )

{
   try
   {
      return myClubMedDB.cancelReservation(resv);
   } catch (Exception e)
   { System.out.println("System Exception in cancelReservation");
      return false;
   }
}

public java.lang.String[] getDates()
{
   try
   {
      String[] dates;
      Vector datesVector = myClubMedDB.getDates();
      dates = new String[datesVector.size()];
      datesVector.copyInto(dates);
      return(dates);
```

```java
        } catch (Exception e)
        { System.out.println("System Exception in getDates");
          return null;
        }
    }

  public Clubs.bargainStruct getBargainInfo(String date)
  {
      try
      {
        return myClubMedDB.getBargainInfo(date);
      } catch (Exception e)
      { System.out.println("System Exception in getBargainInfo");
        return null;
      }
  }

}
```

Listing 37-3. Club Med Server: ClubMedDispenserImpl Class.

```java
// ClubMedDispenserImpl.java

public class ClubMedDispenserImpl
       extends Clubs._ClubMedDispenserImplBase
{
  private int maxObjects = 10;
  private int numObjects = 0;
  private ClubMedStatus[] clubMed =
                     new ClubMedStatus[maxObjects];

  public ClubMedDispenserImpl(java.lang.String args,
                              java.lang.String args[], int num)
  {
    super(name);

    try
    {
      // get reference to orb
      org.omg.CORBA.ORB orb = org.omg.CORBA.ORB.init(args, null);

      // prestart n ClubMed Objects
      numObjects = num;
      for (int i=0; i < numObjects; i++)
```

```
      {
        clubMed[i] = new ClubMedStatus();
        clubMed[i].ref = new ClubMedImpl("ClubMed" + (i+1));
        orb.connect(clubMed[i].ref);
      }
    } catch(Exception e)
    { System.err.println(e);
    }

  }


  public Clubs.ClubMed reserveClubMedObject( )
                   throws Clubs.ClubException
                         {
    for (int i=0; i < numObjects; i++)
    {
      if (!clubMed[i].inUse)
         { clubMed[i].inUse = true;
           System.out.println("ClubMed" + (i+1) + " reserved.");
           return clubMed[i].ref;
         }
    }
    return null;
  }

  public void releaseClubMedObject(
                   Clubs.ClubMed ClubMedObject)
                   throws Clubs.ClubException
  {
    for (int i=0; i < numObjects; i++)
    {
      if (clubMed[i].ref == ClubMedObject)
         { clubMed[i].inUse = false;
           System.out.println("ClubMed" + (i+1) + " released.");
           return;
         }
    }
    System.out.println("Reserved Object not found");
    return;
  }
}
```

Listing 37-4. Club Med Server: ClubMedStatus Class.

```
class ClubMedStatus
{
  ClubMedImpl ref;
  boolean        inUse;

  ClubMedStatus()
  { ref = null;
    inUse = false;
  }
}
```

Listing 37-5. Club Med Server: ClubMedDB Class.

```java
// ClubMedDB.java

import java.net.URL;
import java.sql.*;
import java.util.*;

public class ClubMedDB
{
  Connection con;
  Driver driver = null;
  ResultSet rs;
  PreparedStatement pstmt;

  public void connect(String datasource, String db,
                      String id, String pw)
                      throws Exception
  {
    try
    {
      // Load the jdbc-odbc bridge driver
      Class.forName ("sun.jdbc.odbc.JdbcOdbcDriver");

      String url   = "jdbc:odbc:" + datasource + ";database=" + db;
      System.out.println("Connecting to " + url);
      con = DriverManager.getConnection(url, id, pw);
    } catch(Exception e)
    { System.err.println("System Exception in connect");
      System.err.println(e);
      throw e;
```

```java
    }
}


public void closeConnection() throws Exception
{
  try
  {
    System.out.println("Closing connection");
    con.close();
  } catch (Exception e)
  { System.err.println("System Exception in closeConnection");
    System.err.println(e);
    throw e;
  }
}


public Vector getClubs() throws Exception
{
  try
  {
    Vector clubs = new Vector();
    pstmt = con.prepareStatement("SELECT * FROM Clubs");
    pstmt.execute();
    ResultSet rs = pstmt.getResultSet();
    while (rs.next())
    {
      clubs.addElement(new Clubs.clubStruct(rs.getString(1),
                                            rs.getString(2)));
    }
    pstmt.close();
    con.commit();
    return clubs;
  }
  catch( Exception e )
  { System.err.println("System Exception in getClubs");
    System.err.println(e);
    throw e;
  }
}

public Vector getClubPrices(String club ) throws Exception
{
  try
```

```java
{
   Vector prices = new Vector();
   pstmt = con.prepareStatement(
                        "SELECT " +
                        "WeekDate, AdultPrice, ChildPrice " +
                        "FROM Prices " +
                        "where Club = '" + club + "'");
   pstmt.execute();
   ResultSet rs = pstmt.getResultSet();
   while (rs.next())
   {
     prices.addElement(new Clubs.pricesStruct(rs.getString(1),
                                             rs.getShort(2),
                                             rs.getShort(3)));
   }
   pstmt.close();
   con.commit();
   return prices;
  }
  catch( Exception e )
  { System.err.println("System Exception in getClubPrices");
   System.err.println(e);
   throw e;
  }
}


public int addReservation(String club, Clubs.resvStruct resvData )
            throws Exception
{
  try
  {
   pstmt = con.prepareStatement(
           "SELECT MAX(ResvNo) FROM RESERVATIONS");
   pstmt.execute();
   ResultSet rs = pstmt.getResultSet();
   rs.next();
   int resvNo = rs.getInt(1);
   resvNo = resvNo + 1;

   pstmt = con.prepareStatement(
                "INSERT INTO Reservations " +
                "(ResvNo, Club, WeekDate, LastName, " +
                "FirstName, PartyAdults, " +
                "PartyChildren, TotalFare, PaymentMethod, " +
```

```
                  "PhoneNo, Address, City, State, Zip) " +
                  "VALUES(?, ?, ?, ?, ?, ?, ?, ?, " +
                  "?, ?, ?, ?, ?, ?)");
     pstmt.setInt(    1, resvNo);
     pstmt.setString( 2, club);
     pstmt.setString( 3, resvData.weekDate);
     pstmt.setString( 4, resvData.lname);
     pstmt.setString( 5, resvData.fname);
     pstmt.setShort(  6, resvData.partyAdults);
     pstmt.setShort(  7, resvData.partyChildren);
     pstmt.setString( 8, resvData.totalFare);
     pstmt.setString( 9, resvData.payment);
     pstmt.setString(10, resvData.phone);
     pstmt.setString(11, resvData.address);
     pstmt.setString(12, resvData.city);
     pstmt.setString(13, resvData.state);
     pstmt.setString(14, resvData.zip);
     pstmt.executeUpdate();
     pstmt.close();
     con.commit();
     return resvNo;
   }
   catch( Exception e )
   { System.err.println("System Exception in addReservation");
     System.err.println(e);
     throw e;
   }
 }


public Vector getClubReservations(String club )
              throws Exception
{
   try
   {
     Vector resvSum = new Vector();
     pstmt = con.prepareStatement(
                 "SELECT ResvNo, LastName, FirstName " +
                 "FROM Reservations WHERE Club = '" + club + "' " +
                 "ORDER BY ResvNo ASC");
     pstmt.execute();
     ResultSet rs = pstmt.getResultSet();
     while (rs.next())
     {
       Clubs.resvSummaryStruct resv = new Clubs.resvSummaryStruct();
```

```
        resv.resv  = rs.getInt(1);
        resv.lname = rs.getString(2);
        resv.fname = rs.getString(3);
        resvSum.addElement(resv);
      }
      pstmt.close();
      con.commit();
      return resvSum;
    }
    catch( Exception e )
    { System.err.println("System Exception in getClubReservations");
      System.err.println(e);
      throw e;
    }
}



public Clubs.resvStruct getReservation(int resv )
                    throws Exception
{
  Clubs.resvStruct resvData = new Clubs.resvStruct();
  try
  {
    pstmt = con.prepareStatement(
        "SELECT Club, WeekDate, LastName, " +
        "FirstName, PartyAdults, " +
        "PartyChildren, TotalFare, PaymentMethod, " +
        "PhoneNo, Address, City, State, Zip " +
        "FROM Reservations " +
        "WHERE ResvNo = ?");
    pstmt.setInt(1, resv);
    pstmt.execute();
    ResultSet rs = pstmt.getResultSet();
    rs.next();
    resvData.club          = rs.getString( 1);
    resvData.weekDate      = rs.getString( 2);
    resvData.lname         = rs.getString( 3);
    resvData.fname         = rs.getString( 4);
    resvData.partyAdults   = rs.getShort( 5);
    resvData.partyChildren = rs.getShort( 6);
    resvData.totalFare     = rs.getString(7);
    resvData.payment       = rs.getString( 8);
    resvData.phone         = rs.getString( 9);
    resvData.address       = rs.getString(10);
    resvData.city          = rs.getString(11);
```

```
      resvData.state        = rs.getString(12);
      resvData.zip          = rs.getString(13);
      pstmt.close();
      con.commit();
      return resvData;
    }
    catch( Exception e )
    { System.err.println("System Exception in getReservation");
      System.err.println(e);
      throw e;
    }
}


public boolean cancelReservation(int resv ) throws Exception
{
    try
    {
      pstmt = con.prepareStatement(
            "DELETE FROM Reservations WHERE ResvNo = ?");
      pstmt.setInt( 1, resv);
      pstmt.executeUpdate();
      pstmt.close();
      con.commit();
      return true;
    }
    catch( Exception e )
    { System.err.println("System Exception in cancelReservation");
      System.err.println(e);
      throw e;
    }
}


public Vector getDates() throws Exception
{
    try
    {
      Vector datesList = new Vector();
      pstmt = con.prepareStatement(
              "SELECT DISTINCT WeekDate FROM Prices " +
              "ORDER BY WeekDate ASC");
      pstmt.execute();
      ResultSet rs = pstmt.getResultSet();
      while (rs.next())
```

```java
      {
        String date = rs.getString(1);
        datesList.addElement(date);
      }
      pstmt.close();
      con.commit();
      return datesList;
    } catch( Exception e )
    { System.err.println("System Exception in getDates");
      System.err.println(e);
      throw e;
    }
  }


  public Clubs.bargainStruct getBargainInfo(String date)
                      throws Exception
  {
    Clubs.bargainStruct bargainData = new Clubs.bargainStruct();
    try
    {
      String date1 = date.substring(1,11);
      System.out.println("getBargainInfo("+date1+");");

      pstmt = con.prepareStatement(
          "SELECT Club, AdultPrice " +
          "FROM Prices WHERE (WeekDate = '" + date1 + "') AND " +
          "AdultPrice = (SELECT MIN(AdultPrice) FROM Prices " +
          "WHERE WeekDate = '" + date1 + "')");
      pstmt.execute();
      ResultSet rs = pstmt.getResultSet();
      rs.next();
      bargainData.club          = rs.getString( 1);
      bargainData.adultFare     = rs.getShort( 2);
      pstmt.close();
      con.commit();
      return bargainData;
    } catch( Exception e )
    { System.err.println("System Exception in getBargainInfo");
      System.err.println(e);
      throw e;
    }
  }
}
```

COMPILE THE CLUB MED SERVER

We're now ready to compile the Club Med server. First, we must create the skeletons and stubs. Make sure you've installed VisiBroker for Java. Then go to the appropriate subdirectory and enter the following command at the prompt:

```
prompt> idl2java  ClubMed.idl -no_comments
```

To compile the server code, make sure you've installed Symantec Visual Café (which includes the JDBC package with the JDK 1.1). Then go to the appropriate directory and run the make file. Or, you can type the following commands at the prompt:

```
prompt> javac -d \CorbaJavaBook.2e\classes ClubMedServer.java
prompt> javac -d \CorbaJavaBook.2e\classes ClubMedDispenserImpl.java
prompt> javac -d \CorbaJavaBook.2e\classes ClubMedImpl.java
prompt> javac -d \CorbaJavaBook.2e\classes ClubMedDB.java
```

The -d option tells the compiler to put the (.class) files it creates into the directory we specify—in this case, the \CorbaJavaBook.2e\classes subdirectory.

If all goes well, you should have some compiled Java code—including some stubs and skeletons—that you can now run.

RUNNING CLUB MED

You should already have a fully-populated ClubMed database. If not, follow the instructions in Chapter 35. Next, you must install *ClubMed.html*, the *clubmed.jar* file created for ClubMedBean, and the ClubMedClient applet on your Web server.

Next start the Naming Service as we described in Chapter 7. You can now start the server program by entering the following command:

```
prompt> start java ClubMedServer 10
```

We're telling the **Dispenser** to create a pool of ten server objects. You can change this number to suit your needs.

You're now ready to run as many client programs as you require. You can run multiple client programs from the same machine. Or, you can give each client its own machine. To run each client, first install Netscape Communicator on the client. Then point to your HTML page. You should see the club selection panel. If you've made it this far, congratulations; it was a long journey. Yes, this is a good time to pop a bottle of champagne. You're almost at the finishing line.

CONCLUSION

This is the end of the Club Med Grand Finale that pulls it all together. Are you experiencing CORBA/Java Nirvana? At the least, you now have a working code template for a 3-tier client/server solution that uses CORBA, JavaBeans, and JDBC. You can use Club Med to jump-start your own programs. Hopefully, they'll be as much fun as this one. We still have one more chapter to go before we say goodbye. In the next chapter, we will step back a little and summarize our client/server experiences with CORBA and Java. We will look at the good, the bad, and the ugly.

Chapter 38

CORBA/Java: The Good, the Bad, and the Ugly

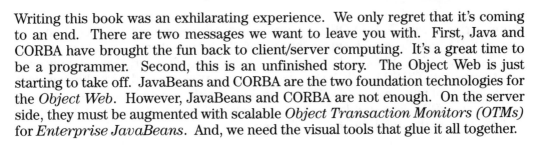

Writing this book was an exhilarating experience. We only regret that it's coming to an end. There are two messages we want to leave you with. First, Java and CORBA have brought the fun back to client/server computing. It's a great time to be a programmer. Second, this is an unfinished story. The Object Web is just starting to take off. JavaBeans and CORBA are the two foundation technologies for the *Object Web*. However, JavaBeans and CORBA are not enough. On the server side, they must be augmented with scalable *Object Transaction Monitors (OTMs)* for *Enterprise JavaBeans*. And, we need the visual tools that glue it all together.

So are Java and CORBA ready for client/server prime time? Almost. The key message you should get from this book is that you can start now. Even in its current incarnation, CORBA/Java provides the best platform for creating Web-based client/server applications today. We don't need to get on a Soapbox to make this claim—the results from Part 4 speak for themselves.

Of course, the applications you write today may end up resembling our Club Med beans instead of the *Shippable Places* that we describe later in this chapter. You may also be using our Object Dispenser instead of an off-the-shelf OTM. But at the end of the day, you will still have the best intergalactic applications on the Web today. In addition, you will have a headstart in developing for the Object Web.

CORBA/Java objects have a long shelf life, so you won't be throwing away code. The distributed object foundation only gets better with time. It's like writing SQL applications today when you know that SQL3 is on its way. Your applications should be upwardly compatible. This is the beauty of a standards-based approach.

In this chapter, we will summarize our experience with CORBA and Java. You can learn quite a bit by writing a programming book of this size that deals with uncharted territory. It's not every day that you get a chance to revisit your work one year later to add another 400 pages of new material. We will tell you the good, the bad, and the ugly. We will then share our vision of what's next for the Object Web. It's like the U.S. highway system—it's perpetually under construction. Finally, you should be warned that this entire chapter is one big parting Soapbox.

SO, WHAT DID WE LEARN?

In this section, we take each of the elements—the client, the server, and the ORB middleware—and tell you the good, the bad, and the ugly. It's the gestalt of our experience with these pieces.

CORBA ORBs: The Good, the Bad, and the Ugly

Our experience with CORBA ORBs was excellent. We are more convinced than ever that CORBA middleware is miles ahead of its competitors—including DCOM, HTTP/CGI, Servlets, RPC, and Sockets. We were pleasantly surprised by how easy it is to integrate CORBA with Java. We were also very pleased with the excellent performance of pure Java ORBs. We are delighted with the vendor implementations of the new CORBA/Java standards. There are also a few negatives we want to share. So let's go over the good, the bad, and the ugly.

CORBA ORBs: The Good

We don't want to turn this section into a diatribe on why ORBs are wonderful. Instead, we will give you our Top-Ten list of the CORBA benefits that we experienced first-hand in this book. Here they are, in no particular order:

- **A solid distributed object foundation:** A CORBA *object reference* is a very powerful unit of distributed service negotiation. It points to an object interface— that is, a set of related methods that operate on an individual object. In contrast, an RPC only returns a reference to a single function. Furthermore, you can aggregate CORBA interfaces via multiple-inheritance. And, CORBA objects are polymorphic—the same call behaves differently depending on the object type that receives it. Of course, RPCs don't support inheritance, polymorphism, or unique objects with state. The bottom line is that a CORBA object reference provides scalpel-like precision; it lets you invoke a set of methods on a specific object. Unique object references are the most efficient way to obtain remote services on the intergalactic network.

■ *Callbacks:* We were able to use CORBA callbacks very effectively to control clients from the server side. You can also use callbacks to create client applications (and applets) that dynamically receive content, state, news, status, alerts, and instructions from their servers.

■ *Excellent CORBA/Java integration:* We were pleasantly surprised by how well CORBA integrates with Java. CORBA interfaces map nicely to their Java counterparts. In addition, Netscape/Visigenic's Caffeine makes CORBA totally seamless to Java programmers. We also like the way VisiBroker was able to seamlessly take advantage of Java threads on the server side. It shows good synergy between CORBA's object activation services and Java's threads. OTMs will be able to do wonders in this new environment.

■ *Excellent Java ORB performance:* Our benchmarks show that pure Java ORBs are able to hold their ground against their more seasoned C++ counter-parts. The JIT compilers helped a lot.

■ *Interoperability with C++ objects:* We were delighted by the seamless interoperation of Java objects with their C++ counterparts using IIOP. It's the cleanest way for Java objects to talk to existing code on the enterprise, and vice versa. CORBA's language-independent and OS-independent foundation makes it a natural player in the heterogeneous world of Java and the Internet.

■ *Dynamic discovery and introspection:* CORBA objects are self-describing and introspective. CORBA's dynamic facilities—including the Trader Service, DII, and Interface Repository—provide a solid foundation for the dynamic discovery and invocation of services on the intergalactic network. They let you create very flexible and agile systems. We're talking about a brave new world where run-time discovery and late-binding become the norm. Clients will register for services. Servers will call them back whenever they have something that matches their clients' needs. Discovery and serendipity are two essential elements in an intergalactic Object Web.

■ *A modern 3-tier client/server foundation:* CORBA objects make ideal server objects in a 3-tier (or n-tier) distributed architecture. They provide a middle-tier, object-to-object infrastructure that you can use to encapsulate data from multiple sources. In addition, you can use CORBA IDL to encapsulate existing systems and connect them to the ORB.

- ***Local/remote transparency:*** A CORBA ORB can run in standalone mode on a laptop, or it can be interconnected with every other ORB in the universe via IIOP's intergalactic services. An ORB can broker interobject calls within a single process, multiple processes running within the same machine, or multiple processes running across networks and operating systems. This is all done in a manner that's transparent to your objects.

- ***A ubiquitous middleware infrastructure:*** Major software companies—including Oracle, IBM, Novell, JavaSoft, and Netscape—have chosen CORBA IIOP as the common way to connect distributed objects across the Internet and intranets. This will create a mass market for software that runs on top of CORBA middleware.

- ***An open standard:*** CORBA is not controlled by a single vendor. Consequently, you will always be able to obtain your ORBs from more than one vendor. For example, we developed the programs in this book using *VisiBroker for Java.* However, we could have just as easily switched platforms—even in midstream—to Iona's *OrbixWeb 3.0* or to JavaSoft's *Java IDL* without significantly impacting our schedule. Finally, CORBA is not platform specific; it runs on all the major hardware platforms and operating systems. Yes, freedom of choice is wonderful! So, it's important for an intergalactic middleware foundation to be open.

We could go on, but we promised to stop after the top ten. Let's go after the bad and the ugly.

CORBA ORBs: The Bad

We did not encounter major problems with CORBA/Java. The bad reads more like a list of what's missing in CORBA/Java ORBs. Here goes:

- ***Where are the rest of the CORBA services?*** We need a complete set of CORBA Services implemented in Java. Of course, there are many more services on the market now than in the previous edition of this book.

- ***Where's MOM?*** MOM stands for *Message-Oriented Middleware.* It provides asynchronous message queues on both the client and server sides. MOM allows clients and servers to function at their own designated times and speeds without necessarily being simultaneously active. ORBs must provide MOM services to support mobile users and to facilitate communications in heterogeneous environments. We need to be able to pass objects by value; we also need to ship CORBA/Java agents using these queues.

We have additional esoteric items on our wish list. For example, we would like to see semantic-level extensions to the CORBA IDL. The idea is that components should be able to interact with each other at the semantic level. To do so, they need ontologies that you can use to create common vocabularies.

CORBA ORBs: The Ugly

After six years in gestation, most of the ugly has been squeezed out of the CORBA ORBs. There aren't too many nasty little secrets left. In the bad old days, we could always depend on a memory leak somewhere to bring a C++ ORB to its knees. It's becoming harder to do so, especially with Java ORBs. The lack of documentation and the lack of a standard *IDL-to-Java* mapping were the two biggest CORBA-related headaches we faced in writing the first edition of this book. We are happy to say that these two problems are gone. The documentation for CORBA/Java ORBs is now first class. The *IDL-to-Java* standard is now out and it has been implemented in record time by all the CORBA/Java ORB vendors. The proof is that we used this new portable standard to develop all the programs in this book (starting with Part 3).

CORBA/Java Clients: The Good, the Bad, and the Ugly

Our experience with CORBA/Java on the client side was good. Yes, you can create very functional clients using JavaBeans today. The tool situation has greatly improved since the first edition of this book. However, we would have liked to see more support for 3-tier client/server visual programming in the current generation of JavaBeans tools. So let's go over the good, the bad, and the ugly.

CORBA/Java Clients: The Good

We're not going to go over the wonders of JavaBeans and applets. Yes, they make wonderful mobile code systems. Instead, let's concentrate on the unique CORBA/JavaBeans client features. Here's our list:

■ ***CORBA works just fine from with applets***. Applets make wonderful downloadable clients. A Java applet can interact directly with CORBA server objects. In addition, CORBA server objects can call back the applet to update its state—the possibilities are only limited by the imagination. Netscape's decision to bundle a CORBA/Java ORB with every browser makes it easier to seamlessly invoke remote CORBA objects from within your browser. In addition, Netscape is providing an architected solution for invoking objects anywhere on the Internet from within your browser. Today, most browsers only let you call objects that live on the same IP port from which your applet was downloaded.

- *You can use CORBA with JavaBeans today.* Eventually, the CORBA and JavaBeans component models will merge, which is a good thing. However, our Club Med and Bargain Hunter beans show that you can do quite a bit with these two technologies today.

- *JavaBeans and JFC have greatly improved Java's looks.* The client in this edition is much more polished than in the previous one. We had a much wider selection of widgets that we could use. All these widgets are now JavaBeans, which means they are toolable. So it's now possible to write mainstream type of front-ends using Java.

- *Visual tools make it easier to develop Java clients.* Over 25 tool vendors now support JavaBeans. They are competing to provide features that make it easier to assemble these beans. In the first edition, we wrote a ton of code to create a platform-independent gridbag layout. In this edition, we told the tools to "make it so." And, they were able to do 90% of the work, which is quite good.

So the story here is that you can use CORBA with JavaBeans today to create some very professional client front-ends. They can either be Java applications or applets. Java client applications perform better than applets, but they're less mobile.

CORBA/Java Clients: The Bad

The bad is the few features that are still missing from the Java client. Also, some of the applet performance numbers got worse in this edition. Here's a short list of problems:

- *Where's the OOUI?* Today's crop of JavaBeans is functional, but it does not provide an *Object-Oriented User Interface (OOUI)*. To become an OOUI, JavaBeans must have drag-and-drop facilities and better support for containers. Both are under construction.

- *What happened to applet performance?* We demonstrated in Part 3 that applet Ping performance got much worse in this edition. It's a step in the wrong direction. Netscape is aware of the problem.

Let's move on to the ugly, where we can continue this discussion.

CORBA/Java Clients: The Ugly

In the previous edition of this book, our main gripe was that AWT was the ugly duckling of user interfaces. It kept Java from looking like the user interfaces of Apple Macintosh, OS/2, Windows 95, or NeXT.

They must have heard us at JavaSoft. So now we have Swing and JavaBeans. Our Java user interfaces don't have to be ugly anymore. That's the good news. Here's the bad news:

■ *We need more stability, please.* The shift from JDK 1.02 to JDK 1.1 was traumatic. We had nine months of turmoil adjusting to the new event model. It took forever to get our components to work with the different tools and browsers. It also took forever for tool vendors to catch up with the new JDK. The enterprise client/server world is used to more stability. You can't go around breaking things and changing APIs every 12 months. Even book authors can't keep up with this hectic schedule. A Java book has a shelf-life of less than a year. Of course, the CORBA world didn't stand still either, as you can see from the massive changes in this edition. We pity the developers.

CORBA/Java Servers: The Good, the Bad, and the Ugly

The big surprise in the first edition of this book was how well Java does servers. We still feel this way. In addition, many more people are now starting to recognize Java's role on the server. CORBA/Java is almost the ideal platform for creating middle-tier server objects. CORBA extends Java's reach to the enterprise and to legacy systems. It also provides a solid server-to-server infrastructure. Enterprise JavaBeans will help bring this technology to the masses. Of course, this picture is not all rosy. You may remember that our 3-tier Debit-Credit benchmark did not perform as well as it should have. The Java VM is very CPU-intensive—JIT compilation eats up tons of MIPs at run time. CORBA also has some shortcomings on the server side, but the story got a lot better with POA. But, we're getting ahead of our story.

CORBA/Java Servers: The Good

You already encountered many of the benefits in the ORB section. So, we will keep this list short. Here are the main benefits CORBA and Java provide on the server side:

■ *A portable operating system for servers:* The Java language offers many operating system features. It lets you write very portable server objects. For example, Java provides advanced threading facilities, automatic garbage collection, and powerful error-handling facilities. Eventually, you may not have to re-target your Java code to obtain these facilities on a variety of server platforms.

■ *A versatile server-to-server infrastructure: Object Transaction Monitors* can use the CORBA bus to coordinate server-side components and to provide fault-tolerance and load-balancing. In addition, they can use IIOP's built-in *Object Transaction Service* to coordinate transactions across components and to manage state at transaction boundaries. You can use this server-to-server bus for intercomponent coordination. For example, you can use it to do publish-and-subscribe, workflow, or to create task forces of cooperating objects.

■ *A toolable and portable server-side component model:* The CORBA 3.0 POA makes the server side of CORBA very portable. Enterprise JavaBeans start out where POA leaves off. They introduce a toolable CORBA/Java component model that supports declarative transactions and security. CORBA OTM vendors can now standardize their components around POA and EJB. These two standards will open up a huge server-side component model.

■ *A solid middle-tier server platform:* We already explained what this means in the ORB section. The message is that CORBA/Java server objects are ideal for encapsulating existing applications and bringing them to the Object Web. They can also bring together data that comes from multiple sources.

CORBA/Java Servers: The Bad

For the last five years, our perennial questions to the ORB vendors have been (and still are):

■ *How do you scale the server side?* We're still looking for an ORB that can manage millions of server objects and their state.

■ *Where's the load-balancing?* We're still looking for an ORB that can distribute server loads across multiple processors and provide a single system image to the clients. The ORB should be able to prestart server objects and cache their state.

■ *Where's the fault-tolerance?* We're still looking for an ORB that provides automatic switchover during failure to an object replica.

In other words, how do you put the server side of the ORB on par with TP Monitors, ODBMSs, and RDBMSs? In the last edition, it finally dawned on us that we were barking up the wrong tree. The ORB vendors are simply communications middleware providers. And, middleware communications providers do not normally deal with these issues. You don't normally purchase a mission-critical server framework from your TCP/IP stack vendor.

So who's going to provide this mission-critical stuff? In this book, we created our own poor man's TP Monitor: the Object Dispenser. However, it appears that over

12 software vendors are now working on CORBA Object Transaction Monitors that also support Enterprise JavaBeans (we list these vendors in the Enterprise JavaBeans chapter). The list includes ORB vendors, TP Monitor vendors, DBMS vendors, and even Web Application Server vendors. So the race is on. In the meantime, use our Object Dispenser.

CORBA/Java Servers: The Ugly

So what makes an ugly server? In our book, it's a server platform that leaves a lot of the infrastructure as an exercise for the customer. This means that we have to reinvent the infrastructure instead of developing our business applications. We think the ORB vendors created a problem by selling ORBs without understanding the mission-critical requirements of the server side. You just can't shift all the burden to your customers. Most of the early CORBA users spent a lot of time and energy trying to get their objects to scale. Yes, ORBs are wonderful, but someone's got to create the code that manages objects on the server side. Of course, this is precisely the problem space that OTMs and EJBs are now addressing. The next time we write a book, we hope to point you to an off-the-shelf commercial product that provides this function (many are in beta).

THE OBJECT WEB VISION AND SHIPPABLE PLACES

In Part 1, we painted a vision of an Object Web. We spoke of *shippable places* that provide a container technology for distributing, caching, and storing groups of related components and their data. In the remainder of this section, we give you a quick overview of this technology and how it plays with CORBA and JavaBeans.

What Is a Shippable Place?

A *place* is a visual ensemble of related components. A *shippable place* is a mobile container of components; it's a place that can be shipped over the Net. Today's user interfaces are centered around a primitive place that represents a desktop. In contrast, shippable places let you interact with multiple places that represent collaborative environments based on real-world models. A place is a mini virtual world. For example, we can have places for 12-year olds, lawyers, or accountants. A place is typically used to display components that represent people and things. For example, places can represent meeting rooms, libraries, offices, homes, stadiums, shopping malls, museums, parks, and auditoriums. People live, work, shop, and visit these places. Things are tools that help us communicate, interact, and work within these places.

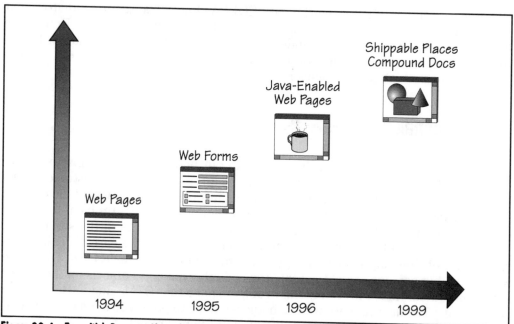

Figure 38-1. From Web Pages to Shippable Places.

A place is implemented as a collection of components stored in a structured file container. You assemble a place by dragging components and dropping them within a visual container, which you then store in a structured file. You should be able to connect to a place via its URL and then download it just like any ordinary Web page. Of course, a place will have a digital signature that guarantees it came from a trusted server. The client will also have to authenticate itself before it can use the downloaded place.

Once the place is secured on your desktop, it will serve as a visual front-end for all kinds of specialized Internet services and business objects. The components within a place will typically communicate with their back-end counterparts using a CORBA ORB. A place is a dynamic assembly of ever-changing data, video feeds, and other live content. The place provides an anchor point on the client that servers can invoke via CORBA callbacks.

You will probably keep the place on your desktop for weeks or months at a time, occasionally refreshing it with newer versions of the components it contains. The place is really one of many alternate desktops. You can also customize a place to reflect your preferences and needs. So, a place is a mobile document that you will store and access over time.

In contrast, a Web page is more transient; it comes and then goes. With Web pages, screen updates are wholesale page replacements that destroy a user's context. In addition, there is no easy way for servers to tell clients that something has changed. Places fix these problems. Note that Marimba's *Castanet* provides some of the elements of shippable places. But it's still a far cry from being a virtual world. To get there, Marimba needs to be augmented with compound documents, portable containers, CORBA callbacks, and JavaBeans.

Figure 38-1 shows the evolution of shippable client front-ends. Web technology made it possible for servers to ship HTML pages to clients where they are displayed in GUI format. The Web then evolved to support HTML-based forms that let clients send data to their servers. With Java, servers can now embed code—in the form of applets—within HTML pages; Java makes Web pages active and smart. Finally, we have shippable places. Like a page, a place can contain Java components. But unlike a page, a place can live on your desktop for as long as you need it. A place also has its own storage, so it can remember your preferences and maintain links to the outside world.

The Future Web Client

Figure 38-2 shows three client models for the Web. In the first model, the browser is the desktop; it assumes that people live within their browsers. This is the current Netscape model of the world (also see the next Briefing Box). In the second model, everything on the desktop is Web-enabled; the idea is that you will be able to access the Web from within any application or component without starting a browser. This is the Microsoft *Windows 98* model. The third model is shippable places; it lets you access the Web from within your places. A place can have multiple concurrent sessions with Web object servers. In addition, multiple places can be concurrently active on the same desktop. The Object Web may end up supporting all three models.

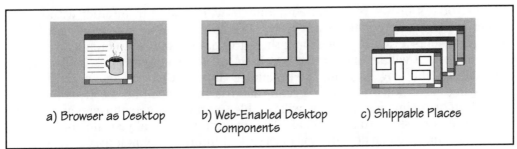

a) Browser as Desktop   b) Web-Enabled Desktop Components   c) Shippable Places

Figure 38-2. The Evolving Web Client Model.

Portable Component Stores

Most of today's Web pages are simply files that get transmitted out of the file system or the Web server and sent down the wire to the client. But increasingly, as

FYI

Component-Based Web Browsers

Briefing

Imagine a Web browser built entirely from components. In addition, imagine that the Web browser itself is a visual container of components. This means that it's a component that also lets you embed other components. So what can you do with such a thing?

For starters, this new kind of browser can provide an integrated visual experience unlike anything you've seen to date. JavaBeans will be able to seamlessly share the visual real estate within a browser's window. You will be able to edit the contents of any component in-place, regardless of how deeply embedded it is within other components. You will also be able to drag-and-drop components not only within the browser but also between the browser and the surrounding desktop. This means that you should be able to embed components within other components and then move them around at will across documents, desktops, and networks.

In today's browsers, components own a static rectangular area within a page. In a compound document browser, components can take any shape, and you can move them around and embed them at will. You should be able to resize components within a browser, zoom in on their contents, and visually rearrange the contents of the page in any way you want. The components will automatically share the document's menu, clipboard, and palette. Everything will look very seamless.

Unlike today's browsers, visual components will be able to interact with each other in many unpredictable ways. For example, you'll be able to drag a URL that represents a CORBA object and then drop it on a button to create an active pushbutton. It will invoke a remote CORBA object when you click on it. You'll be able to shop by dragging merchandise and dropping it in an electronic shopping cart. You'll pay with e-cash that you pull out of an electronic wallet and drop on an invoice. And you will be able to drag an electronic signature and drop it on a message to seal a deal. The imagination is really at the controls in terms of what you can do with this marriage of Internet technology, CORBA, and JavaBeans. ❏

information becomes richer and more finely honed, you want to pull it from other sources. According to Microsoft's Paul Maritz, "Over time most information that gets sent over the Internet will not come out of file systems, but will come out of structured stores."

Simply put, structured containers allow us to store multiple components in a single document, move them as a single unit across networks, cache them where it makes most sense, and store them in document databases. The component store also becomes a unit of defense for an entire set of components. For example, Java JARs let you selectively encrypt a set of components. Finally, the containers can also persistently store a document's context and act accordingly. For example, you can store in a container—along with a set of components—a user's preferences, login state, and the most current visual layout of the document.

In summary, shippable places need component stores so that you can move them around the Web at will. Structured containers are lightweight, shippable object databases that were designed specifically to store, manage, and transport components. We can think of hundreds of ways these structured component containers can be used to create a smarter Object Web. The Java JAR technology (and its manifest) is an embryonic version of this technology.

Jumping Beans

An pioneering example of an infrastructure for shippable places is a product under construction called *Jumping Beans* by Ad Astra Engineering.[1] This alpha product lets you visually construct shippable places from off-the-shelf JavaBeans.

Jumping Beans lets you visually construct an *itinerary* for a place and then dispatch it into cyberspace. Along the way, users can interact with the place as it progresses through its itinerary. You can dynamically add or change the content by adding or removing beans via drag-and-drop. For example, you can drag a signature bean from the palette and drop it on an expense form to authorize a payment.

These places can also be used in heads-down IT applications. The Jumping Beans infrastructure allows IT to deploy client applications (or places) from a centralized location. For example, you can deploy new package-tracking front-end (a place) to 10,000 client machines via a single mouse click.

In Jumping Beans, an *agency* is both a landing pad and launching pad for shippable places. Figure 38-3 shows a screen capture of an itinerary we created for a shippable place. In this case, the shippable place is our **ClubMedBean**. You can mobilize any bean by simply packaging it inside a JAR and then importing it into the Jumping Beans agency. You can use the Jumping Beans designer to assemble new beans from existing beans (the designer is part of the agency). To make a long story

---

[1] The company was started by two of our graduate students—Chris and Mary Rygaard. They mortgaged their house to bring the idea of shippable places to the market. Check them out at *http://www. JumpingBeans.com.*

short, we click on *dispatch* to send our Club Med on its merry way. Figure 38-4 shows the Club Med inside an agency (a landing pad) along the itinerary.

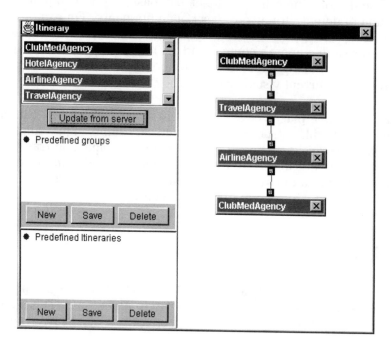

Figure 38-3. Creating a Jumping Beans Itinerary.

Jumping Beans is 100% pure Java; it's built using JFC. Consequently, the runtime is very portable. The application packages the beans inside sealed JARs. It uses certificates and ACLs to control access. The distributed object infrastructure is built on top of a commercial CORBA/Java ORB.

Back to Reality

Two important pieces of this Object Web are here today: CORBA and JavaBeans. This book is living proof that you can use them today to create Web-based, 3-tier client/server applications. These applications are better than anything you can create with any competing form of middleware. Of course, we would have preferred to create a *virtual world* called Club Med where you do everything via drag-and-drop and in-place editing. But we're not quite there yet. The current version of Club Med represents the state-of-the-art in JavaBeans technology. It's as good as it gets today. In a few years, it is likely to become a museum piece. We may all be laughing at how primitive it looks.

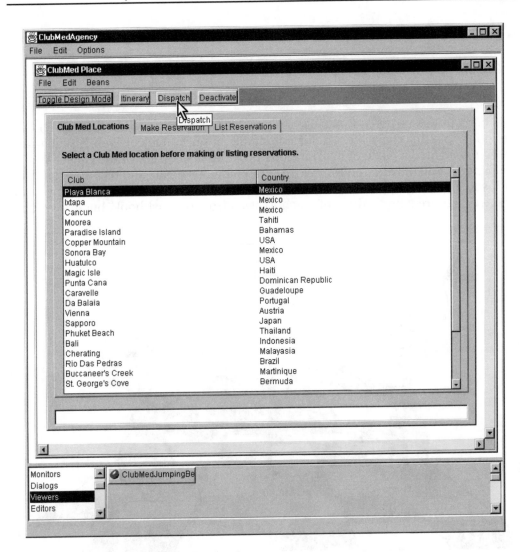

Figure 38-4. Club Med as a Jumping Bean.

However, in a few years, the underlying CORBA/Java architecture will still be intact. It will have become mainstream. Your server objects may become *CORBA Enterprise JavaBeans*. If everything goes well, you will have tossed away our Object Dispenser. You should be able to replace it with a full-blown *Object Transaction Monitor*. So life goes on.

It's Time To Say Good-Bye

The future is bright, fruitful, and positive.

— Bob Marley

This book brings us one notch closer to our final destination—the Object Web. We feel good this time because we did not simply describe Object Web Nirvana—we also implemented a piece of it. This book provides a snapshot of the Object Web at this time. It will only get better. We're scratching our heads and trying to come up with some parting words of wisdom. We'll say good-bye with a final Soapbox on where things are going. Much of it is borrowed from our last book, but it says it all.

Soapbox

Wanted: One Million New Beans

"We need 1,000,000 new JavaBeans." How did we come up with that number? Client/server technology makes it possible to redeploy most of our computer applications on commodity hardware, where the profit margins are razor thin. If we keep re-computerizing the same application base, using PC LANs and intranets instead of mainframes, most of us will end up without jobs. This is because we're going after a downsized pie, where the profits are dramatically lower. If our profits are lower, we cut down on the research that helps us create these new technologies. And IT shops won't get new applications or technology. Everybody ends up losing. It's called the "cannibalizing effect."

Instead, we need to take advantage of client/server technology to extend the boundaries of computerization. In other words, we need to move on to new frontiers like the *Object Web*. But, can we create thousands of new client/server applications quickly to populate these new frontiers? To do that effectively, we need a technology base, standards, and tools. This book makes the case that the technology base, standards, and some solid products are here today. We even have some embryonic tools that can help us create these applications more quickly. However, it's not enough to create the application; it must also be effectively packaged, deployed, and managed.

The Object Web offers the best hope for creating—in record time—new client/server applications that can go where no other applications have gone before. We're excited about the long-term prospects. However, in the short term, we must still write a lot of code with very little help from tools. So we'll be in the doldrums until we can figure out how to unleash the true power of this technology. This is sad—but true. The good news is that after we get over that rough hump, those of us who are still around will be headed straight for a new Gold Rush. ❏

Where to Go for More Information

We compiled the following list of resources to help you find more information on the topics we covered in this book.

CORBA: The OMG Publications

The OMG meets every two months—usually in attractive locations—to continue its standards work. If you can't attend, the best way to find out what's happening is to visit the OMG Web site at http://www.omg.org. OMG publishes three books on the CORBA standard:

- **CORBA: Architecture and Specification** (OMG, 1997). This book covers the CORBA 2.0 ORB, IDL, Interface Repository, and inter-ORB communications.

- **CORBAservices** (OMG, 1997). This book covers the CORBA services.

- **CORBAfacilities** (OMG, 1997). This book covers the CORBA Common Facilities Architecture.

This documentation is available online. You can also call the OMG at 1-508-820-4300 to order any of the above.

CORBA ORB Vendors

We provide a list of the top CORBA ORB vendors (in alphabetical order). We also throw in some comments that you should treat as Soapbox material:

- **BEA Systems**
  ORB name: *ObjectBroker* and *Iceberg*
  http://www.beasys.com/
  Comments: This is the first and most seasoned ORB on the market. It runs on dozens of platforms and scales well. In 1997, BEA acquired *ObjectBroker* from Digital. *BEA Iceberg*—now in beta—is an *Object Transaction Monitor (OTM)* that integrates *ObjectBroker* with *Tuxedo*—the leading TP Monitor on the market (also from BEA). We expect BEA to stake out the high-end of the CORBA server market.

■ **Borland/Visigenic**

ORB name: *VisiBroker*

http://www.visigenic.com/prod

Comments: *VisiBroker for Java* is the leading CORBA/Java ORB. *VisiBroker for C++* is a very fast IIOP-based C++ ORB that runs on multiple platforms. VisiBroker is becoming ubiquitous through its OEM partnerships—it is incorporated in products from Netscape, Oracle, Novell, Sybase, and many others. VisiBroker is also a favorite with tool vendors—it is embedded in many visual tools.

■ **Expersoft**

ORB name: *PowerBroker*

http://www.expersoft.com/

Comments: PowerBroker was picked as the Anderson Consulting ORB in a much publicized bake-off. It is one of the best C++ ORBs on the market.

■ **IBM**

ORB name: *SOM* and *Component Broker*

http://www.software.ibm.com/objects/somobjects/

http://www.software.ibm.com/ad/cb/

Comments: SOM is now part of IBM's *Component Broker*—another CORBA-based OTM. *Component Broker* supports over 10 CORBA services and includes a visual framework for composing CORBA business objects. It also supports instance managers that let you store a CORBA object's state inside DB2.

■ **ICL**

ORB name: *DAIS*

http://www.icl.co.uk/products/dais/home.html

Comments: This is a mission-critical ORB by the UK-based company, *International Computer Limited (ICL)*. It has few features, but it scales well. DAIS is also the first CORBA ORB to implement the OMG Security Service.

■ **IONA**

ORB name: *Orbix* and *OrbixWeb*

http://www.iona.ie/

Comments: Iona is a leading provider of CORBA technology. Its C++ *Orbix* ORB now runs on 20 operating systems—including twelve Unix variants, OS/2, NT, Windows 95, Macintosh System 7.5, OpenVMS, and MVS. Iona's *OrbixWeb V3* is a very complete all-Java ORB. Iona is also a provider of CORBA firewalls, DCOM-to-IIOP bridges, and CORBA-based transaction services. It is widely deployed in IT shops.

- **JavaSoft**
  ORB name: Java IDL
  http://www.javasoft.com/
  Comments: Java IDL is the CORBA/Java ORB that will be embedded in JDK 1.2. It includes a development platform and CORBA-compliant Naming Service. And, it's free.

Books on CORBA

- Thomas Mowbray and Ron Zahavi, **The Essential CORBA: Systems Integration Using Distributed Objects** (Wiley, 1995). This book is on object methodology and design using CORBA. Tom Mowbray previously chaired the CORBA Common Facilities Task Force. So you will get a dose of valuable CORBA insights from reading this book.

- Thomas Mowbray and Raphael Malveau, **CORBA Design Patterns** (Wiley, 1997). This useful book uses design patterns to explain CORBA programming techniques. It is the first design patterns book to cover distributed systems.

- Roger Sessions, **Object Persistence** (Prentice Hall, 1996). This book contains everything you need to know about CORBA's _Persistent Object Service 1 (POS1)_. Roger Sessions was one of POS1's key architects. This standard is being replaced with POS2. However, this book still contains useful insights on object persistence.

- Jon Siegel, et al., **CORBA Fundamentals and Programming** (Wiley, 1996). This book is a CORBA programmer's Bible; it covers multivendor C++ and Smalltalk CORBA ORBs.

- Geoffrey Lewis, et al., **Programming with Java IDL** (Wiley, 1998). This book covers JavaSoft's _Java IDL_. Its authors are the Sun developers of the product.

- Sean Baker, **CORBA Distributed Objects: Using Orbix** (Addison Wesley, 1998). This book covers advanced Orbix features such as filters and thread support. It briefly covers _OrbixWeb_.

- Andreas Vogel and Keith Duddy, **Java Programming With CORBA** (Wiley, 1997). This is another CORBA/Java book.

- Robert Orfali, et al., **Instant CORBA** (Wiley, 1997). This book by your authors is a gentle introduction to CORBA and its services for people who are in a hurry.

COM and DCOM

COM is covered indirectly in about a dozen Visual C++ and ActiveX books on the market. It's also covered in tons of online documentation from Microsoft—including the Win32 SDK. To get the latest on Java and DCOM, visit the following Microsoft Web Sites: http://www.microsoft.com/visualj and http://www.microsoft.com/java/sdk.

Here are some COM-specific books that you may find helpful:

- Kraig Brockschmidt, **Inside OLE 2, Second Edition** (Microsoft Press, 1995). This second edition is still more complete in some places than the "official" Microsoft documentation on OLE.

- David Chappell, **Understanding ActiveX and OLE** (Microsoft Press, 1996). This book is a very gentle guide to OLE and ActiveX. It's prerequisite reading for anyone interested in COM.

- Dale Rogerson, **Inside COM** (Microsoft Press, 1997). This C++ programming book only covers COM.

- Richard Grimes, **Professional DCOM Programming**, (Wrox Press, 1997). This very detailed C++ book covers both COM and DCOM.

- Don Box, **Essential COM** (Addison Wesley, 1998). This is the latest and greatest C++ COM programming book to hit the market. We received it just as we were going to press. It appears to cover COM in depth, but we really haven't had a chance to read it yet.

- Roger Sessions, **COM and DCOM: Microsoft's Vision for Distributed Objects** (Wiley, 1998). Yes, this is the same Roger Sessions who wrote the CORBA Persistence book. This is the first Java/DCOM book on the market; it's also the first book that really covers MTS. As usual, Roger's style is wonderful. Of course, we strongly disagree with some of the positions Roger takes in his new book (but that's life).

Distributed Objects

There are tons of books on object-oriented methodologies and languages. However, very few of these books deal with distributed objects. Here are a few that you may find helpful:

■ David Taylor, **Object-Oriented Information Systems** (Wiley, 1992). This book is a very approachable introduction to objects.

■ Grady Booch, **Object-Oriented Analysis and Design, Second Edition,** (Benjamin-Cummings, 1994). This second edition of Booch's book is superb reading. It's also an introduction but with more emphasis on language constructs, methodology, and notation.

■ Rick Cattell, **The Object Database Standard: ODMG-93** (Morgan Kaufmann). This is the published ODMG standard. To get more information on the Object Database Management Group (ODMG) contact http://www.odmg.org.

■ Oliver Sims, **Business Objects** (McGraw-Hill, 1994). This book provides a general introduction to client/server business objects. Oliver Sims is the principal architect of Newi and an early pioneer of business objects. You should read this book, even if you have no interest in Newi.

■ Orfali et al., **The Essential Distributed Objects Survival Guide** (Wiley, 1996). This book is a gentle introduction to distributed objects and components.

Java

You should always start your Java quest with a visit to the JavaSoft Web Site—http://www.javasoft.com. In addition, there are now hundreds of books on Java. Here are the ones we found to be the most helpful:

■ Cay Horstmann and Gary Cornell, **Core Java 1.1** (Prentice Hall, 1997). This is still our favorite introduction to programming in Java.

■ David Flanagan, **Java in a Nutshell, Second Edition**, (O'Reilly, 1997). This is a must-have reference for Java programmers. It's a very handy guide to the Java classes and interfaces.

■ James Gosling et al., **Java Programming Language, Second Edition** (Addison Wesley, 1998). After you read an introduction—for example, Horstmann—you may want to look at this insightful book by the creator of Java. It will help you consolidate your understanding of the Java language.

■ Rick Cattell et al., **JDBC Database Access With Java** (Addison Wesley, 1997). This book is an introduction to JDBC by the JavaSoft team that developed JDBC.

Client/Server and Transaction Processing

This is a huge topic in its own right. The best place to get started is with our book—**The Essential Client/Server Survival Guide**, Second Edition (Wiley, 1996). This gentle introduction covers all of client/server from the NOS to TP Monitors, ORBs, and the Internet. We also recommend:

- Jim Gray and Andreas Reuter, **Transaction Processing Concepts and Techniques** (Morgan Kaufmann, 1993). This book is the Bible of transaction processing.

- David Vaskevitch, **Client/Server Strategies, Second Edition** (IDG, 1995). Vaskevitch is Microsoft's VP of enterprise computing. This book provides an insider's view of Viper and Microsoft's client/server directions. Most of the meat is in the last part. The rest of the book is mostly about the business aspects of client/server technology. It's worth a read.

- David Linthicum, **Client/Server and Intranet Development** (Wiley, 1997). This book covers all aspects of client/server tools. It also has a good section on 3-tier and TP Monitors.

- Juan Andrade et al., **The Tuxedo System** (Addison Wesley, 1996). This well-written book is an introduction to the Tuxedo TP Monitor; its four authors are the key architects of the Tuxedo system.

- Philip Bernstein and Eric Newcomer, **The Principles of Transaction Processing** (Morgan Kaufmann, 1997). This book provides a good overview of TP Monitors and their underlying technology.

- Jeri Edwards, **3-Tier Client/Server At Work** (Wiley, 1998). This fast-paced book by our coauthor presents eight case studies of some of the largest client/server systems in existence; it provides a ton of insight on how client/server technology is used in the real world.

Index

Java(tm) Development Kit
Version 1.1.5
Binary Code License

This binary code license ("License") contains rights and restrictions associated with use of the accompanying software and documentation ("Software"). Read the License carefully before installing the Software. By installing the Software you agree to the terms and conditions of this License.

1. Limited License Grant. Sun grants to you ("Licensee") a non-exclusive, non-transferable limited license to use the Software without fee for evaluation of the Software and for development of Java(tm) compatible applets and applications. Licensee may make one archival copy of the Software and may re-distribute complete, unmodified copies of the Software to software developers within Licensee's organization to avoid unnecessary download time, provided that this License conspicuously appear with all copies of the Software. Except for the foregoing, Licensee may not re-distribute the Software in whole or in part, either separately or included with a product. Refer to the Java Runtime Environment Version 1.1.5 binary code license (http://java.sun.com/products/JDK/1.1/index.html) for the availability of runtime code which may be distributed with Java compatible applets and applications.

2. Java Platform Interface. Licensee may not modify the Java Platform Interface ("JPI", identified as classes contained within the "java" package or any subpackages of the "java" package), by creating additional classes within the JPI or otherwise causing the addition to or modification of the classes in the JPI. In the event that Licensee creates any Java-related API and distributes such API to others for applet or application development, Licensee must promptly publish an accurate specification for such API for free use by all developers of Java-based software.

3. Restrictions. Software is confidential copyrighted information of Sun and title to all copies is retained by Sun and/or its licensors. Licensee shall not modify, decompile, disassemble, decrypt, extract, or otherwise reverse engineer Software. Software may not be leased, assigned, or sublicensed, in whole or in part. **Software is not designed or intended for use in on-line control of aircraft, air traffic, aircraft navigation or aircraft communications; or in the design, construction, operation or maintenance of any nuclear facility. Licensee warrants that it will not use or redistribute the Software for such purposes.**

4. Trademarks and Logos. This License does not authorize Licensee to use any Sun name, trademark or logo. Licensee acknowledges that Sun owns the Java trademark and all Java-related trademarks, logos and icons including the Coffee Cup and Duke ("Java Marks") and agrees to: (i) to comply with the Java Trademark Guidelines at http://java.sun.com/trademarks.html; (ii) not do anything harmful to or inconsistent with Sun's rights in the Java Marks; and (iii) assist Sun in protecting those rights, including assigning to Sun any rights acquired by Licensee in any Java Mark.

5. Disclaimer of Warranty. Software is provided "AS IS," without a warranty of any kind. ALL EXPRESS OR IMPLIED REPRESENTATIONS AND WARRANTIES, INCLUDING ANY IMPLIED WARRANTY OF MERCHANTABILITY, FITNESS FOR A PARTICULAR PURPOSE OR NON-INFRINGEMENT, ARE HEREBY EXCLUDED. 6. Limitation of Liability. SUN AND ITS LICENSORS SHALL NOT BE LIABLE FOR ANY DAMAGES SUFFERED BY LICENSEE OR ANY THIRD PARTY AS A RESULT OF USING OR DISTRIBUTING SOFTWARE. IN NO EVENT WILL SUN OR ITS LICENSORS BE LIABLE FOR ANY LOST REVENUE, PROFIT OR DATA, OR FOR DIRECT, INDIRECT, SPECIAL, CONSEQUENTIAL, INCIDENTAL OR PUNITIVE DAMAGES, HOWEVER CAUSED AND REGARDLESS OF THE THEORY OF LIABILITY, ARISING OUT OF THE USE OF OR INABILITY TO USE SOFTWARE, EVEN IF SUN HAS BEEN ADVISED OF THE POSSIBILITY OF SUCH DAMAGES.

7. Termination. Licensee may terminate this License at any time by destroying all copies of Software. This License will terminate immediately without notice from Sun if Licensee fails to comply with any provision of this License. Upon such termination, Licensee must destroy all copies of Software.

8. Export Regulations. Software, including technical data, is subject to U.S. export control laws, including the U.S. Export Administration Act and its associated regulations, and may be subject to export or import regulations in other countries. Licensee agrees to comply strictly with all such regulations and acknowledges that it has the responsibility to obtain licenses to export, re-export, or import Software. Software may not be downloaded, or otherwise exported or re-exported (i) into, or to a national or resident of, Cuba, Iraq, Iran, North Korea, Libya, Sudan, Syria or any country to which the U.S. has embargoed goods; or (ii) to anyone on the U.S. Treasury Department's list of Specially Designated Nations or the U.S. Commerce Department's Table of Denial Orders.

9. Restricted Rights. Use, duplication or disclosure by the United States government is subject to the restrictions as set forth in the Rights in Technical Data and Computer Software Clauses in DFARS 252.227-7013(c) (1) (ii) and FAR 52.227-19(c) (2) as applicable.

10. Governing Law. Any action related to this License will be governed by California law and controlling U.S. federal law. No choice of law rules of any jurisdiction will apply.

11. Severability. If any of the above provisions are held to be in violation of applicable law, void, or unenforceable in any jurisdiction, then such provisions are herewith waived to the extent necessary for the License to be otherwise enforceable in such jurisdiction. However, if in Sun's opinion deletion of any provisions of the License by operation of this paragraph unreasonably compromises the rights or increase the liabilities of Sun or its licensors, Sun reserves the right to terminate the License and refund the fee paid by Licensee, if any, as Licensee's sole and exclusive remedy.

To redeem this offer, mail this original coupon (no photocopies, please) along with payment and shipping information to:

Borland International, Inc.
Order Processing
P.O. Box 660005
Scotts Valley, CA 95067-0005

Or call 1-800-932-9994, offer code 1515.

Name _____

Address _____

City _____

State/Province _____ Zip/Postal Code _____

Phone (_____) _____ Fax (_____) _____

Select one:

❑ JBuilder Standard for Windows 95 & Windows NT	CD-ROM	$99.95
❑ JBuilder Professional for Windows 95 & Windows NT (Reg. $799)	CD-ROM	$249.95
❑ JBuilder Client/Server Suite Windows 95 & Windows NT (Reg. $2,499)	CD-ROM	$1,999.00

Method of payment:

❑ Check enclosed (Make checks payable to Borland International, Inc.)

❑ VISA   ❑ MasterCard   ❑ American Express

Card number: __ __ __ __ - __ __ __ __ - __ __ __ __ - __ __ __ __

Expiration date: __ __ / __ __

Subtotal	$ _____
State sales tax*	$ _____
Freight ($10.00 per item)	$ _____
Total order	$ _____

Offer Code 1515

Offer expires October 31, 1998.

This offer good in the U.S. and Canada only. International customers, please contact your local Borland office for the offer in your country. Corporate Headquarters: 100 Borland Way, Scotts Valley, California 95066-3249, 408-431-1000. Internet: http://www.borland.com/ Offices in: Australia (61-2-9248-0900), Canada (905-477-4344), Chile (56-2-233-7113), France (33-1-41-23-11-00), Germany (49-6103-9790), Hong Kong (852-2572-3238), Japan (81-3-5350-9380), Latin American Headquarters in U.S.A. (408-431-1126), The Netherlands (+31 [0] 20 503 5100), Singapore (65-339-8122), Taiwan (886-2-718-6627), and United Kingdom (1-[0800] 973139)

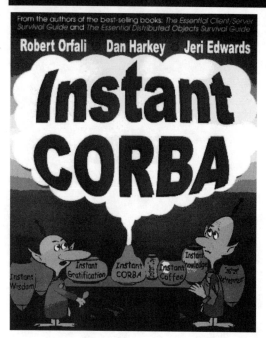

3-Tier Client/Server At Work

Jeri Edwards

With Deborah DeVoe

Transactions per Second

Forward by Robert Orfali

Contents at a Glance

You've heard the theory behind 3-tier client/server. Now learn how to put it into practice. Jeri Edwards takes you on a rare, international tour of eight large companies' client/server applications that are at work in enterprises today.

I may not appear in this book, but I still highly recommend it!

You'll get an insider's peek at these companies' projects. Find out what went right, and what they would do differently next time. You'll learn:

✔ Why 3-tier architectures are key to successful enterprise client/server applications

✔ How to migrate from monolithic, single-tier applications to multi-tier client/server

✔ What today's middle-tier platforms are—including TP Monitors, ORBs, MOMs, and RPCs—and when to use them

✔ What the architectural trade-offs are and how to choose between them

✔ How successful projects are run and what outcomes to expect

✔ Word to the wise: tips from the architects

WILEY

Available at Bookstores Everywhere

For more information visit **http://www.wiley.com/compbooks**
ISBN: 0471-18443-8, 238 pages, 1997, $22.99 US / $32.50 CAN

Your Survival Guide to Client/Server!

Robert Orfali • Dan Harkey • Jeri Edwards

The Essential Client/Server Survival Guide

Second Edition

Completely Updated Award-winning Bestseller

Contents at a Glance

I highly recommend it!

It's as savvy, informative, and entertaining as anything you are likely to read on the subject. Client/server isn't one technology but many—remote SQL, TP, message-oriented groupware, distributed objects, and so on. Like the proverbial blind men feeling the elephant, most of us have a hard time seeing the whole picture. The authors succeed brilliantly in mapping the elephant.

— *Jon Udell, BYTE Magazine*

The scope and depth of topics covered in the Guide, with its straightforward and often humorous delivery, make this book required reading for anyone who deals with computers in today's corporate environment.

— *Bob Gallagher, PC Week*

Absolutely the finest book on client/server on the market today.

— *Richard Finkelstein*
President of Performance Computing

Charmingly accessible.

— *Dr. Jim Gray*
Author of Transaction Processing

WILEY

Available at Bookstores Everywhere

For more information visit **http://www.wiley.com/compbooks**
ISBN: 0471-15325-7, 676 pages, 1996, $32.95 US / $46.50 CAN

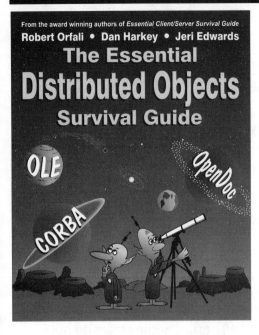